1 MONTH OF
FREE
READING

at

www.ForgottenBooks.com

By purchasing this book you are
eligible for one month membership to
ForgottenBooks.com, giving you
unlimited access to our entire
collection of over 1,000,000 titles via
our web site and mobile apps.

To claim your free month visit:

www.forgottenbooks.com/free54267

ISBN 978-1-5285-6339-0
PIBN 10054267

LECTURES

ON

THE CONSTITUTION

OF

THE UNITED STATES

BY

SAMUEL FREEMAN MILLER, LL.D.

LATE AN ASSOCIATE JUSTICE OF THE SUPREME COURT OF THE UNITED STATES

NEW YORK AND ALBANY
BANKS AND BROTHERS, LAW PUBLISHERS -
1891

Copyright, 1891,

By BANKS & BROTHERS.

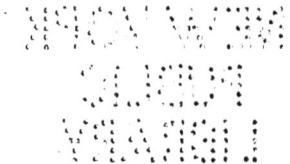

THIS POSTHUMOUS WORK

OF

Mr. Justice Miller

IS RESPECTFULLY DEDICATED

TO THE

CHIEF JUSTICE AND ASSOCIATE JUSTICES

OF THE

SUPREME COURT OF THE UNITED STATES

PREFACE.

THE late Mr. Justice Miller, at his death, left a carefully prepared manuscript of ten lectures upon the Constitution of the United States, which had been read by him before the students of the Law School of the National University, in the city of Washington, during the winter of 1889 and early spring of 1890. These lectures were accompanied by a series of notes, prepared under his direction.

This material, and two other papers by him on cognate subjects — the first an address before the Alumni of the Law Department of the University of Michigan on the 29th day of June, 1887, entitled, "The Constitution and the Supreme Court of the United States"; the other "An Oration delivered at the one hundredth anniversary of the framing and promulgation of the Constitution in Independence Square, Philadelphia, on the 17th day of September, 1887" — have been placed in my hands for arrangement and publication. The address and the oration were published together under Mr. Justice Miller's supervision during his lifetime. The ten lectures are now published for the first time.

It will be easily seen that no editing of these papers, in the ordinary sense of that term, was necessary, beyond the care required in order to ensure the exact reproduction of the thoughts and language of the great judge who has passed away, and the verification of the authorities cited or quoted in the footnotes. The simplicity of style, the directness of statement, the breadth of view, the honesty of purpose, and the discriminating analysis to be found in these papers, must arrest the attention and command the admiration of students of Constitutional History, without extraneous suggestions. I have, accordingly, printed Judge Miller's Lectures as they came to me, and have attached to them the footnotes in the condition in which they were left by him, after properly verifying them.

I have also taken the liberty to add a short note to each of these Lectures, which in each case will explain itself. I have also added a supplemental chapter containing references to minor provisions of the Constitution, not discussed in the Lectures, and an appendix containing (1) a collated copy of the Constitution, with full references to the cases in which it has been construed or discussed; (2) a collated copy of the Articles of Confederation; (3) copies of the Randolph draft for a constitution, and of the Pinckney draft for the same, which were submitted to the convention May 29, 1787, both of which proved to be of substantial use in the discussions which followed in the convention.

I have endeavored to present this work to the profession and the public in a manner worthy of the great judge who has passed away, so far as the limited time given me, and my duties to the court would allow. If there be any serious shortcoming, no one will regret it more than I. It has been to me a labor of love to follow in the footsteps of one whose great intellect, probity, manliness, and directness of purpose were recognized by the whole nation; whose amiable character was admired by all who knew him; and whose friendship I was permitted to enjoy for nearly a quarter of a century.

Mr. Justice Miller was trained in the school of Chief Justice Marshall. When he died, the bar of the Supreme Court passed a series of resolutions to express their estimate of his character, and of the great value of his services to his country. When these resolutions were presented to that court by the Attorney General of the United States, the Chief Justice, in responding, said:

"When he took his seat, the country was in the throes of internecine conflict; when his eyes closed, it was upon a happy, prosperous, and united people, living under the form of government devised by the fathers, the wisdom of whose fabric the event had vindicated. Great problems crowded for solution: the suspension of the habeas corpus; the jurisdiction of military tribunals; the closing of the ports of the insurrectionary States; the legislation to uphold the two main nerves, iron and gold, by which war moves in all her equipage; the restoration of the predominance of the civil over the military authority; the reconstruction measures; the amendments to the Constitution, involving the consolidation of the Union, with the preservation of the just and equal rights of the States, — all these passed in various phases under the jurisdiction of the court, and he dealt with them with the hand of a master.

"While he took his full share in the consideration of every subject of judicial investigation, notably in reference to some, as, for instance, those pertaining to the public lands, yet he chiefly distinguished himself in the treatment of grave constitutional questions, which brought into play the patience, the intuition, the deliberation, the foresight, the intellectual grasp and the breadth of view which characterize all who have deserved the name of statesman. And, as with private controversies, so with those concerning the public and the Government, he sought to go by the ancient ways and never to incur the curse denounced on him who removeth the landmarks. His style was like his tread, massive but vigorous. His opinions, from his first in the second of Black's Reports, to his last in the one hundred and thirty-sixth United States, some seven hundred in number (including dissents), running through seventy volumes, were marked by strength of diction, keen sense of justice, and undoubting firmness of conclusion.

"He had that true legal instinct which qualified him to arrive at the very right of a cause and to apply settled principles to its proper disposition; while to courage was joined an integrity and simplicity that always commanded respect and generally carried conviction. Benignant in temperament, and with a heart full of sensibility, his intercourse with his fellows was so cordial and kindly as to endear him to all who came within the sphere of his influence."

To Gherardi Davis, Esq., of the New York bar, I wish to return my thanks for valuable suggestions in the preparation of these Lectures and Notes for publication; and still more for the full references to decided cases which accompany the copy of the Constitution in the Appendix.

To Hon. J. B. Moore, Assistant Secretary of State, I am indebted for the collated and certified copies of the Constitution, etc., in the Appendix, which cannot but prove interesting to students of constitutional history.

J. C. BANCROFT DAVIS.

WASHINGTON, July 1, 1891.

TABLE OF CONTENTS.

TABLE OF CASES

CITED IN LECTURES AND NOTES.

———◆———

THE FRAMING OF THE CONSTITUTION.[1]

·

——∘∘❀∘∘——

WE are met here to commemorate an event in our progress, in many respects inferior to none in importance in our own history or in the history of the world. It is the formation of the Constitution of the United States, which, on this day, one hundred years ago, was adopted by the Convention which represented the *people* of the United States, and which was then signed by the delegates who framed it, and published as the final result of their arduous labors, — of their most careful and deliberate consideration, — and of a love of country as unmixed with selfishness as human nature is capable of.

In looking at the names of those who signed the instrument, our sentiment of pious reverence for the work of their hands hardly permits us

---

[1] This paper, which leads up to the Lectures delivered by Mr. Justice Miller before the classes in the Law School, is in substance the oration which he delivered on the 17th of September, 1887, at Philadelphia at "the celebration of the one hundredth anniversary of the framing and promulgation of the Constitution." Only such passages are omitted as treat of matters which are again discussed in the Lectures.

to discriminate by special mention of any. But it is surely not in bad taste to mention that the name of George Washington is there as its first signer, and as president of the convention; the man of whom it was afterwards so happily declared by the representatives of a grateful people, that he was "first in war, first in peace, and first in the hearts of his countrymen." He was the first man selected to fill the Chief Executive office of President created by the Constitution; and James Madison, another name found in the list of signers, filled the same office.

James Wilson, of Pennsylvania, John Blair, of Virginia, and John Rutledge, of South Carolina, were made justices of the court established by that instrument, with a large view, among its other functions, of expounding its meaning. With no invidious intent it may be here said that one of the greatest names in American history — Alexander Hamilton — is there as representing alone the important State of New York; his colleagues from that State having withdrawn from the convention before the final vote on the Constitution. Nor is it permissible, standing in this place and in this connection, to omit to point to the name of Benjamin Franklin, the venerable philosopher and patriot; of Robert Morris, the financier of the Revolution; and of Gouverneur Morris, the brilliant scholar and profound statesman.

It is necessary to any just appreciation of the Constitution, whose presentation for acceptance to the people of the United States a hundred years ago on this day we commemorate, that some statement of its origin, and of the causes which led to it, should be made. The occasion requires that this shall be brief.

The war of seven years, which was waged in support of the independence of these States, former provinces of Great Britain, — an independence announced by the Declaration of July 4, 1776, already referred to, — the war which will always be known in the history of this country as the war of the Revolution, was conducted by a union of those States under an agreement between them called Articles of Confederation. Under these articles each State was an integer of equal dignity and power in a body called the Congress, which conducted the affairs of the incipient nation. Each of the thirteen States which composed this confederation sent to Congress as many delegates as it chose, without reference to its population, its wealth, or the extent of its territory; but the vote upon the passage of any law, or resolution, or action suggested, was taken by States, the members from each State, however numerous or however small, constituting one vote, and a majority of these votes by States being necessary to the adoption of the proposition.

The most important matters on which Con- gress acted were but little else than recommendations to the States, requesting their aid in the general cause. There was no power in the Congress to raise money by taxation. It could declare by way of assessment the amount each

State should contribute to the support of the Government, but it had no means of enforcing compliance with this assessment. It could make requisitions on each State for men for the army which was fighting for them all, but the raising of this levy was wholly dependent upon the action of the States respectively. There was no authority to tax, or otherwise regulate, the import or export of foreign goods, nor to prevent the separate States from taxing property which entered their ports, though the property so taxed was owned by citizens of other States.

The end of this war of the Revolution, which had established our entire independence of the crown of Great Britain, and which had caused us to be recognized theoretically as a member of the family of nations, found us with an empty treasury, an impaired credit, a country drained of its wealth and impoverished by the exhaustive struggle. It found us with a large national debt to our own citizens and to our friends abroad, who had loaned us their money in our desperate strait; and worst of all, it found us with an army of unpaid patriotic soldiers who had endured every hardship that our want of means could add to the necessary incidents of a civil war, many of whom had to return penniless to families whose condition was pitiable.

For all these evils the limited and imperfect powers conferred by the Articles of Confederation afforded no adequate remedy. The Congress, in which was vested all the authority that those articles granted to the General Govern-

ment, struggled hopelessly and with constant Lecture I.
failure from the treaty of peace with England, Weakness of Congress under
in 1783, until the formation of the new Consti- them.
tution. Many suggestions were made for enlarging the powers of the Federal Government
in regard to particular subjects. None were
successful, and none proposed the only true
remedy, namely, authority in the National Government to enforce the powers which were entrusted to it by the Articles of Confederation, by
its own immediate and direct action on the people of the States.

It is not a little remarkable that the sugges- Causes which
tion which finally led to the relief, without which led to a change.
as a nation we must soon have perished, strongly
supports the philosophical maxim of modern
times, — that of all the agencies of civilization
and progress of the human race, commerce is the
most efficient. What our deranged finances, our
discreditable failure to pay our debts, and the
sufferings of our soldiers could not force the
several States of the American Union to attempt,
was brought about by a desire to be released
from the evils of an unregulated and burden-
some commercial intercourse, both with foreign
nations and between the several States.

After many resolutions by State legislatures Action of Vir-
which led to nothing, one was introduced by ginia.
Mr. Madison into that of Virginia, and passed
on the twenty-first day of February, 1786, which
appointed Edmund Randolph, James Madison
Jr., and six others, commissioners, " to meet such
commissioners as may be appointed by other

States in the Union, at a time and place to be
agreed, to take into consideration the trade of
the United States; to examine the relative situation and trade of the said States; to consider
how far a uniform system in their commercial
regulations may be necessary to their common
interest and their permanent harmony."

This committee was directed to transmit copies
of the resolution to the several States, with a
letter requesting their concurrence, and proposing a time and place for the meeting. The time
agreed upon was in September, 1786, and the
place was Annapolis. Nine States appointed
delegates, but those of five States only attended.
These were New York, New Jersey, Pennsylvania, Virginia, and Delaware. Four other
States appointed delegates who, for various reasons, did not appear, or came too late. Of course
such a convention as this could do little but
make recommendations. What it did was to
suggest a convention of delegates from all the
States, "to devise such further provisions as
might appear to be necessary to render the Constitution of the Federal Government adequate
to the exigencies of the Union." It also proposed that whatever should be agreed upon by
such a convention should be reported to Congress, and confirmed by the legislatures of all
the States.

This resolution and an accompanying report
were presented to Congress, which manifested
much reluctance and a very unreasonable delay
in acting upon it, and a want of any earnest

approval of the plan. But the proceedings of the Annapolis convention had been laid before the legislatures of the States, where they met with a more cordial reception, and the action of several of them in approving the recommendation for a convention, and appointing delegates to attend it, finally overcame the hesitation of Congress. That body, accordingly, on the 21st of February, 1787, resolved that, in its opinion, "it was expedient that on the second Monday in May next, a convention of delegates, who shall have been appointed by the several States, be held at Philadelphia, for the sole and express purpose of revising the Articles of Confederation; and reporting to Congress and the several legislatures such alterations and provisions therein as shall, when agreed to in Congress, and confirmed by the States, render the Federal Constitution adequate to the exigencies of government and the preservation of the Union."

On the day thus recommended, — May 14th, — delegates from Virginia and Pennsylvania met and adjourned from day to day until the 25th, during which period delegates from other States made their appearance. On that day the delegates of seven States, duly appointed, being present, the convention was organized by the election of General Washington as its president, at the suggestion of Franklin. On the 28th the representation in the convention was increased to nine States; and on the 29th Edmund Randolph, delegate from Virginia, and governor of that State, inaugurated the work of the conven-

LECTURE I.
Congress reluctant to act.

It acts favorably.

The Convention meets.

LECTURE I.
The Convention
meets.

It frames the
Constitution.

tion by a speech in which he presented an outline of a constitution for its consideration.

From this time on, the convention labored
assiduously and without intermission, until, on
the seventeenth day of September, one hundred
years ago, it closed its work by presenting a
completed instrument, which, being subsequently
ratified by the States, became the Constitution
of the United States of America.

Rhode Island not
represented.

All the States except Rhode Island were finally
represented in the convention and took part in
framing the instrument, a majority of the delegates of each State assenting to it. That State
sent no delegate to the convention; and when
the Constitution was presented to it for ratification no convention was called for that purpose
until after it had gone into operation as the
organic law of the National Government. It
was two years before she accepted it and became
in reality a State of the Union.

Reasons for it.

It is a matter for profound reflection by the
philosophical statesman, that, while the most
efficient motive in bringing the other States
into this convention was a desire to amend the
situation in regard to trade among the States,
and to secure a uniform system of commercial
regulation, as necessary to the common interest
and permanent harmony, the course of Rhode
Island was mainly governed by the consideration that her superior advantages of location,
and the possession of what was supposed to be
the best harbor on the Atlantic coast, should *not*
be subjected to the control of a Congress which

was by that instrument expressly authorized "to regulate commerce with foreign nations and among the several States," and which also declared that "no preference shall be given by any regulation of commerce or revenue to the ports of one State over those of another, nor any vessel bound to or from one State be obliged to enter, clear, or pay duties in another."

That the spirit which actuated Rhode Island still exists, and is found in other States of the Union, may be inferred from the fact that at no time since the formation of the Union has there been a period when there were not to be found in the statute-books of some of the States acts passed in violation of this provision of the Constitution, imposing taxes and other burdens upon the free interchange of commodities, discriminating against the productions of other States, and attempting to establish regulations of commerce, which the Constitution says shall only be done by the Congress of the United States.

During the session of the Supreme Court which ended in May last[1] no less than four or five decisions of the highest importance were rendered, declaring statutes of as many different States to be void, because they were forbidden by this provision of the Federal Constitution.

We need not here pursue the detailed history of the ratification and adoption of the Constitution by the States. The instrument itself, and the resolution of Congress submitting it to the

---

[1] October Term, 1886. 118 U. S.–122 U. S.

LECTURE I.
The Constitution
accepted.

States, both provided that it should go into operation when adopted by nine States. Eleven of them accepted it in their first action in the matter. North Carolina delayed a short time, and Rhode Island two years later changed her mind; and thus the thirteen States which had united in the struggle for independence became a nation under this form of government.

And transmitted
to Congress.

Let us consider now the task which the convention undertook to perform, the difficulties which lay in its way, and the success which attended its efforts. In submitting to Congress the result of their labors, the convention accompanied the instrument with a letter signed under its authority by its president, and addressed to the President of Congress. Perhaps no public document of the times so short, yet so important, is better worth consideration than this letter, dated September 17, 1787. From it I must beg your indulgence to read the following extracts : —

"SIR : — We now have the honor to submit to the consideration of the United States in Congress assembled that Constitution which has appeared to us the most advisable. The friends of our country have long seen and desired that the power of making war, peace, and treaties, that of levying money and regulating commerce, and the correspondent executive and judicial authorities, should be fully and effectually vested in the general government of the Union; but the impropriety of delegating such extensive trusts to one body of men" (meaning

Congress) "is evident. Hence results the necessity of a different organization. It is obviously
impracticable in the federal government of these
States to secure all the rights of independent
sovereignty to each, and yet provide for the
interests and safety of all." Again: —

"In all our deliberations on this subject we
kept steadily in view that which appears to us
the greatest interest of every true American,
— *the consolidation of our Union,* in which is
involved our prosperity, felicity, safety, perhaps
our national existence. This important consideration, seriously and deeply impressed on our
minds, led each State in the convention to be
less rigid on points of inferior magnitude than
might otherwise be expected; and thus the Constitution which we now present is the result of
a spirit of amity, and of that natural deference
and concession which the peculiarity of our political situation rendered indispensable."

The instrument framed under the influence of
these principles is introduced by language very
similar. The opening sentence reads: "We,
the people of the United States, in order to form
a more perfect union, establish justice, insure
domestic tranquillity, provide for the common
defence, promote the general welfare, and secure
the blessings of liberty to ourselves and our posterity, do ordain and establish this Constitution
for the United States of America."

This Constitution has been tested by the
experience of a century of its operation, and
in the light of this experience it may be well

to consider its value. Many of its most important features met with earnest and vigorous
opposition. This opposition was shown in the
convention which presented it, and the conventions of the States called to ratify it. In both,
the struggle in its favor was arduous and doubtful, the opposition able and active.

Perhaps the wisdom of this great instrument
cannot be better seen than by reconsidering at
this time some of the most important objections
then made to it. One of these which caused the
opposition of several delegates in the Constitutional Convention, and their refusal to sign it,
was the want of a well-defined bill of rights.
The royal charters of many of the colonies, and
the constitutions adopted by several States after
the revolt, had such declarations, mainly assertions of personal rights and of propositions intended to give security to the individual in his
right of person and property against the exercise of authority by governing bodies of the
State. The Constitution was not void of such
protection. It provided for the great writ of
habeas corpus, the means by which all unlawful
imprisonments and restraints upon personal liberty had been removed in the English and
American courts since Magna Charta was proclaimed; and it declared that the privilege of
that writ should not be suspended, unless in
cases of rebellion or invasion the public safety
should require it. The Constitution also declared that no *ex post facto* law or bill of
attainder should be passed by Congress; and

no law impairing the obligation of contracts by any State. It secured the trial by jury of all crimes within the State where the offence was committed. It defined treason so as to require some overt act, which must be proved by two witnesses, or confessed in open court, for con- viction.

It can hardly be said that experience has demonstrated the sufficiency of these for the purpose which the advocates of a bill of rights had in view, because, upon the recommendation of several of the States made in the act of rati- fying the Constitution, or by legislatures at their first meeting subsequently, twelve amendments were proposed by Congress, ten of which were immediately ratified by the requisite number of States, and became part of the Constitution within two or three years of its adoption.

In the presentation and ratification of these amendments, the advocates of a specific bill of rights, and those who were dissatisfied with the strong power conferred on the Federal Govern- ment, united ; and many statesmen who leaned to a strong government for the nation were will- ing, now that the Government was established, to win to its favor those who distrusted it by the adoption of these amendments. Hence a very slight examination of them shows that all of them are restrictions upon the power of the General Government, or upon the modes of exercising that power, or declarations of the powers remaining with the States and with the people. They establish certain private rights of

persons and property which the General Government may not violate. As regards these last,
it is not believed that any acts of intentional
oppression by the Government of the United
States have called for serious reprehension; but,
on the contrary, history points us to no government in which the freedom of the citizen and
the rights of property have been better protected
and life and liberty more firmly secured.

As regards the question of the relative distribution of the powers necessary to organized
society, between the Federal and State governments, more will be said hereafter.

As soon as it became apparent to the convention that the new government must be a
nation, resting for its support upon the people
over whom it exercised authority, and not a
league of independent States, brought together
under a compact on which each State should
place its own construction, the question•of .the
relative power of those States in the new government became a subject of serious difference.
There were those in the convention who insisted
that in the legislative body, where the most
important powers must necessarily reside, the
States should, as in the Articles of Confederation,
stand upon a perfect equality, each State having but one vote; and this feature was finally
retained in that part of the Constitution which
vested in Congress the election of the President,
when there should be a failure to elect by the
electoral college in the regular mode prescribed
by that instrument. The contest in the conven-

tion became narrowed to the composition of the
Senate, after it had been determined that the
legislature should consist of two distinct bodies,
sitting apart from each other, and voting separately. One of these was to be a popular body,
elected directly by the people at short intervals.
The other was to be a body more limited in
numbers, with longer terms of office; and this,
with the manner of their appointment, was
designed to give stability to the policy of the
Government, and to be in some sense a restraint
upon sudden impulses of popular will.

With regard to the popular branch of the
legislature, there did not seem to be much difficulty in establishing the proposition, that in
some general way each State should be represented in it in proportion to its population, and
that each member of the body should vote with
equal effect on all questions before it. But
when it was sought by the larger and more
populous States, as Virginia, Pennsylvania, and
Massachusetts, to apply this principle to the
composition of the Senate, the resistance of the
smaller States became stubborn, and they refused
to yield. The feeling arising under the discussion of this subject came nearer causing the
disruption of the convention than any which
agitated its deliberations. It was finally settled
by an agreement that every State, however small,
should have two representatives in the Senate of
the United States, and no State should have any
more; and that no amendment of the Constitution should deprive any State of its equal suf-

frage in the Senate without its consent. As the Senate has the same power in enacting laws as the House of Representatives, and as each State has its two votes in that body, it will be seen that the smaller States secured, when they are in a united majority, the practical power of defeating all legislation which was unacceptable to them.

What has the experience of a century taught us on this question? It is certainly true that there have been many expressions of dissatisfaction with the operation of a principle which gives to each of the six New England States, situated compactly together, as much power in the Senate in making laws, in ratifying treaties, and in confirming or rejecting appointments to office, as is given to the great State of New York, which, both in population and wealth, exceeds all the New England States, and nearly if not quite equals them in territory.

But if we are to form an opinion from demonstrations against, or attempts to modify, this feature of the Constitution, or any feature which concerns exclusively the functions of the Senate, we shall be compelled to say that the ablest of our public men, and the wisdom of the nation, are in the main satisfied with the work of the convention on this point after a hundred years of observation. And it is believed that the existence of an important body in our system of government, not wholly the mere representative of population, has exercised a wholesome conservatism on many occasions in our history.

Another feature of the Constitution which
met with earnest opposition was the vesting of
the executive power in a single magistrate.
While Hamilton would have preferred a monarch, with strong restriction on his authority,
like that in England, he soon saw that even his
great influence could not carry the convention
with him. There were not a few members who
preferred in that matter the system of a single
body (as the Congress) in which should be
reposed all the power of the nation, or a council, or executive committee, appointed by that
body and responsible to it. There were others
who preferred an executive council of several
members, not owing its appointment to Congress.

It was urged against our Constitution by
many liberty-loving men, both in the convention
and out of it, that it conferred upon the executive, a single individual, whose election for a
term of four years was carefully removed from
the direct vote of the people, powers dangerous
to the existence of free government. It was
said that with the appointment of all the officers
of the Government, civil and military, the sword
and the purse of the nation in his hands, the
power to prevent the enactment of laws to
which he did not assent, — unless they could be
passed over his objection by a vote of two-thirds
in each of the two legislative houses, — and the
actual use of this power for four years without
interruption, an ambitious man, of great personal popularity, could establish his power dur-

ing his own life and transmit it to his family as a perpetual dynasty.

Perhaps of all objections made to important features of the Constitution this one had more plausibility, and was urged with most force. But if the century of our experience has demonstrated anything, it is the fallacy of this objection and of all the reasons urged in its support.

The objection that the electoral college was a contrivance to remove the appointment of the President from the control of popular suffrage, was, if it had any merit, speedily overcome without any infraction of the Constitution by the democratic tendencies of the people. The electors composing the college, who, it was supposed, would each exercise an independent judgment in casting his vote for President, soon came to be elected themselves on distinct pledges made beforehand, that they would vote for some person designated as a popular favorite for that office. So that at the present time the electors of each State, in sending to the capital their votes for President, do but record the instruction of a majority of the citizens voting in that State. The term of four years for the Presidential office is not now deemed too long by any one, while there are many who would desire that it should be made longer, say seven or ten years.

The power of appointment to office requires the consent of the Senate to its exercise; and that body has asserted its right of refusing that assent so courageously and so freely, that there can be no real fear of its successful use by the President in a manner to endanger the liberty of the country, unless the Senate itself shall be utterly corrupted. Nor can the means for such corruption be obtained from the public treasury, unless Congress in both branches shall become so degenerate as to consent to such use.

Nor have we had in this country any want of ambitious men, who have earnestly desired the Presidency, or, having it once, have longed for a continuation of it at the end of the lawful term. And it may be said that it is almost a custom when a President has filled his office for one term acceptably, that he is to be re-elected, if his political party continues to be a popular majority. Our people have also shown the usual hero-worship of successful military chieftains, and rewarded them by election to the Presidency. In proof of this it is only necessary to mention the names of Washington, Jackson, Harrison, Taylor, and Grant. In some of them there has been no want of ambition, nor of the domineering disposition, which is often engendered by the use of military power. Yet none of these men have had more than two terms of the office. And though a few years ago one of the most largely circulated newspapers of the United States wrote in its paper day after day articles headed "Cæsarism," charging danger to the republic from one of its greatest benefactors and military chiefs, it excited no attention but derision, and deserved no other.

There is no danger in this country from the power reposed in the Presidential office. There is, as sad experience shows, far, far more danger from nihilism and assassination, than from ambition in our public servants.

So far have the incumbents of the Presidency, during the hundred years of its history, been from grasping, or attempting to grasp, powers not warranted by the Constitution, and so far from exercising the admitted power of that office in a despotic manner, that a candid student of our political history during that time cannot fail to perceive that no one of the three great departments of the Government — the Legislative, the Executive, and the Judicial — has been more shorn of its just powers, or crippled in the exercise of them, than the Presidency.

In regard to the function of appointment to office, — perhaps the most important of the executive duties, — the spirit of the Constitution requires that the President shall exercise freely his best judgment and follow his most sincere conviction in selecting proper men.

It is undeniable that for many years past, by the gradual growth of custom, it has come to pass that in the nomination of officers by the President, he has so far submitted to be governed by the wishes and recommendations of interested members of the two Houses of Congress, that the purpose of the Constitution in vesting this power in him, and the right of the public to hold him personally responsible for each and every appointment he makes, are largely defeated. In

other words, the great principle lying at the
foundation of all free governments, that the legislative and executive departments shall be kept
separate, is invaded by the participation of
members of Congress in the exercise of the
appointing power.

History teaches us in no mistaken language
how often customs and practices, which were
originated without lawful warrant and opposed
to the sound construction of the law, have come
to overload and pervert it; as commentators on
the text of Holy Scripture have established doctrines wholly at variance with its true spirit.

Without considering many minor objections
made to the Constitution during the process of
its formation and adoption, let us proceed to
that one which was the central point of contest
then, and which, transferred to the question of
construing that instrument, has continued to
divide statesmen and politicians to the present
time.

The convention was divided in opinion between
those who desired a strong national government,
capable of sustaining itself by the exercise of
suitable powers, and invested by the Constitution with such powers, and those who, regarding
'the Articles of Confederation as a basis, proposed
to strengthen the General Government in a very
few particulars, leaving it chiefly dependent on
the action of the States themselves for its support and for the enforcement of its laws.

Let us deal tenderly with the Articles of Confederation. We should here, on this glorious

LECTURE I.   : anniversary, feel grateful for any instrumentality
Weakness of the
Articles of   which helped us in the days of our earliest strug-
Confederation. (gle.   Very few are now found to say anything
for these Articles, yet they constituted the nom-
inal bond which held the States together during
the war of independence.   It must be confessed
that the sense of a common cause and a common
danger probably did more to produce this united
effort than any other motives.   But the Articles served their purpose for the occasion; and
though, when the pressure of imminent danger
was removed, they were soon discovered to be a
rope of sand, let them rest in a peaceful, honorable remembrance.

Federal and State-   Between those who favored a strong govern-
Right principles
of Construction. ment of the Union and those who were willing
to grant it but little power at the expense of the
States, there were various shades of opinion;
and while it was the prevailing sentiment of the
convention that "the greatest interest of every
true American was the consolidation of the
Union," there were many who were unwilling
to attain this object by detaching the necessary
powers from the States and conferring them on
the National Government.

These divergent views had their effect, both
in the constitutional convention and in those
held for its ratification.   Around this central
point the contention raged, and it was only by
compromises and concessions, dictated by the
necessity of each yielding something for the
common good, — so touchingly mentioned in
the letter of the convention to Congress, — that

the result was finally reached.   The patriotism
and the love of liberty of each party were undis-
puted.   The anxiety for a government which
would best reconcile the possession of powers
essential to the State governments with those
necessary to the existence and efficiency of the
government of the Union, was equal; and the
long struggle since the adoption of the Constitution, on the same line of thought, in its construction, shows how firmly these different views
were imbedded in our political theories.

The party which came to be called the party
of State's Rights has always dreaded that the
alleged supremacy of the national power would
overthrow the State governments, or control
them to an extent incompatible with any useful
existence.   Their opponents have been equally
confident that powers essential to the successful
conduct of the General Government, which either
expressly or by implication are conferred on it
by the Constitution, were denied to it by the
principles of the State's Right party.   The one
believed in danger to the States, from the theory
which construed with a free and liberal rule the
grants of power to the General Government, and
the other believed that such a construction of
the Constitution was consistent with the purpose
and spirit of that instrument, and essential to
the perpetuity of the nation.

If experience can teach anything on the subject of theories of government, the late civil war
teaches unmistakably that those who believed
the source of danger to be in the strong powers

of the Federal Government were in error, and that those who believed that such powers were necessary to its safe conduct and continued existence were in the right. The attempted destruction of the Union by eleven States, which were part of it, and the apparent temporary success of the effort, were undoubtedly due to the capacity of the States under the Constitution for concerted action, by organized movements, with all the machinery ready at hand to raise armies and establish a central government. And the ultimate failure of the attempt is to be attributed with equal clearness to the exercise of those powers of the General Government, under the Constitution, which were denied to it by extreme advocates of State Rights. And that this might no longer be matter of dispute, three new amendments to the Constitution were adopted at the close of that struggle, which, while keeping in view the principles of our complex form of State and Federal government, and seeking to disturb the distribution of powers among them as little as was consistent with the wisdom acquired by a sorrowful experience, confer additional powers on the government of the Union, and place additional restraints upon those of the States. May it be long before such an awful lesson is again needed to decide upon disputed questions of constitutional law.

It is not out of place to remark that, while the pendulum of public opinion has swung with much force away from the extreme point of State's Right doctrine, there may be danger of

·its reaching an extreme point on the other side.
In my opinion, the just and equal observance of
the rights of the States, and of the General Government, as defined by the present Constitution,
is as necessary to the permanent prosperity of
our country, and to its existence for another
century, as it has been for the one whose close
we are now celebrating.

Having considered the objections originally
made to this great work, in the light of its operation for a century, what shall we say of it in
regard to those great features which were more
generally acceptable ? The doctrine of Montesquieu, then in the height of his influence, that
the powers essential to all governments should be
distributed among three separate bodies of magistracy, — namely, legislative, executive, and judicial,—was, as Madison affirms in number XLVII
of the *Federalist*, recognized by the convention
as the foundation of its labors. The apparent
departure from that principle in making the
Senate a participant in the exercise of the appointing power, and the treaty-making power,
works well, because the initiative remains with
the Executive. The power of that body to try
impeachments of public officers for high crimes
and misdemeanors, a function essentially judicial, while it has not produced any substantial
injury, has, perhaps, operated as a safety-valve
in cases of great popular excitement. As an
efficient remedy, it must be conceded to be a
failure.

But the harmony and success with which the

LECTURE I.
Division of
powers into legis-
lative, executive,
and judicial.
three great subdivisions of the organized government of the Constitution have co-operated in the
growth, prosperity, and happiness of this great
people, constitute the strongest argument in favor
of the organic law, which governs them all. It
is the first successful attempt, in the history of
the world, to lay the deep and broad foundations
of a government for millions of people and an
unlimited territory, in a single written instrument, framed and adopted in one great national
effort.

This instrument comes nearer than any of
political origin to Rousseau's idea of a society
founded on social contract. In its formation,
States and individuals, in the possession of equal
rights, — the rights of human nature common
to all, — met together and deliberately agreed to
give up certain of those rights to government
for the better security of others; and that there
might be no mistake about this agreement it was
reduced to writing, with all the solemnities which
give sanction to the pledges of mankind.

Other nations speak of their constitutions,
which are the growth of centuries of government, and the maxims of experience, and the
traditions of ages. Many of them deserve the
veneration which they receive; but a constitution, in the American sense of the word, as
accepted in all the States of North and South
America, means an instrument in writing, defining the powers of government, and distributing
those powers among different bodies of magistrates for their more judicious exercise. The

Constitution of the United States not only did this as regards a national government, but it established a federation of many States by the same instrument, in which the usual fatal defects in such unions have been corrected with such felicity, that during the hundred years of its existence the union of the States has grown stronger, and has received within that Union other States exceeding in number those of the original federation.

It is not only the first important written constitution found in history, but it is the first one which contained the principles necessary to the successful confederation of numerous powerful States. I do not forget, nor do I mean to disparage, our sister, the federal republic of Switzerland: but her continuance as an independent power in Europe is so largely due to her compact territory, her inaccessible mountains, her knowledge of the necessity of union to safety, and the policy of her powerful neighbors which demands of each other the recognition of her rights, that she hardly forms an exception. Switzerland stands to-day — so may she ever stand — as the oldest witness to the capacity of a republican federation of States for sound government, for the security of freedom, and resistance to disintegrating tendencies. When we consider the results of confederation in the Olympic Council, and the Achaian League of ancient history, and in modern times in the States of Holland and the old German Empire, we must admit that the United States

Lecture I. Division of powers into legislative, executive, and judicial.

The success of the new form of government.

LECTURE I.
The success of the
new form of
government. present the most remarkable, if not the only successful, happy, and prosperous, federated government of the world.

Let us consider for a moment the evidence of
this. When the Constitution was finally ratified,
and Rhode Island also accepted it, the Government was composed of thirteen States. It now
numbers thirty-eight. The inhabited area of
those States was found between the Allegheny
Mountains and the Atlantic Ocean, a region
which, when we now look over a map of the
United States, seems to be but the eastern bor-
der of the great republic. Its area now includes
all the territory between the Atlantic and Pacific
Oceans,— a distance of over three thousand
miles east and west, — and between the St.
Lawrence and the Great Lakes on the north and
the Gulf and States of Mexico on the south.
Besides these thirty-eight States, the remainder
of this immense region is divided into eight
Territories, with an organized government in
each, several of which are ready to be admitted
into the Union as States, under a provision of
the Constitution on that subject, and in accordance with the settled policy of the nation.

The thirteen States which originally organized
this Government had a population believed to
be, in round numbers, three millions, many of
whom were slaves. To-day it seems probable
that sixty millions are embraced in the United
States, in which there breathes no soul who owns
any man master.

I have already suggested the impoverished

condition of the country at the close of the Revolutionary war.   To-day I do not hesitate to
make the assertion, that if you count only that
which is real wealth, and not accumulated capital in the shape of evidences of debt, — which
is but a burden upon such property, — I mean,
if you count lands and houses and furniture, and
horses and cattle and jewels, — all that is tangi-
ble and contributes to the comfort and pleasure
of life, — the United States to-day is the wealth-
iest country upon the face of the globe, and is
the only great government which is so rapidly
paying off its national debt that it is begging
its creditors to accept their money not yet due,
with a reasonable rebate for interest.

Under the Government established by this
Constitution we have, in the century which we
are now overlooking, had three important wars,
such as are always accompanied by hazardous
shocks to all governments.   In the first of these
we encountered the British Empire, the most
powerful nation then on the globe, — a nation
which had successfully resisted Napoleon, with
all the power of Europe at his back.   If we did
not attain all we fought for in that contest, we
displayed an energy and courage which commanded for us an honorable stand among the
nations of the earth.

In the second, — the war with Mexico, — while
our reputation as a warlike people suffered no
diminution, we made large accessions of valuable
territory, out of which States have been since
made members of the Union.

The last war, — the recent civil war, — in the number of men engaged in it, in the capacity of the weapons and instruments of destruction brought into operation, and in the importance of the result to humanity at large, must be esteemed the greatest war that the history of the world presents. It was brought about by the attempt of eleven of the States to destroy the Union. This was resisted by the Government of that Union under the powers granted to it by the Constitution. Its results were the emancipation of three millions of slaves, the suppression of the attempt to dissever the Union, the resumption of an accelerated march in the growth, prosperity, and happiness of this country. It also taught the lesson of the indestructibility of the Union, of the wisdom of the principles on which it is founded, and it astonished the nations of the world and inspired them with a respect which they had never before entertained for our country.

I venture to hope that, with the earnest gaze of the wisest and ablest minds of the age turned with profound interest to the experiment of the federative system, under our American Constitution, it may suggest something to relieve the nations of Europe from burdens so heavy that if not soon removed they must crush the social fabric. Those great nations cannot go on forever adding millions upon millions to their public debts, mainly for the support of permanent standing armies, while those armies make such heavy drafts upon the able-bodied men whose productive industry is necessary to the support of the people and of the government.

I need not dwell on this unpleasant subject further than to say that these standing armies are rendered necessary by the perpetual dread of war with neighboring nations.

In the principles of our Constitution by which the autonomy and domestic government of each State are preserved, while the supremacy of the General Government at once forbids wars between the States, and enables it to enforce peace among them, we may discern the elements of political forces sufficient for the rescue of European civilization from this great disaster.

Do I claim for the Constitution, whose creation we celebrate to-day, the sole merit of the wonderful epitome which I have presented to you of the progress of this country to greatness, to prosperity, to happiness, and to honor? Nay, I do not; though language used by men of powerful intellect and great knowledge of history might be my justification if I did.

Mr. Bancroft, the venerable historian, who has devoted a long and laborious life to a history of his country that is a monument to his genius and his learning, says of the closing hours of the convention: "The members were awe-struck at the result of their counsels; the Constitution was a nobler work than any one of them believed possible to devise." And he prefaces the volume of his invaluable history of the formation of the Constitution with a sentiment of Mr. Gladstone, the greatest living statesman of England, who said : " As the British constitution is the most subtle organism which has proceeded from progressive history, so the American Constitution is the most wonderful work ever struck off at a given time by the brain and purpose of man."

And while I heartily indorse this, and feel it impossible to find language in which to express my admiration and my love for the Constitution of the United States, and my profound belief that the wisdom of man, unaided by inspiration, has produced no writing so valuable to humanity, I should fail of a most important duty if I did not say on this public occasion, that no amount of wisdom in a constitution can produce wise government, unless there is a suitable response in the spirit of the people.

The Anglo-Saxon race, from whom we inherit so much that is valuable in our character, as well as our institutions, has been remarkable in all its history for a love of law and order. While other peoples, equally cultivated, have paid their devotion to the man in power, as representative of the law which he enforces, the English people, and we their descendants, have venerated the law itself, looking past its administrators, and giving our allegiance and our obedience to the principles which govern organized society. It has been said that a dozen Englishmen or Americans, thrown on an uninhabited island, would at once proceed to adopt a code of laws for their government, and elect the officers who were to enforce them. And certainly this proposition

is borne out by the early history of our emi-
grants to California, where every mining camp organized into a political body, and made laws for its own government, which were so good that Congress adopted them until they should be repealed or modified by statute.

I but repeat the language of the Supreme Court of the United States when I say that in this country the law is supreme. No man is so high as to be above the law. No officer of the Government may disregard it with impunity. To this inborn and native regard for law, as a governing power, we are indebted largely for the wonderful success and prosperity of our people, for the security of our rights; and when the highest law to which we pay this homage is the Constitution of the United States, the history of the world has presented no such wonder of a prosperous, happy civil government.

Let me urge upon my fellow-countrymen, and especially upon the rising generation of them, to examine with careful scrutiny all new theories of government and of social life, and if they do not rest upon a foundation of veneration and respect for law as the bond of social existence, let them be distrusted as inimical to human happiness.

And now let me close this address with a quotation from one of the ablest jurists and most profound commentators upon our laws, — Chancellor Kent. He said, fifty years ago: "The Government of the United States was created by the free voice and joint will of the people of

America for their common defence and general welfare. Its powers apply to those great interests which relate to this country in its national capacity, and which depend for their stability and protection on the consolidation of the Union. It is clothed with the principal attributes of sovereignty, and it is justly deemed the guardian of our best rights, the source of our highest civil and political duties, and the sure means of our national greatness."

NOTES UPON LECTURE I.

———◦✦◦———

THE Constitution of the United States, like
all systems of government which are permanent,
had its origin in the history and necessities of
the people through whose instrumentality and
for whose benefit it was formed. Driven by
those necessities, the people of the United Colonies assumed and exercised the national powers
of a federative government, before any written
charter was made. The very Act of Separation
assumes this fact. It is not the Declaration of
thirteen individual States, but of "the Representatives of the United States of America, in
General Congress assembled."

In Colonial days more than one effort had
been made to secure a local union of Colonies in
different parts of the country. These doubtless
contributed more or less to the desire for unity
and nationality which eventually found expression in the Constitution.[1]

In 1765 an American Congress assembled at
New York, but it was a deliberative body only,
with no governmental functions, and no powers,
executive or legislative. On the 5th of Sep-

---

[1] Bancroft's History of the United States. Last Revision, vol. 1,
pp. 291, 292; 2 Ib. pp. 74, 75; 6 Ib. pp. 7, 8.

tember, 1774, the first Continental Congress met in Philadelphia. When it adjourned it provided for a second Congress to meet in Philadelphia in the following May. Before that time arrived the battles of Lexington and Concord had taken place.

The Congress of 1775 exercises National powers.   This outbreak of a state of war found in each Colony or Province an organized government with separate functions, exercising a limited sovereignty under the king of Great Britain. Many of the broader powers and functions of National Sovereignty, which the Constitution now places in the government of the United States, then resided in the British king and Parliament. When British sovereignty fell, such powers were assumed and exercised, without question, by the Congress of the United Colonies, before the United States existed as an independent nation; months before the Articles of Confederation were agreed to; years before they became operative by receiving the assent of all the States. They were never enjoyed or exercised by the States separately; and consequently, as an historic fact, independently of theory, they could not have been retained when the States conferred upon the general Government other enumerated powers in the Articles of Confederation.

The United States becomes a nation.   Unconsciously to themselves the people of the United States were absorbed into a new nationality by the very fact of their combined resistance to Great Britain. They carried on war; they officered and maintained armies; they

commissioned vessels of war; they borrowed
money and issued evidences of debt therefor; they created prize courts; they acquired territory and determined what the nature of its civilization should be; they made treaties with foreign powers; and in many ways, both before and after the adoption of the Articles of Confederation, they exercised the highest powers of sovereignty.

This Congress was both the Executive and the Legislature of the Nation. It was the body which framed the Articles of Confederation, and many of its members were also in the Convention which framed the Constitution of the United States. Unless that Constitution is to be construed theoretically, and without regard to the incidents of the national history of which it was the outcome, a knowledge of what that Congress did, derived from historical investigation, must help us in comprehending what sort of a government the framers of the Constitution intended to establish. To cover this whole ground would be to write the legislative history of those eventful fourteen years. I select from all its legislation three subjects: 1, The Appellate Prize Courts; 2, The Treaties negotiated with Foreign Powers; 3, The acquisition of the territory to the northwest of the Ohio, and the exclusion of slavery from it.

1. *Appellate Prize Courts of the Revolution.*

Soon after hostilities began, representatives
of the United Colonies assembled together in

Philadelphia with the purpose of consulting and legislating for the common good. Union existed, though without written charter, and with no means of preventing dissolution. The first object of the Continental Congress, after the battles of Lexington and Concord, was to put a force in the field which would enable the commander-in-chief to hold the enemy in check. But it was soon discovered, in practice, that there was another element in the contest for which no provision, adequate or otherwise, had been made, and which Congress had, perhaps, not taken into consideration.

The people living in the eastern part of Massachusetts, which was then the theatre of war, were to a large extent sailors or fishermen; or in some other way they got their living or their recreation out of maritime pursuits. The commerce of Boston, Providence, New York, and other ports was carried on under the British flag, with British money, to transport British goods. This was an invitation to a maritime people to engage in a maritime war against the enemy's commerce. The invitation was immediately accepted.

Vessels, captured from time to time, were brought into such Massachusetts ports as were not in the enemy's possession; but it was found that no court existed with competent jurisdiction to adjudge them to be lawful prize. The admiralty colonial courts, such as they were, existed under authority derived from a royal commission. This was, of course, not available to the seamen of Massachusetts in the summer of 1775.[1]

To meet this emergency, the Council and House of Representatives of the Province of Massachusetts Bay, on the 1st of November, 1775, enacted a statute which is said to be " remarkable as having been the first which was passed by any of the Colonies for fitting out vessels of marque and reprisal, and for establishing a court to try and condemn the captured vessels of the enemy." [2] The act divided the State into three districts, in each of which it established a Maritime Court, with jurisdiction over prizes, but differing from the Admiralty Court known in International Law, by permitting the facts to be found by a jury.[3] Boston, being occupied by the enemy, was not included in this division; but when the enemy retired, the districts were reorganized, and an appeal was given to the Continental Congress in cases

LECTURE I.
Colonial
Admiralty
Courts.
Massachusetts
Admiralty
Courts.

---

[1] " In each one of the royal colonies in America, as in each of the other colonies of Great Britain, the commission issued to the royal governor usually invested him with the powers of a vice-admiral. . . . Cases of capture arising in the Colonies had naturally gone to these courts. But the vice-admiralty courts were rapidly destroyed by the Revolution. Where the governor had acted as judge, he was now in flight. . . . Nor could judges sit by virtue of commissions from King George to give judgment respecting prizes captured from him. The vice-admiralty courts continued in existence in those places only which were occupied by royal forces." — *The Predecessor of the Supreme Court*, by J. F. Jameson, Ph.D., being Essay 1 in *Essays in the Constitutional History of the United States in the Formative Period*, p. 5, edited by Professor Jameson.

[2] 3 Sparks' Washington, 154, n.

[3] Act of November 1, 1775. Acts and Resolutions of the Province of Massachusetts Bay, vol. 5, p. 436.

LECTURE I.
Massachusetts
Admiralty
Courts.
of vessels fitted out at the charge of the United Colonies.

This act apparently came at once into the hands of General Washington. On the 11th day of the same November in which it was enacted, he sent a copy of it to the President of Congress, and suggested that such a court should "be established by authority of Congress, to take cognizance of prizes made by the Continental vessels," adding, "whatever the mode is which they are pleased to adopt, there is an absolute necessity of its being speedily determined on."

Action of
Washington.

Congress becomes
an Appellate
Court in Prize
Cases.
This letter was, on its receipt, referred to a committee, who on the 23d of the same November, brought in their report. After a debate running over parts of the following two days, a series of resolutions, appended to the report, was adopted and passed. These resolutions authorized the capture of prizes on the high seas; legalized those already made; settled a rate of distribution of prize money (a settlement which was afterwards modified); provided that suits for condemnation should be commenced in the first instance in Colonial Courts, and, further, contained the following section respecting appeals:

"6. That in all cases an appeal shall be allowed to the Congress, or such person or persons as they shall appoint for the trial of appeals, provided the appeal be demanded within five days after definitive sentence, and such appeal be lodged with the Secretary of Congress within

forty days afterwards, and provided the party LECTURE I.
appealing shall give security to prosecute the Congress becomes an Appellate
said appeal to effect ; and in case of the death of Court in Prize
the Secretary during the recess of Congress, then Cases.
the said appeal to be lodged in Congress within
twenty days after the meeting thereof."

When Washington learned of this action, he
wrote to the President of Congress: "The re-
solves relating to captures made by Continental
armed vessels only want a court established for
trial to make them complete. This, I hope, will
soon be done, as I have taken the liberty to urge
it often to the Congress."

This suggestion of Congress was responded to The Colonies
sooner or later by all the Colonies and States confer Appellate Prize Jurisdiction
except New York, whose maritime counties were on Congress.
in the possession of the enemy from the autumn
of 1776 until the close of the war. A detailed
account of this legislation will be found in the
Appendix to Volume 131 of the United States
Reports. It is sufficient here to say that all
the States except New York created prize
courts, and gave an appellate jurisdiction to
Congress from their judgments ; but in nearly
or quite every one, provision was made for a
trial of the facts by a jury, from which great
trouble arose, as we shall see hereafter.

The State Courts, organized under these sev- Decisions of the
eral statutes, evidently had plenty to do. Of their Appellate Prize Courts.
decisions one hundred and nine were reviewed
in the appellate tribunals created by Congress.
The origin of two of these cases is not known.
Three came from New Hampshire ; twenty-six

from Massachusetts; ten from Rhode Island; sixteen from Connecticut; fourteen from New Jersey; eleven from Pennsylvania; five from Delaware; four from Maryland; two from Virginia; twelve from North Carolina; two from South Carolina; and two from Georgia. The first appeal was decided September 9, 1776; the last judgment was rendered May 3, 1787.

Some applications were made to Congress to take original jurisdiction in such cases; but with one exception it refused. Its appellate jurisdiction was exercised at first through special committees, and, later, by a general committee, who soon came to be styled Commissioners. This committee was constantly changing its members, so that it was rarely that two cases were heard by the same committee.

The Articles of Confederation were moving along side by side with these proceedings. They were adopted in November, 1777, and by May 5, 1779, had received the assent of all the States except Maryland, which wisely held back to secure that settlement of the public lands which was eventually made. That State gave its assent in March, 1781.

Before such consent was given a question arose which showed how important it was that a court of appeals in prize cases should be established on a proper basis.

An armed vessel, commissioned by the State of Pennsylvania, captured on the high seas a vessel called the Active, sailing from Jamaica to New York; took it into Philadelphia; and caused it to be libelled in the State Court of Admiralty there. A trial was had by jury, whose verdict was as follows: "One fourth of the net proceeds of the sloop Active and her cargo to the first claimants; three fourths of the net proceeds of the said sloop and her cargo to the libellant and the second claimant as per agreement between them." Judgment was entered on the verdict, from which an appeal was taken to the Commissioners.

The Commissioners, after hearing, reversed the judgment, and directed the court below to issue process commanding the marshal to sell the sloop and her cargo, and to pay the residue remaining after payment of costs, charges, and expenses to the appellants.

The judge of the State Court of Admiralty declined to execute this mandate, on the ground that, under the Pennsylvania Statute creating the court, the jury were to pass upon the facts, and that the reversal above, being a reversal of their verdict, was beyond the competence of the court. Thereupon General Benedict Arnold, who was in command in Philadelphia, wrote to the Commissioners of Appeal that the judge below was "about getting possession of the money with the avowed and declared purpose of standing out obstinately against any orders that may be given. He has issued his orders to the marshal to deliver the amount of sales to him, which is to be done by appointment at nine o'clock to-morrow morning, and posi-

tively declares that no order of the Court of
Appeals shall take it out of his hands or be
obeyed." He added : " Such a daring attempt as
this to evade the justice of the Superior Court,
at a time too when the matter is under consideration, will, I doubt not, apologize for my
troubling you with a request to meet this evening at such time and place as you may think
proper in order to determine upon what process
shall issue at so early an hour to-morrow morning as will tend to the carrying into execution
the decree above."

The Commissioners met, as suggested, and
issued the proposed injunction which was served
on the marshal early on the morning of January
4, while the money was still in his possession ;
but he deposited it in the court below notwithstanding the injunction, and so made return.
The Commissioners, " being unwilling to enter
upon any proceedings for contempt, lest consequences might ensue at this juncture dangerous
to the public peace of the United States," laid
the matter before Congress, which passed the
following resolutions : —

" *Resolved,* That Congress, or such person or
persons as they appoint to hear and determine
appeals from the Courts of Admiralty, have
necessarily the power to examine as well into
decisions on facts as decisions on the law, and
to decree finally thereon, and that no finding of
a jury in any court of admiralty, or court for
determining the legality of captures on the high
seas, can or ought to destroy the right of appeal

and the reëxamination of the facts reserved to
Congress :

" That no act of any one State can or ought
to destroy the right of appeal to Congress in the
sense above declared :

" That Congress is by these United States
invested with the supreme sovereign power of
war and peace :

" That the power of executing the law of
nations is essential to the sovereign supreme
power of war and peace :

" That the legality of all captures on the high
seas must be determined by the law of nations :

" That the authority ultimately and finally to
decide in all matters and questions touching the
law of nations does reside and is vested in the
sovereign supreme power of war and peace :

" That a control by appeal is necessary in order
to compel a just and uniform execution of the
law of nations:

" That the said control must extend as well
over the decisions of juries as judges in courts
for determining the legality of captures on the
sea; otherwise the juries would be possessed of
the ultimate supreme power of executing the
law of nations in all cases of captures, and
might at any time exercise the same in such
manner as to prevent a possibility of being controlled; a construction which involves many
inconveniences and absurdities, destroys an essential part of the power of war and peace
entrusted to Congress, and would disable the
Congress of the United States from giving

satisfaction to foreign nations complaining of a violation of neutralities, of treaties, or other breaches of the law of nations, and would enable a jury in any one State to involve the United States in hostilities; a construction which for these and many other reasons is inadmissible:

"That this power of controlling by appeal the several admiralty jurisdictions of the States has hitherto been .exercised by Congress by the medium of a committee of their own members: .

"*Resolved*, That the committee before whom was determined the appeal from the Court of Admiralty for the State of Pennsylvania, in the case of the sloop Active, was duly constituted and authorized to determine the same."

This disposed of the case, so far as Congress was concerned. It had a subsequent history, however, which is related in the foot-note.[1]

---

[1] After the payment of the money into court, the marshal, by direction of the court, paid it to the Treasurer of the State, he giving a bond of indemnity to the judge. The State neglecting or declining to indemnify the Treasurer, that officer kept possession of it until his death. It was invested in loan office certificates which, after his death, passed to his personal representatives. The owners under the decree of the Congressional Court brought suit in admiralty, after the Constitution came into force, against these representatives. The District Court adjudged that the libellants were entitled to the certificates, with the interest upon them which had been collected. The State of Pennsylvania then set up title to the certificates. In a statute, the preamble to which set up this title and set forth the Eleventh Amendment to the Constitution, and that the suit was in reality one against the State, it was enacted that the executors should pay the money into the State Treasury, and that the Governor should take such steps as he might deem necessary to protect the rights of the State. The District Judge under these circumstances declined to issue process to enforce the decree in favor of the claimants. They applied to the Supreme Court of the United States for a writ of mandamus.

Notwithstanding its action in this case, it
was not until January 15th, 1780, that Congress resolved " that a court be established for
the trial of all appeals from the Courts of
Admiralty in these United States, in cases of
capture, to consist of three judges appointed
and commissioned by Congress, either two of
whom, in the absence of the other, to hold the
said court for the despatch of business; that
the said court appoint their own register; that
the trials therein be according to the usage of
nations, and not by jury;" and "that the said
judges hold their first session as soon as may
be at Philadelphia, and afterwards at such times
and places as they shall judge most conducive
to the public good, so that they do not at any
time sit further eastward than Hartford in
Connecticut, or southward than Williamsburg
in Virginia."

On the 24th day of the following May Congress gave to this court the name of the Court
of Appeals in Cases of Capture; and after that
time, no appeal that had been properly taken
in a State Court, reached the Appellate Court
through the action of Congress.   That body
acted in a few cases, but only to give the court

An alternative writ was issued, to which the judge made return,
setting out the material facts, and saying that, deeming it best not
to embroil the government of the United States with the State of
Pennsylvania, until the Supreme Court should have had an opportunity to pass upon the question, he had acted as he did in order
to enable it to do so. On the authority of *Penhallow* v. *Doane*, 3
Dall. 54, which will be referred to more particularly in the note
to Lecture II, *post*, the court ordered the District Court to enforce
its judgment. This was eventually done, after some difficulty.

a jurisdiction which it could not take under the general law.

In July, 1785, the war being over, Congress refused to continue to grant salaries to these judges. The next year it voted a *per diem* pay while on duty, together with travelling expenses. Thus the predecessor of the Supreme Court of the United States, called into existence by a great public necessity, sank away as the necessity diminished, and finally ceased to exist; and when, in a few years, the new Constitution was made, its framers, learning wisdom from the past, gave to the new Federal Judiciary not only an appellate, but an original and exclusive jurisdiction in Admiralty.

2. *Treaties negotiated by the Continental Congress.*

Congress prepares
a general form
for treaties of
amity and com-
merce.
Five days after the passage of the resolutions inviting the several Colonies to create Courts of Admiralty, and creating a Tribunal for Appeals in Prize Cases, Congress, on the 29th of November, 1775, took another step, in a different direction, which resulted in a still more marked assertion of a federal control over matters which up to that time had been entirely within local disposition. It appointed a " Committee of Secret Correspondence," to correspond with friends of the Colonies in other parts of the world, and to ascertain, if possible, " whether, if the colonies should be forced to form themselves into an independent State, France . . . would enter into any treaty of alliance with

them for commerce or defence, or both." This
resulted in the adoption by Congress, in Sep- Congress prepares a general form
tember following, of a plan for a treaty to be for treaties of
proposed to the King of France.[1] This plan amity and commerce.
contemplated that the Federal Government,
which for yet two years was to exist without
the adoption of any written Articles of Confederation by the States, should assume and
exercise the following important powers:—

    Article 1 provided that Frenchmen should General provis-
" pay no other duties or imposts in the ports " ions contained
of the United States " than the natives thereof," in that form.
and that they might enjoy all "the rights, liberties, privileges, immunities, and exemptions in
trade, navigation, and commerce, in passing
from one part thereof to another, and in going
to and from the same, from and to any part of
the world," which the natives enjoyed. This
proposed surrender to the Federal Government
by the States of their right of control in this
respect was practically carried into effect in the
Treaty of Commerce of 1778 with France (Art.
III);[2] in the Treaty of 1782 with Netherlands
(Art. II);[3] in the Treaty of 1783 with Sweden
(Art. III);[4] and in the Treaty of 1785 with
Prussia (Art. II).[5]

    By Article 5 of the plan the United States
were to engage to protect and defend all vessels
and effects belonging to French subjects, and
to endeavor to recover and restore them, if
taken within the jurisdiction of the United

---

[1] 2 Secret Journals of Congress: Foreign Affairs, 7.
[2] 8 Stat. 14.   [3] 8 Stat. 32.   [4] 8 Stat. 62.   [5] 8 Stat. 84.

LECTURE I.
General provis-
ions contained
in that form.
States or any of them. This provision is
found in Article VI of the Treaty of Commerce of 1778 with France;[1] in Article V of
the Treaty of 1782 with Netherlands;[2] and partially, in Article VII of the Treaty of 1785 with
Prussia.[3]

Droit d'aubaine.
The *droit d'aubaine*, a right claimed by most
sovereigns of that time to confiscate to their
own use the succession of an unnaturalized foreigner dying within their dominions, and which
Montesquieu styled "an absurd right,"[4] Congress, in its plan for a treaty, asked the king of
France to abandon. Article II of the Treaty
of Commerce of 1778,[5] as negotiated, complied
with this request, but accompanied it with a
declaration that Frenchmen should "enjoy on
their part, in all the dominions of the said
States, an entire and perfect reciprocity relative
to the stipulations contained in the present article." The Treaty of 1782 with the Netherlands (Art. VI[6]) gave, in the place of this
abandonment, the right to the Dutch foreigner
residing in the United States, to dispose of his
property there by testament, donation, or otherwise; the right to receive the succession *ab
intestato*, in case there was no will; and the
right for a guardian or tutor to a minor, to act
in his behalf in receiving, keeping, and alienating
his property. This precedent was followed in

---

[1] 8 Stat. 16.   [2] 8 Stat. 34.   [3] 8 Stat. 86.
[4] "Les droits insensés d'aubaine et de naufrage." Esprit des
Lois, xxi, 17.
[5] 8 Stat. 18.   [6] 8 Stat. 36.

the Treaty of 1783 with Sweden (Art. VI);[1] Lecture I.
and in the Treaty of 1785 with Prussia (Art X).[2] Droit d'aubaine.

In many other respects these several treaties, Other provisions
made before the adoption of the Constitution, in these treaties.
and largely upon the suggestions in the plan of
Congress which was promulgated before the
Articles of Confederation were adopted, secured
the assent of the contracting parties to important
principles, some of which were not then universally recognized as constituting part of the
public law which should govern the intercourse
of nations with each other.[3]

The evils of war were lessened by agreements
that, in case it should break out, time should be
given to the citizens of each, in the territories of
the other, to close their business and remove
their properties;[4] or that, should differences
arise, resort should not be had to force until a
friendly application should be made for an
arrangement.[5]

A restraint was imposed upon private war by
provisions forbidding the citizens of either Power
to accept commissions or letters of marque
from enemies of the other Power when at
war;[6] and the acceptance of such commissions

---

[1] 8 Stat. 64.   [2] 8 Stat. 88.

[3] See Treaties and Conventions between the United States and
other Powers, ed. 1889, p. 1221: introductory note.

[4] France, 1778, Art. 20, 8 Stat. 24; Netherlands, 1782, Art. 18,
8 Stat. 42; Sweden, 1783, Art. 22, 8 Stat. 72; Prussia, 1785, Art.
23, 8 Stat. 94.

[5] Morocco, 1787, Art. 24, 8 Stat. 104.

[6] France, 1778, Art. 21, 8 Stat. 24; Netherlands, 1782, Art. 19,
8 Stat. 44; Sweden, 1783, Art. 23, 8 Stat. 74; Prussia, 1785, Art.
20, 8 Stat. 94.

or letters was declared to be an act of piracy, which placed the offender beyond the claim of national protection.

The right of neutrals to carry on and maintain their commerce on the high seas in time of war was recognized.[1] Articles contraband of war were defined and limited;[2] and in the Treaty with Prussia it was even agreed that no articles should be so deemed contraband as to bring about confiscation and loss of property to individuals.[3] And it was further agreed that free ships should make free goods;[4] that neutral goods found in an enemy's ship should not be confiscated if they had been put aboard before the declaration of war, or within such short period thereafter that ignorance of a state of war might fairly be implied.[5]

Precise rules were laid down to be observed in visiting neutral vessels on the high seas,[6] and humane regulations were made respecting vessels on which articles contraband of war should be discovered.[7]

---

[1] France, 1778, Art. 23, 8 Stat. 24 ; Sweden, 1783, Art. 7, 8 Stat. 64 ; Prussia, 1785, Art. 12, 8 Stat. 90.

[2] France, 1778, Art. 24, 8 Stat. 26 ; Netherlands, 1782, Art. 24, 8 Stat. 46 ; Sweden, 1783, Arts. 9, 10, 8 Stat. 64, 66.

[3] Prussia, 1785, Art. 13, 8 Stat. 90.

[4] France, 1778, Arts. 23, 24 ; Sweden, 1783, Art. 7, 8 Stat. 64 ; Prussia, 1785, Art. 12, 8 Stat. 90.

[5] France, 1778, Art. 14, 8 Stat. 20 ; Netherlands, 1782, Art. 12, 8 Stat. 40 ; Sweden, 1783, Art. 14, 8 Stat. 68.

[6] France, 1778, Arts. 12, 25, 27 ; Netherlands, 1782, Arts. 10, 20, 25, 26 ; Sweden, 1783, Arts. 11, 12, 24, 25 ; Prussia, 1785, Arts. 14, 15.

[7] France, 1778, Art. 13 ; Netherlands, 1782, Art 11 ; Sweden, 1783, Art. 13 ; Prussia, 1785, Art. 13.

These early treaties thus uniformly asserted the nationality of the United States not only in their dealings with foreign powers, but in their relations with the several States. The favored nation clause put Prussia on the best footing in the ports of Charleston, Boston, Philadelphia, and New York, no matter what the Legislatures of South Carolina, Massachusetts Pennsylvania, or New York might say. Aliens were permitted to hold personal property and dispose of it by testament, donation, or otherwise, and the exaction of State dues in excess of those exacted from citizens of the State in like cases were forbidden. The right was secured to aliens to frequent the coasts of each and all the States, and to reside and trade there. Resident aliens were assured against State legislation to prevent the exercise of liberty of conscience and the performance of religious worship; and when dying, they were guaranteed the right of decent burial and undisturbed rest for their bodies.[1]

LECTURE I.
Effect of all these provisions upon State Independence.

In 1784 sundry letters from Ministers of the United States in Europe having been referred to a special committee, of which Mr. Jefferson was chairman, Congress, on the recommendation of that committee, by a vote of eight States to two, resolved to instruct their Ministers " that these United States be considered, in all such treaties, and in every case arising under them,

Jefferson's Consular Convention with France.

---

[1] Netherlands, 1782, Art. 4, 8 Stat. 34; Sweden, 1783, Art. 5, 8 Stat. 62; Prussia, 1785, Art. 11, 8 Stat. 90.

as one Nation, upon the principles of the Federal Constitution." [1]

At one time a postal convention was contemplated between France and the United States.
A scheme was submitted by the French minister, which Jay answered by a counter proposal; [2]
but nothing came of it.

In 1788 Mr. Jefferson, as Minister of the
United States in France, concluded a Consular
Convention with that power, which went still
further. It authorized French Consuls, in certain cases, to administer upon the estates of
their deceased countrymen in the several States;
to exercise police powers over French vessels in
American ports; to arrest officers or crews of
such vessels; to require the courts, at a time
when no Federal Courts existed, to aid them in
the arrest of deserters; and it clothed them
with authority, as judges, to decide all differences and disputes arising between their countrymen and the United States. [3]

---

[1] 3 Secret Journals of Congress, 453.

[2] 1 Diplomatic Correspondence, 1783–89, pp. 185, 201.

[3] Consular Convention of 1788 with France, Arts. 5, 8, 9, 12.
In his autobiography Mr. Jefferson gives an account of this convention: "A consular convention had been agreed on in 1784
between Dr. Franklin and the French Government, containing
several articles so entirely inconsistent with the laws of the several
States, and the general spirit of our citizens, that Congress withheld their ratification, and sent it back to me, with instruction to
get those articles expunged, or modified so as to render them
compatible with our laws. The minister unwillingly released us
from these concessions which, indeed, authorized the exercise of
powers very offensive in a free State. After much discussion, the
convention was reformed, in a considerable degree, and was signed
by the Count Montmorin and myself on the 14th of November,

It so happened that this treaty, although
negotiated and signed before the Constitution took effect, had not been ratified when Washington took the oath of office. On the 11th of June, 1789, it was laid before the Senate, for its constitutional action, being the first foreign treaty upon which that body passed. The Secretary of State — then styled Secretary for Foreign Affairs — appeared before the Senate and explained its provisions; and it was unanimously ratified by men, many of whom were fresh from the Convention which framed the Constitution.

That instrument gives to the President power to make treaties by and with the advice and consent of the Senate. This power was conferred, with full knowledge of this repeated exercise by the Continental Congress of its treaty-making power in limitation and curtailment of the power of the States. This may fairly be regarded as a contemporaneous construction of the Constitution by those who framed it.

3. *The Northwest Territory.*

In the acquisition of the territory northwest of the Ohio, and in the legislation which excluded slavery from it, and which provided for its future admission into the Union, as it should become settled, the Congress of the Confederation

---

1788; not, indeed, such as I would have wished, but such as could be obtained with good humor and friendship." — 1 Jefferson's Works, 85.

LECTURE I.
The cession of
the Northwestern
territory, and the
passage of the
Ordinance of 1787. exercised one of the highest attributes of sovereignty in a matter in which no individual State took a separate part. It was the *United* States of America which accepted the deeds of cession, and which thereby acquired a Colonial Empire. In the words of the Legislature of Maryland, enacted before the cession was made, " the sovereignty over the Western territory was vested in the United States as one undivided and independent nation." [1] As such it accepted the cession on the 1st of March, 1784 ; and as such, on the 13th day of July, 1787, it enacted the Ordinance under which five States (Ohio, Indiana, Illinois, Wisconsin, and Michigan) were gradually settled and admitted to the Union. One will search the Articles of Confederation in vain to find authority for such an exercise of power. On the contrary, the Eleventh Article, providing that " Canada, acceding to this confederation, and joining in the measures of the United States, shall be admitted into, and entitled to all the advantages of this Union ; but no other Colony shall be admitted into the same, unless such admission be agreed to by nine States," may be cited argumentatively against such authority.

The powers assumed by the Congress of the Confederation, in enacting the Ordinance of 1787, are now conferred upon Congress by the third section of the Fourth Article of the Constitution.

---

[1] 6 Bancroft's Hist. U. S., last revise, 104.

Thus it is seen that the Statesmen in the Continental Congress felt that they formed part of a National Government, ruling, in its proper sphere, over a Federation of United States, and exercising powers to which each of those States must of necessity be subordinate. The action of Washington, in 1775, in asking Congress to establish Prize Courts with original jurisdiction; the resolutions of Congress in January, 1779, above quoted, regarding prizes and Prize Courts; the action of Congress in the negotiation of the several treaties above referred to, all negotiated without assent of the States, either previously given or subsequently obtained, except as given in the Articles of Confederation as to such as were negotiated after they were agreed to; the assumption of colonial jurisdiction by Congress, and the exclusion of slavery from the acquired territory, all point in this direction.

The simple truth is, that the United States, under the Articles of Confederation, like the United Colonies after the battle of Lexington, existed as a Sovereign Power from the necessities of the emergency. The Colonies were compacted together by the blows of a common enemy. The semi-legislative body, which took the name of Congress, was forced, from the necessities of the case, to assume and exercise Executive Powers which no Colony had ever possessed or exercised. It found precedent for this in English history; and it followed the lines of the race to which its members mainly belonged. In studying the ante-Constitutional

history of the United States, we may often find
Congress weak in action, but never irresolute
or weak in asserting its Federal powers. Before
the Declaration of Independence it claimed and
exercised the National Powers which until then
had been wielded by the king of Great Britain.
When that Declaration was proclaimed, it pressed
this claim with stronger emphasis, if not with
better right.   This power it handed over to the
government of the Confederation, which was in
fact the Congress itself; and that government,
in its turn, deposited the power in the new
Union, as defined by the Constitution.   It is
true that in the interim between the ratification
of the Treaty of Peace, and the adoption of the
Constitution, there was a time when the desire
for union weakened.   After all these powers
had been claimed and exercised by Congress,
after the war was over and success had been
achieved and acknowledged, there came a day
of reckoning, when the debts incurred in prosecuting the war had to be faced and provided
for.   There then came a short hour when the
enemies of the Union had some reason to look
for success; when its friends, in their confidential correspondence, could only hope that this
"epidemic frenzy"[1] would subside.   That day
passed away when the Constitution was adopted.

---

[1] Hamilton to Washington, September 30, 1783.   1 Hamilton's
Works, 402, 403.

II.

THE PRINCIPLES OF CONSTRUCTION
OF THE CONSTITUTION.[1]

————∘o⌐oⵗo∘⌐————

I<small>F</small> we desire to consider the subject of constitutional law, to obtain some idea as to what
is meant by that phrase, and to examine the
elementary doctrines which underlie all written-
constitutions, we can select no better text than
the Constitution of the United States. It is of
all existing foundations of civil government the
most important, as well as the best which the
wisdom of man has yet devised,[2] and its con-

---

[1] In the manuscript notes left by Mr. Justice Miller, this was
Lecture I of the lectures delivered by him before the classes of the
University Law School. It was delivered January 24th, 1890.

[2] Freeman gives four commonwealths which have most perfectly
realized the Federal idea in history.

1. The Achaian League, in the latter days of ancient Greece,
whose most flourishing period comes within the third century.
(B.C. 281–146.)

2. The Confederation of the Swiss Cantons, which, with many
changes in extent and constitution, has endured since the thirteenth
century. (A.D. 1291.)

3. The Seven United Provinces of the Netherlands, whose union
arose in the war of independence against Spain, and lasted in a
republican form till the French Revolution. (A.D. 1579–1795.)

4. The United States of America. History of Federal Government, p. 5.

Jefferson wrote soon after the formation of the Constitution:
" The example of changing a constitution by assembling the wise·

sideration will most clearly and forcibly suggest those general principles upon which not only the institutions, but the preservation and well-being of all constitutional governments depend.

It is first of all necessary to have a clear idea of what is meant by the word "constitution" as applied to the various forms of civil government, before entering upon the rules for the construction and application of its provisions or an exposition of constitutional law. As was well said by Judge Bates, afterwards Chief Justice of the Supreme Court of Missouri, in an argument before that court in the case of *Hamilton v. St. Louis County Court*,[1] "it is easier to tell what a constitution is not, than to tell what it is." As a constitution has relation to the form of a government and to the mode in which its powers are to be exercised, let us consider briefly the nature of the elementary forms under which it can be organized. These are primarily of three kinds, into which both reason and authority agree that all forms of government may be reduced, namely, a monarchy, a democracy, and an aristocracy.[2]

---

men of the state, instead of assembling armies, will be worth as much to the world as the former examples we had given them. The Constitution too, which was the result of our deliberations, is, undoubtedly, the wisest ever yet presented to men." 3 Works, 12.

The basis of the English constitution, the capital principle on which all others depend, is that the legislative power belongs to Parliament alone; that is to say, the power of establishing laws and of abrogating, changing, or explaining them. De Lolme, Constitution of England (London, 1834), p. 49.

[1] 15 Missouri, 3, 13.

[2] Writers have divided governments into various classes. The most usual division is into monarchy, aristocracy, and democracy.

A pure monarchy means a despotism, a gov-

ernment where the supreme power is lodged in the hands of one man, a monarch, an autocrat, or whatever else he may be called, who, in his own discretion, discharges all the functions of the executive, legislative, and judicial departments of the government. He decides controversies between private individuals, makes the laws by which their determination is to be controlled, and executes his own decrees.

A pure democracy is one in which every trans- action of common interest and private justice is brought before the entire body of the people, and they determine what shall be done in the premises; the government "of the people, by the people, for the people." They make and administer the law, they hear and decide cases, and they execute their judgments.

A pure aristocracy is a form of government in which these powers are held and exercised by a few favored individuals, a limited number of prominent men who have become such by their greater wealth or power, or by inheritance.

I am not aware that there exists at this day in any civilized country a pure example of either

---

Grimke, Nature and Tendency of Free Institutions, 7. (Ed. Cincinnati, 1848.)

Freeman says, "A more philosophical division perhaps is that which does not look so much to the nature of the hands in which supreme power is vested, as to the question whether there is any one body or individual which can fairly be called supreme. This is the division of monarchies, aristocracies, and democracies respectively, into absolute and constitutional examples of their respective classes." History of Federal Government, p. 15. See Calhoun's Works, vol. 1, pp. 28, 34.

of these forms of government. The Chinese monarchy is a close approximation to a pure type, Russia is known as an "absolute monarchy," and the history of Athens and Rome shows the former existence there of a near approach to a pure democracy. Perhaps the purest example of an aristocracy was the Venetian Government, which was successfully carried on for a long time, and attained great power. In a modified form an aristocracy may be said to govern to-day in England, but it is united with a monarchy.[1] Indeed, all modern governments in civilized countries are combinations and modifications of these three forms.

The United States
a combination of
the best in each. The United States is a wonderful illustration of their harmonious combination, preserving for the benefit of the people most of the advantages and the best points inherent in each system. We have an executive who is not hereditary, but elective; a legislative body elected by the people; and a judicial body separated from and which may be said to be independent of the other two.[2]

---

[1] As described by Sir William Blackstone and his followers, the British is a despotic government. It is a government without a people. In that government, as so described, the sovereignty is possessed by the Parliament. In the Parliament, therefore, the supreme and absolute authority is vested: in the Parliament resides that uncontrollable and despotic power which in all governments must reside somewhere. The constituent parts of the Parliament are the King's Majesty, the Lords Spiritual, the Lords Temporal and the Commons. The king and these three estates together form the great corporation or body politic of the kingdom. . . . What, then, or where, are the people? Nothing! Nowhere! They are not so much as even the baseless fabric of a vision. From legal contemplation they totally disappear. Mr. Justice Wilson, in *Chisholm* v. *Georgia*, 2 Dall. 419, 462.

[2] "There are two classes of Federal Commonwealths. 1. The

The term "constitution" may be applied, not
improperly, to the guiding principles underlying
all these varying forms of government, whether
they are, or are not, established by any written
instrument.[1] No doubt an intelligent Russian

system of Confederate States, where the central power deals only
with the State governments. 2. The composite State, where the
central power acts directly on citizens." Freeman, History of
Federal Government, 11. To the latter class the United States
belongs, or as expressed in the language of Mr. Justice Johnson : "To me the Constitution appears, in every line of it, to be a
contract, which in legal language may be denominated tripartite.
The parties are the people, the States, and the United States."
Martin v. Hunter's Lessee, 1 Wheat. 304, 373.

[1] The word "constitution" in the time of the Roman Empire
signified a collection of laws or ordinances made by the emperor.
It is so used in the early history of English law ; as, the Constitution
of Clarendon. In its modern use it has been restricted to those
rules which concern the political structure of society. Encyclopædia Britannica, tit. Constitution.

A constitution is the fundamental law of a free country, which
characterizes the organism of the country and secures the rights of
the citizen and determines his main duties as a freeman. Bouvier's Law Dictionary.

The body of fundamental laws, as contained in written documents or established by prescriptive usage, which constitutes the
form of government for a nation, State, community, association, or
society ; as, "The *constitution* of the United States," "The British
constitution." (*Roman Law.*) Decrees of regular authorities, particularly of the emperors. Worcester's Dictionary.

The principles or fundamental laws which govern a State or
other organized body of men, and are embodied in written documents, or implied in the institutions and usages of the country or
society ; organic law. Webster's Dictionary.

"There is one great and happy feature in the Constitution of
the United States"; "provision is made for the admission of new
States upon equal terms with the old ones. For Europe there remained the sad necessity of revolution. For America, the gates of
revolution are shut and barred and bolted down, never again to
be thrown open ; for it has found a legal and peaceful way to intro-
duce every amelioration." Bancroft's History of the Constitution,
1st. ed. vol. 2, p. 334.

France had no parliamentary machinery for effecting desired or

might speak of the constitution of the Russian monarchy, by which he would mean that there were certain limitations upon the power of his sovereign, that there were certain privileges pertaining to the nobility which could not be invaded, that the serfs which belonged to the crown having been emancipated, no power could reinstate the old order of things. These invisible unwritten barriers, surrounding the action of the despot, are comprehended under this use of the word "constitution." [1] No doubt an educated Turk might allude to the constitution of the Turkish Government, by which he would mean

---

needful changes in its constitution, so that the right of revolution, as it was called, became a necessity on the part of those who conceived that they embodied and were in a position to express the popular will.

[1] "Quodcumque ergo imperator per epistolam constituit, vel cognoscens decrevit, vel edicto præcepit, legem esse constat; hæ sunt quæ constitutiones appellantur. Justinian, Inst. Lib. I, tit. 2, pl. 6.

The French "Charte" is the most remarkable of the European constitutions. Like the Magna Charta it was wrested from the king; it was not the act of a popular convention. It is said to be a settled maxim in France that it can never be altered. See Grimke on Nature and Tendency of Free Institutions, p. 129.

Jameson, in his work on Constitutional Conventions, divides political constitutions with reference to the mode in which they originated into two classes, accumulated or cumulative and enacted. p. 75. Those of ancient Rome and England belong to the first class. The Reform Act is considered by the English as much a portion of the constitution as trial by jury, or the representative system, which have never been enacted, but correspond to what Cicero calls *leges natæ*, or "grown law." To the second class belong the Federal constitution and those of the several States; that is, they were at a certain time and by a certain authority enacted as the fundamental law of the body politic. Encyclopædia Americana, tit. Constitution; Hallam's Constitutional History of England; Shepherd's Constitutional Text-Book; Elliot's Debates on the Federal Constitution.

that the sultan was bound to administer justice,
and that he was under many restrictions as to the counsellors with whom he must surround himself as well as to the methods by which he should administer the affairs of the kingdom.[1]

We are all familiar with the frequent allu-
sions made by English statesmen to the British Constitution, which are repeated by every writer on the subject in that country. And they mean what they say; they have in their sense a constitution; that is to say, they have for hundreds of years had a monarchy in which the powers of the sovereign have been confined within very narrow limits, much more restricted in many respects than those confided to the President of the United States under our Constitution. So that the term "constitutional government" has come to be generally used in contradistinction to absolutism. Their judiciary is also independent of the law-making power, which is a parliament composed of the House of Lords and the Commons, the latter of which is elective. It is much older than ours, having begun to exist in times when statesmen were not much accustomed to frame exact definitions; but if the great length of its duration and the admiration

---

[1] Some English writers speak of the constitution of the Turkish Empire. See Hallam's Constitutional History of England.

The emperor of China is bound by ancient laws and customs, and could scarcely, without danger, if he would, disregard the advice or remonstrances of his ministers or the boards of administration. American Cyclopædia, tit. China.

A collection of ecclesiastical regulations appeared in the fourth century, attributed to the apostles, but generally supposed to be spurious, known as "apostolical constitutions."

LECTURE II.
British constitution.

of the English people for it, together with their earnest belief in its value and perpetuity, are evidences of its worth, then it is clear that they have a good constitution.[1]

A constitution is a written instrument, as understood in America.

But in America when we speak of a constitution, we refer to a written instrument, one in which the powers granted and duties imposed by it are reduced to writing.[2] The earliest con-

---

[1] It was during the thirteenth century that first appeared with distinctness that Constitution which has ever since, through all changes, preserved its identity ; of which all the other free constitutions in the world are copies, and which, in spite of some defects, deserves to be regarded as the best under which any great society has ever yet existed during many ages. . . . Yet the present Constitution is to the one of five hundred years ago what the tree is to the sapling, what the man is to the boy. The alteration has been great. . . . A constitution of the Middle Ages was not like one of the eighteenth or nineteenth century, created entire by a single act, and fully set forth in a single document. Macaulay's History of England, vol. 1, pp. 16–28.

The English Constitution is largely unwritten, using the word as we do of unwritten law ; its rules are found in no written document, but depend on precedent modified by a constant process of interpretation. See Encyclopædia Britannica, tit. Constitution. De Lolme says it has, like that of most countries of Europe, grown out of occasion and emergency, and its earliest history is involved in obscurity.

Mr. Gladstone has said with admirable force, "As the British Constitution is the most subtile organism which has proceeded from progressive history, so the American Constitution is the most wonderful work ever struck off at a given time by the brain and purpose of man."

[2] In American constitutional law, the word "constitution" is used in a restricted sense, as implying the written instrument agreed upon by the people of the Union, or any one of the States, as the absolute rule of action and decision for all departments and officers of the government, in respect to all points covered by it ; which must control until it shall be changed by the authority which established it, and in opposition to which any act or any regulation of any such department or officer, or even of the people themselves, will be altogether void. Cooley's Constitutional Limitations, 3.

stitutions for the government of the ancestors of the people who now constitute the United States were the charters of the Colonies; and although those charters were but grants of liberties, rights, and powers from the home government, not in all cases well defined, yet they were reduced to writing under the seal of the kingdom to which they were tributary, and constituted the foundation and the formal statement of the principles on which the colonies administered their own domestic affairs and permitted the officers of the parent government to assist in that administration. They undoubtedly contributed very largely towards the education of the people in those days in ideas of constitutional liberty; and they were in many respects much superior to the much vaunted British Constitution, because they contained limitations upon the legislative power which were not found in the usages of the English Government.[1] They

LECTURE II.

A "constitution" is a written instrument, as understood in America.

Colonial charters.

---

[1] In England there is no written constitution, no fundamental law, nothing visible, nothing real, nothing certain, by which a statute can be tested. In America the case is widely different. Every State in the Union has its constitution reduced to a written exactitude and precision. *Vanhorne's Lessee* v. *Dorrance*, 2 Dall. 304, 308.

The power of the sovereign, "though ample, was limited by three great constitutional principles, so ancient that none can say when they began to exist; so potent that their natural development, continued through many generations, has produced the order of things under which we now live. First, the king could not legislate without the consent of his Parliament. Secondly, he could impose no taxes without the consent of his Parliament. Thirdly, he was bound to conduct the executive administration according to the laws of the land, and, if he broke those laws, his advisers and his agents were responsible." Macaulay's History of England, vol. 1, p. 29.

The principles embodied in the Acts of Settlement and the Bill of Rights are the basis of the English Constitution. De Lolme.

LECTURE II.   also contained assertions of individual rights,
Colonial charters. which were not always fully acknowledged, and
thus not only contributed in that way to educate
the people in a knowledge of their rights and
of the just powers of the government, but also
taught them the necessity and propriety of having such rights and powers fixed by a written
instrument.[1]

Previous attempts   There have been other written constitutions
at written consti-
tutions.   besides these.   Solon drew up a body of laws
for the Athenian State, and Lycurgus one for
Sparta.   Some of the governments of Europe
have attempted to formulate such instruments.[2]
Comprehensive laws or decrees have been called
constitutions, and France may be instanced as
a country which has had something which has

---

[1] The general principles which are the groundwork of modern
constitutions, — principles which were imperfectly known in Europe, and not completely triumphant even in Great Britain, in the
seventeenth century, — were all recognized and determined by the
laws of New England : the intervention of the people in public
affairs, the free voting of taxes, the responsibility of authorities,
personal liberty, and trial by jury, were all positively established
without discussion.   De Tocqueville, Democracy in America, vol. 1,
p. 22 (ed. N. Y. 1838).

[2] Ten or twelve European States have adopted written constitutions, but they have been the gift of some self-constituted lawgiver,
or imposed by bodies of men who very imperfectly represented the
supreme authority of the State.   None of them rest upon the same
firm foundation as ours, the sovereignty of the people.   A written
constitution, emanating from the popular will, while the government was still a monarchy or aristocracy in character, would be a
solecism in politics.   Neither form could survive the adoption of
such an instrument.   If not immediately annihilated, they must
speedily have fallen into decay.   See Grimke on Nature and
Tendency of Free Institutions, pp. 124–128.

The present constitution of Switzerland dates from 1874, on the
basis of the previous one of 1848.

been called such, from the day that Louis XVI LECTURE II.
was overthrown to the present hour.[1] Every Previous attempts at written consti-
successive government established its written tutions.
constitution, and the French people have had
in that length of time enough such documents
to supply the nations of the earth; most of them
probably good ones if they had been able to successfully put them into practice. It is unnecessary here to recall the history of that country;
how with every change in the course of its
affairs they abolished the previous constitution
and established a new one, until thinking people
began to doubt their capacity for self-govern-
ment.

Spain followed France in this course, and although it did not become republican until within
a very recent period, yet under French influence
its people wrung from Ferdinand and Charles
written constitutions, and such an instrument
they have had from that hour to this. They
have, however, frequently risen in rebellion to

---

[1] Napoleon I styled himself Emperor of the French " by the grace
of God and the Constitution of the Empire."

De Tocqueville, in his Democracy in America, says, p. 140:
"In France the constitution is the first of laws "; and on p. 139:
" It is, or is supposed to be, immutable, and the received theory is
that no power has the right to change any part of it " ; and again,
p. 288: " As the king, the peers, and the deputies all derive their
authority from the constitution, these three persons united cannot
alter a law by virtue of which alone they govern. Out of the pale
of the constitution they are nothing."

Charles VII was the first French king who attempted to form a
code for the entire kingdom. Several of his successors had the
same idea. One was prepared and published in 1629, but many
important chapters were added before it assumed the form in which,
as the Code of Louis XV, it represents the status of French jurisprudence at the time of the Revolution.

overthrow their monarch and get another constitution, so that none of them have been permanent or very enduring.[1] It is with sorrow,
and regret also that we see their descendants on
this side of the Atlantic, Spanish republicans
they call themselves, evince scarcely more respect for written constitutions than the country
from which they originally came.[2]

So that it is evident that something more
than a written constitution is essential to the
safety and perpetuity of any government, and
that is, a due reverence by the people for it and
for their laws. All the instruments in the
world, though they were written in letters of
gold upon the most imperishable tablets, will be
but as ropes of sand if the people themselves have
no respect for law or for those who administer it.[3]

[1] But however imperfect European constitutions in their practical enforcement may have been, they work a great advance in
government, not only as an open recognition of certain general
principles in favor of liberty, but as a definite application of them.
See Grimke on Nature and Tendency of Free Institutions, p. 129.

"A written constitution never adds to, but always takes away
from, the power which has previously been exercised." Ib.

[2] The precedent of Federal union given by the English settlements in North America has been followed, though as yet with
little success or credit, by several of the republics which have
arisen among the ruins of Spanish dominion in the same continent.
Freeman, History of Federal Government, 7.

[3] A nation may establish a system of free government, but without the spirit of municipal institutions it cannot have the spirit of
liberty. De Tocqueville, vol. 1, p. 42 (ed. N. Y. 1838). "The Federal
form of government is no panacea for all human ills; a well-planned
constitution at home is no guarantee for wise or honorable conduct
in foreign affairs," and will not hinder among the people the development of the characteristic virtues and vices of a Democratic Federation. Freeman on Federal Government, 325, 326.

The formation of a written constitution is one of the most decisive steps which has been made toward the establishment of free

A constitution, in the American sense of the word, is a written instrument by which the fundamental powers of the government are established, limited, and defined, and by which these powers are distributed among several departments, for their more safe and useful exercise, for the benefit of the body politic. A search for a more satisfactory definition has been in vain, but this language, perhaps, fairly expresses the meaning of the term in this country.[1]

institutions. It implies the exercise of reflection in its highest degree, an ability to frame the most comprehensive rules, and to make application of them to the actual affairs of men. . . . The constitutions of antiquity confounded what we would characterize as political ordinances with the acts of ordinary legislation. This was the case in the code of the Roman decemvirs, and it was equally so in the systems introduced by the Athenian and Spartan lawgivers. Grimke on Free Institutions, Book II, c. I.

[1] What is a constitution ? It is the form of government, delineated by the mighty hand of the people, in which certain first principles of fundamental laws are established. The Constitution is fixed and certain; it contains the permanent will of the people, and it is the supreme law of the land; it is paramount to the will of the legislature, and can be revoked and altered only by the authority that made it. The life-giving principle and the death-dealing stroke must proceed from the same hand. . . . In short, the Constitution is the sun of the political system, around which the legislative, executive, and judicial bodies revolve. Whatever may be the case in other countries, yet in this there can be no doubt that every act of the legislature repugnant to the Constitution is absolutely void. *Vanhorne's Lessee* v. *Dorrance*, 2 Dall. 308.

It is not, however, the origin of private rights, nor the foundation of laws, nor the beginning of a community. It is not the cause, but the consequence of personal and political freedom. It declares those natural and fundamental rights of individuals, for the security and common enjoyment of which governments are established. It is, in a word, the form and framework of political government, devised for the protection of the people, the instrument of their convenience, and is always a limitation upon the governing powers exercised by their agents.

It has been defined to be a system of law established by the sovereign power of a State for its own guidance.

Not everything in detail that a government may do can be embraced in a written document; that would fill a volume like the statutes; but the fundamental principles by which it is to be carried on and maintained are established by it.[1] Certain great powers are specifically granted, but at the same time certain restrictions are thrown around their exercise which are essential under our form of government to the rights of the States, and to the rights of individuals. For example, a person's property cannot be taken for public use without due course of law and just compensation; his life or liberty cannot be taken from him without a fair trial before a court of competent jurisdiction;[2] he shall enjoy the right to a speedy and public trial by an impartial jury of the State and district wherein the crime was committed; he shall be confronted with the witnesses against him, shall have compulsory process for obtaining witnesses in his favor, and shall also have the assistance of counsel for his defence.[3] These are some of the rights defined and secured to those who live under the protection of the Constitution of the United States.

This is a very remarkable instrument in many particulars. Perhaps no more important writing exists in the world to-day, affecting its prosperity and the happiness of its people, outside of

---

[1] In no written constitution which ever existed has there been defined or delegated to officials all the latent powers which lie dormant in every nation, boundless in extent and incapable of definition.

[2] Constitution, Fifth Amendment.

[3] Constitution, Sixth Amendment.

those which are of a religious character. It is,
and has been for many years, the subject of per-petual exegesis by all the lawyers and courts of this country, representing millions of inhabi-tants, great and diverse interests, and very ex-tensive business relations, all of which are more or less affected by its provisions. All the pre-vious instruments known in this country and in the history of its Colonies, such as the charters already referred to, were granted by the ruler or sovereign, and were designed to confer certain rights and regulate the relations of the subjects with their monarch. But this instrument comes from a very different source. It is one in which the people themselves have undertaken to frame an organic law governing the relations of the whole people, as well as of the individual States, to the Federal Government, and to prescribe in many cases the limits and rules of private and personal rights. It is the fundamental law pur-suant to which the government is permanently organized and conducted.[1] Such a document, framed and put into written language, judiciously operative upon the affairs which it is intended to govern, is a rare thing in the history of the world; and it may be said with safety that none has ever been constructed by the wisdom or in-

---

[1] Federal Government may be said to be essentially a compro-mise between two opposite political systems ; an intermediate step. In its most perfect form two requisites have been suggested : the complete independence of each member of the Union in all matters concerning that member only, and that all must be subject to a central power in those matters concerning the whole body of mem-bers collectively.

genuity of man so well adapted to the ends it was intended to subserve, or so successful in the execution of those purposes.[1] It is, therefore, a subject unique in that respect, to which attention is here invited.

This, like all other instruments, when it becomes the subject of comment and construction, must necessarily be looked at in the light of its origin, the purposes which it was intended to accomplish, as well as the evils which it was intended to remedy. A volume would hardly be sufficient to give a complete history of the Constitution of the United States. It will be impossible here to give more than a brief outline of some of the principal reasons for its adoption.

It may, in a word, be said that this Constitution arose out of the condition in which the people of the United States found themselves at the close of the Revolutionary War. Having established their independence of the government of Great Britain, and been recognized as one of the family of nations, they soon found that the compact under which they had successfully achieved that independence, namely, the Articles of Confederation, was utterly inefficient and incompetent to answer the purpose of binding them

---

[1] The examples of Federal constitutions which history supplies are scattered over widely distant ages and countries; they are found among nations widely differing from one another in the amount of their political advancement and general civilization. . . . There is what may be called a certain Federal ideal, which has sometimes been realized in its full, or nearly its full, perfection, while other cases have shown only a more or less remote approximation to it. Freeman on Federal Government, 2.

together and conducting the new nation on its LECTURE II.
pathway to future usefulness.[1] Its defects were Causes which led to its adoption.
many and obvious.[2]

It was found that the Colonies, as they had been previously called, had never really been independent States or Nations. They had been subjects of Great Britain, governed by charters from the Crown, or organized under certain commissions or grants by letters patent, and submitting very largely to the legislation of the English Parliament until certain questions connected with taxation caused them to rebel, not against the king, but against those laws as oppressive and unjust. In the effort at resistance

---

[1] Madison said: "The close of the war brought no cure for the public embarrassments. The States, relieved from the pressure of foreign danger, and flush with the enjoyment of independent and sovereign power, instead of a diminished disposition to part with it, persevered in omissions and in measures incompatible with their relations to the Federal Government, and with those among themselves." 5 Elliot's Debates, 112.

[2] The first number of the Federalist opens with the statement: "After full experience of the inefficacy of the existing Federal Government, you are invited to deliberate upon a New Constitution for the United States of America"; and in No. 15 the author says, "It may perhaps be asked what need there is of reasoning or proof to illustrate a position [the insufficiency of the present Confederation to the preservation of the Union] which is neither controverted nor doubted; to which the understandings and feelings of all classes of men assent; and which, in substance, is admitted by the opponents as well as by the friends of the New Constitution? It must in truth be acknowledged, that however these may differ in other respects, they in general appear to harmonize in the opinion that there are material imperfections in our national system, and that something is necessary to be done to rescue us from impending anarchy. . . . Each State, yielding to the persuasive voice of immediate interest or convenience, has successively withdrawn its support, till the frail and tottering edifice seems ready to fall upon our heads, and to crush us beneath its ruins."

LECTURE II.
Causes which led
to its adoption.
they had united together in a body to make the
struggle successful; so that, although being a
government or nation when they became free,
each individual Colony had never been at any
time a separate and independent State, and yet
none of them recognized any supremacy in any
other State.   The question was, how much
should they grant or yield to the common government which they were about to form in the
common interest of self preservation; for it was
soon discovered that the one which had carried
them through the war, in the paroxysm of patriotism necessary for self-defence, was incapable of
carrying on a successful government after that
impulse was gone.[1]

One of the most pressing evils to be remedied
by the reorganization of the Central Government
was in relation to the collection of revenues for
its support, for it had been found that taxes
could not be successfully collected for that purpose.[2]   Its only reliance during the Revolution-

---

[1] " The radical infirmity of the Articles of Confederation was
the dependence of Congress on the voluntary and simultaneous
compliance with its requisitions by so many independent communities, each consulting more or less its particular interests and convenience, and distrusting the compliance of the others."   Mr.
Madison: 5 Elliot's Debates, 112.

[2] The requisitions of Congress under the Confederation were as
constitutionally obligatory as the laws enacted by the present Congress.   That they were habitually disregarded is a fact of universal
notoriety.   *Cohens* v. *Virginia*, 6 Wheat. 264, 388.

Among the debilities of the government of the Confederation,
no one was more distinguished or more distressing than the utter
impossibilty of obtaining from the States the moneys necessary
for the payment of debts, or even for the ordinary expenses of the
government.   Jefferson's Works, vol. 1, p. 82.

The great office of the Confederation was to demonstrate to the

ary War and down to the year 1789, when the
present form of government was fully organized, was 'by a call or request upon the States for their proportion of the amount necessary for its support.[1] Even during the pendency of the war such calls were responded to very feebly and unequally, and hence that war was fought on credit, leaving an immense debt to be paid at its close. After the enthusiasm of the war had died away, and the independence of the Colonies had been conceded, it was still more difficult to obtain funds in that way, and there was no relief to be had through taxation of the people by the General Government.[2]

Another evil was, that, although it had come to be recognized as one of the nations of the earth, this so-called Central or General Government had no sufficient powers conceded to it by the States in order to properly conduct its affairs with foreign governments. It had no capacity

---

people of the American States the practicability and necessity of a more perfect union. 1 Curtis' Const. 150.

[1] To the purposes of public strength and felicity that Confederacy was totally inadequate. A requisition on the several States terminated its legislative authority. Executive or judicial authority it had none. *Chisholm* v. *Georgia*, 2 Dall. 419, 463.

[2] April 5, 1784, Mr. Jefferson, as chairman of a grand committee, made a report upon the arrears of interest on the public debt, in which he refers to the requisitions that have been made upon the various States, and complains that the payments have been small and slow. Journal of Congress, vol. 9, p. 103.

Madison uses the following terse language, February 25, 1787 : "Our situation is every day becoming more and more critical. No money comes into the Federal treasury; no respect is paid to Federal authority; and people of reflection unanimously agree that the existing Confederacy is tottering to its foundation." 5 Elliot's Debates, p. 106.

LECTURE II.
Causes which led
to its adoption.
to make treaties, except on a limited class of
subjects. It had no means to raise armies and
navies, or to pay the national debt; and no one
could tell how far each State could itself negotiate with other nations, or how soon they would
be subjected, as were the Grecian republics in
the days of the Amphictyonic councils,[1] to the
influence of other nations who might approach
any one of them for the purpose of inducing it
to withdraw from the Union.

But perhaps of all the causes which contributed
to the formation of the new Constitution, one of
the most effective, like some little fretful thing
that seems unimportant but which perpetually
annoys you, was the condition of their foreign
commerce[2] as well as the trade between the

---

[1] The Amphictyons, or association of neighboring tribes or
cities, were the germ of one of the strongest bonds of union by
which the Greek tribes were held together. American Cyclopædia, tit. Amphictyons.

The council not a Federal Government, a union not of cities,
but of tribes. See Freeman on Federal Government, p. 123, for
a full history of its origin and character.

"Philip of Macedon by his intrigues and bribes won over to his
interests the popular leaders of several cities; by their influence
and votes gained admission into the Amphictyonic council; and by
his arts and his arms made himself master of the Confederacy."
The Federalist, No. 18.

[2] The want of a power to regulate commerce is one of the defects
which renders the existing Federal system unfit for the administration of the affairs of the Union. There is no object that more
strongly demands a Federal superintendence. . . . The interfering
and unneighborly regulations of some States, contrary to the true
spirit of the Union, have, in different instances, given just cause
of umbrage and complaint to others; and it is to be feared that
examples of this nature, if not restrained by a national control,
would be multiplied and extended till they became not less serious
sources of animosity and discord, than injurious impediments to
the intercourse between the different parts of the Confederacy.
The Federalist, No. 22.

different States.[1]   The States being practically LECTURE II.
Causes which led
to its adoption. independent of each other had the power of taxing all goods which passed through their borders or entered their ports.   The little State of Rhode Island had in Newport one of the most important ports of entry upon the Atlantic coast, and by levying taxes on importations was getting rich at the expense of its neighbors in the confederacy of States.[2]   The port of Charleston bore the same relation to the southern part of the country, and the port of Norfolk held a like position with reference to Virginia and Maryland.[3]

---

[1] "We are uncertain whether the States generally will come into the proposition of investing Congress with the regulation of their commerce. Massachusetts has passed an act, the first object of which seems to be to retaliate on the British commercial measures, but in the close of it they impose double duties on all goods imported in bottoms not owned wholly by citizens of our States. New Hampshire has followed the example. This is much complained of here, and will probably draw retaliatory measures from the states of Europe, if generally adopted in America, or not corrected by the States which have adopted it." Jefferson's Works, vol. 1, p. 475.

[2] Mr. Hamilton said, February 19, 1783 : "The true objection on the part of Rhode Island was the interference with the impost, with the opportunity afforded by their situation of levying contributions on Connecticut, etc., which received foreign supplies through the ports of Rhode Island: that the true objection on the part of Virginia was her having little share in the debts due from the United States to which the impost would be applied." 5 Elliot's Debates, 52.

[3] "The other source of dissatisfaction was the peculiar situation of some of the States, which, having no convenient ports for foreign commerce, were subject to be taxed by their neighbors, through whose ports their commerce was carried on. New Jersey, placed between Philadelphia and New York, was likened to a cask tapped at both ends; and North Carolina, between Virginia and South Carolina, to a patient bleeding at both arms. The Articles of Confederation provided no remedy for the complaint, which pro-

LECTURE II.
Causes which led
to its adoption.

But that was not all. The trade between the States was heavily taxed, in pursuance of a policy by which each endeavored to lay the burden of raising its revenues upon the others. This has been one of the most difficult things to correct, and efforts in that direction have been made against the attempts to accomplish this object, which have been persistently pursued up to the present time.[1] Many cases have come

---

duced a strong protest on the part of New Jersey, and never ceased to be a source of dissatisfaction until the new Constitution superseded the old." Madison in 5 Elliot's Debates, 112.

[1] Statute of New York granting exclusive navigation of waters within the State. *Gibbons* v. *Ogden*, 9 Wheat. 1.

Statute of Maryland requiring license to sell imported goods. *Brown* v. *Maryland*, 12 Wheat. 419 ; *Ward* v. *Maryland*, 12 Wall. 418.

Statute of Missouri, requiring a like license. *Welton* v. *Missouri*, 91 U. S. 275.

Statute of California imposing a tax upon bills of lading for gold or silver carried out of the State. *Almy* v. *California*, 24 How 169.

Statute of Alabama providing for the registration of the names of steamboat owners, etc. *Sinnot* v. *Davenport*, 22 How. 227.

Statutes of New York and Massachusetts imposing taxes on alien passengers arriving in ports of those States. *Passenger Cases*, 7 How. 283 ; *Henderson* v. *Mayor of New York*, 92 U. S. 259.

Statute of California imposing like taxes. *Chy Lung* v. *Freeman*, 92 U. S. 275.

Statute of New York taxing banks. *Bank of Commerce* v. *New York City*, 2 Black, 620 ; *Bank Tax Case*, 2 Wall. 200.

Statute of Nevada levying a capitation tax upon passengers carried out of the State. *Crandall* v. *Nevada*, 6 Wall. 35.

Statute of Pennsylvania imposing tax upon articles brought into or carried out of the State. *Case of State Freight Tax*, 15 Wall. 232 ; *Philadelphia Steamship Co.* v. *Pennsylvania*, 122 U. S. 326.

Statute of Tennessee imposing a license or privilege tax on sleeping-cars. *Pickard* v. *Pullman Southern Car Co.*, 117 U. S. 34 ; *Tennessee* v. *Same*, 117 U. S. 51.

Statute of Louisiana imposing a license tax on boats. *Moran* v. *New Orleans*, 112 U. S. 69.

before the Supreme Court of the United States LECTURE II.
Causes which led
to its adoption.
involving this question, where State laws of this
character have been held to be invalid because
in conflict with the constitutional power of Congress to alone regulate commerce of that nature.[1]
Notwithstanding for nearly one hundred years
we have had in the Federal Constitution the
declaration that Congress shall have power to
regulate commerce among the several States,
there are at this hour upon the statute books of
almost every State laws violating that provision ;
and there is no doubt that if that clause were
removed to-morrow, this Union would fall to
pieces, simply by reason of the struggles of each
State to make the property owned in other States
pay its expenses.   It was this tendency of each
State to support its Government out of taxes
levied upon the property of other States, or on

Statutes regulating delivery of telegraphic despatches in other
States. *Western Union Telegraph Co.* v. *Pendleton*, 122 U. S.
347 ; *Telegraph Co.* v. *Texas*, 105 U. S. 460.

Statute of Missouri prohibiting bringing certain cattle into the
State. *Railroad Co.* v. *Husen*, 95 U. S. 465.

Statute of Louisiana regulating transportation of passengers,
without distinction of race or color. *Hall* v. *De Cuir*, 95 U. S.
485.

Statute of Tennessee taxing drummers. *Robbins* v. *Shelby
County Taxing District*, 120 U. S. 489. [Cases reviewed.]

Statute of Illinois regulating rates of railroad transportation.
Wabash & St. Louis Railway Co. v. *Illinois*, 118 U. S. 557. [Cases
reviewed.]

[1] Even with this explicit declaration it was yet difficult for men
trained, as were the older lawyers during the early part of this century, to concede the supreme power of Parliament over and above
any court in the land ; — that any law passed by the legislative and
approved by the executive branches of the government could be
set aside upon the mere opinion or judgment of a judicial tribunal.
For this there was no precedent in ancient or modern history.

LECTURE II.
Causes which led
to its adoption.
the produce or merchandise which must go
through one State to another, that more than
any other one thing compelled the formation of
the present Constitution.[1]

An understanding
of these causes a
key to its con-
struction.
The importance of a clear understanding of
these reasons, which were so cogent in its formation, is quite apparent. A very useful key to
the construction of a statute or a constitution is
to inquire what was the evil to be removed, and
what remedy did the new instrument propose;
so that when any question arises requiring a
judicial construction of any of its clauses, it is
important to go back and ascertain the evil that
was intended to be remedied.

The Articles of Confederation by which the
Colonies were bound together were but a rope of
sand; the nation was such only in name.[2] To
make it such in reality, this was the problem

---

[1] Mr. Van Buren said, as early as 1826, in the Senate of the
United States: "There are few States in the Union upon whose
acts the seal of condemnation has not from time to time been placed
by the Supreme Court. The sovereign authorities of Vermont,
New Hampshire, New York, New Jersey, Pennsylvania, Maryland,
Virginia, North Carolina, Missouri, Kentucky, and Ohio, have in
turn been rebuked and silenced by the overruling authority of this
court." 4 Elliot's Debates, 486.

[2] The day is at length arrived when dangers and distresses have
opened the eyes of the people, and they perceive the want of a
common head to draw forth in some just proportion the resources
of the several branches of the Federal union. They perceive that
the deliberative powers exercised by States individually over the acts
of Congress must terminate in the common ruin ; and the Legislatures, however reluctantly, must resign a portion of their authority
or cease to be Legislatures. Letter of James Duane to Washington, January 29, 1781; see 1 Bancroft's History of the Constitution, 283 (orig. ed.).

Hamilton wrote: "The Union has neither troops, nor treasury,
nor government."

which confronted the founders of this Govern-ment, and they came to their work of framing its organic law, with a full view of its impor-tance and the evils to be remedied. They deter-mined that this instrument which they framed should be no such feeble tie. They were insti-tuting a government for the common defence and the general welfare, and they, therefore, no longer spoke of the States individually, who might struggle with each other,[1] but they said: "We, the people of the United States, do ordain this instrument to be our Constitution."[2] It was then that a nation was born.[3]

LECTURE II.

An understanding of these causes a key to its con-struction.

---

[1] The great and radical vice in the construction of the existing Confederation is in the principle of LEGISLATION FOR STATES OR GOVERNMENTS, in their CORPORATE OR COLLECTIVE CAPACITIES, and as contradistinguished from the INDIVIDUALS of which they consist. The Federalist, No. 15.

The decay and failure of the Confederation is graphically described in Curtis' Constitution.

[2] This preamble is constantly referred to by statesmen and jurists, to aid in expounding its provisions. *Chisholm* v. *Georgia*, 2 Dall. 474; 2 Curtis' History of Constitution, pp. 372-376.

It is the essence and epitome of the whole instrument by which this government is ordained and created, and its purposes, author-ity, and duty established. Farrar's Constitution, sec. 5.

The Constitution of the United States was ordained and estab-lished, not by the States in their sovereign capacity, but emphat-ically, as the preamble of the Constitution declares, by "the people of the United States." Story, J., in *Martin* v. *Hunter's Lessees*, 1 Wheat. 326.

[3] The new government was not a mere change in dynasty, or in a form of government leaving the nation or sovereignty the same, and clothed with all the rights, and bound by all the obligations of the preceding one. But when the present United States came into existence under the new government, it was a new political body, a new nation, then for the first time taking its place in the family of nations. Chief Justice Taney, in *Dred Scott* v. *Sandford*, 19 How. 441.

LECTURE II.
Characters of the
framers.

Of course, when the delegates from the various States all came together, they must have had . among them a great deal of discussion about the philosophy of government. Probably no nation, or people, as young as ours then was, ever had so many men thoroughly versed in that direction, or so many who had given vigorous, educated, and trained attention to that science, as were to be found in this country at that time.[1] And, fortunately, society was then in a condition when personal aspirations and malign influences were not, and probably could not be, brought to bear, from the fact that the wisest and best men were sent forward from the various communities to participate in the work of the constitutional convention. In that we have reaped the benefit of the good fortune of our ancestors.

The United States
not a democracy.

It has been common to designate our form of government as a democracy, but in the true sense in which that term is properly used, as defining a government in which all its acts are

---

[1] The convention that formed the Constitution was composed of fifty-five members. It was a body of great and disinterested men, competent, both morally and intellectually, to the work assigned to them. . . . There was certainly a remarkable amount of talent and intellectual power in that body. There were men in that assembly, who, for genius, for statesmanship, and for profound speculation in all that relates to the science of government, the world has never seen overmatched, and they were, happily, the most marked in that assembly for their comprehensive patriotism, their justice, their unselfishness and magnanimity.

Mr. Choate said in 1858 in a lecture on Jefferson, Burr, and Madison: "I dwell on that time from 1780 to 1789 because that was our age of civil greatness. Then first we grew to be one. In that time our nation was born."

performed by the people, it is about as far from
it as any other of which we are aware. As has already been said, a pure democracy is almost unknown, from the difficulty of having all the people participate in the functions of government, which include not only the processes of making the laws, but also the administration of them. Such was that of Athens,[1] the only highly civilized form of democracy that ever existed, where people from the streets, who could gather in the public places of that city, met and decided lawsuits, questions of the right of property, of the life or death of individuals, of the election, punishment, or censure of their officers, of the proprietorship of land, or of making war or preserving peace. This may have seemed well in theory, but history shows that it resulted in a scene of perpetual turmoil. There was little security to life or liberty when the best men in the community were compelled to drink the deadly hemlock, or were banished from their homes. Their intellect was stimulated, and they prized human effort directed in the channels of imagination, of science, and of literature, but it was still far from being a place where personal rights were respected, or

---

[1] In the Athenian republic, the most democratic of the Greek states, when the population and suffrage were most extended, 317 B.C., but 21,000 were entitled to vote out of more than 500,000. . . . Real democracy was first put in practice by the New England Colonies, and to this day the most perfect examples are the New England towns, where the whole adult male population assemble together and decide by their votes their own public affairs. American Cyclopædia, tit. Democracy.

where any man of modern times would have been willing to make his home.

But our forefathers did not adopt any of the forms referred to. They had suffered from the evils of a monarchical as well as an aristocratical system; for England was, a century ago, more of an aristocracy than anything else. A pure democracy was neither possible nor desirable; but still they determined that the people should be felt in the direction of public affairs, and so they constructed what may be called a composite government, a representative republican government, one in which the powers that belong to all sovereignties were divided and placed in different depositories.

The proper division of these powers is of the greatest importance, and they were wisely distributed by the framers of the Constitution among the three branches which have come to be recognized in all good governments as essential to a proper balance of their functions,— the executive, the legislative, and the judicial. The legislative branch enacts the law, the executive enforces it, and the judicial interprets its provisions, both as regards public and private rights, as between the citizens themselves and as between them and the Government of the United States.

This, then, is the Constitution of the United States. It establishes these powers, defines and limits them. It distributes them among these three departments, and then confines them to their proper scope and field of action, in order that there may be a useful and safe administra-

tion for the benefit of all the people, for whom
all governments are instituted.

You will observe, however, that the lines that mark that division are not perfect. Perhaps it is impossible that they should be; it may be desirable that they should be more perfect than they are. As regards the executive, for instance, the powers which properly belong to that branch of the government are not completely vested in the President, for we find that the Senate is required to give its assent to all treaties made by the President before they can be operative. The Senate is also required to confirm all nominations to the higher offices before they become valid appointments.[1] So that these two great duties, of making appointments to office and making treaties, which are usually classed as executive functions of the Government, are to some extent divided in their exercise, as well as in the forms necessary to give them efficacy, between the President, who is the Executive, and the Senate of the United States, which is one of the branches of the legislative department.

So, also, in regard to declaring war and making peace, which in most other countries are held to be exclusively executive functions, and which even under the popular government of Great Britain remains in the Crown alone, they are, under our system, participated in by both the executive and legislative branches.[2] The

---

[1] Constitution, Art. 2, sec. 2, par. 2.

[2] The great disadvantage of the Swiss Confederation was in the power which the cantons formerly had of levying war against each

Constitution says that Congress shall have power to declare war ;[1] the President takes part in that matter only as he is a part of the latter. The laws are required to be signed by him, and it is, therefore, evident that the legislative branch is not entirely separate from the executive, but that it thus becomes an integral part of that department of the Government. If, on the contrary, he does not see fit to sign the bills which have been passed by the Congress, he usually sends them back to the body in which they originated with his reasons and objections thereto. It then requires a two-thirds vote of both branches of the Legislature to enact them into laws over such veto.[2] It is, therefore, apparent that the power of legislation is not confided wholly to the legislative branch of the government.

Perhaps the judicial power is left more nearly intact in the hands of the judiciary than any of the others, but it is not wholly so. The power of framing impeachments and trying them, which is eminently a judicial function, as much so as it is to indict a man and try him for murder, belongs wholly and exclusively to the two branches of the legislative department. The

---

other, and of resisting the Central Government in its method of conducting the foreign policy of the country. This was, however, remedied in the present constitution, which gives the control of the army, foreign affairs, and settlements between cantons, and the management of the police and post-offices, to the Federal Assembly. This body represents all the cantons, and consists of two chambers.

[1] Constitution, Art. 1, sec. 8, par. 11.
[2] Constitution, Art. 1, sec. 7, par. 2.

House of Representatives formulates the charges Lecture II.
or indictment, and the Senate tries and deter- Division of powers.
mines them.[1]

But, after all, those are only exceptions, and
it remains true that, for general and most useful
purposes, the best feature of our Constitution is
that it does make this substantial separation of
power among these three departments.

These departments, under our form of government, are co-ordinate in dignity. Neither of
them is intended, by the theory of our Constitution, to be subjected to the other. The President cannot be compelled to make a treaty, or
to appoint anybody to office that he does not
wish to. The Legislature cannot be compelled
to pass any laws, and it alone can exercise that
function. The judiciary alone can construe
them, when enacted, and enforce them by proper
judgments of the various courts. Mr. Justice
Wayne has advanced this idea in very appropriate terms.[2] "The departments of the Government are legislative, executive, and judicial.
They are co-ordinate in degree to the extent of
the powers delegated to each of them. Each in
the exercise of its power is independent of the
other, but all rightfully done by either is binding upon the others. The Constitution is supreme over all of them, because the people who
ratified it have made it so."[3]

---

[1] Constitution, Art. 1, sec. 2, par. 5 ; Art. 1, sec. 3, par. 6.

[2] *Dodge* v. *Woolsey*, 18 How. 331, 347.

[3] Whenever the political laws of the United States are to be discussed, it is with the doctrine of the sovereignty of the people that
we must begin. De Tocqueville, Democracy in America, vol. 1,
p. 36 (ed. N. Y. 1838).

LECTURE II.
Objections to the
Constitution when
promulgated.

When the Constitution was first framed, it was received by a great many thinking people with much distrust. An examination of the history of the proceedings of the conventions of the States, which were called to ratify and confirm that instrument, and without which it would have had no efficacy, will show that it was fiercely assailed, and that in the debates in regard to its adoption in several of the States the issue was for a long time doubtful.[1] It is well, perhaps, to consider some of the objections to it in the light of a century's experience.[2]

One of the greatest was that it conferred too much power upon the Central or Federal Government, and that it curtailed too largely the powers of the States. It will be remembered that the Colonies had just been emancipated from the parent government. They had worked together but a short time, and that not very

---

[1] Washington wrote to Patrick Henry, September 24, 1787: "I wish the Constitution which is offered had been more perfect; but it is the best that could be obtained at this time, and a door is opened for amendments hereafter. The political concerns of this country are suspended by a thread. The convention has been looked up to by the reflecting part of the community with a solicitude which is hardly to be conceived; and if nothing had been agreed on by that body, anarchy would soon have ensued, the seeds being deeply sown in every soil." Bancroft's History of the Constitution, vol. 2, p. 231.

[2] Richard Henry Lee published a series of papers called "Letters from the Federal Farmer," in which the chief objections to the new constitution were stated: that it created a national legislature where the votes were to be, not by States, but by individuals, whose salaries were to be paid out of the general treasury, thus making them independent of their own States, and that they had an unlimited power of taxation; that too much power was given to the Federal judiciary; that an oath of allegiance was required to the Federal Government, and that no Bill of Rights was included in it.

harmoniously. Each man felt that his own
State was more to him, and that he had a larger
interest in it than he had in the welfare of all
the others, and it is one of the most creditable
as well as remarkable things that the superior
discernment and influence of a few great minds
could overcome these strong prejudices, and so
crystallize the wise provisions of the Constitution into a new form of government, which
has proved so harmonious in its action and permanent in its character. Several of the States
expressed their dissatisfaction by proposing
amendments, under the provision in the instru- The amendments.
ment therefor, and within two years after it was
ratified,[1] Congress passed and referred to the
different States twelve amendments,[2] ten of

---

[1] The Constitution went into operation March 4, 1789. *Owings*
v. *Speed*, 5 Wheat. 420.

[2] The first and second articles, of the twelve proposed and
passed, were never ratified. The first is interesting in view of the
recent strictures, in the press and elsewhere, upon the unwieldy
character of the present House of Representatives, which now consists of 325 members and 8 delegates. [Since this note was written the number has been increased to 356.] The unratified articles
are as follows :

1. After the first enumeration required by the first article of
the Constitution, there shall be one representative for every 20,000
until the number shall amount to 100, after which the proportion
shall be so regulated by Congress that there shall not be less than
100 representatives, nor less than one representative for every
40,000 persons, until the number shall amount to 200 ; after which
the proportion shall be so regulated by Congress that there shall
not be less than 200 representatives, nor more than one representative for every 50,000 persons.

2. No law varying the compensation for the services of senators
and representatives shall take effect until an election of representatives shall have intervened. See Appendix to Annals of 1st
Congress, vol. 2, pp. 1984-5 ; also Hickey's Constitution, p. 35, note.

LECTURE II.
The amendments.

which were ratified finally by the requisite number to make them a part of the Constitution.
These were soon followed by two others, the
eleventh and twelfth, after the ratification of
which it remained unchanged for a period of
more than sixty years.[1]

The objections to
the Constitution.

In those amendments, if they are carefully
examined, may be plainly seen this distrust of
the power of the Central Government,[2] and this

---

[1] At the first Congress after the organization of the Government,
the House proposed seventeen amendments to the Constitution.
These were by the Senate reduced to twelve, and they were then
submitted to the States.

At various times between November, 1789, and March, 1790, ten
of these amendments were ratified by the Legislatures of the following States: New Jersey, North Carolina, Maryland, New Hampshire, Delaware, South Carolina, New York, and Pennsylvania;
one less than three-fourths of the twelve States then in the Union.
Annals of 1st Congress, vol. 2, Appendix. In May, 1790, Rhode
Island came into the Union, and in June her Legislature ratified,
but as there were now thirteen States, three-fourths had not yet
given their assent. Subsequently Vermont was admitted, and in
November, 1791, ratified the amendments; but there were now
fourteen States, and the requisite number had not been obtained.
But in December of the same year, Virginia, one of the original
twelve, gave in her adhesion, and thus the ten amendments became
a part of the Constitution. Annals 2d Congress, pp. 54, 75. These
were the first ten amendments now in the Constitution, and were
declared in force December 15, 1791.

The eleventh was proposed by Congress, March 5, 1794, and
declared in force January 8, 1798; the twelfth, proposed December
12, 1803, and proclaimed September 25, 1804; the thirteenth, proposed February 1, 1865, and proclaimed December 18, 1865; the
fourteenth, proposed June 16, 1866, proclaimed July 20, 1868; and
the fifteenth, proposed February 26, 1869, and proclaimed March
30, 1870.

It was mainly through the efforts of Mr. Madison, who proposed and advocated them, that the first ten amendments were
passed through Congress. 2 Story on the Constitution, sec. 303,
note.

[2] As showing the diversity of opinion existing at the time the
Constitution was finally ratified, it may be worthy of note that two

desire to protect the States from being over- LECTURE II.
whelmed and annihilated by its exercise. The The objections to the Constitution.
contest has continued to the present time. It
would be well for the country if it could be said
that it had been settled by the results of the
recent war, but while it has undergone considerable discussion, it has not been finally determined. It is sufficient to say here, although
others may disagree with this conclusion, that
the experience of a century under the Government as it was then organized has shown that
the danger to its perpetuity and to the people of
this country did not lie in the aggrandizement
of the central authority, but rather in the power
that remained in the several States.

Another objection, second in importance in The executive.

---

hundred and one amendments were proposed in one form or another by the different States in the course of their action upon its
ratification. Of course many of them referred to substantially the
same matter of grievance.

" It is universally understood, it is a part of the history of the
day, that the great revolution which established the Constitution
of the United States was not effected without immense opposition.
Serious fears were extensively entertained that those powers which
the patriot statesmen, who then watched over the interests of our
country, deemed essential to union, and to the attainment of those
invaluable objects for which union was sought, might be exercised
in a manner dangerous to liberty. In almost every convention by
which the Constitution was adopted, amendments to guard against
the abuse of power were recommended. These amendments demanded security against the apprehended encroachments of the
General Government — not against those of the local governments.
In compliance with a sentiment thus generally expressed, to quiet
fears thus extensively entertained, amendments were proposed by
the required majority in Congress, and adopted by the States.
These amendments contain no expression indicating an intention
to apply them to the State governments. This court cannot so
apply them." Chief Justice Marshall in *Barron* v. *Mayor and
Council of Baltimore*, 7 Pet. 243, 250.

the minds of those who were not favorable to
the Constitution as it was submitted for ratification, was that too much power was lodged in
the executive office.[1] It was said to be inconsistent with the genius of the Government which
they were establishing, that any one man should
exercise the extraordinary authority which that
instrument vested in the President of the United
States ; that the appointment of all the officers
of the Federal Government, the distribution of
all its patronage, and the control of its army and
navy, would, in process of time, enable some
man to build up a power that could not be resisted. It was argued that some one would arise
who, by that power and with that inclination,
would destroy the really democratic features of
our government, and finally establish a monarchy in its place.

This belief, though natural enough at that
time, was a very great mistake. The nearer we
approach to individual responsibility in the executive, the nearer will it come to perfection.
It is my deliberate opinion that, of all the three
branches which have been discussed, the execu-

---

[1] " It will always be far more easy for the State governments
to encroach upon the national authorities, than for the National
Government to encroach upon the State authorities. The proof of
this proposition turns upon the greater degree of influence which
the State governments, if they administer their affairs with up-
rightness and prudence, will generally possess over the people ; a
circumstance which at the same time teaches us, that there is an
inherent and intrinsic weakness in all Federal constitutions, and
that too much pains cannot be taken in their organization, to give
them all the force which is compatible with the principles of liberty."
The Federalist, No. 17.

tive has been in time, under the construction Lecture II.
given to the Federal Constitution and its prac- The executive.
tical administration, most shorn of the powers
granted to it thereby. The President of the
United States for the first forty or fifty years
did practically nominate all public officers; he
selected his cabinet himself, and personally
made other appointments, although possibly a
few private friends, and occasionally a member
of Congress or two, may have made suggestions.
But within the memory of many men now living
the time arrived when the' President (as the
gentleman who travelled around the world with
General Grant reports him as saying) only registered the edicts of members of Congress in
making appointments to office; that is to say,
in the function about which the Executive is
mainly employed, he has become subservient to
the legislative branch of the Government. This
objection, therefore, has proved to be without
foundation, and is not now seriously considered
by thoughtful men. Of all the delusive ideas,
or fallacies, that ever entered anybody's brain,
the most unfounded is this — that any President
can ever make himself a perpetual dictator,
either in our time and generation or in those
which are to come.

But the branch of the Government which has The Congress.
grown the most, and which a sagacious man
might perhaps have foreseen would so expand, is
the legislative.[1] Coming more immediately, as it

---

[1] It is without doubt absolutely necessary for securing the constitution of a State to restrain the executive power; but it is still

does, from the people, at least one branch of it, and representing a constituency who look to it as representing them in all their legislation, much is tolerated in it which would not be tolerated in the executive or judicial departments; because the people reason that if their representatives do badly during their present terms they may be turned out at the next election, and they are not, therefore, afraid that they will very greatly exceed their powers.

Weakness of the judicial branch.

The judicial branch is the weakest of all.[1] It has no army. It has no navy, and it has no purse. It has no officers, except its marshals, and they are appointed by the President and confirmed by the Senate. They are the officials to whom its processes are sent, but they may be removed at any time by the Executive. The clerks whom the judges are permitted in some form or another to appoint, have salaries and compensations regulated by the legislature; and a clerk who may receive $20,000 or more in fees must pay all but $3500 of such receipts into the Treasury of the United States.[2] It is then, so far as the ordinary forms of power are

---

more necessary to restrain the legislative. De Lolme, Constitution of England, London, 1834, p. 190.

Montesquieu said that the English constitution would perish when the legislative power becomes more corrupt than the executive.

[1] Montesquieu says: " The judiciary is the weakest of the three departments of the government."

[2] No clerk of a district or circuit court shall be allowed to retain fees, over and above necessary office expenses, in excess of $3500 per annum, [Rev. Stat. sec. 839,] except in California, Oregon, and Nevada, $7000 [sec. 840].

concerned, by far the feeblest branch or depart- LECTURE II.
ment of the Government. It must rely upon the Weakness of the judicial branch.
confidence and respect of the public for its just
weight and influence, and it may confidently be
asserted that neither the country, the people, nor
the other branches of the government, have ever
been found wanting in that respect or confidence.
It is one of the best tributes which can be paid
to the American nation, a tribute which it deserves above all others even of Anglo-Saxon
descent, and one which can be paid to no other
race, that it always submits to the law as expounded by its judiciary. Under all the excitements of bitter contests, involving great financial
interests, power, position, and even political
existence, in fact everything which could be
properly brought within its judicial cognizance,
the people have always felt that their interests
were safely intrusted to its charge. There has
never been a grander phenomenon witnessed in
the history of any country than that which occurred some years since in the State of Maine,
when a body calling itself a legal legislature,
and claiming to be an authorized government,
quietly laid down its functions and dispersed at
the mere opinion of a court that it had no rightful existence.[1]

---

[1] In 1879 there arose a controversy between the Fusionists and
the Republicans in the State of Maine, which was hotly contested,
and the feeling became exceedingly intense and bitter on both
sides. The decision of the Supreme Court of the State of Maine, by
which the organization of the Legislature by the Republicans was
sustained, was rendered on the 16th of January, 1879. See full
history of the origin and conclusion of the difficulty in Appleton's
Annual Cyclopædia, 1879-80.

LECTURE II.
Difficulties of
interpretation.

Of course there are nice questions constantly arising between these various departments of the Government as to the strict lines of demarcation which separate one from the other, and they are frequently of great importance. The fundamental principles by which the various powers of the Government are distributed among them are laid down in the Constitution, which it is the duty of the courts to construe,[1] whenever it shall come before them in a fair judicial proceeding, and they can construe it in no other way. It is a mistake to suppose that the special function for which the Supreme Court of the United States was created was to interpret and construe that instrument. It is, certainly, the special function of the courts to construe it in a judicial proceeding, with parties properly before them; but it is equally the duty of each member of Congress, as well as of the Executive, to make that construction for himself when he is called upon to act, within the sphere of his duty, upon any matter involving a question of constitutional law. It is also true that such member or Executive is bound to consider that in the execu-

Executive construction sometimes necessary.

---

[1] It has been often decided that the Supreme Court is the final arbiter of the meaning of the Constitution. This question has been very fully examined in the cases of *Vanhorne's Lessee* v. *Dorrance*, 2 Dall. 304; *Martin* v. *Hunter's Lessee*, 1 Wheat. 304; *Cohens* v. *Virginia*, 6 Wheat. 264; *Ableman* v. *Booth*, 21 How. 506.

Story, in his treatise on the Constitution, after discussing the question of who is final judge or interpreter in constitutional controversies, says that the appropriate conclusion is that the judicial department of the United States is, in the last resort, the final expositor of the Constitution, as to all questions of a judicial nature.

tion of the law, as between such parties, all other LECTURE II.
branches of the Government must yield to the Executive construction sometimes necessary.
interpretation declared by the courts; yet, when
the question is addressed to his conscience as to
whether he can vote for a proposed measure, or
sign a certain bill which is presented to him, it
is for him to decide, with the best light that he
can obtain, whether the matter is within the constitutional power of the body of which he is a
member.

It will thus be seen how difficult it is to get a
settled construction of this great instrument;
and, since every branch of the Government, when
called upon to act originally, is bound to act on
the judgment which it forms of its own powers,
it is not hard to understand the reason why the
exact relations of the States to the Federal Government should still, in many instances, remain
an open and undecided question. We are, how- Judicial interpretation should be sustained.
ever getting a body of decisions which have
become recognized principles. These interpretations of our organic law have been more often
made by the judicial branch than by all the
others, although largely by them as well, and
have been very clearly brought out in the light
of the events which have arisen to test it. For
example, many points, in regard to which a construction was put upon it during the late insurrection, as to the powers that could be exercised
in such an emergency by the President, by the
War Department, by the Legislature, or by the
Judiciary, all underwent a severe and thorough
investigation, and such construction was thus

practically tested. No man can say that all of
the many decisions have been correct; but yet it
must, in the light of any impartial mind, be
clear that we are completing a construction of
our Constitution, and are deciding a great many
things with regard to it which will remain
forever.

It is very desirable that this should be so.
All loose methods of construing authority are
dangerous, as well as all such as are too limited
to serve the purposes for which they were in-

Principles of in-
terpretation.

tended. The Constitution must be looked at in
the light of the ends it was designed to accomplish, having in view the evils it was intended
to remedy and the benefits it was to exert. We
must examine it in the light of the fact that we
were a dissolving people, which it was designed
anew to bind together in a relation which should
continue forever; that the Confederation was
rapidly falling to pieces for want of power to protect itself;[1] and that one of the main purposes of

---

[1] Upon the report, February 21, 1787, by a majority of one, that
the Confederation needed amendments, and the proposed convention
was the most eligible means of effecting them, many members of
the Congress considered it a deadly blow to the existing Confederation, others as a harbinger of a better one. All agreed and owned
that the Federal Government, in its existing shape, was inefficient,
and could not last long. 5 Elliot's Debates, 96.

" The adoption of the first eleven amendments to the Constitution, so soon after the original instrument was accepted, shows a
prevailing sense of danger at that time from the Federal power.
And it cannot be denied that such a jealousy continued to exist
with many patriotic men until the breaking out of the late Civil
War. It was then discovered that the true danger to the perpetuity
of the Union was in the capacity of State organizations to combine
and concentrate all the powers of the States and of contiguous
States for a determined resistance to the General Government.

this instrument was to give to the Central Government that power. .It must not be forgotten
that the Confederacy, or the government that
existed under the Articles of Confederation,
could only request the States to do a great many
things necessary in order to maintain and carry
on the Federal Government successfully, and
that it was desirable to give the new one the
power of operating directly upon the people
without going through the instrumentality of
the States. We must consider that under the
old order of things the laws were enacted to
take effect through the action of the State legislatures,[1] which ineffective and circuitous method
was to give way to the direct legislation of
Congress; so that the action of the legislative
branch, and concurrently with it the decisions of
the judiciary, should act immediately upon the
people themselves, without the consent, and even
against the wishes, of the States, if it were
necessary.

Unquestionably, this has given great force to the argument, and
added largely to the number of those who believe in the necessity
of a strong National Government." *Slaughter-House Cases,* 16
Wall. 36, 82.

[1] The taxes for paying the proportion needful for charges of war
and other expenses for the common defence, or general welfare,
were to be "laid and levied by the authority and direction of the
Legislatures of the several States." Articles of Confederation, VIII.

The Articles of Confederation were entirely without any provision for enforcing the measures which they authorized Congress
to adopt for the general welfare of the Union. . . . The sole means
it gave to Congress of supplying the treasury of the United States
was to vote what sum was wanted, and call upon the Legislature
of each State to pay in its proportion within a given time. Curtis'
Constitution.

All these things are to be considered when it is sought to determine ·the force and effect of any of its provisions. Like a remedial statute, or a contract between individuals, it must be construed in the light of the times in which it was made, with reference to the evils to be remedied, the good to be effected, and, above all, in the light of the idea that it was made to create a perpetual government of the people, among the people, and by the people.[1]

Another canon of construction which must not be overlooked has reference to the fundamental nature of the novel government which was erected, very much in the nature of an experiment,[2] by the Colonies when they severed the ties which bound them to England. The Federal Government which they founded is one of conceded or granted powers. The State governments are governments authorized to exercise all the powers not prohibited by the Federal Gov-

---

[1] The Constitution was for a new government, organized with new substantive powers, and not a mere supplementary charter to a government already existing. The Confederation was a compact between States, and its structure and powers were wholly unlike those of the National Government. The Constitution was an act of the people of the United States to supersede the Confederation, and not be ingrafted on it, as a stock through which it was to receive life and nourishment. Story, J., in *Martin* v. *Hunter's Lessees*, 1 Wheat. 332.

[2] A constitution adopted with great opposition, the subject of the gravest difference of opinion among the wisest men on its most material points, was quite as likely to fail as its predecessor, the Articles of Confederation, had failed. The field was absolutely untried. Never before had there been such a science in the world as the law of a written constitution of a government. Address of Hon. Edward J. Phelps, in 1879, before the American Bar Association.

ernment or by the Constitution of the United
States.[1] There is a corresponding difference in .construction, therefore, and this difference pervades the Federal and State constitutions throughout the entire catalogue of their powers and the limitations thereon. These need too extended an examination to be considered here, but will be treated under their appropriate heads.

One illustration of the different nature of the powers of the State and Federal Governments is in the authority to punish offences. A State legislature can declare any act of an individual deemed by it to be detrimental to the public good to be an offence, and can prescribe for it a punishment. Whatever that body may conceive to be injurious to the general welfare they can forbid, and if it is done they can punish the infraction of their law by a penalty. But the Federal Government can only punish offences against the powers which it exercises. Having exclusive control of the carrying of the mail,[2] it can punish persons unlawfully interfering therewith in any way. With the power to coin money it has also been given the power to punish the counterfeiting of that coin. Having authority to borrow funds for its needs, it can issue bonds therefor, and can punish the counterfeiters of those bonds, as well as those who

---

[1] The powers not delegated to the United States by the Constitution, nor prohibited by it to the States, are reserved to the States respectively, or to the people. Amendment X.

[2] Congress shall have the power to establish post-offices and post-roads. Constitution, Art. 1, sec. 8, par. 7.

put them in circulation.[1] But the national authority has no power to punish murder or theft in general, because that is within the province of the individual States.

The General Government can levy taxes, but they must be for a defined purpose, such as the payment of the public debt, or of the army and navy of the United States. It has no right to raise money by taxation for religious purposes, or for a thousand things on account of which States may impose taxes and collect them of the people. It has no such power, because, as has already been intimated, it is not granted by the Constitution.[2]

There is no part of the great system of constitutional law in which modern improvements have been greater, and have more steadily progressed in a proper direction, than in that of limitations upon the powers of the legislative and the executive branches of the government.[3]

---

[1] Congress shall have power to borrow money on the credit of the United States. Constitution, Art. 1, sec. 8, par. 2. To provide for the punishment of counterfeiting the securities and current coin of the United States. Id. par. 6.

It is within the constitutional powers of Congress to enact laws to provide for the punishment of the offence of counterfeiting notes of a foreign bank or corporation. *United States* v. *Arjona*, 120 U. S. 479.

Congress shall have power to lay and collect taxes, duties, imposts, and excises; to pay the debts, and provide for the common defence and general welfare of the United States. Constitution, Art. 1, sec. 8, par. 1.

[2] There can be no lawful tax which is not laid for a *public purpose*. See cases cited; *Loan Association* v. *Topeka*, 20 Wall. 655, 664.

[3] The theory of our governments, State and National, is opposed to the deposit of unlimited power anywhere. The executive, the

Both the Federal and the State constitutions of this country are full of them.[1] Under the boasted constitution of Great Britain there are many instances in which a man has been condemned to death by its Parliament without any reference to any statute or law existing at the time authorizing such a proceeding. By virtue of the omnipotent power reposed in the king and the Parliament of that country a man might lose his life, his property be taken from him, and his blood become so attainted that even his children could not inherit it.[2]

Our constitutions are limited in many such respects. No government in this country would undertake to deprive a man of his liberty or property, much less his life, without the authority of an already existing law.[3] So in regard to

---

legislative, and the judicial branches of these governments are all of limited and defined powers. *Loan Association* v. *Topeka*, 20 Wall. 655, 663.

[1] " The Executive, in our governments, is not the sole, it is scarcely the principal, object of my jealousy. The tyranny of the Legislatures is the most formidable dread at present, and will be for many years." Letter of Jefferson to Madison, March 15, 1789; Jefferson's Works, vol. 3, p. 5.

[2] See the instance of attainder of Lord Seymour, in 1548-9, whom according to the policy of that age the Duke of Somerset thought it necessary to crush by a bill of attainder. He was in his turn also prosecuted in the same manner within a few months after the execution of his victim. Hallam's Constitutional History of England, vol. 1, p. 39 (London, 1855). See also the attainder of the Earl of Strafford by the Long Parliament in 1640. 2 Ib. 103. Bills of attainder were by no means uncommon in England, especially under Henry VIII.

The subject of bills of attainder is discussed at length, both in the opinion of the court and the dissent thereto, in *Cummings* v. *Missouri*, 4 Wall. 277, and *Ex parte Garland*, 4 Wall. 333.

[3] No bill of attainder or *ex post facto* law shall be passed by

private property taken for public uses. All governments exercise this right; but while it is done by others without any fixed rule in regard to compensation, all of our constitutions, both Federal and State, provide that private property shall not be so taken without just compensation.[1] Indeed, the tendency of all changes in constitutional governments, both in this country and in all others where sound principles of political economy are taught and discussed, is to the further protection of private rights as against the governing power, which represents the entire body politic.

There is another change going on in this country, which, whether it shall turn out to be so worthy of praise or not, remains for time to settle; that is, the tendency to popularize suffrage and to extend the elective principle to a vast number of offices not formerly within its purview. But it is difficult to believe that, in

---

Congress (Constitution, Art. 1, sec. 9, par. 3), or by a State (Art. 1, sec. 10, par. 1).

No State shall make or enforce any law that shall abridge the privileges or immunities of citizens of the United States, nor shall any State deprive any person of life, liberty, or property without due process of law, nor deny to any person within its jurisdiction the equal protection of the laws. Constitution, Amendment XIV, sec. 1.

Nor shall private property be taken for public use without just compensation. Amendment V.

[1] In nearly all of the constitutions of the various States of the Union provision has been made substantially of this character, and in most cases in the exact language of the Federal Constitution. It usually occurs in what is designated as the Bill of Rights prefatory to the main body of the instrument. See Charters and Constitutions of the United States (Ben: Perley Poore, Washington, 1878), containing the complete texts of all the constitutions of the States.

any country where the people are governed by Lecture II.
laws made by legislatures, the basis upon which Extension of the suffrage.
the representation stands can be too large. It
may, however, be doubted whether the elective
principle can safely be applied to that class of
officers, especially the judicial, whose duty it is
to enforce the laws.

The importance of a thorough knowledge of A knowledge of the Constitution essential to a lawyer.
constitutional law to those who propose here-
after to practise the profession of the law in this
country can hardly be exaggerated. The time
has been, and until very recently, that a lawyer
might attain a great practice and a very high
reputation in the State courts, and some of the
first reputations in the country have been so
made, without ever having practised at all in
the Federal courts, or having his attention called,
except perhaps incidentally, to this subject, or
the matters we have been discussing. But that
period in the history of the country has passed.
The time has come when the Constitution and
laws of the United States are not the mere theoretical object of the thoughts of the statesman,
the lawyer, or the man of affairs; for the operations of its Government now reach to the recesses
of every man's business, and force themselves
upon every man's thoughts.

The history of the events which led to the
recent War of the Rebellion, and of the times
subsequent thereto, taught the people of this
country, in a manner which it is to be hoped
will never again be necessary, that this Government within its sphere is supreme, and that its

LECTURE II.
A knowledge of
the Constitution
essential to a
lawyer.
sphere is a very extensive and pervading one. Leaving out of the question now all that took place under the period of reconstruction, many other matters have come into play in the operations of the Federal Government which were previously almost unknown.

An illustration of this is to be seen in the internal revenue system, under which, during the years immediately succeeding the Rebellion, almost every species of property, occupation, and pursuit, and many things which had scarcely acquired the name of property or occupation, were taxed by the Federal Government to pay the interest and principal of the debt incurred in that war, as well as for the expenses of the Government, largely increased by its operations. Those statutes, and the taxes which were laid under them, even if everybody was willing to submit to them cheerfully, required construction. They were new to the country. When the laws were put into operation the officers themselves were frequently very much perplexed to know what they meant, and the Government, desiring that no person should be injured, was ready, and afforded opportunities, to have the laws tested by courts of justice. A man had but to pay his taxes, and take an appeal to the commissioner who had supervision of those matters. If he failed there he could sue the man who collected them, and recover if they were illegally assessed. The number of suits growing out of this class of cases was immense, and has been so ever since the internal revenue system was established. The list of articles subject to taxation

has been very largely decreased, but it is probable that a very large sum, possibly approaching one hundred millions of dollars, which sum has been largely exceeded every year since the establishment of the present system in 1863, will always be raised annually in this country by the taxation imposed by the Federal Government on spirits, tobacco, and malt liquors.[1]

But it is not only when a suit is brought, or is to be brought, that the lawyer is called upon to understand these things, or to give counsel in regard to this jurisdiction and these laws. He is very often consulted as to what a party should do where no suit is contemplated. Neither is this knowledge necessary or useful only in the large business centres; but the system permeates the entire country, so that the remotest village lawyer may be called upon to advise upon questions of constitutional or statutory construction, or as to the manner in which the laws are enforced by the officials charged with that duty.

It may also be noted that the bankruptcy laws have greatly modified the existing system of enforcing contracts or collecting debts, in the case of persons who fail to meet their engagements, or to pay for want of ability to do

---

[1] For annual statistics of internal revenue receipts of the United States from March 4, 1789, to June 30, 1886, see Spofford's American Almanac, 1887.

Many decisions of controverted questions on this subject, which were referred to the Attorney General of the United States, are collated in the Digest of Opinions of Attorney General, tit. Internal Revenue.

LECTURE II.
A knowledge of
the Constitution
essential to a
lawyer.
so. Those laws are administered under Federal statutes, and not only under an act of Congress, but under the rules of practice prescribed and adopted for the courts of the. United States.[1] The lawyer who does not know when a man has committed an act of bankruptcy, or who does not know how to institute a proceeding in such a court, can hardly expect to receive a full share of practice in any community.

In addition to this the admiralty jurisdiction of the Federal courts has, within the last few years, by constructions placed upon it by those courts, received an immense increase in its extent. Down to 1851 it was held to be limited in fact to the seaboard, if not actually to the sea. It extended no further on the rivers

---

[1] Congress shall have power . . . to establish . . . uniform laws on the subject of bankruptcies throughout the United States. Constitution, Art. 1, sec. 8, par. 4.

See acts of April 4, 1800, 2 Stat. 19, c. 19; December 19, 1803, 2 Stat. 248, c. 6; August 19, 1841, 5 Stat. 440, c. 9; and March 2, 1867, 14 Stat. 517, c. 176. A State may, however, pass a bankrupt law, provided there is no act of Congress conflicting with it. *Sturges* v. *Crowninshield*, 4 Wheat. 122.

As to what is a bankruptcy, see opinion of Judge Catron delivered in the Circuit Court *In re Klein*, 1 How. 277. The whole subject was elaborately considered by the Supreme Court of New York in *Kunzler* v. *Kohaus*, 5 Hill, 317, and *Sackett* v. *Andross*, 5 Hill, 327.

By the act of Congress, approved June 7, 1878, 20 Stat. 99, c. 160, the bankruptcy law of 1867, 14 Stat., 517, c. 176, and all supplementary acts, incorporated in the Revised Statutes, sections 4972 to 5132, were repealed, to take effect September 1, 1878. Pending cases were not, however, affected. A strong effort has been made to secure another national act of a similar character, and one has been past the Senate, but failed of action in the House.

For rules of court in bankruptcy, see Desty's Federal Procedure, p. 337.

than the tide ebbed and flowed. But the Supreme Court of the United States has since decided that it extended to all navigable streams;
that it was a system of laws intended to have
operation upon the interests of navigation; that
whether it took place upon salt or fresh water
was entirely immaterial, and that the Constitution of the United States, when it declared that
the Federal courts should have jurisdiction in
admiralty, meant that they should have jurisdiction in all that class of cases which heretofore
had been called admiralty cases, whether they
grew out of salt water transactions or of engagements and acts upon fresh water.[1]

The decision of this principle has made the
subject of questions concerning the carrying
trade by steamboats upon our rivers and lakes
one of much interest to every lawyer throughout the great interior of this country. Every
steamboat becomes, in regard to suits concerning its transactions or its contracts, as well as
in regard to torts committed by its officers, subject to the admiralty jurisdiction of the courts
of the United States. By an act of Congress
passed in the earliest history of the country,
where the action is, strictly speaking, an admiralty case; that is, one known and recognized

---

[1] In the case of *The Thomas Jefferson*, 10 Wheat. 428, it was
decided that the jurisdiction of the courts of admiralty in the
United States was limited to the ebb and flow of the tide; but in
The Genessee Chief v. *Fitzhugh*, 12 How. 443, it was held that it
was not limited to the tide waters, but extends to all public navigable lakes and rivers where commerce is carried on between different States, or with a foreign nation. See Notes upon this Lecture.

Lecture II.
A knowledge of
the Constitution
essential to a
lawyer.
as belonging to the ancient jurisdiction of admiralty in England and on the Continent, the Federal courts have exclusive jurisdiction, and it cannot be exercised by the State courts.[1] If a lawyer, therefore, expects to have a large practice in any part of the country now, he must know something of admiralty law and its jurisdiction and application.

It is evident, therefore, that the discussion of the principles which have been outlined has something more than a mere theoretical value, not only to every lawyer, but to every citizen living under the authority and protection of a constitutional government. Questions of constitutional law, especially in regard to the Constitution of the United States, have become matters of common occurrence in the courts. Whether it is that the Congress of the United States has taken a more liberal view of its powers than formerly, or whether it is that the people are more disposed to question the exercise of its powers, may be open to question, but certain it is that hardly any act of that body in modern times can be brought to bear upon an individual, to which he is reluctant to assent, that he does not attempt to raise the question of its constitutional power to pass it. Our books of reports, both State and Federal, are thus filled

---

[1] The original jurisdiction in admiralty exercised by the District Courts, was regulated by the act of September 24, 1789, 1 Stat. 73, c. 20, and enlarged by the act of February 26, 1845, 5 Stat. 726, c. 20. It is exclusive in those courts, not only of other Federal courts, but of the State courts also. *The Hine* v. *Trevor*, 4 Wall. 555, 569.

with decisions upon questions of constitutional law.

With the rapid progress of this country in wealth, and its growth in population and power, it is but natural that there should be a great increase in litigation. Out of the multiplication of corporations of all kinds, and the changes in the methods for the transportation of persons and property, which have taken place within a few years, have arisen a vast number of suits before almost entirely unknown, involving also new principles of construction and application.

The Federal Government is exercising to some extent its powers over this subject of transportation, under the clause of the Constitution of the United States which declares that Congress shall have the right to regulate commerce with foreign nations, with the Indian tribes, and among the several States.[1] State legislatures are constantly enacting laws for the promotion of their purposes, for the raising of money, or for the protection of what they consider their individual rights, which are supposed to be in conflict with this right of Congress to regulate commerce among the States; and the Supreme Court of the United States has been flooded in recent years with questions concerning the power of the States to pass laws regarding tax-

---

[1] Congress shall have power to regulate commerce with foreign nations, and among the several States, and with the Indian tribes. Constitution, Art. 1, sec. 8, par. 3.

See "an act to regulate commerce," generally known as the Interstate Commerce Act, approved February 4, 1887, 24 Stat. 379, c. 104.

ation, and other matters supposed to infringe upon the rights of individuals as citizens of the Federal Government.[1]

By the recent amendments to the Constitution, adopted since the War of the Rebellion ended,[2] new questions of constitutional law, involving the relations sustained by the Federal Government to the States and their people, have been raised, and are constantly arising, which require attentive consideration. A mass of people, several millions in number, who were not theretofore citizens of the United States, have been made such by those amendments. That class of people who were declared by the Dred Scott decision,[3] in 1856, to have no rights

---

[1] The cases on this subject are so numerous that attention need now only be directed to several of the most recent, in which the previous decisions and history of the matter are referred to.

Interstate commerce cannot be taxed at all by a State. *Robbins* v. *Shelby County Taxing District*, 120 U. S. 489.

A prosecution of a citizen and resident of New York for selling by sample in the State of Maryland without a license held to be constitutional under the commerce clause of the Federal Constitution. *Corson* v. *Maryland*, 120 U. S. 502.

A State statute, which levies a tax upon the gross receipts of railroads for the carriage of freight and passengers into, out of, or through the State, is a tax upon commerce among the States, and therefore void. *Fargo* v. *Michigan*, 121 U. S. 230.

See also very full reference to previous cases and authorities in *Wabash, St. Louis & Pacific Railway Co.* v. *Illinois*, 118 U. S. 557.

Mr. Garfield said in the House of Representatives : " Chief Justice Marshall, that great judge who found the Constitution paper, and made it a power, who found it a skeleton, and clothed it with flesh and blood. By his wisdom and genius, he made it the potent and beneficent instrument for the government of a great nation." Record, 46 Congress, p. 2390.

[2] Amendments XIII, XIV, and XV.

[3] *Dred Scott* v. *Sandford*, 19 How. 393.

which a white man was bound to respect, have
come to have all the legal or civil rights which
a white man has.

Attorneys and courts are frequently called
upon to construe the Constitution of the United
States, and the laws passed in pursuance thereof,
as well as to determine questions of the conflict of State constitutions and laws therewith.
Any lawyer may at any time be called upon to
advise about all of these questions which have
been so briefly suggested, and to put in operation
the machinery of the law of the Federal Government for the protection of the rights of his
client. No branch of the law is of more importance to the counsellor, the statesman, or the
citizen, than a thorough acquaintance with the
Constitution and laws of the Federal Government, as they are administered, and as they
affect the rights of the people.

In this connection may be appropriately cited
the words of Chancellor Kent, one of the most
able and accomplished writers upon legal topics
that this country ever produced, which, delivered a half century ago, derive added force from
the great historical events which have occurred
since he passed away.

"The Government of the United States was
erected by the free voice and joint will of the
people of America for their common defence and
general welfare. Its powers apply to those
great interests which relate to this country in
its national capacity, and which depend for
their stability and protection on the consolida-

tion of the Union.   It is clothed with the principal attributes of political sovereignty, and it is justly deemed the guardian of our best rights, the source of our highest civil and political duties, and the sure means of national greatness." [1]

---

[1] 1 Kent's Commentaries, 201.

NOTES UPON LECTURE II.

FROM the very beginning of the Government LECTURE II. Federal and States' rights theories of construction. there have been two theories for the construction of the Constitution. The thorough-going Federalist on the one hand, insists that it must be construed with reference to the circumstances which made it necessary, and with a just conception of the objects which its framers desired to accomplish by it. Hence he contends that the delegated powers are to be construed liberally, and that implied powers are to be assumed when necessary to fully carry delegated powers into effect. On the other hand, the strict States' rights man plants himself upon the Tenth Amendment, as the people's contemporaneous construction, and contends that the National Government is a government with delegated powers only, and that the Instrument of delegation should be construed strictly.

If I understand the views of Justice Miller, Weight to be given to judicial construction. while his personal sympathies were undoubtedly in the main with the Federalists, he belonged to neither school. He was of the opinion that the powers of the Central Government are, in the end, practically to be settled by the judiciary; and that judicial decisions upon constitutional questions are entitled to the respect which those

LECTURE II.
Weight to be
given to judicial
construction.

decisions receive in questions of law. Although he admits that the Executive must act according to its own light when new questions arise, he inclines to the view that, under the Constitution, the Supreme Court is the proper interpreter of that instrument; and that its interpretation, especially when repeatedly given, ought to have controlling weight.

It may be objected to this theory that the judiciary has been at different times, on both sides of many questions of constitutional law; as for instance on the constitutional limits of admiralty jurisdiction, and on the constitutionality of the Legal Tender Act. Nevertheless it must be true that a power of authoritative interpretation is lodged somewhere. We have seen in the outcome of the doctrine first announced in the *Dartmouth College Case*,[1] how a theory of construction, novel when propounded, may, as time rolls on, commend itself and be universally accepted. Judicial interpretation can become necessary or possible only when private interests are in litigation; but when the same question often recurs, and is as often decided in the same way, an accepted rule of construction comes at last into force. It is in the courts alone that opportunity is given for such repeated consideration and reconsideration of a constitutional question; and hence their decisions should have persuasive weight.

Prior to the adoption of the Constitution,

---

[1] 4 Wheat. 518.

there being no Federal judiciary (with the exception of the Prize Courts), Congress itself set
the limit to its own powers by its executive and
legislative acts. In the Note to Chapter I, taking as a starting-point the fact that the Constitution was the historic outcome of various efforts at
nationality during preceding years, an attempt
was made to learn from history what construction Congress at that time put upon its own powers. We saw it forced by necessity to assume
functions of sovereignty which had dropped from
the hands of the king of Great Britain, and to
exercise them repeatedly and without question
prior to the adoption of any Articles regulating
the relations between it and the individual States.
We saw Congress, after the adoption of those
Articles, receive the cession of an empire, and
determine the character of its civilization, without having received in the Articles authority to
do so. These exercises of sovereign power, growing out of the necessities of the people of the
whole United States, were unquestioned when
made, and have not been doubted since. The
most extreme Federalist must admit, however,
that such a rule of construction is loose and
dangerous, and that it should be resorted to only
in case of necessity.

The Constitution gave to the people a judiciary to protect it against an abuse of its
powers by either co-ordinate branch of the Government, on the one hand; and, on the other
hand, to recognize as just and constitutional an
exercise of power assailed as unconstitutional.

LECTURE II.
Weight to be
given to judicial
construction.

Although the Supreme Court of the United States has become one of the recognized great law courts of the world, whose decisions on questions of law, civil and international, are everywhere regarded with the highest respect, it is not too much to say that its greatest and its most important work has been done in the settlement of disputed points of constitutional law. Persons not familiar with its reports have little conception of the amount of time, of labor, and of thought which has been expended upon this subject.

Out of the mass of decisions, running through one hundred and forty volumes, I select four subjects as specially illustrating the fundamental principle of construction which appears to have prevailed throughout the hundred years. The first of these cases related to the Appellate Prize Courts of the Revolution, and the judgment was rendered in the early part of the first quarter of the century. The second subject was the acquisition of Louisiana, which was sustained judicially in the second quarter. The third relates to admiralty jurisdiction, which was extended by the legislature, and the extension judicially sustained, in the third quarter. The fourth is the legislation making the promises of the United States a legal tender, which was finally sustained by the Supreme Court near the close of the fourth quarter of the century.

1. *The Judgments of the Appellate Prize Courts.*

The validity of these judgments came before Lecture II. the court at the February Term, 1795,[1] on the Action of the Supreme Court on following facts. In April, 1776, Congress agreed the judgments of upon a form of commission to commanders of the Prize Courts of the Confedera- private vessels of war, and such a commission was tion. issued to Joshua Stackpole of New Hampshire, as commander of the McClary. In October, 1777, while in command of that vessel, he captured the brigantine Susanna on the high seas, and carried her into the port of Portsmouth for condemnation as lawful prize. The legislature of New Hampshire had, on the 3d of July, 1776, created a Prize Court, with a right of appeal to the Continental Congress when the capture was made by an "armed vessel fitted out at the charge of the United Colonies," and in other cases to the Superior Court of the State. Congress had, as we have already seen, taken appellate jurisdiction in many such cases before the date of the capture.

The Susanna and her cargo were libelled in the Maritime Court of New Hampshire, and condemned as lawful prize and ordered to be sold. An appeal to Congress was claimed from this decree and was refused. The claimants then took an appeal to the Superior Court of New Hampshire, which was granted, and the judgment below was affirmed there. The claimants took an appeal to Congress from this judgment, which was not allowed; but they

---

[1] *Penhallow* v. *Doane*, 3 Dall. 54.

LECTURE II.
Action of the
Supreme Court on
the judgments of
the Prize Courts
of the Confedera-
tion.
nevertheless lodged their petition there in October, 1778, within the prescribed time, asking
Congress to hear the appeal.   Congress decided,
after discussion, to take jurisdiction ; and, after
hearing the parties, reversed the judgment of
the court below in September, 1783.

After the organization of the Federal judiciary
under the Constitution, the representatives of
these appellants instituted proceedings in admiralty in the District Court of the United States
in New Hampshire to enforce the judgment
of the Appellate Court, citing in the owners
of the McClary; and, as the result of the proceedings, the libellants obtained a judgment for
upwards of $38,000. This was the case brought
for review to the Supreme Court by writ of error.
It is plain that it involved the question of the
jurisdiction of the Court of Appeals over the appeal in October, 1778, when the petition of the
appellant was presented. Judgment was announced January 24, 1795, the judges delivering
their opinions *seriatim*. The court consisted of
Mr. Jay, Chief Justice (who was absent); Mr.
Cushing of Massachusetts; Mr. Wilson of Pennsylvania ; Mr. Blair of Virginia ; Mr. Iredell of
North Carolina ; and Mr. Paterson of New Jersey. Mr. Paterson, Mr. Blair, and Mr. Wilson
were members of the convention which framed
the Constitution.

Mr. Justice Paterson, speaking first, divided
the question of the jurisdiction of the Appellate
Prize Court into two branches ; (1) acts done
before the adoption of the Articles of Confederation in 1781; (2) acts done after that time.

In respect of the first he said: "The powers LECTURE II.
Action of the
Supreme Court on
the judgments of
the Prize Courts
of the Confedera-
tion. of Congress were revolutionary in their nature, arising out of events, adequate to every national emergency, and co-extensive with the object to be attained. Congress was the general, supreme, and controlling council of the nation, the centre of union, the centre of force, and the sun of the political system. To determine what their powers were, we must inquire what powers they exercised. Congress raised armies, fitted out a navy, and prescribed rules for their government; Congress conducted all military operations, both by land and sea; Congress emitted bills of credit, received and sent ambassadors, and made treaties; Congress commissioned privateers to cruise against the enemy, directed what vessels should be liable to capture, and prescribed rules for the distribution of prizes. These high acts of sovereignty were submitted to, acquiesced in, and approved of by the people of America. . . . There was but one war, and one sovereign will to conduct it. The danger being imminent and common, it became necessary for the people or Colonies to coalesce and act in concert in order to divert or break the violence of the gathering storm; they accordingly grew into union, and formed one great political body, of which Congress was the directing principle and soul."

On the second point he said: "The Court of Appeals, in September, 1783, decided upon the point of jurisdiction, either directly or incidentally; for, after a full hearing, they decreed that the sentences passed by the superior and inferior

LECTURE II.

Action of the
Supreme Court on
the judgments of
the Prize Courts
of the Confedera-
tion.

courts of New Hampshire should be reversed
and annulled, and the property be restored. This
decree, being made by a court constitutionally
established, of competent authority and the highest jurisdiction, is conclusive and final."

Mr. Justice Iredell said: "When acts were
passed by the Parliament of Great Britain,
which were thought unconstitutional and unjust,
and when every hope of redress by separate
applications appeared desperate, there was conceived the noble idea, which laid the foundation
of the present independence and happiness of
this country, (though independence was not
then in contemplation,) of forming a common
council to consult for the common welfare of
the whole, so far as an opposition' to the measures of Great Britain was concerned. . . . Each
province appointed as many or as few deputies
as it pleased, at its own discretion, which was
not objected to, because the members of Congress
did not vote individually, but the votes given in
Congress were by provinces, as they afterwards
were, (subsequent to the Declaration of Independence, and until the present Constitution of the
United States was formed,) by States. The
powers of Congress, at first, were indeed little
more than advisory; but, in proportion as the
danger increased, their powers were gradually
enlarged, either by express grant, or by implication arising from a kind of indefinite authority,
suited to the unknown exigencies that might
arise. That an undefined authority is dangerous, and ought to be intrusted as cautiously as

possible, every man must admit; and none could Lecture II.
Action of the
Supreme Court on
the judgments of
the Prize Courts
of the Confedera-
tion. take more pains than Congress for a long time
did, to get their authority regularly defined by
a ratification of the Articles of Confederation.
But that, previously thereto, they did exercise,
with the acquiescence of the States, high powers
of what I may, perhaps, with propriety, for distinction call external sovereignty is unquestionable. . . . Whether among these powers
comprehended within their general authority,
was that of instituting courts for the trial of all
prize causes, was a great and awful question;
a question that demanded deep consideration,
and not perhaps susceptible of an easy decision.
That in point of prudence and propriety, it
was a power most fit for Congress to exercise, I
have no doubt. I think all prize causes whatsoever ought to belong to the national sovereignty.
. . . This is a consideration of no small weight
to induce an inference that they actually possessed it when their powers were so indefinite,
and when it seems to have been the sense of all
the States that Congress should possess all the
incidents to external sovereignty."

Mr. Justice Blair said : "The immediate question is, whether Congress had a right to exercise,
by themselves, by their committees, or by any regular court of appeals by them erected, an appellate
jurisdiction, to affirm or reverse a sentence of a
State court of admiralty, in a question whether
prize or no prize. If they possessed such an
authority, it must be derivative, and its source,
either mediately or immediately, the will of the

LECTURE II.
Action of the
Supreme Court on
the judgments of
the Prize Courts
of the Confedera-
tion.
people. Usurpation can give no right. . . .
They raised an army; they appointed a commander-in-chief with other general and field officers; they modelled the army, disposed of the
troops, emitted bills of credit, pledged the confederated Colonies for the redemption of them,
and, in short, acted in all respects like a body
completely armed with all the powers of war;
and at all this I find not the least symptom of
discontent among all the confederated States,
or the whole people of America; on the contrary,
Congress were universally revered, and looked
up to as our political fathers and the saviours
of their country. . . . I am therefore of opinion that those acts of New Hampshire which
restrain the jurisdiction of Congress, being contrary to the legitimate powers of Congress, can
have no binding force; and that, under the
authority of Congress, an appeal will lay from
the courts of admiralty of that State to the court
of Commissioners of Appeals."

Mr. Justice Cushing said: "I concur with the
rest of the court, that the Court of Appeals,
being a court under the Confederation of 1781
of all the States, and being a court for 'determining finally appeals in all cases of capture,'
and so being the highest court, the dernier resort
of all such cases, their decision upon the jurisdiction and upon the merits of the cause, having
heard the parties by their counsel, must be final
and conclusive. . . . As to the original question of the powers of Congress respecting captures . . . I have no doubt of the sovereignty

of the States, saving the powers delegated to Congress, being such as were ' proper and necessary ' to carry on, unitedly, the common defence in the open war that was waged against this country, and in support of their liberties, to the end of the contest."

As we have already seen,[1] this unanimous ruling, although the different judges reached their conclusions by different methods of reasoning, was followed by the court fourteen years later, Mr. Chief Justice Marshall giving the opinion.[2]

Thus it was determined, as an historic fact, that in 1779 Congress had the power to create a Prize Court with jurisdiction over judgments of State courts, even in violation of the laws of a State, provided the subject of the judgment was national in character; and that rights of property acquired under this legislation were to be upheld by courts of the United States existing under the Constitution, and to be protected by its civil authorities. The court practically adopted the language of the Resolutions of Congress passed in 1779, at a time when no power had been conferred upon it by a written instrument, that "Congress or such person or persons as they appoint" "have *necessarily* the power" to exercise full appellate jurisdiction in such cases, and that "no act of any one State can or ought to destroy" it. Here was first announced,

---

[1] See *ante*, p. 46.
[2] *United States* v. *Peters*, 5 Cranch, 115.

LECTURE II.
Action of the
Supreme Court on
the judgments of
the Prize Courts
of the Confedera-
tion.

Acquisition of
Louisiana.

and in the most concrete form, that doctrine of implied powers, which has had so great influence in shaping the destinies of the United States.

2. *The Acquisition of Louisiana.*

Mr. Jefferson, under whom the acquisition was made, held views on its constitutionality which are well known. He said : " This treaty must, of course, be laid before both Houses, because they have important functions to exercise respecting it. They, I presume, will see their duty to their country in ratifying and paying for it, so as to secure a good which would otherwise probably be never again in their power. But I suppose they must then appeal to *the nation* for an additional article to the Constitution, approving and confirming an act which the nation had not previously authorized. The Constitution has made no provision for our holding foreign territory, still less for incorporating foreign nations into our Union. The Executive, in seizing the fugitive occurrence which so much advances the good of their country, have done an act beyond the Constitution." [1]

On the 30th of the same month he wrote to Mr. Lincoln, the Attorney General, who had given an opinion favorable to the constitutionality of the measure, that " the less that is said about any constitutional difficulty the better. Congress should do what is necessary *in silence.*

---

[1] Jefferson to Breckenridge, August 12, 1803. 4 Jefferson's Works, 500.

I find but one opinion as to the necessity of
shutting up the country for some time." [1]

Mr. Gallatin, however, who was the Secretary of the Treasury at that time, was of a different opinion. He said : " Does any constitutional objection really exist? . . . To me it would appear, (1) that the United States, as a nation, have an inherent right to acquire territory ; (2) that whenever that acquisition is by treaty, the same constituted authorities, in whom the treaty-making power is vested, have a constitutional right to sanction the acquisition." [2]

The average view of the Federalists is probably expressed by Josiah Quincy, then a member of Congress : " The clause in the Constitution giving the power to Congress to admit into the Union other States, had unquestionably sole reference to the admission of States within the limits of the original territory of the United States. No original document, argument, or treatise, at the time of the formation of the Constitution, can be adduced to give color to the opinion that it was intended to extend to territories then belonging to foreign powers, beyond the limits of the original thirteen States. Mr. Jefferson himself was so convinced of this fact, that he declared, previous to the purchase of Louisiana, that it could not be done, except by receiving the sanction of the several States, without a violation of the Constitution. . . .

---

[1] 4 Jefferson's Works, 505.

[2] Gallatin to Jefferson, January 13, 1803. 1 Gallatin's Works, 112.

" Notwithstanding the perfect conviction of his own mind on this point, as he unequivocally declared (a fact well known at that time and subsequently publicly demonstrated), he yielded to the solicitations and influence of his partisans, silenced his conscientious scruples, and, holding in his hand the omnipotence of the present party power, consented to give his sanction to the violation of the Constitution by admitting Louisiana into the Union, without receiving or asking the consent of the several States." [1]

Congress adopted Mr. Gallatin's theory of construction rather than that of Mr. Jefferson and Mr. Quincy. On the 31st October, 1803,[2] it authorized the President to take possession of the ceded territory, and extended the laws of the United States over it; on the 20th February, 1811,[3] it passed an enabling act, under which Louisiana was, on the 8th April, 1812, admitted into the Union.[4] This treaty, and these laws, and individual rights created under them, have been recognized by the Supreme Court.[5]

In thus construing the Constitution, the statesmen of 1802 only followed in the footsteps of the statesmen of 1787, who accepted the cession

---

[1] Life of Josiah Quincy, 91.

[2] 2 Stat. 245.   [3] 2 Stat. 641.   [4] 2 Stat. 701.

[5] *Mahew* v. *Thatcher*, 6 Wheat. 129 ; *Soulard* v. *United States*, 4 Pet. 511 ; *Livingston* v. *Story*, 9 Pet. 632 ; *Livingston* v. *Story*, 11 Pet. 351 ; *Story* v. *Livingston*, 13 Pet. 359 ; *United States* v. *D'Auterive*, 10 How. 609 ; *Montault* v. *United States*, 12 How. 47 ; *United States* v. *Rillieux*, 14 How. 189 ; *United States* v. *King*, 7 How. 833 ; *United States* v. *Turner*, 11 How. 663 ; *Mackey* v. *United States*, 10 Pet. 340 ; *Pollard* v. *Files*, 2 How. 591 ; *Foster* v. *Neilson*, 2 Pet. 253.

of the Northwest Territory. The question and
the doubt with Louisiana grew out of the silence
of the Constitution; but the Articles of Confederation were equally silent. Nor could the
fact that, in the one case, the cession was made
by individual States of the Union, and, in the
other, by a Foreign Power, affect the nature of
the constitutional question. In the one case
Congress, and in the other the Executive, assumed that the power of such acquisition was
impliedly given to a sovereign, though not in
terms delegated; and in each case the action
has been approved by the people and sustained
by the courts.

The acquisition of Florida[1] followed that of
Louisiana. Texas came next, but by a different
process. It was admitted as a State while still
foreign territory.[2] The cession of California[3]
by treaty, and then of Alaska[4] followed. Meanwhile a treaty of the United States gave to
Great Britain[5] a tract of territory claimed by
the State of Maine; and another treaty gave to
the same power[6] a large tract claimed by the
United States in the Northwest and on the
shores of the Pacific.

In *American Insurance Co.* v. *Canter,*[7] Chief
Justice Marshall, delivering the opinion of the

---

[1] Treaty of February 22, 1819, with Spain. 8 Stat. 252.
[2] 5 Stat. 797.
[3] Treaty with Mexico, February 2, 1848. 9 Stat. 922.
[4] Treaty with Russia, March 30, 1867. 15 Stat. 539.
[5] Treaty with Great Britain, August 9, 1842. 8 Stat. 572.
[6] Treaty with Great Britain, June 15, 1846. 9 Stat. 869.
[7] 1 Pet. 511, 542.

court, said: "The Constitution confers absolutely on the Government of the Union, the powers of making war and of making treaties; consequently that Government possesses the power of acquiring territory, either by conquest or by treaty. The usage of the world is, if a nation be not entirely subdued, to consider the holding of conquered territory as a mere military occupation, until its fate shall be determined at the treaty of peace. If it be ceded by the treaty, the acquisition is confirmed, and the ceded territory becomes a part of the nation to which it is annexed. . . . The same act which transfers their country, transfers the allegiance of those who remain in it."

3. Extension of the Admiralty Jurisdiction of the Courts of the United States.

The second section of the Third Article of the Constitution provides that the judicial power shall extend " to all cases of admiralty and maritime jurisdiction."

The Supreme Court has held that this language referred to the general system of maritime law which was familiar to the lawyers and statesmen of the country when the Constitution was adopted.[1]   In an early case, admiralty jurisdiction was invoked in Kentucky, to enforce a claim of a hand for wages earned on a steamboat running from a port in Kentucky up the river Missouri; but the court said: " In the

---

[1] *The Lottawanna*, 21 Wall. 558.

great struggles between the courts of the com- mon law and the admiralty, the latter never attempted to assert any jurisdiction except over maritime contracts ; . . . nor could it rightfully exercise any jurisdiction, except in cases where the service was substantially performed, or to be performed, upon the sea, or upon waters within the ebb and flow of the tide.[1] This was affirmed and reasserted by the court.[2] And it can hardly admit of a doubt that the framers of the Constitution by the term 'admiralty,' understood admiralty as its jurisdiction was defined by English law ; and that the adjective 'maritime' related to tidal waters."

As the commerce of the lakes and internal rivers expanded, it was found that the admiralty and maritime jurisdiction as thus settled and defined, did not meet the necessities of the country. Congress accordingly, on the 26th of February, 1845, passed an act "extending the jurisdiction of the District Courts to certain cases upon the lakes and navigable waters connecting the same."[3] The court, at December Term, 1851, held this statute to be within the constitutional power of Congress.[4] It said, among other things : "The only objection made to this jurisdiction is that there is no tide in the lakes or the waters connecting them ; and it is said that the admiralty and maritime jurisdic-

---

[1] *The Thomas Jefferson*, 10 Wheat. 428.

[2] *American Ins. Co.* v. *Canter*, 1 Pet. 511 ; *The Orleans*, 11 Pet. 175 ; *United States* v. *Coombs*, 12 Pet. 72.

[3] 5 Stat. 726, c. 20.   [4] *The Genesee Chief*, 12 How. 443.

tion as known and understood in England and this country at the time the Constitution was adopted, was confined to the ebb and flow of the tide. . . . In England, undoubtedly, the writers upon the subject, and the decisions in its courts of admiralty, always speak of the jurisdiction as confined to tide water. . . . At the time the Constitution of the United States was adopted, and our courts of admiralty went into operation, the definition which had been adopted in England was equally proper here. In the old thirteen States, the far greater part of the navigable waters are tide waters. . . . It is evident that a definition that would at this day limit public rivers in this country to tide-water rivers is utterly inadmissible. . . . The lakes and the waters connecting them are undoubtedly public waters, and we think are within the grant of admiralty and maritime jurisdiction in the Constitution of the United States."

Twenty-two years later the court, speaking of this, said that the court had " felt itself at liberty to recognize the admiralty jurisdiction as extending to localities and subjects which were prohibited to it in England, but which fairly belong to it on every ground of reason when applied to the peculiar circumstances of this country."[1] The most extreme States' right theorist cannot doubt that this decision was in accordance with the true interests — it is not too strong to say the absolute necessities — of the nation.

---

[1] *The Lottawanna*, 21 Wall. 558.

4. *The Legal Tender Decisions.*

By the act of February 25, 1862, 12 Stat. 345, c. 33; the joint resolution of January 17, 1863, 12 Stat. 822; and the act of March 3, 1863, 12 Stat. 709, c. 73, all passed during the civil war, Congress made provisions for issues of the notes of the United States, to be a legal tender, receivable in payment of private debts. It was further provided that these notes, as they should come into the treasury, might be reissued from time to time, and, if mutilated so as to be unfit for use, might be replaced by a new issue.

At December Term, 1869, this provision was pronounced to be unconstitutional by a majority of the court.[1] The opinion was delivered by Chief Justice Chase, Justices Nelson, Clifford, and Field concurring in the opinion and judgment, and Justice Grier concurring in the judgment. Justice Miller delivered a dissenting opinion, in which Justices Swayne and Davis concurred.

The majority did not doubt the power to issue notes which should become a currency in circulation: its doubt was "as to the power to declare a particular class of these notes to be a legal tender in payment of preëxisting debts." On this point they said: "We confess ourselves unable to perceive any solid distinction between such an act and an act compelling all citizens to accept, in satisfaction of all contracts for money, half, or three-quarters, or any other proportion less than the whole, of the value actually due

[1] *Hepburn* v. *Griswold*, 8 Wall. 603.

according to their terms. It is difficult to conceive what act would take private property without process of law if such an act would not. We are obliged to conclude that an act making mere promises to pay dollars, a legal tender in payment of debts previously contracted, is not a means appropriate, plainly adapted, really calculated to carry into effect any express power vested in Congress; that such an act is inconsistent with the spirit of the Constitution, and that it is prohibited by the Constitution."

The dissenting opinion said: "The legal tender clauses of the statutes under consideration were placed emphatically, by those who enacted them, upon their necessity to the further borrowing of money and maintaining the army and navy. . . . The history of that gloomy time, not to be readily forgotten by the lover of his country, will forever remain, the full, clear, and ample vindication of the exercise of this power by Congress. . . . Undoubtedly it is a law impairing the obligation of contracts made before its passage; but, while the Constitution forbids States to pass such laws, it does not forbid Congress."

At December Term, 1870, the question came again before the court,[1] when the decision in *Hepburn* v. *Griswold* was reversed. The opinion of the court, concurred in by Justices Swayne, Davis, and Miller, was delivered by Mr. Justice Strong. Mr. Justice Bradley delivered a concur-

---

[1] *Knox* v. *Lee*, 12 Wall. 457.

ring opinion. Chief Justice Chase delivered a Lecture II.
dissenting opinion in which Justice Nelson con- Legal tender decisions.
curred. Justice Clifford and Justice Field each
delivered a dissenting opinion.

The question was again before the court at
December Term, 1883, when the decision in
Knox v. *Lee* was reaffirmed, Justice Field being
the only dissenting judge.[1]

By an act passed in 1875, "to provide for the
resumption of specie payments,"[2] Congress had
directed that these notes as retired should be
cancelled. By the act of May 31, 1878,[3] it terminated such retirement, and directed the reissue
of such notes when paid into the treasury. The
court, in its opinion, delivered by Justice Gray,
Justice Field only dissenting, said : " A constitution, establishing a frame of government, declaring fundamental principles, and creating a
national sovereignty, and intended to endure
for ages and to be adapted to the various crises
of human affairs, is not to be interpreted with
the strictness of a private contract. The Constitution of the United States, by apt words of
designation or general description, marks the
outlines of the powers granted to the national
Legislature ; but it does not undertake, with the
precision and detail of a code of laws, to enumerate the subdivision of those powers, or to
specify all the means by which .they may be
carried into execution. . . . The words ' to

---

[1] *Legal Tender Cases*, 110 U. S. 421.
[2] 18 Stat. 296, c. 15.
[3] 20 Stat. 87, c. 146.

borrow money,' as used in the Constitution, to designate a power vested in the National Government, for the safety and welfare of the whole people, are not to receive that limited and restricted interpretation and meaning which they would have in a penal statute, or in an authority conferred, by law or by contract, upon trustees or agents for private purposes. . . . Congress has the power to issue the obligations of the United States in such form, and to impress upon them such qualities as currency for the purchase of merchandise and the payment of debts, as accord with the usage of sovereign governments. The power, as incident to the power of borrowing money and issuing bills or notes of the Government for money borrowed, of impressing upon those bills or notes the quality of being a legal tender for the payment of private debts, was a power universally understood to belong to sovereignty, in Europe and America, at the time of the framing and adoption of the Constitution of the United States. The governments of Europe, acting through the monarch or the legislature, according to the distribution of powers under their respective constitutions, had. and have as sovereign a power of issuing paper money as of stamping coin."

Although this carefully considered decision put at rest further judicial discussion of the question, it has not passed unquestioned by those who deny that the Constitution gives such a power to Congress. The opponents put their case on the ground that the question was directly before the Convention and fully discussed there ;

and that the Convention, with full knowledge of what it was doing, refused to grant the power to Congress. Consequently, they say, no such power can be implied. This contention is maintained by Mr. Bancroft in a pamphlet entitled " A Plea for the Constitution," published in 1886, the latest original work of his long life. He sums up the historical argument thus : —

" Madison, agreeing with the journal of the convention, records that the grant of power to emit bills of credit was refused by a majority of more than four to one. Eleven men took part in the discussion ; and every one of the eleven, whether he spoke for or against the grant of the power, Gouverneur Morris, Pierce Butler, James Madison, Nathaniel Gorham, George Mason, John F. Mercer, Oliver Ellsworth, Edmund Randolph, James Wilson, George Reed, and John Langdon, each and all, understood the vote to be a denial to the Legislature of the United States of the power to emit paper money. . . . The evidence is perfect ; no power to emit paper money was granted to the Legislature of the United States.

" By refusing to the United States the power of issuing bills of credit, the victory over paper money was but half complete. The same James Wilson who, twelve days before, with Oliver Ellsworth had taken a chief part in refusing to the United States the power to emit paper money, and the same Roger Sherman who, in 1752, had put forth all his energy to break up paper money in Connecticut, jointly took the lead. The first draft of the Constitution had forbidden the States to emit bills of credit without the consent of the Legislature of the United States; on the 28th of August they jointly offered this motion: 'No State shall coin money, nor emit bills of credit, nor make anything but gold and silver coin a tender in payment of debts,' making the prohibition absolute. Roger Sherman, animated by zeal for the welfare of the coming republic of countless millions, exclaims in the debate: 'This is the favorable crisis for crushing paper money.' His word was the will of the convention, and the States, by a majority of eight and a half against one and a half — that is, by more than five to one — forbade the State, under any circumstances, to emit bills of credit. This is the way in which our Constitution shut and barred the door against paper money, and crushed it.

"Nothing is wanting to the perfect strength of the truth that the Constitution put an end to paper money in all the United States, and in all the several States."

It is of little consequence, however, on which side the truth of this historical issue lies. The court of final resort has settled that this great power exists in Congress, not by special grant, but as a necessary adjunct of sovereignty; just as the Congress of the Confederation, and the Supreme Court held as to Prize Courts. This has been done after a fluctuation of opinion, running through a series of years. If judicial

determination of a question, over which the Lecture II.
court has jurisdiction, is to have any weight, Legal tender decisions.
the point must be regarded as settled. Those
who are opposed to the issue of such paper must
endeavor to convert Congress to their way of
thinking.

The Supreme Court has often had occasion to Implied powers.
consider the subject of these implied powers.
Its decisions, as a whole, are substantially in
harmony with each other. In the opinion of
Chief Justice Marshall in *McCulloch* v. *Maryland*, it is said : —

" This Government is acknowledged by all to
be one of enumerated powers. The principle
that it can exercise only the powers granted to
it, would seem too apparent to have required to
be enforced by all those arguments, which its
enlightened friends, while it was depending before the people, found it necessary to urge; that
principle is now universally admitted. But the
question respecting the extent of the powers
actually granted, is perpetually arising, and will
probably continue to arise, so long as our system
shall exist. In discussing these questions, the
conflicting powers of the General and State governments must be brought into view, and the
supremacy of their respective laws, when they
are in opposition, must be settled.

" If any one proposition could command the
universal assent of mankind, we might expect it
would be this, that the Government of the Union,
though limited in its powers, is supreme within
its sphere of action. This would seem to result,

necessarily, from its nature. It is the government of all; its powers are delegated by all; it
represents all, and acts for all. Though any one
State may be willing to control its operations, no
State is willing to allow others to control them.
The nation, on those subjects on which it can act,
must necessarily bind its component parts."

"We admit, as all must admit, that the
powers of the Government are limited, and that
its limits are not to be transcended. But we
think the sound construction of the Constitution
must allow to the national legislature that discretion, with respect to the means by which the
powers it confers are to be carried into execution, which will enable that body to perform the
high duties assigned to it in the manner most
beneficial to the people. Let the end be legitimate, let it be within the scope of the Constitution, and all means which are appropriate, which
are plainly adapted to that end, which are not
prohibited, but consist with the letter and spirit
of the Constitution, are constitutional." [1]

In *Hepburn* v. *Griswold*, Chief Justice Chase,
referring to these words of Chief Justice Marshall, said: "The rule for determining whether
a legislative enactment can be supported as an
exercise of an implied power, was stated by
Chief Justice Marshall, speaking for the whole
court in the case of *McCulloch* v. *The State of
Maryland*, and the statement then made has
ever since been accepted as a correct exposition

---

[1] *McCulloch* v. *Maryland*, 4 Wheat. 316, 405, 421.

of the Constitution. His words were these :
'Let the end be legitimate, let it be within the
scope of the Constitution, and all means which
are appropriate, which are plainly adapted to
that end, which are not prohibited, but consist
with the letter and spirit of the Constitution,
are constitutional.' And, in another part of
the same opinion, the practical application of
this rule was thus illustrated. 'Should Congress, in the execution of its powers, adopt
measures which are prohibited by the Constitution, or should Congress, under the pretext
of executing its powers, pass laws for the accomplishment of objects not intrusted to the Government, it would be the painful duty of this
tribunal, should a case requiring such a decision
come before it, to say that such an act was not
the law of the land. But where the law is not
prohibited, and is truly calculated to effect any
of the objects intrusted to the Government, to
undertake here to inquire the degree of its necessity, would be to pass the line which circum-
scribes the judicial department, and tread on
legislative ground.'

"It must be taken, then, as finally settled, so
far as judicial decisions can settle anything,
that the words, 'all laws necessary and proper
for carrying into execution,' powers expressly
granted, or vested, have, in the Constitution, a
sense equivalent to that of the words, laws, not
absolutely necessary, indeed, but appropriate,
plainly adapted to constitutional and legitimate
ends ; laws not prohibited, but consistent with

the letter and spirit of the Constitution; laws really calculated to effect objects intrusted to the Government." [1]

---

[1] *Hepburn* v. *Griswold*, 8 Wall. 603, 614, 615.

III.

THE EXECUTIVE BRANCH OF THE GOVERNMENT.[1]

———oo༄ꕔ༄oo———

CONSTITUTION, ARTICLE II, SECTION 1. The executive Power shall be vested in a President of the United States of America. He shall hold his Office during the Term of four Years, and, together with the Vice-President, chosen for the same Term, be elected, as follows:

Each State shall appoint, in such Manner as the Legislature thereof may direct, a Number of Electors, equal to the whole Number of Senators and Representatives to which the State may be entitled in the Congress: but no Senator or Representative, or Person holding an Office of Trust or Profit under the United States, shall be appointed an Elector.

The Electors shall meet in their respective states, and vote by ballot for President and Vice-President, one of whom, at least, shall not be an inhabitant of the same state with themselves; they shall name in their ballots the person voted for as President, and in distinct ballots the person voted for as Vice-President, and they shall make distinct lists of all persons voted for as President, and of all persons voted for as Vice-President, and of the number of votes for each, which lists they shall sign and certify, and transmit sealed to the seat of the government of the United States, directed to the President of the Senate; —The President of the Senate shall, in presence of the Senate and House of Representatives, open all the certificates and the votes shall then be counted; —

---

[1] This is Lecture II of the Lectures delivered before the classes of the University Law School.

III.

The person having the greatest number of votes for President, shall be the President, if such number be a majority of the whole number of Electors appointed ; and if no person have such majority, then from the persons having the highest numbers not exceeding three on the list of those voted for as President, the House of Representatives shall choose immediately, by ballot, the President. But in choosing the President, the votes shall be taken by states, the representation from each state having one vote ; a quorum for this purpose shall consist of a member or members from two-thirds of the states, and a majority of all the states shall be necessary to a choice. And if the House of Representatives shall not choose a President whenever the right of choice shall devolve upon them, before the fourth day of March next following, then the Vice-President shall act as President, as in the case of the death or other constitutional disability of the President. The person having the greatest number of votes as Vice-President, shall be the Vice-President, if such number be a majority of the whole number of Electors appointed, and if no person have a majority, then from the two highest numbers on the list, the Senate shall choose the Vice-President ; a quorum for the purpose shall consist of two-thirds of the whole number of Senators, and a majority of the whole number shall be necessary to a choice. But no person constitutionally ineligible to the office of President shall be eligible to that of Vice-President of the United States.[1]

The Congress may determine the Time of chusing the Electors, and the Day on which they shall give their Votes ; which Day shall be the same throughout the United States.

No Person except a natural born Citizen, or a Citizen of the United States, at the time of the Adoption of this Constitution, shall be eligible to the Office of President ; neither shall any Person be eligible to that Office who shall not have attained to the Age of thirty-five Years, and been fourteen Years a Resident within the United States.

In Case of the Removal of the President from

---

[1] This paragraph contains the text of the Twelfth Amendment, which was a substitution for the original clause in the Constitution, and came into force in 1804.

Office, or of his Death, Resignation, or Inability to LECTURE III. discharge the Powers and Duties, of the said Office, the same shall devolve on the Vice-President, and the Congress may by Law provide for the Case of Removal, Death, Resignation, or Inability, both of the President and Vice-President, declaring what Officer shall then act as President and such Officer shall act accordingly, until the Disability be removed, or a President shall be elected.

The President shall, at stated Times, receive for his Services a Compensation, which shall neither be encreased nor diminished during the Period for which he shall have been elected, and he shall not receive within that Period any other Emolument from the United States, or any of them.

Before he enter on the Execution of his Office, he shall take the following Oath or Affirmation : —

"I do solemnly swear (or affirm) that I will faith-"fully execute the Office of President of the United "States. and will to the best of my Ability, preserve, "protect and defend the Constitution of the United "States."

SECTION 2. The President shall be Commander in Chief of the Army and Navy of the United States, and of the Militia of the several States when called into the actual Service of the United States ; he may require the Opinion, in writing, of the principal Officer in each of the executive Departments, upon any Subject relating to the Duties of their respective Offices, and he shall have Power to grant Reprieves and Pardons for Offences against the United States, except in Cases of Impeachment.

He shall have Power, by and with the Advice and Consent of the Senate, to make Treaties, provided two thirds of the Senators present concur ; and he shall nominate, and by and with the Advice and Consent of the Senate, shall appoint Ambassadors, other public Ministers and Consuls, Judges of the supreme Court, and all other Officers of the United States, whose Appointments are not herein otherwise provided for, and which shall be established by Law: but the Congress may by Law vest the Appointment of such inferior Officers, as they think proper, in the President alone, in the Courts of Law, or in the Heads of Departments.

The President shall have Power to fill up all Vacancies that may happen during the Recess of the

Senate, by granting Commissions which shall expire at the End of their next Session.

SECTION 3. He shall from time to time give to the Congress Information of the State of the Union, and recommend to their Consideration such Measures as he shall judge necessary and expedient; he may, on extraordinary Occasions, convene both Houses, or either of them, and in Case of Disagreement between them, with Respect to the Time of Adjournment, he may adjourn them to such Time as he shall think proper; he shall receive Ambassadors and other public Ministers; he shall take Care that the Laws be faithfully executed, and shall Commission all the officers of the United States.

SECTION 4. The President, Vice-President and all civil Officers of the United States, shall be removed from Office on Impeachment for, and Conviction of, Treason, Bribery, or other high Crimes and Misdemeanors.

The Executive.

You are all familiar with the main principle of all written constitutions in the American form of government, that the powers of government are reposed in three distinct and separate bodies of magistracy. These are, the legislative or law making power, the executive or law enforcing power, and the judiciary, which construes the laws and administers the rights of citizens as among themselves, and as they relate to contests with the Government.

For the subject matter of the present lecture I have selected that part of the Constitution of the United States which is devoted to the executive branch. This is found in Article Two of that instrument. The first and second paragraphs of the first section are as follows:

"1. The Executive power shall be vested in a President of the United States of America. He shall hold his office during the term of four years, and, together with the Vice-President, LECTURE III. chosen for the same term, be elected as follows : The Executive.

" 2. Each State shall appoint, in such manner as the Legislature thereof may direct, a number of Electors, equal to the whole number of Senators and Representatives, to which the State may be entitled in the Congress : but no Senator or Representative, or person holding an office of trust or profit, under the United States, shall be appointed an Elector."

In 1804 the Twelfth Amendment, the text of which will be found at the head of this lecture, was adopted, and substituted in the place of the third paragraph of Article II.

The manner of electing the President of the United States was a subject of very grave consideration in the Convention which framed the Constitution, and several propositions which had apparently at one time the sanction of a majority of that body were changed and modified before the final adoption of the rule here stated. As originally adopted, and as it now exists, it was supposed that the body of electors interposed between the State legislatures and the presidential office would exercise a reasonable independence and fair judgment in the selection of the chief Executive of the National Government, and that thus the evil of a President selected by immediate popular suffrage on the one side, and the opposite evil of an election by the direct vote of the States in their legislative bodies on the other, would both be avoided. A very short experience, however, demonstrated that these

electors, whether chosen by the legislatures of
the States, as they were originally, or by the
popular suffrage of each State, as they have
come to be now, or by limited districts in each
State, as was at one time the prevailing system,
are always but the puppets selected under a
moral restraint to vote for some particular person who represented the preferences of the appointing power, whether that was the legislature,
or the more popular suffrage by which the legislature itself was elected. So that it has come
to pass that this curious machinery is only a
mode of casting the vote, to which a State is
entitled in the election of President, in favor of
that candidate who is the favorite of the majority of the people, entitled to vote for the more
popular branch of the State legislature in each
State.

This system has given rise on more than one
occasion to serious difficulties in ascertaining
who has been really elected President, and
seems, if it ever had any useful purpose, to have
long become an obstruction and a stumbling-
block in the way of some sounder and wiser
system. A change has often been talked of
and canvassed in Congress and in the public
journals, but the difficulty of agreeing on any
other system, which Congress may present as an
amendment to the Constitution, has thus far led
to the failure of all attempts to make such change.

I do not propose to take up any more of your
time by a discussion of the manner of electing
the President.

The experience of nearly a hundred years of
government under this Constitution has produced in the minds of many thinking men and
able statesmen a belief that the term of four
years prescribed for the office of President is too
short. The great disturbance of public tranquillity produced by the recurring election of a
President once in four years, the enormous patronage which belongs to the presidential office,
stimulating all the activities, and many of the
most evil passions, of the human heart, and the
fact that this struggle, owing to the shortness
of the period between one election and another,
is always going on more or less by way of preparation for that event, leaving the public mind
at no time open to that calmness which is necessary to a just consideration and appreciation
of the measures of government policy which
ought to influence their votes, are strong arguments for this belief. As we shall see hereafter,
it is the duty of the President to suggest to the
legislative body and recommend for their consideration measures of public policy which must
more or less affect the prosperity and happiness
of the entire people. If he were assured, by the
length of the period for which he would hold
the office, of a sufficient time in which his measures, if enacted, could be fairly judged on their
merits, or his recommendations, whether enacted
or not, could have the just estimation of the
public sentiment, that independence and faith-
ful expression of his convictions, which can only
make such recommendations useful, would have

a fair support in these considerations; while, if he be desirous of a re-election, as has proved to be almost universal, or if having no desire for re-election he has that reasonable wish to retire with a favorable estimate of his conduct, which is natural to all men, he would be much influenced by these considerations to recommend that which was policy rather than that which was wise, and to frame his conduct in accordance with his view of what the public would say at the time, rather than what might be their estimate, after a long and calm consideration.

In opposition to these views it has been urged that a President elected for a long period would, by the use of the patronage at his disposal, by the arts of the politician and the great influence which he would be enabled to exert over the popular voice by the exercise of power for a lengthened period, always be able to secure a re-election; and it would be in the end equivalent to holding the office for life. Probably some period longer than four years and shorter than ten would be found to remove the principal objections to the present short term without incurring the dangers incident to a longer one.[1]

---

[1] It was at first proposed to make the term of office of the Executive seven years, and it so stood in the first draft of the Constitution. This was, however, altered upon the report of a committee by a vote of ten States against one fixing the period at four years, which was finally adopted.

It was also, at one time, proposed to fix the term of the Executive during good behavior, and this was supported by Madison, Jay, and Hamilton, among others, although the latter afterward changed his views somewhat. See 2 Story, Constitution, sec. 1436 (4th ed.), 281 and note.

The qualifications which make a person eligible to the office of President are found in 'paragraph four of the first section of this article,
which reads as follows —:

"No person except a natural born citizen, or
a citizen of the United States, at the time of
the adoption of this Constitution, shall be eligible to the office of President; neither shall any
person be eligible to that office who shall not
have attained to the age of thirty-five years, and
been fourteen years a resident within the United
States."

In regard to this nothing more need be said
on this occasion.

In order to secure his freedom of action and
independence of the legislative branch of the
Government, paragraph six provides for his compensation or salary in the following language:

"The President shall, at stated times, receive
for his services, a compensation, which shall
neither be increased nor diminished during the
period for which he shall have been elected, and
he shall not receive within that period any other
emolument from the United States, or any of
them."

This provision, in some respects similar to

Jefferson, in 1813 wrote as follows: "I am for responsibilities
at short periods, seeing neither reason nor safety in making public
functionaries independent of the nation for life, or even for a long
term of years. On this principle I prefer the Presidential term of
four years, to that of seven years, which I myself had at first suggested, annexing to it, however, ineligibility forever after; and I
wish it were now annexed to the second quadrennial election of
President." 6 Jefferson's Works, 213.

that in regard to the judges, is a wise one. They exempt the two other branches of the Government, the executive and the judicial, from an undue control by the legislative branch, which has the power of the administration of the finances of the Government, the appropriation of money to pay for its expenses, and the regulation of the salaries of all officers. It thus secures, so far as a fixed compensation can do it, the independence of these two other departments.[1]

In the second and third sections of this article we find the definition of the powers, duties, and obligations of the President of the United States. They read as follows : —

"SECTION 2. The President shall be commander-in-chief of the army and navy of the United States, and of the militia of the several States, when called into the actual service of the United States ; he may require the opinion,

---

[1] The difference between the provision, in this regard, to the President and that in regard to the judges of the United States courts is this: the salary of a judge cannot be diminished during the continuance of his office ; that of the President can be neither increased nor diminished during the period for which he shall have been elected. This provision is construed as applicable only to the term in which the law is enacted making the increase. On the 3d of March, 1873, Congress, by the Legislative, Executive, and Judicial Appropriation Act, passed that day, 17 Stat. 485, c. 226, provided for a general increase of salaries, including the salaries of the President and the Justices of the Supreme Court. President Grant approved the bill. His first term of office expired the next day, and he at once entered upon his second term. On the 20th of January, 1874, Congress repealed so much of this act "as provide for the increase of the compensation of public officers and employés, whether members of Congress, delegates, or others, except the President of the United States and the Justices of the Supreme Court."

in writing, of the principal officer in each of the executive departments, upon any subject relating to the duties of their respective offices, and he shall have power to grant reprieves and pardons for offences against the United States, except in cases of impeachment.

" He shall have power, by and with the advice and consent of the Senate, to make treaties, provided two-thirds of the senators present concur; and he shall nominate, and by and with the advice and consent of the Senate, shall appoint ambassadors, other public ministers, and consuls, judges of the Supreme Court, and all other officers of the United States, whose appointments are not herein otherwise provided for, and which shall be established by law; but the Congress may by law vest the appointment of such inferior officers as they think proper, in the President alone, in the courts of law, or in the heads of departments.

" The President shall have power to fill up all vacancies that may happen during the recess of the Senate, by granting commissions which shall expire at the end of their next session.

" SECTION 3. He shall, from time to time, give to the Congress information of the state of the Union, and recommend to their consideration such measures as he shall judge necessary and expedient; he may, on extraordinary occasions, convene both Houses, or either of them, and in case of disagreement between them, with respect to the time of adjournment, he may adjourn them to such time as he shall think proper; he

shall receive ambassadors and other public ministers; he shall take care that the laws be faithfully executed and shall commission all of the
officers of the United States."

A critical examination of the powers thus
conferred on the President would hardly justify
the jealousy and dread which many of the
wisest statesmen of the period of the formation
of the Constitution entertained on that subject.
With the exception that he shall be commander-
in-chief of the army and navy, and of the militia
of the several States when called into the actual
service of the United States,[1] and the power of
appointment to office, there is little to justify
such fear; and when we consider that Congress
alone can declare war, and thus put the commander-in-chief in a position for any dangerous
use of the military arm of the Government, that
the co-operation of the Senate is necessary to
the appointment of all the other officers of the
army and navy below the President, that the
consent of that body is essential to the confirmation of all the civil officers which the President
may nominate or appoint, and that the appointment of the largest body of these officers may,
by an act of Congress, be taken away from the
President and vested in the courts of law or

---

[1] The question was raised during the War of 1812 whether the
right to command the militia could be delegated by the President
when they were called into the public service. President Washington, however, called out the militia during the Pennsylvania insurrection of 1794, and they acted under the orders of the governor
of Virginia, to whom the chief command was given during his
absence. Rawle on the Constitution, 193.

heads of departments, there would seem to be
but little reason to dread an undue exercise of
the grant of power to the President, under this
provision of the Constitution.

The experience of a century of the operations of
the Government has shown that, while the growth
of the country in territory, in population, in wealth,
and in power has added largely to the patronage
of the Executive in the way of appointments to
office and to the importance of those offices, and
while the frequent accession of successful and
popular military chiefs to the Presidency, some
of whom were men of arbitrary disposition, and
well inclined to the exercise of all the power
which the Constitution gave them, and who
have shown in every instance a disposition for a
continuance in power by seeking or accepting a
re-election, there has never been the slightest
danger to the liberties of the country, or of an
overthrow of the existing institutions, or of any
material infraction of the general principles of
constitutional government from this quarter. In
fact, of all the three branches of the constitutional government of the United States, the
Executive has been the most crippled, confined,
and limited in its practical use, during the period
mentioned of the power really conferred on it.

The power of appointment to office, which
was originally considered the great source of
danger, has, by a practice not to be commended,
and at variance with the letter and spirit of the
Constitution, been largely controlled in the hands
of the President by the two branches of the

Legislature. The exercise of this restraint by the Senate, in its right to refuse its consent to nominations made to it by the President, is not to be complained of. It is a power which the Constitution reposes in that body and which though often used with a disposition to conform to the wishes of individual members of the Senate (called " the courtesy of the Senate "), rather than looking to the public good and the fitness of the nominee, has, perhaps, on the whole been exercised with prudence and forbearance. But the disposition of the members of the House of Representatives, in which senators have often joined, to impose their individual wishes upon the President as entitled to paramount weight in his selection for appointments to office, stands on no such favorable foundation, and the pressure from this source, which has unfortunately been submitted to by successive Presidents, has almost passed into an informal rule of action, — a rule which has encroached upon the powers clearly committed by the Constitution to the President, and which, when submitted to, tends to destroy the exercise of that sound judgment and freedom of choice which that instrument, for wise purposes, intended to repose in the President. Indeed, if there is any wisdom in the fundamental proposition of constitutional law, that the functions of the executive, legislative, and judicial bodies should be kept separate, that wisdom is most manifest in the provision which is intended to repose exclusively in the President the power of appointment

to office, except so far as the consent of the
Senate may be required. The interference of
the more popular branch of the legislative body
in this function, and the great influence which it
has acquired, and which the members use as a
means of political influence to secure their own
re-election, is a pernicious practice and at war
with the manifest purpose of the Constitution.

Perhaps the third clause of the second section,
in regard to the power of the President to fill
vacancies that may happen during the recess of
the Senate, has given rise in recent years to more
controversy than any other, and is the one as to
which the executive power has been more frequently charged with a purpose to exceed its
just limits than any other.[1] The question of the
right of removal from office, and the conditions
under which it may be exercised by the President alone, has been a much controverted matter
from the beginning of the Government to the
present time; and when the legislative body, and
especially the Senate, have been of the opposite
party in politics to the President, it has given
rise to considerable controversy. It may be considered as settled, however, by the practice of
the Government, and by a fair construction of
the Constitution, that the President has, especially in the recess of the Senate, the right to
remove any officer whose appointment is dependent upon the Executive. But since this
provision of the Constitution requires that the

---

[1] See Note at the end of this Lecture.

LECTURE III.
The Executive.
Power to fill
vacancies during
recess of Senate.
commissions granted by the President in the recess of the Senate shall expire at the end of the next session, and the implication is still stronger that appointments made while the Senate is in session must be then submitted to it for its consent, there would seem to be no question that the President should, when these commissions are granted during its recess, notify the Senate of the removal which he has made, and of the appointment by which he has filled the office. And there can be as little doubt that, unless the Senate consents to the new appointment, or to some other new appointment, during its session next succeeding the removal, this action of the Senate must be construed as a disapproval by that body of the removal of the officer, or of the person who has been nominated to fill the place.

In the unfortunate event of the President and the Senate being unable to agree upon any other person than the original incumbent to fill the vacancy, before the end of the session of the Senate, it has been insisted by many statesmen, and particularly by members of the Senate, that this operates as a restoration of the officer removed to the place which he held. The tenure of office law, passed by the Congress of the United States over the veto of President Johnson, is framed upon this principle. So far at least was this principle acted on, that the President could not, after the adjournment of the Senate, to whom such nomination had been or should have been made, fill the office with any

other person; but, in the language of that act,
"such office shall remain in abeyance, without any salary, fees, or emoluments attached thereto, until the same shall be filled by appointment by and with the advice and consent of the Senate." This statute has not been received with entire satisfaction by considerate statesmen and constitutional lawyers. It was made in the heat of ill-feeling, as a curb upon President Johnson, during his long and bitter controversy with both branches of Congress, which ultimately led to the preferring of articles of impeachment against him by the House of Representatives, and to a protracted trial upon the same.

This perhaps is not the time nor the place to express my opinion upon the nature of that controversy: but I think it clear that, while the right of removal remains in the President, he can put no one in the place thus made vacant for a longer period than the end of the next succeeding session of the Senate; and that, whether by failure to nominate some person to fill the place during that session of the Senate, or by the refusal of the Senate to give its assent to such nomination, the office is, at the end of that session, vacant; and that an effort of the President to keep in office the man of his choice by reappointment under such circumstances is, at least in spirit, a violation of the Constitution. The functions of the President and of the Senate in relation to appointments to office are so clearly stated in the Constitution that it would not seem to be necessary that any question should arise about it. The initiative is with the President, the right to nominate and refer that nomination to the Senate is with him, and the Senate can have no right to dictate to him whom he shall nominate. Their right is one of approval or disapproval. When they have exercised that right, the President has as little authority to make other efforts to impose the same nominee upon the Senate, or to continue him in office, as that body would have to interfere with the President's choice among all eligible persons to such office. Hence any attempt, by giving the commission to the same person who had been rejected by the Senate, after the expiration of its session, or to renominate the same person to the Senate after its rejection during the same session, is equally opposed to the spirit, if not to the letter of the Constitution, and to the just right of either the President or the Senate to exercise the functions and powers which the Constitution confers upon either of them.

The power of the President as commander-in-chief of the army and navy has in practice never been exercised by the President's taking immediate command of the army or the navy during the existence of actual hostilities; so that, in that sense, no President has ever been commander-in-chief when the army immediately confronted an enemy. Such authority as the President has exercised under this constitutional provision has been almost exclusively through the Secretary of War and the Secretary of the Navy, offices created among others by an act of the first ses-

sion of the Congress, which distributed the exercise of the executive functions among several
departments, at the head of each of which was
placed a minister, called usually a "Secretary."
And so strong and prominent to the public eye has
been the control of these secretaries in the operations of the army and navy, in the few wars of
an important character which we have had during the existence of the government, that the
influence of the President in the actual movements of the army and navy has been hardly
perceptible. Whether in case a war should occur
during a period when the incumbent of the executive office is a man who has had experience
in the command of armies, and with a good
military reputation, it would be judicious for
him to place himself at the head of the army,
or to conduct its campaigns, or to be present
and directing in battle, or whether public sentiment would tolerate such a course of action, is
extremely doubtful.

In the recent Civil War, which, if we look to
the number of men engaged in it, or to the number destroyed by it, or to the magnitude of the
resources brought to bear in its prosecution on
both sides, or to the destructive power of arma-
ments and weapons, or the advanced skill of the
military art, is perhaps the greatest war that
history has to describe, the Secretary of War
looms up as a figure whose importance as regards the successful issue of that war is hardly
exceeded, if it be equalled, by any person holding
any office or command in the armies of the

United States. Indeed, the name of Edwin M.
Stanton, who, though a civilian and until the
period of the war a private citizen, will go down
to posterity as the great war minister of the
greatest war in the world's history.

In all this, however, the secretaries of the
War Department, as also the heads of all the
other departments, are but executive ministers
and agents, discharging the functions of the executive office, under the control and with the
consent of the President. How far President
Lincoln actually interposed his own will and his
own judgment in the conduct of this war will
perhaps never be fully known, though it is well
understood that on many important occasions,
and in great emergencies, he enforced his judgment in many ways; mainly, however, in displac-
ing commanders of large armies and appointing
others, until success established his own confidence and the confidence of the public in a few
great military leaders.

Pardons.
One of the powers intrusted to the President
by this second section is that of granting reprieves and pardons for offences against the
United States, except in cases of impeachment.
This useful power could nowhere be more appropriately lodged than with the chief executive
officer of the Government. It is one which does
not affect the public generally, and by reason of
the limited criminal jurisdiction of the Government of the United States does not call for
much comment of a public character. It is
derived from the history of our British ances-

tors; and, in the absence of any more particular definition of it than is found in this short sentence of the Constitution, so far as it has become the subject of public discussion or of judicial decision, reliance has been had mainly upon the nature and character of the power as exercised by the Crown of Great Britain. The power, therefore, in this general sense is almost unlimited; is vested exclusively in the President; and is not subject to the interference of Congress.[1]

It has been officially decided that it may be exercised as well before the trial as after conviction.[2] It also includes the power to commute sentences.[3] It may be granted upon conditions.[4] This grant of power carries with it the power to release from fines, penalties, and forfeitures which accrue from the offence.[5]

An act of Congress which attempted to destroy the effect of a pardon by the President of persons engaged in the rebellion, who were claimants in the courts of the United States, under the Captured and Abandoned Property Act, was held by the Supreme Court to be unconstitutional.[6] The original act, which authorized per-

---

[1] A pardon reaches both the punishment prescribed for the offence and the guilt of the offender; and when the pardon is full it releases the punishment and blots out of existence the guilt, so that in the eye of the law the offender is as innocent as if he had never committed the offence. *Ex parte Garland*, 4 Wall. 333, 380.

[2] 6 Opinions Attorneys General, 20.

[3] *Ex parte William Wells*, 18 How. 307.

[4] *United States* v. *Wilson*, 7 Pet. 150, 161.

[5] *Osborn* v. *United States*, 91 U. S. 474.

[6] *United States* v. *Klein*, 13 Wall. 128.

sons whose property had been seized as captured and abandoned during the war, and sold, and the proceeds paid into the treasury, to make a claim for it in the Court of Claims and recover the money, required that proof should be made that the claimant had been loyal to the Government during the war. The Supreme Court had in a case previous to this declared that the pardon of the President dispensed with the necessity of this proof of loyalty. To counteract the effect of this decision Congress, on the 12th of July, 1870,[1] enacted that such proof of loyalty was necessary to the recovery in the Court of Claims, irrespective of the effect of any executive proclamation, pardon, amnesty, or other act of condonation or oblivion. The Supreme Court held that this statute was designed to destroy the effect which the Constitution of the United States intended to give to a pardon by the President, and thus infringed the constitutional power of the Executive. The court uses the following language : —

"Now it is clear that the Legislature cannot change the effect of such a pardon any more than the Executive can change a law. Yet this is attempted by the provision under consideration. The court is required to receive special pardons as evidence of guilt and to treat them as null and void. It is required to disregard pardons granted by proclamation on condition, though the condition has been fulfilled, and to deny them their legal effect. This certainly

---

[1] 16 Stat. 235, c. 251.

impairs the executive authority and directs the court to be instrumental to that end." [1]

The wisdom of exempting cases of impeachment from this pardoning power in the hands of the President will be very obvious when we come to consider that the main object of the impeachment is to remove the person from office; and that this right of removal would exist in the President without the necessity of impeachment; and that, in all cases, the officer impeached, except it be the President himself, is one who, if he belong to the executive branch of the government, is exercising power under the control of the President, and whom the President may for many reasons be willing to protect from punishment by his pardon.

The power of the President to make treaties, in which the concurrence of two-thirds of the senators present when the treaty is voted on shall be necessary, is one which is essentially of an executive character, and which can only be wisely executed under the control of the executive head of the Government. The requirement of two-thirds of the Senate for the final ratification of such treaty made by the President, or his ministers, shows the jealousy of the influence of foreign nations in our domestic policy which was so prevalent at the time the Constitution was adopted. This was evidenced in other respects; as in the forbidding of the acceptance of titles

---

[1] 1 *United States* v. *Klein*, 13 Wall. 128, 148. This general doctrine is subject to some limitations and restrictions. See Note at the end of this Lecture.

of nobility by any officer of the Federal Government, or of any presents.   This jealousy, which
at the time of the formation of the Constitution,
in the weakness of our Government, seems justifiable, has perhaps long passed away since the
Government has grown so wealthy and powerful,
and its offices so valuable ; and it is impossible
to conceive now of an officer of the Government
being in any way bribed or influenced by considerations of honor or profit, coming from other
nations, to disregard the interests of his own
Government by favoring the conflicting interests
of any foreign government.

A question of some interest has arisen in regard to the power of the President and the Senate to make a treaty with a foreign nation which
shall be, according to the declaration of the Constitution, the supreme law of the land, in cases
to which, by other provisions of the Constitution,
it would seem that the concurrence of the House
of Representatives is essential to the making of
a valid law.   This question, which has occasionally vexed the legislative bodies of both Houses
of Congress from the beginning of the Government, but in regard to which any serious difficulty has been averted by the wisdom and forbearance of the House of Representatives, is too
large to be entered upon on this occasion, and is
perhaps too complex to justify your serious consideration of it at this time.[1]

Duty to communi-
cate information
to Congress.
The duty of the President under section three,
to give to Congress information of the State of

_____

[1] 1 See Note at the end of this Lecture.

the Union, and recommend to their consideration such measures as he shall judge necessary
and expedient, is one of very great importance.
In the early history of the Government this duty
was generally performed by a personal interview
between the Executive and the two Houses of
Congress, assembled to listen to him; but since
Mr. Jefferson's time, whose skill and facility in
composition induced him to discharge this function by written messages to Congress, this course
has been invariably followed. Very few public
events are looked to with more interest by the
people at large, as well as all those engaged in
the administration of the Government, than the
annual message which the President sends to
Congress at the beginning of each session.
These messages are generally considered as
defining the policy of the Executive in regard
to the administration of public affairs falling
within this branch of the Government, as also
with regard to such legislation as he thinks the
good of the country requires at the hands of
Congress. These messages have had a varying
degree of power in the influence which they
have exerted upon the legislation of Congress.
In years past the recommendations of the President were held to represent the opinions of the
political party by whom he was elected, and of
which he was the recognized leader, and to have
almost a controlling influence over the members
of that party in the two branches of the Legislature. So that, in those times, a recommendation of the President in regard to a matter of

political policy, when the two Houses of Congress were in accord with him in party politics,
was almost omnipotent. In more recent years
the frequent recurrence of the fact that a majority of the Senate might be found on one side
of such party divisions, and of the House of Representatives on the other, has tended very much
to diminish the influence of such Presidential
recommendations, as well as the constantly
recurring fact that, in regard to such measures
the President does not represent in all instances
the entire or unanimous opinion of his own
party, in which in one House or the other there
may be divisions on such subjects.

Power to call
extra sessions of
Congress.
The power of the President to convene both
Houses, or either of them, on extraordinary
occasions, has been rarely exercised, and certainly has not been abused during the history of
the Government. The principal exercise of this
power has been in proclamations by which the
President has called the Senate together at the
close of a session of Congress, for the purpose
of considering appointments to office, and sometimes treaties.

As to the general provisions that he shall take
care that the laws be faithfully executed, any
comment which would be useful would extend
this. lecture beyond the limit which necessity
imposes.

The only other provision of this Second Article of the Constitution to which I deem it necessary to call your attention, is found in section
four, which declares : —

"The President, Vice-President, and all civil officers of the United States, shall be removed from office, on impeachment for, and conviction of, treason, bribery, or other high crimes and misdemeanors."

The general principles on which an impeachment of any officer of the Government may be conducted is prescribed by other provisions of the Constitution. The substance of them is that the House of Representatives, acting in the character of a grand inquest of the nation, may frame and prefer articles of impeachment, constituting the charges on which he shall be tried before the Senate. These articles are delivered to the Senate, which, by the other provisions of the Constitution, shall make arrangements for the trial. At the trial, by an exceptional provision of the Constitution in regard to the President when he is impeached, the Chief Justice of the Supreme Court of the United States shall preside; which is not required or permitted in the impeachment of any other officer of the Government. The conviction of the party tried in any such impeachment can only be declared by a vote of two-thirds of the senators, and judgment only extends to removal from office, and a disqualification of the person convicted from holding any other office of honor or profit under the Government of the United States.

In the history of the Government under the Constitution, but a single effort to impeach a President has ever been made. The case of President Johnson, against whom the House preferred articles of impeachment, was tried in 1868, and the prosecution failed of conviction on any of the specifications charged against him. Whatever may have been the justice of the charges made against President Johnson, looking back as we now do with much of the asperity of the time at which it took place removed, it may safely be said that the failure to convict him was mainly to be attributed to the belief in the minds of many senators that the charges, if true, were not of a character for which impeachment is provided in the Constitution, and not from a want of belief in the truth of some of those charges. It may also be said that, in view of the invitation which a successful result in that effort to convict and remove him would have held out in future times to exasperated majorities in the legislative body, opposed to the President and his manner of exercising the functions with which he is charged by the Constitution, to get rid of a President against whom such personal hostility existed, the country is fortunate in the fact that the great impeachment failed. A certain degree of security in the stability of his power for the short period for which he is elected is absolutely essential to the successful and conscientious discharge of executive duties by the President; and the easy exercise of the power of impeachment and a frequent recurrence to it might impress upon him, if the causes of impeachment were not of the profoundest gravity, a hesitation and a want of courage in the conscientious discharge of his duties which

would be in many cases disastrous to the public
service.

There remains to be considered a very important duty imposed upon the President by the
Constitution, by which in effect he becomes a
part of the legislative power of the nation.
This is to be found in paragraph two, of section
seven of the first Article, and is commonly called
the veto power. It reads as follows : —

"Every bill, which shall have passed the
House of Representatives and the Senate, shall,
before it become a law, be presented to the
President of the United States; if he approve,
he shall sign it, but if not he shall return it,
with his objections, to that House in which it
shall have originated, who shall enter the objections at large on their journal, and proceed to
reconsider it. If, after such reconsideration, two-
thirds of that House shall agree to pass the bill,
it shall be sent, together with the objections, to
the other House, by which it shall likewise be
reconsidered, and if approved by two thirds of
that House, it shall become a law. But in all
such cases the votes of both Houses shall be
determined by yeas and nays, and the names of
the persons voting for and against the bill shall
be entered on the journal of each House, respectively. If any bill shall not be returned by the
President within ten days (Sundays excepted)
after it shall have been presented to him, the
same shall be a law, in like manner as if he had
signed it, unless the Congress, by their adjourn-

ment, prevent its return, in which case it shall not be a law." [1]

Of the wisdom of this part of the Constitution, it is not my purpose to speak. Upon each occasion of its exercise the anger of those who have supported the measure which the President disapproves has been aroused, and ill-natured and inconsiderate remarks upon such occasions, would lead to the belief that this provision is very generally disliked; but after all, the infrequency of its exercise, and the wisdom with which it has generally been done, has led to its approval by wise and considerate men not influenced by passion, and its tolerance by the public has grown with the increasing years of the existence of the Government.

In fact, there are those who are anxious for an amendment to the Constitution by which the President may be permitted to exercise this veto. power, in regard to specific items or parts of a bill presented to him without being compelled to approve or reject the bill as a whole, while there are objectionable parts in it which could be separated and disapproved by him. [2] Such is the constitution of the State of New York in regard to the power of the governor; and other States have recently adopted the same principle.

It has been contended that the only proper occasion for the President to deny his approval by a message to Congress, refusing to sign a bill, is, when the bill is not in his judgment

---

[1] See Note at the end of this Lecture.   [2] Ib.

within the constitutional power of the Legislature In such case it has been thought to be
his duty to interpose his objection, and the doctrine has been advanced with much earnestness,
that on no other account is he justified in setting
up his opposition to the more popular legislative
branch of the Government.

This view, however, has not been accepted in
modern times, and Presidents within the last
thirty or forty years have apparently exercised
the veto power with as much freedom in regard
to questions of mere expediency and wisdom of
legislation, as of constitutional invalidity. Undoubtedly there is a just medium on this subject,
and it is probable that a sound view would be
that the occasion which requires or justifies the
President in returning without his approval a
bill passed by both Houses of Congress, with his
objections thereto, should be of a grave and serious character, and the measure itself one of much
public importance. There remains to the President, in all cases, the alternative of declining to
sign, and failing to veto a bill, and thus permitting it by the lapse of ten days, without any
action on his part, to become a law of the land
upon the sole responsibility of its passage by the
Senate and House of Representatives. This has
been done occasionally by Presidents, and it is
rather curious that of the many bills presented
to the Executive for his approval, of the propriety of which he must have serious doubts and
in regard to which he might be unwilling to

interpose this power reposed in him. alone, he has so seldom resorted to the expedient of inaction, leaving the responsibility with the legislative branch proper of the Government.

NOTES UPON LECTURE III.

1. *The Appointing Power.*

The difficulty in regard to appointments which Judge Miller suggests, began in the very beginning of the new government. At an early day in his first term Washington wrote to a friend who had solicited an office for another: "From the moment when the necessity had become more apparent, and, as it were, inevitable, I anticipated, with a heart full of distress, the ten thousand embarrassments, perplexities, and troubles, to which I must again be exposed in the evening of a life already nearly consumed in public cares. Among all these anxieties, I will not conceal from you, I anticipated none greater than those which were likely to be produced by applications for appointments to the different offices which would be created under the new government. Nor will I conceal that my apprehensions have already been but too well justified. Scarcely a day passes in which applications of one kind or another do not arise; insomuch that, had I not early adopted some general principles, I should before this time have been wholly occupied in this business. As it is, I have found the number of answers which I have been necessitated to give in my own hand, an almost insupportable burden to me.[1]"

2. *Appointments to Vacancies during the Recess.*

Vacancies during
the recess.
    A question has been made as to the power of the President to fill an office during the recess of Congress, which was created by the legislative body at its session immediately before that recess. In practice this has been frequently done ; and the better opinion would seem to be that it has been rightfully done.

3. *Heads of Executive Departments.*

Heads of Executive Departments.
    " There can be no doubt that the President, in the exercise of his executive power under the Constitution, may act through the head of the appropriate executive department. The heads of departments are his assistants in the performance of his executive duties, and their official acts, promulgated in the regular course of business, are presumptively his acts. That has been many times decided by this court."[2]

But when the action required of the President is judicial in character, not administrative, as when the duty is imposed upon him of reviewing the proceedings of Courts Martial, he must himself consider the proceedings laid before him, and decide personally whether they ought to be carried into effect.[3] But this judgment, although

---

[1] Sparks's Life of Washington, 454.
[2] *Runkle* v. *United States*, 122 U. S. 543, 557.   [3] Ib.

his personal act in fact, and not presumptively, Lecture III.
need not be attested by his sign manual, in order Heads of Executive Departments.
to be effective.[1]

4. *Pardons.*

In *Hart* v. *United States* the effect of a par- Pardons.
don on the right to sue in the Court of Claims
was again before the court. Hart, who was a
resident in Texas, joined the insurgents in April,
1861, " and then and afterwards furnished them
with supplies, money, and means of transportation to carry on their invasion and campaign
into New Mexico. On the 3d of November,
1865, the President granted to him a full pardon and amnesty for all offences committed by
him, arising from participation, direct or implied,
in the rebellion. Hart claimed certain sums as
due to him for flour, corn, and forage delivered
to the United States before April 13, 1861, and
certain sums for flour, corn, and forage delivered
after that date."

" The Court of Claims applied to those demands of the claimant which accrued before
April 13, 1861, the provisions of joint resolution. No. 46, approved March 2, 1867, 14 Stat.
571, now embodied in section 3480 of the
Revised Statutes, forbidding the payment of
claims against the United States, 'which accrued
or existed prior to the thirteenth day of April,
A.D. eighteen hundred and sixty-one, in favor of
any person who promoted, encouraged, or in any

---

[1] *United States* v. *Page*, 137 U. S. 673, 678, by Chief Justice
Fuller.

manner sustained the late rebellion,' etc., and
further providing that no pardon should 'authorize the payment of such account, claim, or
demand, until this resolution is modified or
repealed.'

"It was urged before the Court of Claims that
the pardon and amnesty granted by the President to Hart on the 3d of November, 1865, 'for
all offences committed by him arising from participation, direct or implied, in the rebellion,'
operated to set aside the provisions of the joint
resolution as to him and his claims. The court
held otherwise. Its view was that Hart was
guilty of numerous acts for which he could, on
conviction, have been punished in his person and
his property, and that the pardon freed him from
liability for those offences; that his disability to
receive from the United States a debt due to him
was not a consequence attached to or arising out
of any such offence; that it grew out of the fact,
stated in the joint resolution, that he had been
a public enemy; that every disability which a
state of war imposed upon him was removed by
the cessation of the war; that it needed no pardon to effect that result; that, as the pardon
conferred upon him no new right, so the joint
resolution did not take from him anything which
the pardon had conferred; that it did not, like
the legislation considered in *United States* v.
Klein, 13 Wall. 128, attempt to prescribe to the
judiciary the effect to be given to a pardon, in
regard to a matter to which the pardon extended,
but merely forbade certain debts to be paid, un-

til Congress should otherwise order; and that a LECTURE III.
creditor of the United States can only be paid in Pardons.
accordance with the provision of the Constitution (Art. I, sec. 9, subd. 7), which declares that
'no money shall be drawn from the treasury,
but in consequence of appropriations made by
law.' . . . We are of opinion that the judgment
of the Court of Claims was right." [1]

5. *Treaties providing for payment of moneys.*

Whether a treaty, providing for the payment Treaties provid-
of money by the United States, makes it obliga- ing for payment of moneys.
tory upon Congress to pass the necessary appro-
priation, is a question that has been more than
once mooted.

When the treaty of 1794 with Great Britain,
known as Jay's Treaty, was sent to the House
by President Washington, that body, on the
motion of Mr. Edward Livingston, asked the
President to transmit to it a copy of the instructions to Mr. Jay, and of the correspondence and
documents relating to the treaty. This motion
was resisted by the Federalists, on the ground
that the treaty had become the supreme law,
and that the House had no jurisdiction over a
question which had been settled elsewhere under
the Constitution. Notwithstanding the opposition the resolution was adopted. In reply the
President said: " Having been a member of the
General Convention, and knowing the principles
upon which the Constitution was formed, I have

---

[1] *Hart* v. *United States*, 118 U. S. 62, 64, 65, 66.

ever entertained but one opinion on this subject,
and from the first establishment of this Government to this moment, my conduct has exemplified that opinion; that the power of making
treaties is exclusively vested in the President,
by and with the advice and consent of the Senate, provided two-thirds of the senators present
concur; and that every treaty so made and promulgated thenceforward becomes the law of the
land. . . . As, therefore, it is perfectly clear
to my understanding that the assent of the
House of Representatives is not necessary to the
validity of a treaty; as the treaty with Great
Britain exhibits in itself all the objects requiring
legislative provision, and on these the papers
called for can throw no light, and as it is essential to the due administration of the Government
that the boundaries fixed by the Constitution
between the different departments should be preserved — a just regard to the Constitution and
to the duty of my office, under all the circumstances of this case, forbid a compliance with
your request." [1]

The House replied to this by resolving that
when it made application to the Executive for
information it was not necessary "that the purpose for which such information may be wanted,
or to which the same may be applied, should be
stated in the application." [2]   This may have been
the work of Madison, who wrote Jefferson, " The
absolute refusal was as unexpected as the tone

---

[1] Annals 1st Session, 4th Congress, 761, 762.
[2] Annals 1st Session, 4th Congress, 771, 772.

and tenor of the message are improper and
indelicate."[1] After a long and animated debate,
the House resolved, by a vote of 51 to 48, that
legislation ought to be had for carrying the
treaty into effect.[2]

Similar questions came up in 1803, when Mr.
Jefferson asked appropriations for carrying out
the treaty for the purchase of Louisiana. Congress granted the money.[3]

In 1816 the Senate passed an act to carry
into effect the commercial convention of 1815,
with Great Britain. The substance of this act
was that so much of any existing act as might
be contrary to the provisions of the convention
should be deemed and taken to be of no effect.
The House passed an act, reënacting, *seriatim*,
the provisions of the treaty. Each body refused
to recede. The Senate maintained that, as the
treaty was operative of itself, the act should be
declaratory only. The House contended that
legislation was necessary. A committee of conference was appointed, Rufus King being chairman on the part of the Senate and John Forsyth
on the part of the House. The principle of the
settlement was thus stated to the House by Forsyth: "Your committee understood the committee of the Senate to admit the principle
contended for by the House, that whilst some
treaties might not require, others may require
legislative provision to carry them into effect;
that the decision of the question how far such

---

[1] Madison to Jefferson, April 4, 1796. 2 Madison's Writings, 89.
[2] Annals 1st Session, 4th Congress, 1291.
[3] 2 Wharton's Int. Dig. 19.

provision was necessary must be founded upon the peculiar character of the treaty itself." [1] The bill agreed upon was enacted. [2]

In 1843 a commercial treaty was concluded with the German States containing provisions in regard to rates of duties. The Senate Committee on Foreign Relations made an adverse report on the ground of the " want of constitutional competency" to make it; and the Senate laid the subject indefinitely on the table. Mr. Calhoun, then Secretary of State, said: " If this be a true view of the treaty-making power, it may be truly said that its exercise has been one continual series of habitual and uninterrupted infringements of the Constitution. From the beginning, and throughout the whole existence of the Federal Government, it has been exercised constantly on commerce, navigation, and other delegated powers." [3]

The subject was again before Congress when the bill making appropriations for the purchase of Alaska was under consideration. It was elaborately discussed in the House. In the end that body accepted a report from a conference committee containing a resolution with a preamble reciting that " the stipulations of the treaty cannot be carried into full force and effect, except by legislation to which the consent of both Houses is necessary." [4]

---

[1] Introductory note, Treaties and Convention of the United States with other powers, orig. ed. p. 944.

[2] 3 Stat. 255, c. 22.   [3] 2 Wharton's Int. Dig. 20, 21.

[4] Introductory note, Treaties and Conventions, orig. ed. p. 944. See also 2 Wharton's Int. Dig. 21.

6. *Opinions by Heads of Departments.*

Such opinions have been required in two not- Lecture III.
Opinions by heads of departments.
able instances.

In April, 1793, President Washington sent a circular letter to each member of his cabinet stating that "the posture of affairs in Europe, particularly between France and Great Britain, places the United States in a delicate situation, and requires much consideration as to the measures which it will be proper for them to observe in the war between those powers." He asked to have the questions considered preparatory to a meeting the next day, when he should expect to receive "the result of their reflections." [1] Thirteen questions were enclosed [2] relating to the issue of a proclamation of neutrality, to the then relations between France and the United States, and to the binding force of treaties with France concluded during the War of the Revolution.

Mr. Jefferson has left an account of the meeting of the cabinet in which these questions were answered *seriatim* and individually.[3] "It was determined by all, on the first question, that a proclamation shall issue, forbidding our citizens to take part in any hostilities on the seas, with or against any of the belligerent powers; and warning them against carrying to any such powers any of those articles deemed contraband, according to the modern usage of nations; and

---

[1] 10 Sparks' Washington, 337.
[2] 10 Sparks' Washington, 533.
[3] 9 Jefferson's Works, 142.

enjoining them from all acts and proceedings
inconsistent with the duties of a friendly nation
towards those at war.   On the second question,
' Shall a minister from the Republic of France
be received ? ' it was unanimously resolved that
he shall be received.   The remaining questions
were postponed for further consideration." [1]

In August, 1873, this constitutional power was
again exercised by President Grant.   He sent
to each member of his cabinet seven questions
on the subject of expatriation, and received letters in reply from all.   With his annual message
to Congress on the following December he transmitted this correspondence, saying: " I invite
the earnest attention of Congress to the existing
laws of the United States respecting expatriation
and the election of nationality by individuals.
. . . Persons who have never resided within the
United States have been enabled to put forward
a pretension to the protection of the United
States against the claim to military service of
the government under whose protection they
were born and have been reared.   In some cases
even naturalized citizens of the United States
have returned to the land of their birth, with
intent to remain there, and their children, the
issue of a marriage contracted there after their
return, and who have never been in the United
States, have laid claim to our protection when
the lapse of many years had imposed upon them
the duty of military service to the only government which had ever known them personally.

---

[1] 10 Sparks' Washington, 534.

. . . For my own guidance, in determining such LECTURE III.
Opinions by heads
of departments. questions, I required (under the provisions of the Constitution) the opinion in writing of the principal officer in each of the executive departments upon certain questions relating to this subject. The result satisfies me that further legislation has become necessary. I therefore commend the subject to the careful consideration of Congress, and I transmit herewith copies of the several opinions of the principal officers of the executive departments, together with other correspondence and pertinent information on the same subject." [1]

7. *Power to approve an act after the adjournment of Congress.*

On the 3d of March, 1863, Congress passed Approval of an act of Congress after its adjournment. " an act to provide for the collection of abandoned property, and for the prevention of frauds in insurrectionary districts within the United States." On the 4th of March that Congress was adjourned *sine die* under the Constitution, and that act had not received the signature of the President. On the 12th of the same March (within the ten days) President Lincoln signed it, and it was printed with the other acts of that Congress.[2]

Under its operation a large amount of property came into the possession of the Executive; but it was not thought wise to attempt to administer upon it in the courts, without a recognition by the law-making power, which

---

[1] Foreign Relations, 1873, pp. vi, vii, 1185.   [2] 12 Stat. 820, c. 120.

LECTURE III.
Approval of an
act of Congress
after its adjourn-
ment.
should practically amount to its reënactment. Accordingly Congress, on the 20th of July, 1864, passed "an act in addition to the several acts concerning commercial intercourse between loyal and insurrectionary States, and to provide for the collection of captured and abandoned property, and the prevention of frauds in States declared in insurrection. This statute practically reënacted the previous act with amendments, and thus disposed of the difficulty."[1]

8. *Partial Veto.*

Partial veto.
President Grant, in his annual message of December 1, 1873, recommended the adoption of an amendment to the Constitution, "To authorize the Executive to approve of so much of any measure passing the two Houses of Congress as his judgment .may dictate, without approving the whole; the disapproved portion or portions to be subjected to the same rules as now, to wit, to be referred back to the House in which the measure or measures originated, and, if passed by a two-thirds vote of the two Houses, then to become a law without the approval of the President." He added: "I would add to this a provision that there should be no legislation by Congress during the last twenty-four hours of its sitting, except upon vetoes, in order to give the Executive an opportunity to examine and approve or disapprove bills understandingly." Congress took no action on this recommendation.

---

[1] 13 Stat. 375, c. 225.

IV.

THE SEPARATE POWERS OF THE SEN-ATE AND THE HOUSE OF REPRE-SENTATIVES.[1]

——oo⟩o⟨oo——

ARTICLE I, SECTION 5. Each House shall be the LECTURE IV. Judge of the Elections, Returns and Qualifications of its own Members, and a Majority of each shall consti-tute a Quorum to do Business ; but a smaller Number may adjourn from day to day, and may be authorized to compel the Attendance of absent Members, in such Manner, and under such Penalties as each House may provide.

Each House may determine the Rules of its Pro-ceedings, punish its Members for disorderly Behav-iour, and, with the Concurrence of two-thirds, expel a Member.

Each House shall keep a Journal of its Proceed-ings, and from time to time publish the same, except-ing such Parts as may in their Judgment require Secrecy; and the Yeas and Nays of the Members of either House on any question shall, at the Desire of one-fifth of those Present, be entered on the Journal.

Neither House, during the Session of Congress, shall, without the Consent of the other, adjourn for more than three days, nor to any other Place than that in which the two Houses shall be sitting.

ARTICLE I, SECTION 2, PARAGRAPH 5. The House of Representatives shall chuse their Speaker and other Officers ; and shall have the sole Power of Impeach-ment.

ARTICLE I, SECTION 7. All Bills for raising Reve-nue shall originate in the House of Representatives ;

[1] This is Lecture III of the Lectures delivered before the classes of the University Law School.

IV.

but the Senate may propose or concur with Amendments as on other Bills.

EXTRACT FROM THE TWELFTH AMENDMENT. The person having the greatest number of votes for President, shall be the President, if such number be a majority of the whole number of Electors appointed ; and if no person have such majority, then from the persons having the highest numbers not exceeding three on the list of those voted for as President, the House of Representatives shall choose immediately, by ballot, the President. But in choosing the President, the votes shall be taken by states, the representation from each state having one vote ; a quorum for this purpose shall consist of a member or members from two-thirds of the states, and a majority of all the states shall be necessary to a choice. And if the House of Representatives shall not choose a President whenever the right of choice shall devolve upon them, before the fourth day of March next following, then the Vice-President shall act as President, as in the case of the death or other constitutional disability of the President.

ARTICLE I, SECTION 3, PARAGRAPHS 4, 5 and 6. The Vice-President of the United States shall be President of the Senate, but shall have no Vote, unless they be equally divided.

The Senate shall chuse their other officers, and also a President pro tempore, in the Absence of the Vice-President, or when he shall exercise the Office of President of the United States.

The Senate shall have the sole Power to try all Impeachments. When sitting for that Purpose, they shall be on Oath or Affirmation. When the President of the United States is tried, the Chief Justice shall preside: And no Person shall be convicted without the Concurrence of two-thirds of the Members present.

ARTICLE II, SECTION 4. The President, Vice-President and all civil Officers of the United States, shall be removed from Office on Impeachment for, and Conviction of, Treason, Bribery, or other high Crimes and Misdemeanors.

ARTICLE II, SECTION 2, PARAGRAPH 2. He [the President] shall have Power, by and with the Advice and Consent of the Senate, to make Treaties, provided two-thirds of the Senators present concur ; and he shall nominate, and by and with the Advice and

Consent of the Senate, shall appoint Ambassadors, LECTURE IV.
other public Ministers and Consuls, Judges of the
supreme Court, and all other Officers of the United
States, whose Appointments are not herein otherwise
provided for, and which shall be established by Law:
but the Congress may by Law vest the Appointment
of such inferior Officers, as they think proper, in the
President alone, in the Courts of Law, or in the
Heads of Departments.

OF the powers conferred upon the General Congress.
Government by the Constitution of the United
States much the most important are those given
to the legislative body. Many if not nearly all
of the powers of the executive and judicial
branches of the Government are regulated in
the manner of their exercise by the laws enacted
by this body, called the Congress.[1] It is made
to consist of two branches, the Senate and the
House of Representatives; and there is confided
to the President a limited right to control the
action of these two Houses by the exercise of
the veto power. Each House of Congress has

---

[1] In England, from whence most of our legal principles and legislative notions are derived, the authority of Parliament is tran-
scendant and has no bounds. . . . It can change and create afresh
even the constitution of the kingdom and of Parliament itself.
It can, in short, do everything that is not naturally impossible.
Vanhorne's Lessee v. *Dorrance*, 2 Dall. 304, 307.

It is a fundamental principle with English lawyers, that Parliament can do everything except making a woman a man, or a man
a woman. De Lolme, Constitution of England, p. 135.

The first meeting of the Commons in a separate body, as an
independent branch of Parliament, was in 1306, the 34th year of
Edward I. Prior to this time they had met with the nobles and
the clergy and had been outvoted, but they thenceforth assumed
the power to act independently upon proposed legislation, and
especially in the enactment of tax laws. This was the beginning
of the growth of the dominant influence of the House of Commons
in the English Government of to-day.

certain powers of its own which it exercises independently of the other, and it is to these that I propose to call your attention.

Article I, section 5, declares that : —

"Each House shall be the judge of the elections, returns, and qualifications of its own members, and a majority of each shall constitute a quorum to do business; but a smaller number may adjourn from day to day, and may be authorized to compel the attendance of absent members, in such manner, and under such penalties, as each House may provide.

" Each House may determine the rules of its proceedings, punish its members for disorderly behavior, and, with the concurrence of two-thirds, expel a member.

Separate powers of each House.

" Each House shall keep a journal of its proceedings, and, from time to time, publish the same, excepting such parts as may, in their judgment, require secrecy; and the yeas and nays of the members of either House, on any question, shall, at the desire of one-fifth of those present, be entered on the journal.

"Neither House during the session of Congress, shall, without the consent of the other, adjourn for more than three days, nor to any other place than that in which the two Houses shall be sitting."

Qualifications of members.

It will be observed that while these provisions give to each House the same powers, and impose upon each the same limitations, they are to be exercised separately and independently. " Each House shall be the judge of the elections, returns,

and qualifications of its own members." This
provision necessarily refers all contested elections, and all questions about the eligibility of members of Congress, to the House to which they belong; but it seems from the experience of the past to have been one of those principles adopted from the English House of Commons which has not worked well with our institutions, and which the House of Commons itself has been compelled to abandon. Contested elections are now by the law of England tried before the judiciary, and the judgment of the court is conclusive upon the subject. It is conceded on all hands that justice is in this way more nearly administered with accuracy, than it was under the former system. Both in that country and this under the former method the result of a contested election has been very generally forecast by a knowledge of the relations of the parties contesting to the political majority or minority of the House in which the contest is carried on. As this is a constitutional provision, however, there exists no power in the legislature, without an amendment of that instrument, to refer these contested cases to the judiciary. The increasing number of contested election cases arising out of frauds supposed to be perpetrated at the elections themselves, the investigation of which is always difficult, and the uncertainty of a fair and impartial decision by the Senate or House before whom the matter may come, render it very doubtful whether the entire provision on this subject is of any value.

Very few controversies, if any, have arisen in either body concerning the qualifications of its members. It was at one time a question somewhat mooted whether the States could add to the qualifications which the Constitution has prescribed for members of the Senate or the House of Representatives; but it is now conceded that these must be determined by the Constitution alone, because, although it may be conceivable that Congress might make some conditions or limitations concerning the eligibility of its members, it has not been done, and the constitutional qualifications alone regulate that subject.

Power to compel attendance.
The power to compel the attendance of absent members is one which unfortunately it is often necessary to call into operation. In the House of Representatives the "call of the House," which is the phrase for the method used in compelling each member to be present, is one which in every session is frequently resorted to, and is always tedious and almost fruitless in its results. The stately Senate resorts to this measure more rarely, but it has been found occasionally necessary, even there. The penalties for such absence have in practice usually amounted to nothing; the absentees are generally brought in, under the custody of the sergeant-at-arms, and make an apology which is accepted.

Rules.
The provision that each House may determine the rules of its proceedings has led to the adoption of two systems, differing widely from each other, in each of the bodies. The main basis,

however, on which those rules have been con-
structed is Jefferson's Manual, a work prepared by him mainly from the historical precedents in the English House of Commons. These rules have become by many changes and amendments very numerous. The Senate, being a much smaller body than the House, and professing to proceed upon principles of courtesy which allow every member to speak upon any question as long as he may desire, most of the business of that branch of the Legislature is done under a kind of general consent. In the House of Representatives, on the contrary, the greater numbers of that body, and the difficulty of restraining its members, and making them conform to any set of regulations, have led to a very complex and troublesome set of rules. With a good knowledge of them an experienced member, who has served in that body during several terms of Congress, may obtain a very great advantage in the conduct of the business of the House. Many of these rules, indeed, in the opinion of intelligent members and outside observers, are better calculated to embarrass than to facilitate the progress of business, and a member familiar with them and their bearing upon all subjects of legislation which may arise is often enabled to get the House into inextricable confusion, and retard or suspend its proceedings entirely. It is obvious, therefore, that these rules could be very much improved by a careful revision.

The punishment of members for disorderly behavior has generally been by resolutions expressing the disapprobation of the House to which the member belonged, or by a reprimand to the disorderly party by the presiding officer thereof under the direction of that body; but both of these punishments, as well as the expulsion of a member which requires two-thirds, have been of rare occurrence and have never been exercised, it is believed, without sufficient grounds, although this has been questioned in regard to some cases of expulsion at the beginning of the recent war on account of the supposed treasonable practices or utterances of certain Senators.

Each House shall keep a journal of its proceedings, and, from time to time, publish the same, excepting such parts as may, in their judgment, require secrecy. The journals of both Houses of Congress have undoubtedly been faithfully kept since the beginning of the Government; and but rarely has any portion been withheld from publication, except that which relates to the secret sessions of the Senate when engaged in its function of considering treaties or nominations to office sent to it by the President. Very recently a strenuous effort has been made to abolish the secret sessions in which these matters have been considered, by a resolution of the Senate itself. Thus far it has failed; and in regard to treaties it is certainly wise that, while they are yet incomplete and matters of negotiation between the two nations proposing to make them, the discussions of a body like the Senate should not be bruited abroad.

The provision that " the yeas and nays of the
members of either House, on any question, shall,
at the desire of one-fifth of those present, be
entered on the journal," whether wise or unwise,
is the fruitful source of a great waste of time.
It may be very well doubted whether the call of
the yeas and nays in the House of Representatives, which necessarily consumes a great deal
of time, is not resorted to more for that purpose
than any other, thereby frequently defeating a
measure which a majority of the House is prepared to pass.   It may be of some advantage in
the way of compelling members to spread their
names upon the record as having voted for or
against any particular proposition, and thereby
holding them responsible to the public sentiment
of their constituents.   Where this is the conscientious object and motive in calling for the yeas
and nays it is probably unobjectionable, and in
the enactment of laws of great public importance it is desirable, for many reasons, that the
votes of members should be recorded.   No doubt
this was the object of the Constitution in authorizing a call of the yeas and nays upon the request of one-fifth of the members present, and
this requirement of one-fifth seems to be a necessity to prevent the frittering away of the time
of the legislative body at the request of a single
member.

The requirement that " neither House, during
the session of Congress, shall, without the consent of the other, adjourn for more than three
days, nor to any other place than that in which

LECTURE IV.
Limitation in
power of separate
adjournment.

the two Houses shall be sitting," is of obvious necessity to prevent either branch of the Congress from breaking up its sessions. If one House could adjourn itself to a different place it would practically be an end to that session of Congress ; or if one House could adjourn of its own motion without the other, for two or three weeks at a time, the obstruction of the public business would be very great, and there would be an impossibility of the co-operative action contemplated by the Constitution. In practice, the three days' limit is reached by one or both branches of Congress very frequently during a long session, when an adjournment is had over from Thursday until Monday.

Separate powers
of the House.

These are the provisions which apply equally to each House of Congress, and are obligatory upon both. We now come to consider certain powers and functions which are reposed in one House and not in the other. Of these we will begin with the House of Representatives.

The Speaker.

Article I, section 2, declares that " the House of Representatives shall choose their Speaker and other officers, and shall have the sole power of impeachment." In the use of the word which designates the presiding officer of that body the convention which framed the Constitution adopted, as it has done in so many other instances, the language of the law of England in regard to the presiding officer of the House of Commons. While there is in the Constitution no very definite description of the powers which may be exercised by the Speaker of the House, that

office has become, by the practice and the rules
of the House, the repository of more unrestricted power than any other officer of the Government of the United States possesses. The Speaker appoints all the committees of that body, whether those prescribed by the general rules of the House or special committees for particular occasions. He not only appoints these committees, but he nominates their chairmen; although he does this, of course, with reference to the opinions of the members of the committee, so far as they may be known, in regard to matters which will come before them. It is also customary to make up these committees, with regard to the political affiliations of the members who are to compose them, in such a manner as to give a majority upon each committee to the party to which the Speaker himself belongs; and in regard to particular measures which may be brought to the attention of the House, the Speaker, if he is aware of their character, may so arrange the committee, to which they will be referred, as to secure action in accordance with his own views of the subject under consideration. As the influence of the reports and action of these committees has grown greater and greater with the increasing number of the members of the House of Representatives, the power of the Speaker in thus securing in advance a committee which will act according to his views is hard to over-estimate. In the pressure of business in the House, which is always very great, the recognition of a member by the Speaker, or his failure

to so recognize him when he rises upon the floor, often determines the fate of an important measure ; and this recognition, which formerly was supposed to be impartial and the actual result of the Speaker's eye first falling upon the member whom he recognized, has come to be in modern times a matter of prearrangement and understanding between the Speaker and the members who desire to be heard. All this makes him almost the absolute arbiter of the important legislation which is crowded into the latter part of a session of Congress.

The House of Representatives, by the character of its organization under the Constitution of the United States, consists of the same body of men for two years, and a term of Congress has come to be treated as the same as that of the members, whose term of office commences on the fourth of March and continues for two years thereafter. It is this body which elects a Speaker, and he is elected for the term of that Congress. There is, therefore, a new Speaker elected at the beginning of every Congress. It is creditable to the characters of the Speakers who have presided over that body, and to the discretion of the respective Houses that elected them, that it is rare that a Speaker has only served a single term. They have generally been re-elected for several terms, as long as they themselves remained in Congress and their party in the majority, or chose to seek a re-election. Undoubtedly this grows largely out of the fact that the necessity and value of experience in a

Speaker is felt by all the members; and perhaps
it may be said also that, subject to certain recognized obligations to the political party who elected him, the Speaker has .generally been found to be impartial toward the members, and just in his rulings on matters submitted to him.

The other officers of the House of Represent- atives, beside the Speaker, are the clerk, the sergeant-at-arms, doorkeeper, postmaster, and perhaps others of inferior grade. These require no comment at the present time, except to say that they are almost invariably selected at a caucus of the dominant party held a day or two before the organization of the House. It has happened once or twice in the history of the Government, the contest for the office of Speaker being so close and so bitter, that, no candidate receiving a majority of the whole number of votes, the struggle was prolonged for several weeks at the beginning of the session, during which the House could do nothing.

The House also has the sole power of im- peachment.[1] The Constitution provides else-

---

[1] " It is not disputed that the power of originating the inquiry, or, in other words, of preferring the impeachment, ought to be lodged in the hands of one branch of the legislative body ; will not the reasons which indicate the propriety of this arrangement strongly plead for an admission of the other branch of that body to a share of the inquiry ? The model from which the idea of this institution has been borrowed, pointed out that course to the convention. In Great Britain it is the province of the House of Commons to prefer the impeachment, and the House of Lords to decide upon it. Several of the State constitutions have followed the example. As well the latter, as the former, seem to have regarded the practice of impeachments as a bridle in the hands of the legislative body upon the executive servants of the Government. Is not this the true light in which it ought to be regarded ? " The Federalist, No. 64. Dawson's ed. : No. 65, Hallowell ed.

where, to which we have already referred in these lectures, that the President, and all the other officers of the Government, may be removed from office by impeachment for high crimes and misdemeanors. The process of impeachment, which is here provided for, can only begin in the House of Representatives. This is done by that House formulating charges in the nature of an indictment against the officer intended to be impeached, upon inquiry into the matters which they propose to include within such impeachment. No other body has the right to prefer these articles or charges. In doing this the House of Representatives discharges a function in the nature of that exercised by a grand jury. Nor does its connection with the proceedings cease with the mere formulation of the charges and the presentation of them to the Senate, which is the body that tries the impeachment. The prosecution of the case before the Senate by the introduction of evidence, the argument of the cause, and all the other machinery for the conviction of the defendant, is submitted to the control of the House. That body usually appoints a special committee, called a committee of managers, who conduct the prosecution. They may be, and in important cases are, aided by counsel who are not members of the committee, nor even members of the House; but this matter is within the control of the House, and such counsel are employed by its authority.

The most important trial of this class which

has ever taken place in this country was that of
President Johnson, which has already been referred to. This power of impeachment has not
been exercised very frequently, probably not
nearly so often as it would have been but for
the limited tenure of most of the officers of the
Federal Government. The process is tedious
and expensive, and the requirement of a two-
thirds majority in order to convict, renders it
generally inefficient. As most of the officers of
the Government have a term fixed to the enjoyment of their offices, it has been usually thought
wiser to let the limitation effect the removal,
than to engage in this costly and unsatisfactory
process of impeachment.

"All bills for raising revenue shall originate
in the House of Representatives;[1] but the Senate
may propose or concur with amendments, as on
other bills."[2]

This is a very important function of legislation, as it is now construed by the House, to be
reposed exclusively in that body. As we would

---

[1] The House of Representatives can not only refuse, but they alone can propose the supplies requisite for the support of Government. They, in a word, hold the purse; that powerful instrument by which we behold, in the history of the British constitution, an infant and humble representation of the people gradually enlarging the sphere of its activity and importance, and finally reducing, as far as it seems to have wished, all the overgrown prerogatives of the other branches of the government. This power over the purse may, in fact, be regarded as the most complete and effectual weapon, with which any constitution can arm the immediate representatives of the people for obtaining a redress of every griev-ance, and for carrying into effect every just and salutary measure. The Federalist, No. 57, Dawson's ed.: No. 58, all other editions.

[2] Constitution, Art. 1, sec. 7, par. 1.

naturally understand the meaning of the term "revenue" at the present day, the expression "bills for raising revenue" would have reference to laws for the purpose of obtaining money by some form of taxation or other means of raising the necessary funds to be used in supplying the wants of the government, paying its expenses, and discharging its debts. The appropriation of that money, which is always necessarily done by virtue of an act of Congress, would seem to be quite a different thing from the laws prescribing how the money shall be raised. In practice, however, the House of Representatives has insisted that, not only shall it originate all bills of ways and means for raising revenue, for which purpose there is a committee appointed in that body called the "Committee on Ways and Means," but it has also claimed that all the appropriation bills, and especially the annual appropriation bills, which are prepared each year to meet the current expenses of the Government during the succeeding fiscal year, shall originate in that body; and it has, therefore, a standing "Committee on Appropriations." This has been the practice now for so long a time that it may be doubted whether it will be seriously questioned.

The Senate, however, has never given its full assent to this proposition, but has, on the contrary, from time to time originated bills appropriating money for specific purposes; although it is not believed that it has for a great many years attempted to act upon any of the general

appropriation bills until they have been sent to Lecture IV.
that body from the House. At the present time Revenue bills.
there is no apparent connection between a bill for
raising money and an appropriation bill to spend
that money. The revenues of the country are
derived from a system of permanent taxation,
which year after year brings into the treasury
of the United States, by its continued operation,
sufficient means to pay all the expenses of the
Government, as well as the interest on its public
debt; and it is not necessary that every year, or
even at every term of the Congress, there should
be a new law for the raising of revenue, but it
is required that there should be a law every
year appropriating the money thus placed in the
treasury to the needs of the Government. It is
difficult to see, under this clause of the Constitution, how it is, when no new law is necessary
to raise revenue, that the act appropriating or
directing how the revenue already raised, which
exists or is expected to exist in the treasury,
shall be appropriated, can be properly called a
bill for raising revenue. Undoubtedly the adop- Difference be-
tion of this article into the Constitution, and the tween English and American
construction which has been given to it, is the practice in this
result of the practices of our English ancestors. matter.
The Commons of England came into existence
as an efficient power in the government of that
country by virtue of the necessity there was for
them to make contributions, called subsidies,
and taxes, which they gave to the King for his
support and for that of his government. This
at first was done at odd times, and but infre-

quently, the King relying in early days upon his own revenues to support his regal station and his authority. But as these became inadequate, and wars with foreign nations demanded more money and treasure or property than the King could command, he was by necessity compelled to call upon his subjects to aid him by contributions from their substance. This he did by calling together certain prominent and leading men in the country who represented their own classes and the citizens of the towns, who voted a voluntary supply, or contribution, or subsidy (for it was called by all of these names), which they appropriated to the support of the King and his government. These votes and gifts of the Commons they were very jealous about. They would not permit the King himself to levy these taxes or contributions without their consent given in public in solemn form; and it may be remarked that the revolution in which King Charles lost his life was the result of an attempt on his part to do this. Neither would they permit the House of Lords to vote these taxes or supplies. Hence, as the necessity for resorting to the Commons for the support of the government grew greater and greater, the tenacity with which they clung to the right to have this done by their own voluntary action became stronger and stronger.[1]

---

[1] The Commons, through its nominees, the ministry, has absorbed the greater part of the power of the Crown, and more and more reduced the other House to a position of secondary importance.

These contributions were at first voted at considerable intervals, and the bill or law by which they were given was both a bill to raise revenue and to appropriate that revenue when raised. They, therefore, came to be called appropriations, or bills of supply, and perhaps revenue bills. They have retained that name to the present time in England, as well as in most of the States of the Federal Union. The annual appropriation bills in Great Britain, and in this country in most of the States, are called "bills of supply." In England a familiar term also is "The Budget," and this budget, while voting the money necessary for the support of the Government, almost always contains some modification of the system of taxation; they are united together, and they are in fact bills which appropriate the money, and establish the sources at the same time from which it shall be raised. It is undoubtedly in analogy to that system, as furnishing the true meaning of this clause of the Constitution, that the phrase "bills for raising revenue" in that instrument has come to be construed to include both bills of appropriation and bills for establishing or raising revenue; although they may be very different in character, and the bill for an appropriation may contain no element incident to the raising of revenue.

It is singular that so little comment is to be found upon this clause of the Constitution by those who have made that instrument the subject of their consideration; and there is but little reference to it in the debates of the two Houses

LECTURE IV.
Difference be-
tween English
and American
practice in this
matter.

of Congress or in the discussions at the time the
Constitution was framed and adopted. It seems to
have been assumed, and probably a hundred years
ago it was the usual custom, that appropriation
bills were accompanied by more or less legislation on the subject of the means of raising revenue. But at the present time, under our settled
system of financial operation, although there is,
of course, a necessity for regulating the expenditures of the Government and therefore prepar-
ing the appropriation bills to meet its expenses
according to the means which are at the command of Congress, there is, in fact, a very remote connection between a bill for the raising
of revenue and the ordinary bills appropriating
the revenue already raised to the support of the
Government.

Election of Presi-
dent when there
is no election by
the people.

In some respects the most important duty,
devolved upon the House of Representatives
exclusively by the Constitution, is that which
was originally found in Article II, section 1,
paragraph 3, of that instrument, but for which
the Twelfth Article of the amendments has since
been substituted. This Article, after amending
in some respects the clumsy provision as it
originally stood concerning the appointment of
electors, and their choice of a President, declares
that " the person having the greatest number of
votes for President shall be the President, if such
number be a majority of the whole number of
electors appointed, and if no person have such
majority, then, from the persons having the
highest numbers, not exceeding three, on the list

of those voted for as President, the House of
Representatives shall choose immediately, by
ballot, the President. But in choosing the
President, the votes shall be taken by States,
the representation from each State having one
vote ; a quorum for this purpose shall consist of
a member or members from two-thirds of the
States, and a majority of all the States shall be
necessary to a choice. . And if the House of Representatives shall not choose a President, whenever the right of choice shall devolve upon them,
before the fourth day of March next following,
then the Vice-President shall act as President, as
in case of the death, or other constitutional disability of the President."

As this provision stood in the original Constitution, each elector cast two votes, and the person receiving the largest number of such votes
was to be President, and the one the next largest
was to be Vice-President. This made no provision for distinctive votes for President and
for Vice-President, the result of which was that
at the end of President John Adams' administration, when the electors came to cast their votes,
it was found that Mr. Jefferson and Mr. Burr had
an equal number of votes, though it has been
said that in the popular canvass which resulted
in the election of these electors, it had always
been understood that Mr. Jefferson was supported
for President by those who voted for Mr. Burr
as Vice-President. The result, however, of this
tie was that the election went to the House of
Representatives under the provision in the orig-

inal Constitution, and not under the ones which we have just cited from the Twelfth Article of the amendments, and a long and bitter contest ensued in that body before Mr. Jefferson was finally elected President, and Mr. Burr Vice-President.

A similar event under this Twelfth Article occurred at the expiration of Mr. Monroe's administration, when neither of the candidates who were voted for by the electors received a majority of the electoral votes. General Jackson received a plurality; Mr. John Quincy Adams received the next highest number, and then came Mr. Crawford and Mr. Clay. The election by the House, taken by States, resulted in the choice of Mr. Adams.

Although this mode of electing a President, by which, as in the case last cited, the plurality of the electoral vote and a very large plurality of the popular vote was for one man, while another was elected President by the House of Representatives, has never met with general public approval, yet it remains unaltered in the objectionable feature mentioned, and but little effort has ever been made to change it. In fact the whole subject of the manner of electing a President has never been satisfactory to the general public, and only the difficulty of proposing a system which would meet with the general approval of the States, to which it would have to be submitted, has prevented some material modification of it. The manner of counting the votes is left ambiguous in many respects,

and in the case of the contest between Mr.
Hayes and Mr. Tilden was a subject of great
anxiety and even danger from a public disturbance of the peace, which was only averted by
the novel expedient of an electoral commission
to report upon the condition of the electoral
votes cast.

Reverting now to the exclusive powers vested
in the Senate, that which relates to the selecting
of its officers, as found in Article I, section 3,
will be seen to differ somewhat from that of the
House of Representatives. Paragraphs 4, 5 and
6 read as follows : —

" 4. The Vice-President of the United States
shall be President of the Senate, but shall have
no vote, unless they be equally divided.

" 5. The Senate shall choose their other officers, and also a President *pro tempore*, in the
absence of the Vice-President, or when he shall
exercise the office of President of the United
States.

" 6. The Senate shall have the sole power to
try all impeachments. When sitting for that
purpose, they shall be on oath or affirmation.
When the President of the United States is
tried, the Chief Justice shall preside ; and no
person shall be convicted without the concurrence of two-thirds of the members present."

It will thus be seen that the presiding officer
of the Senate is the Vice-President of the United
States, not selected from among the senators,
nor by them, and that his principal function in
the scheme of the Government is this duty of

presiding over the Senate. The office as thus established was probably supposed to be one of much dignity and of some power, especially in regard to the appointment of committees, standing or others. The practice of the Senate, however, for many years past has been, under the domination of all political parties in it, to select by a majority vote of the entire body its committees and their chairmen. This is altogether true of the regular standing committees. If the presiding officer of the Senate is ever authorized to appoint the members of a special committee, it is by virtue of the express delegation of that power in the resolution providing for such committee.

The limited power of the Vice-President to cast a vote in the case of an equal division of the Senate has been rarely called into exercise, and the office itself, except for the event unfortunately too often occurring in the history of our Government of his succession to the Presidential office by the death of its incumbent, would be one merely of dignity and respectability. In the case of the death of the Vice-President, or his accession to the office of President of the United States, or his temporary absence, the Senate elects a president *pro tempore*, from among its own members, who exercises all the functions of the Vice-President in relation to that body, except that of giving a casting vote in case of an equal division. This he does not do because he does not lose his right to vote as a senator by becoming the presiding officer of that body.

One of the most important powers confided
to the Senate is that of trying impeachments.
As already suggested, this power has been
rarely called into operation when we consider
that it is the only mode of removing from his
place an officer of the Government during the
term of office for which he is elected or appointed, except so far as that power may be
reposed in the President as a part of his power
of appointment to office. In other cases, which
are by far the most numerous, where it would
be important to remove an officer, it can only
be done by impeachment. The result of this
has been that the expense, the delay, the cumbersome method of the process of impeachment,
and the interference which it causes with the
other functions of the Senate while the trial
is in progress, have all contributed to give
immunity to men in high offices who ought to
have been removed for the good of the service
to which they belonged.

The Senate in trying an impeachment sits as
a court, its members take a new oath or affirmation as such, and when the President of the
United States is to be tried the Chief Justice of
the Supreme Court is to be the presiding officer.
No conviction shall be had without the concurrence of two-thirds of the members present, and
in case of a conviction the punishment, if it can
be called punishment, shall extend no further
than to removal from office, and disqualification
to hold and enjoy any office of honor, trust, or
profit, under the United States thereafter.

The uncertainty as to what must be the nature of the offences which will justify a conviction on trials of impeachment is another reason why it is so seldom resorted to.   Article II, section 4, declares that " The President, Vice-President, and all civil officers of the United States, shall be removed from office, on impeachment for, and conviction of, treason, bribery, or other high crimes and misdemeanors."

Treason and bribery are easily understood, but no satisfactory definition has ever been given or generally accepted of the phrase " or other high crimes and misdemeanors."

The most important power of the Senate, however, in which the House of Representatives has no part, is that in which it is called to assist in the performance of functions properly executive in connection with the President of the United States.   These are the making of treaties, and the appointments to office.   The second paragraph of section 2, of Article II, of the Constitution joins the Senate and the President in the execution of these two powers.   It declares that the President " shall have power, by and with the advice and consent of the Senate, to make treaties, provided two-thirds of the Senators present concur ; and he shall nominate, and by and with the advice and consent of the Senate, shall appoint ambassadors, other public ministers, and consuls, judges of the Supreme Court, and all other officers of the United States, whose appointments are not herein otherwise provided for, and which shall be established by law ; but the Con-

gress may by law vest the appointment of such
inferior officers as they think proper, in the
President alone, in the courts of law, or in the
heads of departments."

All treaties, therefore, made by this country
with any foreign power, require, in the first
place, the action of the executive branch of the
Government, and then the advice and consent of
the Senate. To make this advice and consent
operative, two-thirds of the senators present,
when a treaty is passed upon, must concur in its
approval. The consent of the Senate also is
necessary, though not requiring two-thirds of
that body for that purpose, to the confirmation
of such officers as shall be nominated to it by
the President for ambassadors, other public
ministers and consuls, judges of the Supreme
Court, and all other officers of the United States
whose appointments are not otherwise provided
for, and which shall be established by law. It
will be seen that this provision confers upon the
Senate a power of the greatest importance and
magnitude in the conduct of the affairs of the
Government, although it is true that the President in this conjoint action with the Senate has
the initiative. He makes the treaty before it is
submitted to the Senate for its consent thereto,
and he selects the individuals whom he will
nominate to office before their names are sent to
the Senate for its concurrence. Although the
language of the clause that "he shall have
power, by and with the advice and consent of
the Senate, to make treaties," would imply that

the negotiation of a treaty with a foreign nation in the first instance, would be an act in which the advice of the Senate would be asked, and though the Senate has in a few instances been advised with, and has made suggestions concerning treaties before they were signed by the officers of the governments initiating them, yet the practice has almost uniformly been that the treaty has been first reduced to form and signed by the ministers authorized to negotiate it, before it has been submitted to the Senate for its approval.

The Senate, however, has exercised freely its prerogative, in cases where treaties have been thus submitted to it, of suggesting amendments which would put the treaty in such form as to meet its views, or of refusing its consent altogether. The other power of the Senate, to confirm or reject nominations to office, has also been freely exercised and freely commented upon. Grave differences of opinion exist as to the authority of the President where such nominations are rejected. The power conferred by this clause of the Constitution is too important, too far-reaching, and presents too many questions of magnitude and of every day occurrence to justify me in entering any further into its consideration than I have done at this time.

NOTES UPON LECTURE IV.

1. *Impeachment.*

"Impeachment was taken, not directly from English usage, but rather from the Constitutions of Virginia (1776), and Massachusetts (1780), which had, no doubt following the example of England, established this remedy against culpable officials." [1] It is a cumbersome process, and very apt to fail. A competent observer says that it " is the heaviest piece of artillery in the congressional arsenal, but, because it is so heavy, it is unfit for ordinary use. It is like a hundred-ton gun, which needs complex machinery to bring it into position, an enormous charge of powder to fire it, and a large mark to aim at. Or, to vary the simile, impeachment is what physicians call a heroic medicine, an extreme remedy, proper to be applied against an official guilty of political crimes, but ill adapted for the punishment of small transgressions." [2]

Seven persons have been impeached. Of these, five were acquitted; one a President of the United States, one a Justice of the Supreme Court, one a District Judge, one a Senator, and

---

[1] Note 2, Bryce's American Commonwealth, vol. 1, p. 47.
[2] 1 Bryce's American Commonwealth, 208.

one a Secretary of War.   Two District Judges have been convicted.[1]

2. *The Budget.*

The budget.   " This name is applied to an account of the ways and means by which a minister of finance purposes to defray the expenditure of the State. In the United Kingdom the Chancellor of the Exchequer, usually in April, lays before the House of Commons a statement of the actual results of revenue and expenditure, in the past finance year ending March 31, showing how far his estimates have been realized, and what surplus or deficit there has been in the income as compared with the expenditure.   This is accompanied by another statement in which the Chancellor gives an estimate of what the produce of the revenue may be in the year just entered upon, supposing the taxes and duties to remain as they were in the past year, and also an estimate of what the expenditure will be in the current year.   If the estimated revenue, after allowing for normal increase of the principal sources of income, be less than the estimated expenditure, this is deemed a case for the imposition of some new, or the increase of some existing tax or taxes. On the other hand, if the estimated revenue shows a large surplus over the estimated expenditure, there is room for remitting or reducing some tax or taxes, and the extent of this relief is generally limited to the amount of surplus

---

[1] 1 Bryce's American Commonwealth, 106, 227.

realized in the previous year. The Chancellor
of the Exchequer has to take Parliament into
confidence on his estimates both as regards revenue and expenditure; and when the taxation
and expenditure obtain the assent of Parliament,
the results as thus adjusted become the final
budget estimate for the year."[1]

3. *The Speaker.*

The enormous power which the Speaker of
the House of Representatives wields over the
legislation of Congress, which Mr. Justice Miller has so forcibly pointed out, is not enjoyed
by the presiding officer of that great body in
England from whence the office and its title are
derived.

" In the House of Commons the Speaker is a
member, elected to that office at the desire of
the Crown, and confirmed by the royal approbation, given in the House of Lords. A similar
office seems to have existed as early as the reign
of Henry III, when Peter de Montfort signed
and sealed an answer of the Parliament to Pope
Alexander, *vice totius communitatis;* but the
title Speaker was first given to Sir T. Hunger-
ford, in the reign of Edward III. The Speaker
of the House of Commons presides over the
deliberations of the House, and enforces the
rules for preserving order; he puts the question,
and declares the determination of the House.
As the representative of the House, he communi-

---

[1] Encyclopædia Britannica, tit. Budget.

cates its resolutions to others, and conveys its thanks or its censures. He is thus the mouth-piece of the House, whence his title seems to be derived. He issues warrants in execution of the orders of the House for the commitment of offenders, for the issue of writs, the attendance of witnesses, the bringing up prisoners in custody, etc. The mace is borne before him by the sergeant-at-arms when he enters or leaves the House; when he is in the chair, it is left on the table, and it accompanies him on all State occasions. He cannot speak or vote on any question, but on an equality of voices he has the casting vote. Both by ancient custom and legislative declaration, he is entitled to take precedence of all commoners." [1]

4. *Treaties.*

Treaties.

The treaties made by the United States with foreign powers have had their full share in shaping the destiny of the nation ; and hence the power in this respect reposed in the Senate is one of great importance.

In the notes to Lecture I, the treaties concluded before the adoption of the Constitution were considered. It was also seen that the municipal operation of every treaty is subject to be modified or abrogated by legislation of Congress. It only remains to notice some of the principal treaties, concluded under this power, and this notice of necessity must be confined to a few, and be very brief.

---

[1] Chambers' Encyclopædia, tit. Speaker.

The treaty known as Jay's Treaty was the
most important concluded during the administration of President Washington. He found, on
becoming President, Great Britain occupying all
the principal military stations within our territory on our northern frontier, from Oswego to
Detroit, and even penetrating, with its military
forces, into the interior of the State of Ohio.
Spain was in possession of Natchez and was aim-
ing at Vicksburg. The two powers soon after
took up arms against France, in the wars of the
French Revolution, and Great Britain began to
seize, condemn, and confiscate our commerce on
the high seas, on frivolous and illegal pretences,
and to drag American seamen from American
ships, and force them into British service.
France, on the other hand, was represented in
the United States by a rash and imprudent
envoy, who was persistent in his efforts to drive
the United States into the controversy on the
side of France. Washington felt that the country needed rest, and was determined to remain
neutral if it were possible to do so. With this
view he sent Chief Justice Jay to London, to
settle matters with England. Jay concluded
there on the 19th of November, 1794, the treaty
which has since borne his name. It provided
for the withdrawal of the British garrisons; for
joint commissions to determine the claims of
British subjects against the United States and
of American citizens against Great Britain; for
the payment of the judgments, and for various
other things; but it did not provide for an

abandonment by Great Britain of the illegal claims under which the acts complained of had been committed. This caused great excitement in the United States, and became the rallying-point of those who opposed the ratification of the treaty, and who desired to force the United States into the war on the side of France.

The treaty was ratified however, and I repeat here what was said some years ago: "It is the judgment of history that, with all its shortcomings, it was a wise measure. We came out of the war of independence poor; with a great debt; with a depreciated paper currency emitted by the States, and emitted by authority of Congress; with a paralyzed business, and with a narrow ribbon of population along the shores of the Atlantic, of uncongenial pursuits, with great difficulties of communication, and with no common historical traditions prior to the war. With the greatest difficulty, the aversion to a stronger Central Government was overcome. The Constitution started its operation in time of peace, among a people, a large minority of whom, if not an actual majority, was averse to it. Jay's Treaty secured a certainty of a longer time of peace for it to take root and grow. If we had not concluded that treaty, we might have been bound in honor to go to war with England at that time. I cannot see what the result of such a war would have been; but I can see that, by putting off taking part in the great struggle for eighteen years, we secured precious time for the people to become accustomed and attached to the new form of government, and on this is Lecture IV. founded the opinion that the measure, however Jay's Treaty. intrinsically defective, was a wise turning-point in our history."[1]

This treaty introduced the custom of interna- Settlement of in. tional arbitration of private claims, which has ternational claims by treaty. now become so common. Some sixty years ago it was said by the Baron de Barante, in the French Chamber of Peers, while discussing the bill for the overdue instalments on the French Convention of 1831, that "the United States, when the laws of neutrality are violated with respect to them, do not go to war. . . . Without beginning hostilities they protest, quietly present their claims, and when the time comes that their good will is needed, or their friendship sought, they profit by the occasion, and cause the settlement of the private claims, the payment of which had been contested or deferred."[2]

. It is impossible to overestimate the impor- Treaty ceding tance of the Treaty of April 30, 1803, with Louisiana. France, ceding Louisiana. "History fully justifies the wisdom of a measure, acquiring the mouth of the Mississippi. Jay's Treaty and this treaty had a marked influence on the political history of the country. They mainly contributed to wrest the Federal Government from the hands of those who favored the adoption of the Constitution, and place it in the hands of those

---

[1] Cyclopædia of Political Science, etc., tit. Treaties of the United States.

[2] Treaties and Conventions, with other powers. Introductory note, p. 941, orig. ed.

LECTURE IV.
Treaty ceding
Louisiana.

who opposed it. They thus converted a jealous and astute oligarchy in the South from opponents into supporters of the new form of government, and made it their interest to preserve it during the long years that they held power. When the day of change at last came, the Constitution had ceased to be an experiment. It had traditions in the national heart deep enough to protect it."[1]

Treaty of Ghent.

The Treaty of Ghent, signed December 24, 1814, which made peace with Great Britain, is remarkable for two things: First, that it made no provision for settling the principal causes of the war: Second, that by it the United States lost valuable rights in the Fisheries. After resisting Great Britain's construction of that treaty in this respect, a construction in my judgment manifestly erroneous, Mr. Munroe finally accepted it in the Treaty of 1818. This decision has been the cause of much trouble since.

Treaty ceding
Florida.

Treaty ceding
California.

By the Treaty of February 22, 1819, with Spain, we acquired the Floridas; and by the Treaty of Guadalupe Hidalgo, terminating the Mexican War, we acquired California. The first of these treaties promised, in its operation, to perpetuate the power of the slave-holding States in the republic, especially when it was fortified, in this respect, by the annexation of Texas; but the second operated to overcome the influence of the first; and to restore to the non-slave-

---

[1] Encyclopædia of Political Science, etc., tit. Treaties of the United States.

holding States the healthy influence of liberty and freedom.

LECTURE IV.
Treaty ceding
California.

The treaty known as the Clayton-Bulwer Treaty, concluded in 1850, dispossessed Great Britain of an important military, naval, and political position on the Isthmus, at a time when the relative strength of the two powers was very different from what it is now; and, as construed by the United States, contains no continuing engagements to embarrass them. It made possible the canal which is now in course of construction across Nicaragua.

Clayton-Bulwer treaty.

The naturalization treaties negotiated by Mr. Bancroft with the several German States, put an end to the feudal doctrine of perpetual allegiance, and laid the foundation for similar treaties with other States.

Naturalization treaties.

The Treaty of Washington of 1871 with Great Britain resulted in the settlement of the Alabama claims in accordance with the demands of the United States; in the settlement of the water boundary between the United States and Vancouver Island upon the line claimed by the United States; and in an adjustment of the Fishery question, which proved to be temporary and unsuccessful.

Treaty of Washington.

During the century several commercial treaties have been made, affecting the legislation of Congress in regard to customs duties. As the Constitution places this matter within the control of the House of Representatives to originate, such treaties were long received with disfavor in the House. Recent legislation, how-

Commercial treaties.

ever, seems to indicate a change of opinion on this subject, and a disposition on the part of the House of Representatives to concede to the treaty-making power the right to settle the rates of customs duties.

The settlement of international postal rates by treaty or convention, and the international arrangements for the surrender of fugitives from justice, are modern applications of the treaty-making power to produce most useful results.

V.

THE POWER OF TAXATION.[1]

———•o╎•╎oo———

ARTICLE I, SECTION 8, PARAGRAPH 1. The Congress shall have Power to lay and collect Taxes, Duties, Imposts and Excises, to pay the Debts and provide for the common Defence and general Welfare of the United States ; but all Duties, Imposts and Excises shall be uniform throughout the United States ;

ARTICLE I, SECTION 7, PARAGRAPH 1. All Bills for raising Revenue shall originate in the House of Representatives ; but the Senate may propose or concur with Amendments as on other Bills.

ARTICLE I, SECTION 9, PARAGRAPH 4. No Capitation, or other direct, Tax shall be laid, unless in Proportion to the Census or Enumeration hereinbefore directed to be taken.

ARTICLE I, SECTION 10, PARAGRAPH 3. No State shall, without the Consent of Congress, lay any Duty of Tonnage, etc.

IT has been said that the Federal Government is one of granted or conceded powers.[2] This

Power of taxation.

---

[1] This is Lecture IV of the Lectures delivered before the classes of the University Law School.

[2] "The Government of the United States can claim no powers which are not granted to it by the Constitution, and the powers actually granted must be such as are expressly given, or given by necessary implication." Story, J., in *Martin v. Hunter's Lessee*, 1 Wheat. 304, 326.

The distinction between the power of taxation and the power to regulate commerce existed before the Revolution ; the former was asserted to belong to the internal polity of the Colonies, while the latter was conceded to be a proper exercise of the imperial authority.

The essential principle of the American Revolution was that

227

being so, even the most cursory examination of
the Constitution of the United States, which is
the great charter upon which it was founded
and is still carried on, will show that among all
the powers given by that instrument none are
more important than those vested in the legislative body, or Congress. Without attempting
any general or very elaborate exposition of all
those powers, let us briefly consider some of
those most important and useful, among which
your attention is more particularly directed to
that of taxation.[1]

The first clause of section 8, of Article I,
declares that: —

---

they who pay the taxes should control the levying of them. The
right is thus wedded to the power, and representation and taxation
become correlatives.

The principle was early asserted that taxation by Parliament in
any Colony, without its consent, was tyranny. It had been the
inspiration of Magna Charta, and was to be the force which im-
pelled the Colonies to the Revolution. The exclusive power of taxation was claimed by Virginia in 1623; and treaty was made with
the Parliament of the Commonwealth of England in March, 1651,
which declared that the Virginia colonists were as free as the English subjects; that their assembly should transact all their own
affairs, and taxes should not be imposed, or forts or garrisons maintained in that Colony without their consent. Massachusetts asserted
the same doctrine in 1636, and it was reiterated in other Colonies.

[1] The power is not judicial. Its collection may involve the
exercise of judicial and executive functions. Blackwell on Tax
Titles, 26.

It is as incompetent for the Legislature to confer the power to
tax upon the judiciary as upon the executive. *Hardenburg* v.
Kidd, 10 California, 402.

This power of taxation belongs in this country to the legislative
sovereignty, State and national. It is not only not one of the
inherent powers of the court to levy and collect taxes, but it is an
invasion by the judiciary of the Federal government of the legislative functions of the State Government. *Heine* v. *Levee Commissioners*, 19 Wall. 655, 661.

"The Congress shall have power to lay and collect taxes, duties, imposts and excises, to pay the debts and provide for the common defence and general welfare of the United States;[1] but all duties, imposts and excises shall be uniform throughout the United States."

It may be noted that the language is "to lay and collect taxes, duties, imposts and excises," and then there comes a comma, after which it continues, "to pay the debts and provide for the common defence and general welfare of the United States."[2] Whether this latter clause

---

[1] This language was not novel. Compare the objects of union among the States as stated in the Articles of Confederation. In Article III it is "for their common defence, the security of their liberties, and their mutual and general welfare." In Article VIII "all charges of war, and all other expenses that shall be incurred for the common defence, or general welfare" shall be defrayed out of a common treasury. Similar language is used in the Ninth Article.

A government ought to contain in itself every power requisite to the full accomplishment of the objects committed to its care, and the complete execution of the trusts for which it is responsible; free from every other control, but a regard to the public good, and to the sense of the people. The Federalist, No. 31 (Hallowell ed.).

[2] In the transcript of the Constitution as printed in the Revised Statutes, p. 19, there is only a comma after the word "excises," which was the end of the clause in the first draft when reported in the convention, a semicolon only appearing after the following word "States." The same is also true of the carefully corrected copy found in Hickey's Constitution. It would appear, therefore, that the proper value to be attached to this clause and its true meaning, as intended by the wise and learned framers of this instrument, are best exemplified by considering the latter part of the clause as a limitation upon the power given by the opening words. Story in his work on the Constitution prints it in the same way, but remarks, section 912, that in the revised draft in the convention there was a semicolon and paragraph as in the other cases; that it so stands now in some copies, and it is said so stands in the official copy, with a semicolon interposed. In the Federalist this

was put there as a distinctive power, or as a limitation upon the power of taxation, has been a question much controverted. Not being a distinct clause by itself, it would seem probable that these words are a limitation upon the purposes for which taxes may be laid and collected.[1] At one time I did not concur in this peculiar manner of punctuating this instrument by commas and semicolons, without a period coming in between the opening words of this eighth section, "Congress shall have power," and the eighteenth clause with which it concludes. This clause, however, in regard to paying the debts and providing for the common defence and general welfare, constitutes a proper qualification of the power to collect taxes, and in what may be called the same sentence is followed by the limitation requiring all duties, excises, and im-

---

punctuation is referred to, and, referring to the complaint that the language amounts to an unlimited commission to exercise every power which may be alleged to be necessary, it is asked "what color can the objection have when the specification of the objects alluded to by these general terms immediately follows; and is not even separated by a longer pause than a semicolon?" Federalist, No. 41, Hallowell ed. ; 40 Dawson's ed.

[1] This view was concisely and strongly presented by Mr. Jefferson in his opinion on the Bank of the United States, February 15, 1791. He says : "To lay taxes to provide for the general welfare of the United States, that is to say, "to lay taxes *for the purpose* of providing for the general welfare." For the laying of taxes is the *power*, and the general welfare the *purpose* for which the power is to be exercised. They are not to lay taxes *ad libitum for any purpose they please ;* but only *to pay the debts or provide for the welfare of the Union.* In like manner, they are not *to do anything they please* to provide for the general welfare, but only to *lay taxes* for that purpose." 7 Jefferson's Works, 557. And the same construction has been placed upon this language by other eminent men of that period. Hamilton, Gerry, Ellsworth, and others.

posts to be uniform ; so that it seems probable that the meaning is that Congress shall
have power to lay these taxes and collect them
in order "to pay the debts and provide for the
common defence and general welfare." [1]

The importance in the study of constitutional
law of this subject of the power of taxation, as
exercised by both the Federal and State governments, can hardly be overestimated. It would
be curious and interesting to examine into the
origin, growth, and progress of methods of taxation as a means of carrying on the business of
government, but it is unnecessary to go further
back than the feudal ages to note the fact that
no taxes were needed then to carry on the public institutions. The monarch, king, duke, or
other sovereign of a particular district or country was generally the owner of a large proportion of the soil. The men who cultivated it
were his villeins, serfs, or tenants. The theory
of English land tenures to-day is, that the orig-

---

[1] The Government of the Union is a Government of the people ;
it emanates from them ; its powers are granted by them ; and are
to be exercised directly on them and for their benefit. Though limited in its powers, it is supreme within its sphere of action. If the
end be legitimate, and within the scope of the Constitution, all the
means which are appropriate, which are plainly adapted to that
end or not prohibited, may constitutionally be employed to carry
it into effect. *McCulloch* v. *Maryland*, 4 Wheat. 316.

Congress is authorized to lay and collect taxes, etc., to pay the
debts, and provide for the common defence and general welfare of
the United States. . . . Congress is not empowered to tax for those
purposes which are within the exclusive province of the States.
Gibbons v. *Ogden*, 9 Wheat. 1, 199.

Taxation purely in aid of personal or private objects is beyond
the legislative power and an unauthorized invasion of private right.
Loan Association v. *Topeka*, 20 Wall. 655, 662.

inal title is in the king, and that everybody who has an interest in the land is a tenant. There is no such thing known in England, though it may be in some other countries, as an allodial title; that is, one which is absolute, such as we have in this country, to the ownership of the soil.[1] Out of this fact come many of the difficulties American students find in regard to the doctrines pertaining to estates and tenancies. Our laws have been freed from a large part of those intricacies and traditional requirements, which were the outgrowth of centuries of development among our English ancestors regarding the holding of land, but their influence still embarrasses our judicial system.

A sovereign who owned all the land of a country, and who could impose such terms as he pleased on the people who cultivated it, naturally did not need any taxes, in the ordinary use of that term. It was customary, however, to take rents, and generally services, in addition to the revenues derived by the prince from his own large domain, which was cultivated by his own servants. He was also attended by a retinue of followers, his feudatories, sub-tenants, or lords, who each had their following. War was made

---

[1] In England all land is held mediately or immediately of the king, and there is no allodial tenure. The greatest dominion recognized over property by the English law is expressed by the words "tenancy in fee simple." In America, however, the title of land is essentially allodial. In New York, Pennsylvania, Connecticut, Virginia, Michigan, and perhaps other States, lands have been declared to be allodial and free from every vestige of feudal tenure. 4 Kent. Com. 2.

by the prince calling on those who owed him allegiance to come forward with their followers, and by thus joining together their forces form an army with which the sovereign could take the field. Many a kingdom was won or lost by the failure of the feudatory chiefs to come forward to fight in response to such a call. Each was generally expected to bear his own expenses, while the cost of the Central Government the king paid himself. He was, indeed, but little more than a superior chief.

We cannot, however, trace the history of those customs farther at this time than to say, that the great revolution in England, by which the constitutional rights of the people were finally established, wherein Charles I lost his head and James II had to flee the country, was caused by a question of taxation. The old methods, to which reference has been made, for getting the means of maintaining the public authority had become exhausted. The king had not soil or country enough to furnish means for his proper support, and that of his government, and so he had gradually come to receive assistance from the people by the House of Commons voting him certain concessions, as they called them, out of the wealth of the country every two or three years, which was called their free offering.

This was the free offering of the Commons and not of the Lords.

This fact is the origin of that provision in the Constitution of the United States declaring that "all bills for raising revenue shall originate in the House of Representatives" (Art. I, sec. 7, par. 1), which body, under our political system, may be compared with the English House of Commons. That more nearly representative and popular body, in comparison with the House of Lords, was very jealous of its dignity and prerogatives. The Commons, claiming to represent the people, said, in effect, that what they gave to support the government was their money; that the prince could not get it unless they voted it, and that they did not propose to allow the Lords to originate a bill declaring that they raised the money without their assistance.[1]

Questions growing out of taxation, the methods by which it should be levied, and its collection enforced, have always been troublesome, and they have frequently led to public disturbances and even to prolonged wars. Out of the taxation of tea, and the taxation by means of stamps, imposed upon the American Colonies by Great Britain, arose the difficulties which culminated in the revolution that secured their independence. But after a while it came to be understood, at least in all civilized nations, that government must be carried on, not by the revenue derived from the domain of the sovereign or money belonging to him, but by contri-

---

[1] All bills for granting money must have their beginning in the House of Commons; the Lords cannot take this object into their consideration but in consequence of a bill presented to them by the latter. De Lolme, Constitution of England, p. 59, ed. London, 1834.

butions from the people. A tax is a contribution,
and the modern and free governments organized
for the benefit of society, must depend upon
them for their support. The definition by both
Webster and Story is that "a tax is a contribution imposed by government on individuals for
the service of the State." [1]

When, therefore, the members of the convention assembled from the various States, for the
purpose of forming an organic law for the government of the new nation, which was intended
to be permanent in its character, the very first
power that they conferred upon Congress was
that of laying and collecting taxes, duties, imposts, and excises, for the purpose (if it may be
so construed) of paying the debts and providing
for the common defence and general welfare.
It will be observed that it does not say "all
taxes," because in another clause of the same
instrument it is said that "no capitation, or
other direct tax shall be laid, unless in proportion to the census or enumeration," directed to
be taken. Art. I, sec. 9, par. 4. It has been
a troublesome question to determine what was

---

[1] Taxes are defined as being the enforced proportional contribution of persons and property, levied by the authority of the State
for the support of the government, and for all public needs. They
are the property of the citizen, demanded and received by the
government to be disposed of to enable it to carry into effect its
mandates, and to discharge its manifold functions. Cooley on
Taxation, 1.

The power to tax is granted for the benefit of the whole people,
and none have any right to complain if the power is fairly exercised
and the proceeds properly applied to discharge the obligations for
which the taxes were imposed. — *North Missouri Railroad Co.* v.
Maguire, 20 Wall. 46, 60.

LECTURE V.
Our provisions
derived from
England.
Capitation tax.

meant by the expression "direct taxes" as distinguished from other taxes.

A "capitation tax" is, of course, so much a head, and must be levied according to the population, as determined by the census. It can be levied in no other way. But it is not so easy to determine what is a "direct tax."

Direct tax.

The question has been before the Supreme Court of the United States several times, and has been the subject of comment in both Houses of Congress. One principle upon which all have agreed is, that a direct tax must be made upon each State in proportion to its population. When a direct tax is laid, as was done in the beginning of the late war, and was the case shortly after the organization of our Government, the amount of money to be raised is first ascertained, then the population of each State is taken, according to the last census, after which it is a simple matter of division to find out the proportion or quota due from each State. A statute is then passed, declaring that each State shall pay to the Federal Government so much money, according to their ascertained proportion of the whole amount which it is proposed to raise.

But suppose the State does not pay it? In regard to this it may be said that in all instances where a direct tax has been laid, except in the case of some of the States engaged in the late rebellion, the obligation has been promptly assumed, and each State has taken its own means of collecting the sum for which it was assessed.

This amount was then paid into the national LECTURE V.
treasury. But during that contest the States Direct tax.
that did not sympathize with the loyal side did
not want to help the Federal Government by
raising money for its use. Congress, therefore,
passed a law appointing commissioners, whose
duty it was to go into those States as fast as
they were subjugated, following up the armies,
and ascertain the value of the landed estate as
reported by their own tax officers. The assessment was then levied against this real property,
and in many cases it was sold to pay the amount
required. Growing out of these transactions
extensive controversies have arisen and many
suits to determine whether the provisions under
which those things were done were such as to
make the sales valid.

Under the provisions already quoted the question then came up as to what is a "direct tax,"
and also upon what property it is to be levied,
as distinguished from any other tax. In regard
to this it is sufficient to say that it is believed
that no other than a capitation tax, of so much
per head, and a land tax, is a direct tax within
the meaning of the Constitution of the United
States. All other taxes, except imposts, are
properly called excise taxes. Direct taxes, within
the meaning of the Constitution, are only capitation taxes as expressed in that instrument,
and taxes on real estate.[1]

---

[1] *Springer* v. *United States*, 102 U. S. 586.

Mr. Justice Chase said in 1796: "I am inclined to think, but
of this I do not give a judicial opinion, that the direct taxes con-

LECTURE V.
Excise tax.

An excise tax is one which is assessed upon some article of personal property, or money, or something which is exhausted in the use. It is one which from its essence and nature must be paid in fact by the buyer, or the last man who buys and uses the property, because whoever has it at the time when the tax is levied upon it adds that amount to the selling price when he comes to dispose of it, until the property is consumed. It is a tax upon consumption. It was at one time doubted by some whether the late income tax was an excise or a direct tax, and a case to test this question was taken to the Supreme Court of the United States. It was, however, abandoned. It is now entirely clear that the former view was the correct one, and

A tax on incomes
an excise tax.

that the amount assessed upon incomes was in the nature of an excise tax.

The next words of the phrase under discussion are "duties, imposts, and excises." [1] The first

templated by the Constitution, are only two ; namely, the capitation or poll tax, simply without regard to property, profession, or any other circumstance ; and a tax on land.   I doubt whether a tax by a general assessment of personal property within the United States is included within the term direct taxes."   The same opinion was expressed by Mr. Justice Paterson.   In that case it was decided that a tax on carriages was not a direct tax. *Hylton* v. *United States*, 3 Dall. 171, 175.

A tax on the income of an insurance company has been held not to be a direct tax, but a duty or excise. *Pacific Ins. Co.* v. *Soule*, 7 Wall. 433, 444.

A tax of ten per centum upon the circulation of State banks was held not to be a direct tax.   *Veazie Bank* v. *Fenno*, 8 Wall. 533.

[1] Paterson, J., said: "What is the natural and common or technical and appropriate meaning of the words duty and excise, it is not easy to ascertain.   They present no clear and precise idea to the mind.   Different persons will annex different significations to the terms." *Hylton* v. *United States*, 3 Dall. 171, 176.

two, so far as this Constitution is concerned, may be considered as implying the same thing, except that the word "imposts" means more properly a duty or tax upon goods imported from abroad, whereas there might be exports, a tax upon which would be a duty. The Constitution, however, in another place forbids the Federal Government levying any tax or duty upon articles exported from any State (Art. I, sec. 9, par. 5.), so that there can be no tax upon exports, and the words "duties" and "imposts" practically mean the same thing.

"All duties, imposts, and excises," or all taxes that are not direct, are required to be "uniform throughout the United States." What is meant by that word "uniform" has become a matter of very great importance, because the States have begun, of late years, to adopt that principle in their constitutions, and to require that their taxes shall be levied with regard to the restriction of uniformity. So that the question has frequently arisen as to what was a proper definition of that term.

Does it mean that all property that is taxed shall be at the same rate or ratio? That would perhaps be a natural inference at first thought. That is, if horses, wagons, and land are taxed, then the same per cent of value must be assessed upon the horses and wagons as upon the land. The result of this principle would be that, as a very heavy rate is imposed upon whiskey, any other article upon which it is thus proposed to raise a revenue would have to be taxed in the same high proportion. This rate has frequently been as much as two hundred per cent of its original value — much larger than most articles could bear.

The greater part of the money that is raised to support the Government by taxation is raised by duties upon imports from abroad. But the articles which are imported are taxed very differently. For example, silk may be taxed at sixty cents on the dollar of its value. Coffee may be taxed ten cents on the dollar of its value. Are these uniform? If they are not, then very few of our tax laws are valid.

We are, however, relieved from any difficulty in regard to that question, by the peculiar language in which the provision is stated, "but all taxes, imposts, and excises shall be uniform throughout the United States." They are not required to be uniform as between the different articles that are taxed, but uniform as between the different places and different States. Whiskey, for instance, shall not be taxed any higher in the State of Illinois, or Kentucky, where so much of that article is produced, than it is in Pennsylvania. The tax must be uniform on the particular article; and it is uniform within the meaning of the constitutional requirement if it is made to bear the same percentage over all the United States.

That is manifestly the meaning of this word, as used in this clause. The framers of the Constitution could not have meant to say that the Government, in raising its revenues, should not

be allowed to discriminate between the articles
which it should tax.

This conclusion has come to be accepted as the well-settled construction of this clause in regard to uniformity, and it bothers the State authorities now more than the Federal officers. The people in the States are every day resisting the collection of taxes, upon the ground that they are not uniform, although imposed under their own statutes. The better opinion seems to be that what is meant by the use of that term in such statutes is not uniformity as to place. They operate only upon one State, and when they use the words "taxes must be uniform," they mean uniform with regard to the subject of the tax.

This has been productive of some trouble. A State might wish to tax whiskey and tobacco higher than a man's plough or corn-field; and this might be prevented by confining the meaning of this language within too narrow bounds. The difficulties in the way of this construction have, however, been very largely obviated by the meaning of the word "uniform," which has been adopted, holding that the uniformity must refer to articles of the same class. That is, different articles may be taxed at different amounts, provided the rate is uniform on the same class everywhere, with all people, and at all times.

Take, for instance, the case of a license. If everybody in any particular class is required to pay a certain license, — if all lawyers are taxed $25 a year, if all merchants are taxed $100 a

LECTURE V.
Uniformity of
taxation.

year, if all saloon-keepers are taxed $200 a year, — then it is uniform, because it imposes the same burden upon every man of the same class, and who comes within the circle of its well-defined limits. This interpretation may be a little strained, but probably it has arisen from the necessity of enabling the Legislature to levy taxes according to common sense, if not altogether with regard to strict uniformity.

Limits of the taxing power.

One of the most interesting, as well as important, of the branches into which this subject naturally divides, is that in regard to the limits of the taxing power. In this country it is everywhere accompanied by the necessity that the tax shall be imposed for a public use. No State government, nor that of the United States, nor any other authority professing a regard for the rights of the people, is at liberty to take money out of their pockets for any other than a public purpose. Whenever it can be discovered that a tax is levied for something that cannot properly be called such, it may be successfully resisted by all the measures that the law allows in courts of justice.[1]

---

[1] " The power to tax is the strongest and most pervading of all the powers of government, reaching directly or indirectly to all classes of people. It was said by Chief Justice Marshall, in the case of *McCulloch* v. *Maryland*, 4 Wheat. 316, 431, that the power to tax is the power to destroy. A striking instance of the truth of the proposition is seen in the fact that the existing tax of ten per cent imposed by the United States on the circulation of all other banks than the national banks, drove out of existence every State bank of circulation within a year or two after its passage. This power can as readily be employed against one class of individuals and in favor of another, so as to ruin the one class and give unlim-

It is very difficult in a general way, in a Lecture V. government like ours, to say in any particular Taxes levied for public uses. instance where an act of Congress has authorized a certain tax to be levied, under which any money has been collected, paid into the treasury of the United States, and distributed under other acts of the legislative branch by its proper officials, has been levied or collected for any other than a public use. Sometimes the use may not be approved by sound public sentiment; nevertheless it is necessary to give the legislative body the benefit of the presumption that they acted in the exercise of a reasonable discretion, when they profess to have levied the tax for a public purpose.

In some cases, however, States, counties, and municipalities, which have a subordinate right of taxation, have so far departed from that principle that taxes levied by them have been enjoined. Perhaps the greatest number of contests which have originated in regard to this subject have had relation to taxes imposed for the purpose of assisting in the construction of railroads.

---

ited wealth and prosperity to the other, if there is no implied limitation of the uses for which the power may be exercised. To lay with one hand the power of the Government on the property of the citizen, and with the other to bestow it upon favored individuals to aid private enterprises and build up private fortunes, is none the less a robbery because it is done under the forms of law and is called taxation. This is not legislation. It is a decree under legislative forms. . . . We have established, we think beyond cavil, that there can be no lawful tax which is not laid *for a public purpose.*" *Loan Association v. Topeka,* 20 Wall. 655, 664.

Taxes are burdens or charges imposed by the Legislature upon persons or property to raise money for public purposes. Cooley on Constitutional Limitations, 479.

If a private individual should ask the municipality of Washington to levy a tax to enable him to build a road from his house out to the Soldier's Home, in the outskirts of the city, which, when completed, should belong to him, and across which he could put up gates at any time at his own pleasure, everybody would see at once that it was not for public but for private use. There is not a judge in the District of Columbia who would not enjoin the collection of a tax so assessed and levied upon the people.

On the other hand, a tax levied to keep up the streets and roads in the city and county, which everybody travels and uses, is a tax for a public use; and although there has been a great deal of litigation in the courts for the purpose of getting rid of these taxes, and stubborn resistance made to their collection, yet it has been upon the ground of their alleged inequality or improper levy or assessment; not that the Government had not the authority to levy them for such public thoroughfares.

But the main difficulty arises when we come to the case of a corporation, which has built a road by the expenditure of its own funds. That road so built belongs to it, and it has a right to compel everybody who travels over it or uses it to pay for such service or privilege. This fare which it receives is its compensation therefor, and goes into its hands for its own purposes, whether it be large or small in amount. It is true that the property which has thus come into existence belongs to the corporation in one sense,

and yet in another it is one in which the public
have an interest. The people, by whom the
right to construct such a road must first have
been granted, are entitled to its use as a highway under reasonable regulations for the protection of the rights of all persons concerned.
The corporation cannot refuse to carry any person who properly presents himself to be carried.
It must maintain the usual and suitable means
of doing a carrying business. It is generally
authorized to exercise the right of eminent
domain in order to acquire the land on which
its road may be built, and although it must pay
a reasonable compensation therefor, yet it is a
public function which cannot be exercised unless
it be authorized by some constitutional provision
or the act of some legislative body. It is, therefore, said in some senses to be a public body,
and proposals to take stock in it by a State or a
county are one of the great sources from which
controversies arise.

Many such political bodies, in their great
enthusiasm for public improvements, have over-
burdened themselves with obligations for the
purpose of assisting in the construction of railroads, which they afterwards found it almost
impossible to meet when the day of payment
arrived. So they sometimes attempted, more or
less directly, to repudiate these debts, and one
of the ways in which they tried to do this was
by alleging that the assessment of a tax for
their liquidation was void, because it was not
for a public purpose.

They said, in effect, that the corporation received their money, collected its tolls, and appropriated the profits growing out of its business to
its own private uses, such as the payment of
dividends to its stockholders, or the improvement of its plant. On the other hand, the
municipal body alleged that the road could not
have been built without the power of eminent
domain, and even when it was built it was not
permitted to retain absolute control of its management; that it was subjected to certain regulations as to the carriage and accommodation
of passengers, as well as its rates therefor, and
could not reject one man and carry another at
its own pleasure, and that it was also bound to
keep its road in good order; that it was not,
in fact, for all purposes private property, but
possessing a public character was subject to
public supervision.[1]

It is now pretty well settled that building a
railroad with money collected by taxation, by a
State, county, or town, is an appropriation of
such a tax for a public use, and therefore a law
imposing or authorizing it is valid. On the
other hand, a contribution to build a saw mill,
or a steam mill, or anything of that kind, was
not made for a public use, and a tax levied for
such purpose was void.[2] The same question has
also been discussed and decided in several other
similar cases. "It must be for a public object,

---

[1] *Pittsburgh & Connellsville Railroad Co.* v. *Southwestern Pennsylvania Railway Co.*, 77 Penn. St. 173.

[2] *Loan Association* v. *Topeka*, 20 Wall. 655.

clearly superior and paramount, or to which preference is expressly given by law or the Constitution, in order to make the right clear to seize and condemn land." [1]

The United States being a limited form of government, one of the restrictions to which it is subject is in regard to its power to levy taxes. The States may levy them for a great many purposes for which Congress cannot, because to the States belong all of the powers not delegated to Congress.[2] Hence, while the Constitution of the United States has nowhere been amended by any limitation of its taxing power, there has scarcely been a State constitutional convention in half a century that has not imposed some restriction upon the power of the State to levy taxes.

There is, also, another matter concerning this power of taxation that deserves attention. It will be noted that the Constitution of the United States has placed several limitations upon the general power, and that some of them are implied. One of its provisions is that neither the President of the United States (Art. II, sec. 1, par. 6), nor a judge of the Supreme or inferior courts (Art. III, sec. 1), shall have his salary diminished during the period for which he shall have been elected, or during his continuance in office. It is very clear that when Congress, during the late war, levied an income tax, and

---

[1] *United States* v. *Chicago*, 7 How. 185, 195. See also *Pumpelly* v. *Green Bay Co.*, 13 Wall. 166.

[2] Art. X, Amendments to Constitution.

placed it as well upon the salaries of the President and the judges of the courts as those of other people, that it was a diminution of them to just that extent.

The judges were patriotic, however, and did not raise the question, although Chief Justice Taney filed with the Clerk of the Supreme Court an opinion stating that it was unconstitutional and ought not to be paid. Yet everybody did pay their taxes, and possibly they could not have helped themselves if they had tried, because the accounting officers would have deducted the amount of the tax from the salary before paying it. Even after the war this tax of five per cent upon these salaries was deducted and paid. But about that period Mr. Boutwell, who was then Secretary of the Treasury, of his own accord took up the question, investigated it, and came to the conclusion that this tax was void so far as these officers were concerned. He, therefore, returned the money to the President and to each of the judges, which had been paid under that statute, and this they naturally thought was a very fair judicial construction of the constitutional provisions relating to that subject.[1]

---

[1] A tax upon the salary of an officer, to be deducted from what would otherwise be payable as salary, is a diminution of his compensation; and in the cases of the President and judges of the Supreme Court and inferior courts of the United States, such diminution would fall within the prohibition of the Constitution, if the act levying the tax was enacted during the official term of the President or of the judge affected thereby. See Opinion of Attorney General Hoar, October 23, 1869, 13 Opinions Attorneys General, 161.

But it is also well settled that an act reducing the compensation

But the main limitations upon the power of
taxation, found in the Constitution of the United
States, are upon the States. One of these is that
"no State shall, without the consent of Congress,
lay any imposts or duties on imports or exports,
except what may be absolutely necessary for
executing its inspection laws." Art. I, sec. 10,
par. 2.[1]

The several States just after the close of the
Revolutionary War commenced with almost a
fury to tax everything belonging to any other
State that came within their jurisdiction, and
what is known as the commerce clause of the
Constitution, which declares that "Congress shall
have power to regulate commerce with foreign
nations and among the several States, and with
the Indian tribes," was the result of the necessity of preventing each individual State from
embroiling itself in all sorts of quarrels in regard to its commercial relations with its neigh-

---

or salary of a statutory officer is valid in the absence of any constitutional prohibition, although he may have entered upon his term
of service, and that such an act violates no contract rights. That
there is no express or implied contract for the permanence of the
salary, is shown by the constitutional provision making an exception of certain officials, such as the judges. Cases cited in Black
on Constitutional Prohibitions, §§ 96, 97, pp. 116, 117. But after
services have been rendered under a law, resolution or ordinance,
which fixes the rate of compensation, there arises an implied contract to pay for this service at that rate. This contract is a completed contract. Its obligation is perfect and rests on the remedies
which the law itself gives for its enforcement. *Fisk* v. *Jefferson
Police Jury*, 116 U. S. 131.

[1] It is well settled that the States cannot exercise this authority
in respect to any of the instrumentalities which the General Government may create for the performance of its constitutional functions. *Austin* v. *Aldermen*, 7 Wall. 694, 699.

bors, and going on to pass statutes levying taxes of one kind or another upon everything brought within its borders. The result of this course would have been clearly disastrous to the whole people, as well as to the Federal Government that it was proposed to erect, in place of the Confederation under which the Colonies had emerged from the perils of war.[1]

The additional restriction relating to this subject, besides that found in the commerce clause, is that above quoted, prohibiting any State, without the consent of Congress, from laying any imposts or duties on imports or exports. This language implies that they may do it if Congress consents. Such exceptions granted by that body have been of rare occurrence. In the early days there were a few statutes passed, giving the consent of Congress to the imposition of limited duties in order to enable the States to improve their harbors.

The same clause of the Constitution also excepts by its specific terms such as may be absolutely necessary for executing the inspection laws of the particular State, but that has never amounted to much, and the only question of any importance that has ever arisen about the taxa-

---

[1] The author of the Federalist, No. 7, refers to the situation of New York, as compared with that of Connecticut and New Jersey, as affording an example of the opportunities which some States had of rendering others tributary by commercial regulations; and said that New York would neither be willing nor able to forego the advantage of levying duties on importations, a large part of which must necessarily be paid by the individuals of the other two States in the capacity of consumers.

tion of imports or exports has been whether the
words applied to articles carried between the
States.

It has been held[1] that the word "imports,"
as used in this clause, did not apply to articles
imported or transported from one State into
another, and that they were not imports or exports within the meaning of the Constitution;
that it only referred to articles imported from
foreign countries into the United States. The
latter was a case in which Alabama had passed
a statute taxing all the whiskey imported into
the State. It was insisted that it was an import, and consequently its tax in that way was
forbidden by the clause now under discussion.
The court, however, held that it was not an
import, and the tax was not void for that reason.
A similar tax for the same rate or amount had
been levied upon all whiskey produced in Alabama, and the statute was, therefore, not void
because there was no discrimination against the
commerce of any other State.

An important question was also raised in the
Supreme Court of the United States in regard
to the cotton tax. During the war a tax was
imposed upon that staple, and about twenty millions of dollars were raised by its means. Its
collection was resisted on the ground that it was
a tax upon exports, and the argument was that,
as four-fifths of all the cotton raised in the country was in fact exported, therefore a tax on

---

[1] *Woodruff* v. *Parham*, 8 Wall. 123; *Hinson* v. *Lott*, 8 Wall. 148.

LECTURE V.
The cotton tax.

cotton was necessarily a tax on exports. The argument on the other side was that when the cotton was actually exported, then any amount levied upon it would be a tax upon exports, but that it could not be assumed that all the cotton raised in this country was to be exported.

Tax on interstate commerce.

The Supreme Court was divided upon that question, and it stood in that way until the October Term, 1885,[1] when the subject was again discussed, and the following language used : —

"Goods, the product of a State, intended for exportation to another State, are liable to taxation as part of the general mass of property of the State of their origin, until actually started in course of transportation to the State of their destination, or delivered to a common carrier for that purpose; the carrying of them to, and depositing them at, a depot for the purpose of transportation is no part of that transportation.

"When goods, the product of a State, have begun to be transported from that State to another State, and not till then, they have become the subjects of interstate commerce, and, as such, are subject to national regulation, and cease to be taxable by the State of their origin."

This principle was afterwards reasserted and affirmed.[2]

There is another restriction of the same class that may be noted in this connection, and which has been the subject of a great deal of comment in the Supreme Court of the United States. It

---

[1] *Coe* v. *Errol*, 116 U. S. 517.

[2] *Turpin* v. *Burgess*, 117 U. S. 504.

is to be found in the following language : " No Lecture v.
State shall, without the consent of Congress, lay Tax on interstate
commerce.
any duty of tonnage." Art. I, sec. 10, par. 3.

· The meaning of this expression, as may be Tonnage tax.
gathered from the numerous decisions in that
court, undoubtedly is, that vessels coming from
abroad, or engaged in navigation among the
States, or even if plying entirely within the
boundaries of and owned by citizens of a single
State, shall not be taxed, as vessels, for the
privilege of navigating the inland waters of
the country, or coming into any of its ports.
In *State Tonnage Tax Cases*,[1] the court held
that "although taxes levied, as on property, by
a State, upon vessels owned by its citizens, and
based on a valuation of the same, are not prohibited by the Federal Constitution, yet taxes
cannot be imposed on them by the State at so
much per ton of registered tonnage." Such
taxes are within the prohibition of the clause
under consideration.

The word " tonnage " was used by the framers
of the Constitution, because at that day and time
it was the customary mode of measuring the
value of a ship. A vessel was said to be of so
many tons burden, which meant that it was
worth so much money, carried so much freight,
and, therefore, the method generally adopted of
imposing a tax upon its tonnage was the readiest
way to fix the amount which that species of
property should pay. But the Constitution forbids any tonnage tax, and so the Supreme Court

---

[1] 12 Wall. 204.

has been called upon over and over again to decide what that means.

After much discussion it has about settled down to mean this: that if a man living in Louisiana owns a steamboat, it is liable to be taxed like any other property that he may possess there, and if a tax is levied upon it, measured by its capacity, which is called tonnage, that is not a tonnage tax. But when a vessel enters the port of New Orleans from abroad, or from some point up the river, and lands at a wharf, or moors out in the middle of the stream, and the city or State demands that it shall pay a tax for every time that is done, it is in fact a tonnage tax within the meaning of the constitutional provision, because it is a tax on the privilege of navigating the river and entering the harbor. It cannot be evaded by not measuring it by the ton, or by calling it by some other name. A reasonable charge may be made for services actually rendered,[1] but this great privilege of the

---

[1] "A charge for services rendered, or for conveniences provided, is in no sense a tax or a duty. It is not a hindrance or impediment to free navigation. The prohibition to the State against the imposition of a duty of tonnage was designed to guard against local hindrances to trade and carriage by vessels, not to relieve them from liability to claims for assistance rendered and facilities furnished for trade and commerce. It is a tax or a duty that is prohibited: something imposed by virtue of sovereignty, not claimed in right of proprietorship. Wharfage is of the latter character. Providing a wharf to which vessels may make fast, or at which they may conveniently load or unload, is rendering them a service. . . . What was intended by the second clause of the tenth section of the first article was to protect the freedom of commerce and nothing more, . . . and therefore the prohibition should be so construed as to carry out that intent." *Packet Co.* v. *Keokuk*, 95 U. S. 80, 84, 87.

In a later case the Supreme Court said that a duty of tonnage is

free navigation by all persons of the waters of LECTURE V.
this country is thus secured against interference Tonnage tax.
on the part of the individual States of the Union.[1]
In a recent case decided in 1886,[2] may be
found a full review of all the principal cases
upon this subject, together with a full exposition of the doctrines upon which this clause of
the Constitution rests. The State of Louisiana
had required by a statute that each vessel passing a quarantine station should pay a certain
fee for examination as to her sanitary condition.
This was held to be a part of the quarantine
system, and a compensation for services rendered
to the vessel, and not a tax within the meaning

---

a charge for the privilege of entering or trading or lying in a port
or harbor, while wharfage is a charge for the use of a wharf. They
are not the same thing. *Transportation Co.* v. *Parkersburg*, 107
U. S. 691.

The fact that the rates of wharfage charged are graduated by the
size or tonnage of the vessel is of no consequence, and does not
make it a duty of tonnage in the sense of the Constitution and the
acts of Congress. *Cannon* v. *New Orleans*, 20 Wall. 577 ; *Packet
Co.* v. *Catlettsburg*, 105 U. S. 559.

[1] The State of Illinois legislated for the construction of locks
on the Illinois River, and created a Board of Commissioners who
prescribed certain tolls for the passage of vessels, which were fixed
at so much per ton according to the tonnage measurement of the
vessels and the freight carried. The court held that this was
simply a mode of fixing the rate according to the size of the vessel
and the amount of property carried, and was in no sense a duty of
tonnage within the prohibition of the Constitution. It said : "A
duty of tonnage within the meaning of the Constitution is a charge
upon a vessel, according to its tonnage, as an instrument of commerce, for entering or leaving a port, or navigating the public
waters of the country ; and the prohibition was designed to prevent
the States from imposing hindrances of this kind to commerce
carried on by vessels." *Huse* v. *Glover*, 119 U. S. 543, 549.

[2] *Morgan's Steamship Co.* v. *Louisiana Board of Health*, 118
U. S. 455.

of the Constitution concerning tonnage taxes imposed by the States.

In addition to the specific restrictions which are fixed by constitutional or statutory authority, there are implied limitations upon the power of taxation which grow out of the nature of things. It was a terse statement of a great truth which was made by Chief Justice Marshall in the great case, in regard to the United States Bank,[1] that the power to tax, where unlimited, involves the power to destroy. This may at first appear to have been a rather strong statement, but it was not. Any government or municipality possessing unlimited power to tax any property, any business, or any man, can drive that property, that business, or man out of the community. This is true, because it can make the tax equal to all that he earns, or all that he is capable of earning, or equal to all the property that he has. So that the Chief Justice was not stating it too strongly when he said that the unlimited power of taxation was the power to destroy.[2]

This expression was used in reference to the United States Bank, when the State of Maryland undertook to tax its circulation; for if the State could tax that part of its business at all, it could drive the bank out of the State, at least so far as circulation was concerned. Then if the State taxed the circulation, it could tax the deposits

---

[1] *McCulloch* v. *Maryland,* 4 Wheat. 316.

[2] The right of taxation, where it exists, is necessarily unlimited in its nature. It carries with it inherently the power to embarrass and destroy.'' *Austin* v. *Aldermen,* 7 Wall. 694, 699.

of the bank, and could thus force it to withdraw
entirely from its jurisdiction.   That was one of
the great cases arising early in the history of
the establishment of our institutions, in which
very important constitutional questions came up
for consideration, which it was essential to the
future peace and prosperity of the country, as
well as to insure the perpetuity of the new Government, then only in its experimental stage,
should be wisely and permanently settled.   It
was decided in that case, that the State had no
power to tax the bank, because it was the instrument of the United States, and a State could not
tax anything which the United States required
for its use in the administration of the Government, or "any of the constitutional means
employed by the Government of the Union to
execute its constitutional powers." [1]

It was also held that the bonds of the United Income from
bonds of the
United States not
taxable by States.
States could not be taxed, such a power being
inconsistent with the constitutional power of the
Government to borrow money, as enabling the
State to exclude such securities from its mar-
kets.[2] So they are not taxed to-day, and cannot
be taxed by a State, even indirectly by a tax
on valuation.[3] So also of United States notes,

---

[1] See *McCulloch* v. *Maryland*, 4 Wheat. 316.   The principle of
exemption is, that the State cannot control the National Government within the sphere of its constitutional powers, for there it
is supreme, and cannot tax its obligations for payment of money
issued for purposes within that range of powers, because such taxation necessarily implies the assertion of the right to exercise such
control.

[2] *Bank of Commerce* v. *New York*, 2 Black, 620.

[3] *Bank Tax Case*, 2 Wall. 200.

LECTURE V.
Income from
bonds of the
United States not
taxable by States.
Salaries of United
States officers not
taxable by States.
although issued as currency, they are yet national obligations and exempt from State taxation.[1]

Neither can any State authority tax the salaries or emoluments of officers of the United States,[2] or of any of the institutions now called national banks; but Congress put into their charters, originally, a provision permitting the shares to be taxed, at the home of the person who owned them, by including them in the valuation of the personal property of the person or corporation to whom they belonged, at the place where the bank was located. (An act to provide a national currency, secured by a pledge of the United States bonds, and to provide for the circulation and redemption thereof. Approved June 3, 1864.[3]) To guard against the destruction of the banks, however, by the States, or unjust discrimination even in the exercise of that privilege, it was declared by that statute that such taxes shall not exceed the rates imposed upon the shares in any of the banks organized under the authority of the State

---

[1] *Bank of New York* v. *Supervisors*, 7 Wall. 26.

Chief Justice Marshall said: "The tax on Government stock is thought, by this court, to be a tax on the contract, a tax on the power to borrow money on the credit of the United States, and consequently repugnant to the Constitution." *Weston* v. *City of Charleston*, 2 Pet. 449, 469.

[2] The compensation of an officer of the United States is fixed by a law made by Congress. It is in its exclusive discretion to declare what shall be given, and any law of a State imposing a tax upon the office, diminishing the recompense, is in conflict with the law of the United States which secures the allowance to the officer. *Dobbins* v. *Erie County Commissioners*, 16 Pet. 435.

[3] 13 Stat. c. 105, § 41, pp. 99, 112.

where such association was located, or upon
other moneyed capital in the hands of individuals.

The shareholder is thus protected from undue impositions by providing that everybody else, under like circumstances, must be taxed as much as he is, or in the same proportion. This is fully considered in *McCulloch* v. *Maryland*, *supra*.[1] See also *Osborn* v. *United States Bank*,[2] and the case of *Weston* v. *Charleston*, *supra*,[3] in which the city council of Charleston undertook to tax Government bonds in the hands of some of its citizens. It was there held that this could not be done, because "the American people have conferred the power of borrowing money on the Government, and by making that Government supreme, have shielded its action in the exercise of that power, from the action of the local governments. The grant of the power, and the declaration of supremacy, is a declaration that no such distraining or controlling power shall be exercised."

A great many decisions have been made to settle this doctrine. The States have been fertile in constantly devising many means to tax banks, if possible, and the recent volumes of reports of the Supreme Court are full of cases having relation to such attempts, and the discussions which they have elicited. One case which may be referred to in this connection is that of the *People* v. *Weaver*.[4] The State of New York passed a

---

[1] 4 Wheat. 316.　　　　[3] 2 Pet. 449.
[2] 9 Wheat. 738.　　　　[4] 100 U. S. 539.

law declaring that whenever a man listed his personal property for taxation, he might except out of it an amount equal to all the debts he owed, which should not be taxed. The Legislature then passed another law stating that the first should not apply to shares of national banks. This the courts held to be unconstitutional. If the owner of one or more shares in a national bank was not to be allowed to deduct what he owed from the amount of his taxable property, in which those shares were included, then other persons could not be allowed to take out what they owed in the taxation of their personal property.

Indiana unsuccessfully tried the same thing,[1] and there have been many attempts by different States to tax banks in violation of this clause of the Constitution, and of the statutes of the United States. See also *Cummings* v. *The Merchants' National Bank.*[2]

There is another rather curious instance where the States have been forbidden, by the decisions of the courts, to use the power of taxation. It was first discussed in the case of *Crandall* v. *Nevada*,[3] where the principle was declared that every man in this broad country had a right to travel all over it, for purposes of business or pleasure, regardless of State lines, and that no state could levy a tax upon him for that privilege. The State of Nevada attempted to compel certain transportation companies within its

---

[1] *Evansville Bank* v. *Britton*, 105 U. S. 322.   [2] 101 U. S. 153.
[3] 6 Wall. 35.

boundaries to make a report of every passenger
that they carried through the State, for each of
which they were required to pay one dollar. Of
course this was practically a tax upon the passenger, because it was simply added to his fare
by the companies. In one instance the payment
was resisted, and the matter came up in the
usual way to the Supreme Court of the United
States, where the statute was declared to be
unconstitutional and void. If this had been the
extent of the effect of the declaration of this
principle, it would have been comparatively
unimportant, for the total amount collected by
the State of Nevada was not very large; but it
so transpired that the State of New Jersey had
been for many years collecting a similar tax
upon every passenger who passed through that
State on a railroad, and as the traffic was very
heavy the amount was correspondingly important, almost enough in fact to pay the expenses
of the State government. But that tax col-
lapsed with the anouncement of that decision,
and no attempt has been made to collect it
since.[1]

---

[1] Another question which has been the subject of contention was
whether the legislature of a State could so relinquish the right to
impose taxes on property within its jurisdiction that it could not
be revoked by a future one. One of the first cases in which this
was considered was *State of New Jersey* v. *Wilson*, 7 Cranch, 164,
holding that a legislative act declaring certain lands which should
be purchased for the Indians should not, thereafter, be subject to
any tax, constituted a contract which could not be rescinded by a
subsequent legislative act. Bradley, J., in *Given* v. *Wright*, 117
U. S. 648, 655, says that the Supreme Court does not feel disposed
to question that decision, although it was held that by acquiescence

for a long period the right to the privilege might be lost. But this
construction will be taken strictly against the grantee.

The power of taxation is an attribute of sovereignty and is essential to every independent government. The whole community is
interested in retaining it undiminished, and has a right to insist
that its abandonment ought not to be presumed in a case in which
the deliberate purpose of the State to abandon it does not appear.
Delaware Railroad Tax, 18 Wall. 206.   An illustration of this rule
is found in *Vicksburg &c. Railroad Co.* v. *Dennis*, 116 U. S. 665,
where the road and fixtures of the company, by its charter, were
exempt from taxation for ten years after its completion, but this
was held not to exempt the road and fixtures from taxation *before*
its completion.

To support the exemption, there must be an adequate consideration, otherwise it is a mere spontaneous concession on the part of
the legislature, not constituting a contract, and may be revoked
at will. *Rector of Christ's Church* v. *County of Philadelphia*, 24
How. 300.

NOTES UPON LECTURE V.

U_{NDE}R the head of the power of taxation Mr.
Justice Miller groups two distinct subjects in
this lecture : (I) The powers confided by the
Constitution to the United States ; and (2) the
powers which that instrument withholds from
the States. He has also alluded to (3) cases in
which the courts of the United States interfere
to compel the imposition of local taxes in the
States.

The cases under each of these heads are numerous. For many years scarcely a volume of
the reports has been issued which has not contained one or more of them. Little or no good
could come from an extended examination of
them ; indeed such an examination would be
impracticable within the limits to which this
note is necessarily confined. It will be sufficient
to briefly refer to a few of the leading cases,
some of which Mr. Justice Miller has not noticed.

1. *The Federal Power of Taxation.*

In an early case the question was raised Federal power of
whether Congress had the power to tax the Dis- taxation.
trict of Columbia ; and it was held that the
power to levy and collect taxes, duties, imposts,
and excises was coextensive with the territory

263

of the United States.[1] But, if a public enemy
conquers and occupies a portion of the United
States, the portion so occupied becomes foreign
territory, so far as revenue laws are concerned;
and the subsequent restoration of the authority
of the United States over it does not change
the character of past transactions.[2] On the other
hand, the conquest and military occupation of
foreign territory by the United States leaves it
foreign country for revenue purposes.[3]

The exercise by Congress during the civil
war of its power to impose direct taxes upon
real estate within the States did not create a liability, upon the part of the States in which the
land was situated, to pay the tax.[4] The power
to tax was exercised upon the property of private individuals within the State. In the great
taxation during and immediately after the civil
war, questions were sometimes raised whether a
particular tax was a direct tax or an impost or
excise. A succession tax was held to be the latter.[5]

The provision that duties, imposts, and excises shall be uniform throughout the United
States is complied with if the tax operates with
the same effect in all places where the subject
of it is found. There is no want of uniformity
simply because the thing taxed is not equally
distributed in all parts of the United States.[6]

---

[1] *Loughborough* v. *Blake*, 5 Wheat. 317.
[2] *United States* v. *Rice*, 4 Wheat. 246.
[3] *Fleming* v. *Page*, 9 How. 603.
[4] *United States* v. *Louisiana*, 123 U. S. 32.
[5] *Scholey* v. *Rew*, 23 Wall. 331.
[6] *Head Money Cases*, 112 U. S. 580.

There are some things which are not proper LECTURE V. subjects of Federal taxation, as, for instance, Federal power of taxation. the revenues of a municipal corporation.[1]

2. *Restraints upon State Taxation.*

The State can authorize the taking of indi- Restraints upon vidual property by taxation only for public uses State power of taxation. and purposes. Hence it cannot confer upon its municipal corporations power to create debts to be paid by taxation, when the money is to be used for private objects.[2]

It cannot part with its general power to tax, because that power is essential to the exercise of its sovereignty and the performance of its duties. But it can by contract part with a portion of this sovereign power for a consideration which it accepts as sufficient. When, in incorporating a private corporation, the State exempts the property of the corporation from taxation, or limits the amount of taxation to be imposed upon it, subsequent legislation, imposing a higher rate of taxation than the charter permits, is invalid.[3] But such legislation is looked upon with jealousy, and construed strictly by the courts. The immunity will not be recognized, unless granted in terms too plain to be mistaken.[4] It is a privilege belonging only to the corporation named, and will not pass to its successor, unless

---

[1] *United States* v. *Railroad Company*, 17 Wall. 322.

[2] *Cole* v. *La Grange*, 113 U. S. 1, and cases cited in the opinion.

[3] *New Orleans* v. *Houston*, 119 U. S. 265.

[4] *Chicago & Burlington Railroad* v. *Guffey*, 120 U. S. 569; *S. C.* 122 U. S. 561.

the intent of the statute thereto is clear and express.[1]

The power of making such a contract is confined to private corporations. The power of taxation on the part of a municipal corporation is not private property, or a vested right of property in its hands. The conferring of such power is an exercise by the Legislature of a public and governmental power, which cannot be imparted in perpetuity, and is always subject to revocation, modification, and control, and is not the subject of contract.[2]

Real estate and personal property of the United States situated within the limits of a State;[3] evidences of debt issued by the United States held by a citizen of a State;[4] franchises conferred by Congress upon a corporation created by it, to be exercised within a State;[5] and agencies employed by the United States in carrying into effect the powers vested in it by the Constitution,[6] cannot be subjected to taxation by the States, without the consent of Congress. The State taxation of national banks, too, is con-

---

[1] *Morgan* v. *Louisiana*, 93 U. S. 217; *Wilson* v. *Gaines*, 103 U. S. 417; *Louisville & Nashville Railroad* v. *Palmes*, 109 U. S. 244; *Memphis & Little Rock Railroad* v. *Railroad Commissioners*, 112 U. S. 609; *Pickard* v. *East Tennessee, Virginia & Georgia Railroad*, 130 U. S. 637; *Yazoo & Miss. Valley Railroad* v. *Thomas*, 132 U. S. 174.

[2] *Williamson* v. *New Jersey*, 130 U. S. 189.

[3] *Van Brocklin* v. *Tennessee*, 117 U. S. 151; *Wisconsin Central Railroad* v. *Price*, 133 U. S. 496.

[4] *Weston* v. *Charleston*, 2 Pet. 449; *Bank* v. *Supervisors*, 7 Wall. 26.

[5] *California* v. *Central Pacific Railroad Co.*, 127 U. S. 1.

[6] *Osborn* v. *Bank of the United States*, 9 Wheat. 738.

trolled and regulated by Congress.[1] So, too, a LECTURE V.
State income tax cannot be imposed upon the Restraints upon State power of
salary of an officer of the United States.[2] taxation.

The legislation of the State of Virginia, first
making its consolidated bonds receivable in payment of taxes, and then repudiating that contract, has been the subject of much litigation.
The cases were reviewed at length at October
Term, 1889, and it was held that the statute
constituted a contract between the State and the
holders of bonds and coupons issued under it,
which was materially impaired by the subsequent legislation; and that although no proceedings could be instituted by holders against
the Commonwealth or its executive officers to
control them in the exercise of their official
functions, yet that, on the other hand, proceedings could not be taken on behalf of the State
to molest holders on account of such taxes when
payment of them had been tendered in such
coupons, and the taxpayer held himself continu-
ally ready to pay them in such coupons.[3]

---

[1] There are many cases on this point. It is sufficient to refer
to *Mercantile Bank* v. *New York*, 121 U. S. 138, where the subject
is discussed.

[2] *Dobbins* v. *Erie County*, 16 Pet. 435.

[3] *McGahey* v. *Virginia*, 135 U. S. 662. "This case, with seven
others, reported under this title, grew out of the legislation of the
State regarding coupons of the same character as those involved in
the Virginia coupon cases. Mr. Justice Bradley, delivering the
unanimous opinion of the court, after a full and exhaustive review
and analysis of the decisions in those cases and others like them,
presented a summary of the propositions established by those
decisions, which cannot be well abridged, as follows:

"'First, That the provisions of the act of 1871 constitute a
contract between the State of Virginia and the lawful holders of

By far the larger class of cases touching the constitutional restriction of the power of taxation in the States relates to its interference with the powers in respect of commerce which the Constitution has reposed in the Federal Government. This subject, which we shall find considered more at length when we reach the Lecture upon the Regulation of Commerce, has been also touched upon by Judge Miller in this lecture. It is necessary to add to what he has said only a reference to a few of the later cases.

The doctrine of *Brown* v. *Maryland*,[1] that a

---

the bonds and coupons issued under and in pursuance of said statute;

" ' Second, That the various acts of the General Assembly of Virginia passed for the purpose of restraining the use of said coupons for the payment of taxes and other dues to the State, and imposing impediments and instructions to that use, and to the proceedings instituted for establishing their genuineness, do in many respects impair the obligation of that contract, and cannot be held to be valid or binding in so far as they have that effect;

" ' Third, That no proceedings can be instituted by any holder of said bonds or coupons against the Commonwealth of Virginia, either directly by suit against the Commonwealth by name, or indirectly against her executive officers to control them in the exercise of their official functions as agents of the State;

" ' Fourth, That any lawful holder of the tax-receivable coupons of the State, issued under the act of 1871 or the subsequent act of 1879, who tenders such coupons in payment of taxes, debts, dues and demands due from him to the State, and continues to hold himself ready to tender the same in payment thereof, is entitled to be free from molestation in person or goods on account of such taxes, debts, dues or demands, and may vindicate such right in all lawful modes of redress, — by suit to recover his property, by suit against the officer to recover damages for taking it, by injunction to prevent such taking where it would be attended with irremediable injury, or by a defence to a suit brought against him for his taxes or the other claims standing against him.' " Mr. Justice Lamar, in *Pennoyer* v. *McConnaughby*, 140 U. S. 1.

[1] 12 Wheat. 419.

State statute, requiring all importers and dealers in imported goods to take out a license and pay a license fee therefor, is repugnant to the Constitution, and for that reason void, has been steadily followed since, and has been applied to commerce "among the several States," commonly known as interstate commerce. Below will be found references to a few of the many cases.[1]

In *Philadelphia & Southern Steamship Co.* v. *Pennsylvania,* 122 U. S. 326, it was held that a State tax could not be constitutionally imposed upon the gross receipts of a steamship company, incorporated under its laws, which were derived from the transportation of persons and property by sea, between different States, and to and from foreign countries. In *State Freight Tax Case,* 15 Wall. 232, it was held that interstate commerce cannot be taxed at all, even though the same amount of tax should be laid on domestic commerce, or that which is carried on solely within the State. In *Welton* v. *Missouri,* 91 U. S. 275, it was held that a statute of Missouri which required the payment of a license tax by peddlers,

Restraints upon State power of taxation.

---

[1] *Henderson* v. *New York,* 92 U. S. 259 ; *People* v. *Compagnie Générale Transatlantique,* 107 U. S. 59 ; *Welton* v. *Missouri,* 91 U. S. 275 ; *The Passenger Cases,* 7 How. 283 ; *State Freight Tax,* 15 Wall. 232 ; *Walling* v. *Michigan,* 116 U. S. 446 ; *Philadelphia & Southern Steamship Co.* v. *Pennsylvania,* 122 U. S. 326 ; *Pensacola Telegraph Co.* v. *Western Union Telegraph Co.,* 96 U. S. 1 ; *Ratterman* v. *Western Union Telegraph Co.,* 127 U. S. 411 ; *Western Union Telegraph Co.* v. *Alabama,* 132 U. S. 472 ; *Asher* v. *Texas,* 128 U. S. 129 ; *Robbins* v. *Shelby County Taxing District,* 120 U. S. 489 ; *Leloup* v. *Port of Mobile,* 127 U. S. 640 ; *Corson* v. *Maryland,* 120 U. S. 502.

peddling goods within the State, which were not
its growth, produce, or manufacture, and which
required no such payment and license from a
person peddling within the State similar goods,
the growth, produce, or manufacture of Missouri,
was repugnant to the Constitution; and also
that the non-exercise by Congress of its power
to regulate commerce among the States was
equivalent to a declaration that it should be
free from restrictions. In *Asher* v. *Texas*, 128
U. S. 129, it was held that a State law exacting a license tax to enable a person within the
State to solicit orders and make sales there for
a person residing within another State was void;
affirming *Robbins* v. *Shelby County Taxing District*, 120 U. S. 489. And in *Pensacola Telegraph Co.* v. *Western Union Telegraph Co.*, 96
U. S. 1, affirmed and followed in several subsequent cases, it was held that a tax cannot be
imposed by a State upon a telegraph company
which has accepted the provisions prescribed by
Congress (Rev. Stat. tit. LXV), based upon receipts derived from messages received or sent
without the State.

In a recent case a New York statute essentially modifying, in the taxpayer's favor, previous
laws of limitation concerning lands sold for non-
payment of taxes, was attacked as unconstitutional. The new statute enacted that no action
should thereafter be maintained to compel the
execution or delivery of a lease upon a sale for
taxes, etc., made more than eight years prior to
its date, unless commenced within six months

after that date, and that, on the expiration of
that six months, the lien of certificates of purchase on which no lease had been taken or no
action commenced should cease and determine.
It was held by the Supreme Court that there
was nothing in the Constitution of the United
States which prevented the Legislature of New
York from prescribing a limitation for the bringing of suits where none had previously existed,
or from shortening the time within which suits
should be commenced to enforce existing rights
under the tax sales, provided the time prescribed
by the new law was a reasonable one.[1]

3. *Power in Federal Courts to compel Municipal Taxation in a State.*

On pages 243–246, *ante*, Mr. Justice Miller
has referred to the many issues of the bonds of
municipal corporations in aid of the construction of railroads and other private enterprises,
which have been a fertile source of litigation
during the past twenty years.

Although this class of cases, as a whole, in
one aspect belongs to the subject treated of in
Lecture XI, on the impairment of the obligation of contracts, in another and narrower relation they should be classified here.

It is now well settled that the implied power
of a municipal corporation to borrow money to
enable it to execute the powers expressly conferred upon it by law, if it exist at all, does

---

[1] *Wheeler v. Jackson,* 137 U. S. 245.

not authorize it to create and issue negotiable securities, to be sold in the market, and to be taken by the purchaser freed from equities which might be set up by the maker.[1] Also that a grant to a municipal corporation of power to appropriate money in aid of the construction of a railroad, accompanied by a provision directing the levy and collection of taxes to meet such appropriation, and prescribing no other mode of payment, does not authorize the issuing of negotiable bonds in payment of such appropriation.[2]

With this class of cases, many in number, confining the power of municipal corporations in respect to the issue of negotiable securities to the powers expressly conferred upon it by statute, we have nothing to do in this connection.

There are, however, a class of cases, in which such a power was exercised by the municipality in payment of subscriptions to aid in the construction of railroads, either under an unequivocal grant from the State legislature, or under a statute of the State which, as interpreted by its highest court, contained such a grant. Bonds issued under such circumstances were widely scattered; and when default was made in their payment, suits were commenced which finally found their way to the Supreme Court. When they reached that stage, it had been developed in some of them that the highest court of the State had reversed its ruling in regard to the power of the municipality to issue such bonds, and that bonds, valid under

---

[1] *Merrill* v. *Monticello*, 138 U. S. 673, and cases there cited.
[2] *Concord* v. *Robinson*, 121 U. S. 671.

its rulings when issued, would be held invalid, if the new ruling of the same court should be followed. It also appeared that powers of municipal taxation which existed at the time of the original issue of such bonds, had been modified or changed by State legislation to the injury of the holders of such bonds.

With regard to the change of ruling in the State court, the Supreme Court, by Chief Justice Waite, said : —

"Until long after the issue of the bonds now in question, the law was treated by the courts and the people as valid and constitutional. No lawyer, asked for a professional opinion on that subject, could have hesitated to say that it had been settled. It would seem as though every question, which could be raised, had in some form, directly or indirectly, been presented and decided. . . . We are, then, to consider whether, under these circumstances, we must follow the later decisions to the extent of destroying rights which have become vested under those given before. As a rule, we treat the construction which the highest court of a State has given to a statute of the State, as part of the statute, and govern ourselves accordingly; but where different constructions have been given to the same statute at different times, we have never felt ourselves bound to follow the later decisions, if thereby, contract rights, which have accrued under earlier rulings, will be injuriously affected. . . So far as this case is concerned, we have no hesitation in saying that the rights of the parties are to be determined according to the law, as it was judicially construed to be when the bonds in question were put on the market as commercial paper."[1]

In regard to the legislation modifying the taxing power, it is held that, "when a contract is made with a municipal corporation, upon the faith that taxes will be levied, legislation repealing or modifying the taxing power of the corporation, so as to deprive the holder of the contract of all adequate and efficacious remedy, is within the inhibition of the Constitution:" and that "a judgment creditor of a municipal corporation, entitled by his original contract to be paid out of specific tax levies, which agreement the corporation fails to comply with, is entitled, in mandamus proceeding, to a writ ordering the levy and collection of a sufficient tax to pay his judgment according to the assessment roll of the year in which the levy was made."[2]

---

[1] *Douglass v. County of Pike*, 101 U. S. 677, 685, 686, 687; *Scotland County v. Hill*, 132 U. S. 107, 112. See also *Burgess v. Seligman*, 107 U. S. 20, 33, 34, where the subject is fully considered.

[2] *Nelson v. St. Martin's Parish*, 111 U. S. 717. See also *United States v. Clark County*, 96 U. S. 211; *Knox County Court v. United States*, 109 U. S. 229; *Macon County v. Huidekoper*, 134 U. S. 332. In all these cases a writ of mandamus was granted. See also *United States v. Macon*, 99 U. S. 582, where one was refused.

VI.

NATURALIZATION AND CITIZENSHIP.[1]

ARTICLE I, SECTION 8, PARAGRAPH 4. The Con- LECTURE VI. gress shall have Power . . . to establish an uniform Naturalization rule of Naturalization . . . throughout the United and citizenship. States.

ARTICLE IV, SECTION 2. The Citizens of each State shall be entitled to all Privileges and Immunities of Citizens in the several States.

ARTICLE XIV OF THE AMENDMENTS, SECTION I. All persons born or naturalized in the United States, and subject to the jurisdiction thereof, are citizens of the United States and of the State wherein they reside. No State shall make or enforce any law which shall abridge the privileges or immunities of citizens of the United States. . . .

LAST evening we took up the first clause of section 8 of Article I of the Constitution of the United States, which has reference to taxation. This evening I will call your attention to the fourth clause, which is as follows: "To establish a uniform rule of naturalization, and uniform laws on the subject of bankruptcies, throughout the United States."

Naturalization is the process by which a citizen, or subject of a foreign nation or kingdom, is made a citizen of the United States.

Definition of naturalization.

---

[1] This is Lecture V of the Lectures delivered before the classes of the University Law School.

LECTURE VI.
Definition of
naturalization.

It is evident that the Constitutional Convention thought that it was important that this process should be placed under the exclusive control of the Federal Government and not of the States. There are certain rights, privileges, and duties belonging to a citizen of a State, which do not belong to a foreigner resident within the State. Among these it is said that allegiance and protection are correlative obligations. If you are a citizen or subject of a country (and I employ the words " citizen " and " subject" as they are distinctively used in monarchical countries, the former being more commonly used to designate the relation where free or republican institutions exist, and the latter where a monarchy is established), then, in either instance, there are the correlative obligations between yourself on the one side, and the government or the monarch on the other. The citizen or subject owes allegiance, which signifies the loyal devotion and support due from him to the government under which he lives; and, in return, that government owes him protection in a great many ways, too numerous for me to undertake to detail at this time. Naturalization, then, is the process of conferring on, or imparting to, a foreigner, who does not yet owe that allegiance, and who has no right to that protection, the right to protection, and the obligations of allegiance.

Citizenship of the
United States.

Before you can understand what a man gets by being naturalized in this country, you must have an idea of what it is to be a citizen. Citizenship in the United States was for many years

a thing of very imperfect definition. The term occurs several times in the Constitution, in which citizens of the different States, as well as of the United States, are spoken of. It long remained a matter of considerable doubt what constituted citizenship of the United States. It was maintained by many statesmen, up to the time of the adoption of the Fourteenth Amendment, that there was no such distinctive character as " a citizen of the United States ; " that, on the contrary, the designation of " a citizen of a State " had been long known and understood, and as such, and by virtue of that fact, the person was a citizen of the United States. But that, you will at once see, left out all the good people who lived in the District of Columbia, for they were not citizens of any State ; and it also left out all the residents of the Territories, for they were citizens of no State. It was also asserted that it left out, and probably it did, all the Indians in this country, whether connected with some tribe or not ; and the statesmen who lived in the slave-holding States vehemently maintained that it left out as well all the slaves. Possibly it was true ; I am not prepared to say ; but they also insisted that it left out all the free colored population.

. In various ways it became a matter of considerable consequence whether that view was to be generally accepted. For instance, if a citizen of the District of Columbia, or a negro, while travelling abroad, was arrested by a foreign government, and appealed to this Government for protection as a citizen of the United States, the foreign power could reply that he was not such a citizen, and could not assert the same rights as if he were a white man, a citizen of a State, and therefore a citizen of the United States. Among the good as well as evil things that the late rebellion has brought about, is a constitutional definition of this word "citizen." It is impossible to get a clear idea of what naturalization means without knowing what citizenship is; and I will therefore turn your attention to the Fourteenth Amendment to the Constitution of the United States, where that term is now clearly defined, and its meaning placed beyond all question. This it was intended to do, as well as to put at rest the question of the civil status of the negro.

This amendment is divided into several sections, the first of which relates to this subject.

"Sec. 1. All persons born or naturalized in the United States, and subject to the jurisdiction thereof, are citizens of the United States and of the State wherein they reside. No State shall make or enforce any law which shall abridge the privileges or immunities of citizens of the United States; nor shall any State deprive any person of life, liberty, or property, without due process of law; nor deny to any person within its jurisdiction the equal protection of the laws."

Looking at that section critically, you will see that citizenship of the United States and citizenship of a State are distinctly spoken of as sepa-

rate things, although the mode of ascertaining
who is a citizen of the United States is to some extent through citizenship of a State. It is not necessary, however, that a man should be a citizen of a State in order to be a citizen of the United States. If he is born or naturalized in the United States, and subject to its jurisdiction, he is a citizen of the United States, and being such a citizen he is, by virtue of the clause above quoted, necessarily a citizen of the State in which he resides. There is, therefore, no difficulty now in determining what is citizenship of the United States.

In regard to the use of the word " jurisdiction " in the phrase, " All persons born or naturalized in the United States, and subject to the jurisdiction thereof," it may be remarked, that a child of a foreign ambassador, born within the limits of the United States, is not subject to its jurisdiction within the meaning of the language just quoted. He remains a foreigner and a subject of the kingdom or country which is represented by his father, and the same is true of all other diplomatic representatives. If a stranger or traveller passing through, or temporarily residing in this country, who has not himself been naturalized, and who claims to owe no allegiance to our Government, has a child born here which goes out of the country with its father, such child is not a citizen of the United States, because it was not subject to its jurisdiction.

This Amendment, of course, includes all the black people. They are born in the United

LECTURE VI.
The Fourteenth
Amendment.
States and subject to its jurisdiction ; they are, therefore, all citizens. Indeed, the main purpose of this Amendment to the Constitution was to make the fact plain that the black population within our borders were citizens of this country. The Indian tribes were not, however, included; and it has been decided by the Supreme Court of the United States that an Indian did not become a citizen without naturalization, by virtue of this clause of the Fourteenth Amendment.[1]

Citizenship is exclusive of sex or age.
It would seem almost useless to say that the word " citizen " does not pertain alone to adult males, but I have found so many persons who thought that citizenship and the right to vote were in some way connected and identical, that I have thought it proper to remind you that citizenship has no relation to age or sex. A child the moment it enters the world is a citizen, and a woman is a citizen. Consequently they have rights, although the privilege of voting may not be one of them, which are pertinent to and grow out of the fact of this citizenship of the United States. The object, then, of naturalization, in regard to which the Constitution says that Congress shall have power to establish a uniform rule, is to confer upon those persons who do not have it this right of citizenship.

Naturalized citizens.
The process by which a person becomes naturalized will be found prescribed in sections 2165 to 2174 of the Revised Statutes of the United States. I will not read them to you

---

[1] *Elk* v. *Wilkins*, 112 U.S. 94.

here, but will only state the general purport of
the statute on that subject. In the first place,
it is provided that a person must have lived in
the United States five years before he can become a citizen. I am speaking now of persons
who arrive here at adult age; there are other
provisions for those who come here as minors,
whose naturalization is to some extent governed
by that of the father. At any time after a
person enters this country he can go before a
court of competent jurisdiction, and make a declaration that he intends or desires to become a
citizen of the United States. That declaration
becomes a matter of record in the court where
it is made, and the applicant is thereupon furnished with a copy of this record containing his
name, description, and declaration.

The courts which have been given by acts of
Congress jurisdiction over this subject are not
alone those of the United States: but all the
courts of the States and of the United States,
which are courts of record, have the power to
conduct these proceedings for the naturalization
of aliens. After five years' residence within the
United States the party can go to the same court,
or to another court having this jurisdiction, produce his certificate declaring his intention to
become a citizen, and take an oath to perform
the duties of a citizen of the United States, that
he is well affected towards its Government, and
that he renounces all allegiance to any foreign
country, kingdom, or potentate. He then proves,
or tries to prove, in the best way he can, by

LECTURE VI.
Naturalized citi-
zens.

competent witnesses, his five years' residence, and that he is a man of good moral character. If he establishes these facts to the satisfaction of the court, it makes an order that he. is a citizen, which is recorded, and also gives him a certificate which is always evidence of his citizenship. If it is lost he can at any time obtain a copy of it from the court where the original proceedings were had.

What is gained by
naturalization.

Why should a man become naturalized? What does he gain by it, or what does he loose by not thus becoming a citizen? In the first place, if he does not become a citizen he will not have the right to call upon this Government for protection, whenever he may be in another country. A great deal of the trouble about naturalization in this country has arisen from the fact, which you have no doubt observed in the newspapers, that some one is constantly popping up all over Europe, charged with some dereliction, and claiming that the United States must protect him because he has become one of its citizens. This protection is always given, and generally secures a fair consideration of the case. In almost any country, and even in England, if the evidence of citizenship had been established early enough, the consul or minister would have interposed and seen that the man had a fair trial, that it was not a sham, that there was no oppressive tyranny exercised towards the accused, and that the rules of law were fairly observed. Of course the representative of our Government could not compel the court to do anything it did not see

proper to do, or step out of the way to control
the trial; but he would stand by and see that the person who sought his aid had a fair trial. If he became satisfied in any case that a person so accused did not have a fair trial, or was oppressively tried, or was denied witnesses or counsel or any of the ordinary rights of a prisoner on trial, he would communicate that fact to the proper department of the United States; which, while it would not perhaps interpose in the trial, would yet make itself heard by the authorities of the country in which the trial was had, and that hearing would amount to something. That is one of the protections which it is the correlative duty or obligation of this Government to extend in return for that of allegiance on the part of the citizen.

Another instance in which this right of citizen- ship, as acquired by naturalization, has been quite effectual in securing protection and has been often invoked, but most frequently by former German subjects, is where persons who have come to this country and become naturalized have returned for pleasure or business to the country to which they formerly owed allegiance, and have been there seized and drafted into the military service of that government. Most of these cases have occurred where a German State has alleged that the man in question had, before he left Germany, contracted an obligation to perform military service under its law requiring every man of a specified age and capacity to serve in some military organization for a certain

Lecture VI.
German claims to
military duty by
Germans natural-
ized here.

number of years. This was required of every man, or every man in turn, by a certain allotment or by a draft. These men, in regard to whom the controversies arose, had, by that process and under that law, as it was supposed and asserted, become designated and liable to this period of service. Having emigrated before it was performed, or perhaps before they were called on to serve, when they returned, and their presence became known to the authorities who administered these laws, they were seized, placed under military control, and required to perform this compulsory military service. The question then arose. Here was a citizen of the United States by our laws, who had renounced all allegiance to the German power, who according to our laws owed it no allegiance, and was bound to render it no service. He had become one of our citizens and claimed that, being a citizen of the United States, no other country or government, when he was about his peaceable business, or because he happened to be within its limits, should be permitted to draft him into its military service. We have had a great deal of trouble on this subject. The resistance of the German Government to our claims was long, troublesome, and vexatious. Generally where we could find the man, trace him up, and make proper remonstrances, the authorities would release him rather than have a difficulty about it; nevertheless, all the time asserting their right to enforce obedience if they thought proper to do so.[1]

---

[1] See Note upon this Lecture.

A very interesting historical case, that of Lecture VI. Martin Koszta, of which perhaps some of you The Koszta case. may have read, was the subject, some thirty or forty years ago, of a great deal of newspaper comment, while Mr. Marcy was Secretary of State. Koszta was an Austrian subject who came over to this country and became natural- ized, or, rather, had so far begun the process that he had made his declaration of intention to do so, of which he had a certificate. It may be that he had been long enough a resident of the United States to have procured the second order admitting him as a citizen had he applied for it, but that seemed to be about the only defect on our side of the case. While matters were in that condition he went, not to Europe, but to Smyrna, a town under Turkish dominion, and was there seized by an Austrian vessel, or the Austrian consul found him and took him by force on board of an Austrian vessel. He managed, however, before he was taken out of the harbor, to communicate with the captain of an American vessel of war which was lying in the same port. This officer demanded the re- lease of Koszta, but the Austrian commander refused to comply. Thereupon the American officer trained his guns upon the Austrian vessel with the declaration that if he attempted to leave the port with that man on board he would blow his vessel to pieces. The courage of the American captain, and perhaps the superior size of his guns, compelled the Austrian officer to deliver up the prisoner, which he did, not to the captain of our vessel, but to the authorities of the port. He was, as a matter of fact, turned over to the Turkish authorities. The matter then became the subject of a long diplomatic correspondence, mainly carried on here between Mr. Marcy and Chevalier Hulseman, the Austrian Minister to the United States, which finally ended in the Turkish authorities being allowed to deliver the subject of this controversy into our hands; but our right to demand him was not acknowledged; and that refusal was the source of some disagreements between the respective governments.[1]

The governments of Europe for a long time denied, and some of them do still, the right of a man to expatriate himself. They denied his right to abandon his allegiance to the king or monarch in whose country he was born, and to transfer that allegiance or his home and residence to another country. A more remarkable case than even that of Koszta arose in this country with regard to the same thing. Very shortly after our Government was organized under the Constitution, these naturalization laws were passed by the United States; and Irish, Scotch, and English subjects of Great Britain began to pour into this country, naturalize themselves, and thus become citizens. This went on without much question until the wars between Napoleon and England made the matter of securing a sufficient number of fighting

---

[1] See the Note to this Lecture.

men a very important one for the latter country; for, while England had a great deal of
money and subsidized other nations of Europe to
fight Napoleon, it was troubled all the time to
get sailors and soldiers. It was a small kingdom, with an abundance of funds but a scar-
city of fighting material. We, in the meantime,
after the War of the Revolution, had built up a
little navy, of which, though small, we felt very
proud, and it proved its worth when the War of
1812 broke out, because it was made up of good
fighting material. Our sailors at that time were
mostly natives of Ireland, England, or Scotland.
There were not many of our population that
went into the business of sailor soldiers; and on
our merchant vessels the sailors were nearly all
foreigners, mostly English. England was then
frequently in great distress for sailors, often
needing more than it could raise; because it
was in the habit of carrying on war by blockad-
ing the enemies' ports, which required a large
number of vessels and sailors to man them.
The British Government, therefore, assumed the
right, wherever they could find a man who was
born upon the soil of the British Isles, without
regard to what ship or what soil he was at the
time upon, to impress him into their own service. This claim of right was not of much consequence within the limits of the United States,
because no officer of the English Government
could come here and assert it upon our soil or in
our ports; but when they undertook to board
· our ships upon the seas, claiming for their war

vessels the right to search every merchant vessel, not only of our country but of all other
countries, and abusing that right of search by
taking our sailors out of those merchant vessels by the wholesale and transferring them to
their men of war, our Government remonstrated.
There were also serious grievances with France
about which we remonstrated ; but neither country paid much attention to our complaints.
Our worst grievance, however, and the one
which bore hardest upon us, was the seizing of
naturalized citizens of the United States out of
our ships upon the high seas, and putting them
into the service of British men-of-war. This
roused the spirit of our people, and did more to
bring about the War of 1812 than any other one
thing. You have no doubt all heard of the cry
of "Free Trade and Sailor's Rights." This did
not mean free trade in the modern sense of
opposition to a protective tariff, but the free
right to trade on the seas ; it stood for the right
of our vessels to go where they pleased, without
fear of search, and for the freedom of all our
citizens on board of those vessels. That great
war, fought through four years, with much loss
of treasure and some humiliation, but a great
deal of glory, closing with the battle of New
Orleans, was mainly to support this doctrine.
It was to maintain the proposition that when
a man came over to this country and became a
naturalized citizen, no other government had a
right to recapture him ; it was waged in favor
of the doctrine of self-expatriation, the right to

leave one country, go to another, and there be-
come a citizen, if that other would accept him as such, and in doing so to throw off all allegiance to the country of his nativity. But although that was the great controversy in that war, it did not decide the question finally. In fact, after both countries were tired of fighting, we made a treaty of peace in which that matter was left unsettled. The British did not give up this right which they had claimed; we got something the better of them in regard to some disputes as to boundaries and fisheries and other questions which were settled, yet the main question remained undetermined. From that time we have gone on while these troubles have been pending, those with Germany about their military claims, and a great many others of a similar character, negotiating, writing, and talking, the Government of this country all the time asserting this absolute right without concession, until nearly all the governments of the world, even if they have not adopted it as international law, have in the main abandoned the idea that a man cannot expatriate himself. Where they have not done that they have made treaties with the United States recognizing that right, which amounts to about the same thing. We have treaties now with nearly all nations which concede it, and only one subject of difference remains. That is the German question, to which I have referred, whether a man who has left his native country, where the law imposes an obligation on the subject to serve in some

military organization for a certain period, can be compelled to render those services if he returns thither as a naturalized citizen of the United States. It is still asserted that if he goes back to the land of his birth, the government of which he was before a subject has a right to compel him to perform those services, except where they have yielded that right by treaty. This has now, I think, been substantially done, and that is one of the rights which a man acquires by naturalization.[1]

Another right, perhaps the next in importance, is the right to inherit property. It was the law of England that no alien could inherit any real estate in the English dominions, nor could he transmit any real estate, nor any such estate go through him, but to do this he must be a native citizen. It was said that an alien had no inheritable blood with regard to real estate. This rule, however, had no relation to personal estate. That doctrine of the common law became, and is, except as modified by statute or treaty, the doctrine of the States of this Union; the title to real estate being a matter which is prescribed in each State by its own laws, and not governed by the laws of the Congress of the United States. It is one of the effects of this constitutional provision, and one of the purposes for which it was made, that Congress should prescribe a uniform rule of naturalization, which should be effective in all

---

[1] See the Note to this Lecture.

the States, and a rule by which any foreigner or alien might become a citizen. Now, when by that process of naturalization he was declared a citizen, he became entitled in any State, where he might be, to inherit property and transmit it by descent the same as any native citizen. That was also one of the advantages of naturalization.

Another benefit which has been much talked of, but which does not amount to a great deal, is that of the right of voting, as many of the States have prescribed as a qualification for voting, that the man must be at least a citizen of the State where he offers to vote. That is not the case in all of the States, but it is true of most of them. Some of the Western States, I think Minnesota, and perhaps Wisconsin, where there are large numbers of Swedes, Germans, and Norwegians, have provisions in their statutes that a man may vote by reason of his residence without regard to citizenship; but the majority of the constitutions of the States of the Union require that the voters shall be citizens. By this operation of naturalization, and by the Constitutional Amendment which I have read, the alien becomes a citizen of whatever State he may select as his residence at the time. That is one of the valuable things attaching to naturalization.

There have been times when it was a question whether this power to prescribe a rule of naturalization was an exclusive power in the Congress of the United States, or whether it was one that the States might also exercise. That

Lecture VI.

Right to inherit real estate.

Right of suffrage.

The Federal laws on this subject are exclusive.

question, however, has been practically settled by the fact that the United States has had a law on the subject for some eighty or ninety years, which, when it was enacted, necessarily became the exclusive law in regard to that matter, because the power given to the Congress is "to establish a uniform rule of naturalization . . . throughout the United States." This means that the law which Congress establishes is the law of all the States and Territories and places where naturalization can take place. It is, therefore, practically an exclusive power with which the individual States cannot deal.

There have not been a great many decisions in our courts upon this subject of naturalization, because, as I observed a while ago, it has been rather an international question than one of dispute among ourselves. In the case of *Osborn* v.

The Bank of the United States,[1] however, the Supreme Court of the United States, in an opinion delivered by Chief Justice Marshall, made the following remarks upon the subject of a naturalized citizen : —

" He becomes a member of the society, possessing all the rights of a native citizen, and standing, in the view of the Constitution, on the footing of a native. The Constitution does not authorize Congress to enlarge or abridge those rights. The simple power of the national Legislature is to prescribe a uniform rule of naturalization, and the exercise of this power exhausts it, so far as

---

[1] 9 Wheat. 738, 827.

respects the individual. The Constitution then
takes him up, and, among other rights, extends
to him the capacity of suing in the courts of the
United States, precisely under the same circumstances under which a native might sue. He is
distinguishable in nothing from a native citizen,
except so far as the Constitution makes the distinction."

The Constitution of the United States having,
therefore, defined what citizenship is, and removed it out of the domain of controverted
questions of constitutional law, having prescribed
what constitutes citizenship of the United States,
and what citizenship of a State, and having
alluded to them in distinct terms, it has become
a question what are distinctively the rights of a
citizen of the United States, and what are the
rights of a citizen of a State. That question
came up very soon after the adoption of the
Fourteenth Amendment, in what are called the
Slaughter House Cases. It was insisted there
that the rights which the Constitution, or this
Amendment, conferred on a citizen of the United
States, were all those of a fundamental character,
which regard the relations of a citizen to the
society in which he lives; but the court, after
very grave consideration, in an opinion which I
had the honor to deliver, held that not to be a
sound view of the matter; that the State in its
relation to its citizens, and the citizens in their
relation to the State, were interchangeably bound
with regard to those laws which go to make up
the rights which are protected by law: the right

of marriage; the right of the descent of property; the right to the control of children; the right to sue for property, and to have it protected; and, in general, the protection of life, liberty, and the pursuit of happiness, — these were all founded in the relation between the State and its citizens.

The Constitution gave Congress no right to interfere with that great body of the rights of the citizen. He has a right to look to that government, as I have told you, for protection in all foreign countries wherever he might travel, on the high seas or the sands of Africa, in Europe or in Australia, wherever a ship floats, or a traveller can go. He has a right to call on the United States for protection wherever he may be outside of its lines or territories. He has also the right, as I told you in a previous lecture, to travel all over this country free from any tax, assessment, or interruption in his passage from one part of the country to another. He has the right of petition granted to him by the Constitution of the United States. He has the right to the use of the mails of the United States; he has, in short, a right to everything which that great Government gives or concedes to anybody, and these are his rights as a citizen of the United States. They are numerous; they are great; they are valuable. So it may also be said of his rights as a citizen of a State: they are numerous; they are great; they are important. The one affects one class of relations, and the other affects another class. The citizen owes an allegiance to the United States, and he owes an allegiance to his State. He is bound to obey Lecture VI. · the laws of his State, and he is bound to refrain Righ s of a Citizen. t from all criminal practices denounced by those z laws. He is bound to pay his taxes to support the government of the State, and he is bound as well to pay the taxes due from him to the United States; to fight for that Government if called upon, or to fight for his State, and even to give his life, if need be, for his citizenship of the United States. He is bound to be governed by the United States in all of his relations with foreign States. If he wishes to travel in a foreign State, and desires protection, the United States will give him a passport, which a State is not permitted to do. If he wants to take part in the administration of the Government of the United States, either as an officer, member of Congress, contractor, or builder; if he wants his river improved, if he wants the postal railway extended, if he wants a new post-office, or any one of a thousand such things, he must go to the Federal Government. It is the business of a lifetime to define the relations of a man to that Government, or his relations to the State in which he belongs; but they all grow out of, and constitute this doctrine of allegiance and protection. He owes his allegiance first, to the Government of the United States, because he is first of all a citizen of that Government; second, to his State, because he becomes a citizen of that State, after being a citizen of the United States, by his residence.

I hope, gentlemen, while I do not wish any of

you the misfortune of turning out politicians, that you will read and consider this subject dispassionately, neither assuming, on the one hand, that the Federal Government has a right to sweep away a State as so much rubbish, nor that any of the States, have a right to rise up and overthrow the great Government of the United States, which is our guardian and protector, and in which, after all, are united our brightest hopes and greatest interests.

NOTES UPON LECTURE VI.

THE relations between the individual and the State throughout Christendom; (Russia perhaps excepted,) have been* vastly modified by the influence of the naturalization laws and treaties of the United States.

LECTURE VI. Wide influence of the American doctrine of citizenship.

When the war of the American Revolution broke out, the feudal relation still prevailed between the sovereign and the subject, modified to some extent by the progress of civilization, and by the influences of modern thought. The duties of the subject and the rights of the sovereign under that system sprang from occupation of the soil by the former under tenure from the latter, either by the actual tenant, or by the lord to whom he was feudally attached.

The feudal system.

In this respect feudalism differed from the civil law. The Roman citizen's rights came from the State, of which he formed an integral part. The common sovereignty was lodged in the people as a whole. " The Emperor Julian said that States are immortal, that is, that they may be so : because a People is that kind of body which consists of separate elements, but is subject to one name, and has *one habit*, as Plutarch says as one spirit, Paulus. This spirit or habit in a people is the full and perfect common

Roman law.

297

participation of civil life ; the first production of
which is the sovereignty, the bond by which the
State is held together, the vital breath drawn by
so many thousands, as Seneca speaks.' ¹'

Relations of the
citizen to the
State in America.
Thus, in the social system which prevailed
under the civil law, the citizen was but an integral part of the State ; while, under the feudal
system he was the subject of the sovereign, who
was master of the soil. Under the American
system his duties to the·State survive, marked
and defined, however, by positive law ; but he
has the right to determine for himself who shall
be that sovereign, and in whose service those
duties shall be performed.

The first act of Congress, pointing towards its
subsequent policy in the matter of citizenship, is
to be found in the Articles of Confederation.

The Fourth Article of the Articles of Confederation provided that, "the better to secure and
perpetuate mutual friendship and intercourse
among the people of the different States in this
Union, the free inhabitants of each of these
States, paupers, vagabonds, and fugitives from
justice excepted, shall be entitled to all privileges and immunities of free citizens in the several States."

Of this the historian says : " In the republics
of Greece, citizenship had in theory been confined to a body of kindred families, which formed
an hereditary caste, a multitudinous aristocracy:
Such a system could have no permanent vital-

---

¹ Grotius, De jure Belli et Pacis, Lib. 2, c. 9, § 3. Whewell's ed.
Cambridge, 1853, vol. 2, p. 2.

ity; and the Greek republics, as the Italian LECTURE VI.
Interstate citizen-
ship estab^lished
by the Articles of
Confederation. republics in after ages, died out for want of citizens. America adopted the principle of the all-embracing unity of society. As the American territory was that of the old thirteen Colonies, so the free people residing upon it formed the free people of the United States. . . . That which gave reality to the Union was the article which secured to 'the free inhabitants' of each of the States 'all privileges and immunities of free citizens in the several States.' Congress appeared to shun the term 'people of the United States.' It is nowhere found in their Articles of Confederation, and rarely and only accidentally in their votes; yet by this act they constituted the free inhabitants of the different States one people. . . . Congress, while it left the regulation of the elective franchise to the judgment of each State in the Articles of Confederation, in its votes and its treaties with other powers, reckoned all the free inhabitants, without distinction of ancestry, creed, or color, as subjects or citizens. But America, though the best representative of the social and political acquisitions of the eighteenth century, was not the parent of the idea in modern civilization that man is a constituent member of the State of his birth, irrespective of his ancestry. It was already the public law of Christendom." [1]

This provision of the Articles of Confederation was incorporated into the Constitution; and to

---

[1] Bancroft's History, Last Revise, vol. 5, pp. 200, 206, 207.

it was added the power to establish a uniform
system of naturalization. Congress exercised
this power in March, 1790.[1] Under this act,
two years' previous residence was required.
This was repealed in January, 1795, and a previous declaration of intention after an at least
three years' residence was required, and a residence of at least five years before naturalization.[2]
Further changes were made from time to time,
and the law as it now stands is codified in the
Revised Statutes of the United States.[3]

Relation of the
naturalized citi-
zen to the govern-
ment of his native
country.
These laws, however, led up to the doctrine
of expatriation and citizenship as now understood ; but that doctrine was not accepted by
other powers, and was by no means insisted
upon, in its full extent, by our own political
officers.

In the wars of the French revolution and the
French empire, Great Britain, as Mr. Justice
Miller points out, entirely disregarded them.
In the midst of the negotiations for peace
which terminated in the Treaty of Ghent, Mr.
Alexander Baring, when urged by Mr. Gallatin
to lend his official influence to the conclusion of
a treaty on the basis desired by the United
States, answered : " I must freely confess that,
highly as I value a state of peace and harmony
with America, I am so sensible of the danger to
our naval power from anything like an unrestricted admission of your principles, that I
should almost incline to think it safer to consider

---

[1] 1 Stat. 103, c. 3.   [3] Rev. Stat. §§ 2165–2174.
[2] 1 Stat. 414, c. 20.

an American as an inevitable concomitant of a French war, and to provide for it accordingly."[1] And when the treaty of peace was made and promulgated, it was found to contain absolutely nothing about this dispute, which, as Mr. Justice Miller has justly said, was one of the main causes of the war.

LECTURE VI. Relation of the naturalized citizen to the government of his native country.

Meanwhile, as this country increased in population, largely in consequence of emigration, the same old question arose, but in a different form, as pointed out by Mr. Justice Miller. The Prussian army, which was still kept up practically on the basis devised by Stein after the battle of Jena, demanded military duty from Prussians who had been to America, and had been naturalized there as citizens of the United States, and had returned to Prussia. To a person who, under such circumstances claimed his protection as Minister of the United States at Berlin, Mr. Wheaton answered, declining to interfere, upon the ground that, on the applicant's return to his native country, his former nationality reverted. Mr. Everett and Mr. Webster substantially agreed with Mr. Wheaton. Mr. Cass took a somewhat more advanced position; but until the spring and summer of 1868, the question may be fairly regarded as an open one.

On the 22d of February in that year Mr. Bancroft concluded at Berlin the first of a series of such treaties, a list of which will be found in

The naturalization treaties.

---

[1] Baring to Gallatin, M., Ms. Department of State. Notes and Treaties (ed. 1889) p. 1327.

the margin: [1] and, on the 27th of the following
July, Congress enacted that "the right of expatriation is a natural and inherent right of all
people, indispensable to the enjoyment of the
rights of life, liberty, and the pursuit of happiness"; that, "in the recognition of this principle this government has freely received emigrants
from all nations, and invested them with the
rights of citizenship"; and that "all naturalized
citizens of the United States, while in foreign
States, shall be entitled to, and shall receive
from this Government, the same protection of
persons and property, that is accorded to native
born citizens in like situations and circumstances." [2]

The Koszta case. It was some twenty years before the conclusion of these treaties and the passage of this
act, that the case of Martin Koszta, to which
Justice Miller refers, took place. This was subsequently explained and qualified by the Department of State. Just prior to and during the
Cuban insurrection of 1869, 1870, many Cubans
declared their intention to become citizens of the

---

[1] Austria: concluded September 20, 1870.
   Baden: concluded July 19, 1868.
   Bavaria: concluded May 26, 1868.
   Belgium: concluded November 16, 1868.
   Denmark: concluded July 20, 1872.
   Ecuador: concluded May 6, 1872.
   Great Britain: concluded May 13, 1870.
   Great Britain (supplemental):   concluded February 23, 1871.
   Hesse: concluded August 1, 1868.
 * North German Union: concluded February 22, 1868.
   Sweden and Norway: concluded May 26, 1869.
   Württemberg: concluded July 27, 1868.

[2] 15 Stat. 223, c. 249.

United States, and, after doing so, returned to LECTURE VI.
Cuba. It became a practical question whether The Koszta case.
the United States were to assume to protect these
men against the barbaric severity of the Volun-
teers, who dominated Cuba at that time. The
department said : " Mr. Marcy was very careful
in his elaborate letter concerning Martin Koszta,
not to commit this Government to the obligation,
or to the propriety, of using the force of the
nation for the protection of foreign born persons
who, after declaring their intention to become at
some future time citizens of the United States,
leave its shores to return to their native country. . . . He took especial care to insist that
the case was to be judged, not by the municipal
laws of the United States, not by the local laws
of Turkey, not by the conventions between Turkey and Austria, but by the great principles of
international law. . . . It has been repeatedly
decided by this department that the declaration
of intention to become a citizen does not, in the
absence of treaty stipulations, so clothe the individual with the nationality of this country, as
to enable him to return to his native land without being necessarily subject to all the laws
thereof." [1]

Some further official correspondence with
regard to this class of cases, as illustrating the
difficulties with which the Government has to
contend in dealing with them, may not be inappropriate.

---

[1] Session Ex. Doc. 108, 2d Session, 41st Congress, p. 202.

LECTURE VI.
Naturalizations to
escape military
service. Action of
President Grant.
The questions with Germany, to which Justice Miller alludes, growing out of the military service laws of Prussia and of the Empire, were largely the cause of the questions propounded by President Grant to the members of his Cabinet, to which allusion was made in the notes to Lecture III. Since the naturalization treaties went into operation matters have moved on with less friction than before. Native born Germans, who seek naturalization here solely for the purpose of escaping the performance of their duties to their native land, without a purpose or intent of doing their duty as citizens here, have found that the United States expect them to make their home here as a condition of protection: while, on the other hand, such Germans as honestly cast their fortunes in with us, receive the national protection against the claims of the government of their native land as efficiently as it is given to native born citizens.

Simultaneously with the letter of President Grant, calling for the opinions of his Cabinet, the Secretary of State addressed a circular to the Ministers of the United States at Berlin, Rome, and Paris, inquiring, among other things, "the number of Americans whose residence in Germany [Italy] [France] has been of long continuance, or seems to be indefinite in its intended duration." Mr. Bancroft, the then Minister at Berlin, answered: "Of Americans whose residence in Germany has been of long continuance, or seems to be indefinite in its intended duration, I estimate the number at 10,000, and that num-

ber rather on the increase." Mr. Marsh, the
then Minister, addressed a circular to the Consuls in Italy and received from them detailed
reports which footed up 225. He added: " I
have no means for ascertaining the number of
Italians and other foreigners naturalized in the
United States, now residing in Italy; but though
it is doubtless considerably smaller than during
and soon after the rebellion, I think it must
still amount to several hundred." Mr. Washburne reported from Paris that "the number of
resident Americans in France does not increase,
but, on the other hand, rather diminishes."

Shortly before these inquiries were made a
correspondence took place between the Legation
at Paris and the Department of State, which
may have been instrumental in causing the investigation. Mr. Washburne wrote for instructions in two cases.

The first he stated as follows: Madame Pepin, who applies on behalf of her son, a young man
eighteen years of age, to have some papers from
the legation, stating that he is an American
citizen, and is to be protected as such. His case
is as follows: John Pepin, the husband and
father, was a Frenchman by birth. When a
young man he emigrated to the United States,
was educated in Kentucky, and became a naturalized citizen, residing in New Orleans. In
1850 he returned to France, leaving some property in New Orleans, which is still held by his
family, he having died several years ago. After.
his return to this country he married a French-

LECTURE VI.
Status of natural-
ized citizens who
reside perma-
nently in their
native land.
woman, by whom he had a daughter, now twenty years of age, and the son above spoken of. He never returned to the United States to live, but made France his residence up to the time of his death. The boy in question has never been to the United States, though the mother and daughter went there two years ago, and the mother obtained a passport from the State Department as an American citizen. She says that the boy got a passport two years ago from the United States Minister in London, but that he had lost it."

To this the Secretary of State answered: "Pepin, the son of a naturalized Frenchman, who returned to France and died there, was never in this country. . . . It would seem quite possible that, were it not for his desire to avoid the duties required by French law, he would perhaps never have dreamed of calling himself an American; that he would remain in France and avoid all duties to the United States; that he would call himself a citizen of the United States and avoid all duties to France."

The second case was this: "A man and his wife, Americans by birth, came to Paris forty years ago, and have lived here ever since. This has become their permanent home, and they have never had any intention of returning to the United States. Several of their children have been born here, and have never been to the United States, and never expect to go, and never want to go. The question is, are these children citizens of the United States, and is the

Government of the United States bound to protect them as such?"

To this Mr. Fish answered: "In the other case an American, whose name is withheld, has lived with his family forty years in France, has reared his children there, has never proposed to return to the United States, and his children have never been to the United States, and never expect to go, and never want to go."

And to the inquiries in both cases the Secretary said: "In each of these cases there is a presumption of a purpose of expatriation so strong that, until it can be rebutted to your satisfaction, you will be justified in concluding that the persons respectively are not entitled to your intervention to protect them against the operation of the laws of the country which they have selected as the place of their residence."[1]

The political department of the Government has made some rulings on this subject since the negotiation of the treaties, which deserve notice.

The treaty with North Germany calls for an uninterrupted residence of five years in the United States before the naturalized citizen is entitled to the immunities guaranteed by it. It is held that the recital in the record of the naturalization proceedings that the applicant had resided continuously in this country for more than five years does not conclude the United States as to that fact.[2] A similar decision has been made as to the treaty with Austria.[3]

---

[1] Foreign Relations, 1873, vol. 1, pp. 249, 260, 261.
[2] 1 Treaties and Conventions (ed. 1889) p. 1264. [3] Ib. p. 1265.

Cases arise, from time to time, where persons who, by the laws of the United States, are declared to be citizens of the United States, are also, by the law of some other country, held to allegiance in that country. In this class may be included persons born out of the limits and jurisdiction of the United States, whose fathers were, at the time of their birth, citizens of the United States. Such a case being submitted to Attorney General Hoar, that officer held that it was not competent for the United States to interfere with the rights of a foreign nation to the government and control of persons claimed to be its subjects, so long as they were residing in such foreign country.[1]

Any one desiring to see the condition of the statutes and laws of the various powers in regard to this interesting subject will find it discussed at length in Calvo.[2]

---

[1] 13 Opinions Attorney General, 89.
[2] 1 Droit International, liv. 8.

VII.

THE JUDICIAL POWER OF THE UNITED STATES.[1]

ARTICLE III, SECTION 1. The judicial Power of the United States, shall be vested in one supreme Court, and in such inferior Courts as the Congress may from time to time ordain and establish. The Judges, both of the supreme and inferior Courts, shall hold their Offices during good Behavior, and shall, at stated Times, receive for their Services, a Compensation, which shall not be diminished during their Continuance in Office.

SECTION 2. The judicial Power shall extend to all Cases, in Law and Equity, arising under this Constitution, the Laws of the United States, and Treaties made, or which shall be made, under their Authority; —to all Cases affecting Ambassadors, other public Ministers, and Consuls ;—to all Cases of admiralty and maritime Jurisdiction ; — to Controversies to which the United States shall be a Party ;—to Controversies between two or more States ; — between a State and Citizens of another State ;— between Citizens of different States, — between Citizens of the same State claiming Lands under Grants of different States, and between a State, or the Citizens thereof, and foreign States, Citizens or subjects.

In all Cases affecting Ambassadors, other public Ministers and Consuls, and those in which a State shall be Party, the supreme Court shall have original Jurisdiction. In all the other Cases before mentioned, the supreme Court shall have appellate Jurisdiction, both as to Law and Fact, with such Exceptions, and under such Regulations as the Congress shall make.

---

[1] This is Lecture VI of the lectures delivered before the classes of the University Law School.

The Trial of all Crimes, except in Cases of Impeachment, shall be by Jury ; and such Trial shall be held in the State where the said Crimes shall have been committed ; but when not committed within any State, the Trial shall be at such Place or Places as the Congress may by Law have directed.

SECTION 3. Treason against the United States, shall consist only in levying War against them, or in adhering to their Enemies, giving them Aid and Comfort. No Person shall be convicted of Treason unless on the Testimony of two Witnesses to the same overt Act, or on Confession in open Court.

The Congress shall have Power to declare the Punishment of Treason, but no Attainder of Treason shall work Corruption of Blood, or Forfeiture except during the Life of the Person attainted.

ARTICLE VII OF THE AMENDMENTS. In Suits at common law, where the value in controversy shall exceed twenty dollars, the right of trial by jury shall be preserved, and no fact tried by a jury shall be otherwise re-examined in any Court of the United States, than according to the rules of the common law.

ARTICLE XI OF THE AMENDMENTS. The Judicial power of the United States shall not be construed to extend to any suit in law or equity, commenced or prosecuted against one of the United States by Citizens of another State, or by Citizens or Subjects of any Foreign State.

Judicial power.

I HAVE before alluded to the division which the Constitution makes of the powers to be exercised by the National Government into three departments : the legislative, executive, and judicial. That in which students of law will probably be most interested in having an exposition of its powers is the latter, to which attention will now be directed.[1]

My text, after the manner of the clergy, is

---

[1] Courts of justice have been described as an institution framed for the purpose of putting an end to the practice of private war. Without the instrumentality of judicial tribunals, society would be a prey to perpetual civil dissensions.

the third of the three main articles of the Constitution, into which it is divided, the first being
devoted to the legislative, the second to the executive, and the third to the judicial; following
which are some provisions establishing private
rights, concerning the two Houses of Congress,
and several amendments touching other subjects.

Article Third reads as follows : —

"Sec. 1. The judicial power of the United
States shall be vested in one Supreme Court,
and in such inferior courts as the Congress may
from time to time ordain and establish. The
judges, both of the Supreme and inferior courts,
shall hold their offices during good behavior,
and shall, at stated times, receive for their services a compensation, which shall not be diminished during their continuance in office.

"Sec. 2· The judicial power shall extend to
all cases, in law and equity, arising under this
Constitution, the laws of the United States, and
treaties made, or which shall be made, under
their authority; to all cases affecting ambassadors, other public ministers, and consuls; to all
cases of admiralty and maritime jurisdiction; to
controversies to which the United States shall
be a party; to controversies between two or
more States; between a State and citizens of
another State; between citizens of different
States; between citizens of the same State
claiming lands under grants of different States,
and between a State, or the citizens thereof, and
foreign States, citizens, or subjects.

"In all cases affecting ambassadors, other public ministers, and consuls, and those in which a State shall be party, the Supreme Court shall have original jurisdiction. In all the other cases before mentioned, the Supreme Court shall have appellate jurisdiction, both as to law and fact, with such exceptions and under such regulations as the Congress shall make.

"The trial of all crimes, except in cases of impeachment, shall be by jury; and such trial shall be held in the State where the said crimes shall have been committed; but when not committed within any State, the trial shall be at such place, or places, as the Congress may by law have directed.

" Sec. 3. Treason against the United States shall consist only in levying war against them, or in adhering to their enemies, giving them aid and comfort. No person shall be convicted of treason, unless on the testimony of two witnesses to the same overt act, or on confession in open court.

" The Congress shall have power to declare the punishment of treason, but no attainder of treason shall work corruption of blood, or forfeiture, except during the life of the person attainted." [1]

---

[1] In this connection should be read Article XI of the Amendments: "The judicial power of the United States shall not be construed to extend to any suit in law or equity, commenced or prosecuted against one of the United States by citizens of another State, or by citizens or subjects of any foreign State."

Mr. Justice Story says, after quoting these provisions: "Such is the language of the article creating and defining the judicial power of the United States. It is the voice of the whole American people solemnly declared, in establishing one great department of that government, which was, in many respects, national, and in

Attention is first called to the second section,
and the first thing that requires or justifies any
criticism is as to the use of the words "judicial
power."

What is judicial power? It will not do to
answer that it is the power exercised by the
courts, because one of the very things to be determined is what power they may exercise. It
is, indeed, very difficult to find any exact definition made to hand.[1] It is not to be found in
any of the old treatises, or any of the old English authorities or judicial decisions, for a very
obvious reason. While in a general way it may
be true that they had this division between legislative and judicial power, yet their legislature
was, nevertheless, in the habit of exercising a
very large part of the latter. The House of
Lords was often the Court of Appeals, and Parliament was in the habit of passing bills of

---

all, supreme. It is a part of the very same instrument which was
to act not merely upon individuals, but upon States; and to deprive them altogether of the exercise of some powers of sovereignty, and to restrain and regulate them in the exercise of others."
Martin v. *Hunter's Lessee*, 1 Wheat. 304, 328.

[1] "Judicial power" is the authority vested in the judges.
Bouvier Law Dictionary.

As to what is meant by the phrase "judicial power," see *Cal-
lanan* v. *Judd*, 23 Wisconsin, 343, 349. Also charge of Judge
Nelson to grand jury of the Circuit Court, 1851, that it is the power
conferred upon courts in the strict sense of that term; courts that
compose one of the great departments of the government; and not
power judicial in its nature, or *quasi* judicial, invested from time
to time in individuals, separately or collectively, for a particular
purpose and limited time. 1 Blatchford, 635. *Gilbert* v. *Priest*, 65
Barb. 444, 448.

The power to hear and determine a cause is jurisdiction; it is
coram judice, whenever a case is presented which brings this power
into action. *United States* v. *Arredondo*, 6 Pet. 699, 709.

LECTURE VII.
What is judicial
power?
attainder as well as enacting convictions for treason and other crimes.[1]

Judicial power is, perhaps, better defined in some of the reports of our own courts than in any other place, and especially so in the Supreme Court of the United States, because it has more often been the subject of comment there, and its consideration more frequently necessary to the determination of questions arising in that court than anywhere else. It is the power of a court to decide and pronounce a judgment and carry it into effect between persons and parties who bring a case before it for decision.[2]

A case is necessary to its exercise.

This power " shall extend to all *cases* " of a particular character, which is specified. Before there can be any proper exercise of it a " case "

---

[1] The distinction between judicial and political power is so generally acknowledged in the jurisprudence both of England and of this country, that we need do no more than refer to some of the authorities on the subject. *Nabob of Carnatic* v. *East India Co.*, 1 Ves. Jr. 371, 375, 393; *S.C.* 2 Ves. Jr. 56, 60; *Penn* v. *Lord Baltimore*, 1 Ves. Sen. 444, 446, 447; *New York* v. *Connecticut*, 4 Dall. 4, 6; *Cherokee Nation* v. *Georgia*, 5 Pet. 1; *Rhode Island* v. *Massachusetts*, 12 Pet. 657. They are all in one direction. *State of Georgia* v. *Stanton*, 6 Wall. 50, 71.

In the early ages of the English system, however, the line between the judiciary and the legislature was not distinctly marked, and Parliament, consisting of one great chamber, in which sat both lords and commons, not only made but also interpreted the laws. But it has now long been settled in England that the interpretation of statute law belongs to the judiciary alone, and in this country they have claimed and obtained an equal control over the construction of constitutional provisions. Sedgwick on Const. Law, 18.

[2] Judicial power is never exercised for the purpose of giving effect to the will of the judge; always for the purpose of giving effect to the will of the Legislature; or, in other words, to the will of the law. *Osborn* v. *Bank of the United States*, 9 Wheat. 738.

must be presented in court for its action.[1] A case implies parties, an assertion of rights, or a wrong to be remedied. The decisions of the Supreme Court of the United States, as well as those of other courts, contain many definitions of what it is. A reference to Paschal's Annotated Constitution will give many of them, and their leading features. Perhaps there is none better than in the language of Chief Justice Marshall: "A case arises, within the meaning of the Constitution, when any question respecting the Constitution, treaties, or laws of the United States has assumed such a form that the judicial power is capable of acting on it."[2]

In this connection it is proper to endeavor to correct the erroneous impression that prevails in the minds of many persons with regard to the power of the Supreme Court of the United States as the expounder of the Constitution. It has been asserted in popular treatises, in public speeches, and political harangues, that the Supreme Court of the United States is the final expounder of that instrument, that it was made

LECTURE VII.

A case is necessary to its exercise.

Functions of the court as interpreting the Constitution.

---

[1] In order to entitle the party to the remedy a case must be presented appropriate for the exercise of judicial power ; the rights in danger must be rights of persons or property ; not merely political rights, which do not belong to the jurisdiction of a court, either in law or equity. *State of Georgia* v. *Stanton*, 6 Wall. 50, 76.

When a right is asserted by a party before a court in the manner prescribed by law, it then becomes a *case* to which the judicial power extends. This includes the right of both parties to the litigation ; and the case may be said to *arise* whenever its correct decision is dependent upon the construction of the Constitution, laws, or treaties of the United States.

[2] *Osborn* v. *Bank of the United States*, 9 Wheat. 738, 819.

LECTURE VII.
Functions of the
court as interpret-
ing the Constitu-
tion.
for that purpose, and that it is one of its primary functions. But it has been over and again held by that court, that all it can do in that regard is to decide such questions as involve a construction of its provisions, and only those when they are brought before it in a suit between proper parties. In some cases these parties have been very dignified ones. The United States and great States have appeared before its bar, but in the great majority of cases, where it has been called upon to construe the Constitution of the United States, it has been in a conflict between individuals, wherein the validity of some law, or the determination of some right asserted by one party and denied by the other, must be settled by the authority of this great fundamental charter. So this court only does, in its higher position as the last court to which such cases can be brought, what every other court in the United States has to do, whether it be a State or a Federal court. It only decides such cases as arise in the progress of ordinary litigation.[1]

It may also be noted, before passing from the consideration of this part of the clause, that the judicial power "shall extend to *all* cases" aris-

---

[1] This clause enables the judicial department to receive jurisdiction to the full extent of the Constitution, laws, and treaties of the United States, when any question respecting them shall assume such a form that the judicial power is capable of acting on it. That power is capable of acting only when the subject is submitted to it by a party who asserts his rights in the form prescribed by law. It then becomes a case. Marshall, C. J., in *Osborn* v. *Bank of the United States*, 9 Wheat. 738, 819.

ing under the circumstances specified. That is LECTURE VII.
to say, to all cases where a right exists under Functions of the
court as interpret-
the Constitution, or under a treaty which shall ing the Constitu-
be made under the authority of the Federal Gov- tion.
ernment. The Federal power extends over, and
covers all such cases, and they are properly
within the jurisdiction of its courts.[1]

This extension of power over all cases is, however, qualified by the words immediately following "in law or in equity." These cases must
be in law or in equity, with the exception of admiralty, as to which there is a separate clause
further on in the section. Under this provision
an attempt has been made to exclude a very
large class of cases arising in the State and
other courts, which were of an anomalous character. Some actions where remedies were given
by peculiar modes of proceeding, by summary
proceedings, by attachment, and others at variance with the common law, were said not to be
suits at law, and yet did not come under any
head of equity jurisprudence. But the decisions
of the Supreme Court of the United States are
abundant to the effect that, with the exception
of admiralty, all modes of procedure for the
assertion of rights must be arranged under the
one class or the other, either law or equity,
within the meaning of this clause.[2]

---

[1] The judicial department is authorized to decide all cases, of
every description, arising under the Constitution or laws of the
United States. *Cohens* v. *Virginia*, 6 Wheat. 264, 382.

[2] This clause extends the jurisdiction of the court to all cases
described, without making in its terms any exception whatever,
and without any regard to the condition of the party. If there be

Equity is a limited jurisdiction which has grown up by the side of the common law, which is in some sense a restriction of, and departure from that law. There is not much difficulty as to what are cases in equity, and it is sufficient to say, that the Federal courts have held that all the cases that are neither properly cognizable in admiralty or equity are, within this clause of the Constitution, cases at law. Indeed, the Supreme Court have held, as they have been compelled to do, that when the Federal courts come to administer the rights or the remedies claimed under what I may venture to term the improvements in the modes of procedure which have been adopted by the codes of the various States, in most of which equity and law have been consolidated, as well as under many new statutes giving new rights, appointing new modes of procedure, and fixing new remedies, they must range the actions in those courts upon the equity or law side as the nature of the right asserted, or the remedy given may require. They do this, as equity is understood and was understood in the English courts at the time of the Revolution.[1] Their equity jurisdiction is

---

any exception, it is to be implied against the express words of the article. · · · A case in law or equity consists of the right of one party, as well as of the other, and may be truly said to arise under the Constitution or a law of the United States, whenever its correct decision depends on the construction of either. Chief Justice Marshall, in *Cohens* v. *Virginia*, 6 Wheat. 264, 378.

[1] The equity jurisdiction of the courts of the United States is independent of the local law of any State, and is the same in nature and extent as the equity jurisdiction of England from which it is derived. Therefore it is no objection to this jurisdiction that there

independent of the local law of any State, and no rules at law or in equity, which have been adopted in any State court, can abolish the separate and distinct jurisdiction. That must be administered on the chancery side of the Federal court which has taken charge of it.[1]

One of the distinctions necessary to be noted in this regard is that another provision of the Constitution declares that in suits at common law, where the value in controversy exceeds twenty dollars, every one shall have a right to a trial by a jury.[2] The right of trial by jury is

---

is a remedy under the local law. *Gordon* v. *Hobart*, 2 Sumner, 401.

The remedies in courts of the United States are to be, at common law or in equity, not according to the practice of State courts, but according to the principles of common law and equity, as distinguished and defined in that country from which we derive our knowledge of those principles. *Robinson* v. *Campbell*, 3 Wheat. 211, 222.

It is not enough that there is a remedy at law; it must be plain and adequate, or in other words, as practical and as efficient to the ends of justice and its prompt administration, as the remedy in equity. *Boyce's Executors* v. *Grundy*, 3 Pet. 210, 215; *United States* v. *Howland*, 4 Wheat. 108.

[1] Although the forms of proceedings in the State courts have been adopted in the District court, yet the adoption of the State practice must not be understood as confounding the principles of law and equity, nor as authorizing legal and equitable claims to be blended together in one suit. The Constitution of the United States, in creating and defining the judicial power of the General Government, establishes this distinction between law and equity ; and a party who claims a legal title must proceed at law, and may undoubtedly proceed according to the forms of practice in such cases in the State courts. But if the claim is an equitable one, he must proceed according to rules which this court has prescribed [under the authority of the act of August 23, 1842], regulating proceedings in equity in the courts of the United States. *Bennett* v. *Butterworth*, 11 How. 669.

[2] In suits at common law, where the value in controversy shall exceed twenty dollars, the right of trial by jury shall be preserved,

LECTURE VII.
Right of trial by
jury at common
law.
no part of the system of equity jurisprudence, and therefore, in order to give proper effect to all of these provisions, the Federal courts have been compelled to keep separate and distinct cases at law and cases in equity.[1]

When a case
arises under the
Constitution.
Proceeding farther in the consideration of the language of this clause we first note that these cases are those " arising under this Constitution." That is to say, a case arises under the Constitution whenever some constitutional right is denied, some right which this instrument gives, whether it be a right to property, a right of liberty, a right to vote, or any other right which can be traced to this Constitution. If that right be infringed, denied, or imperilled, it can be brought into the courts of the United States by virtue of this provision.[2]

This is also true of the laws of the United States. These cases are also those "arising under . . . the laws of the United States." The Constitution itself is a very general instrument.

---

and no fact tried by a jury shall be otherwise re-examined in any court of the United States, than according to the rules of the common law. Amendment VII.

[1] The courts of the United States are required, both by the Constitution and the acts of Congress, to observe the distinction between legal and equitable rights, and to enforce the rules and principles of decision appropriate to each. *Fenn* v. *Holme*, 21 How. 481.

[2] It is only where the rights of persons or property are involved, and when such rights can be presented under some judicial form of proceedings, that courts of justice can interpose relief. This court can have no right to pronounce an abstract opinion upon the constitutionality of a State law. Such law must be brought into actual, or threatened operation upon rights properly falling under judicial cognizance, or a remedy is not to be had here. Dissenting opinion of Justice Thompson, in *Cherokee Nation* v. *Georgia*, 5 Pet. 1, 75.

The rights which it confers and the duties which

it imposes, are stated in very general language ; but these rights and duties, and the obligations growing out of them, have been put into full operation and defined and perfected by statutes, which we designate the laws of the United States.[1] Whenever, therefore, an individual has a claim or right under a statute of the United States, which he seeks to enforce, we see that this can be done by — and that the proper place to seek the power to accomplish it is in — some one of the different branches of the judicial department of the Government of the United States.[2]

This power extends also to all cases arising under "treaties made, or which shall be made under their authority," as to which some observations may properly be made. A treaty always means a compact or convention between two independent nations or governments. Independence, or at least some degree of it, is necessary

---

[1] The Constitution (Art. 1, sec. 8, par. 18) gives Congress the power " To make all laws which shall be necessary and proper for carrying into execution the foregoing powers, and all other powers vested by this Constitution in the Government of the United States, or in any department or officer thereof." One of these powers is the judicial, embracing civil and criminal cases alike.

The provision that it shall extend to " all cases " embraces civil actions and criminal prosecutions. Both are equally within that power. *Tennessee* v. *Davis*, 100 U. S. 257.

[2] The jurisdiction vested in the courts of the United States . . . shall be exclusive of the courts of the several States. Rev. Stat. § 711.

Congress gave to the Circuit and District Courts of the United States, during and immediately after the close of the rebellion, jurisdiction over many questions which had been previously left entirely within the control of the State courts.

in order that the treaty may exist between the parties who make it. From these principles the conclusion has been reached that so far as the treaty itself is a national obligation to be enforced by the action of the States who made it, either by war, by negotiation, by modification, or by appeals to the States, the courts have nothing to do with it. In that case, they must follow and abide by what the Government proper does upon that subject, or what, in the language of the Supreme Court of the United States, are called the political branches of the Government having charge of that relation.[1]

But a treaty may be the foundation of a private right, and then it becomes a subject of judicial action, as does any other private right.[2]

---

[1] "This court (in *Foster* v. *Neilson*, 2 Pet. 253, 307) did not deem the settlement of boundaries a judicial, but a political question — that it was not its duty to lead but to follow the action of the other departments of the Government; that when individual rights depended on national boundaries, 'the judiciary is not that department of the Government to which the assertion of its interests against foreign powers is confided, and its duty commonly is to decide upon individual rights according to those principles which the political department of the nation has established.'" These views are reiterated in *United States* v. *Arredondo*, 6 Pet. 699, 711.

But this right must be a legal one : the judicial power does not extend to all questions which may arise under the Constitution, laws, and treaties, because they are frequently political in their character, and must be decided by other departments of the Government. Chief Justice Marshall says: "The judiciary is not that department of the Government to which the assertion of its interests against foreign powers is confided; and its duty commonly is to decide upon individual rights, according to those principles which the political departments of the nation have established." *Foster* v. *Neilson*, 2 Pet. 253, 306.

[2] A treaty is the supreme law of the land. *Hauenstein* v. *Lynham*, 100 U. S. 483. Its operation cannot be interfered with or in any way limited by a State, and it overrides State laws in conflict with it. *Baker* v. *Portland*, 5 Sawyer, 566.

This subject has been well considered in the case of the *United States* v. *Rauscher*,[1] who was returned from Great Britain to this country in pursuance of a demand of the President, on the charge of murder. He was tried, and a verdict of guilty rendered by the jury upon a charge of inflicting cruel and unusual punishment upon one of the seamen of the vessel on which he was an officer. He denied the authority of the court to try him for this, or for any other offence, except that for which he had been surrendered in the extradition proceedings. The Supreme Court in response to questions certified to it by the judges of the Circuit Court, held that this contention was sound, and that the treaty would, in the event that he was either acquitted, or not tried for the offence for which he had been extradited, give him a right to be set at liberty and allow him a reasonable time to return to Great Britain. The court, referring to the *Head Money Cases*, quoted from its language in that case in reference to the character of a treaty as a law of the land, as follows : —

"A treaty is primarily a compact between independent nations. It depends for the enforcement of its provisions on the interest and the honor of the governments which are parties to it. If these fail, its infraction becomes the subject of international negotiations and reclamations, so far as the injured party chooses to

---

[1] 119 U. S. 407.

seek redress, which may in the end be enforced by actual war. It is obvious that with all this the judicial courts have nothing to do and can give no redress. But a treaty may also contain provisions which confer certain rights upon the citizens or subjects of one of the nations residing within the territorial limits of the other, which partake of the nature of municipal law, and which are capable of enforcement as between private parties in the courts of the country. An illustration of this character is found in treaties which regulate the mutual rights of citizens and subjects of the contracting nations, in regard to the rights of property by descent or inheritance, when the individuals concerned are aliens. The Constitution of the United States places such provisions as these in the same category as other laws of Congress, by its declaration that ' this Constitution and the laws made in pursuance thereof, and all treaties made or which shall be made under authority of the United States, shall be the supreme law of the land.' A treaty then, is a law of the land, as an act of Congress is, whenever its provisions prescribe a rule by which the rights of the private citizen or subject may be determined. And when such rights are of a nature to be enforced in a court of justice, that court resorts to the treaty for a rule of decision for the case before it, as it would to a statute."[1]

" The treaty of 1842 being therefore the

---

[1] *Head Money Cases,* 112 U. S. 580, 598. See also *Chew Heong* v. *United States,* 112 U. S. 536, 540, 565.

supreme law of the land, of which the courts LECTURE VII.
are bound to take judicial notice, and to enforce Cases arising under treaties.
in any appropriate proceeding the rights of
persons growing out of that treaty, we proceed
to inquire, in the first place, so far as pertinent
to the questions certified by the circuit judges,
into the true construction of the treaty." [1]

Passing on in the consideration of this section, we note that the judicial power not only
extends to cases arising under the Constitution
and laws of the United States, and treaties made
under its authority, but is directed to specific
classes of cases. The text here assumes another
form of expression. Heretofore it has been
dealing with the subject matter of the suit or
with the nature of the controversy. Now it
speaks of cases affecting classes of people. Let
us consider them in their order.

" The judicial power shall extend . . . to all Cases affecting ambassadors.
cases affecting ambassadors, other public min-
isters, and consuls." Every diplomatic representative, such as an ambassador, or a minister or a
consul at one of our various ports, has a right to
have any case affecting his rights tried in a
Federal court. This is true, no matter what
his grade or rank, and some of these diplomatic
gentlemen have very high sounding titles, such
as Minister Plenipotentiary and Envoy Extraordinary. The reason for this provision is easy to
be understood. These persons are the representatives of foreign governments, independent

---

[1] *United States* v. *Rauscher*, 119 U. S. 407, 419.

LECTURE VII.
Cases affecting
ambassadors.

nations, and should not, therefore, be subjected to the power of individual States who have no relation to those governments. Cases in which they are concerned can only be brought before the courts of the United States, who can look into the matters at issue and right them.

Admiralty and
maritime juris-
diction.

It shall also be extended "to all cases of admiralty and maritime jurisdiction." [1] That is a very peculiar thing to be in this Constitution. I suppose the reason it was put there was that it was considered to be in the nature of an international relation, coming immediately, as it does, in juxtaposition with the clause relating to ambassadors and other public ministers and consuls. Doubtless that is why it was taken out from State jurisdiction and placed within the power of the Federal judiciary; for, although admiralty cases do not involve any law or statute of the United States, nor the Constitution of the United States, nor any treaty, yet at the time the Constitution was framed, the admiralty jurisdiction was supposed to be limited, as it was in England, to traffic on the ocean, and the affairs of vessels, seamen, and navigators upon the tidal waters of the country. It was thus thought to be only properly cognizable by the courts of the Central Government.[2] In connec-

---

[1] In the Federalist, No. 80, it is said: "The most bigoted idolizers of State authority have not thus far shown a disposition to deny the National Judiciary the cognizance of maritime causes. These so generally depend on the laws of nations, and so commonly affect the rights of foreigners, that they fall within the considerations which are relative to the public peace."

[2] The exclusive cognizance of all cases of this character was

tion with this view of the subject it may be well
to note also, that this particular provision is an
interpolation of a clause regarding the matter
of jurisdiction among those which concern the
character of the parties.

At this point the word " cases " is dropped, as
well as the subject matter of jurisdiction, and

---

vested in the District Courts by this clause and the judicial act
of 1789. No attempt was made, however, to define the meaning of
the terms or to fix the limits of their jurisdiction. Very few cases
came to the Supreme Court involving these questions up to 1840,
but the principle was established that the true test of the jurisdiction of a court of admiralty was whether the vessel was engaged,
substantially, in maritime navigation, upon the tidal waters of the
country. *The Steamboat Orleans* v. *Phœbus*, 11 Pet. 175.

To give jurisdiction the cause of action must have arisen upon
waters affected by the tide. The District Court was held not to
have jurisdiction of a suit for wages earned on a voyage from Kentucky up the Missouri River and back. *The Thomas Jefferson*, 10
Wheat. 428. [1825].

In other cases following the jurisdiction of admiralty courts
was limited to tide waters, or where the influence of the tide was
at all felt. *The Planter*, 7 Pet. 324; *United States* v. *Coombs*,
12 Pet. 72.

In the case of a collision upon the Mississippi River, ninety
miles above New Orleans, but within the ebb and flow of the tide,
it was held that the expression in the Constitution was neither
limited to nor to be interpreted by, what were cases of admiralty
jurisdiction in England when the Constitution was adopted by the
States of the Union, and that in cases of tort or collision as far up
a river as the tide ebbs and flows, although it may be *infra corpus
comitatus*, courts of admiralty have jurisdiction. *Waring* v. *Clarke*,
5 How. 441. [1847]. See also *The Lexington*, 6 How. 344; *St.
John* v. *Paine*, 10 How. 557; *The New Jersey*, 10 How. 586.

By the act of February 26, 1845, Congress extended the
jurisdiction to the great lakes, 5 Stat. 726, and the tide-water
restriction was entirely abandoned by the Supreme Court in *The
Genesee Chief*, 12 How. 443, extending the jurisdiction to all public
navigable lakes and rivers where commerce is carried on between
different States or with a foreign nation. This doctrine was defined
and reaffirmed in *The Magnolia*, 20 How. 296; *The Eagle*, 8 Wall.
15; *The Montello*, 11 Wall. 411; *Miller* v. *Mayor of New York*,
109 U. S. 385.

the section proceeds to give jurisdiction by a description of the persons or parties who may come before the Federal courts. The judicial power shall extend "to controversies to which the United States shall be a party." Whenever the United States is a party in a suit the Federal courts may have jurisdiction; that is, courts acting under the Federal power. They are tribunals established under the authority of Congress, and in those courts alone can the United States be sued.[1] These courts take jurisdiction of suits in which the United States sues to recover property or taxes, of suits upon the bonds of defaulting officers, of prosecutions for claims against the United States, and many other cases in which the General Government sues in the forum of its own creation.

The judicial power is next extended "to controversies between two or more States."[2] There never has been a tribunal known in history,

---

[1] Except where Congress has provided that the United States cannot be sued. *United States* v. *Lee*, 106 U. S. 196.

[2] The effect of the want of this power is aptly illustrated in the language of the Federalist, No. 21, regarding the American Confederacy which then existed. "The next most palpable defect of the subsisting Confederation, is a total want of a SANCTION to its laws. The United States, as now composed, have no power to exact obedience, or punish disobedience to their resolutions, either by pecuniary mulcts, by a suspension or divestiture of privileges, or by any other constitutional means. There is no express delegation of authority to them to use force against delinquent members; and if such a right should be ascribed to the Federal head, as resulting from the nature of the compact between the States, it must be by inference and construction, in the face of that part of the second article, by which it is declared, 'that each State shall retain every power, jurisdiction, and right, not *expressly* delegated to the United States in Congress assembled.'"

anterior to the formation of this Constitution, LECTURE VII.
which had jurisdiction, in the full sense of that Controversies
between States.
word, of controversies between States.[1] The old
Amphictyonic Council among the Greeks might
possibly have been called a court or tribunal in
some sense, but certainly not in the broad way
in which the term is applied to the Supreme
Court of the United States. That council could

---

[1] In the Germanic Confederation there was a tribunal in some
respects resembling the Supreme Court of the United States. The
Chamber of Wetzlar, or Westphalia, possessed exclusive jurisdiction in deciding upon disputes between members of the Empire.
But it had no power to execute its decisions. The laws operated
not upon individuals, but upon States; and the sentence of the
supreme judicial tribunal had no higher effect. The consequence
was that it became necessary to resort to force, and to this end the
Empire was divided into circles, the entire military force of which
was at the disposal of the Emperor, to enable him to execute the
sentence of the court against a refractory member. Under the new
constitution of 1815 a different organization took place. If the
rights of one State are invaded by another State, the injured party
must choose one of three members of the diet, selected by the
defendant; or if the defendant neglected to select, the diet is bound
to name them. And the court of final resort in the State of the
member thus chosen decides the case. And if the party against
whom the judgment is pronounced does not obey, military force is
resorted to, to coerce submission. There does not appear to have
been any judicial tribunal, either under the old or new constitutions, for the purpose of settling disputes between the States and
the Confederacy. The diet, or national legislature, seems to have
possessed this power. The American system stands alone amid
the institutions of the world, and although it was a natural consequence of the adoption of the perfect form of confederation, yet as
this species of government is a work of the greatest refinement, and
the result of a very high state of civilization, the organization of
the national judiciary may be pronounced one of the greatest
achievements which political science has made. Grimke on Free
Institutions, p. 389, Cincinnati, 1848.

In the Federalist, No. 80, reference is made to the Imperial
Chamber of Maximilian, which is said to have been a court invested
with authority to decide finally all differences among the members
of the Germanic body.

meet and hear the complaints of the Greek States against each other, and in that forum they could complain of each other's acts. Upon such hearing the council could recommend what could be done, but it had no power to carry its determinations into effect. The Constitution of the United States, however, creates a court which can not only hear and determine all controversies between different States, of which it is given original jurisdiction, but can also bring them before it by process, as it can bring the humblest citizen, and declare its judgment, which it has usually been able to enforce.[1]

Controversies
between a State
and citizens of
another State.

It also extends to controversies "between a State and citizens of another State."[2] That is to say, while a State cannot sue one of its own citizens in the courts of the United States, it can sue those of other States. As this Constitution stood at the time it was adopted, a citizen of one State could sue another State in the Federal courts, but as soon as a case of that kind origi-

---

[1] That a person cannot sue his own State, except under some State law, is well settled. *Hans v. Louisiana*, 24 Fed. Rep. 55. [See 134 U. S. 1, for the action of the Supreme Court on this case.]

[2] Nor can that be accomplished by indirect means which cannot be done directly. The history of Article XI of the Amendments to the Constitutions, and the causes which led to its adoption, are reviewed in the case of *New Hampshire v. Louisiana*, 108 U. S. 76, and it was decided that unless the State prosecuted consents, that amendment prohibits the court from entertaining jurisdiction of a case in which one State seeks relief against another State on behalf of its citizens, in a matter in which the State prosecuted has no interest of its own; that one State cannot create a controversy with another State, within the meaning of that term as used in the judicial clauses of the Constitution, by assuming the prosecution of debts owing by the other State to its citizens.

nated in which a State found its dignity infringed and it was seen that a State could be brought into court by any one, a requisite number of States modified this provision by declaring that it should not apply to suits by citizens of one State against another State. The jurisdiction is now between States, which was discussed in a preceding paragraph, and between a State and citizens of another State when the State is plaintiff.[1]

We now come to controversies " between citizens of different States." Here is, as it has turned out, the largest source of the jurisdiction of the Federal courts. In the previous part of this section the right to sue in the Federal

LECTURE VII.
Controversies between a State and citizens of another State.

Between citizens of different States.

---

[1] The impression prevailed after the adoption of the Constitution in 1789 that a citizen of one State or an alien might sue a State. Hamilton refers to this, and denies it, in the Federalist, No. 81. Madison and Marshall both denied its existence in the course of the debates on the Constitution in Virginia. It was, however, maintained in *Chisholm* v. *Georgia*, 2 Dall. 419, in 1793. William Vassal, a British subject, soon after brought a suit in the Supreme Court to set aside a confiscation of his property in Massachusetts. Process was served on the governor of the State, John Hancock. The General Court was convened by him, and the authority questioned. It was argued that such suit was contrary to the principles of the Federal Government. It decided that the Federal Constitution should be amended in this respect, and in 1794 a senator from that State introduced in the Senate of the United States, and secured the adoption of the Eleventh Amendment by that body. It was declared in force January 8, 1798. The cases of Chisholm and Vassal were never prosecuted to judgment, and no attempt has been since made to so use the power of the court against a State at the suit of an individual.

The amendment is as follows: " The judicial power of the United States shall not be construed to extend to any suit in law or equity, commenced or prosecuted against one of the United States by citizens of another State, or by citizens or subjects of any foreign State." Constitution, Art. XI of Amendments.

courts was granted in any action arising under
the Constitution, laws, and treaties of the United
States, without regard to the citizenship or residence of the parties thereto ; but here it is the
character of the party which gives the right to
sue without reference to the nature of the matter at issue. A class of persons is here designated who can bring suits in the Federal courts,
no matter what may be the cause of action. It
may arise on a promissory note, out of an assault
and battery, or from any other matter which
can become the subject of a judicial investigation. A person residing in Maryland can sue
in the courts of the United States a person
residing in Virginia, and e converso, and so of
other States. If a person has the qualification
of citizenship in one State, and his adversary
has it in another State, the suit can be brought
in the Federal courts.

The reason for this, as has been frequently
said by commentators and by courts, was the
fear in the minds of the makers of the Constitution that the local prejudice likely to arise in
favor of a man sued in the courts of his own
State would result in unfair decisions against his
non-resident adversary. Suppose, for illustration, that one party who is living in Boston
brings a suit against a man residing in New
Orleans. It was supposed that the popularity
or the home influence, of the man who was thus
sued in New Orleans, and possibly some irrita-
tion or ill-feeling against citizens of another
State, might stand in the way of the just

determination of the claim of the man from Boston.

So, also, seeing that the Constitution had provided that the man so sued for an amount exceeding twenty dollars in value might demand a trial by a jury, and considering that the jury might be affected by this class of prejudices, it was thought wise that a tribunal that was supposed to be impartial should be provided, and one which did not owe its appointment or compensation to the State in which the case was tried. It was thought that a court owing its allegiance to, and receiving its commission from the United States, would be a safer tribunal than a court which was commissioned by a State, which could be influenced by a vote of a majority of its citizens, and might be swayed more or less in its decisions from the absolute principles of justice.[1] It was for these reasons that this provision was placed in the Constitution, and it has been and is to-day, in the ratio of four to one, the source of controversies, suits, and cases in the courts of the United States.

---

[1] One great object in the establishment of the courts of the United States and regulating their jurisdiction was, to have a tribunal in each State, presumed to be free from local influence; and to which all who were non-residents or aliens might resort for legal redress. *Gordon* v. *Longest*, 16 Pet. 97.

"In the argument the court has been admonished of the jealousy with which the States of the Union view the revising power intrusted by the Constitution and laws to this tribunal. To observations of this character the answer uniformly has been that the course of the judicial department is marked out by law. We must tread the direct and narrow path prescribed for us. As this court has never grasped at ungranted jurisdiction, so it never will, we trust, shrink from that which is conferred upon it." Chief Justice Marshall, in *Fisher* v. *Cockerell*, 5 Pet. 248.

Lecture VII.

Citizens of the same State claiming lands under grants of different States.

The next class of cases to which the judicial power extends is one that depends partly upon the citizenship of the party and partly upon the character of the particular issue. It relates to controversies " between citizens of the same State claiming lands under grants of different States." [1] Virginia, at one time, claimed a large part of what was known as the Northwestern Territory. Connecticut had a grant of land which is included in the State of Ohio, what is called the " Western Reserve," with probably a population of·a quarter of a million. It was supposed that where there were grants under the authority of different States there would be controversies. This provision was, therefore, introduced here for the purpose of giving the Federal courts jurisdiction of that class of cases. [2]

Between a State, or its citizens, and foreign states or citizens.

Finally, it is extended to controversies, " between a State, or the citizens thereof, and foreign states, citizens, or subjects." Every foreign state, or any of its citizens, is entitled to sue any of our citizens in the Federal courts, and if a citizen of this country can get service of process upon them, he has a right to sue them in the same tribunals. [3]

---

[1] These are the only instances in which the proposed Constitution directly contemplates the cognizance of disputes between the citizens of the same State. The Federalist, No. 80.

[2] See case of *Pawlet* v. *Clark*, 9 Cranch, 292, relating to grants by the States of New York and Vermont. If the controversy is founded upon the conflicting grants of different States, the judicial power of the courts of the United States extends to the case, whatever may have been the equitable title of the parties prior to the grant. See grants by Kentucky and Virginia, in *Colson* v. *Lewis*, 2 Wheat. 377.

[3] The courts of the United States have jurisdiction in a case

These are the characteristics of the parties who may bring suits in the various courts of the
United States, and these are the classes of cases,
as well as the nature of the controversies, which come within their jurisdiction. But before this could be exercised in regard to the largest part of them, an act of Congress was required to create the courts for that purpose.[1] Therefore it was that immediately after the organization of the Government, Congress did create courts, define their constitution, and regulate their administration. It is, however, a noteworthy fact that up to within a very few years a large body of this judicial power, which is within the con-

---

between citizens of the same State if the plaintiffs are only nominally plaintiffs for the use of an alien. *Browne* v. *Strode*, 5 Cranch, 303. It must appear from the record that the opposite party is a citizen. *Jackson* v. *Twentyman*, 2 Pet. 136. An Indian tribe or nation located within the United States is not a foreign state within the meaning of this clause. *Cherokee Nation* v. *Georgia*, 5 Pet. 1.

[1] The great act, commonly called the " Judiciary Act," and entitled " An Act to establish the Judicial Courts of the United States," passed September 24, 1789, 1 Stat. 73, c. 20, originated in the Senate. One member of the committee which reported it, Oliver Ellsworth, afterwards became a Chief Justice of the Supreme Court, and another member, William Paterson, an Associate Justice of the same court. Five of its members had also been deputies to the convention which framed the Constitution. It may be said that the authors of this act, as well as the Congress which adopted it, were adherents of the political party which held that it was indispensable to the peace and unity of the country that the authority of the Federal Government should be extended as far as it could be constitutionally. So it has been considered, and justly so, as an authoritative and contemporaneous exposition of the limits of the judicial power of the General Government. Chief Justice Marshall says, in *Cohens* v. *Virginia*, 6 Wheat. 264, " Congress seems to have intended to give its own construction to this part of the Constitution in the twenty-fifth section of the Judiciary Act, and we perceive no reason to depart from that construction."

LECTURE VII.
Between a State,
or its citizens, and
foreign states or
citizens.

trol of Congress under these provisions of the Constitution, was vested in no court at all, and consequently could not be exercised by a Federal court.[1]

Limitations imposed by Congress.

Limitations have also, from time to time, been fixed by Congressional action upon the classes of cases in regard to which jurisdiction has been vested in the courts of the United States. At the present time this limitation is a very large one. For instance, no suit can be brought in those courts where the amount in controversy does not exceed two thousand dollars in value, with the exception of patent, and revenue or admiralty cases, and criminal prosecutions. In regard to those matters suits may be brought without reference to value, but in all other actions brought by a citizen of this country the amount in controversy must exceed this specified limit.[2]

The Act of March 3, 1875.

It was not until March 3, 1875, that Congress finally passed a law which authorized all cases arising under the Constitution, or laws of the United States, and treaties made under their authority, to be brought in the Federal courts,

---

[1] Congress may legislate authorizing the removal from State to Federal courts of criminal as well as civil cases. This has been partially done. Act of February 4, 1815, 3 Stat. 198, c. 31, § 8; Act of March 2, 1833, 4 Stat. 632, c. 57; March 3, 1863, 12 Stat. 755, c. 81, § 5; July 13, 1866, 14 Stat. 171, c. 184, § 67. This subject was considered at length in *Tennessee* v. *Davis*, 100 U. S. 257.

[2] It has often been decided that the sum in controversy in a suit is the damages claimed in the declaration; whether it be an original suit in the Circuit Court of the United States, or brought there by petition from a State court. *Gordon* v. *Longest*, 16 Pet. 97.

thus giving them concurrent jurisdiction with the State courts.[1] Previous to that date, if a party had a right under the Constitution, the laws, or treaties, but had not the requisite citizenship, he had to first go before a State court. After he had carried his case through all the State tribunals, up to the highest, then the question which concerned the Federal jurisdiction might, if it was decided against him, be brought by a writ of error up to the Supreme Court of the United States. But that class of cases may now, by the act of 1875, be brought originally in the Circuit Courts of the United States.

LECTURE VII.
The Act of March 3, 1875.

These comments upon the second section of the third article of the Constitution have been made before taking up the first section, because it defines or marks out the judicial power of the United States by providing to what cases it may extend. It is, therefore, of primary importance to the student of the legal principles upon which our Government is founded.

The first section provides, in its opening clause, that this judicial power of the United States, which we have been discussing, " shall be vested in one Supreme Court,[2] and in such inferior

---

[1] An act to determine the jurisdiction of Circuit Courts of the United States, and to regulate the removal of causes from State courts, and for other purposes. Approved March 3, 1875. 18 Stat. 470.

[2] The origin of this provision is described by Hamilton, in the Federalist, No. 81. He says that contrary to the general supposition of many persons who represented it to be novel and unprecedented, it is but a copy of the constitutions of New Hampshire,

LECTURE VII.
The Act of March
3, 1875.
The Supreme
Court.

courts as the Congress may, from time to time, ordain and establish."

There can, therefore, be but one such court, but one which is supreme.[1] The establishment of that great tribunal is positively required by this provision, while, in that which follows, the establishment of inferior courts is left to the discretion of Congress.

The Supreme Court, once in existence, cannot be abolished, because its foundation is not in an act of the legislative department of the Government, but in the Constitution of the United States.[2] It is true, an act of Congress was

---

Massachusetts, Pennsylvania, Delaware, Maryland, Virginia, North Carolina, South Carolina, and Georgia, and he applauds the wisdom of committing the judicial power, not to a part of the Legislature, but to distinct and independent bodies of men.

[1] The court of errors, or of cassation, in France, is the highest judicial tribunal in the kingdom. The principle on which, until recently, it proceeded, was this: If the judgment of an inferior court was reversed, the case was sent back to be tried again. If the court below persisted in its error, and the case was again appealed, and the court above reaffirmed the judgment before pronounced, it was sent back a second time. But if the inferior court still persevered in its error, the decree of the court of cassation no longer afforded the governing rule. The Legislature was then appealed to to settle the law by a declaratory act. But the absurdity of the scheme, the temptation which it held out to the legal tribunals to resist the judgment of the highest court, and to unsettle all the principles of law, produced so much mischief, that in 1837 the English and American procedure was adopted ; and the determination of the court of cassation is now final, and absolutely binding upon all other tribunals. Grimke on Nature and Tendency of Free Institutions, p. 390 (Cincinnati, 1848).

[2] Chief Justice Taney, in the last judicial paper which he prepared, wrote as follows: "The Supreme Court does not owe its existence or its powers to the legislative department of the Government. It is created by the Constitution, and represents one of the great divisions of power in the Government of the United States, to each of which the Constitution has assigned its appro-

necessary to define the number of judges which
should constitute that court, as well as to limit
their jurisdiction and provide for their compensation;[1] but that once done, the existence of
the court is an established fact. It cannot be
abolished, nor its judges legislated out of existence,[2] although it has been forcibly urged, and

---

priate duties and powers, and made each independent of the other
in performing its appropriate functions. The power conferred on
this court is exclusively judicial, and it cannot be required or
authorized to exercise any other. . . . The existence of this court
is therefore as essential to the organization of the Government
established by the Constitution as the election of a President or
members of Congress. It is the tribunal which is ultimately to
decide all judicial questions confided to the Government of the
United States. No appeal is given from its decisions, nor any
power given to the legislative or executive departments to interfere
with its judgments or process of execution." *Gordon* v. *United
States*, 117 U. S. (Appendix), 699, 700.

[1] The act approved April 29, 1802, 2 Stat. 156, made the Supreme
Court to consist of a Chief Justice and six Associates, which number was increased to eight by an act approved March 3, 1837, 5 Stat.
176, c. 34. Rev. Stat. sec. 673.

[2] Animadverting upon the great power of the Supreme Court,
Mr. Van Buren said in the Senate in 1826 : " It has been justly
observed that there exists not upon this earth, and there never did
exist, a judicial tribunal clothed with powers so various and so
important as the Supreme Court. . . . Not only are the acts of
the national Legislature subject to its review, but it stands as the
umpire between the conflicting powers of the General and State
governments. That wide field of debatable ground between those
rival powers is claimed to be subject to the exclusive and absolute
dominion of the Supreme Court. . . . In virtue of this power, we
have seen it holding for naught the statutes of powerful States,
which had received the deliberate sanction, not only of their Legislatures, but their highest judicatories, composed of men venerable
in years, of unsullied purity, and unrivalled talents — statutes
on the faith of which immense estates had been invested, and the
inheritance of the widow and the orphan were suspended. You
have seen such statutes abrogated by the decision of this court,
and those who had confided in the wisdom and power of the State
authorities plunged in irremediable ruin, — decisions final in

probably with truth, that all the other courts can, by legislative act, be abolished, and their powers conferred on other courts, or subdivided in different modes.

Judges hold office
during good be-
havior.
The concluding clause of the first section fixes still more clearly the status of these judicial officers. "The judges, both of the Supreme and inferior courts, shall hold their offices during good behavior, and shall, at stated times, receive for their services a compensation, which shall not be diminished during their continuance in office.[1]

The judges of the Supreme Court, as we have just seen, cannot be legislated out of office, whatever might be the result as to the other judges of the United States if the inferior courts

---

their effect and ruinous in their consequences. I speak of the power of the court, not of the correctness or incorrectness of its decisions. With that we have nothing to do.

But this is not all. It not only sits in final judgment upon our acts, as the highest legislative body known to the country — it not only claims to be the final arbiter between the Federal and State governments, but it exercises the same great power between the respective *States* forming the great confederacy and their own *citizens*. . . . Add to the immense powers of which I have spoken [the regulation of commerce and the power to determine the validity of all legislative acts] those of expounding treaties, . . . of deciding controversies between the States and the citizens of the different States ; and the justice of the remark will not be questioned, that there is no known judicial power so transcendently omnipotent as that of the Supreme Court of the United States.'' 4 Elliot's Debates, 485.

[1] Chief Justice Taney wrote a letter dated February 15, 1863, in which the position was taken that the act of Congress which imposed a tax of three per cent, so far as it applied to the judges of the Supreme Court, was an unconstitutional diminution of their salaries ; and that they could not be diminished by taxation or otherwise. This letter was ordered by the court on the 10th of March, 1863, to be recorded in its minutes. Tyler's Life of Taney, 432.

were abolished. None of these officers shall be removed during good behavior, nor when the Legislature has once fixed their compensation, can it be diminished during the term of the judge then in office.[1]

There is an obvious reason for that. As has been before remarked, the judicial branch of the Government is the weakest of all.[2] It has

---

[1] Marshall said in the Virginia Convention of 1829 : "The judicial department comes home in its effects to every man's fireside ; it passes on his property, his reputation, his life, his all. Is it not to the last degree important that he should be rendered perfectly and completely independent, with nothing to control him but God and his conscience ? I have always thought, from my earliest youth till now, that the greatest scourge an angry heaven ever inflicted upon an ungrateful and a sinning people was an ignorant, a corrupt, or a dependent judiciary."

"In the general course of human nature, a power over a man's subsistence amounts to a power over his will." The Federalist, No. 79.

[2] The author of the Federalist, No. 78, quotes this sentiment in the strong language of Montesquieu: "Of the three powers [the legislative, executive, and judicial], the judiciary is next to nothing." Spirit of Laws, vol. 1, p. 186. He proceeds to say that the judiciary has no influence over either the sword or purse ; no direction either of the strength or of the wealth of society, and can take no active resolution whatever ; and that it is incontestably the weakest of the three departments of power ; that it can never attack with success either of the other two, and that all possible care is requisite to enable it to defend itself against their attacks.

"While by the Constitution the judicial department is recognized as one of the three great branches among which all the powers and functions of the Government are distributed, it is inherently the weakest of them all. Dependent as its courts are for the enforcement of their judgments upon officers appointed by the Executive and removable at his pleasure, with no patronage and no control of the purse or the sword, their power and influence rest solely upon the public sense of the necessity of the existence of a tribunal to which all may appeal for the assertion and the protection of rights guaranteed by the Constitution, and by the laws of the land, and on the confidence reposed in the soundness of their decisions and the purity of their motives." United States v. Lee, 106 U. S. 196, 223.

neither the purse nor the sword. It is dependent upon annual appropriations for the bread upon which its judges live. The courts are dependent upon the President to furnish marshals to execute their decrees. If, then, they are to administer the Constitution according to its true spirit, as the protectors and guardians of the weak against the strong, and to uphold the righteous cause against the encroachments of injustice, they must be shielded by guarantees of the needful independence in order that they may act impartially.[1] The makers of this wonderful instrument which we are considering, were perfectly aware of the waves of passion which frequently run through the legislative and executive branches of the Government. They knew that these judicial bodies would be called upon occasionally to point out what the Constitution means; that it might even become necessary to declare that certain enactments of Congress were void and of no effect, because they were

---

[1] Mr. Justice Johnson remarked, in the case of *Martin v. Hunter's Lessee*, 1 Wheat. 304, 381, "God forbid that the judicial power in these States should ever, for a moment, even in its humblest departments, feel a doubt of its own independence."

And Hamilton says in the Federalist, No. 78, "The complete independence of the courts of justice is peculiarly essential in a limited constitution."

[2] "This principle, which has been the subject of so much deserved eulogy, was derived from the English constitution. The English judges anciently held their seats at the pleasure of the king, and so does the lord chancellor to this day. It is easy to perceive what a dangerous influence this must have given to the king in the administration of justice, in cases where the claims or pretensions of the crown were brought to bear upon the rights of a private individual. . . . The Act of Settlement of 12 and 13 Wm. III. c. 2, established the commissions of the judges *quamdiu se bene gesse-*

unconstitutional,[2] and that they might thus pro-
voke virulent hostility and popular prejudice.
So they said that their salaries should not be
diminished, because they were not in accord
with the legislative or executive departments
of the Government, or in sympathy with the
prevalent currents of popular feeling in the community. And they went further and said also
that these judges should not be turned out of
office, but should remain as long as they lived,
provided they behaved themselves.[1]

I am not going to discuss now the question
of how well they have behaved. Their opinions
and actions have become a part of the public
history of this great land. If they are guilty
of misconduct the same instrument which pro-

---

rint. The excellence of this provision has recommended the adoption of it by other nations of Europe." 1 Kent Com. 292, 293.

The Americans have acknowledged the right of judges to found
their decisions on the Constitution, rather than on the laws. In
other words, they have left them at liberty not to apply such laws
as may appear to them to be unconstitutional. I am aware that a
similar right has been claimed, but claimed in vain, by courts of
justice in other countries; but in America it is recognized by all
the authorities. De Tocqueville, vol. 1, p. 80, (ed. 1838, N. Y.).

"There is no position which depends on clearer principles, than
that every act of a delegated authority, contrary to the tenor of the
commission under which it is exercised, is void. No legislative act,
therefore, contrary to the Constitution, can be valid." The Federalist, No. 78.

[1] A most ancient precedent in favor of the establishment of
an independent judiciary is the statute of Alfonso V of Aragon, in
1442, providing they should continue in office during life, removable
only on sufficient cause by the king and Cortes united. Prescott's
History of Ferdinand and Isabella, vol. 1, p. 108. Introduction,
sec. 2, p. 74 (5th ed. London, 1849).

And it is the best expedient which can be devised in any government to secure the steady, upright, and impartial administration
of the laws. The Federalist, No. 78.

LECTURE VII.
Judges hold office
during good be-
havior.
tects them in the proper administration of their
duties, provides the means by which the personal responsibility for their misbehavior may be
brought home to them. The only mode for
determining that is by impeachment. If found
guilty they may be removed from office, and
thenceforth disqualified to hold or enjoy any
office of honor, trust, or profit under the United
States. One judge of the Supreme Court of the
United States went through that process, but he
came out unhurt.[1]

We have thus far only considered the first
paragraph of the second section. We come now
to the second paragraph, which provides that
" in all cases affecting ambassadors, other public
ministers, and consuls, and those in which a
State shall be a party, the Supreme Court shall
have original jurisdiction." [2]

That is to say, there are some classes of cases
where a litigant need not go through the forms
of the lower courts; it is not necessary that his
claim or right be passed upon by the District or
Circuit Courts, or any other tribunal; but if he

---

[1] Samuel Chase, appointed by President Washington an Associate Justice of the Supreme Court in 1796, was impeached in 1804,
at the instigation of John Randolph, for various alleged arbitrary,
oppressive, and unjust acts and conduct on the bench. [Trial,
vol. 1, pp. 25–103.] He was arraigned in 1805, but was acquitted
after a long trial. He died June 19, 1811. See Lanman's Biog.
Annals ; Trial of Judge Chase ; Annals of 8th Congress, 2d Session,
pp. 81–676.

[2] The Supreme Court has original jurisdiction only in the two
classes of cases mentioned in this clause. The appellate jurisdiction extends to all other cases within the judicial power of the
United States. See cases reviewed in *Ex parte Yerger*, 8 Wall.
85, 95.

be an ambassador, a public minister, or consul, Lecture VII.
or if a State be a party (provided it be in the Original jurisdiction of the
capacity of plaintiff, unless sued by another Supreme Court.
State), then the action may be brought at once
in the Supreme Court of the United States in
its original jurisdiction. Of course these classes
of persons are not very large, nor will the cases
in which a State is a party ever be very great,
so that the number of suits coming within the
original jurisdiction of that court has always
been and will always continue to be very small.
It never amounts to more than eight or ten
cases upon the docket of any one term.

The word "original" does not appear elsewhere in the Constitution, and is used in this
clause in contradistinction to what is termed its
"appellate" jurisdiction. Under the latter head
comes the great mass of cases to which the power
of the Federal Government extends. The concluding clause of the paragraph is as follows:
"In all the other cases before mentioned, the
Supreme Court shall have appellate jurisdiction,
both as to law and fact, with such exceptions,
and under such regulations, as the Congress
shall make."

The Congress, therefore, can control very Its appellate
jurisdiction.
largely the appellate jurisdiction of the United
States Supreme Court. It has done so, by passing laws at various times regulating that jurisdiction.[1] One of its earliest enactments upon

---

[1] It is essential to the jurisdiction of the Supreme Court of the
United States over the judgment or decree of a State court, that it
shall appear that one of the questions mentioned in the statute

the subject was, that no ordinary suit between individuals could come to the Supreme Court for revision unless the amount involved was over two thousand dollars. It is now five thousand dollars, and it has been urged that this should be enlarged to ten or twenty thousand dollars, either by the creation of some intermediate appellate tribunal, or otherwise. This is proposed in order that the Supreme Court may be relieved from the consideration of a great number of less important matters which are brought to its attention, and so that only cases involving great amounts, as well as certain other cases where the Constitution of the United States is involved, or where there is a conflict between State and Federal authority, shall go up to that court under the head of its appellate jurisdiction.[1]

The third paragraph of the second section provides that "the trial of all crimes, except in cases of impeachment, shall be by jury," and concludes by directing where such trial shall be held. This subject will be more appropriately treated in some observations which will be made concerning the system of trial by jury. The

---

must have been raised and presented to the State court; that it must have been decided by the State court against the right claimed or asserted by the plaintiff in error, under the Constitution, treaties, laws, or authority of the United States, or that such a decision was necessary to the judgment or decree rendered in the case. *Murdock* v. *City of Memphis*, 20 Wall. 590.

[1] The jurisdiction does not depend upon the amount of any contingent loss or damage which one of the parties may sustain by the decision against him, but by the amount in dispute between them. *Ross* v. *Prentiss*. 3 How. 771.

cases in which impeachment is the proper method of procedure is also separately considered under its appropriate head.

The third and last section of Article III is devoted to defining what is treason, and pointing out certain restrictions upon the power of the courts to convict of that offence. Congress is given the power to declare what punishment shall be meted out to the offender, "but no attainder of treason shall work corruption of blood, or forfeiture, except during the life of the person attainted." This subject will also be more appropriately considered in connection with others of the same general character.

It will thus be seen that the Constitution of the United States has created a judicial department of this Government as one of its three great branches, to which it has exclusively delegated all judicial power,[1] with the exception of the trial of impeachments. It prescribes with wonderful clearness the classes and kinds of suits which may be brought before it; it defines the persons who are privileged to sue, either in its highest forum or in its lower grades, and marks out the method in which trials are to be had.

To this department is confided the judicial power of the Government.[2] It is perhaps true

---

[1] In cases arising during the reconstruction period, the extent and essential character of the judicial power, and its relation to the legislative and executive functions of the Government, were discussed at length. *Georgia* v. *Stanton*, 6 Wall. 50 ; *United States* v. *Lee*, 106 U. S. 196.

[2] The judicial power of the United States, considered with ref-

LECTURE VII.
The courts are
the judicial de-
partment of the
Government.
Definition of "ju-
dicial power."
that the lines which separate the legislative and
the judicial power are sometimes not very clearly
defined, but they are becoming more and more
so.   That is a judicial power which, in a controversy, decides the right to property between
citizens or proper parties.   Such a determination is not a legislative power.   If a legislature,
or at least such a body acting within the dominion of the Government of the United States,
should undertake to declare that certain property which belonged to A should become the
property of B, it would be an invasion of the
judicial function, and therefore wholly inopera-
tive and void.[1]   No court would hesitate to declare that such a determination was within the
province of the courts alone; that the legislature
could not effect it, because of this separation of
the judicial and legislative powers which is made
by the Constitution.[2]

---

erence to its adaptation to the purposes of its creation, is one of
the most admirable and felicitous structures that human governments have exhibited.   Curtis' Constitution.

[1] There is nothing in the Constitution of the United States
which forbids the legislature of a State to exercise judicial functions.   *Satterlee* v. *Matthewson*, 2 Pet. 413.   A legislature cannot,
however, declare what the law was, but what it shall be. — *Ogden*
v. *Blackledge*, 2 Cranch, 272.

A resolution by the legislature of Tennessee, that a criminal
should be discharged by a court, was held to be an unwarranted
assumption of power on the part of the legislature, and void.
State v. *Fleming*, 7 Humphreys, 152.

The legislature cannot grant a new trial, or direct the court to
order it.   *De Chastellux* v. *Fairchild*, 15 Penn. St. 18.

[2] The power vested in the American courts of justice of pronouncing a statute to be unconstitutional, forms one of the most
powerful barriers which has ever been devised against the tyranny
of political assemblies.   De Tocqueville, Dem. in America, vol. 1,
p. 83 (ed. N. Y.) 1838.

It is true that the Executive may, under certain circumstances, invade the personal rights of
the individual, as regards his liberty. It has
been done in cases of emergency; it may be
done again. The privilege of the writ of *habeas
corpus* may be suspended, when, in cases of
rebellion or invasion, the public safety may require it. The President, or the executive officers,
may order a man into imprisonment, provided
the necessity of the case warrants such action.
But in all these cases they are bound to be careful to exercise their power within the law.[1]

The highest judicial power in England is subordinate to the legislative power, and bound to obey any law that Parliament may
pass, although it may, in the opinion of the court, be in conflict
with the principles of Magna Charta or the Petition of Rights.
Taney, C. J., in *Gordon* v. *United States*, 117 U. S. 699.

But in the United States, if a legislative act oppugns a constitutional principle, the former must give way, and be rejected on the
score of repugnance. In such case it will be the duty of the court
to adhere to the Constitution, and to declare the act null and void.
The Constitution is the basis of legislative authority ; it lies at the
foundation of all law, and is a rule and commission by which both
legislators and judges are to proceed. *Vanhorn's Lessees* v. *Dorrance*, 2 Dall. 304.

[1] The provisions in the constitutions and laws of the various
States by which the right to the writ of *habeas corpus* has been
secured to the people, incorporated the substance of the famous act
of 31 Car. II, c. 2, which has frequently been termed the second
Magna Charta of Great Britain. The right to suspend this writ in
the United States is expressly confined to cases of rebellion or invasion, where the public safety may require it. Mr. Jefferson was
opposed to the suspension in any case whatever of the " eternal
and unremitting force of the *habeas corpus* laws."

This subject was earnestly debated during the late civil war, but
very few cases were ever brought to the attention of the courts.
Perhaps the most important was *Ex parte Merryman*, Taney's,
C. Ct., Decisions, 246. Merryman was arrested May 26, 1861, in
the State of Maryland by a military force acting under the orders
of General Cadwallader and confined in Fort McHenry. Chief
Justice Taney, sitting at chambers, issued a writ of *habeas corpus*,

LECTURE VII.
Habeas corpus.

Whenever they act arbitrarily, and thus infringe the rights of any man by creating a law for themselves, in violation of the restrictions which both the Constitution and the laws have thrown around private rights, they invade the judicial functions and powers of the United States, and the courts will set that man at liberty, if their mandates are observed.[1]

---

but the officer to whom it was directed refused to produce the petitioner on the ground that he had been arrested for treason, and that the President of the United States had suspended the writ for the public safety. Chief Justice Taney simply filed his opinion, holding the petitioner entitled to be set at liberty, on the ground that Congress was the only power that could authorize a suspension of the privilege of the writ, and issued an attachment which the officers in charge of the fort would not permit to be served.

It was with the tacit consent or permission of Congress that the power was exercised during the rebellion by the President to suspend the action of this writ. March 3, 1863, Congress, however, determined to definitely regulate the matter, and passed an act which, among other things, gave the President the right, during the existing rebellion, to suspend the writ, whenever in his judgment the public safety might require it. 12 Stat. 755.

[1] The constitutional provision that no person shall be deprived of life, liberty or property without due process of law, nor private property be taken for public use without just compensation, relates to those rights whose protection is peculiarly within the province of the judicial branch of the Government. See examination of cases, showing that the courts extend protection when the rights of property are unlawfully invaded by public officers. *United States* v. *Lee*, 106 U. S. 196.

NOTES UPON LECTURE VII.

FOLLOWING the example set by Mr. Justice Miller in this lecture, I will first consider some general subjects, applicable alike to all cases arising under any grant of judicial power, and then consider each grant separately, so far as may be advisable after the full treatment of these subjects in the lecture.

1. *Courts are created for Judicial Purposes only.*

The purpose of the framers of the Constitu-tion to divide the powers of the Government into three branches, executive, legislative, and judicial, might have been frustrated, so far as the judiciary were concerned, but for its power to protect itself by pronouncing any law impos-ing other duties upon it, to be an infringement of its constitutional rights.

As early as 1792 Congress made such an attempt. The Judiciary Act of 1789 had gone into effect, the districts and circuits had been created, the judges had been appointed, and the new courts found themselves with little to do. On the 23d of March, 1792, Congress enacted a law " to provide for the settlement of the claims of widows and orphans barred by the limitations

Attempts to im-pose non-judicial duties upon the courts.

LECTURE VII.
Attempts to im-
pose non-judicial
duties upon the
courts.

heretofore established, and to regulate the claims to invalid pensions." [1]

This act imposed upon courts of the United States the duty of hearing applications for pensions, and of deciding whether the applicant should be put upon the list. It made a Pension Bureau of a court that was practically without judicial employment.

The Circuit Court for the District of New York, consisting of Chief Justice Jay, Mr. Justice Cushing, and Judge Duane, the District Judge, on the 5th of the following April, after consideration, unanimously held : —

"That, by the Constitution of the United States, the Government thereof is divided into three distinct and independent branches, and that it is the duty of each to abstain from, and to oppose, encroachments on the other; that neither the legislative nor the executive branches can constitutionally assign to the judicial any duties but such as are properly judicial, and to be performed in a judicial manner; and that the duties assigned to this circuit, by this act, are not of that description, and that the act itself does not appear to contemplate them as such, inasmuch as it subjects the decisions of these courts, made pursuant to those duties, first to the consideration and suspension of the Secretary at War, and then to the revision of the Legislature; whereas, by the Constitution neither the Secretary at War, nor any other

---

[1] 1 Stat. 243, c. 11.

executive officer, nor even the Legislature, are
authorized to sit as a court of errors on the judicial acts or opinions of this court." They held, however, that they could proceed as commissioners to perform these duties.

In the District of Pennsylvania, the Circuit Court, consisting of Justices Wilson and Blair of the Supreme Court, and Judge Peters of the District Court, on the 18th April, 1792, addressed a letter to the President, declining to proceed : "1st, because the business directed by this act is not of a judicial nature." "2d, because, if upon that business the court had proceeded, its *judgments* (for its *opinions* are its judgments) might, under the same act be revised and controlled by the Legislature, and by an officer in the executive department."

Mr. Justice Iredell and Judge Sitgreaves, District Judge of North Carolina, sitting in Circuit Court, addressed a letter from that circuit to the President on the 8th of June, 1792, setting forth substantially the same thing.[1]

On the 17th of February, 1794, the question came before the Supreme Court in a case which was not reported at the time, but which was made the subject of a note, subsequently prepared by Mr. Chief Justice Taney, and inserted at the end of *United States* v. *Ferreira*[2] by his direction.[3]

This case was heard in circuit at New Haven, on May 3, 1792, before Chief Justice Jay, Mr.

---

[1] *Hayburn's Case*, 2 Dall. 408 ; 409, note.
[2] 13 How. 40.
[3] *United States* v. *Yale Todd*, 13 How. 52, note.

LECTURE VII.
Attempts to im-
pose non-judicial
duties upon the
courts.
Justice Cushing, and Judge Law, the District Judge. They adhered to the decision of the Circuit Court of New York, except that, on reflection, they did not think they could act out of court as commissioners.

Chief Justice Taney, in his note, sums up the result of all the opinions as follows : —

"1. That the power proposed to be conferred on the Circuit Courts of the United States, by the act of 1792, was not judicial power within the meaning of the Constitution, and was, therefore, unconstitutional, and could not lawfully be exercised by the courts:

"2. That as the act of Congress intended to confer the power on the courts as a judicial function, it could not be construed as an authority to the judges composing the court to exercise the power out of court as commissioners:

"3. That money paid under a certificate from persons, not authorized by law to give it, might be recovered back by the United States."

He further adds: "In the early days of the Government, the right of Congress to give original jurisdiction to the Supreme Court, in cases not enumerated in the Constitution, was maintained by many jurists, and seems to have been entertained by the learned judges who decided *Todd's Case*. But discussion and more mature examination have settled the question otherwise ; and it has long been the established doctrine; and we believe now assented to by all who have examined the subject, that the original jurisdiction of this court is confined to the cases speci-

fied in the Constitution, and that Congress can-LECTURE VII.
Attempts to im-
pose non-judicial
duties upon the
courts.
not enlarge it. In all other cases its power
must be appellate."

The same questions were afterwards discussed
in *Gordon* v. *United States*,[1] on an appeal from
the Court of Claims; and in *United States* v.
Jones,[2] explanatory of that case. The cases
settle the principle that courts created by law
to exercise the judicial power conferred by the
Constitution of the United States are purely
judicial bodies.

The converse of this proposition does not hold
good as to legislative bodies, existing under the
laws of the United States. At October Term,
1857, it was held by a majority of the Supreme
Court that a territorial statute of Oregon, dissolving the bonds of matrimony between a husband and his wife, (the husband being a resident
of Oregon, the wife and children residents in
Ohio where they had been left by the husband
under promise that he would return or send for
them, and the statute being enacted on the
husband's application, without knowledge of the
wife,) was an exercise of the legislative power of
the territory on a rightful subject of legislation,
according to the prevailing judicial opinion of
the country, and the understanding of the legal
profession at the time when the act of Congress establishing the territorial government was
enacted (August 15, 1848).[3]

---

[1] 2 Wall. 561 ; 117 U. S. 697.
[2] 119 U. S. 477.
[3] *Maynard* v. *Hill*, 125 U. S. 190.

LECTURE VII.
Attempts to im-
pose non-judicial
duties upon the
courts.

So extreme a case as this, where manifest in-justice was done under the form of law, shows that legislatures ought not to exercise judicial powers; or, at least, if they do exercise them, should be required to cite in all interested parties before they do it.

2. *How far the Laws of the Place of Trial prevail.*

The courts of the United States are neces-sarily held within the domains of forty-four independent States; to say nothing of the Ter-ritories and the District of Columbia. The subjects of controversy which they have to adjudicate upon generally grow out of as many different systems of law, and are tried in locali-ties having as many different systems of practice.

On this subject the Revised Statutes of the United States have made some provisions which are printed in the margin.[1]

---

[1] "SEC. 722. The jurisdiction in civil and criminal matters, con-ferred on the District and Circuit Courts by the provisions of this title, and of title "Civil Rights," and of title "Crimes," for the protection of all persons in the United States in their civil rights, and for their vindication, shall be exercised and enforced in con-formity with the laws of the United States, so far as such laws are suitable to carry the same into effect; but in all cases where they are not adapted to the object, or are deficient in the provisions necessary to furnish suitable remedies and punish offences against law, the common law, as modified and changed by the constitution and statutes of the State wherein the court having jurisdiction of such civil or criminal cause is held, so far as the same is not incon-sistent with the Constitution and laws of the United States, shall be extended to and govern the said courts in the trial and disposi-tion of the cause, and, if it is of a criminal nature, in the infliction of punishment on the party found guilty."

"SEC. 914. The practice, pleadings, and forms and modes of pro-

The adoption of State systems of remedy LECTURE VII.
stops, however, when they conflict with the Local law : when
Constitution ; as, for instance, the blending of prevailing.
remedies at law and in equity, so as to deprive
a litigant of 'his constitutional right to a trial
by jury, where his remedy is a remedy at common law. This question has often arisen. In a
late case[1] from Mississippi, the opinion of the
court was delivered by Mr. Justice Field. He said :

"The general proposition, as to the enforcement in the Federal courts of new equitable
rights created by the States, is undoubtedly correct, subject, however, to this qualification, that
such enforcement does not impair any right conferred, or conflict with any inhibition imposed,
by the Constitution or laws of the United States.
Neither such right nor such inhibition can be in
any way impaired, however fully the new equitable right may be enjoyed or enforced in the
States by whose legislation it is created. The
Constitution, in its Seventh Amendment, declares that "in suits at common law, where the
value in controversy shall exceed twenty dollars,
the right of trial by jury shall be preserved."
In the Federal courts this right cannot be dispensed with, except by the assent of the parties entitled to it, nor can it be impaired by

---

ceeding in civil causes, other than equity and admiralty causes, in
the Circuit and District courts, shall conform, as near as may be, to
the practice, pleadings, and forms and modes of proceeding existing
at the time in like causes in the courts of record of the State within
which such Circuit or District courts are held, any rule of court to
the contrary notwithstanding."

[1] *Scott* v. *Neely*, 140 U. S. 106.

any blending with a claim, properly cognizable at law, of a demand for equitable relief in aid of the legal action or during its pendency. Such aid in the Federal courts must be sought in separate proceedings, to the end that the right to a trial by a jury in the legal action may be preserved intact."

"The Code of Mississippi gives to a simple contract creditor a right to seek in equity, in advance of any judgment or legal proceedings upon his contract, the removal of obstacles to the recovery of his claim caused by fraudulent conveyances of property. There the whole suit, involving the determination of the validity of the contract, and the amount due thereon, is treated as one in equity, to be heard and disposed of without a trial by jury. It is not for us to express any opinion of the wisdom of this law, or whether or not in its operation it is more advantageous in the interests of justice than an entire separation of proceedings at law from those for equitable relief. It is sufficient that under the statute of the United States such separation is required in the Federal courts, and by the Constitution, in cases at common law, a right to a trial by jury is secured to the defendant."

As to the more essential matter, the law which is to determine the rights of the parties to the controversy, the rule in this respect is thus stated by Mr. Justice Bradley in a carefully considered opinion : [1]

---

[1] *Burgess* v. *Seligman*, 107 U. S. 20, 33, 34.

" The existence of two co-ordinate jurisdictions LECTURE VII.
in the same Territory is peculiar, and the results $\begin{smallmatrix}\text{Local law: how}\\\text{construed.}\end{smallmatrix}$
would be anomalous and inconvenient but for
the exercise of mutual respect and deference.
Since the ordinary administration of the law is
carried on by the State courts, it necessarily hap-
pens that, by the course of their decisions, certain rules are established which become rules of
property and action in the State, and have all
the effect of law, and which it would be wrong
to disturb. This is especially true with regard
to the law of real estate and the construction of
State constitutions and statutes. Such established rules are always regarded by the Federal
courts, no less than by the State courts themselves, as authoritative declarations of what the
law is. But when the law has not been thus
settled, it is the right and duty of the Federal
courts to exercise their own judgment; as they
also always do in reference to the doctrines of
commercial law and general jurisprudence. So,
when contracts and transactions have been entered into, and rights have accrued thereon
under a particular state of the decisions, or
when there has been no decision of the State tribunals, the Federal courts properly claim the
right to adopt their own interpretation of the
law applicable to the case, although a different
interpretation may be adopted by the State
courts after such rights have accrued. But even
in such cases, for the sake of harmony and to
avoid confusion, the Federal courts will lean
towards an agreement of views with the State

courts, if the question seems to them balanced
with doubt. . . . As, however, the very object
of giving to the National courts jurisdiction to
administer the laws of the States in controversies between citizens of different States was to
institute independent tribunals, which it might
be supposed would be unaffected by local prejudices and sectional views, it would be a dereliction of their duty not to exercise an independent
judgment in cases not foreclosed by previous
adjudication." [1]

3. *The Right to Trial by Jury.*

Trial by jury.
This constitutional right, so far as it relates
to civil cases, has been sufficiently considered.
In regard to persons accused of criminal offences
before a police court, without a jury, it was
held at October Term, 1887, that the Police
Court of the District of Columbia was without
constitutional power to try, convict, and sentence
to punishment a person accused of a conspiracy
to prevent another person from pursuing his
calling and trade anywhere in the United States,
and to boycott, injure, molest, oppress, intimidate, and reduce him to beggary and want,
although the Revised Statutes relating to the
District of Columbia provide that, " Any party
deeming himself aggrieved by the judgment of
the police court may appeal to the Supreme
Court " of the district : as the provisions of the

---

[1] See *Hardin* v. *Jordan*, 140 U. S. 371 ; *Mitchell* v. *Smale*, 140
U. S. 406 ; *St. Louis* v. *Rutz*, 138 U. S. 226 ; *Barney* v. *Keokuk*,
94 U. S. 324 ; *Packer* v. *Bird*, 137 U. S. 661.

Constitution relating to trial by jury are in force LECTURE VII.
in the District of Columbia.[1] Trial by jury.

.. It is held that the Sixth Amendment providing for the trial in criminal prosecution by a jury of the State and district wherein the crime shall have been committed, has reference only to offences against the United States committed within a State.[2]

4. Ambassadors, other Public Ministers, and Consuls.

The statute which regulates this jurisdiction Suits by ambassa-
is section 687 of the Revised Statutes. "It dors, etc.
[the Supreme Court] shall have exclusively all such jurisdiction of suits or proceedings against ambassadors, or other public ministers, or their domestics, or domestic servants, as a court of law can have consistently with the law of nations; and original, but not exclusive, jurisdiction of all suits brought by ambassadors, or other public ministers, or in which a consul or vice-consul is a party."

These provisions are plenary. When such a suit appears upon the docket, and this privilege is claimed either by plaintiff or defendant, the first question to be passed upon is whether he is entitled to it. It has seemed to me that there is, and from the nature of the case can be, but one class of evidence that can establish this fact. Whether a person is or is not a diplomatic rep-

---

[1] Callan v. Wilson, 127 U. S. 540.
[2] Cook v. United States, 138 U. S. 157.

resentative or consular agent of a foreign power, accepted as such by our Government, is a political fact to be established by the certificate of the. Secretary of State. He may have been accepted as such yesterday, and may not be so accepted to-day. The Department of State is the only place where absolutely correct information on the subject can be had. It seems to me that the courts ought, in every case, to insist upon this as the best evidence, to show what the political department of the Government has determined as to the status of the individual. The courts, however, have not gone quite to this extent. In a recent case it is said : " We do not assume to sit in judgment upon the decision of the Executive in reference to. the public character of a person claiming to be a foreign minister, and therefore have the right to accept the certificate of the Department of State that a party is or is not a privileged person, and cannot properly be asked to proceed upon argumentative or collateral proof." [1]

5. Admiralty and Maritime Jurisdiction.

Nothing further need be said on this point except that it has recently been held that since the passage of the act of June 19, 1886, 24 Stat. 79, this jurisdiction is extended over cases of limited liability on the navigable rivers of the United States.[2]

---

[1] *In re Baiz*, 135 U. S. 403, 432.
[2] *In re Garnett*, Petitioner, 140 U. S. 000.

6. *Controversies between a State and Citizens.*

The history of the Eleventh Amendment and its application to some recent cases[1] is fully set forth by Judge Miller. In a still more recent case it was held that, although this amendment applies, in terms, only to suits against a State by citizens of another State, or by citizens or subjects of any foreign state, yet that a State cannot, without its own consent, be sued in a Circuit Court of the United States, upon a suggestion that the case is one arising under the Constitution and laws of the United States.[2]

Mr. Justice Bradley, in delivering the opinion of the court, said: "Looking back from our present standpoint at the decision in *Chisholm* v. *Georgia*, we do not greatly wonder at the effect which it had on the country. Any such power as that of authorizing the Federal judiciary to entertain suits by individuals against the States, had been expressly disclaimed, and even resented by the great defenders of the Constitution, whilst it was on trial before the American people." And then, after quoting the views of Hamilton in the Federalist, No. 81, and referring to the dissenting opinion of Justice Iredell, he said: "Looking at the subject as Hamilton did, and as Mr. Justice Iredell did, in the light of history and experience, and the established order of things, the views of the

---

[1] *New Hampshire* v. *Louisiana*, 108 U. S. 76.
[2] *Hans* v. *Louisiana*, 134 U. S. 1.

latter were clearly right, as the people of the United States, in their sovereign capacity, subsequently decided." [1]

In the course of the century which has elapsed, especially in the latter part of it, many attempts have been made to enforce, in the courts of the United States, private rights against a State, by suing its officers.

A mass of authority has been created by this litigation, which is admirably and lucidly reviewed by Mr. Justice Lamar.[2] He says: —

"It is well settled that no action can be maintained in any Federal court by the citizens of one of the States against a State, without its consent, even though the sole object of such suit be to bring the State within the operation of the constitutional provision which provides that 'no State shall pass any law impairing the obligation of contracts.' This immunity of a State from suit is absolute and unqualified, and the constitutional provision securing it is not to be so construed as to place the State within the reach of the process of the court. Accordingly, it is equally well settled that a suit against the officers of a State, to compel them to do the acts which constitute a performance by it of its contracts, is, in effect, a suit against the State itself.

"In the application of this latter principle two classes of cases have appeared in the deci-

---

[1] This subject is further treated in Lecture VIII, on the Supreme Court of the United States.

[2] *Pennoyer* v. *McConnaughty*, 140 U. S. I.

sions of this court, and it is in determining to
which class a particular case belongs that differing views have been presented.

"The first class is where the suit is brought
against the officers of the State, as representing
the State's action and liability, thus making it
though not a party to the record, the real party
against which the judgment will so operate as
to compel it to specifically perform its contracts.[1]

"The other class is where a suit is brought
against defendants who, claiming to act as
officers of the State, and under the color of an
unconstitutional statute, commit acts of wrong
and injury to the rights and property of the
plaintiff acquired under a contract with the
State. Such suit, whether brought to recover
money or property in the hands of such defendants, unlawfully taken by them in behalf of the
State, or for compensation in damages, or, in a
proper case where the remedy at law is inadequate, for an injunction to prevent such wrong
and injury, or for a mandamus, in a like case,
to enforce upon the defendant the performance
of a plain, legal duty, purely ministerial, is not
within the meaning of the Eleventh Amendment an action against the State.[2]

---

[1] *In re Ayers*, 123 U. S. 443; *Louisiana* v. *Jumel*, 107 U. S.
711; *Antoni* v. *Greenhow*, 107 U. S. 769; *Cunningham* v. *Macon
& Brunswick Railroad*, 109 U. S. 446; *Hagood* v. *Southern*, 117
U. S. 52.

[2] *Osborn* v. *Bank of the United States*, 9 Wheat. 738; *Davis* v.
Gray, 16 Wall. 203; *Tomlinson* v. *Branch*, 15 Wall. 460; *Litch-
field* v. *Webster County*, 101 U. S. 773; *Allen* v. *Baltimore & Ohio
Railroad*, 114 U. S. 311; *Board of Liquidation* v. *McComb*, 92
U. S. 531; *Poindexter* v. *Greenhow*, 114 U. S. 270.

"It is not our purpose to attempt a review of all, or even many, of these decisions, as to do so intelligently would unnecessarily protract this opinion, and in this connection, would subserve no useful purpose. It will be sufficient, perhaps, to refer to some of those which this case most nearly resembles."

Then, after referring to the cases cited in the margin,[1] he continued : —

"The dividing line between the cases to which we have referred and the class of cases in which it has been held that the State is a party defendant, and, therefore, not suable, by virtue of the inhibition contained in the Eleventh Amendment to the Constitution, was adverted to in *Cunningham* v. *Macon & Brunswick Railroad*,[2] where it was said, referring to the case of *Davis* v. *Gray : 'Nor was there in that case any affirmative relief* granted by ordering the governor and land commissioner *to perform any act towards perfecting the title of the company.'* Thus holding, by implication, at least, that affirmative relief would not be granted against a State officer, by ordering him to do and perform acts forbidden by the law of his State, even though such law might be unconstitutional.

"The same distinction was pointed out in

---

[1] *Osborn* v. *Bank of the United States*, 9 Wheat. 738, 859 ; *New Hampshire* v. *Louisiana*, 108 U. S. 76 ; *In re Ayers*, 123 U. S. 443 ; *Davis* v. *Gray*, 16 Wall. 203 ; *Board of Liquidation* v. *McComb*, 92 U. S. 531 ; *Poindexter* v. *Greenhow*, 114 U. S. 270 ; *Allen* v. *Baltimore & Ohio Railroad Co.*, 114 U. S. 311 ; *McGahey* v. *Virginia*, 135 U. S. 662.

[2] 109 U. S. 446.

Hagood v. *Southern*, which was held to be, in effect, a suit against the State, and it was said : ' A broad line of demarcation separates from such cases as the present, in which the decrees require, *by affirmative official action* on the part of the defendants, *the performance of an obligation which belongs to the State in its political capacity,* those in which actions at law or suits in equity are maintained against defendants who, while claiming to act as officers of the State, violate and invade the personal and property rights of the plaintiffs under color of authority, unconstitutional and void.' [1]

" The cases in which suits against officers of a State have been considered as against the State itself, and, therefore, within the inhibition of the Eleventh Amendment to the Constitution, and those in which such suits were considered to be against State officers, as individuals, were elaborately reviewed and distinguished in the recent case of *In re Ayers*.[2] That case came before us on application for *habeas corpus* by the attorney general of Virginia, the auditor of the State, and the commonwealth's attorney for Loudoun County in that State, who were in the custody of the United States marshal for the Eastern District of Virginia, for contempt of court, in disobeying a restraining order of the Circuit Court of the United States for that district, commanding them not to institute and prosecute certain suits in the name of the State of Virginia, required to be brought by the statutes

---

[1] 117 U. S. 52, 70. [2] 123 U. S. 443.

of the State. The suit in which the restraining
order was issued was nominally against certain
officers of the State, but this court held that it
was, in effect, a suit against the State itself, and,
therefore, in violation of the Eleventh Amendment to the Constitution. And that such being
true, the acts and proceedings of the Circuit
Court in that suit were null and void for all
purposes; and the prisoners were discharged.
In delivering the opinion of the court, Mr. Justice
Matthews, referring to the class of cases in which
it had been adjudged that the suit was against
State officers in their private capacity, and not
against the State, said: 'The vital principle in
all such cases is that the defendants, though professing to act as officers of the State, are threat-
ening a violation of the personal or property
rights of the complainant, for which they are
personally and individually liable. . . . This
feature will be found, on an examination, to
characterize every case where persons have been
made defendants for acts done or threatened by
them as officers of the government, either of a
State or of the United States, where the objection has been interposed that the State was the
real defendant, and has been overruled.'[1]

"In *Hans* v. *Louisiana*[2] the general rule on
this subject was concisely stated by Mr. Justice
Bradley in the following terms: 'To avoid mis-
apprehension it may be proper to add that,
although the obligations of a State rest for their

---

[1] 123 U. S. 500, 501.   [2] 134 U. S. 1, 20, 21.

performance upon its honor and good faith, and cannot be made the subjects of judicial cogni- zance unless the State consents to be sued, or comes itself into court; yet where property or rights are enjoyed under a grant or contract made by a State, they cannot wantonly be invaded. Whilst the State cannot be compelled by suit to perform its contracts, any attempt on its part to violate property or rights acquired under its contract, may be judicially resisted; and any law impairing the obligation of contracts under which such property or rights are held is void and powerless to affect their enjoyment.'

7. *Inferior Courts.*

This grant of power refers to courts of the United States, established by law, under the provisions of the Constitution. About these nothing more need be said. A word may be added, however, concerning some courts, created under authority of Congress, but not held to be courts of the United States under the grant of judicial power under the Constitution.

As long ago as 1828, it was held in an opinion delivered by Chief Justice Marshall, that a territorial court was not "a constitutional court, in which the judicial power conferred by the Constitution on the General Government can be deposited," but a legislative court, "created in virtue of the general right of sovereignty which exists in the Government, or in virtue of that clause which enables Congress to make all needful rules and regulations respecting the territory belonging to the United States.[1] " The District Court of Alaska has just been held to be a court of this stamp,[2] Justices Field, Gray, and Brown dissenting, but not on this point.

A recent opinion by Mr. Justice Field holds the Consular courts established in foreign countries by Congress under grants of rights of exterritoriality to the United States by treaty, to be valid courts, and that the statutes establishing them do not infringe the Constitution. The opinion says : —

" The framers of the Constitution, who were fully aware of the necessity of having judicial authority exercised by our consuls in non-Christian countries, if commercial intercourse was to be had with their people, never could have supposed that all the guarantees in the administration of the law upon criminals at home were to be transferred to such consular establishments, and applied, before an American who had committed a felony there could be accused and tried. They must have known that such a requirement would defeat the main purpose of investing the consul with judicial authority." " By the Constitution a government is ordained and established 'for the United States of America,' and not for countries outside of their limits. The Constitution can have no operation in another country." [3]

---

[1] *American Insurance Co.* v. *Canter,* 1 Pet. 511, 546.

[2] *McAlister* v. *United States,* 141 U. S. Act of May 17, 1884, 23 Stat. 24, c. 53.

[3] *In re Ross,* Petitioner, 140 U. S. 453.

When the Roman Empire fell, the influence of its wonderful system of law remained. Even the common law traces to Rome the principles on which it is grounded. But when the Turks conquered Constantinople, the Twelve Tables and the Institutes gave place to the Koran as a system of law. The unwillingness of the powers of Europe to submit their subjects to such a system — or want of system — of jurisprudence, led to the establishment of consular courts in Ottoman countries, with civil and criminal jurisdiction over the subjects or citizens of the nationality to which the particular capitulation was granted. The first was made to France, from which circumstance all Christians in the Ottoman dominions came to be called Franks.

As intercourse with Asia grew, the same system of consular courts, with extraterritorial jurisdiction, was adopted there.

These concessions proved to be of great importance to Americans residing in those countries. Congress created consular courts to exercise the granted powers, both civil and criminal. In the latter it was a necessity that proceedings should be instituted against persons accused of murder, without the intervention of a grand jury, and that they should be tried without a petit jury. Some strict constructionists in Congress and elsewhere questioned the constitutionality of such proceedings. This decision of the Supreme Court, announced by Mr. Justice Field, has set at rest all such questions.

Somewhat akin to this is the jurisdiction which a District Court of the United States may acquire over crimes committed on Guano Islands, by reason of the offender being brought first into the district.[1]

---

[1] Rev. Stat. § 5576. *Jones* v. *United States*, 137 U. S. 202.

VIII.

THE SUPREME COURT OF THE UNITED STATES.

————∘∘⟩∘⟨∘∘————

ARTICLE III, SECTION 1. The judicial power of the United States, shall be vested in one supreme Court, and in such inferior Courts as the Congress may from time to time ordain and establish. The judges, both of the supreme and inferior Courts, shall hold their Offices during good Behavior, and shall, at stated Times, receive for their services, a Compensation, which shall not be diminished during their Continuance in Office.

SECTION 2. The judicial Power shall extend to all Cases, in Law and Equity, arising under this Constitution, the Laws of the United States, and Treaties made, or which shall be made, under their authority; — to all Cases affecting Ambassadors, other public Ministers and Consuls; — to all Cases of Admiralty and maritime Jurisdiction; — to Controversies to which the United States shall be a Party; — to Controversies between two or more States; — between a State and Citizens of another State; — between Citizens of different States; — between Citizens of the same State claiming Lands under Grants of different States, and between a State, or the Citizens thereof, and foreign States, Citizens or Subjects.

In all Cases affecting Ambassadors, other public Ministers and Consuls, and those in which a State shall be Party, the supreme Court shall have original jurisdiction. In all the other Cases before mentioned, the supreme Court shall have appellate jurisdiction, both as to Law and Fact, with such Exceptions, and under such Regulations as the Congress shall make.

· ARTICLE XI OF THE AMENDMENTS. The Judicial Power of the United States shall not be construed to·

373

LECTURE VIII.

extend to any suit in law or equity, commenced or prosecuted against one of the United States by Citizens of another State, or by Citizens or Subjects of any Foreign State.

The Supreme Court.

I HAVE selected a subject for this address [1] in which I trust the young gentlemen present, who have just graduated, will feel an interest as great as their seniors in the profession of the law. It is one which ought to engage the thoughts and reflections of every member of the legal profession in the United States, and it has been chosen because my own familiarity with the topic will, I trust, enable me to say something valuable in regard to the highest judicature in this country. My subject is " The Supreme Court of the United States."

This court may be regarded in many respects, to consider each one of which would consume more time than is permissible upon an occasion like this. There are, and might be discussed separately, its jurisdiction, the *personnel* of its organization, the history of the men who have occupied places upon its bench, a review of the great cases decided by it, and a general outlook upon the principal events in its career.

Its judicial history.

Upon the present occasion I propose to consider the history of the court with relation to its effect upon the course of the General Government, and in doing this I can best illustrate my meaning and better interest my listeners by

---

[1] This lecture was delivered by Mr. Justice Miller before the Alumni of the Law Department of the University of Michigan on the 29th of June, 1887, as an Address at the semi-centennial celebration of the founding of the University.

a reference to some of its decisions upon great
constitutional questions that have influenced,
and in some instances controlled, the course
of the other two great departments of the
Government.

The framers of the Constitution of the United
States were governed by the principle that the
powers which belong to all governments could be
most safely and satisfactorily exercised by their
division among three separate branches or departments, to one or the other of which, in the
main, they were all distributed. These departments are called the executive, the legislative,
and the judicial. The line, however, is not perfect which divides the powers exercised by each
of them from those of the others. The President, or the Executive, takes part in the making of laws by his signature to them, or by his
refusal to sign them, in which event a two-thirds
vote of the Legislature is required to make the
act a law. The Senate partakes in the executive function by its power to confirm or reject
treaties made by the President, as well as his
nominations to office; and the power to try impeachments, which is essentially judicial in its
nature, is also given to that body. Yet, notwithstanding these departures from the general
principle, it remains true that the great executive functions of the Government in this country
are given to the President, the legislative to
Congress, and, more rigidly than in either of the
other cases, the judicial to the courts of the
United States.

LECTURE VIII.
The Supreme
Court is the head
of the judicial de-
partment.
Of the judicial department of the Government the Supreme Court is the head and representative, and to it must come for final decision all the great legal questions which may arise under the Constitution, the laws, or the treaties of the United States. It is to this court, and to some detached portions of its history of nearly one hundred years, that I propose to call your attention.

It has been said of this court, that the Constitution created it for the purpose of construing that instrument. The popular idea to-day is that such is the primary and most important object of its existence. To some extent this may be so, but it is undoubtedly true that the judicial function of administering justice as a court of law between certain classes of litigants, and upon certain subjects of dispute, is the duty in which it is principally engaged. In the administration of this duty questions must occasionally arise in regard to the validity of the laws enacted by the Congress of the United States, or of a State, or of an act of the executive department of the Government, as to whether such law or action is in conformity to or in violation of the Constitution of the United States; and the court must in such cases give judicial construction to that instrument. Such construction, being by the highest law tribunal of the country, is to be received as the law, not only of that particular case, but the rule of action for all inferior judicial tribunals in all cases of a like character.

As it is also desirable that there should be uniformity of construction upon all important questions arising under the Constitution, the decisions of no other body in the organization of the Government are likely to command the same influence, in producing that result, as those of the Supreme Court. And as the same questions may time after time be brought before it, and will in general be decided in the same way, its decisions constitute a body of precedents which naturally come to command the respect of all other tribunals, and to be generally received as the true construction of the organic law of the nation, upon the points thus determined.

Lecture VIII.
Decisions of the Supreme Court construing the Constitution.

It is not strictly true that these decisions are in all cases binding upon the executive and the legislative branches of the Government. In certain classes of cases every man who takes an oath to support the Constitution of the United States must find himself in the presence of embarrassing questions, in regard to which his action must be governed by his own conviction of the duties which it imposes upon him. Still it may be said that in the history of the Government, during a period of nearly a century since its organization, it has been exceedingly rare that a principle of constitutional law has been distinctly laid down by the Supreme Court, which has not come to be recognized as the true sense of that instrument.

Not strictly binding upon the other departments.

The act of Congress under which the organization of this court took place was approved

Organization of the court.

September 24, 1789. It provided for the appointment of a Chief Justice, and five Associate Justices, who should constitute the court. The first judges appointed under this law were John Jay of New York, Chief Justice; and John Rutledge of South Carolina; James Wilson of Pennsylvania; William Cushing of Massachusetts; Robert Harrison of Maryland; and John Blair of Virginia, Associate Justices.

Jay served as Chief Justice from 1789 to 1795, when he resigned. During this period, however, he was Minister of the United States to England. And, as showing that this high judicial office was not in that early time considered incompatible with the discharge of the functions of other offices, it may be mentioned that, when Marshall was appointed and confirmed as Chief Justice in 1801, he was Secretary of State in the Cabinet of President John Adams, and, though commissioned and taking his seat upon the bench, he continued to discharge the duties of the secretaryship until the end of that administration, a period of two or three months.

On the resignation of Jay, in 1795, John Rutledge was appointed Chief Justice, received his commission, and took his seat in court, but, not being confirmed by the Senate, Oliver Ellsworth was appointed in 1796. He served as Chief Justice until December, 1799, when he resigned.

John Marshall was appointed to the position of Chief Justice in 1801, and served a period of thirty-four years, until he died in 1835. After his death Roger B. Taney was appointed to the

vacant place in 1836, and held it until he died
in 1864, after a service of twenty-eight years. With the additional statement that Chief Justice Chase succeeded him, and presided for nine years, when he died, and was succeeded by the present Chief Justice Waite, I am compelled to close what I have to say with regard to the personal organization of the court.[1] It will be noted that for a period of sixty-two years continuously the court was presided over by two Chief Justices, which may be supposed to have aided very much in the stability and uniformity of its course of decisions.

Very early in the history of the court a question came before it of much importance, which was fully considered at the time, and in which great public interest was felt. Its decision caused the adoption of an amendment to the Constitution of the United States, the Eleventh. It arose in the case of *Chisholm* v. *The State of Georgia*.[2]

This was an action of *assumpsit*, instituted in the Supreme Court of the United States, under its original jurisdiction, at the August Term, 1792, and was decided at the February Term, 1793. The State of Georgia, which was supposed to be brought before the court by the service of the writ upon its Governor and its Attorney General, refused to make any general appearance, but presented by its attorneys, In-

---

[1] Chief Justice Waite died March 23, 1888. Chief Justice Fuller was commissioned July 20, 1888.

[2] 2 Dall. 419.

gersoll and Dallas, a written remonstrance and protestation against the exercise of jurisdiction in this case. The question thus presented was, whether a common law action of *assumpsit* could be sustained against a State in the Supreme Court of the United States by a citizen of another State.

The action was commenced under the second section of the Third Article of the Constitution, providing that the judicial power of the United States shall among other matters extend to controversies between a State and citizens of another State, and that the Supreme Court shall have original jurisdiction in all cases in which a State shall be a party. Chisholm, being a citizen of North Carolina, began his action under this provision against the State of Georgia in the Supreme Court of the United States. The judges delivered separate opinions.

Iredell of North Carolina, who had succeeded Harrison of Maryland as a member of the court, delivered a very learned one, the main object of which seemed to be to show that, inasmuch as States had never been held liable to action at common law, the State in this case could not be sued in an action of *assumpsit*, however it might be in regard to other matters of litigation. The other judges, on the contrary, all agreed in the proposition, that the provision of the Constitution, just recited, made a State liable to be sued for any legal cause of action, in law or in equity, in the Supreme Court of the United States by a citizen or citizens of another State.

This proposition, which, as Mr. Randolph, the

Attorney General of the United States who argued the case for Chisholm, said, was so un- popular that he had been warned against the consequences of his pressing it upon the court, was received with very great disfavor. The result was that Congress immediately proposed the Eleventh Amendment to the Constitution, • which was ratified by the States as soon as they had an opportunity to vote upon it. That amendment is as follows : —

" The judicial power of the United States shall not be construed to extend to any suit in law or equity, commenced or prosecuted against one of the United States by citizens of another State, or by citizens or subjects of any foreign State."

It is a little remarkable that, notwithstanding the unanimity of the court upon this question, a different opinion had been expressed by Mr. Hamilton in No. 81 of the Federalist. In reply- ing to the objection that this provision of the Constitution subjected a State to be sued for its debts or obligations, he says : —

" It has been suggested that an assignment of the public securities of one State to the citizens of another would enable them to prosecute that State in the Federal courts for the amount of those securities, a suggestion which the follow- ing considerations prove to be without founda- tion."

He then goes on to show that it is inherent in the nature of sovereignty not to be amenable to suit without its consent, and that this is the

general sense and the general practice of mankind; that this provision of the Constitution
can only be construed to authorize a State to
bring a suit against citizens of other States in
the Federal courts, and does not authorize a suit
against the State by the citizen of another State.

Mr. Madison and Mr. Marshall, one or both
of them, made the same suggestion in the Convention of the State of Virginia, called to pass•
upon the adoption of the Constitution.

The amendment just quoted was supposed to
have settled the question of the suability of a
State upon its obligations or for its debts in any
other mode than that to which the State should
give its express consent, and that the courts of
the United States had no jurisdiction to entertain such suits. But curiously enough, after the
lapse of ninety years, the suggestion of Hamilton in regard to the assignment by creditors of
a State, who could not themselves sue in the
Federal courts, to parties who could sue the
State in those courts, has been acted upon.

In the cases of New Hampshire v. Louisiana,
and New York v. Louisiana, reported in 108
U. S. 76, this precise question was brought up.
Although the jurisdiction to sue a State in the
courts of the United States by the citizens of
another State, or by citizens or subjects of any
foreign State, was abolished by the Eleventh
Amendment, there yet remained the right of
one State to sue another. Certain creditors,
therefore, of the State of Louisiana, who could
not sue that State themselves, transferred by

assignment the evidence of their indebtedness, some to the State of New Hampshire and others to the State of New York, and these States brought suits in the Supreme Court of the United States against the State of Louisiana upon those obligations.

LECTURE VIII.
New Hampshire v. *Louisiana*, 108 U. S. 76.

The court, after a very elaborate argument, decided that these actions could not be sustained; that "the evident purpose of the amendment, so promptly proposed and adopted, was to prohibit all suits against a State by or for citizens of other States, or aliens, without the consent of the State to be sued," and that "one State cannot create a controversy with another State, within the meaning of that term as used in the judicial clauses of the Constitution, by assuming the prosecution of debts owing by the other State to its citizen."

At the same term there was presented to the court in its appellate jurisdiction an effort to force the State of Louisiana to pay some of the same kind of debts out of the money in its treasury. This was a proceeding in *mandamus* against the treasurer of the State to compel him to pay them out of the funds in his hands as such officer, and by a bill in chancery to enjoin the payment of the same money to other creditors.

Louisiana v. *Jumel*, 107 U. S. 711.

Both of these were held to be forbidden by the Constitution, because they were substantially suits against the State.[1]

---

[1] *Louisiana* v. *Jumel*, 107 U. S. 711.

LECTURE VIII.
Louisiana v.
Jumel, 107 U. S.
711.

And though there have been some differences in court upon the question of how far an action against an officer of a State may be held to be a suit against the State, so as to come within the principle of the Eleventh Amendment to the Constitution, excluding the jurisdiction of the Federal courts, yet the main proposition has been steadily sustained, that if it be essentially a suit against the State the Federal courts cannot entertain it. In view of the many millions of dollars of indebtedness of the States, which they refuse to pay, the importance of the original decision, which evoked the constitutional amendment forbidding the States to be sued in the Federal courts, is readily to be perceived.

Another judgment of the Supreme Court a little later, rendered at the February Term, 1803, which has been very far-reaching in its influence upon the other departments and other officers of

Marbury v. Madi-
son, 1 Cranch, 137. the Government, was made in the case of *Marbury* v. *Madison*.[1]

I have already said that Marshall, although Chief Justice of the Supreme Court, had continued to act as Secretary of State until the close of John Adams's administration, when the latter was succeeded by Jefferson. The commissions of certain officers, signed and sealed by the President, and ready for delivery, were left in the office of the Secretary of State, which the succeeding Secretary, Mr. Madison, refused to deliver to the parties thus commissioned. The

---

[1] 1 Cranch, 137.

result of this was that Mr. Marbury, who was LECTURE VIII.
one of these parties, commissioned as a justice of *Marbury v. Madison*, 1 Cranch, 137.
the peace of the District of Columbia, and whose
appointment had been approved by the Senate,
having demanded the delivery of his commission,
applied to the Supreme Court for a writ of *mandamus* to compel its delivery.

The opinion in the case was delivered by Marshall himself, as Chief Justice, and was concurred in by the whole court. It is very lengthy,
and an exhaustive discussion of the power of a
court of law to compel officers by the writ of
mandamus to discharge duties which it is clear
they are bound to perform, and in regard to
which they have no discretion. The court decides that since the commission was signed and
sealed by the President of the United States,
and the appointment approved by the Senate,
there was no authority in the President or Secretary of State to withhold it; that the duty to
deliver it to the person entitled to it was clear
and unquestionable, and that this duty could be
enforced by any court having jurisdiction of the
case.

The court, however, came to the conclusion
that this was not a case in which it had any
original jurisdiction, and it therefore could not
issue the writ. But it was also held that such
jurisdiction was in the local courts of the District
of Columbia, who had authority to issue the
writ to any officer within the District who refused to perform a duty merely ministerial in its
character, in regard to which he could exercise

no judgment, and that this was of that class of cases.

The immense importance of this decision, though in some respects *obiter*, since the court declared in the end that it had no jurisdiction of the case, may be appreciated when it is understood that the principles declared, which have never since been controverted, subjected the ministerial and executive officers of the Government, all over the country, to the control of the courts, in regard to the execution of a large part of their duties. Its application to the very highest officers of the Government, except perhaps the President himself, has been illustrated in numerous cases in the courts of the United States, and in the reports of the Supreme Court. Perhaps one of the latest and most instructive

of these is the case of *United States* v. *Schurz*,[1] decided at October Term, 1880.

It appears that Mr. Schurz, as Secretary of the Interior, after a patent for lands had been granted, signed by the President of the United States, and recorded in the Register of Patents, issued an order to the Commissioner of the General Land Office that he should withhold the instrument, and not deliver it to the person named in it. The land department of the Government had been in the habit, after patents for lands were issued, and even after they had been delivered, of recalling them at their own option and revoking them. In many instances, even after

---

[1] 102 U. S. 378.

they had been sent to the local land office for
delivery to the proper parties, they had been re-
called while there, and thus their owners had
been put to great inconvenience and trouble.

An action for a writ of *mandamus* to compel
Mr. Schurz to deliver this patent was brought
in the name of the United States on relation of
the party applying for the writ, who was the
grantee of the land. The Supreme Court held
that after the patent had been signed, sealed, and
recorded there no longer remained in the officers
of the Government any power over the title, or
any right to retain, and to refuse to deliver the
patent. They therefore authorized the issuing
of a writ by the Supreme Court of the District.

This decision was founded upon *Marbury* v.
Madison, and upon its reasoning, as many other
decisions have been; and the power of the courts
in the class of cases described in that opinion —
namely, those in which a duty is imposed by law
upon an officer of the Government to do a specific
act, in regard to which he has no discretion, and
which act is simply and purely ministerial in its
nature to compel their performance, has been
well established, and is one of the most useful
principles of Federal jurisprudence.

During the long Chief Justiceship of Marshall,
many cases of public and political importance,
having a large influence over the course of the
Government and very materially guiding the
action of the executive and legislative departments, came up for consideration. I must only
select such of these as I consider most impor-

LECTURE VIII.
United States v.
Schurz, 102 U. S.
378.

McCulloch v.
Maryland,
4 Wheat. 316.

tant, and which can be touched upon within the limits of this discourse.

The next of these to which I shall call your attention is *McCulloch* v. *Maryland*, decided in 1819, and reported in 4 Wheat. 316. It involved the question of the power of the General Government to create a national bank, with branches in the States, capable of issuing circulating notes. Such a bank had been created under Hamilton's administration of the treasury, and its charter expired about the commencement of the war of 1812. A recharter was refused under the influence of the strict construction rule of Virginia politics in regard to the power of Congress to create such a bank. Mr. Madison himself, who was then President, was opposed to it, it is said, upon that ground. But the disastrous condition of the public credit, and the general financial ruin which followed the close of that war, induced Congress to charter a new bank. This was done in 1816, and received the assent of Mr. Madison.

The introduction into the States of this institution, by branches of the principal bank, especially with the power of issuing circulating notes, was unpopular in many of them, and attempts were made to resist their business operations. Among these the State of Maryland assessed a tax upon the circulating notes of the bank, which in effect was intended to drive them from the State. In the attempt to enforce this law, the Court of Appeals of Maryland affirmed the validity of the statute of that State establishing

the tax. McCulloch, the party sued, thereupon LECTURE VIII.
brought the case by a writ of error to the Su- *McCulloch* v. *Maryland,*
preme Court of the United States. 4 Wheat. 316.

The opinion takes a very wide range with regard to the nature and power of the Federal Government, and the principles of construction of the Constitution. It is one of the ablest of the opinions delivered by Chief Justice Marshall, and has often been referred to and followed in subsequent cases.

The court held that Congress had power to incorporate such a bank; that although there was no express grant of such power, or of authority to create any corporation, yet, as one of the appropriate means of exercising the powers of the Government in regard to the collection and disbursement of its revenues and the transfer of them from one point to another, the institution of this bank, with the right to establish its branches and offices of discount and deposit within a State, and to issue circulating notes, was an appropriate means of carrying into effect the powers expressly given by the Constitution to the Government of the Union.

It therefore held that no State had any authority by taxation or otherwise to impede the necessary and proper action of this bank, an instrumentality which Congress deemed necessary in carrying on the general operations of the Government of the United States connected with the treasury. "If," said the court, "the right of the State to tax the means employed by the General Government be conceded, the declaration that the Constitution and laws made in pursuance thereof, shall be the supreme law of the land, is empty and unmeaning declaration."

The number of the Justices at this time had been increased to seven, and their opinion was unanimous.

Just prior to the expiration of the charter of this bank in 1836, the question of its renewal became one of absorbing public interest. The then President of the United States, General Jackson, brought all his influence and popularity to bear to prevent a renewal of its charter, and the question entered into the partisan politics of the day more largely than any other, and to some extent continued to do so until the late war. The Congress of 1836 passed the bill for the recharter of the bank, but President Jackson vetoed it, largely on the ground that it was unconstitutional. It may be said, however, that the prevailing sentiment of the country, and especially of its leading statesmen, has been in the main favorable to the constitutionality of the United States Bank ; and no decision of the Supreme Court, or of any other court of the United States, has ever impugned or denied the correctness of the principle upon which McCulloch v. Maryland was decided.

It is a matter of interest, which I cannot forbear to mention here, that the present national bank system, which in my judgment, and in that of many thinking men, statesmen and financiers, is the best that the world has ever

seen, originated during the midst of the civil LECTURE VIII.
war with the Secretary of the Treasury who *McCulloch* v.
Maryland,
afterwards came to Marshall's place, as Chief 4 Wheat. 316.
Justice of the Supreme Court of the United
States.

It is unnecessary for me to point out to this
intelligent audience the great influence which
that decision of the Supreme Court has exercised over the material and financial prosperity
of this country. Had the decision been, that
there existed in this Government no power to
create a national currency, or to provide for a
national banking system, the disastrous effects
upon the business prosperity of the people can
hardly be imagined. Those who are old enough
to have gone through the State bank and wild-
cat systems of paper money prevalent a few
years since in this country, can bear feeling testimony to the value of a so-called national bank
system.

Another decision of the court, made in the *Dartmouth Col-*
same year, and perhaps at the same term, is that *lege* v. *Woodward,*
4 Wheat. 518.
of *Dartmouth College* v. *Woodward.*[1]

It may well be doubted whether any decision
ever delivered by any court has had such a pervading operation and influence in controlling
legislation as this. The legislation, however, so
controlled, has been that of the States of the
Union. The decision is founded upon that clause
of the Constitution which declares " That no
State shall make any law impairing the obligation of contracts." [2]

---

[1] 4 Wheat. 518.   [2] Art. I, sec. 10.

LECTURE VIII.
Dartmouth Col-
lege v. Woodward,
4 Wheat. 518.
Dartmouth College existed as a corporation
under a charter granted by the British Crown to
its trustees in New Hampshire, in the year 1769.
This charter conferred upon them the entire
governing power of the college, and among other
powers that of filling up all vacancies occurring
in their own body, and of removing and appointing tutors. It also declared that the number of
trustees should forever consist of twelve, and no
more.

After the Revolution, the Legislature of New
Hampshire passed a law to amend the charter,
to improve and enlarge the corporation. It increased the number of trustees to twenty-one,
gave the appointment of the additional members
to the Executive of the State, and created a
board of overseers to consist of twenty-five persons, of whom twenty-one were also to be appointed by the Executive of New Hampshire.
These overseers had power to inspect and control the most important acts of the trustees.

The Supreme Court, reversing the decision of
the Superior Court of New Hampshire, held that
the original charter constituted a contract between the Crown, in whom the power was then
vested, and the trustees of the college, which
was impaired by the act of the Legislature above
referred to. The opinion, to which there was
but one dissent, establishes the doctrine that the
act of a government, whether it be by a charter
of the Legislature or of the Crown, which creates
a corporation, is a contract between the State
and the corporation, and that all the essential

franchises, powers, and benefits conferred upon LECTURE VIII. the corporation by the charter become, when *Dartmouth College* v. *Woodward*, accepted by it, contracts, within the meaning of 4 Wheat. 518. the clause of the Constitution referred to.

I cannot here go into the great argument by which this proposition was supported, nor enter into a minute statement of the class of subjects which by the rulings of this case became contracts protected by the Constitution. The opinion has been of late years much criticised, as including with the class of contracts whose foundation is in the legislative action of the States, many which were not probably intended to be so included by the framers of the Constitution. And it is undoubtedly true that the Supreme Court itself has been compelled of late years to insist in this class of cases upon the existence of an actual contract by the State with the corporation, when relief is sought against subsequent legislation.

The main feature of the case, namely, that a Statutory contracts. State can make a contract by legislation, as well as in any other way, and that in no such case shall a subsequent act of the Legislature interpose any effectual barrier to its enforcement, where it is enforceable in the ordinary courts of justice, has remained. The result of this principle has been to make void innumerable acts of State legislatures, intended in times of disastrous financial depression and suffering, to protect the people from the hardships of a rigid and prompt enforcement of the law in regard to their contracts, and to prevent the States from repealing, abrogating, or avoiding by legislation contracts entered into with other parties.

This decision has stood from the day it was made to the present hour as a great bulwark against popular effort through State legislation to evade the payment of just debts, the performance of obligatory contracts, and the general repudiation of the rights of creditors. I cannot even refer here to the numerous decisions by the Supreme Court of the United States, of the subordinate courts of the Government, and the highest courts of the States themselves, in which, under the influence of this decision, the principle of the Constitution that no State shall pass any law impairing the obligation of contracts has been upheld for the protection of those contracts.

With the case of *Gibbons* v. *Ogden*,[1] which has always been considered a leading one, commenced a series of decisions which has continued down to the term of the court just ended, construing the third clause of section 8, Article I, of the Constitution of the United States. The
language of this clause is that " Congress shall have power to regulate commerce with foreign nations, and among the several States, and with the Indian tribes."

There has not been, during the history of the Government, any serious question or difficulty about the exercise of the power by Congress to regulate commerce with the Indian tribes. The

---

[1] 9 Wheat. 1.

few laws which that body has found it necessary
to pass in regard to trade and intercourse with
the Indians have given rise to very few controversies before the courts. The power to regulate commerce with foreign nations has necessarily occupied the attention of the legislative
body, and the questions arising under it have
principally been as to the construction of the
statutes, with an occasional contest as to the
power to regulate immigration into the various
States from foreign countries.

But, as regards the regulation of commerce
among the States, Congress has signally failed
in providing any general system, or in enacting
any very important laws upon the subject. In
point of fact, the commerce in existence which
could be regulated with any profit, or called for
it at the time the Constitution was formed, was
that upon the ocean, carried on by sailing vessels,
and it was not until the origin of the steamboat,
making the great rivers of the country equal in
carrying capacity to seas, with the superadded
power of steam to make them useful, that interstate commerce became a matter of much consequence. Afterwards the invention of railroads
increased the magnitude of this kind of traffic,
so that in relative importance to foreign commerce it is now so much superior that I dare
not, without consulting the statistics, undertake
to state what it is.

Very soon after the introduction of the steamboat, whose use was accompanied by great dangers in the navigation of the interior rivers of

the country, Congress began to legislate upon
the subject, and finally established, some forty
or fifty years ago, a system of laws regulating
their construction and navigation. The various
acts passed from time to time also required that
the masters and pilots of these vessels should be
regularly examined as to their qualifications and
licensed by officers appointed by the General
Government. They also prescribed with great
minuteness what safeguards they should keep on
board in the way of life-saving implements and
small boats, and limited the number of passengers, thus taking special care of their comfort
and safety.

But in relation to railroads, whose owners
were corporations under charters from the different States of the Union, such legislation as
was needful has been left by Congress to the
States who chartered them, or through whose
territory they extended.

This inaction of the Congress of the United
States, which it was asserted could alone establish regulations for the control of railroads in
conducting transportation of persons and property through more States than one, thus coming
within the definition of the phrase " interstate
commerce," has at length been superseded by a
very important statute, called the Interstate
Commerce Law, passed at the recent session.
These railroad corporations, the necessity and
value of which to meet the wants of this great
country grew so rapidly, asserted for a long
time that by virtue of the charters granted

them by the States, they were exempt from nearly all legislative control over their business, their contracts, or the manner in which their transportation should be conducted.

In the cases of *Munn* v. *Illinois*,[1] *Chicago, Burlington & Quincy Railroad* v. *Iowa*,[2] and *Peik* v. *Chicago & Northwestern Railroad*,[3] decided at the same time, it was held by the Supreme Court that as common carriers they were subject to appropriate regulation of the manner in which their business should be conducted, by legislative authority. But these decisions left undecided the question how far this legislative power of regulation belonged to the States, and how far it was in the Congress of the United States.

The case of *Gibbons* v. *Ogden*, above referred to, originated in an attempt of the State of New York to pass laws which affected free navigation upon the Hudson River by steamboats. With the idea of rewarding Fulton and Livingston for the invention by the former of the new method of propulsion by steam, a statute was passed giving to them the exclusive right of navigating that river with boats thus propelled. Other persons coming into the business of transportation with boats of a similar character, contested this right to such exclusive privilege, and were sued for infringing it in those waters.

The questions arising in that case were argued with great ability, Mr. Webster being one of the counsel engaged in the case, and one

---

[1] 94 U. S. 113.   [2] 94 U. S. 155.   [3] 94 U. S. 164.

of the best considered opinions of the court was delivered by Chief Justice Marshall. It is not important here to detail the substance of that argument; but the two questions that were mostly discussed related to the following conclusions which were reached by the court : —

First. That this statute was an exercise of the power of regulating commerce among the States, which had been confided to Congress by the Constitution.

Second. That inasmuch as Congress had passed laws authorizing the licensing of vessels for the coasting trade, which authorized them to navigate all the waters within the jurisdiction of the United States capable of being used for that purpose, this act was an exercise of the power conferred by the clause of the Federal Constitution concerning commerce among the States, and that Congress having occupied the field by its own legislation, this necessarily excluded the action of the State upon the subject.

While the opinion of the court undertakes to ascertain what kind of commerce must be regulated exclusively by Congress, it also seems to concede that there may be a class of regulations affecting it, when carried on between the States, which would be valid in the absence of any action by Congress. But the case rested in the end upon the proposition that such a principle could not be applied to the case then before the court, because Congress had acted upon the subject, having passed a law or made a regula-

tion which was inconsistent with the statute of
the State of New York granting this exclusive
privilege to Livingston and Fulton.

In the subsequent case of *Willson* v. *Black-*
bird Creek Marsh Co.,[1] the principle was laid
down, that in a class of cases, local in their
character, regulations affecting interstate commerce may be enacted by the States in the absence of the exercise of that power by Congress.
That proposition, which in a subsequent stage
of the history of the court was very much controverted, and upon which it had been divided
until within recent years, has led to much uncertainty as to the validity of laws passed by
the States of the Union. This doubtful condition of affairs can hardly yet be considered to
be at an end. The great necessity of some well-
defined rule in regard to these matters, in the
absence of any Congressional regulation of commerce, is evinced by the fact that scarcely a
session of the Supreme Court of the United
States has passed within the last twenty-five
years, in which some case has not been brought
before it, wherein the validity of laws passed by
the States of the Union, or ordinances of municipalities made under the authority of some
State laws affecting commerce, has not been
brought up and controverted, and become the
subject of serious consideration.

I venture to hope, however, that some of the
decisions discussing these questions, made during

---

[1] 2 Pet. 245.

the term of the court just expired, have brought
it to a substantial unanimity upon these subjects,
and have established a reasonable degree of precision in the definition of the regulations of interstate commerce exclusively within the control
of Congress, and what legislation remains to the
States where Congress has taken no action in
regard to the matter. *Wabash, St. Louis &c.
Railway* v. *Illinois;*[1] *Fargo* v. *Michigan;*[2] *Philadelphia & Southern Steamship Co.* v. *Pennsylvania.*[3]

The importance of the subject, and the necessity of a true construction of this clause of
the Constitution, may be seen when we consider
the trouble among the States between the time
of the closing of the revolutionary war and the
adoption of that instrument, in regard to their
interstate commerce, and to burdens and ob-
structions placed upon it by each of the States
for what they regarded as their own interest,
without reference to the general good. Indeed,
these considerations were among the principal,
if not the most weighty, which induced its formation. And the cases to which I have referred
as coming before the Supreme Court of the
United States, are ample evidence of what the
States would now do, if they had the power, in
crippling the interstate commerce of this country, by imposing burdens upon its exercise; and
the efforts of the States, endeavoring to shift
the burden of taxation from their own shoulders

---

[1] 118 U. S. 557.   [2] 121 U. S. 230.   [3] 122 U. S. 326.

and impose it upon the property, rights, and interests of others could only end in the destruction of the Union and the total suppression of the free and valuable commerce now carried on between the States.

The relations of the Indian tribes to the States and to the Federal Government have often been before the Supreme Court of the United States, whose judgments have largely influenced the course of legislation by Congress, as well as the States, in regard to those tribes. The first case involving those relations was that of the *Cherokee Nation* v. *Georgia*,[1] in which the court, considering the general subject, held that these tribes, although occupying a semi-independent position, which enabled them to make treaties with the United States, were neither States of the Union nor foreign States, in the sense of the Constitution, which confers jurisdiction upon the Supreme Court in controversies between a State or the citizens thereof and foreign States, citizens, or subjects. It declared that these tribes were, owing to their peculiar conditions, wards and pupils of the nation, and largely under its control.

In the succeeding case of *Worcester* v. *Georgia*,[2] the same proposition is advanced, and it was held that they were independent of the laws and government of the State within which they might as a tribe be located. This latter case was one in which the State of Georgia, having

LECTURE VIII. Importance of these decisions, especially as affecting inter-state commerce.

The Indians.

Cherokee Nation v. Georgia, 5 Pet. 1.

Worcester v. Georgia, 6 Pet. 515.

---

[1] 5 Pet. 1.   [2] 6 Pet. 515.

LECTURE VIII.
Worcester v. Georgia, 6 Pet. 515.

passed a statute extending the jurisdiction of its laws over the Cherokee lands, indicted and imprisoned Worcester, a missionary of some Christian church, who had settled among those Indians, for a violation of a law of the State. He was convicted by the State courts and sent to prison. On a writ of error to the Supreme Court of the United States it was held that the State courts of Georgia had no jurisdiction over the Indian tribes, or the land which they had held in possession from time immemorial.

This principle seems to have settled the independence of those tribes of State legislation and State jurisdiction generally, but it afterwards came to be questioned what power the Government of the United States or Congress could exercise over such Indians. This matter came up in *United States* v. *Kagama*.[1] The whole

United States v. *Kagama*, 118 U.S. 375.

subject there was fully reviewed, and the proposition finally established that "while the Government of the United States has recognized in the Indian tribes heretofore a state of semi-independence and pupilage, it has the right and authority, instead of controlling them by treaties, to govern them by acts of Congress; they being within the geographical limit of the United States, and being necessarily subject to the laws which Congress may enact for their protection and for the protection of the people with whom they come in contact. The States have no such power over them as long as they maintain their tribal relations."

---

[1] 118 U. S. 375.

This settled a difficult and vexatious question, and one very important to the Indians themselves as well as to the citizens of the United States who are brought in contact with them.

LECTURE VIII.
United States v. Kagama, 118 U. S. 375.

Perhaps the two most important decisions of the Supreme Court that have been delivered in many years grew out of the agitation of the subject of slavery. The long and continued discussion of that topic, in and out of Congress, commencing at a time not within the memory of any one in this audience, and prolonged up to the close of the late civil war, which was the cause of that war, the most destructive that the history of mankind presents, almost necessarily brought before the great judicial tribunal of the nation grave questions in regard to the constitutional power of Congress over the subject. With the exception, however, of *Prigg* v. *Pennsylvania* [1] (in which an act of Congress to enable the owners of fugitive slaves who had fled from service and got beyond the borders of the State in which such owners resided, was held to be a proper exercise by Congress of the provisions of the Constitution for the return of persons held to service in the States to which they belonged, and which itself excited much comment), the Dred Scott decision[2] overshadowed all others on the subject, in the importance of the principles which it laid down, and in the immense influence which it had upon the history of the country.

Slavery. Fugitive slaves.

Prigg v. *Pennsylvania*, 16 Pet. 539.

The *Dred Scott Case*, 19 How. 393.

Dred Scott, a slave, having been taken from

---

[1] 16 Pet. 539.   [2] *Dred Scott* v. *Sandford*, 19 How. 393.

the State of Missouri, in which laws authorizing slavery prevailed, by his master with his family into the Territory of Minnesota, in which slavery was forbidden, was afterwards carried back by that master to the State of Missouri. Scott asserted that having been voluntarily carried by his master into a government where slavery was not recognized, he thereby became a free man, and that Sandford, his owner, in exercising restraint over his personal liberty was a trespasser. He therefore brought suit to establish his freedom, and the case came in regular order in the Supreme Court of the United States, which, after some controversy in regard to the jurisdiction of that court, finally decided that it had jurisdiction to entertain the appeal. It then proceeded to decide the question of the effect of the residence of Scott, with the consent of his master, in the free Territory of Minnesota. It held that there existed no power in the Congress of the United States to pass any laws for the government of a Territory of the United States, by which owners of slaves could be prevented from carrying them there and making it their residence, and still retaining the same power and control over their slaves which they had in the States where slavery was established.

This decision was made very soon after Congress had passed a statute for the organization of territorial governments for Kansas and Nebraska, and the question whether slavery should be excluded from those Territories or not by the act agitated the public mind to a degree perhaps

unknown since the formation of the Constitution. To pass a law recognizing as valid the
institution of slavery in these Territories was
not only a violation of the strongest feelings of a
large portion of the people of the United States,
but it was necessarily a repeal of what was called
the compromise on that subject at the time that
the Territory of Missouri was admitted as a State.
At that time the same excited controversy existed, and was only settled by a provision that
in future, slavery should not exist north of a
line corresponding with the southern line of
Missouri, extending westward, namely, the par-
allel of 36° 30′ north latitude. The decision in
the *Dred Scott Case*, that Congress had no power
to pass any law forbidding slavery in any of the
Territories of the United States, from which it
necessarily resulted that the Missouri Compromise law was unconstitutional, added to the
flames of popular excitement.

I do not need to go over the history of the
contest which led to the attempted secession of
eleven of the slave States of the Union, and to
the civil war of four years which followed this
effort to secede. The unparalleled excitement
of the public mind, brought about by the act
organizing the Territories of Kansas and Nebraska, which repealed the Missouri Compromise
law, so far from being mitigated by the Dred
Scott decision, added fuel to the flame. It was
charged that the decision was merely a partisan
effort to aid in the establishment of slavery in
the rich soil of Kansas, and it added force to

LECTURE VIII.
The *Dred Scott*
Case, 19 How. 393.
the determined purpose of those opposed to the further progress of slavery, to prevent it. If that statute had not been passed it is not within the capacity of human wisdom to tell how long the great contest over human slavery within the limits of the United States might have been postponed.

This decision has never been reconsidered in the Supreme Court of the United States. Its operation upon public opinion was to incite to additional ardor the efforts of those who desired the emancipation of the slaves; and, although the decision itself was of no value and only precipitated the evils which it was intended to avoid, the civil war brought about by these events resulted in the abolition of slavery throughout the entire extent of the United States, and, of course, the Dred Scott decision became a useless incumbrance in the reports of that court.

The Thirteenth
Amendment.

At the close of the war the public sentiment of those who had conducted it to a successful termination required certain amendments to the Constitution, the first of which, the Thirteenth, established the abolition of slavery forever within all the dominions over which the United States had jurisdiction. It was soon found, however, that the sudden gift of freedom to over four millions of human beings, who had been slaves, and who were unprepared by education or training to assert their rights or protect themselves against those who had been their masters for generations past, required some additional safeguards in the Constitution, which would operate as a protection to them against those masters, or the acts of the States themselves readmitted into the Union. This induced the passage of the Fourteenth Amendment, which declared all these former slaves to be now citizens of the United States, and entitled to all the privileges and immunities of such citizens. It further enacted provisions for the equality of rights of all persons, intending thereby to secure the rights of this depressed race, and to protect them from unjust and unequal laws which might be passed by the States for the purpose of their oppression.

A short experience seemed to prove that even these two amendments, the one abolishing slavery and the other with the provisions mentioned, were inadequate to secure the purpose which the people had in view, that of guaranteeing equal rights to all persons, including former slaves. The Fifteenth Amendment was therefore passed, which declared that no discrimination in regard to the right of suffrage should be made in any State on account of race, color, or previous condition of servitude.

These three amendments to the Constitution, the Thirteenth, Fourteenth, and Fifteenth, were rapidly passed through Congress and ratified by the States. They have been the subject of many decisions of the Supreme Court of the United States, with regard to their construction and their effect upon enactments of the State legislatures, which have been supposed to be in conflict with them. The most important of

these cases, and perhaps the first one which
came before the court, and which, by reason of
the questions involved and the course of the
argument, required a construction of all three
of these amendments, were *The Slaughter
House Cases,* so called, reported in 16 Wall.
36. They grew out of an act of the legislature of Louisiana, passed since it had been
recognized as a State of the Union after the
close of the civil war. This statute, assuming
to regulate the business of slaughtering animals
for food within the limits of the city of New
Orleans, and of the landing of live animals as
they came into the city, created a corporation
upon which it conferred the exclusive right of
killing animals for food within that city. It
directed the place where they should be landed,
the place where they should be slaughtered,
made full and complete regulations for the main-
tenance of a public slaughter-house by this corporation, at which all butchers must slaughter
the animals whose flesh they intended to sell,
required this corporation to provide all the conveniences necessary for this purpose, and made
proper restrictions upon the price which should
be charged therefor.

After a while the butchers of the city, who
considered this monopoly an invasion of their
personal rights, brought suit to enjoin the exercise of this authority by the slaughter-house
company. The case came finally to the Supreme
Court of the United States, upon the ground
that by the three amendments to the Con-

stitution, to which I have just referred, the
exercise of this power by a State legislature is
forbidden. The whole subject was very fully
argued in that court, and the range of discussion was very wide.

At the close of the civil war there were many very wise and patriotic statesmen who had come to the conclusion that the powers left with the States in the original formation of the Constitution, by which they were enabled to combine and organize into a formidable confederacy for the overthrow of the Government and the destruction of the Union, had been the source of a protracted and terrible war, which was just terminated by the re-establishment of the General Government in all its original powers. They therefore felt, that, in the amendments to the Constitution which were deemed necessary for the reconstruction of this Union, which if not broken was very much shattered, these powers of the States should be curtailed in their capacity to bring about another such catastrophe. Many of these men were in Congress when the resolutions for these amendments were adopted, and proposed to the States for their ratification. The members of · that body undoubtedly differed among themselves as to the effect to be attained, and the manner in which it was to be accomplished by these three amendments. When this case came up, the first in which the Supreme Court was called upon to construe them, the opinions of the judges, of lawyers, and of statesmen, were divergent in regard to the principles which should govern that construction.

These views are represented in the opinions filed in the case mentioned, the opinion of the court being fully concurred in by five of the judges. The court, after speaking of the fact that the civil war disclosed that the true danger to the perpetuity of the Union was in the capacity of the States to organize, combine, and concentrate all the powers of a State and all contiguous States to resistance to the General Government, said: —

"Unquestionably this has given great force to the argument, and added largely to the number of those who believe in the necessity of a strong National Government. But, however pervading this sentiment, and however it may have contributed to the adoption of the amendments we have been considering, we do not see in those amendments any purpose to destroy the main features of the general system. Under the pressure of all the excited feeling growing out of the war, our statesmen have still believed that the existence of the States with powers for domestic and local government, including the regulation of civil rights — the rights of person and property — was essential to the perfect working of our complex form of government, though they have thought proper to impose additional limitations on the States, and to confer additional power on that of the United States. But whatever fluctuations may be seen in the history of public opinion on this subject during

the period of our national existence, we think it
will be found that this court, so far as its functions required, has always held with a steady
and an even hand the balance between State
and Federal power, and we trust that such may
continue to be the history of its relation to that
subject so long as it shall have duties to perform
which demand of it a construction of the Constitution, or of any of its parts." [1]

Although this decision did not meet the approval of four out of nine of the judges on
some points on which it rested, yet public sentiment, as found in the press and in the universal
acquiescence which it received, accepted it with
great unanimity; and although there were in-
timations that in the legislative branches of the
Government the opinion would be reviewed, and
criticised unfavorably, no such thing has occurred in the fifteen years which have elapsed
since it was delivered. And while the question
of the construction of these amendments, and
particularly the Fourteenth, has often been before the Supreme Court of the United States,
no attempt to overrule or disregard this elementary decision of the effect of the three new constitutional amendments upon the relations of
the State governments to the Federal Government has been made; and it may be considered
now as settled that, with the exception of the
specific provisions in them for the protection of
the personal rights of the citizens and people of

LECTURE VIII.
Construction of
amendments in
*The Slaughter
House Cases.*

---

[1] *Slaughter House Cases*, 16 Wall. 36, 82.

the United States, and the necessary restrictions
upon the power of the States for that purpose,
with the additions to the powers of the General
Government to enforce those provisions, no substantial change has been made. The necessity
of the great powers, conceded by the Constitution originally to the Federal Government, and
the equal necessity of the autonomy of the
States and their power to regulate their domestic
affairs, remain as the great features of our complex form of government.

The only other decision of the Supreme Court
to which I shall call your attention is that of
Kilbourn v. *Thompson*, 103 U. S. 168. It is
principally remarkable as establishing the right
of a party to recover damages for an unlawful
imprisonment by the express order of the House
of Representatives. That body, as well as the
Senate, had been in the habit of calling witnesses before them to testify in regard to various
matters concerning which an investigation had
been ordered by one or the other of those bodies.
They also seem to have exercised without hesitation the power to punish by fine and imprisonment any witness who refused to answer
questions which, by order of the particular body
authorizing the investigation, had been propounded to him, and without much if any regard to the limitation upon their right to
exercise this power.

Under a resolution, which recited that the
Government was a creditor of the banking firm
of Jay Cooke & Company, then in bankruptcy

by the decree of the District Court of the United
States for the Eastern District of Pennsylvania,
and that settlements had been made adverse to
the interests of the United States in that court,
a special committee of the House of Representatives was appointed by the Speaker to inquire
into the matter, together with the history of a
real estate pool, in which that firm was said to
be involved. In the progress of the investigation Mr. Kilbourn, who was a real estate dealer
in the city of Washington, was called before the
committee and required to make statements in
regard to his dealings with various persons who
had had transactions with him, and to produce
his books for the general inspection of the committee. He declined to do this, and being brought
before the House he was ordered to make answer.
Still further declining, the House ordered him to
be imprisoned, and that the Speaker issue his
warrant to the sergeant-at-arms to commit him
for contempt.

Mr. Kilbourn was held in confinement under
this order for some time, but was finally released
on a writ of *habeas corpus* issued by the Chief
Justice of the Supreme Court of the District of
Columbia. He then brought suit against the
sergeant-at-arms, by whom he was kept in
prison, and against the members of the committee who were active in procuring the order
of the House for his punishment. On a de-
murrer to the answer of the defendants, which
set up this order of the House as their defence,
the Supreme Court of the District of Columbia

held the answer to be good; but on a writ of error to the Supreme Court of the United States that decision was reversed.

The opinion goes into a thorough examination of the history of this class of questions in various cases before the House of Commons of Great Britain, which were afterwards carried to the courts of that country, and comes to the conclusion that, while in that country, by reason of the history of the Parliament, and of its original possession of full judicial powers, the House of Commons could punish for contempt, there is no inherent authority in any purely legislative body, apart from that remnant of judicial power remaining in the Parliament, to punish parties for offences of that character.

Referring to the Constitution of the United States, under which alone Congress, as an entire body or either branch of it, could exercise any such power, it is declared that there is a total absence of any general grant of such authority; but inasmuch as each branch of Congress had certain specific powers to make orders which required the examination of witnesses, that in that class of cases, where a witness refused to testify, the House could enforce this duty by fine and imprisonment as a punishment for contempt. Those occasions were limited to such cases as punishment of its own members for disorderly conduct, or failure to attend sessions, or in cases of contested elections, or in regard to the qualifications of its own members, or in case of an

effort to impeach an officer of the Government,
and perhaps a few others.

It was held that neither House had any right
to organize an investigation into the private
affairs of a citizen, and that, except in a case in
which the Constitution expressly conferred upon
the one body or the other powers which were
in their nature somewhat judicial, and which
required the examination of witnesses, they possessed no power to compel by fine or imprisonment, or both, the attendance of such witnesses,
and answers to interrogatories which did not
relate to some question of which it had jurisdiction.

This decision, which ultimately resulted in the
recovery of a large judgment by Mr. Kilbourn
against the sergeant-at-arms, which sum was
paid by an appropriation made by the Congress
of the United States out of the Treasury, was
everywhere received with satisfaction. It has
been followed in the States of the Union where
similar questions have constantly arisen, and is
undoubtedly, on account of the assertion by it of
the right of the citizen to be protected against
the legislative body, and to be proceeded against
for any offence only in the judicial branch of the
Government, one of the most important that
has been made in recent years. It is also important as being in some sense a direct control
by the Supreme Court of the United States over
the decisions and acts of one of the branches of
the legislative department of the Government,
made without authority of the law.

It is proper also to observe that the court decided that the members of the committee who had propounded these questions to Kilbourn, and at whose instance the House passed the resolution for his imprisonment, were not liable to his action for damages, on the ground that what they did came within the constitutional provision that "senators and representatives . . . shall in all cases, except treason, felony, and breach of the peace, be privileged from arrest during their attendance at the session of their respective Houses, and in going to and returning from the same ; and for any speech or debate in either House, they shall not be questioned in any other place." Art. I, sec. 6.

This court, of which we have been speaking, whether we take the character of the suitors that are brought before it, or the importance of the subjects of litigation over which it has final jurisdiction, may well be considered one of the highest that the world has ever seen. It has the power to bring States before it, States which some of our politicians have been in the habit of considering sovereign, not only when they come voluntarily, but by judicial process they are subjected, in certain classes of cases, to the judgment of the court. Whatever these States may have been at the time of the formation of the Constitution, they now number their inhabitants by millions, and in wealth and civilization are equal to many of the independent sovereignties of Europe.

The subject matter of which this court has jurisdiction is the construction and exposition of the Constitution of the United States, which controls the affairs of sixty millions of people. Its every-day business, almost, is to pass upon the question of conflicting rights and jurisdictions between the States and the United States, and between the laws framed by each of this class of political bodies. Its judges hold their offices for life, unless removed by impeachment. But one attempt has been made in the history of the Government to impeach a member of that court, and that effort failed.

LECTURE VIII.
No danger to be apprehended from the exercise of the power to construe the Constitution.

It has been said that these powers may be dangerous to the people, and to the other departments of the Government, but the answer to this is both true and perfect. The judicial branch of the Government, of which the Supreme Court is the head, is the weakest of all the three great departments into which the power of the nation is divided. It has no army, it has no navy, and it has no purse. It has no patronage, it has no officers, except its clerks and marshals, and the latter are appointed by the President and confirmed by the Senate. They are the officers to whom its processes are sent for the enforcement of its judgments, but they may be removed at any time by the Executive. The clerks, whom the judges in some form or other are permitted to appoint, have salaries or compensation regulated by the legislature. The clerk who may receive $20,000 or more, in fees, must pay all but $3500 of such receipts into the

LECTURE VIII.
No danger in the
exercise by the
Court of its power
to construe the
Constitution.

Treasury of the United States. The judges themselves are dependent upon appropriations made by the legislature for the payment of the salaries which support them while engaged in the functions of their office.

It is, then, so far as the ordinary forms of power are concerned, by far the feeblest branch or department of the Government. It must rely upon the confidence and respect of the public for its just weight and influence, and it may be confidently asserted that neither with the people, nor the country at large, nor the other branches of the Government, have there ever been found wanting that respect and confidence. It is one of the best tributes which can be paid to the American nation, a tribute which it deserves above all others, even of Anglo-Saxon descent, and which can be paid to no other race, that it always submits to the law as expounded by its judiciary. In all the excitements of bitter contests, involving great financial interests, power, position, and even political existence, in fact everything which could properly be brought within its judicial cognizance, the people have always felt that their interests were safely intrusted to its charge.

That the court may long continue to deserve this confidence, as it has for the past hundred years, must be the desire of every patriotic citizen.

NOTES UPON LECTURE VIII.

Mr. Justice Miller's treatment of the sub- ject of this lecture is so thorough, and his reference to cases so recent, as to leave little to be said. The subjects will be considered in the order in which they are treated in the lecture.

1. *Detail of a Justice to other duties.*

In addition to the cases of Chief Justice Jay and Chief Justice Marshall, referred to by Mr. Justice Miller, there have been two notable instances, in more recent days, of the detail, if I may call it so for want of a better word, of justices of the Supreme Court to the performance of duties outside of the judicial power imposed upon them by the Constitution.

In January, 1871, the British Cabinet made confidential approaches to the Government of the United States with a view to ascertain whether some practicable way could not be found for disposing of the pending questions between the two governments, including the Alabama Claims, the Fisheries, and the Oregon boundary. This resulted in an agreement to organize a joint commission, which should be charged with dealing with these subjects; and

419

LECTURE VIII. on the 9th of February, just one month after
Detail of a justice the negotiations opened, President Grant nomi-
to other duties.
nated to the Senate five commissioners on the
part of the United States, of whom one was
"Samuel Nelson, an associate justice of the
Supreme Court of the United States." The
message with the nominations was accompanied
by a brief on "Plurality of Offices" for the use
of the Senate. The first among several cases
given was that of Mr. Jay; and it was said that
he was nominated to the Senate "as Envoy
Extraordinary of the United States on the 16th
of April, 1794; was confirmed on the 19th of
that month; went to London, and there signed
the treaty known as Jay's Treaty on the 29th
of November, 1794; arrived in New York on
the 28th of May, 1795; and resigned the office
of chief justice on the 29th of the following June."

I trust it will not be thought improper for
me to add a fact within my own knowledge,
that Mr. Justice Nelson proved to be a most
valuable member on that commission. His counsels were always judicious, and his views were
generally adopted by his colleagues. His labors
there lasted until after the end of that term of
court, and with them closed the work of a long
and honorable career of public service. He was
retired at his own request in the following
autumn, and died in December, 1873.

The second instance of such detail was brought
about by the Act of January 29, 1877,[1] under

_____

[1] 19 Stat. 227, c. 37.

which the Electoral Commission was established LECTURE VIII.
Detail of a justice
to other duties. to decide "all questions upon or in respect of double returns" in the Presidential election of that year. This body consisted of five members of the Senate, five members of the House, and five associate justices of the Supreme Court, of whom Mr. Justice Miller was one. It is unnecessary to make further references to so recent an historic fact.

2. *Suits against a State.*

The provision in the Constitution conferring
upon the Federal courts judicial power in " controversies between two or more States" was adopted from the Articles of ·Confederation, which provided, in Article IX, that, " The United States in Congress assembled shall also be the last resort on appeal in all disputes and differences, now subsisting or that may hereafter arise, between two or more States concerning boundary, jurisdiction, or any other cause whatever." Elaborate provisions were made for regulating the exercise of this jurisdiction which need not be described. This power was invoked six times during the existence of the Confederation; but in only one case were the proceedings carried to final judgment. All were questions of territorial jurisdiction.

The first in date related to the sovereignty over the territory now known as Vermont, then claimed by New York on the one hand, and New Hampshire on the other. The settlers and occupiers of the soil drove out the New York

officials by force in 1775, and refused to recognize any authority in New Hampshire. The
State of New York initiated proceedings in
Congress under the Articles of Confederation.
The State of New Hampshire responded, but
the actual settlers refused to come into court,
although censured by Congress. We have the
authority of Mr. Hamilton[1] for saying that
their attitude caused some anxiety. Vermont
had made up its mind to be independent.
Massachusetts assented to the recognition of its
independence in 1781; New Hampshire followed in the same year; New York in 1790;
and the controversy was closed, without a judicial determination, by its admission into the
Union in 1791.[2]

The controversy between Virginia and Pennsylvania as to the boundary line between them
was before Congress in 1779 by its own initia-
tion. It does not appear that either State invoked its interference. It was settled between
the parties by mutually agreeing to and running, on the face of the soil, the line now
known as "Mason and Dixon's line."

The controversy between Pennsylvania and
Connecticut concerning the sovereignty of lands
on the east branch of the Susquehanna, is the
only one that was ever brought to trial and
judgment under the Articles of Confederation.
An account of the proceedings is given in the
Appendix to volume 131 of the United States
Reports, at pages liv.–lviii.

---

[1] Federalist, No. 7.   [2] 1 Stat. 191.

In the proceedings instituted by the State of
New Jersey against the State of Virginia in
1784, the apparent object was to prevent Congress from accepting the cession by New York, Virginia, and Connecticut of the Northwestern lands. Nothing was done beyond the presentation of the petition.

The dispute between Massachusetts and New York was carried to the point of selecting judges to be appointed by Congress, and was then settled by the parties.

That between South Carolina and Georgia reached the same point, and got no farther, if the record is to be trusted. It is apparently the same controversy which was settled by an agreement between the parties, which will be found in *South Carolina* v. *Georgia*, 93 U. S. 5, 6.

It was found both convenient and just to have a tribunal vested with jurisdiction to determine such controversies; and so, when the Constitution was adopted, it contained a provision that the judicial power should extend to controversies between two or more States.

In *Hans* v. *Louisiana*, 134 U. S. 1, which was an action against the State of Louisiana brought by one of its citizens to recover on coupons annexed to bonds of the State, it was held that a State could not, without its consent, be sued in a Circuit Court of the United States, upon a suggestion that the case was one arising under the Constitution and laws of the United States; and *Chisholm* v. *Georgia*, 2 Dall. 419, com-

mented on by Judge Miller in this chapter, was
substantially overruled, the court saying that the
views of Mr. Justice Iredell, who dissented from
the judgment, "were clearly right."

3. *Some Recent Cases additional to those cited
by Mr. Justice Miller.*

Mandamus.

In *Dunlap* v. *Black*[1] the question before the
court was whether mandamus should issue to the
Commissioner of Pensions, commanding him to
increase a pension. Mr. Justice Bradley reviewed
at length the cases of *Marbury* v. *Madison*,[2] *Kendall* v. *United States*,[3] *Decatur* v. *Paulding*,[4] *United
States* v. *Schurz*,[5] and others, and as a result of
the examination laid down this rule: "The court
will not interfere by mandamus with the executive officers of the Government in the exercise
of their ordinary official duties, even where those
duties require an interpretation of the law, the
court having no appellate power for that purpose; but when they refuse to act in a case at
all, or when, by special statute or otherwise, a
mere ministerial duty is imposed upon them,
that is, a service which they are bound to perform without further question, then, if they refuse, mandamus will be issued to compel them."

---

[1] 128 U. S. 40.   [2] 1 Cranch. 137.
[3] 12 Pet. 524.   [4] 14 Pet. 497.
[5] 102 U. S. 378. See also *Brashear* v. *Mason*, 6 How. 92; *Goodrich* v. *Guthrie*, 17 How. 284; *Commissioner of Patents* v. *Whiteley*,
4 Wall. 522; *Georgia* v. *Stanton*, 6 Wall. 50; *Gaines* v. *Thompson*,
7 Wall. 347; *Butterworth* v. *Hoe*, 112 U. S. 50.

The recent cases relating to interstate com- LECTURE VIII.
merce will be referred to more at length in connec- Interstate com-
tion with Lecture IX. The latest case referred to merce.
by Mr. Justice Miller is *Philadelphia & Southern
Steamship Co.* v. *Pennsylvania.*[1] The leading
cases since that time are recited in the note
below.[2] The great number of them is an evidence of the importance of the subject, and of
the pertinacity, alluded to more than once by
Mr. Justice Miller, with which the States try to
get round this provision of the Constitution, and
secure for themselves some advantages in violation of its spirit.

In *Cook* v. *United States*[3] the statutes relating Indians.
to the organization of the Indian Territory, and
more especially the courts of the United States
and their criminal jurisdiction within it, are
reviewed at length, both in the arguments and
in the opinion. In *Gon-shay-ee's Case*[4] it was
held that the Act of March 3, 1885,[5] was enacted

---

[1] 122 U. S. 326.

[2] *Sands* v. *Manistee River Improvement Co.*, 123 U. S. 288; *Smith*
v. *Alabama*, 124 U. S. 465; *Pembina Mining Co.* v. *Pennsylvania*,
125 U. S. 181; *Bowman* v. *Chicago & Northwestern Railway Co.*,
125 U. S. 465; *California* v. *Central Pacific Railroad Co.*, 127 U. S.
1; *Ratterman* v. *Western Union Tel. Co.*, 127 U. S. 411; *Leloup*
v. *Port of Mobile*, 127 U. S. 640; *Kidd* v. *Pearson*, 128 U. S. 1;
Nashville, Chattanooga &c. Railway Co. v. *Alabama*, 128 U. S. 96;
Stoutenburgh v. *Hennick*, 129 U. S. 141; *Pennsylvania Railroad
Co.* v. *Miller*, 132 U. S. 75; *Western Union Telegraph Co.* v. *Ala-
bama*, 132 U. S. 472; *Leisy* v. *Hardin*, 135 U. S. 100; *Lyng* v.
Michigan, 135 U. S. 161; *McCall* v. *California*, 136 U. S. 104;
Norfolk & Western Railroad Co. v. *Pennsylvania*, 136 U. S. 114;
Minnesota v. *Barber*, 136 U. S. 313; *Brimmer* v. *Rebman*, 138 U. S.
78; *Pullman's Palace Car Co.* v. *Pennsylvania*, 141 U. S. 18;
Crutcher v. *Kentucky*, 141 U. S. 47.

[3] 138 U. S. 157.   [4] 130 U. S. 343.   [5] 23 Stat. 385, c. 341, § 9.

to transfer to Territorial courts established by the United States the jurisdiction to try the crimes described in it[1] when sitting as and exercising the functions of a Territorial court, and not of a Circuit or District Court of the United States; and in *Mayfield's Case*[2] it is held that a member of the Cherokee nation, committing the crime of adultery in territory assigned to that tribe, is not subject to trial for that crime by the courts of the United States.

In *Clay* v. *Field*[3] it appeared that two persons were partners in working a plantation in Tennessee. One of them died before the civil war, and the other retained possession of it in good faith, and also of all the slaves upon it, and continued to operate it for what he thought was for the interest of the deceased as well as himself. The war broke out, the plantation was in the theatre of the conflict, and at its close the slaves were free. In view of all the circumstances, the court decided that the surviving partner was not accountable for the value of the slaves, but that he was accountable for the fair rental value of the property, including the slaves while they were slaves.

In *Baiz' Case*, 135 U. S. 403, the petitioner Baiz, being sued in the Circuit Court of the United States for the Southern District of New York, set up a constitutional privilege, as a diplomatic representative, to be exempt from the

---

[1] Murder, manslaughter, rape, assault with intent to kill, and larceny.

[2] 141 U. S. 107.   [3] 138 U. S. 464.

jurisdiction of that court. Evidence was offered on both sides in the Supreme Court. This claim being overruled, he applied to the Supreme Court for a writ of prohibition or mandamus to restrain the Circuit Court from exercising further jurisdiction in the case. It was held that, in the absence of a certificate from the Secretary of State that he was such a representative, he was not entitled to the immunity from suit except in the Supreme Court which is granted to such persons by the Constitution. It was also held that, on such an application, the respondent was called upon to produce any evidence within his knowledge to overcome the petitioner's proof of his privilege ; and that the court could accept the certificate of the Department of State upon the question at issue, and was not required to proceed upon argumentative or collateral proof.

In *Cooper's Case*, 138 U. S. 404, on an appli- cation for a writ of prohibition to restrain the District Court of the United States for the District of Alaska from issuing process upon a decree condemning a vessel for illegally capturing seals, the court held that it had jurisdiction, and granted leave to file the petition for the writ.

In *Neagle's Case*, 135 U. S. 1, argued and decided after this lecture was delivered, the subject of the protection which the Constitution affords to the court when exercising the judicial power conferred upon it was elaborately considered, the opinion of the court being written by

Mr. Justice Miller. The headnotes of the case,
as reported, which were also written by him,
embody all the propositions of law bearing
upon the subject, which were discussed and
decided by the court, and also make a sufficiently full statement of the facts to enable the
student to understand exactly what was before
the court and decided by it. The material propositions in those headnotes are the following:—

"By virtue of Rev. Stat. §§ 606, 610, the justices of the Supreme Court of the United States
are allotted among the nine circuits, to each
one of which a judge is assigned; and the latter section makes it the duty of each judge to
attend the Circuit Court in each district of the
circuit to which he is allotted, and thereby imposes upon him the necessity of travelling from
his residence to the Circuit Court which he is to
attend, and from each place in that circuit where
the court is held to the other places where it is
held. *Held*, that, while a judge is thus travelling to or from those places, he is as much in
discharge of his duty as when listening to and
deciding cases in open court, and is as much
entitled to protection in the one case as in the
other.

"While there is no express statute authorizing
the appointment of a deputy marshal, or any
other officer, to attend a judge of the Supreme
Court when travelling in his circuit, and to
protect him against assaults or other injury, the
general obligation imposed upon the President

of the United States by the Constitution to see
that the laws be faithfully executed, and the
means placed in his hands, both by the Constitution and the laws of the United States, to enable
him to do this, impose upon the executive department the duty of protecting a justice or
judge of any of the courts of the United States,
when there is just reason to believe that he will
be in personal danger while executing the duties
of his office.

"An assault upon a judge of a court of the
United States, while in discharge of his official
duties, is a breach of the peace of the United
States, as distinguished from the peace of the
State in which the assault takes place.

"Under the provisions of Rev. Stat. § 788, it is
the duty of marshals and their deputies in each
State to exercise, in keeping the peace of the
United States, the powers given to the sheriffs
of the State for keeping the peace of the State;
and a Deputy Marshal of the United States,
specially charged with the duty of protecting
and guarding a judge of a court of the United
States, has imposed upon him the duty of doing
whatever may be necessary for that purpose,
even to the taking of human life.

"United States officers and other persons, held
in custody by State authorities for doing acts
which they were authorized or required to do by
the Constitution and laws of the United States,
are entitled to be released from such imprisonment; and the writ of *habeas corpus* is the appropriate remedy for that purpose.

"David Neagle, a Deputy Marshal of the United States for the District of California, was brought by writ of *habeas corpus* before the Circuit Court of that district, upon the allegation that he was held in imprisonment by the sheriff of San Joaquin County, California, on a charge of the murder of David S. Terry. He alleged that the killing of Terry by him was done in pursuance of his duty as such deputy marshal in defending the life of Mr. Justice Field, while in discharge of his duties as Circuit Judge of the ninth circuit. On the trial of this writ in the Circuit Court it entered an order discharging the prisoner, finding that he was in custody for an act done in pursuance of a law of the United States, and was imprisoned in violation of the Constitution and laws of the United States. The case being brought up to the Supreme Court by appeal, this court, on examining the voluminous testimony, arrived at the conviction that there was a settled purpose on the part of Terry and his wife, amounting to a conspiracy, to murder Mr. Justice Field, on his official visit to California in the summer of 1889 ; that this arose from animosity against him on account of judicial decisions made in the Circuit Court of the United States for the Northern District of California in a suit or suits to which they were parties; that the purpose which they had of doing Mr. Justice Field an injury became so well and so publicly known, that a correspondence ensued between the marshal and the district attorney of that district and the Attor-

ney General of the United States, the result of
which was that Neagle was appointed a deputy marshal for the express purpose of guarding Mr. Justice Field against an attack by Terry and his wife which might result in his death; that such an attack did take place; that Neagle, being there for the said purpose of affording protection, had just reason to believe that the attack would result in the death of Mr. Justice Field unless he interfered; and that he did justifiably interfere by shooting Terry while in the act of assaulting Mr. Justice Field, whom he had already struck two or three times. *Held,*

"(1) That Neagle was justified in defending Mr. Justice Field in this manner;

"(2) That in so doing he acted in discharge of his duty as an officer of the United States;

"(3) That having so acted, in that capacity, he could not be guilty of murder under the laws of California, nor held to answer to its courts for an act for which he had the authority of the laws of the United States;

"(4) That the judgment of the Circuit Court, discharging him from the custody of the sheriff of San Joaquin County, must therefore be affirmed."

This case, from the novelty of the questions involved, and from the character and eminence of the distinguished jurist assaulted by Terry, naturally excited the greatest attention throughout the country. There was some difference of opinion between members of the bar before the argument. The elaborate opinion of the court,

however, closed the doors against further discussion; and it has been accepted as affording
to the court only the measure of protection to
which it is justly entitled.

Mr. Justice Miller brings his treatment of the
Thirteenth, Fourteenth, and Fifteenth Amendments only to *The Slaughter House Case.* There
have been many decisions upon these amendments, made since that case, in which some one
of them has been the subject of controversy
and of construction. These cases are grouped
together in the supplementary paper, No. XIII,
in which the subjects not discussed elsewhere
are treated.

IX.

REGULATION OF COMMERCE AMONG THE STATES.[1]

—∘o⟩✕⟨o∘—

ARTICLE I, SECTION 8, PARAGRAPH 3. The Con- LECTURE IX.
gress shall have Power . . . To regulate Commerce
with Foreign Nations, and among the several States,
and with the Indian Tribes.

THE text of this discourse is one of the most Regulation of commerce among States. important of the powers delegated to Congress by the Constitution of the United States. It is provided in Article I, section 8, paragraph 3, of that instrument, as follows : —

" The Congress shall have power, . . . to regulate commerce with foreign nations, and among the several States, and with the Indian tribes."

You would scarcely imagine, and I am sure The importance of this power. you do not know, unless you have given some consideration to the subject, how very important is that little sentence in the Constitution. It was the want of any power to regulate commerce, as between the States themselves, and with foreign nations, which as much, and I am not sure but I am justified in saying more, than any

---

[1] This lecture is Lecture VII of the Lectures delivered before the classes at the University Law School.

433

one thing, forced the States to form the present Constitution in lieu of the Articles of Confederation under which they had won their freedom and established their independence. It is difficult now for us to fully appreciate how strong was the tendency to separate, to quarrel, and to bring their adverse interests into collision, which grew out of the want of any general power in the Federal Government, as it then existed, to control the commercial relations of the States with each other. A slight examination in the records which remain to us of the conditions, circumstances, and the discussions which preceded the formation of the Constitution, will be of service in enabling us to better understand this subject.

One of the earliest and most significant was a resolution of the Virginia legislature of January 21, 1786. The Convention that framed the present Constitution assembled in the year 1787, so that this resolution was passed but a little over a year before its meeting. It was proposed to confer, by the action of the separate States composing the Confederation, additional power on the then Congress of the United States. This was a most pressing question, the necessity was urgent, and the legislature of Virginia thus expressed its desire that there should be greater power placed in the hands of the National Government. The resolution reads as follows : —

"Resolved, that Edmund Randolph, James Madison Jr., Walter Jones, St. George Tucker, and Merriweather Smith, Esquires, be appointed

commissioners, who or any three of whom shall Lecture IX
meet such commissioners, as may be appointed Action of Virginia In 1786.
in the other States of the Union at a time and
place to be agreed on, to take into consideration
the trade of the United States; to examine the
relative situations and trade of said States; to
consider how far a uniform system in their commercial regulations may be necessary to their
common interest and their permanent harmony;
and to report to the several States such an act
relative to this great object as, when unanimously ratified by them, will enable the United
States, in Congress, effectually to provide for
the same." [1]

Mr. Madison was undoubtedly the author of Mr. Madison.
that resolution, and he was afterwards a member of the Convention which framed the Constitution. That was the only resolution passed at
that time, so that it is evident that more than a
year before that Convention was finally called,
the trade and commerce of the country occupied
a prominent place in the minds of the Virginia
legislature, as well as in the thought of this distinguished statesman, together with the prominent idea that there should be such regulation
of that commerce as might be beneficial to all
the States, with a power to control it placed in
the central authority, weak though it then was.
With the same end in view Oliver Ellsworth Mr. Ellsworth.
of Connecticut, a distinguished man of that day,
a member of the Constitutional Convention, and

---

[1] 5 Elliot's Debates, 113 (Madison Papers).

one of the early Chief Justices of the Supreme Court of the United States, had urged upon the people of his State to send delegates to the Convention which was to consider the subject of a Federal Constitution. His main argument was that the people of his State were suffering from the imposts laid upon their commerce by the States of New York and Rhode Island, each of which had fine harbors and ports of entry. Having succeeded in getting a Constitution adopted with this provision in it, he was then elected to the State convention which should approve or reject it. In the opening of the discussion in that body, in the first speech that was made, he made use of this remarkable language : —

"Our being tributaries to our sister States is in consequence of the want of a Federal system. The State of New York raises £60,000 or £80,000 a year by impost. Connecticut consumes about one-third of the goods upon which this impost is laid, and consequently pays one third of this sum to New York. If we import by the medium of Massachusetts she has an impost, and to her we pay a tribute." [1]

The Federalist, that remarkable series of papers published by Hamilton, Madison, and Jay, while the ratification of the Constitution was pending before the people in their State conventions, contains, of course, the principal arguments in favor of the adoption of that instrument. To that, therefore, all persons

---

[1] 2 Elliot's Debates, 189.

engaged in construing the Constitution of the United States naturally look for a contemporaneous exposition of it by the distinguished statesmen of that period, two of whom were engaged in its formation, and who had no superiors at that time in the public service. In the seventh number of that series of articles the author, in speaking of the evils of a divided condition of the States, says: —

" The competitions of commerce would be another fruitful source of contention. The States less favorably circumstanced would be desirous of escaping from the disadvantages of local situation, and of sharing in the advantages of their more fortunate neighbors. Each State, or separate confederacy, would pursue a system of commercial polity peculiar to itself. This would occasion distinctions, preferences, and exclusions, which would beget discontent. The habits of intercourse, on the basis of equal privileges, to which we have been accustomed from the earliest settlement of the country, would give a keener edge to those causes of discontent, than they would naturally have, independent of this circumstance. *We should be ready to denominate injuries those things which were in reality the justifiable acts of independent sovereignties consulting a distinct interest.*" [1]

Again the following language is used: —

" The opportunities which some States would have of rendering others tributary to them, by

---

[1] The Federalist, No. 7 (Hamilton).

commercial regulations, would be impatiently submitted to by the tributary States. The relative situation of New York, Connecticut, and New Jersey, would afford an example of this kind. New York, from the necessities of revenue, must lay duties on her importations. A great part of these duties must be paid by the inhabitants of the two other States in the capacity of consumers of what we import. New York would neither be willing, nor able, to forego this advantage. Her citizens would not consent that a duty paid by them should be remitted in favor of the citizens of her neighbors." [1]

The subject is recurred to again in the twenty-second letter : —

" The interfering and unneighborly regulations of some States, contrary to the true spirit of the union, have, in different instances, given just cause of umbrage and complaint to others ; and it is to be feared that examples of this nature, if not restrained by a national control, would be multiplied and extended till they became not less serious sources of animosity and discord, than injurious impediments to the intercourse between the different parts of the confederacy." [2]

Here follows a sentence remarkable as almost a prophecy of what we have seen and known in our day : —

" The commerce of the German Empire is in

---

[1] The Federalist, No. 7.   [2] Ib. No. 22.

continual trammels, from the multiplicity of the Lecture IX
The Federalist. duties which the several princes and States exact upon the merchandises passing through their territories, by means of which the fine streams and navigable rivers with which Germany is so happily watered, are rendered almost useless." [1]

Now we know that Germany submitted to German Zoll-
verein. that condition of affairs until some fifty or sixty years ago, when that portion since called North Germany, with Prussia as the dominant power, formed what they called the Zollverein.[2] This was a commercial union between about a dozen of those States, Dukedoms, and Principalities, by which it was arranged that travellers and goods of all kinds might pass entirely through their

---

[1] The Federalist, No. 22, quoting from the Encyclopædia, art. Empire.

[2] The Zollverein had its origin in a customs convention between Prussia and the Grand Duchy of Hesse in 1828 ; and other states, as they gradually became convinced of the advantages afforded by a general customs frontier, joined it from time to time during the succeeding forty years. The following table shows the progressive territorial limits of the Zollverein, which may be regarded as the precursor of the present German Empire : —

Years.	States entering During the Various Periods.	Area Square Miles.	Population of the Union States.
1828	Prussia, Hesse (Grand Duchy) .	112,000	13,295,254
1831	Hesse-Cassel	115,300	15,090,075
1834	Bavaria, Würtemberg, Saxony, Thuringia, etc.	163,900	23,478,120
1844	Brunswick, Luxembourg, etc. .	171,900	28,498,136
1851	Hannover, Oldenburg	191,800	32,559,055
1868	Schleswig-Holstein, Lauenburg, Mechlenburg	205,500	38,277,939
1871	Alsace-Lorraine	209,251	40,677,950

Encyclopædia Britannica, vol. 10, 455 (9th ed.).

territories with but one inspection and one set of duties. I am not familiar with the details of the treaty, but, as we all know, its practical result was to bring together all the North German States in a union for all commercial transactions. That condition of affairs had existed but a few years when war broke out between Prussia and Austria. The entire North German Confederacy, if it could be so called, joined Prussia in this war, in which that country was successful, and they then established a still more intimate relation, forming themselves into one kingdom or government. They then extended their Zollverein, but not their unity of government, to South Germany, which included Bavaria and Würtemberg, each of which was a rather large kingdom in its territorial extent among those small principalities. So intimate, however, was this commercial relation that those two governments followed Prussia in the subsequent war with France, and at the end of that war the present German Empire was organized. All this grew out of the original commercial union, called the Zollverein, adopted to prevent discriminating duties and other troubles which arise when the business relations of neighboring territories are interrupted by independent laws and regulations.

In the paper No. 41 of the Federalist there is another reference to this subject, written before the adoption of the Constitution, in which the same idea is expressed.

" The defect of power in the existing confederacy to regulate the commerce between its several members, is in the number of those which have been clearly pointed out by experience. To the proofs and remarks which former papers have brought into view on this subject, it may be added, that without this supplemental provision, the great and essential power of regulating foreign commerce would have been incomplete and ineffectual. A very material object of this power was the relief of the States which import and export through other States, from the improper contributions levied on them by the latter. Were these at liberty to regulate the trade between State and State, it must be foreseen that ways would be found out to load the articles of import and export, during the passage through their jurisdiction, with duties which would fall on the makers of the latter, and the consumers of the former. We may be assured by past experience, that such a practice would be introduced by future contrivances ; and both by that and a common knowledge of human affairs, that it would nourish increasing animosities, and not improbably terminate in serious interruptions of the public tranquillity." [1]

Lecture IX. Importance of this clause in the Constitution.

A further indication of the importance which the States attached to this matter is to be found in the fact that Rhode Island was between two and three years in ratifying the Constitution, after all the other States except North Carolina had acted upon the subject. Your attention

Legislation of Rhode Island.

---

[1] The Federalist, No. 41 (Dawson's ed.) ; No. 42 all other editions.

may not have been called to the reason which governed Rhode Island in that matter, but history shows that it was on account of the importance which that State attached to this power to regulate the commerce that would naturally seek its ports.   It possessed in Newport one of the finest harbors on the whole Atlantic coast, and a very large part of the imports into the northern States of the Union from abroad went through that town.   There was, of course, a heavy tax laid upon such importations, so that this little State and its principal city were paying their expenses and living a jolly life off of the imposts collected on goods that went through its ports to Connecticut, Massachusetts, New Hampshire, and the adjoining States, for consumption.

The experience of the country since the adoption of the Constitution has shown how wise were its framers in including this particular clause which we are now considering within its provisions.   From the case of *Gibbons* v. *Ogden*, 9 Wheat. 1, 189, argued in the Supreme Court of the United States in 1824, down to the present time, there have been many judicial decisions upon this subject, in which acts of the States were held void which were intended to infringe that provision of the Constitution, and which attempted to impose upon the property and goods of citizens of other States the burdens which the citizens of the States making the enactments ought themselves to bear.   The case of *Gibbons* v. *Ogden*, in which the opinion was delivered by Chief Justice Marshall, arose under a statute of the State of New York which seemed to be intended as a liberal concession on account of an invention of great public value. That State granted to Robert R. Livingston and Robert Fulton, the inventor of the steamboat, the exclusive right of navigating all the waters within its jurisdiction with boats moved by fire or steam for a term of years. This included the waters of the Hudson River, which were then relatively more important than they now are, because there were no railroads or canals. The defendant Gibbons employed two steamboats, running between New York and Elizabethtown in the State of New Jersey, in violation, as it was claimed, of this exclusive privilege. An injunction was therefore sought to restrain him from using those boats, although they had been duly enrolled and licensed under acts of Congress. The case came by due process into the Supreme Court of the United States, where it was held that the statute of the State of New York was a regulation of commerce between the States, and therefore repugnant to the clause of the Constitution which we are now considering, authorizing Congress to regulate commerce among the several States.

From that time until the present the efforts of the individual States to take advantage of their opportunities to impose duties, taxes, restraints, and burdens upon the property of citizens of other States passing through or brought into them have been the source of the continued exercise

LECTURE IX.
Legislation of New York.

Legislation of Maryland.

of the jurisdiction of the Supreme Court of the United States, where such laws have in almost every instance been declared void. For example, the statute in the case of *Guy* v. *Baltimore,* 100 U. S. 434, was an old sinner, and made a very clever attempt to conceal the evil. It appeared that the city of Baltimore owned some of the wharves in that city at which vessels coming to that port landed : probably not all, but some of them, and imposed a certain tax for the use of those wharves. This was begun a great many years ago, and was done by an act of the General Assembly of Maryland, passed in 1827, and regulations made thereunder by the city authorities, which provided in effect that all articles of merchandise brought into that city and landed at its wharves, which were the produce of the State of Maryland, should pay no fees on account of their use, but that all similar articles brought into that port from any other State should pay a tax for the use of the wharf upon which it was landed. Of course it was a small affair, the main business at these wharves being the landing of chickens, eggs, potatoes, cabbages, oysters, and other articles of food and things of that kind, so that the sum that any one little sailing vessel had to pay did not amount to much. Nobody, therefore, resisted its payment until a few years ago, when a man was at last found who would stand it no longer. In 1876 Guy, a resident citizen of Accomac County in the State of Virginia, landed his vessel at one of the public wharves, and when this tax was demanded of him refused to pay it. So they sued him, and by regular process through their courts the case came at last into the Supreme Court of the United States. That court said that it did not matter if this tax had been collected for so many years, it was nevertheless a regulation of commerce which the State could not make or authorize, because this tax was not a compensation for the use of the city's property, but was a mere expedient or device to foster the domestic commerce of Maryland by means of unequal and oppressive burdens upon the industry and business of other States. It was invalid as a regulation of commerce. It was not merely intended to raise money for the use of a wharf, — that they had a right to do, and if they had laid a reasonable tax for its use and laid it alike upon the produce which came from every State in the Union, it would have been a valid tax; but it was evident that it was intended by this statute to make the produce and goods of Virginia, which lies right alongside, as well as that of the adjacent States of New Jersey and Delaware, which came into this port for a market, pay a tax to keep up the wharves and wharfage system of that port, while permitting the entry of goods and produce from the State of Maryland free of any such imposition. This was held to be a regulation of commerce, and though of nearly sixty years' standing, to be void.

If you will take the Constitution of the United States and read it, or that part of it in immediate connection with this paragraph, you will see that the position which it occupies in that instrument indicates the place it occupied in the thought of the Convention which framed it. Article I is devoted to the organization and powers of the legislative branch of the Government, consisting of the Senate and House of Representatives. Section eight of the Article contains the specific grants of power made to the Congress. The first one of these is a grant to raise money by taxation for the support of the Government; the second is an authority to borrow money for the same purpose, and the third, out of about fifteen in number, is this clause concerning the regulation of commerce.

We must next, in order to ascertain with any philosophical nicety what is meant by this clause, take some of its parts into the field of definition. And first let us consider, what is commerce? You remember that the commerce to be regulated by Congress is that "with foreign nations, and among the several States, and with the Indian tribes;" but the word "commerce" is applicable to all these, and it is essential to have some idea as to what is meant by the word. It is defined in *Gibbons* v. *Ogden*, as well as in some later cases, but it is difficult to give in any one sentence its entire meaning as employed in the Constitution. The ordinary meaning is trade and traffic — intercourse between different peoples; and that will perhaps answer for our purpose as a general definition of the word as used in this clause. But traffic and

trade are composed of a great many elements
so far as the means are concerned by which and
the persons by and between whom they are
carried on.

That element of commerce which has been
the most frequent subject of legislation by the
Congress of the United States, and which has
perhaps received more frequent consideration in
the courts than any other, is what may be
called "transportation." In *Gibbons* v. *Ogden*
the eminent Chief Justice made a very elaborate
argument to prove that navigation was one of
the principal elements of commerce, which was
perhaps necessary for him to do in that day
although it is a proposition which it would certainly not be thought necessary now to establish by precedents or authorities. In fact we
have gone further than that, and we have said
that the transportation of goods and passengers
is commerce. And in that view, in the case of
the *Clinton Bridge*, reported in 1 Woolworth,
150, in 1867, in which I had the honor of delivering the opinion of the court, it was held,
though I believe it has sometimes been doubted
since, that since the railroads of the country
had almost superseded the use of vessels and
water carriage, they, as a means of transportation, constituted an element of commerce, and
that it was within the power of Congress to
regulate that element. There is this limitation
to that, however, that since these railroads are
generally chartered by States, and many of them
run only within the borders of a single State,

the transportation or commerce over them is
said to be not commerce with foreign nations,
not commerce among the several States, and not
commerce with the Indian tribes, and, therefore, not subject to regulation by Congress.
But many of these roads run through several
States, and most of them make arrangements
to continue the transportation of their freight
over other lines. A large part of the transportation of freight and passengers in this country
from the Pacific to the Atlantic coast, and *vice
versa*, is done in one vehicle and by one continuous passage. It is my opinion that such
traffic is subject to regulation by Congress. The
judgment rendered in that case was affirmed by
the Supreme Court of the United States, but
the argument which I have presented here, and
which I used in the case below as a part of my
opinion, was not fully adopted. The question
was whether the Congress of the United States
had power to authorize one of these railroads
to build a bridge across the Mississippi River at
the town of Clinton, where two roads, one on
each side, met, and where it was necessary to
have a bridge. I held that Congress having
passed a statute authorizing it to be built, and
declaring what the size and height of the bridge
and the width between its piers should be, the
act was within the power of Congress because
it was a regulation of commerce. The Supreme
Court sustained me in that, although some of
the judges may have based their decision upon
the fact that it was a bridge across a naviga-

ble stream, and therefore within the control of Congress. My decision in that case has often been quoted in Congress; various committees having charge of the question of the regulation of railroad traffic have considered the subject, and although no bill has passed both Houses, yet bills substantially based upon that idea have at different times passed each House, and generally the reports of the committees having them in charge have made reference to that opinion.

LECTURE IX.
What is commerce?

Having ascertained, then, what commerce is, and what are some of its elements, which may be the subject of the action of Congress, or of the attempted action of the States, we next come to consider what it is to "regulate" commerce. You will observe from the extracts quoted from the Federalist, and still more if you study the history of the formation of the Constitution, that the word "regulate" was one much more frequently used in those days than it is now; undoubtedly our forefathers used it in a larger and wider sense than it would be generally used at this time. But we have in *Gibbons* v. *Ogden*, that magazine of constitutional law upon this subject, a definition by Chief Justice Marshall of what it is to regulate commerce, which perhaps can never be excelled in its brevity, accuracy, and comprehensiveness. He says that "to regulate commerce is to prescribe the rule by which commerce is to be governed." Commerce being intercourse and traffic between people, to regulate it is to prescribe rules by which it shall be conducted.

What it is to "regulate" commerce.

It is said in *Cooley* v. *Port Wardens of Phila-delphia*, 12 How. 299, that it is the power to regulate the instruments of commerce; that " it extends to the persons who conduct navigation as well as to the instruments used." In pursuance of that view the Congress of the United States has applied the power which it has under that clause to regulate commerce to a method of intercourse which had no existence when the Constitution was framed. By this I mean the internal commerce of the country, among the States and on its great rivers, by means of steamboats, for it was nearly forty years after the Constitution was adopted before a steamboat was successfully used to take part in the actual transportation of goods and the navigation of the waters of the country. Before that time, however, Congress had applied its powers to the regulation of sailing vessels, both foreign and domestic. The next year after the adoption of the Constitution it passed two statutes, one called the " registry law," which applied exclusively to vessels engaged in foreign trade, and the other called the " enrolment law," which had application alone to coasting and other vessels engaged in the domestic trade. Congress also passed statutes: indeed, it was a part of those statutes, that all those vessels should be licensed, and that they should take out their licenses from the officers of the custom houses where they were built, or where their owners resided. In fact, it may be briefly stated that the whole system of the navigation laws of the United States is

founded on that simple clause giving Congress
the power to regulate commerce.

Since steamboats came into successful operation Congress has been busy, and profitably so,
in passing laws concerning and regulating their
use on the interior waters of the country. It
has passed laws prescribing the number of passengers that each one of these boats may carry in
proportion to the space which they have for their
accommodation, and providing heavy penalties
for any excess in the number of passengers carried beyond the limit permitted by law. It has
also enacted statutes requiring them to keep on
board certain life-preserving and life-saving implements, of which there is a great variety, some
circular, some square, some of cork, and some
filled with air. These are all arrangements prescribed by Congress under this same clause of
the Constitution.

These statutes also require that these vessels
shall be inspected. The smallest vessel that
navigates a river by steam as well as the largest
that navigates the ocean is required, whether
belonging to the United States service or to an
individual, to be inspected and to have put up
and exhibited in their cabins a certificate of that
inspection, which must be renewed at appropriate intervals. These provisions are all intended for the safety of the passengers and
crews, and to provide against danger to human
life. It is also provided that on the inland
waters of the country the pilot and engineer
must be examined by suitable commissioners

located in the principal cities of the Union. Any
steamboat owner who employs a pilot or engineer
who has no license is liable to a penalty, and any
man who undertakes to serve as a pilot or engineer
without such license is liable to a similar penalty.
So that you will see that there has been a great
deal of use made of this power which is conferred
by this clause of the Constitution.

Another matter having reference mainly to
the foreign commerce of the United States has
been the subject of consideration in our courts.
I allude to laws concerning the landing of passengers who are foreigners in our ports. For
more than fifty years the States within which
the principal ports of entry are situated have
struggled to in some way levy a tax upon every
human being not a citizen of the United States
who landed in one of those ports. This tax
they endeavored to collect from the officers of
the vessels bringing such passengers, under the
pressure of heavy penalties for failure to pay
such impositions. Such laws have over and
over again been declared by the Supreme Court
to be unconstitutional and void, because they
are an attempt at a regulation of foreign commerce ; because the terms upon which subjects
and citizens of foreign nations shall land in the
United States are not fit matters for State legislation ; because, under the theory upon which
our Government is based, the central authority
must deal with the sovereigns of those subjects,
as well as answer to them for any wrong done
to them under the laws of nations ; and because

such laws are essentially and from their very nature, of that class of legislation or action which
is international in its character and which must,
therefore, be regulated and· acted upon by the
Federal Government alone so far as foreign
powers are concerned, and cannot be intrusted
to any one or more of the individual States of
the Union. But often as that doctrine has been
declared by the Supreme Court of the United
States, beginning with the *Passenger Cases*, 7
How. 283, in 1849, down to those which have
been recently delivered, still the States continue
this effort to tax passengers and freight and
seek to avoid in some way or another the force
and effect of the constitutional provision concerning commerce and its regulation.

There is one other question connected with
this topic which has been much mooted in the
Supreme Court, and that is, whether there may
not exist in the States a co-ordinate power to
regulate commerce of certain kinds in the absence of any action by Congress on the subject..
It has been a vexed question in the court
whether there is any such limited field of State
legislation, or for State legislative power, in
regard to any subject which can be fairly called
a regulation of commerce. But I think that it
is now the established doctrine that there is a
class of subjects having the elements of commerce, both foreign and domestic and interstate,
which may be acted on and in regard to which
rules may be prescribed by the States so long as
Congress does not choose to occupy the field and

pass laws upon the same subject. The principal cases upon that subject are rather numerous, but I will give you some of them. *Gibbons* v. *Ogden,* 9 Wheat. 1, 189; *Willson* v. *Blackbird Creek Co.,* 2 Pet. 245; *Cooley* v. *The Board of Wardens of the Port of Philadelphia,* 12 How. 299; *Gilman* v. *The City of Philadelphia,* 3 Wall. 713; *Crandall* v. *Nevada,* 6 Wall. 35; *Pound* v. *Turck,* 95 U. S. 459, 462; *Packet Co.* v. *Catlettsburg,* 105 U. S. 559.

These are cases involving some local matter, yet in its nature a regulation of commerce, in regard to which the States concerned have attempted to pass, and have passed laws whose validity was disputed under this clause of the Constitution. They have come in this way before the Supreme Court of the United States, where they have been held to be valid. I can do no more now than to state what I have deduced as the result of these cases. The doctrine was for the first time clearly stated in *Cooley* v. *The Board of Wardens,* and it has been repeatedly affirmed since in the same court. It may be thus stated: That the power to regulate commerce is one which includes many subjects various and quite unlike in their nature; that whenever subjects of this power are in their nature national, or require one uniform system or plan of regulation, they may be justly held to belong to that class over which Congress has the exclusive power of legislation; but that local and limited matters, not national in their character, which are most likely to be wisely provided for by such

diverse rules as the localities and the authorities LECTURE IX.
of the different States may deem applicable, Co-ordinate
powers of the
may be regulated by the legislatures of those States.
States in the absence of any act of Congress
upon the same subject. Of course when Congress does legislate, as it has a right to do, that
excludes the legislation of the States and renders it void so far as it may interfere or conflict
with the statutes of the United States.

It may be useful to suggest here one or two
of the classes into which this subject may be
divided. One is pilotage, which was under consideration in *Cooley* v. *The Board of Wardens.*
Almost all the seaports of the United States
have found it necessary to make rules and laws
constituting and regulating a system of pilotage. Pilotage.
By these provision has been made for putting
upon the great ocean steamships and other vessels before they reach the bar, which exists in
most of our harbors, a pilot who is familiar with
the coast and the channel, so that they may be
brought safely into port. This dispenses, of
course, with any pilot the vessel may have on
board, whether competent or not. The reason
for this is that it has been found necessary, in
order to make proper compensation to these
pilots and support a sufficient number of them
to do the business, to require by law that every
vessel shall take a pilot; and they have gone
further, no doubt under a necessity inherent in
the system, and have required that the vessel
entering a port shall take the first pilot who
offers himself when it comes within the limits

where the pilot-laws operate. This is because these pilots must go out and cruise about before the harbor, and stay there regardless of the weather, so that all vessels may avail themselves of their services, and it is therefore provided that they must be taken in the order in which they present themselves. Most of the States, however, have a provision in their laws that if a vessel has a pilot of her own, or for any other reason chooses to dispense with the services of the first pilot who offers himself, such vessel shall pay to that pilot one-half of the usual fees, which are established by the local regulations of the different States, or by their legislative bodies. This is a system that requires different rules and provisions in New York from what has been found necessary in New Orleans, and it has therefore been held that the laws of the States upon that subject are valid. It has been contended that all compulsory pilotage should be abolished, and a bill to accomplish that object has been reported from the Committee on Commerce of the Senate of the United States. If such a bill should pass it would not be necessary for a vessel to take a pilot whether she wanted him or not. This is an apt illustration of the power of Congress to act upon a subject which, if left untouched by it, would fall within the power of the State legislatures.

Another is wharfage rules and rates. So different are the localities where vessels land, the nature of the ground, and the condition of the

wharves, that it generally has been conceded
that the places and times at which such landings may be made and the rates of wharfage shall be left to local regulation. Yet, undoubtedly, they are so far regulations of commerce, that if Congress should at any time interfere and pass a law upon the subject it would be controlling.

Another class, which has been frequently be- fore the Supreme Court, involves matters like ·that discussed in the case of the Clinton Bridge, that is, of bridges over navigable streams. Such streams are within the control of Congress, absolutely. We may say in regard to every stream in the United States capable of being used as an aid to commerce for the navigation of any craft whatever, that Congress has a right to regulate its use. But, in the building of railroads across the country it was necessary that they should cross many streams, some of them navigable, and it was found to be to the interest of commerce that they should be bridged. This was sometimes done with drawbridges, but their piers were somewhat in the way, and rafts and steamboats often struck against them. So, some of the States authorized the building of bridges, and the courts of the United States have held that if there be no unreasonable use of the power of crossing the stream, the States may authorize the building of bridges in the absence of any action by Congress. There are now bridges over the Ohio, the Mississippi, indeed over all the streams crossed by railroads in this country, of which perhaps one-half are authorized by some act of Congress, most of the others by the States, and some by both. In some cases there was a State law allowing the bridge to be built which Congress ratified. It has been sometimes said in regard to this subject that the power of Congress is in abeyance and can be exercised by the States in the absence of Congressional action.

The language of the clause of the Constitution which we are considering, declaring that Congress shall have power "to regulate commerce with foreign nations, among the several States, and with the Indian tribes," thus points out three different classes of commerce placed within the control of that body. It has pretty fairly performed its duty so far as passing laws regulating commerce with foreign nations and the Indian tribes is concerned; but until recently almost entirely ignored its duty in regard to its regulation among the several States of the Union. The result of this failure of Congress to prescribe rules for the government of com-

merce, which is the power of regulation, has been that the States, under pretence of exercising the power to pass laws concerning this subject, where Congress had not acted upon it, have been themselves making perpetual efforts to exercise forbidden powers at the expense of other States. The power to regulate commerce of course carries with it the auxiliary powers of the courts of the United States to enforce the laws which Congress may enact thereunder, and also the power of the Supreme Court to declare null and void regulations and statutes in contravention of those laws or of the Constitution, in order that all citizens may be protected from unconstitutional laws or regulations upon this subject sought to be enforced by the States. So the Federal courts, and particularly the Supreme Court of the United States, have been the theatre of a contest between certain States of the Union and citizens of other States who have thought themselves injured by State laws affecting commerce. ·That the courts established under the Constitution of the United States necessarily have a power of a judicial character, coextensive with the enforcement of the laws which Congress has a right to make and with the needful protection of the citizens of the Federal Union against laws made under a usurpation of power by the States, in the absence of any action by Congress on the subject, would hardly seem to need any argument. I will, however, refer to the expression used in that remarkable case of *Gibbons* v. *Ogden,* where it is said that " wherever commerce among the States goes the judicial power of the United States goes to protect it from invasion by State legislatures." 9 Wheat. 191.

There are many cases reported in the decisions of the Supreme Court discussing the attempted exercise of power by the State legislatures over this subject, principally devoted to commerce among the States. As an evidence of the persistence of some of the States in this attempt to transcend their powers, I quote the

LECTURE IX.
State laws in conflict with this provision.

LECTURE IX.
State laws in con-
flict with this pro-
vision.
headnotes of the opinion in *People* v. *Compagnie Générale Transatlantique*, 107 U. S. 59, delivered in 1882, on the subject of the landing of passengers at one of the larger ports of the United States. The syllabus contains a sufficient synopsis of the opinion to indicate the persistent effort made by some States to pass laws which they are forbidden to pass, for the purpose of raising taxes from people over whom they never had any right of taxation.

" 1. The statute of New York of May 31, 1881, imposing a tax on every alien passenger who shall come by vessel from a foreign country to the port of New York, and holding the vessel liable for the tax, is a regulation of foreign commerce, and void. *Henderson* v. *Mayor of New York*, 92 U. S. 259, and *Chy Lung* v. *Freeman*, 92 U. S. 275, cited, and the rulings therein made reaffirmed.

" 2. The statute is not relieved from this constitutional objection by declaring in its title that it is to raise money for the execution of the inspection laws of the State, which authorize passengers to be inspected in order to determine who are criminals, paupers, lunatics, orphans, or infirm persons, without means or capacity to support themselves, and subject to become a public charge, as such facts are not to be ascertained by inspection alone.

" 3. The words 'inspection laws,' 'imports' and 'exports,' as used in cl. 2, sec. 10, Art. I, of the Constitution have exclusive reference to property.

"4. This is apparent from the language of cl.
1, sec. 9, of the same article, where, in regard
to the admission of persons of the African race,
the word 'migration' is applied to free persons,
and 'importation' to slaves."

The point here made is that the Constitution
declares that "no State shall, without the consent of Congress, lay any imposts or duties on
imports. or exports, except what may be absolutely necessary for executing its inspection
laws." After the Supreme Court of the United
States decided in the *Passenger Cases*, in 1849,
that passengers were not imports, and could not,
therefore, be taxed in that way, and after the
decision in *Henderson* v. *Mayor of New York*,
92 U. S. 259, in 1875, that an amended law
intended to get rid of that decision was unconstitutional, the legislature passed the law of
1881, and by calling it an inspection law undertook to get rid of the prohibition against the
regulation of commerce by a State. This effort
was declared by that opinion to be an unsuccessful one.

There are many cases, however, reported in
the decisions of the Supreme Court which uphold the powers exercised by the State legislatures as coming within the rule in *Cooley* v. *The
Board of Wardens*, above referred to. Among
those where the State laws have been supported
are the cases of *Willson* v. *The Blackbird Creek
Marsh Co.*, 2 Pet. 245; *Gilman* v. *Philadelphia*,
3 Wall. 713, and others above cited.

Willson v. *The Blackbird Creek Marsh Co.*

LECTURE IX.
State laws in con-
flict with this pro-
vision.
was a case where a small stream emptying into Delaware Bay, and navigable for ten or fifteen miles into the interior of the country, had been dammed with a view to improving its utility and draining the water from the surrounding swamps. The authority under which this was done was held not to be an act regulating commerce which was forbidden by the Constitution, being of a mere local and limited character, until Congress should pass some law on the subject. That was the first case in which the doctrine was clearly stated.

In *Gilman* v. *Philadelphia* a bridge was built across the Schuylkill River in the city of Philadelphia, within its present limits, below a wharf which had been long used and to which vessels of a very large class had been accustomed to go. It was decided that the necessities of a bridge at that point for the use of the great travel of the city were so great that its authorization by the legislature of Pennsylvania, being of a strictly local character and not interfering with general commerce, came within the rule in *Cooley* v. *The Board of Wardens*, and was, until Congress forbade it, a legitimate exercise of power.

In other cases, rather more numerous, various acts of the State legislatures have been held void as infringing upon the power to regulate commerce exclusively belonging to Congress. *Gibbons* v. *Ogden*, 9 Wheat. 1, 186; *Brown* v. *Maryland*, 12 Wheat. 419; *Crandall* v. *Nevada*, 6 Wall. 35; *Case of the State Freight Tax*, 15

Wall. 232; *Woodruff* v. *Parham*, 8 Wall. 123; LECTURE IX.
Welton ·v. *State of Missouri*, 91 U. S. 275; State laws in conflict with this provision.
Western Union Telegraph Co. v. *Texas*, 105 U. S.
460; *Railroad Co.* v. *Husen*, 95 U. S. 465.

Perhaps a clearer idea may be had of the
principles upon which these State laws have
been held to be infringements of the power
vested in Congress by the Constitution by stating briefly the substance of one or two of the
most remarkable of these cases.

In *Crandall* v. *Nevada*, 6 Wall. 35, it ap- Review of principal cases. *Crandall* v. *Nevada*.
peared that the State of Nevada had enacted
a statute that every person who passed through
its territory by any of the ordinary modes of
public conveyance should pay to the State one
dollar for that privilege. That is the way the
Supreme Court construed the act. But the
statute was artfully drawn, as all such statutes
are, and it provided that every railroad, stage,
or other company engaged in the business of
transportation, should pay to the State one dollar for every person that they carried through
the State. It has, however, long been decided,
and it is very obvious, that such a tax levied on
a carrier is really a tax on the passenger, for
the carrier of course makes him pay that much
more for carrying him through the State or for
his conveyance whether it is by land or water.
As remarked by the Supreme Court in *Hender-* *Henderson* v. *New York*.
son v. *The Mayor of New York*, 92 U. S. 259,
in the *Passenger Cases*, and some others, a tax
demanded of a vessel for landing a passenger,
coming from a European shore, in the harbor

of New York, is in its effect clearly a tax upon the passenger, because the master of the vessel puts that tax into his charge before he takes the passenger on his vessel at the European port, wherever it may be. So in this case, it was unquestionably a tax upon the passenger for the simple privilege of going through the State. The Supreme Court of the United States held that to be void, and the act was thereafter never enforced.

That decision, which probably would not have affected but a few thousand dollars a year so far as the State of Nevada was concerned, had the effect to break up a system of taxing passengers by railroads that run into the city of Washington. The State of Maryland had for twenty years exacted from the Metropolitan Branch of the Baltimore and Ohio Railroad Company a tax of half a dollar for every passenger carried over that road, but the practice was stopped by that decision. The State of New Jersey had taxed all the passengers which passed through its strip of territory extending as a barrier between the city of New York and the West and South, and that custom was also broken up by that decision.

In *Welton* v. *The State of Missouri*, 91 U. S. 275, it was shown that that State had by legislative enactment authorized the city of Saint Louis, among other things, to tax peddlers. In the exercise of that power, however, the city taxed only those peddlers who came within its borders to sell goods from other States, and did not tax

those who in that city sold only the goods or
produce of the State of Missouri. This was
very clearly a regulation of commerce prejudi-
cial to other States and favorable to the merchants of Saint Louis, designed to compel every
man who came within its limits to sell the produce of any other State to pay a tax regulated
by its discretion, because if it could levy a tax
of one dollar it might increase it to one hundred dollars. The Supreme Court held that to
be a regulation of commerce among the States.
If a peddler came there from New York, Cincinnati, or Chicago, to sell goods that he had
bought in those cities, and was compelled by the
State of Missouri to pay a tax for the privilege,
when the man living in that State was not taxed
for selling the produce or goods of that State,
it was manifestly a regulation of commerce un-
favorable to other States of the Federal Union.
It was, therefore, held to be void.

The question of the taxation of non-resident
peddlers has arisen in the District of Columbia,
but since the acts of Congress govern here, the
District not being a State, and the authority
under which a peddler can be taxed in this city
must originate in Congress, which has a right to
regulate its commerce, it is not clear how the
courts can do much in regard to the grievance.

Another case illustrating the point in question
is that of *Railroad Co.* v. *Husen*, 95 U. S. 465.
There was a statute passed by the State of
Missouri with regard to a disease which was
supposed to infest Texan cattle coming into and

going through Missouri, and which was regarded as infectious. I am not prepared to say that if the statute had been strictly limited to the exclusion of cattle having that disease, or if it had provided proper means for ascertaining what cattle were diseased, and when that was ascertained had directed them to be turned back or segregated so that the disease should not be further propagated, it would not have been valid. But Missouri, like other States attempting to operate on this class of subjects, declared that no cattle from the State of Texas should come into that State at all, until they had been kept long enough to prevent any danger of contagion. The statute in effect amounted to an entire prohibition on the railroads from carrying cattle from Texas through the State of Missouri, and the Supreme Court of the United States held it to be unconstitutional.

Perhaps the case of the *Western Union Telegraph Co.* v. *Texas*, 105 U. S. 460, more fully illustrates what is and what is not permissible on the part of the several States, than any other which has been decided by the Supreme Court. That State attempted to levy a tax of one cent upon every message received at or sent from any telegraph office located within its limits. Without going into the circumstances of the case in detail, it may be simply remarked that the telegraph company contested the validity of the act on the ground that it was unconstitutional, being a regulation of commerce. The question came before the Supreme Court and they held that the

very terms of the commerce clause of the Constitution imply that there is a commerce with
which Congress has no right to interfere, and
which the States, therefore, have the right to
regulate. It will be observed that " commerce
with foreign nations," and " among the several
States," and " with the Indian tribes," leaves a
large body of commerce, which has been defined
as trade, traffic, and intercourse, conducted between citizens of the same State, entirely beyond
the control of Congress. It has always been
conceded in the discussions in the Supreme Court
that with this great body of commerce, consisting of trade between citizens of the same State,
Congress could not interfere, and that the Constitution did not affect the power of the State
to regulate and control it. The business of the
company was the forwarding of messages, of
which undoubtedly a large number were sent
from some point or office of the company in the
State of Texas to some other point or office
within the same State. Naturally, also, a very
large number of these messages went from that
State into others, as well as came from others
into the State of Texas. If the latter was commerce at all, it was " commerce among the several
States ; " for another definition which has been
given of the matter shows that the nations,
States, and tribes designated in this clause of
the Constitution do not mean those bodies in the
aggregate. For example : the State of Tennessee
has no commerce with the State of Kentucky
lying adjacent to it ; the United States as a body

has no commerce with England. It simply means commerce, traffic, and intercourse between the citizens or subjects of those nations, States, or tribes; so that when a man in Liverpool sells an article to a man in New York that is commerce with a foreign state. The same is true as to citizens of different States of the Union, or as to an American citizen and a member of an Indian tribe. It follows from these observations that, as regards the tax of one cent levied upon the telegraph company for every message received or delivered in the State of Texas, some portion of it might be valid, because levied upon messages transmitted wholly within the limits of the State, belonging to what may be called State commerce or internal commerce, which is not affected by the clause under consideration. On the other hand, a large portion of the tax would be levied upon messages coming from or going into other States, which would be, if commerce at all, " commerce among the several States." I will quote the language of the Chief Justice in the opinion in this case, confirmatory of what has been before stated, that railroad and steamboat transportation is as much commerce as that which takes place in sailing vessels, the only known method of water carriage at the time the Constitution was adopted.

" In *Pensacola Telegraph Co.* v. *Western Union Telegraph Co.*, 96 U. S. 1, this court held that the telegraph was an instrument of commerce and that telegraph companies were subject to the regulating power of Congress in respect to

their foreign and interstate business. A tele- LECTURE IX.
graph company occupies the same relation to Review of principal cases.
commerce, as a carrier of messages, that a rail-
road company does as a carrier of goods. Both
companies are instruments of commerce, and
their business is commerce itself." *Telegraph
Co.* v. *Texas,* 105 U. S. 460, 464.

The opinion then goes on to decide that so
much of the law levying that tax as concerned
messages coming into the State of Texas or
going out of it to other States was void, and
that if the State wanted to tax messages sent
by private parties, and not by agents of the Government of the United States, from one place to
another exclusively within its own jurisdiction,
it could do so, but that it could not under the
law in question tax messages between different
States.

Only a few words need be said in regard to com- Commerce with the Indian tribes.
merce with the Indian tribes. Of course they
were relatively much more powerful, and they
themselves more numerous, at the time the Constitution was adopted than now, and commerce
and personal intercourse with them was a matter
of much more importance. They are still, however, a great expense to the Government, and
occupy even at this day, as they have always
done, a great deal of public attention, an important place in the legislation of Congress and in
the action of the departments. Very early after
the formation of the Constitution Congress took
up the subject of intercourse with the Indian
tribes and passed laws, supposed to be judicious,

restraining them, forbidding white people to settle among them, and made a special effort to prevent the use of intoxicating liquors and to exclude them from their reservations. Congress had the power under that clause of the Constitution to prohibit or license trade, to prohibit or license personal intercourse, and it passed laws upon that subject. This power of Congress to regulate commerce with these tribes, as the Supreme Court has said in several instances, is one which may be exercised with regard to the tribes in their localities, in the territories or within organized States, and also with regard to a member of a tribe who abides by the tribal relation. It has no restriction to locality, but wherever a tribe is found, however large or small, wherever there is an Indian who belongs to a tribe, this power of Congress attaches, whether it be in a State of the Union or upon the plains of the territories of the West. A short extract from the case of *United States* v. *Holliday*, 3 Wall. 407, 417, will perhaps give you a clearer view of the relation which Congress sustains to the Indian tribes than any statement which I might make. The court was considering an act forbidding the sale of liquor to Indians in charge of an agent appointed by the Government. The offence complained of in that case took place within the organized State of Minnesota, without the limits of the reservation on which the Indian tribe lived. The objection was raised that the power of Congress did not extend there, but that the Indian was

within the territory of a State which had the
right to regulate its sale. The court said : —

" If the act under consideration is a regulation
of commerce, as it undoubtedly is, does it regulate that kind of commerce which is placed
within the control of Congress by the Constitution. The words of that instrument are :
'Congress shall have power to regulate commerce with foreign nations, and among the
several States, and with the Indian tribes.'
Commerce with foreign nations, without doubt,
means commerce between citizens of the United
States and citizens or subjects of foreign governments, as individuals. And so commerce with
the Indian tribes means commerce with the
individuals composing those tribes. The act
before us describes this precise kind of traffic or
commerce, and therefore comes within the terms
of the constitutional provision. Is there anything in the fact that this power is to be exercised within the limits of a State, which renders
the act regulating it unconstitutional ? In the
same opinion to which we have just before referred, [*Gibbons* v. *Ogden*,] Judge Marshall, in
speaking of the power to regulate commerce
with foreign states, says : ' The power does not
stop at the jurisdictional limits of the several
states. It would be a very useless power if it
could not pass those lines.' ' If Congress has
power to regulate it, that power must be exercised wherever the subject exists.' It follows
from these propositions, which seem to be in-
controvertible, that if commerce, or traffic, or

intercourse, is carried on with an Indian tribe, or with a member of such tribe, it is subject to be regulated by Congress, although within the limits of a State. The locality of the traffic can have nothing to do with the power. The right to exercise it in reference to any Indian tribe, or any person who is a member of such tribe, is absolute, without reference to the locality of the traffic, or the locality of the tribe, or of the member of the tribe with whom it is carried on. It is not, however, intended by these remarks to imply that this clause of the Constitution authorizes Congress to regulate any other commerce, originated and ended within the limits of a single State, than commerce with the Indian tribes."

In that case one of the Indians concerned belonged in the State of Michigan, was authorized to vote in that State by its laws, and had so voted at county and town elections. He also owned property there, and, therefore, it was argued that he could not be the subject of any regulation of commerce with the Indian tribes. The answer to this proposition is, in the language of the opinion, that "neither the Constitution of the State, nor any act of its legislature, however formal or solemn, whatever rights it may have conferred on those Indians or withheld from them, could withdraw them from the influence of an act of Congress which that body has the constitutional right to pass concerning them. Any other doctrine would make the legislation of the State the supreme law of the

land instead of the Constitution of the United
States."

It is, however, proper to say that it was ascertained that this Indian still so far retained his tribal relation that he drew his share of the annuities belonging to the tribe, and that he was among the number of those that an Indian agent was appointed to look after as members of that tribe. The court held in that case, following a long course of previous decisions, that in a matter which constituted a kind of political relation between the Government of the United States and some other nation or tribe, the court would follow the action of what may be termed the political branch of the Government, that is, the Executive, the Congress, and the Departments.

NOTES UPON LECTURE IX.

———◦◆◦———

LECTURE IX.
Cases decided
since this lecture
was written. IT is apparent that this lecture was written
some years since. It contains no reference to a
single case decided since 107 U. S. (October Term,
1882), although far more cases involving a consideration of this clause of the Constitution have
been decided since then, than during any period
of the same number of years since the court was
organized. The footnote below gives a list of
the more important of these cases.[1]

---

[1] *Miller* v. *New York*, 109 U. S. 385 ; *Moran* v. *New Orleans*,
112 U. S. 69 ; *Foster* v. *Kansas*, 112 U. S. 201 ; *Head Money Cases*,
112 U. S. 580 ; *Cardwell* v. *American Bridge Company*, 113 U. S.
205 ; *Cooper Manufacturing Co.* v. *Ferguson*, 113 U. S. 727 ;
Gloucester Ferry Company v. *Pennsylvania*, 114 U. S. 196 ; *Brown*
v. *Houston*, 114 U. S. 622 ; *Fisk* v. *Jefferson Police Jury*, 116 U. S.
131 ; *Stone* v. *Illinois Central Railroad*, 116 U. S. 347 ; *Stone* v.
New Orleans & Northeastern Railroad, 116 U. S. 352 ; *Walling*
v. *Michigan*, 116 U. S. 446 ; *Coe* v. *Errol*, 116 U. S. 517 ; *Pickard*
v. *Pullman Southern Car Co.*, 117 U. S. 34 ; *Tennessee* v. *Pullman
Southern Car Co.*, 117 U. S. 51 ; *Spraigue* v. *Thompson*, 118 U. S.
90 ; *Morgan's Steamship Co.* v. *Louisiana*, 118 U. S. 455 ; *Wabash
&c. Railway Co.* v. *Illinois*, 118 U. S. 557 ; *Robbins* v. *Shelby
County Taxing District*, 120 U. S. 489 ; *Corson* v. *Maryland*, 120
U. S. 502 ; *Fargo* v. *Michigan*, 121 U. S. 230 ; *Philadelphia &
Southern Steamship Co.* v. *Pennsylvania*, 122 U. S. 326 ; *Western
Union Telegraph Co.* v. *Pendleton*, 122 U. S. 347 ; *Mugler* v. *Kan-
sas*, 123 U. S. 623 ; *Smith* v. *Alabama*, 124 U. S. 465 ; *Willamette
Iron Bridge Co.* v. *Hatch*, 125 U. S. 1 ; *Bowman* v. *Chicago &
Northwestern Railway Co.*, 125 U. S. 465 ; *California* v. *Central
Pacific Railroad Co.*, 127 U. S. 1 ; *Ratterman* v. *Western Union
Telegraph Co.*, 127 U. S. 411 ; *Leloup* v. *Port of Mobile*, 127 U. S.

474

A selection from some of the points in the headnotes of a few of these cases will show their importance.

1. *Generally.*

As to those subjects of commerce which are local or limited in their nature or sphere of operation, the State may prescribe regulations until Congress assumes control of them. As to those national in character, and requiring uniformity of regulation, the power of Congress is exclusive; and until Congress acts, such commerce is entitled to be free from State exactions.[1]

The clause in the Constitution which confers upon Congress the power to regulate commerce among the several States leaves to the States, in the absence of congressional legislation, the power to regulate matters of local interest, which affect interstate commerce only incidentally; but the power of Congress over interstate commerce is exclusive wherever the matter is national in character, or admits of a uniform system or plan of regulation. So long as Congress passes no law to regulate interstate commerce of the nature and character which makes its jurisdiction exclusive, its refraining from

---

640 ; *Kidd* v. *Pearson*, 128 U. S. 1 ; *Asher* v. *Texas*, 128 U. S. 129 ; *Stoutenburgh* v. *Henrick*, 129 U. S. 141 ; *Western Union Telegraph Co.* v. *Alabama*, 132 U. S. 472 ; *Louisville, New Orleans &c. Railway Co.* v. *Mississippi*, 133 U. S. 587 ; *Leisy* v. *Hardin*, 135 U. S. 100 ; *McCall* v. *California*, 136 U. S. 104 ; *Norfolk & Western Railroad Co.* v. *Pennsylvania*, 136 U. S. 114 ; *Minnesota* v. *Barber*, 136 U. S. 313 ; *Crowley* v. *Christensen*, 137 U. S. 86 ; *Brimmer* v. *Rebman*, 138 U. S. 78.

[1] *Gloucester Ferry Co.* v. *Pennsylvania*, 114 U. S. 196.

action indicates its will that commerce shall be free and untrammelled.[1]

The transportation of persons and property between States is commerce of a national character, requiring uniformity of regulation.[2]

The prohibition of the Constitution against State laws impairing the obligation of contracts applies to implied contracts as well as to express contracts.[3]

Interstate commerce by corporations is entitled to the same protection against State exactions which is given to such commerce when carried on by individuals.[4]

A State act which imposes limitations upon the power of a corporation, created under the laws of another State, to make contracts within the State for carrying on commerce between the States, violates that clause of the Constitution which confers upon Congress the exclusive right to regulate that commerce.[5]

The power to regulate commerce, interstate and foreign, vested in Congress, is the power to prescribe the rules by which it shall be governed, that is, the conditions on which it shall be conducted; to determine when it shall be free, and when subject to duties or other exactions.[6]

When goods, the product of a State, have

---

[1] *Brown* v. *Houston*, 114 U. S. 622.

[2] *Gloucester Ferry Co.* v. *Pennsylvania*, 114 U. S. 196.

[3] *Fisk* v. *Jefferson Police Jury*, 116 U. S. 131.

[4] *Gloucester Ferry Co.* v. *Pennsylvania*, 114 U. S. 196.

[5] *Cooper Manufacturing Co.* v. *Ferguson*, 113 U. S. 727.

[6] *Gloucester Ferry Co.* v. *Pennsylvania*, 114 U. S. 196.

begun to be transported from that State to Lecture IX. another State, and not till then, they become Generally. the subjects of interstate commerce, and, as such, are subject to national regulation, and cease to be taxable by the State of their origin. Goods on their way through a State, from a place outside thereof to another place outside thereof, are in course of interstate or foreign transportation, and are subjects of interstate or foreign commerce, and are not taxable by the State through which they are passing, even though detained within that State by low water, or other temporary causes.[1]

Interstate commerce cannot be taxed at all by a State, even though the same amount of tax should be laid on domestic commerce, or that which is carried on solely within the State.[2]

The question whether, when Congress fails to provide a regulation by law as to any particular subject of commerce among the States, it is conclusive of its intention that that subject shall be free from positive regulation, or that, until Congress intervenes, it shall be left to be dealt with by the States, is one to be determined from the circumstances of each case as it arises.[3]

A burden imposed upon interstate commerce is not to be sustained simply because the statute imposing it applies alike to the people of all the States, including the people of the State enacting it.[4]

---

[1] *Coe* v. *Errol*, 116 U. S. 517.

[2] *Robbins* v. *Shelby County Taxing District*, 120 U. S. 489.

[3] *Bowman* v. *Chicago & Northwestern Railway Co.*, 125 U. S. 465.

[4] *Minnesota* v. *Barber*, 136 U. S. 313.

2. *Bridges over Navigable Streams.*

A bridge erected over the East River in New York, in accordance with authority derived from Congress and from the legislature of New York, is a lawful structure, which cannot be abated as a public nuisance.[1]

In the absence of legislation by Congress, a State may authorize a navigable stream within its limits to be obstructed by a bridge or highway;[2] but Congress has plenary powers respecting such streams and is not concluded, by anything that may have been done under State authority, from assuming entire control, abating any erections that may have been made, and preventing any other from being made except in conformity with such regulations as it may impose.[3]

3. *Steamships.*

A tax upon the gross receipts of a steamship company incorporated under its laws, which are derived from the transportation of persons and property by sea, between different States and to and from foreign countries, is a regulation of interstate and foreign commerce, in conflict with the exclusive power of Congress under the Constitution.[4]

---

[1] *Miller* v. *New York*, 109 U. S. 385.

[2] *Cardwell* v. *American Bridge Company*, 113 U. S. 205.

[3] *Willamette Iron Bridge Co.* v. *Hatch*, 125 U. S. 1.

[4] *Philadelphia & Southern Steamship Co.* v. *Pennsylvania*, 122 U. S. 326.

4. *Railroads.*

A privilege tax of fifty dollars per annum on Lecture IX. every sleeping car or coach used or run over a Railroads. railroad in Tennessee, and not owned or run by the railroad on which it was run or used, was held to be void so far as it applied to the interstate transportation of passengers carried over railroads in Tennessee into or out of or across that State, in sleeping cars owned by a corporation of Kentucky, and leased by it to Tennessee corporations, the latter receiving the transit fare, and the former the compensation for the sleeping accommodations.[1]

A State statute requiring locomotive engineers on railroad trains to obtain licenses from the State before being permitted to run trains within the State is not a regulation of commerce when applied to engineers on through trains coming into the State from another State, or going from it to another State.[2]

A State statute which levies a tax upon the gross receipts of railroads for the carriage of goods and passengers into, out of, or through the State, is a tax upon commerce among the States, and therefore void. The States cannot be permitted, under the guise of a tax upon business within their borders, to impose a burden upon commerce within the States, when the business so taxed is itself interstate commerce.[3]

---

[1] *Pickard* v. *Pullman Southern Car Co.,* 117 U. S. 34.

[2] *Smith* v. *Alabama,* 124 U. S. 465.

[3] *Fargo* v. *Michigan,* 121 U. S. 230.

LECTURE IX.
Railroads.

Congress has authority, in the exercise of its power to regulate commerce among the several States, to construct or authorize the construction of railroads across the States and Territories of the United States; and the franchises thus conferred cannot, without its permission, be taxed by the States.[1]

5. *Quarantine.*

Quarantine.

States may enact quarantine laws which amount to regulations of commerce, though not intended to be so, and maintain them until Congress acts in the matter by covering the same ground, or by forbidding State legislation.[2]

6. *Tax on Commerce.*

Tax on commerce.

A municipal ordinance of the city of New Orleans to establish the rate of license for professions, callings, and other business, which assesses and directs to be collected a tax from persons owning and running towboats to and from the Gulf of Mexico and the city of New Orleans is a regulation of commerce among the States, and is an infringement of the provisions of Article 1, section 8, paragraph 3, of the Constitution.[3]

The act of Congress of August 3, 1882, "to regulate immigration," which imposed upon the owners of steam or sailing vessels bringing passengers from a foreign port into a port of the United States, a duty of fifty cents for every

---

[1] *California* v. *Central Pacific Railroad Co.*, 127 U. S. 1.
[2] *Morgan's Steamship Co.* v. *Louisiana*, 118 U. S. 455.
[3] *Moran* v. *New Orleans*, 112 U. S. 69.

such passenger, not a citizen of this country, was Lecture IX.
a valid exercise of the power to regulate com- Tax on commerce.
merce with foreign nations.[1]

The business of receiving and landing of passengers and freight is incident to their transportation, and a tax upon such receiving and landing is a tax upon transportation and upon commerce, interstate or foreign, involved in such transportation.[2]

7. Telegraphs.

A State statute intended to regulate, or to Telegraphs.
tax, or to impose a restriction upon the transmission of persons, or property, or telegraphic messages, from one State to another, is not within that class of legislation which a State may enact, in the absence of legislation by Congress; and such statutes are void, even as to the part of such transmission within the State.[3] The judgment in this case was announced on the 25th of October, 1886, Mr. Justice Miller delivering the opinion of the court. It is not too much to say that it was the immediate cause of the passage of the "act to regulate commerce," commonly known as the Interstate Commerce Act.[4]

The reserved police power of a State under the Constitution, although difficult to define,

---

[1] *Head Money Cases,* 112 U. S. 580.

[2] *Gloucester Ferry Company* v. *Pennsylvania,* 114 U. S. 196.

[3] *Wabash, St. Louis &c. Railway* v. *Illinois,* 118 U. S. 557.

[4] 24 Stat. 379, c. 104; amended March 2, 1889, 25 Stat. 855, c. 382.

does not extend to the regulation of the deliv-ery at points without the State of telegraphic messages received within the State; but the State may, within the reservation that it does not encroach upon the free exercise of the pow-ers vested in Congress, make all necessary pro-visions in respect of the buildings, poles, and wires of the telegraph companies within its jurisdiction, which the comfort and convenience of the community may require.[1]

A single tax assessed under the laws of a State upon receipts of a telegraph company, which were partly derived from interstate com-merce and partly from commerce within the State, and which were capable of separation, but were returned and assessed in gross and without separation or apportionment, is invalid in propor-tion to the extent that such receipts were derived from interstate commerce, but is otherwise valid.[2]

8. *Spirituous Liquors.*

A State law prohibiting the manufacture and sale of intoxicating liquors is not repugnant to the Constitution of the United States.[3]

A State cannot, for the purpose of protecting its people against the evils of intemperance, enact laws which regulate commerce between its people and those of other States of the Union,

---

[1] *Western Union Telegraph Co.* v. *Pendleton*, 122 U. S. 347.

[2] *Ratterman* v. *Western Union Tel. Co.*, 127 U. S. 411. See also *Leloup* v. *Port of Mobile*, 127 U. S. 640; *Western Union Tel. Co.* v. *Alabama*, 132 U. S. 472.

[3] *Foster* v. *Kansas*, 112 U. S. 201.

unless the consent of Congress, express or im- LECTURE IX.
Spirituous
liquors.
plied, is first obtained.[1]

The sale of spirituous liquors by retail and in
small quantities may be regulated or prohibited
by State legislation, without violating the Constitution or laws of the United States.[2]

9. *Discriminating License Taxes.*

The act of the legislature of Tennessee pro- Discriminating
license taxes.
viding that "all drummers and all persons not
having a regular licensed house of business in
the taxing district of Shelby County, offering
for sale or selling goods, wares, or merchandise
therein, by sample, shall be required to pay to
the county trustee the sum of $10 per week, or
$25 per month for such privilege," applies to
persons soliciting the sale of goods on behalf of
individuals or firms doing business in another
State; and, so far as it applies to them, it is a
regulation of commerce among the States, and
violates the provision of the Constitution, which
grants to Congress the power to make such
regulations.[3]

10. *Discriminating Taxes.*

A tax imposed by a State statute upon an oc- Discriminating
taxes.
cupation which necessarily discriminates against

---

[1] *Bowman* v. *Chicago & Northwestern Railway Co.*, 125 U. S.
465. See *Mugler* v. *Kansas*, 123 U. S. 623; *Kidd* v. *Pearson*, 128
U. S. 1; *Leisy* v. *Hardin*, 135 U. S. 100; *Crowley* v. *Christensen*,
137 U. S. 86.

[2] *Crowley* v. *Christensen*, 137 U. S. 86.

[3] *Robbins* v. *Shelby County Taxing District*, 120 U. S. 489. See
also *Corson* v. *Maryland*, 120 U. S. 502; *Asher* v. *Texas*, 128 U. S.
129; *Stoutenburgh* v. *Hennick*, 129 U. S. 141; *McCall* v. *California*,
136 U. S. 104.

LECTURE IX.
Discriminating
taxes.

the introduction and sale of the products of another State, or against the citizens of another State, is repugnant to the Constitution of the United States.[1]

11. *Food Inspection.*

Food inspection.

A law providing for the inspection of animals, whose meats are designed for human food, cannot be regarded as a rightful exercise of the police power of the State, if the inspection prescribed is of such a character, or is burdened with such conditions, as will prevent the introduction into the State of sound meats, the product of animals slaughtered in other States.[2]

The Virginia statute of February 18, 1890, makes it unlawful to offer for sale, within the limits of that State, any beef, veal, or mutton from animals slaughtered one hundred miles or more from the place at which it is offered for sale, unless it has been previously inspected and approved by local inspectors appointed under that act. It fixes the inspector's compensation at one cent a pound, to be paid by the owner of the meats. It does not require the inspection of fresh meats from animals slaughtered within one hundred miles from the place in Virginia at which such meats are offered for sale. The act was held to be void, as being in restraint of commerce among the States, and as imposing a discriminating tax.[3]

---

[1] *Walling* v. *Michigan*, 116 U. S. 446.

[2] *Minnesota* v. *Barber*, 136 U. S. 313.

[3] *Brimmer* v. *Rebman*, 138 U. S. 78.

X.

THE RIGHT OF TRIAL BY JURY.[1]

————oo:o:oo————

ARTICLE I, SECTION 9, PARAGRAPH 2. The Privilege of the Writ of Habeas Corpus shall not be suspended, unless when in Cases of Rebellion or Invasion
the public Safety may require it.

ARTICLE III, SECTION 2, PARAGRAPH 1. The judicial Power shall extend to all Cases, in. . . Equity,
arising under this Constitution, the Laws of the
United States, and Treaties made, or which shall be
made, under their Authority.

ARTICLE III, SECTION 2, PARAGRAPH 3. The trial
of all Crimes, except in Cases of Impeachment, shall
be by Jury; and such Trial shall be held in the State
where the said Crimes shall have been committed; but
when not committed within any State, the Trial shall
be at such Place or Places as the Congress may by
Law have directed.

ARTICLE V OF THE AMENDMENTS. No person shall
be held to answer for a capital, or otherwise infamous
crime, unless on a presentment or indictment of a
Grand Jury, except in cases arising in the land or
naval forces, or in the Militia, when in actual service
in time of War or public danger; nor shall any person be subject for the same offence to be twice put in
jeopardy of life or limb; nor shall be compelled in
any Criminal Case to be a witness against himself,
nor be deprived of life, liberty, or property, without
due process of law; nor shall private property be
taken for public use, without just compensation.

ARTICLE VI OF THE AMENDMENTS. In all criminal
prosecutions, the accused shall enjoy the right to a

---

[1] C'est donc le jury civil qui a réellement sauvé les libertés de
l'Angleterre. De Tocqueville.

485

LECTURE X.

speedy and public trial, by an impartial jury of the State and district wherein the crime shall have been committed, which district shall have been previously ascertained by law, and to be informed of the nature and cause of the accusation ; to be confronted with the witnesses against him ; to have compulsory process for obtaining Witnesses in his favour, and to have the Assistance of Counsel for his defence.

ARTICLE VII OF THE AMENDMENTS. In suits at common law, where the value in controversy shall exceed twenty dollars, the right of trial by jury shall be preserved, and no fact tried by a jury shall be otherwise re-examined in any Court of the United States than according to the rules of the common law.

The Constitution founded upon English law.

[1]No one familiar with the common law of England can read the Constitution of the United States without observing the great desire of the Convention which framed that instrument to make it conform as far as possible with that law. One would suppose that the leaders of a revolutionary movement of eight years' duration or more, the purpose of which was to emancipate the newly formed States from the dominion of Great Britain, would have come out of that struggle with resentments arising from a sense of injury at the hands of that government which would have created a prejudice against its laws and their system of administration. On the contrary, it seems obvious from the instrument which they produced as the fundamental and organic law of a new government for a new country, that their attachment for the old laws and even for the old general form of political government remained almost unaffected.

---

[1] This is Lecture VIII delivered before the classes of the University Law School.

To look at the general outlines organizing the new government into its various branches, there is but little departure from that of the English government. The President, the Senate, and the House of Representatives correspond in essential features with the King, Lords, and Commons of Great Britain. And although there was a necessity arising from the bringing together of thirteen different States into one general government, with a recognition of many of ꝸthe most important powers of government left in the States themselves, to vary in some respects the powers which were confided to the President, the Senate, and the House of Representatives from those which had by immemorial usage come to be the powers of the King, the House of Lords, and the House of Commons of Great Britain, yet the analogy is very close. It has often been said that Mr. Hamilton, who perhaps of all other men in the Convention which framed this Constitution most strongly impressed his views upon that instrument, desired a still closer conformity to the British model in the matter of stronger powers in the Federal Government, and especially in the Senate and Executive.

The first great nation of the earth which succeeded us in the process of revolution and forming a new government, namely, the French, acted in a very different manner. They abolished at one blow the existence of the King, or of any recognized power which represented the functions of the Crown. They reposed all the power

LECTURE X.
The Constitution founded upon English law.

Unsuccessful French attempts at framing constitutions.

Lecture X.
Unsuccessful
French attempts
at framing con-
stitutions.

of the government in a single body elected directly by the people. They also abolished during the course of their revolutionary proceedings their entire body of civil law, and substituted therefor a new code called the "Code Napoleon," which has been supposed by many jurists to be the ablest code of laws ever formed for the government of a people. The instability of the government which resulted from this action of the French people and of all governments formed by that nation since the revolution of 1793, may well be used as an argument against such violent and sudden changes. Certainly if any deduction on that subject is to be made from the success and stability given to a new government by its adherence to the best maxims of the old one out of which it was formed, the history of the United States presents that argument in its best form.

English features
retained in the
Constitution.

Not only did the framers of the new Constitution follow as well as they might the general polity of the English system, but they evinced an ardent desire to preserve the principles which had been accepted as part of the general administration of the law among our ancestors. This is shown in many of the provisions of the Constitution. Among others, the article concerning the judicial powers of the new government establishes its jurisdiction as extending to all

Distinction be-
tween law and
equity.

cases in admiralty, and in law, and in equity, thus recognizing the English separation of these three classes of legal controversies as being governed by a separate jurisdiction. At least such

has been the construction placed upon that instrument by the courts of the country without
much question. It has been repeatedly decided
that the jurisdiction in equity, which was a very
peculiar one under the English system of legal
administration, remains in the courts of the
United States as it was at the time they separated from that country, and that one of the
distinctive features of the difference between
law and equity, namely, that at law there is a
right to a trial by jury, and in equity there is
none, has continued to the present day. And
it is a very grave question, one which has never
been brought to the attention of the courts,
because Congress has never attempted to exercise any such authority, whether the Congress
of the United States can make any change in the
equitable jurisdiction of the courts of the United
States, and if so, to what extent it can be done.

Another very important instance in which the
venerable maxims of the common law have been
thought worthy of a place in the organic law of
this country, is that concerning the writ of
habeas corpus, the great writ by which a person
unjustly imprisoned may cause himself to be
brought before the proper judicial tribunal, and
have the nature, cause, and legality of that imprisonment inquired into. Among the limitations imposed by section 9 of Article I, is
the declaration that "the privilege of a writ of
habeas corpus shall not be suspended, unless
when in cases of rebellion or invasion, the public
safety may require it."

LECTURE X.
Right of trial by
jury.

Of a similar character, and perhaps of much more importance, is the subject to which I invite your attention this evening as it is found in the Constitution, namely, that of the right of trial by jury. This right has been the subject of such inquiry into its origin and history, and of such glowing eulogy by all those who believe in the beauties of the common law, and by many who do not, as well as of criticisms upon its value, which have become more frequent in modern times, that I must rely upon your general reading upon this subject without myself entering upon its discussion.[1]

The jury system
of England.

Grand jury.

The jury system of the English at the time of the adoption of our Constitution divided itself into two branches. One of these was called the grand jury, whose purpose and function was to make inquiry as to crimes committed in the county, and presentments to the court of such charges as they thought proper growing out of that investigation; and also when indictments for crimes were submitted to them by the law officers of the government, it was their duty to pass upon them by endorsing them as true bills, or ignoring them as not supported by the

---

[1] In 1215 personal rights were secured to the subject by Magna Charta, which declared : "No freeman shall be taken or imprisoned, or be disseized of his freehold or liberties, or free customs, or be outlawed or exiled, or any otherwise damaged, nor will one pass upon him, nor send upon him, but by lawful judgment of his peers, or by the law of the land." 2 Inst. 45.

Lord Coke says in his comments upon this clause that it "hath the first place, because the liberty of a man's person is more precious than all the rest which follows."

facts before them. This grand jury consisted of a number of jurors, varying from twelve or fifteen to twenty-four, but the concurrence of twelve of that number was always required in making a presentment or finding an indictment.

The other form of jury is the one before which the trial actually takes place " This means the examination before a competent tribunal, [the jury,] according to the laws of the land, of the facts put in issue for the purpose of determining such issue."[1]

This jury has always been composed, at least in modern times, of twelve men, and its finding of issues presented to it can only be made by the concurrence of all the twelve. These jurors are supposed to be impartial, and the manner of their appointment or selection has been prescribed by acts of Congress as regards trials in the Federal courts, and by statutes of the States so far as trials in the State courts are concerned, with a view to secure this object. Whether it is in the power of Congress to modify this system by prescribing a jury of less than twelve men, or by giving validity to a verdict which represents less than the whole number of twelve, are questions which have never been decided because Congress has never attempted to vary this rule. There have been decisions of various courts that this could not be done, that the word "jury" as used in the Constitution means "ex vi termini," a tribunal of twelve men,

---

[1] *United States* v. *Curtis*, 4 Mason, 232.

and that its verdict must be unanimous to be the verdict of a jury under the Constitution. The question, so far as I am aware, has never been decided by the Supreme Court because no law has ever been passed by Congress to vary or change the common law rule. In no other way could it come before that court.

The right of trial by jury has relation to civil cases and to prosecutions for crimes. The original Constitution contained no specific reference to such trial in civil cases, but the Seventh Article of the Amendments reads as follows: —

" In suits at common law, where the value in controversy shall exceed twenty dollars, the right of trial by jury shall be preserved ; and no fact, tried by a jury, shall be otherwise re-examined in any court of the United States, than according to the rules of the common law."

It has relation to
the common law
as understood in
England.

The first thing to be observed about this Article is that it prescribes this mode of trial in " *suits at common law.*" It does not use the same words as the clause extending the judicial power " to all cases *in law* and equity." It is to be inferred, therefore, that trial by jury, as imposed by the Constitution, has relation to the common law as it was understood in England and to the right to such a trial in that class of cases. This distinction may be important in regard to a class of cases where a summary remedy is given by a statute, which is itself a departure from the common law and at variance with it. How far in this anomalous class of cases, which, while they may be said to be cases at law, as distinguished from cases in equity, are not "suits at common law," the parties would have a right to demand a trial by jury, it is not my purpose at present to inquire. Nor is it material why the sum of twenty dollars was established as the line above which the Constitution gave the right to a trial by jury and did not do so below it.

This Article of the Amendments to the Constitution, as well as all of the others from one to eight inclusive, applies to the powers exercised by the Government of the United States, and not to those of the States. This has been repeatedly decided.[1]

But while the effect given by this Article as to a fact tried by a jury has relation to such effect in the courts of the United States, it applies equally to verdicts found by juries in the State courts; that is to say, that in a court of the United States a fact once found by a jury of a State court or of a Federal court shall not be re-examined in any other manner than according to the rules of the common law. This conclusiveness given to the verdict of a jury is in accordance with the common law of England, and is an additional evidence of the sanctity with which the right of trial by jury is held both in that country and this. Let it also be observed that this Article does not prescribe as an arbitrary rule to the courts that all cases *must* be tried by a jury which are suits at com-

Lecture X.

It has relation to the common law as understood in England.

It applies only to the United States.

Effect of a verdict.

___

[1] *Livingston* v. *Moore*, 7 Pet. 469; *The Justices* v. *Murray*, 9 Wall. 274; *Edwards* v. *Elliott*, 21 Wall. 532.

mon law and exceed twenty dollars in value, but that it is the *right* of any party to such a suit to have a trial by a jury if he demands it. The parties can waive this right[1] and submit the case to the court without a jury, in which case the judgment of the court would be equally binding as if there had been a verdict of a jury; and in practice in this country, both in the Federal and State courts, a very large proportion of the trials of issues of fact are by the judge or judges of those courts without the aid of a jury. In the Federal courts the consent of all the parties concerned is essential to the validity of

---

[1] Though this right to a trial by jury embraces all suits not in equity or admiralty (*Parsons* v. *Bedford*, 3 Pet. 433) ; yet parties may waive the right (*Bond* v. *Brown*, 12 How. 254 ; *Morgan* v. *Gay*, 19 Wall. 81 ; *Baylis* v. *Travellers' Ins. Co.*, 113 U. S. 316 ; *Flanders* v. *Tweed*, 9 Wall. 425 ; *Henderson's Distilled Spirits*, 14 Wall. 44 ; *Phillips* v. *Preston*, 5 How. 278) ; and in a suit in equity the court may not only find the facts itself without impairing the right of trial by jury, but it may disregard the findings of fact by a jury, if it thinks them wrong (*Basey* v. *Gallagher*, 20 Wall. 670). So, too, the mode of proceeding in the Court of Claims, under the statutes, is constitutional. *McElrath* v. *United States*, 102 U. S. 426. This constitutional provision, so far as it relates to civil actions, is a restriction only upon courts of the United States. *Edwards* v. *Elliott*, 21 Wall. 532, 557. State courts are not forbidden, even by the provisions in the Fourteenth Amendment as to " due process of law." *Walker* v. *Souvinet*, 92 U. S. 90.

This guaranty of trial by jury is as operative in time of war as in time of peace ; is equally binding upon rulers and people, at all times and under all circumstances. Military commissions organized during the late civil war, in a State not invaded and not engaged in rebellion, in which the Federal courts were open and in the proper and unobstructed exercise of their judicial functions, had no jurisdiction to try, convict, or sentence, for any criminal offence, a citizen who was not a resident in a rebellious State, nor a prisoner of war, nor a person in the military or naval service, and Congress could not invest them with that power. *Ex parte Milligan*, 4 Wall. 2.

this form of trial. Indeed it had been decided LECTURE X.
prior to the act of Congress of 1865[1] that there Effect of such a judgment.
could be no writ of error or appeal to a judg-
ment of an inferior court in a suit at common
law in which the parties had submitted the case
to the court without a jury, because, as was held
by the Supreme Court of the United States, such
judgment was in effect but a mere arbitration.
But by that statute where the parties waive a
jury by a stipulation in writing, the finding of
the court upon the facts, which might be either
general or special, was to have the same effect
as the verdict of a jury, and the judgment
might be reviewed by the Supreme Court upon
a writ of error or upon appeal, the review extending to the sufficiency of the facts found to
support the judgment, and to such exceptions
as might have been taken and presented by a
bill of exceptions during the progress of the
trial.[2] These provisions of the act of 1865 are
embodied in sections 649 and 700 of the Revised
Statutes of the United States.

The language of this Article is that "no fact How judgments
tried by a jury shall be otherwise re-examined on a verdict could be re-examined at
in any court of the United States, than accord- the common law.
ing to the rules of the common law." The
common law admitted of but two modes of
re-examining the verdict of a jury. One of
these was by a motion for a new trial in the
same proceeding, and usually in the same court in

---

[1] 13 Stat. 501, c. 86, § 4.
[2] *Norris* v. *Jackson*, 9 Wall. 125.

LECTURE X.

How judgments
on a verdict could
be re-examined at
the common law.

which the verdict was rendered. The other was by some supervisory or appellate court which had jurisdiction upon a writ of error in certain classes of cases to set aside the verdict and grant a new trial.

These two modes of re-examining a verdict and affirming it or setting it aside proceeded upon somewhat different principles. The court of original jurisdiction, in which the case was tried, had an almost unlimited power of setting aside the verdict for errors of law committed by the court itself during the progress of the trial, for insufficiency of the evidence to sustain the verdict of the jury, and for other causes so numerous and varying that they cannot even be enumerated here; but it may be said that the power of the court in that proceeding, upon a proper showing, to re-examine the verdict, was only governed by a sound legal discretion. The re-examination by an appellate court on a writ of error, or in any other mode by which such a case was carried to a superior court for review, extended only to errors of law committed by the court in the progress of the case, and which were presented by the record and by bills of exception. By this restriction the appellate court was forbidden at common law to enter into an examination of the weight of evidence and the soundness of the verdict of the jury, except as that was affected by some matter of law presented in the course of the trial. In the case of *Parsons* v. *Bedford*, 3 Pet. 433, 448, Mr. Justice Story, representing the court, says: —

"The only modes known to the common law, LECTURE X.

How judgments on a verdict cou'd be re-examined at the common law. to re-examine such facts, are the granting of a new trial by the court where the issue was tried, or to which the record was properly returnable; or the award of a *venire facias de novo,* by an appellate court, for some error of law which intervened in the proceedings. The judiciary act of 1789, c. 20, § 17, has given to all the courts of the United States 'power to grant new trials in cases where there has been a trial by jury, for reasons for which new trials have usually been granted in the courts of law.' And the appellate jurisdiction has also been amply given by the same act (§§ 22, 24) to this court, to redress errors of law; and for such errors to award a new trial, in suits at law which have been tried by a jury."

The whole opinion in this case may be read by you with profit as explaining the objects and purposes of this amendment to the Constitution. See also *Insurance Co.* v. *Comstock,* 16 Wall. 258, 269, where the following language is used by the court:—

"Two modes only were known to the common law to re-examine such facts, to wit: the granting of a new trial by the court where the issue was tried or to which the record was returnable, or, secondly, by the award of a *venire facias de novo* by an appellate court for some error of law which intervened in the proceedings."

As showing the extent to which this doctrine of the sacredness of a verdict, in a case which was once tried by a jury, even in the State

LECTURE X.
How judgments
on a verdict could
be re-examined at
the common law.
courts, has been carried, when the same case has been brought into a court of the United States, your attention is called to the case of *The Justices* v. *Murray*, 9 Wall. 274. It was there held that an act of Congress which provided for the removal of a judgment in a State court, where the cause had been tried by a jury, to the Circuit Court of the United States for a retrial of the facts and the law, was unconstitutional on account of the Article now under consideration, because such removal implied the necessity of a re-examination of the facts already found by the jury in the State court.

The only other observation I have to make in regard to the effect of the Constitution of the United States as governing trials in civil actions is that it has been contended that by the Fourteenth Amendment the right of trial by jury in the States is guaranteed to every person by the phrase, " Nor shall any State deprive any person of life, liberty, or property, without due process of law." This question was presented, examined, and decided otherwise in *Hurtado* v. *California*, 110 U. S. 516.

Article III, section 2, paragraph 3, is as follows : —

" The trial of all crimes, except in cases of impeachment, shall be by jury ; and such trial shall be held in the State where the said crimes shall have been committed ; but when not committed within any State, the trial shall be at such place, or places, as the Congress may by law have directed."

And, as intimately connected with the same subject, Articles V and VI of the Amendments are here presented. LECTURE X. The Fourteenth Amendment.

"Article V. No person shall be held to answer for a capital, or otherwise infamous crime, unless on a presentment or indictment of a grand jury, except in cases arising in the land or naval forces, or in the militia, when in actual service, in time of war, or public danger; nor shall any person be subject, for the same offence, to be twice put in jeopardy of life or limb; nor shall be compelled, in any criminal case, to be a witness against himself, nor be deprived of life, liberty, or property, without due process of law; nor shall private property be taken for public use, without just compensation. The Fifth Amendment.

"Article VI. In all criminal prosecutions, the accused shall enjoy the right to a speedy and public trial, by an impartial jury of the State and district wherein the crime shall have been committed, which district shall have been previously ascertained by law; and to be informed of the nature and cause of the accusation; to be confronted with the witnesses against him; to have compulsory process for obtaining witnesses in his favor; and to have the assistance of counsel for his defence." The Sixth Amendment.

You will see that the paragraph in Article III, above quoted, differs in its language from that which we have already considered in regard to trial by jury in civil cases as prescribed by Article VII of the Amendments. In the latter Article it is the mere right to demand the trial by

jury which is guaranteed, and the parties may
waive that right either by express agreement or
by failing to demand a jury, while the language
used in Article III is peremptory that "the trial
of all crimes, except in cases of impeachment,
shall be by jury." This language excludes all
other modes, whether with or without the consent of the party. A party may, however, confess his guilt by a plea of guilty, and judgment
may be passed upon that plea, yet if there is an
issue of fact which has to be tried, that trial can
only be by a jury. Indeed it has been argued with
a good deal of earnestness and plausibility that
in criminal cases by virtue of that clause of the
Constitution the jury are made the judge both of
the facts and the law, and have a right upon
their own view of what the law of the cases may
be, without regard to the decisions of the court
on the subject, to find a verdict. This contention has been supposed to be supported by the
conceded fact that a verdict of not guilty, ac-
quitting the party of the crime charged, has in
practice always been held to be final, and that
the court could not set aside such a verdict and
subject the party to a new trial. Such action
has, however, been founded upon that provision
of Article V of the amendments, which declares
that no person shall "be subject, for the same
offence, to be twice put in jeopardy of life or
limb," it having been held that on a verdict of
acquittal, however erroneous, the party has been
put in jeopardy within the meaning of that
clause of the Constitution. It is, however, the

doctrine of the present day, established by numer- Lecture X.
ous authorities, that in a trial for a crime against But in the U S. courts the jury
the United States, the jury are legally bound in must accept the
law and in conscience to be controlled by the law from the court.
law which may be applicable to such a case as
laid down by the court before whom the issue is
tried.[1]

The exception of cases of impeachment from Impeachment.
those which- must be tried by a jury demands
but a moment's attention. Other clauses of the
Constitution provide that all officers of the
Government, from the President down, may be
removed from office by impeachment, for treason,
for felony, and other high crimes and misdemeanors. They provide that this impeachment
shall be instituted by charges preferred by the
House of Representatives, and that the issues
shall be tried by the Senate of the United States;
that it shall require two-thirds of the senators
present to authorize a verdict of guilty, and
that the punishment shall only extend to removal
from office and a disqualification for the future
to hold any office of honor or profit under the
Government of the United States. This does
not preclude a trial in the ordinary courts for
any of the crimes which may be charged in the
articles of impeachment.

This section of the Third Article of the Constitution then goes on to declare that the trial
of all crimes, with the exception of cases of im-

---

1 *United States* v. *Morris*, 1 Curtis, 23 ; *United States* v. *Shive*,
1 Baldwin, 510 ; *United States* v. *Battiste*, 2 Sumner, 240.

peachment, which we have above considered, " shall be by jury; and such trial shall be held in the State where the said crimes shall have been committed; but when not committed within any State, the trial shall be at such place, or places, as the Congress may by law have directed."

Place of trial.

We have here, in this declaration, that the trial shall be held in the State where the crime shall have been committed, another evidence of the disposition of the Convention to adhere to what they supposed to be the safeguards of the common law. It was a part of the common law that every man charged with a crime should be tried by a jury of the vicinage, which vicinage was held to be the local jurisdiction of the hundred, or shire, or by whatever name the tribunal was called, which could try the offence. And though it has long since been discovered that the knowledge which the neighbors where the offence was committed might have of the crime itself, and of the character of the party charged, and the feeling which they might entertain on the subject, are in reality to a large extent disqualifications for the exercise of the functions of a juror, yet it is an undoubted fact that the principle of the trial by a jury of the vicinage was founded on these considerations. This policy of the common law, and the feeling that no man charged with a crime against the Government of the United States should be carried away from the State where the crime was committed, and tried in some other State, even though it was in

a court of the United States, lay at the founda- Lecture x.
tion of this provision of the Constitution. The Place of trial.
mention of crimes "not committed within any
State" had reference to those committed upon
the high seas, in the Territories of the United
States and in the forts, arsenals, and other
places, the jurisdiction in regard to which has
been ceded to the Federal Government. In this
class of cases Congress may prescribe the place
where the trial shall be had.

The Fifth Article of the Amendments, which An infamous
declares that "No person shall be held to answer crime within the meaning of the
for a capital, or otherwise infamous, crime, unless Fifth Amend-
on a presentment or indictment of a grand jury," ment.
is one which has recently attracted the consideration of the courts. It has become quite
common for the prosecuting officers of the Government to file informations against parties for
offences against the United States, and to proceed to a trial on the charges presented in those
informations without any action by a grand
jury thereon. The question then presented is
whether the charges thus preferred constitute
infamous crimes. There is no difficulty in holding that all crimes for which the punishment is
death are infamous crimes within the meaning
of this clause of the Constitution, and no attempt
has been made in the Federal courts to prosecute a person for any such offence in any other
way than by an indictment by a grand jury.
But a very large class of offences against the
laws of the United States have recently been
prosecuted on information, where the party

Lecture X.

An infamous
crime within the
meaning of the
Fifth Amend-
ment.

charged has taken the ground that the offence charged was an infamous crime within the meaning of this clause of the Constitution, and could only be tried under an indictment or presentment of a grand jury. There has been great difficulty in deciding what was meant a hundred years ago by the phrase "infamous crime," which is used in this constitutional amendment. That difficulty is not diminished by the fact of the obscurity of the language itself as construed by what is known of the laws and usages of our ancestors at that time, in connection with the fact that both State and Federal legislation in regard to crimes may have made that infamous since which would not have been so considered then. While there are several decisions reported from the Circuit Courts of the United States on this subject, the question never came directly before the Supreme Court until recently.[1]

The opinion of the court in *Wilson's Case* shows the difficulty of arriving at any satisfactory and exclusive definition of the phrase "infamous crimes;" but after an examination of all the sources of light upon that subject the court held that " for the reasons above stated, having regard to the object and the terms of the first provision of the Fifth Amendment, as well as to the history of its proposal and adoption, and to the early understanding and practice under it,

---

[1] *Ex parte Wilson*, 114 U. S. 417 ; *United States* v. *Petit*, 114 U. S. 429.

this court is of opinion that the competency of
the defendant, if convicted, to be a witness in
another case is *not* the true test ; and that no
person can be held to answer, without presentment or indictment by a grand jury, for any
crime for which an infamous punishment may
be imposed by the court.

" The question is whether the crime is one for
which the statutes authorize the court to award
an infamous punishment, not whether the punishment ultimately awarded is an infamous one.
When the accused is in danger of being subjected
to an infamous punishment if convicted, he has
the right to insist that he shall not be put upon
his trial, except on the accusation of a grand
jury." [1]

The court also said that " deciding nothing
beyond what is required by the facts of the case
before us, our judgment is that a crime, punishable by imprisonment for a term of years at
hard labor, is an infamous crime, within the
meaning of the Fifth Amendment of the Constitution." [2] These views are adopted at the same
time and governed the decision of the case of the
United States v. *Petit ;* and in *Mackin* v. *United
States,* 117 U. S. 348, it is held that all crimes
punishable by imprisonment in a State prison
or penitentiary are infamous. Of course these
cases decide no more than what was before the
court, and many other crimes may be found to
be infamous than those which are punishable by

---

[1] *Ex parte Wilson,* 114 U. S. 417, 426.   [2] Ib. 429.

LECTURE X.
An infamous
crime within the
meaning of the
Fifth Amend-
ment.

hard labor in the penitentiary. But the principles laid down in that opinion may serve in a
general way as a guide in the decision of future
cases. Such decisions must, however, depend in
each case upon the facts peculiar to it.

Offences by per-
sons in the land
or naval forces or
militia in actual
service.

There is an exception in regard to the necessity of finding a presentment or indictment by
a grand jury in crimes against the United States
of those " arising in the land or naval forces, or
in the militia, when in actual service, in time of
war or public danger." The reason for this
was that soldiers of the regular forces of the
United States, or of the militia when called into
the service of the General Government, could
not with convenience be tried by a jury. The
necessity for strict discipline and subordination
in the military service required that there should
be prompt and speedy action in regard to all
offences committed therein. From time immemorial our ancestors had subjected persons so
engaged to trial by military courts of various
kinds, and it was supposed by the framers of the
Constitution that these courts, proceeding by
their own methods, which were well understood,
and inflicting punishments appropriate to the
offences committed, would answer all the purposes of securing the rights of the persons
charged with such offences, considering also the
inconvenience and impossibility of convening
grand juries and petit juries from men in civil
life to try military offences, or any others, committed by officers or soldiers of the army of the
United States. These considerations it was

thought justified the departure from the general rule.

LECTURE X.

Offences by persons in the land or naval forces or militia in actual service.

As regards offences committed by persons in the militia the exception was limited to those "in actual service, in time of war, or public danger." And this has relation to what I said to you the other evening as to the power of the President under the second section of the Second Article as the commander-in-chief of the militia of the several States, when called into the actual service of the United States. The militia is spoken of in other parts of the Constitution, and always has reference to a body of citizens of the States, organized under State authority into military divisions, subject to officers appointed by the States, and which may be called into the service of the Federal Government on special occasions mentioned in the Constitution. Therefore, if a person who is a member of the militia is charged with a crime against the United States, he cannot be proceeded against without an indictment or presentment of a grand jury unless he be " in the actual service of the United States " and " in time of war or public danger."

Article VI of the Amendments opens with a declaration that " in all criminal prosecutions the accused shall enjoy the right to a speedy and public trial." It may be supposed that this right thus placed in the foreground of one of these Articles would be considered a right of the gravest importance, but I am not aware of any act of Congress designed to secure it to a person so accused. In the absence of any such legislation this right of a speedy trial as guaranteed by this provision must depend upon the control which the courts exercise over their prosecuting officers, by requiring them to proceed within a reasonable time to the trial when the accused so desires, but it is to be feared that the spirit of this constitutional provision has not always been enforced in favor of accused persons.

The trial, it is also declared, shall be "public," which was a wise provision, designed to prevent secret trials from which the public could be excluded, where the jury and the witnesses alone would be present with the officers of the court, and where any injustice that might be done to the prisoner could be covered up and kept from public notice.

The provision that this trial shall be "by an impartial jury of the State and district wherein the crime shall have been committed," we have already considered, to which is added that this "district shall have been previously ascertained by law." The object of this was to prevent the party from being taken out of the district or State for trial, and also to prevent such a change of the boundaries of a district by an act of Congress after the commission of the offence as might subject the prisoner to a trial in a part of the country less favorable to him than that in which the offence was committed.

The remaining provisions of this Article are among the most important rights which are guaranteed by the Constitution to a person charged with offences against the United States.

He shall be "informed of the nature and cause

of the accusation," so that he may know precisely what is charged against him. If the offence be prosecuted by indictment or presentment the instrument must contain a clear statement of the nature and character of the accusation and of the offence for which the prisoner is to be tried. He can be tried for no other offence than that thus charged. He has a right to be specifically informed of the exact nature of the violation of law for which he is to undergo a trial. The importance of this cannot well be questioned, and the books of reports are filled with decisions of what is necessary to be stated in such indictment and presentment, and in regard to the particularity and precision with which the charges shall be set out. A discussion, however, of the rules which have been established on this subject, would occupy more time than the present occasion justifies.

The accused is also "to be confronted with the witnesses against him;" that is to say, that no evidence shall be brought against him on his trial made up of depositions or affidavits or hearsay statements, but that the witnesses by whom his guilt is to be established shall be brought face to face with him in order that he may see them and hear them, witness their manner of testifying, and so that either by himself or his counsel they may be subjected to such cross-examination as he may consider of benefit to his interests.

He is also "to have a compulsory process for

obtaining witnesses in his favor," that is to say, that, however poor he may be, or however unable to pay the expenses of such witnesses as he may deem necessary, the court shall issue its process to compel their attendance for examination upon the trial.

And lastly, he is entitled "to have the assistance of counsel for his defence." Whether this provision requires the Government to provide him with counsel, it is not necessary for us now to inquire. The occasion for that provision in the Constitution undoubtedly was that up to a period long subsequent to its adoption a prisoner on trial in an English court accused of an offence against the Government was not entitled to the aid of counsel in the progress of his trial, except in a very limited degree, even when he was ready to pay for the same and such counsel was ready to act. This disgrace upon the English system of criminal jurisprudence was not removed until 1836.

NOTES UPON LECTURE X.

1. *Definition of "Trial by Jury."*

THE references to the reported cases upon the subject of trial by jury come down to volume 117 of the United States Reports, leaving but little to be added. Before doing this I venture to quote, from a standard authority, a definition of the English and American jury, as distinguished from all other judicial modes for investigating disputed facts. The Encyclopædia Britannica,[1] in its article "Jury," says : —

"The essential features of trial by jury, as practised in England and countries influenced by English ideas, are the following : The jury are a body of laymen, selected by lot to ascertain, under the guidance of a judge, the truth in questions of fact arising either in a civil litigation or in a criminal process. They are generally twelve in number, and their verdict, as a general rule, must be unanimous. Their province is strictly limited to questions of fact, and within that province they are still further restricted to the exclusive consideration of matters that have been proved by evidence in the course

---

[1] Encyclopædia Britannica (9th ed.), vol. 13, p. 783, tit. Jury.

of the trial. They must submit to the direction
of the judge as to any rule or principle of law
that may be applicable to the case; and even in
deliberating on the facts, they receive, although
they need not be bound by, the directions of the
judge as to the weight, value, and materiality of
the evidence submitted to them. Further, according to the general practice, they are selected
from the inhabitants of the locality within which
the cause of action has arisen, or the crime has
been committed, so that they bring to the discharge of their duties a certain amount of independent local knowledge, an element in the
institution which is by no means to be ignored.
. . . What is the origin of this very remarkable and characteristic system? That is a question which has engaged the attention of many
learned men. The fullest discussion of the subject is contained in Forsyth's 'Trial by Jury,'
published in 1852." [1]

2. *Origin of the Jury System.*

It may not be inappropriate to refer very
briefly to Mr. Forsyth's excellent work, which
deserves all that the writer in the Encyclopædia
says, to see how and where the jury originated,
and how far it has been adopted into other
systems of law.

The distinctive characteristic of the system is
this: That the jury consists of a body of men

---

[1] History of Trial by Jury, by William Forsyth, M.A. London,
1852.

taken from the community at large, summoned
to find the truth of disputed facts, who are quite
distinct from the judges or court. They are to
decide upon the effect of the evidence, and thus
assist the court to pronounce a right judgment;
but they have nothing to do with the sentence or
judgment which follows the verdict. They are
not, like the judges, members of a class, charged
with the duty of judicial inquiry; they are taken
from varied pursuits to make a special inquiry,
and return to their ordinary avocations when
the labor is over. This distinguishes the system
from the Geschwornen-Gerichte of Germany,
from the Scandinavian courts, Norwegian, Swed-
ish, and Danish, and from the Anglo-Saxon
courts, to each of which speculation has traced
it. Even identity in details does not necessarily
imply identity in origin, when history shows it
to be most improbable — as Mr. Forsyth shows
in a note in which he says: "The most remarkable approximation to our own institution seems
to have existed at an early period in Russia for
the trial of criminal cases. In the French trans-
lation of M. Karamsin's *Histoire de Russie*, we
find the following: *Le plus ancien code des lois
russe porte que douze citoyens assermentés discu-
tent suivant leur conscience les charges qui pèsent
sur un accusé, et laissent aux juges le droit de dé-
terminer la peine.*" [1]

Courts existed in England in the Anglo-Saxon
period, presided over by a reeve, or judge, who

---

[1] Forsyth on Trial by Jury, 37 n.

Lecture X.
How the system
grew up in Eng-
land.

had no voice in the decision, and the number of
persons who sat as judges (or jurors) was frequently twelve, or some multiple of that number; but it was not until the establishment of
the assize in the time of Henry II, after these
Saxon elements had been continued in force
under the Anglo-Normans, that the institution
of the jury was produced. There the jury is
first found in its distinct form, although the elements of which it was composed were familiar
to the jurisprudence of the time.

Before that time, and in the early Norman
reigns, it was the practice to decide controversies
by appealing to the knowledge of the neighbor-
hood where the parties resided and the land
lay. There was no difference in principle between such inquests and the recognitions by the
knights of assize.

Passing by the constitutions of Clarendon
(1164), the statute of Northampton (1176), and
Magna Charta (1215), we find in a note in
Forsyth an account of the earliest record extant
of a trial by a regularly constituted *jurata*,
respecting the right to the custody of the Hospi-
tal of St. Julian at Southampton. Twenty-four
jurors were summoned; twelve acted, and gave
their verdict for the king "*in cujus rei testi-
monium*," they affixed their seals.[1]

During all this time the jury were both witnesses and jurors, rendering their verdicts on
their personal knowledge respecting the matter

---

[1] Forsyth on Trial by Jury, 149 n.

in dispute, without hearing witnesses. The Lecture X.
change to the present mode was made gradually. How the system grew up in England.
By the time of "the reign of Edward III trials
by jury in criminal cases were nearly, if not
quite, the same as at the present day. . . .
Although the qualification of previous knowledge on the part of jurors empanelled to try a
a prisoner had long fallen into desuetude, the
fiction was still kept up by requiring them to
be summoned from the hundred where the crime
was alleged to have been committed, until the
passing of Stat. 6, Geo. IV, c. 50, by which the
sheriff is now obliged to return for the trial of
any issue, whether civil or criminal, twelve good
and lawful men *of the body of his county* qualified according to law."

As late as the time of Queen Elizabeth it was
the custom in civil actions for the successful
party to entertain the jury at dinner. "The
party with whom they have given their sentence
giveth the enquest their dinner that day most
commonly, and this is all they have for their
labour, notwithstanding that they come, some
twenty, some thirty, or forty miles or more, to
the place where they give their verdict; all the
rest is of their own chuze." [1]

The jury system was brought by emigrants How the system came to this country.
to this country, to Canada, to Australia, to South
Africa, and wherever colonies have been planted
by British emigrants. It extended to Scotland;
but there, the Scottish system of law, derived

---

[1] Forsyth on Trial by Jury, 242 n.

LECTURE X.
How the system
came to this
country.

from the civil law, authorized the finding in criminal cases of a verdict of " not proven " when the jury were not prepared to find either " guilty " or " not guilty," like the " *non liquet* " in the Roman law.[1] The jury was introduced into France in 1789 in criminal cases, but not in civil cases; in Belgium in 1830; in Sardinia in 1850, from whence it has extended into Italy, and in Germany. De Tocqueville says of it, " Le jury est, avant tout, une institution politique. . . . L'homme qui juge au criminel est donc réellement le mâître de la société. Or l'institution du jury place le peuple lui-même, ou du moins une classe de citoyens, sur le siège du juge. L'institution du jury met donc réellement la direction de la société dans les mains du peuple, ou de cette classe." " Le jury qui semble diminuer les droits de la magistrature, fond réellement son empire : et il n'y a pas de pays où les juges soient aussi puissans que ceux où le peuple entre en partage de leurs priviléges."

---

[1] " There [in Rome] we find a presiding judge, who was either the *prætor*, or a *judex questionis* specially appointed by him, and a body of *judices* taken from a particular class, . . . whose duty it was to determine the fact of the guilt or innocence of the accused. At the close of the evidence they were said to be *missi in consilium* by the judge, that is, told ' to consider their verdict,' and to each were given three tablets marked respectively with the letters A. for *Absolvo*, C. for *Condemno*, and N. L. for *Non Liquet*, one of which he threw into an urn, and the result of the trial was determined by the majority of the letters that appeared." Forsyth, pp. 12, 13.

3. *Decisions on these Clauses in the Constitution.*

The Constitution, as has been seen, makes LECTURE IX. three provisions in regard to trial by jury.

The first is in Article III, Section 2, Paragraph 3, and relates only to the trial of crimes.

The second is Article VI of the Amendments, and also relates only to criminal prosecutions.

The third is in Article VII of the Amendments, and relates to suits at common law.

A. *Generally.*

At a trial by jury in a court of the United Generally. States, the judge may express his opinion upon the facts. The expression of such an opinion, when no rule of law is incorrectly stated, and all matters of fact are ultimately submitted to the determination of a jury, cannot be reviewed by writ of error. In this respect the powers of the courts of the United States are not controlled by State statutes forbidding judges to express any opinion on the facts.[1]

B. *In Criminal Cases.*

The provision in the Fifth Amendment, that Criminal cases. "no person shall be held to answer for a capital or otherwise infamous crime, unless on a presentment or an indictment of a grand jury," is jurisdictional, and no court of the United States has authority to try a prisoner without indictment or presentment in such cases.[2]

---

[1] *Vicksburg & Meridian Railroad* v. *Putnam*, 118 U. S. 545. See also *St. Louis, Iron Mountain, & Southern Railway* v. *Vickers*, 122 U. S. 360; and *Williams* v. *Conger*, 125 U. S. 397.

[2] *Ex parte Bain*, 121 U. S. 1.

In some of the States a juror who has formed an opinion of the case from reading the newspaper is not competent to sit upon the jury which tries a person accused of committing a crime; and by his doing so it would cease to be an impartial jury. But in Illinois he is not thereby disqualified if he can swear that he believes that he can fairly and impartially render a verdict on the evidence. The statute which authorizes him in such case to sit upon the jury is held not to deprive the accused of his right to trial by an impartial jury.[1]

The provision in Article III of the Constitution that "the trial of all crimes, except in cases of impeachment, shall be by jury," is to be construed in the light of the principles which, at common law, determined whether or not a person accused of crime was entitled to be tried by a jury; and, thus construed, it embraces not only felonies punishable by confinement in the penitentiary, but also some classes of misdemeanors the punishment of which may involve the deprivation of the liberty of the citizen.[2]

The provisions in the Constitution relating to trial by jury are in force in the District of Columbia.[3]

A person accused of a conspiracy to prevent another person from pursuing a lawful avocation, and by intimidation and molestation to reduce him to beggary and want, is entitled,

---

[1] *Spies* v. *Illinois*, 123 U. S. 131.
[2] *Callan* v. *Wilson*, 127 U. S. 540.   [3] Ib.

under the provisions of the Constitution, to a Lecture x.
trial by jury.[1] Criminal cases.

A Circuit Court of the United States, upon the commission of a contempt in its presence, may, upon its own knowledge of the facts, without further proof, without issue or trial by jury, immediately proceed to determine whether the facts justify punishment, and to inflict such punishment therefor as the law allows.[2]

A statute of Utah provided that every person guilty of murder in the first degree shall suffer death, or, upon the recommendation of the jury, be imprisoned at hard labor in the penitentiary for life, at the discretion of the court. It was held that it was the duty of the court, when a person was on trial, charged with the commission of murder in the first degree, to inform the jury of their right, under the statute, to recommend imprisonment for life at hard labor, in the place of death, and that failure to do so was error.[3]

In a very recent case these provisions relating to the place of trial came before the Supreme Court. A murder was committed in 1888 in the parallelogram of land south of Kansas and Colorado known as " No Man's Land." This tract was not at that time included within any organized judicial district of the United States, but in March, 1889, a court was established over it, with jurisdiction over offences previously

---

[1] *Callan* v. *Wilson*, 127 U. S. 540.

[2] *Ex parte Terry*, 128 U. S. 289.

[3] *Calton* v. *Utah*, 130 U. S. 83.

committed. The persons alleged to have committed the murder were tried and convicted. Their case being brought to the Supreme Court for review, it was there held that the statute was intended to act retroactively; that such a provision was not unconstitutional; that the provision in Article III of the Constitution respecting the trial of crimes "not committed in any State" imposed no restriction as to the place of trial, except that it could not take place until Congress should designate the place, and might take place at any locality which should have been designated by Congress previous to the trial; that the provision in the Sixth Amendment respecting the place of trial had reference only to offences against the United States committed within a State; and that the act fixing the place of trial was in no sense an *ex post facto* law.[1]

If the trial court makes the decision of a motion for a new trial depend upon a remission of the larger part of the verdict, this is not a re-examination by the court of facts tried by the jury in a mode not known at the common law, and is no violation of the Seventh Article of Amendment to the Constitution.[2]

C. *In Civil Cases.*

Civil cases.

In regard to the right to a jury in civil cases, it is a right which may undoubtedly

---

[1] *Cook* v. *United States*, 138 U. S. 157.

[2] *Arkansas Valley Land & Cattle Co.* v. *Mann*, 130 U. S. 69.

be waived, and which is constantly waived
in practice. But, unless waived, it cannot be
taken away.

The restriction is to be found in the Seventh Amendment, and it relates to "suits at common law, where the value in controversy shall exceed twenty dollars." It was to that extent a restriction upon the power of Congress, but did not limit the power of the State governments in respect to their own citizens.[1]

Several of the States have exercised their reserved right to curtail the right of trial by jury in civil cases.

The Constitution, in the second section of Article III, provides that the judicial power of the Federal Government shall extend to all cases in law and equity, arising under the Constitution, the laws of the United States, etc. The difference between law and equity was well settled when the Constitution was adopted, and the provisions of the Seventh Amendment relating to suits at the common law, had no application to suits in equity in the courts of the United States.

In process of time, as new States have been organized, and new legislation had under new influences, the terms of pleading have been modified and changed, and the dividing line between equity and law, and the corresponding remedies, have been likewise changed and modified in

---

[1] *United States* v. *Cruikshank*, 92 U. S. 542, 552, and cases cited on page 552.

many States. The forms of proceedings in State courts having been adopted in the courts of the United States, held within the States respectively, these changes in equity jurisdiction naturally found an expression and formed the subject of litigation in cases pending in the Federal courts. In an early case Chief Justice Taney said " the adoption of the State practice must not be understood as confounding the principles of law and equity, nor as authorizing legal and equitable claims to be blended together in one suit." [1] In a very late case the cases are reviewed, and it was held that a Federal court could not take jurisdiction in Mississippi of a bill in equity to subject the property of the defendants to the payment of a simple contract debt of one of them, in advance of any proceedings at law, either to establish the validity and amount of the debt, or to enforce its collection, although that might be done in a State court under the provisions of the code of that State.[2]

---

[1] *Bennett* v. *Butterworth*, 14 How. 669, 674. See also *Hipp* v. *Babur*, 19 How. 271; *Lewis* v. *Cocks*, 23 Wall. 466; *Killian* v. *Ebbinghaus*, 110 U. S. 568; *Buzard* v. *Houston*, 119 U. S. 347; *Thompson* v. *Railroad Companies*, 6 Wall. 134; *Hutchins* v. *King*, 1 Wall. 53; *Holland* v. *Challen*, 110 U. S. 15; *Whitehead* v. *Shattuck*, 138 U. S. 146.

[2] *Scott* v. *Neely*, 140 U. S.

XI.

IMPAIRMENT OF THE OBLIGATION OF CONTRACTS.[1]

—∘○∶◉∶○∘—

ARTICLE I, SECTION 10. No State shall enter into any Treaty, Alliance, or Confederation; grant Letters of Marque and Reprisal; coin Money; emit Bills of Credit; make any Thing but gold and silver Coin a Tender in Payment of Debts; pass any Bill of Attainder, ex post facto Law, or Law impairing the Obligation of Contracts, or grant any Title of Nobility.

LECTURE XI.

THE topic for this discourse is taken from section 10, Article I, of the Constitution of the United States, which reads as follows: —

Laws impairing the obligation of contracts.

"No State shall enter into any treaty, alliance, or confederation; grant letters of marque and reprisal; coin money; emit bills of credit; make anything but gold and silver coin a tender in payment of debts; pass any bill of attainder, *ex post 'facto* law, or law impairing the obligation of contracts, or grant any title of nobility."

Out of that important sentence I have selected for a more careful consideration the words, " or law impairing the obligation of contracts."

---

[1] This Lecture was Lecture IX of the Lectures delivered before the classes of the University Law School.

LECTURE XI.   The first Article of the Constitution begins
Laws impairing
the obligation of   with provisions concerning the organization of
contracts.   the two houses of the legislative body, the Senate
and the House of Representatives, and then sec-
tion eight in affirmative language confers certain
express powers upon the Congress of the United
States, that is to say, upon the Federal Government, or the General Government, of the Union,
as distinguished from the States, and the people
of the States.   In section nine certain limitations
are laid down in regard to the power of the
Federal legislature.   Among other things it is
provided that it shall not pass any bill of attainder, or any *ex post facto* law, and through a
number of negotiations states what shall not be
done by the Congress of the United States, or
by the National Government.

This limitation is   In section ten, above quoted, limitations are
upon the States.   imposed upon the individual States, the language
being that "no State" shall do any of the things
which are here prohibited.

Bills of credit.   In passing, it may be remarked that the phrase
"emit bills of credit" was for a long time the
subject of judicial and political controversy.   It
was questioned whether it did not prevent any
State from issuing bonds, or chartering banks of
issue, but the better opinion seems to be, (and it
was so decided in 1830, by Chief Justice Marshall[1]) that to "emit bills of credit" meant
to issue in the name of the State some form of
certificates of indebtedness which were "intended

---

[1] *Craig* v. *The State of Missouri*, 4 Pet. 408, 432.

to circulate through the community, for its or- Lecture XI.
dinary purposes, as money, which paper was Bills of credit.
redeemable at a future day," and that if such
was not the purpose their issue would not come
within this clause.

No State is permitted to " make anything but Legal tender.
gold and silver coin a tender in payment of
debts." The object of this provision was to correct what had grown to be an enormous evil at
that time, that of a debased paper currency, in
connection with the further prohibitions against
any State passing any *ex post facto* law, or law
impairing the obligation of contracts, in order to
prevent the scaling of debts or the authorization
of their payment in a depreciated and worthless
paper. This was thought to be necessary because it was seen that statutes of the States
passed for that purpose would constitute one of
the great hindrances to the collection and payment of honest debts.

In approaching this subject the following Circulating
quotation from Mr. Bancroft's " History of the medium when the Constitution was
Constitution of the United States " will be of framed.
service in getting a better knowledge of the condition of the times when that instrument was
framed. The whole work is the most valuable
contribution to the history of the period preceding the time when it was adopted and subsequent thereto, that has yet been written. The
author, speaking of the events which went before the formation of the Constitution, says.—

" The thirteen American States had a larger
experience of the baleful consequences of paper

LECTURE XI.
Circulating
medium when the
Constitution was
framed.

money than all the world besides. As each of them had a legislation of its own, the laws were as variant as they were inconvenient and unjust. The shilling had differing rates from its sterling value to an eighth of a dollar. The confusion in computing the worth of the currency of one State in that of another was hopelessly increased by the laws which discriminated between different kinds of paper issued by the same State; so that a volume could hardly hold the tables of the reciprocal rates of exchange. Moreover, any man loaning money or making a contract in his own State or in another, was liable at any time to loss by some fitful act of separate legislation. The necessity of providing effectually for the security of private rights and the steady dispensation of justice, more, perhaps, than anything else, brought about the new Constitution."[1]

History of this
clause in the Con-
stitution.

One of the earliest of the Constitutions proposed for the confederated States contained provisions for some of the items mentioned; for instance, as to coining money, emitting bills of credit, and passing *ex post 'facto* laws. That branch of the instrument had been passed over and committed to the charge of the committee on revision and style. For the purpose of preventing any interference with contracts the Convention had relied very largely upon the clause prohibiting the passage of any *ex post 'facto* law. The original draft had nothing in it about impairing the obligation of contracts when it was

---

[1] Bancroft's Hist. Const., vol. 1, book 2, c. 6; author's Last Revise, vol. 6, p. 167.

submitted to the committee. It was supposed that the expression " *ex post ʹfacto* law" neces- sarily included all laws bearing upon past trans- actions, and that, therefore, with this prohibi- tion inserted against the passage of *ex post ʹfacto* laws, no State could pass any law impairing a contract already made. Another extract from the same work will be of interest in this connec- tion.

" It has already been told how the delegates from Connecticut had agreed among themselves ' that the legislatures of the individual States ought not to possess a right to make any laws for the discharge of contracts in any manner different from the agreement of the parties.' Stringent clauses in the Constitution already prohibited paper money. For the rest, King, as we have seen, proposed a clause forbidding the States to interfere in private contracts; but the motion had been condemned as reaching too far, and instead of it, at the instance of Rutledge, the Convention denied to the States the power ' to pass bills of attainder or *ex post ʹfacto* laws.' In this manner it was supposed that laws for closing the courts, or authorizing the debtor to pay his debts by more convenient instalments than he had covenanted for, were effectually prohibited. But Dickinson, as we have seen, after consulting Blackstone, mentioned to the House that the term *ex post ʹfacto* related to criminal cases only; and that restraint of the States from retrospective laws in civil cases would require some further provision. Before

LECTURE XI.
History of this
clause in the Con-
stitution.
an explanatory provision had been made, the
section came into the hands of the committee
on revision and style.   That committee had no
authority to bring forward any new proposition,
but only to make corrections of style.   Gouverneur Morris retained the clause forbidding *ex
post ¥facto* laws; and, resolute not 'to counte-
nance the issue of paper money and the conse-
quent violation of contracts,' he of himself
added the words: 'No State shall pass laws
altering or impairing the obligation of contracts.'   The Convention reduced the explanatory words to the shorter form: 'No State shall
pass any law impairing the obligation of contracts.'   In this manner an end was designed
to be made to barren land laws, laws for the in-
stalment of debts, and laws closing the courts
against suitors.   Sherman and Ellsworth, in
their official letter recommending the Constitution to Connecticut, explained the intent of the
Convention by saying: 'The restraint on the
legislatures of the several States respecting
emitting bills of credit, making anything but
money a tender in payment of debts, or impairing the obligation of contracts by *ex post ¥facto*
laws, was thought necessary as a security to
commerce, in which the interest of foreigners
as well as of the citizens of different States may
be affected.' " [1]

I do not say that these words providing that
no State shall pass any law "impairing the obli-

---

[1] Bancroft's History of the Const. of the U. S., vol. 2, book 3,
c. 11; author's Last Revise, vol. 6, pp. 361, 362.

gation of contracts" are the most important in LECTURE XI.
the Constitution. I do not believe it; but they Importance of this provision.
have certainly been more frequently called into
operation in the courts than any other single
clause of that instrument, because they come
into immediate connection with the great volume of business and traffic dependent upon the
sacredness of contracts. Your critical attention
is called to these few words, almost every one
of which has received a construction by the
judicial department of the Government, and
almost every one of which is important.

The first point of interest is that " no State"
shall pass any such law. There is no such prohibition upon the United States, or Congress,
contained in the Constitution. In the limitations upon the power of the Federal Government, contained in the ninth section of Article
I, it will be noted that Congress is also forbidden to pass any bill of attainder, or any *ex post
facto* law. But there the prohibition stops, and
nothing is said about impairing the obligation of
contracts. Indeed that could not have been forbidden consistently with other powers vested by
that instrument in Congress; for section eight,
clause four, confers upon Congress the power to
establish " uniform laws on the subject of bankruptcies throughout the United States.' Of
course, any system of bankruptcy with which
we are familiar, however it may be in continental Europe, includes a discharge of the
debtor from his debts, and a distribution of his
property among his creditors. It, therefore,

LECTURE XI.
Importance of
this provision.

necessarily implies the power of impairing the obligation of a contract, and even the discharge of it altogether.

The legal tender
act constitutional
although it im-
paired existing
contracts.

So the legal tender statute, which declared that the Treasury notes of the United States should be lawful tender in payment of any debt due to the Government or between individuals, except for customs duties, necessarily impaired the obligation of a contract, because at the time the contract was made no man was bound to take anything but gold and silver. The contract was to pay coin dollars, and therefore when Congress authorized the debtor to pay it in legal tender notes it impaired the obligation of his contract. Yet that law has been held to be constitutional, although there are people who doubt it. I am not one of these, however; and I have no doubt that Congress had the power, in the emergency which then existed, to declare those notes a legal tender for the payment of debts.

The prohibition is
against State
legislation.

It will be further noted that the language is that no State shall pass "any law" impairing the obligation of contracts. This means that it is a statute of a State which is forbidden, or something which is equivalent to such a statute, possessing the same dignity and character, and passed or enacted by the authority of the State. It is unnecessary to go into details in regard to this point, for it has been repeatedly decided by all the courts with which I am familiar before whom the subject has come, that it must be either a Constitution or a statute of a State which impairs such an obligation to bring it Lecture XI. within the meaning of these words used in the The prohibition is against State Federal Constitution. A judicial decision by legislation. the courts of a State that a certain contract is good or bad, is valid or invalid, is of this or that character, is not a "law" passed by a State, as has sometimes been supposed. It is not true, therefore, that every decision of a State or other court, adverse to the assertion of the rights of a promisee or claimant under a contract, violates this provision of the Constitution. What is meant is that after the contract has been made no State shall make a law which impairs its force, and it does not mean anything more than that.

It has been held several times in the Supreme Court of the United States that no mere decision of a State court, or inferior Federal court, on the subject of the validity of a contract, or the mode of its discharge, is within the meaning of this provision, unless it be founded upon a statute or constitution of a State passed subsequent to the making of the contract.[1]

The Constitution of a State, or any act of its Existing State laws enter into all contracts. legislature, in existence at the time a contract is made, becomes thereby a part of that contract. It is a universal rule that every contract is made with a view to the laws extant at the place of execution, which become a part of it, and by the aid of which it is to be read and expounded.

---

[1] *Railroad Co.* v. *Rock*, 4 Wall. 177; *University* v. *People*, 99 U. S. 309, 320; *Railroad Co.* v. *McClure*, 10 Wall. 511; *Knox* v. *Exchange Bank*, 12 Wall. 379.

LECTURE XI.
Existing State
laws enter into
all contracts.

Therefore no statute in existence at the time it was made could be a law impairing its obligation, within the meaning of the Constitution, because it would be a part of the contract itself.

This is well set forth in a case[1] in which the question raised was whether a contract was not void, within the meaning of this clause, by reason of some legislation antecedent to its execution, but the court said: "The inhibition of the Constitution is wholly prospective. The States may legislate as to contracts thereafter made, as they may see fit. It is only those in existence when the hostile law is passed that are protected from its effects." It is clear, therefore, that the constitutional provision applies only to statutes passed after the contract is made.

The Dartmouth
College Case.

There have been numerous efforts by individual States at different times to make certain classes of contracts subject to future legislation. The celebrated Dartmouth College Case[2] was the earliest which decided that a charter granted to a private corporation was a contract between the corporation and the State which granted it. The result of that decision was that many statutes, which it had been supposed the State legislatures could repeal or modify, were found to be of such a character that they could not be changed.

Reservation
clauses in acts of
incorporation.

This principle, as applied to the efforts of the legislature of the States to escape the force of

---

[1] *Edwards* v. *Kearzey*, 96 U. S. 595, 603.
[2] *Dartmouth College* v. *Woodward*, 4 Wheat. 513.

this constitutional provision, was recently examined by this Court.

The legislatures commenced by making what
they called "reservation clauses" in all their
acts of incorporation, which reserved to the legislature the power of making alterations, amendments, or of repealing those statutes, and many
of the States went so far as to pass a general
law that all acts of incorporation should be
subject to repeal, modification, or alteration by
the legislature. The argument, which has been
sustained, was that, since these charters were
granted with this provision in them, either specifically stated or contained in the general law
under which the corporation was organized, it
thus became a part of the contract, and such
charters could be repealed, altered, or modified.
Therefore, any such action on the part of the
legislature could not be a violation or impairment of the obligation of a contract, since the
permission to do it was a part of the contract.
This court said : —

" A short reference to the origin of this reservation of the right to repeal charters of corporations may be of service in enabling us to decide
upon its office and effect when called into operation by the legislative exercise of the power.

"As early as 1806, in the case of *Wales* v.
Stetson, 2 Mass. 143, the Supreme Court of that
State made the declaration 'that the rights
legally vested in all corporations cannot be controlled or destroyed by any subsequent statute,
unless a power for that purpose be reserved to

the legislature in the act of incorporation.'
Trustees of Dartmouth College v. *Woodward*,
Wheat. 518, decided in 1819, this court a
nounced principles on the subject of the p
tection that the charters of private corporatic
were entitled to claim, under the clause of
Federal Constitution against impairing the o
gation of contracts, which, though received at
the time with some dissatisfaction, have never
been overruled in this court. The opinion in
that case carried the protection of the constitutional provision somewhat in advance of what
had been decided in *Fletcher* v. *Peck*, 6 Cranch,
87, and the preceding cases, and held that it
applied not only to contracts between individuals,
and to grants of property made by the State to
individuals, or to corporations, but that the rights
and franchises conferred upon private as distinguished from public corporations by the legislative acts under which their existence was
authorized, and the right to exercise the functions
conferred upon them by the statute, were, when
accepted by the corporators, contracts which the
State could not impair.

"It became obvious at once that many acts of
incorporation which had been passed as laws of
a public character, partaking in no general sense
of a bargain between the States and the corporations which they created, but which yet conferred
private rights, were no longer subject to amendment, alteration, or repeal, except by the consent
of the corporate body, and that the general control which the legislatures creating such bodies

had previously supposed they had the right to
exercise, no longer existed. It was, no doubt,
with a view to suggest a method by which the
State legislatures could retain in a large measure
this important power, without violating the provision of the Federal Constitution, that Mr. Justice
Story, in his concurring opinion in the *Dartmouth
College Case*, suggested that when the legislature
was enacting a charter for a corporation, a provision in the statute reserving to the legislature
the right to amend or repeal it must be held to
be a part of the contract itself, and the subsequent exercise of the right would be in accordance
with the contract, and could not, therefore, impair its obligation. And he cites with approval
the observations we have already quoted from
the case of *Wales* v. *Stetson*, 2 Mass. 143.

" It would seem that the States were not slow
to avail themselves of this suggestion, for while
we have not time to examine their legislation
for the result, we have in one of the cases cited
to us as to the effect of a repeal, *McLaren* v.
Pennington, 1 Paige, 102, in which the legislature of New Jersey, when chartering a bank with
a capital of $400,000 in 1824, declared by its
seventeenth section that it should be lawful for
the legislature at any time to alter, amend, and
repeal the same. And Kent, 2 Com. 307, speaking of what is proper in such a clause, cites as
an example a charter by the New York legislature, of the date of February 25, 1822. How
long the legislature of Massachusetts continued
to rely on a special reservation of this power in

LECTURE XI. each charter as it was granted, it is unnecessary
Reservation to inquire; for in 1831 it enacted as a law of
clauses in acts of
incorporation. general application, that all charters of corporations thereafter granted should be subject to
amendment, alteration, and repeal at the pleasure
of the legislature, and such has been the law ever
since.

"This history of the reservation clause in acts
of incorporation supports our proposition, that
whatever right, franchise, or power in the corporation depends for its existence upon the granting clauses of the charter, is lost by its repeal." [1]

Retroactive laws. The objectionable feature of the legislation
which we have discussed, where a legislative body
attempted to exercise some authority over existing
contracts, was that it was retrospective or retroactive, the two words being almost synonymous,
the first meaning looking backwards or behind
and the other acting backwards, being intended
to operate upon some past transaction.

It is not all retrospective laws, however, that
are forbidden by this clause of the Constitution,
but only such as impair the obligation of a contract. *Ex post facto* laws are also forbidden in
the same clause, but, as before explained, that
term is only applied to criminal laws and procedure, and has no reference to contracts. There
is a large class of retrospective legislation which
is constitutional, not inconsistent with the principles above laid down, and sometimes necessary
and proper, relating to rights not dependent

---

[1] *Greenwood* v. *Freight Co.*, 105 U. S. 13, 19, 21.

upon contract or affecting the individual by increasing his liability to a criminal prosecution.
It will be observed, however, that this class of
statutes is not favored, nor is it large, but that
there is a class of legislation retrospective in its
character, which is not forbidden by the Constitution, having no relation to contracts or to
crimes, should not be overlooked.

Perhaps the best illustration of a valid retrospective law to be found in the reported decisions
of the Supreme Court of the United States, not
amenable to the objections already set forth, is
contained in *Satterlee* v. *Matthewson*, 2 Pet. 380,
decided in 1829. That was a case where a
judgment had been rendered in a court of Common Pleas of the State of Pennsylvania, in favor
of the plaintiff, who claimed land occupied by the
defendant as a tenant under what was known
as a " Connecticut title." This was reversed by
the Supreme Court of the State on the ground
that the relation of landlord and tenant could
not subsist under such a title. Before the second trial took place the legislature passed a law
which said that the relation of landlord and
tenant could exist in such cases, and on the retrial, judgment being given for the plaintiff, it
was, on the strength of this statute, affirmed.
The case was then brought to the Supreme Court
of the United States under the idea that this
statute of the State of Pennsylvania was either
an *ex post facto* law, or a law impairing the
obligation of contracts, within the meaning of
the clause of the Constitution we are now con-

sidering. That court held, however, that it did not affect the obligation of a contract, nor was it an *ex post facto* law, and that it was not, therefore, repugnant to the Constitution of the United States, for "retrospective laws which do not impair the obligation of contracts, or partake of the character of *ex post facto* laws, are not condemned or forbidden by any part of that instrument." The opinion was delivered by Mr. Justice Washington, one of the ablest judges this country ever produced. He was over thirty years upon the bench of the Supreme Court of the United States at a period when very few of the associate justices delivered opinions. His four volumes of Circuit Court reports are also the most valued of any of those reports in existence, and are very difficult to obtain. He said in that case: —

"The objection, however, which was most pressed upon the court, and relied upon by the counsel for plaintiff in error, was that the effect of this act was to divest rights which were vested by law in Satterlee. There is certainly no part of the Constitution of the United States which applies to a State law of this description; nor are we aware of any decision of this, or of any Circuit Court, which has condemned such a law upon this ground; provided its effect be not to impair the obligation of a contract."[1]

In 1834 Mr. Justice Story, delivering the opinion of the court, said: "It is clear that this

---

[1] 2 Pet. 413.

court has no right to pronounce an act of the
State legislature void, as contrary to the Constitution of the United States, from the mere fact
that it divests antecedent vested rights of property. The Constitution of the United States does
not prohibit the States from passing retrospective
laws generally, but only *ex post facto* laws." [1]

He then goes on to state that the latter phrase
"is not applicable to civil laws, but to penal
and criminal laws;" so it will be seen that it is
not every retrospective law which is forbidden
by the Constitution of the United States as
impairing the obligation of contracts.

Proceeding then in order with the critical What is the obligation of a con-
tract?
examination of this short sentence, every word
of which is important and has been the subject
of judicial consideration, we come next to inquire, what is the "obligation" of a contract,
which no State shall pass any law to impair?
This is necessary as a preliminary to considering what it is that impairs it, for it is this obligation which cannot be impaired by the State.
It has often been the subject of definition by the
courts. In a recent case [2] may be found the following language : —

"'Obligation' is defined to be 'the act of oblig-
ing or binding; that which obligates; the binding power of a vow, promise, oath, or contract.'
. . . The obligation of a contract includes everything within its obligatory scope. Among these
elements nothing is more important than the

---

[1] *Watson* v. *Mercer*, 8 Pet. 88, 110.
[2] *Edwards* v. *Kearzey*, 96 U. S. 595, 600.

LECTURE XI.
What is the obli-
gation of a con-
tract?

means of enforcement. This is the breath of its
vital existence. Without it, the contract, as
such, in the view of the law, ceases to be, and
falls into the class of those 'imperfect obligations,' as they are termed, which depend for
their fulfilment upon the will and conscience of
those upon whom they rest. The ideas of right
and remedy are inseparable."

In ordinary language, there is a moral and
a legal obligation to do what we promise to do,
and it is familiar thought and speech to draw
the distinction between a moral and a legal
obligation. The moral one addresses itself to
the conscience, to the sense of duty, to the sense
of right and wrong. As observed in the last
quotation there is a binding power in a vow;
there is a moral obligation to do anything which
one promises to do, unless it is something wrong
or wicked. A consideration is the essence of all
legal contracts, and of all those obligations which
do not depend upon it but rather upon the faith
due to yourself and your own sense of moral
right, and which address themselves to your own
conscientious determination to do what you have
said you would do, neither the law nor the Constitution takes any cognizance. So far as the
law is concerned the obligation of a contract is
the means by which the law enforces a legal
duty, and it is that with which the law and the
Constitution deals. In this sense the obligation
of a contract consists in the authority or power
which the law gives to enforce its performance,
or to give a remedy for its non-performance.

The next thing in proper sequence to consider Lecture XI.
is what it is to "impair" this obligation, which What impairs the
obligation of a
is at once the means and the remedy given by contract?
the law to compel a man to perform his contracts, or in case of failure forces him to make
proper compensation in damages. It follows
that to impair this obligation by a State law is
in some way to weaken or diminish the power
which the courts had when the contract was
made to enforce it, if enforceable specifically, or
to give remedy by damages for failure to perform it.

It is needless here to advert to the difference
between specific performance and damages for
non-performance. In a very limited class of
cases only are contracts capable of being specifically enforced by the court, such as conveyance
of real estate, and some others, where the judicial power can take hold of a man and compel
him to do what he has promised. In much the
larger number of cases at law the remedy is by
way of damages in a money judgment for not
performing the thing promised. A State statute
or law that impairs the obligation of a contract
must be one which takes away the remedy for
its violation. It may take away all remedy, or
the most valuable one extant at the time the
contract was made by which to secure its specific
enforcement, or damages for its non-performance. Accordingly we find that nearly all the
long list of cases that have come into the courts
for relief against State laws and statutes, on the
ground that they had the effect of impairing

LECTURE XI.
What impairs the
obligation of a
contract?
the obligation of a contract, have had relation to enactments abolishing or changing the remedy for any infringement of such contract.

It is not every change of remedy, however, which impairs the obligation we are considering. It is not necessary that the legislature should always permit the same remedial forms to remain because contracts are in existence at the time it is thought advisable to change the mode by which a suitor may obtain relief. The amalgamation of the common law with the chancery system of procedure in different States is no impairment of the remedy if it can still be obtained by petition, or by any mode of procedure which is left. Indeed, the true line of distinction, between the change which impairs the obligation of a contract and that which does not, is found in considering whether such change of remedy leaves a sufficient and efficient remedy or provides a new and adequate one in its place.

This question has frequently been before the Supreme Court, and perhaps the best expression of its views on this subject is to be found in a recent case,[1] in which the language of the court is as follows : —

" If a particular form of proceeding is prohibited, and another is left or is provided which affords an effective and reasonable mode of enforcing the right, the obligation of the contract is not impaired."

That was a case where the notes of the Bank

---

[1] *Tennessee* v. *Sneed*, 96 U. S. 69, 74.

of Tennessee had, when it was chartered in
1838, been made receivable for taxes by the
State of Tennessee, which was interested as part
owner in the bank. During the period immediately succeeding the rebellion the State wanted
to get rid of the necessity of redeeming or
allowing these notes to be used in the payment
of taxes, and a statute was passed on that subject in 1873. At that time the remedy by mandamus existed, and if the tax receiver refused to
take the banknotes for taxes the party offering
them could apply to the proper court and by
writ of mandamus have the tax receiver brought
before the court, compelled to accept them, and
give a receipt. The statute, however, which
abolished the remedy by mandamus made provision for another, to wit, that if the notes were
not received by the tax collector à suit might be
brought against him which should be defended
by the State, and, in case the plaintiff obtained
a judgment, that the money should be paid to
him out of the treasury of the State. The
Supreme Court of the United States held that
this latter remedy was a better one than the
former, for " a suit at law to recover money unlawfully exacted was as speedy, as easily tried,
and less complicated than a writ of mandamus,"
and was therefore a better proceeding for the
purpose. It gave to the complainant a sufficient
remedy, and was not therefore a law that impaired the obligation of a contract.

. Statutes of limitations also present an instance in which it has been supposed that there

was an infringement of this clause of the Constitution. The cases in which that subject was discussed show very clearly the distinction and real
difference between a law which impairs the obligation of a contract and one which does not.
Suppose, for example, that the ordinary period
of limitation within which an action may be
brought upon a promissory note is ten years,
but the legislature chooses to shorten it, as most
of them have, to five or six years. Such a statute would not be held void, as contrary to the
constitutional provision we are considering, if
it gave the plaintiff a reasonable time within
which to bring his suit before it took effect,
although it would be if the remedy were at
once extinguished.

In some instances statutes have been passed
declaring that hereafter no remedy shall exist
on contracts where the right of a claim has already run five years. Now, inasmuch as some
of those contracts may have already been past
due for five years, that would be cutting off all
such cases absolutely, without giving any time
under the new statute within which to bring
suit, and in so far as these statutes have had
that effect they have been held to be unconstitutional. These statutes of limitation, although
they diminished the period within which a complainant is bound to sue, were, as early as the
case of *Sturges* v. *Crowninshield*,[1] which was
decided in 1819, declared not to impair the

---

[1] 4 Wheat. 122.

obligation of contracts; but in the recent case of Terry v. *Anderson*,[1] the subject is reviewed at length, and the distinction above taken suggested. The headnote of that case correctly states the doctrine decided by the court as follows : —

LECTURE XI.

Statutes of limitations.

" An enactment reducing the time prescribed by the statute of limitations in force when the right of action accrued, is not unconstitutional, provided a reasonable time be given for the commencement of a suit before the bar takes effect."

A very remarkable instance may be noted in this connection of a law operating upon a remedy, which was supposed to impair the obligation of a contract, but which was held by the Supreme Court not to have that effect; that is, the abolition of imprisonment for debt. At the time the Constitution of the United States was adopted it is probable that imprisonment, as a means of enforcing the collection of a judgment, was the law of every State in the Union. And yet soon after that, every State had abolished that method of compelling the collection of debts. Of course, when this was done, at different times in the different States, there were in existence many debts which had arisen under contracts made before that statute was passed. In such cases it is somewhat difficult to see how the Supreme Court came to the conclusion which they reached at that time, that those laws did not impair the obligation of such contracts. It

Abolition of imprisonment for debt.

---

[1] 95 U. S. 628.

LECTURE XI.
Abolition of imprisonment for debt.

is hard to imagine a more stringent mode of compelling a man to pay his debts than seizing him and putting him in prison, unless corporal punishment is inflicted upon him. That right of arrest and imprisonment the creditor then had, and yet the Supreme Court in one or two well considered opinions, though not without dissent, held that the right to imprison a man was not a part of his contract, nor a part of the remedy that belonged to it when it was made.

The case which first announced this doctrine, although the question was not directly in issue, was that of *Sturges* v. *Crowninshield, ubi supra.* It was afterwards put directly in issue in a case[1] in which the opinion of the court was delivered by Justice Thompson, Justice Washington dissenting. It was again affirmed in 1835.[2]

Exemptions from execution.

Having thus discussed the various classes of statutes which have been held not to impair the obligation of contracts, although at one time supposed to do so, let us now examine those which do impair them. The latter have often been the subject of earnest contention in the courts. One of the first to be considered is a class of enactments known in this country as exemption laws, which exempt a certain amount of the property of a debtor from a forced judicial sale, either by execution or decree of the court. The enactment of these statutes was commenced, probably in every State in the Union, after the adoption of the Constitution, and has been con-

---

[1] *Mason* v. *Haile*, 12 Wheat. 370.
[2] *Beers* v. *Haughton*, 9 Pet. 329.

tinued in pursuance of a liberal policy of which
everybody has come to approve. At first the value and amount of the property exempted was very small; such as beds and bedding and the cooking utensils of the family. These were generally the first articles exempted from a forced sale for debt. Afterwards their scope was enlarged to exempt the library of the lawyer, as well as the surgeon's implements and books, and gradually extended to larger amounts of personal property, as for instance, exempting from sale all the household furniture of a family. Then in some of the States they proceeded to exempt the homestead, as it is called. In nearly all of the Western States the house in which the debtor resides, together with the land on which it stands, have been brought within the purview of these statutes. This homestead is exempted either by a description of the quantity of land which it is permitted to cover, or by some limitation in its value, such as that it shall not exceed $1000, or $3000, or $5000 in value, or go beyond one acre or forty acres.

There is, however, one difficulty inherent in these various modes of exempting the homestead. As for instance, where the exemption is by a description of the quantity which may be allowed without reference to its value, great injustice has frequently resulted. A debtor might have $100,000 which his creditors could not touch where such an exemption was in force.

So far as these laws, or any of them, have had the effect to operate upon contracts in existence when they were passed they have been uniformly held by the Supreme Court of the United States, as well as by nearly all the other courts before whom the question has come, to be forbidden by the clause of the Constitution we are now considering. To the extent that they impair the obligation of contracts, or hinder the creditor from collecting his debt, they benefit the debtor and place him in a better position at the expense of the creditor, and so are repugnant to this clause of the Constitution. It matters not whether the sum involved be large or small, every law which has this effect in regard to past contracts, or those in existence when the law took effect, is void. As to future contracts the exemption becomes a part of the contract and therefore the law which is passed by the State is valid as to them. This is in brief a statement of the principles which may be deduced from a consideration of the cases in which this class of statutes has been considered.

Redemption laws. Another class of statutes, bearing a strong analogy to those we have just been considering, are called redemption laws. These relate to lands and houses sold under execution for debt. Most of the States of the Union have provided that when land is sold under execution the debtor shall have a certain time given him within which to pay the sum for which it sold, with costs and interest, and thus redeem it. So far as these statutes applied to contracts in existence at the time they were passed, they have been held to impair the obligation of con-

tracts. This they clearly do, for they allow the Lecture XI.
debtor a certain time, in some cases a year or Redemption laws.
more, after the time at which the creditor could
have otherwise collected his debt, thus extending
the time, compelling him to buy in the property,
and permitting the debtor to redeem.[1]

Another class of enactments of the same char- Appraisement laws.
acter are called appraisement laws, and are very
common in the Western States. All of these
statutes, it will be observed, are made in the
interest of struggling debtors, and show the
consideration which the legislatures have had,
especially in the new and poorer communities
of the West, for those who are struggling with
the hardships and vicissitudes incident to the
development of a new State in the wilderness.
An appraisement law is one which provided that
in case of an execution being levied upon the
real, and in some cases the personal estate of
the debtor, he was authorized to demand of the
proper officer that it should be appraised. This
meant to have a certain value put upon it, and
the method by which this should be done — generally by two or three disinterested persons —
was pointed out. If upon being brought to a
sale the property should not bring two-thirds, or
three-fourths, or one-half, or whatever proportion the legislature might determine, of its
appraised value, there would be no sale. In
other words, the bids for the property must
approximate within a certain limit of the value

---

[1] *Bronson* v. *Kinzie*, 1 How. 311; *Howard* v. *Bugbee*, 24 How.
461; *McCracken* v. *Hayward*, 2 How. 608.

put upon it in the manner prescribed by the statute, or else it could not be sold. It will be seen that this might effectually prevent the creditor from ever realizing his debt, especially where the only property owned by the debtor happened to be real estate. It might be so valued that the creditor, or the purchaser, would have to pay a great deal more than it was worth if he bought it. Perhaps nobody else will buy it. Perhaps the creditor does not wish to buy it, and does not want it. He may, like many men, have more land than he wants, and may not wish to take any more for his debt. At any rate it was not his contract, and it is impairing its obligation whenever one of these appraisement laws or redemption laws interferes to make a harder rule than existed at the time the indebtedness was contracted, so that the collection of the debt is made more difficult than it otherwise would have been.

There is still another class of statutes belonging to the same general category, known as the stay laws. Whenever there is a time of commercial and financial disturbance prevailing, when business is at a stand-still and there is every indication of a panic, when people are in debt and property is low in value, the debtor is very apt to imagine that, if he can get an extension of time, he will be enabled to realize upon his property and pay his indebtedness without a sacrifice. This idea has prompted one of the most frequent attempts on the part of the State legislatures to aid their own citizens in those

straits, by passing stay laws which were obnox-
ious to the true intent and meaning of this
clause of the Constitution. These were laws by
which it was provided that the creditor should
not have an execution as soon as judgment was
rendered, or within the time that the law
allowed when the contract was made, but extended the time or stayed the execution, as it
was said, for months and sometimes for years.

One of the best exemplifications of this kind
of a statute was one which was passed in Kentucky about 1822, during a period of great
financial distress which came on after the war
with Great Britain. That State, like all the
others at that time, had created State banks,
which furnished the only circulating medium ·
the country then had. One of those banks,
chartered by the State, and in which it was interested as the owner of a large portion of the
stock, was called the Bank of the Commonwealth of Kentucky. When this financial crisis
came its notes began to depreciate in value;
they went down to fifty cents on the dollar, and
they probably would have gone down to nothing
if the State had not been interested in the bank.
They remained the only currency in circulation
in the State. Gold and silver had practically
disappeared, and the United States Bank had
not yet sent out its branches. At this juncture
the legislature passed a statute providing that
when a man recovered a judgment, if the debtor
offered to pay him in the notes of the Bank of
the Commonwealth at par, or in common par-

lance at their face value, the creditor had a right to take them or to refuse them; but if he refused such offer that fact was to be entered upon the records of the court and he could have no execution to make his judgment for two years. In other words, it was a stay of execution unless the creditor would accept payment in money or notes only worth fifty cents on the dollar.

The passage of that act led to one of the most remarkable judicial and political struggles ever known in any country, but which it will be impossible to discuss in detail at this time. It may be remarked, however, that it involved two great constitutional questions, the substance of which may be briefly stated.

The first one was whether that stay law was forbidden by the provision of the Constitution we are now considering. A case involving this question came before the Court of Appeals of Kentucky, which held that the statute did impair the obligation of contracts, and was, therefore, void as to those in existence when it was passed. It thus nullified the law which had been passed under the pressure of public clamor, and was intended as a means of relief to many who could not meet their obligations or keep their contracts. But not to be thus thwarted, the legislature of the State met immediately after this decision and passed a statute abolishing that Court of Appeals and creating another in its stead. Now the Constitution of the State of Kentucky is almost identical in language with that of the United States, so far at least as Lecture XI. regards the power of the legislature over the Stay laws. courts. The Federal Constitution says that "the judicial power of the United States shall be vested in one Supreme Court, and in such inferior courts as the Congress may, from time to time, ordain and establish." This has always been held by good constitutional lawyers to mean that, while Congress may abolish all the inferior courts, may change them, or give them different names and jurisdictions, yet the one Supreme Court of the United States it cannot abolish or change, otherwise than by adding to its members. This was the doctrine laid down by the old Court of Appeals of Kentucky. The Constitution of that State provided that there should be a Court of Appeals, and such inferior courts as the legislature might from time to time ordain. This Court of Appeals held that the law abolishing it was unconstitutional; so they sat with their clerk, their marshal, and other officers, in their own room, and proceeded to consider all business that came before them. In pursuance, however, of the new law, the governor of the State appointed another set of judges as a new Court of Appeals, who organized, selected a clerk and marshal, and proceeded to decide such cases as were brought before them.

This was the serious condition of affairs that then existed, arising out of the determination to enforce this stay law which had been passed by the legislature of the State. The matter then

LECTURE XI.
Stay laws.

came before the people at the next election for members of the legislature; and, with some of the most remarkable exhibitions of learning and ability that any young State ever had, these subjects were canvassed on the stump, in the papers, by pamphlets and magazines, and the whole country was aroused by them, involving as they did not only the validity of the decision of the Court of Appeals, as well as its very existence, but the upholding of this important stay law. First it was relief and anti-relief, and then it was new-court and old-court. At the ensuing election, by a very considerable majority, men were elected who decided for the old court, and left it in the full possession of all its powers; so that was the end of stay laws in the State of Kentucky.

What is a con-
tract?

In the consideration of this clause of the Constitution there remains only the principal word of the sentence, the "contract" itself. It is probably unnecessary to undertake here to define a contract in general, or even what it is within the meaning of that instrument. The general subject is one of the most important in the study of the law, and about which no true lawyer can ever know too much. The recent work on this subject by Wharton, in two volumes, is, I am inclined to think, the best and most philosophical, as well as the one best suited to the American lawyer and student, of any treatise on contracts with which I am acquainted. He gives several pages to the different definitions to be found in the laws and treatises of

continental Europe, the ancient Roman law,
and in the reported decisions of the courts of this country. A reference to that treatise, therefore, will be more satisfactory than any brief definition which might be attempted here, and will give also many appropriate citations for further investigation.

It has seemed probable to many judges and lawyers who have considered this clause of the Constitution that it was not designed by the framers of that instrument to do anything more than protect private contracts, those between individuals, and those between individuals and private corporations, that is, not municipal corporations, but those organized for purposes of profit; and if it were now an original question, it is by no means certain but that this would be held to be a sound view of it. But those eminent men who at an early day had the duty of defining the meaning of this provision thought otherwise. They held it to apply very largely to contracts made by a State, and not only to those made by it, but to contracts arising out of State statutes and legislation.

The first case[1] on this subject before the *Fletcher v. Peck*, 6 Cranch, 87. Supreme Court of the United States came from Georgia. That State, under an act passed in 1795, sold to a number of individuals a large tract of the unappropriated public lands within its limits, and which belonged to it. The purchasers came forward, paid their money, and

---

[1] *Fletcher* v. *Peck*, 6 Cranch, 87.

took the patent, which the State authorized, from the proper officer. A few years afterward it was alleged that the passage of the statute was obtained by fraud and misrepresentation on the part of those purchasers, and the legislature passed an act annulling that contract, setting aside the sealed conveyance, and authorizing the sale of the same land to other individuals, which was accordingly done. These two parties, each with a title, or a supposed title, from the State of Georgia, came before the Supreme Court of the United States in the ordinary way. The first purchasers of the land in question claimed that the second statute was a law impairing the obligation of their contract with the State of Georgia, and the Supreme Court, in a very learned opinion by Chief Justice Marshall, held that it was so; that the State was bound by its contracts as well as an individual, and could no more impair its obligation by a subsequent statute than an individual could defeat his sale of property by a declaration that the sale was invalid. That, however, was a case very fairly in the nature of a bargain. The State had sold the land, got the money and made a deed which the grantees held so that it was not going very far to say that this was a case of bargain and sale. It was an ordinary contract, and one of the parties to it could not pronounce it invalid even though that party was a sovereign State.

In a subsequent case[1] the State of New Hampshire undertook to turn out the professors,

---

[1] *Dartmouth College Case*, 5 Wheat. 518.

faculty, and trustees of Dartmouth College by Lecture XI.
an act of the legislature and substitute others Dartmouth College Case, 5 Wheat. 518.
in their stead. The old trustees resisted, and
the case came to the Supreme Court of the
United States on the proposition that that act
of the legislature was invalid as impairing the
obligation of a contract. The contract which
they set up was that, in the colonial times, the
king by a royal charter had invested the college with certain rights and privileges, which
had been accepted. It was held that in cases
where a charter was granted to a corporation,
even where it was organized for educational
purposes, on the faith of which private citizens
had invested money, which charter had been
accepted by the corporation and its trustees, it
constituted a contract between the State and
the trustees, or other parties, which was within
the protection of this clause of the Constitution,
and could not be impaired by a subsequent statute of the State.

That decision took the country a good deal
by surprise, because it meant that, whenever a
corporation is chartered by a statute or act of
the legislature, or by the crown, and certain
rights are granted to it and accepted, on which
it acts, that constitutes a contract directly between the State and the corporation which the
State cannot repeal. It is an interesting chapter in the legal history of this country to consider how, after this decision was rendered, the
States sought to, and did practically, avoid the
worst effects of it, by putting into all statutes

granting corporate privileges and powers, the
condition that the charter should be subject to
amendment, alteration, or repeal at the pleasure
of the legislature. This, of course, entered into
and became a part of the contract, which was
not, therefore, violated or impaired by a subsequent statute abolishing or changing the corporation.

Having thus considered the different parts of
this important clause of the Constitution, let us
briefly look at the class of contracts which have
been most frequently brought before the courts
on the allegation that subsequent statutes have
impaired their obligation. These are not generally private contracts. The nature, character,
and general principles governing those between
man and man have come to be so well understood, as well as what it is to impair their
obligation, that they are now somewhat rarely
met with in the court of last resort. It is still
rarer that any State legislature attempts to
impair or change the nature of a private contract. Most of the cases that now come to the
Supreme Court of the United States, involving a
consideration of this subject, are those in which
a State has sought to get rid of a promise or
statute or grant made by it, and which other
parties have accepted, and where it has sought
to do this by some new statute which impairs
the obligation of that contract.

A large portion of the contracts which the
States have sought to modify, alter, or impair,
have related to the creation of corporations and

grants to them of certain powers. In this cate- Lecture XI.
gory are included railroad, transportation, insur- Charters of incorporation.
ance, and other companies. All of these depend
for their existence on State statutes, and the
States have often endeavored to get some relief
against what they have said and done, by impairing the obligation of the contract they have
made with the incorporators.

Another class of cases more frequently brought Exemptions from taxation.
before the Supreme Court now than any other is
that of contracts made by some State in regard
to taxation. The reason for this is very obvious.
The burden of taxation has grown much greater
since the war, and is frequently very heavy. An
immense amount of money has been collected
to pay off the public debt, which is being rapidly
decreased. The obligations which have been
incurred by States, counties, and towns, and
other municipal corporations, by borrowing
money both in Europe and the United States,
render the taxation necessary to meet the interest and principal upon this enormous indebtedness, a heavy burden upon everybody who has
property upon which it can be levied. It is but
natural that those whose taxes are large enough
to make it an object for them to fight about it,
litigate, and try to avoid their payment as long
as possible.

In many cases the States have passed statutes
favoring certain parties in regard to taxation.
In the early days of the West, when there was
but little money in circulation, the States frequently passed laws chartering banks and other

corporations, because they were anxious to get
the capital which would naturally come to them
from the East or Europe for investment, and for
the purposes of business in that country. So in
granting the charters they often offered induce-
ments to capitalists in the way of relief from
taxation. Some of the States excepted banking
houses and bank bills: in some cases this was
for a period of years, in some the circulation
alone was excepted, in others the stock alone,
and in still others the capital of the bank as distinguished from the shares of the stockholders.
Innumerable statutes of this character were
passed to induce people to start banks. But
after a while the banks became rich, the communities were in a flourishing condition, and
the people saw that a very large amount of capital in this way escaped taxation. The legislatures that chartered these banks had long since
passed away, and the new ones, who did not
know them, passed laws that they should be
taxed. Of course those whose privileges were
infringed would not submit without a struggle.
So these questions were made the subject of litigation, and there are a number of cases in the
Supreme Court of the United States in which
they have been discussed.

Capitalists knew very well what they were
doing when they contracted with a State under
the form of a statute that they should not be
taxed at all, or only a certain per cent and no
more. When it came to exceed that in the
community they rebelled, said it was unjust, and

tried to escape its payment by every means in their power. Of course those who did not share in these privileges claimed that everybody in the community should be treated alike, and insisted that these exceptions were not valid. Indeed, it may be generally said that every total or limited exemption from taxation, either for all time or for a limited period, some later legislature has by subsequent legislation attempted to break down.

The first question that arises in regard to the subject is, had the States the constitutional power to pass the first statute of exemption? Has a legislature sitting in the State of Pennsylvania or Maryland to-day a right to bargain with a taxpayer that he shall never pay a tax, or that he shall not be taxed for fifty years at a higher rate than one per cent on his business or property? Can it in that manner forestall a succeeding legislature, elected in that State, and bind their hands so that they shall not be able to impose a tax which shall be equal on everybody, or increase the taxes of these parties?

There are some general principles relative to this subject which I deem it proper here to make the subject of brief remark. The power of taxation is not given for the private benefit of anybody. Taxation is, in this country and in all civilized countries, the lifeblood of the existence of the government. Without it there could be no officers paid, no legislature elected, no laws enforced. When you undertake to cripple and tie up this power of taxation in an organized

LECTURE XI.
Exemptions from taxation.
A legislature cannot limit the taxing power of · its successor.

government, it is equivalent to putting a ligature around an artery of a living body.

There are a great many intelligent and able lawyers in this country, and there has always been in the Supreme Court of the United States more than one justice, who have thought it not within the constitutional power of one legislature to limit the taxing power of a succeeding one. I have no hesitation in saying that I am one of those. As late as 1869 Chief Justice Chase, Justice Field, and myself made a dissent on that subject.[1]

There has never been a time in the history of the court when there was not a dissenting justice who did not believe in the validity of that class of subsequent legislation; but the majority of the court has always held that these contracts were within the power of the legislatures to make, were binding on them as well as the State, and that, when subsequent legislatures sought to impair them, they were protected by the clause of the Constitution which we have been considering.

The theory upon which these decisions have been based is that the State is a corporation, and that all statutes passed by it which invite persons to invest their capital upon the promise of certain privileges granted, which are formally accepted by the grantees and acted upon, constitute a contract between the State and those parties. I concur with this statement of a general prin-

---

[1] *Washington University* v. *Rouse*, 8 Wall. 439, 441.

ciple when it is applied to anything which a Lecture XI.
State may properly do ; that is to say, that any A legislature cannot limit the
contract about a matter which is within their taxing power of
power comes within this reasoning and should its successor.
be·protected. But where the power is wanting,
as it is above intimated is my opinion in regard
to limiting future taxation, of course this argument would not apply.

Perhaps I cannot do better at this point than
to quote from the opinion that I had the honor
to deliver in regard to this subject of taxation
in its relations to the clause of the Constitution
now under discussion. The following language
was there used : —

"As we have already said, since the legislature which passed the act of 1865 had the power
to make a contract which should not be subject
to repeal or modification by one of the parties to
it without the consent of the other, the main
question here is, did they intend to make such a
contract ?

" The principal function of a legislative body
is not to make contracts, but to make laws.
These laws are put into a form which, in all
countries using the English language, and in-
heriting the English common law, is called a
statute.

" Unless forbidden by some exceptional constitutional provision, the same authority which
can make a law can repeal it. The Constitution
of the United States has imposed such a limitation upon the legislative power of all the States,
by declaring that no State shall pass any law

LECTURE XI.
A legislature
cannot limit the
taxing power of
its successor.

impairing the obligation of a contract. The
frequency with which this court has been called
on to declare State laws void, because they do
impair the obligation of contracts, shows how
very important and far reaching that provision is.

"It may safely be said that in far the larger
number of cases brought to this court under that
clause of the Constitution, the question has been
as to the existence and nature of the contract,
and not the construction of the law which is supposed to impair it; and the greatest trouble we
have had on this point has been in regard to what
may be called legislative contracts, — contracts
found in statute laws of the State, if they existed
at all. It has become the established law of this
court that a legislative enactment, in the ordinary
form of a statute, may contain provisions which,
when accepted as the basis of action by individuals or corporations, become contracts between
them and the State within the protection of the
clause referred to of the Federal Constitution.

"The difficulty in this class of cases has
always been to distinguish what is intended by
the legislature to be an exercise of its ordinary
legislative function in making laws, which, like
other laws, are subject to its full control by
future amendments and repeals, from what is
intended to become a contract between the State
and other parties when the terms of the statute
have been accepted and acted upon by those
parties. This has always been a very nice
point; and, when the supposed contract exists
only in the form of a general statute, doubts

still recur, after all our decisions on that class of questions.

"These doubts are increased when the terms of the statute relate to a matter which is in its essential nature one of exclusive legislative cognizance, and which at the same time requires money or labor to be expended by individuals or corporations. In such cases the legislature may be supposed to be merely exercising its power of regulating the burdens which are to be borne for the public service, in which case it could be modified from time to time as legislative discretion might determine; or it might be a contract founded on a fair consideration moving from the party concerned to the State, and which in that case would be beyond the power of the State to impair. Statutes fixing the taxes to be levied on corporations, partake in a striking manner of this dual character, and require for their construction a critical examination of their terms, and of the circumstances under which they are created.

"The writer of this opinion has always believed, and believes now, that one legislature of a State has no power to bargain away the right of any succeeding legislature to levy taxes in as full a manner as the Constitution will permit. But, so long as the majority of this court adhere to the contrary doctrine, he must, when the question arises, join with the other judges in considering whether such a contract has been made."[1]

---

[1] *New Jersey* v. *Yard*, 95 U. S. 104, 113, 114, 115.

NOTES UPON LECTURE XI.

LECTURE XI.
Impairment of
contracts.

THIS lecture, like the lecture upon the Regulation of Commerce, was evidently prepared some years ago, and has not been brought down by incorporating into it the later decisions. The latest case cited in it is from 105 U. S. So far as it comes it is thorough; and nothing is left for the editor to do except to take up the Reports at volume 106, and note the more important cases from that time on to the close of volume 140.

In deciding whether a State statute of incorporation created a contract, and whether a subsequent statute of the State, as construed by its courts, impaired that contract, the Supreme Court is not governed by previous decisions of the States, unless they are so firmly established as to have become a rule of property.[1]

The right to demand reimbursement from a municipal corporation for damages caused by a mob is not founded on contract; and the fact that a statutory right to demand such reimbursement has passed into a judgment does not convert the obligation into such a contract as is contemplated in the provision in the Constitu-

---

[1] *Louisville & Nashville Railroad* v. *Palmes*, 109 U. S. 244.

566

tion that no State shall pass any law impairing the obligation of contracts. The term contract, as used in the Constitution, signifies the agreement of two or more minds, for considerations proceeding from one to the other, to do or not to do certain acts.[1]

When a contract is made with a municipal corporation upon the faith that taxes will be levied, legislation repealing or modifying the taxing power of the corporation, so as to deprive the holder of the contract of all adequate and efficacious remedy, is within the inhibition of the Constitution. A judgment creditor of such a corporation, entitled by his contract to be paid out of specific tax levies, is further entitled, in mandamus proceedings, to a writ ordering the levy and collection of a sufficient tax to pay his judgment.[2]

The power of a State legislature to make a contract which, under the Constitution, cannot be modified or abrogated, does not extend to subjects affecting public health or public morals.[3]

The Funding Act of March 30, 1871, of the State of Virginia, and the issue of coupon bonds under it, constituted a valid contract between the State and the holders of the coupons that the coupons should be receivable at and after maturity for all taxes, debts, dues, and demands due the State, which the legislature of Virginia

---

[1] *Louisiana* v. *Mayor of New Orleans*, 109 U. S. 285.

[2] *Louisiana ex rel. Nelson* v. *St. Martin's Parish*, 111 U. S. 716.

[3] *Butchers' Union Co.* v. *Crescent City Live Stock Co.*, 111 U. S. 746.

was not at liberty to rescind or modify without the assent of the holders of the coupons.[1]

When a statute attaches a fixed compensation to a public office during the whole term of service of a person legally filling the office and performing the duties thereof, a complete, implied obligation arises to pay for the services at the fixed rate, which can be enforced by the remedies which the law then gives; and, as the prohibition of the Constitution against State laws impairing the obligations of contracts applies to implied contracts, it is not within the power of the State, by a change in its Constitution, to take away existing powers of taxation so as to deprive the incumbent of the means of collecting his salary.[2]

The remedy subsisting in a State when and where a contract is made and is to be performed is a part of its obligation. Any subsequent statute of the State which so affects that remedy as substantially to impair and lessen the value of the contract is forbidden by the Constitution, and is void. When it is a material part of a contract between a municipal corporation and the holders of its bonds that the creditor should always have the right to a special tax, to be levied and collected under laws then in force, in the same manner as county taxes at the same time might be levied, it is not within the power

---

[1] *Virginia Coupon Cases*, 114 U. S. 269. See also *McGahey v. Virginia*, 135 U. S. 662; *Hucless v. Childrey*, 135 U. S. 709; and *Vashon v. Greenhow*, 135 U. S. 713.

[2] *Fisk v. Jefferson Police Jury*, 116 U. S. 131.

of the legislature to repeal the existing laws, Lecture XI. and substitute for them statutes regulating the Impairment of contracts. assessment and collection of such taxes in a way which is not a legal equivalent.[1]

The provision in the Constitution in regard to the impairment of contracts is aimed at the legislative power of the State, and not at decisions of its courts, or acts of executive or administrative boards or officers, or doings of corporations or individuals. Hence the Supreme Court has no jurisdiction of a writ of error to the highest court of a State on the ground that the obligation of a contract has been impaired, unless some legislative act of the State is upheld by the judgment sought to be reviewed.[2]

The provision in the Constitution of West Virginia of 1872, that property of a citizen of the State should not " be seized or sold under final process issued upon judgments or decrees heretofore rendered, or otherwise, because of any act done according to the usages of civilized warfare in the prosecution of the ' war of the rebellion' by either of the parties thereto," does not impair the obligation of a contract within the meaning of the Constitution of the United States when applied to a judgment previously obtained, founded on a tort committed as an act of public war.[3]

The exemption of a railroad corporation, in-

---

[1] *Seibert* v. *Lewis*, 122 U. S. 284.

[2] *New Orleans Water Works* v. *Louisiana Sugar Refining Co.*, 125 U. S. 18.

[3] *Freeland* v. *Williams*, 131 U. S. 405.

corporated by a State, from future general legislation of the State, either in its Constitution or by an act of its legislature, cannot be admitted to exist, unless it is expressly given, or unless it follows by an implication equally clear with express words.[1]

The fifteenth section of the act of the legislature of New York, approved June 6, 1885, provides that no action or special proceeding shall thereafter be maintained against the city of Brooklyn, or the Registrar of Arrears of that city, to compel the execution or delivery of a lease upon any sale for taxes, assessments, or water rates, made more than eight years prior to the above date, unless commenced within six months after that date, and notice thereof filed in the office of the Registrar of Arrears; also, that that officer shall, upon the expiration of such six months, cancel in his office all sales made more than eight years before the passage of the act, upon which no lease had been given, and no action commenced and notice thereof filed, within the period limited as aforesaid, and that thereupon the lien of all such certificates of purchase should cease and determine.

On these facts the court held (1) That this section was not repugnant to the clause of the Constitution of the United States forbidding a State to pass any law impairing the obligation of contracts, or to the clause declaring that no State shall deprive any person of property with-

---

[1] *Pennsylvania Railroad Co.* v. *Miller*, 132 U. S. 75.

out due process of law; (2) That, consistently LECTURE XI.
with those clauses, the legislature might prescribe Impairment of
contracts.
a limitation for the bringing of suits where none
previously existed, as well as shorten the time
within which suits to enforce existing causes of
action should be commenced, provided, in each
case, a reasonable time, taking all the circumstances into consideration, be given by the new
law for the commencement of suit before the
bar took effect.[1]

On December 12, 1883, the city of Sioux City,
in Iowa, by ordinance, conferred on a street railway company, incorporated December 6, 1883,
under the general laws of Iowa, the right of
operating a street railway, with the requirement that it should pave the street between the
rails. Subsequently, under an act of 1884, the
city, by ordinance, required the company also to
pave the street for one foot outside of the rails,
and assessed a special tax against it for the cost
of the paving outside of the rails. On these
facts it was held that there was no contract
between the company and the State or the city,
the obligation of which was impaired by the
laying of the tax: and that, under section 1090
of the Code of Iowa, which was in force when
the company was incorporated, its franchise was
subject to such conditions as the legislature
should thereafter impose as necessary for the
public good.[2]

---

[1] *Wheeler* v. *Jackson*, 137 U. S. 245.
[2] *Sioux City Street Railway Co.* v. *Sioux City*, 138 U. S. 98.

A ferry connecting Wheeling with Wheeling Island was licensed at an early day in Virginia. Subsequently a general law of that State prohibited the courts of the different counties from licensing a ferry within a half a mile in a direct line from an established ferry. Still later the defendant purchased the ferry and its rights. On these facts the court held (1) That the general law of Virginia had in it nothing in the nature of a contract; (2) That the transfer of the existing rights from the vendor to the vendee added nothing to them.[1]

An executive agency, created by a statute of a State for the purpose of improving public highways, and empowered to assess the cost of its improvements upon adjoining lands, and to put up for sale, and buy in for a term of years for its own use, any such lands delinquent in the payment of the assessment, does not, by such a purchase, acquire a contract right in the land so bought which the State cannot modify without violating the provisions of the Constitution of the United States. Such a transaction is matter of law and not of contract, and as such is not open to constitutional objections. Even as to third parties an assessment is not a contract in the sense in which the word is used in the Constitution of the United States.[2]

---

[1] *Wheeling & Belmont Bridge Co.* v. *Belmont Bridge Co.*, 138 U. S. 287.

[2] *Essex Public Road Board* v. *Skinkle,* 140 U. S. 334.

XII.

LIMITATIONS UPON THE POWERS OF STATES.[1]

————•o⦂⦁⦂o•————

ARTICLE I, SECTION 8, PARAGRAPH 18. The Con- LECTURE XII.
gress shall have power . . .

. To make all Laws which shall be necessary and
proper for carrying into Execution the foregoing
Powers, and all other Powers vested by this Constitution in the Government of the United States, or in
any Department or Officer thereof.

ARTICLE I, SECTION 10. No State shall enter into
any Treaty, Alliance, or Confederation; grant Letters
of Marque and Reprisal; coin Money; emit Bills of
Credit; make any Thing but gold and silver Coin a
Tender in Payment of Debts; pass any Bill of Attainder, ex post facto Law, or Law impairing the Obligation of Contracts, or grant any Title of Nobility.

No State shall, without the consent of the Congress,
lay any Imposts or Duties on Imports or Exports, except what may be absolutely necessary for executing
its inspection Laws: and the net Produce of all
Duties and Imposts, laid by any State on Imports or
Exports, shall be for the Use of the Treasury of the
United States; and all such Laws shall be subject to
the Revision and Controul of the Congress.

No State shall, without the Consent of Congress,
lay any Duty of Tonnage, keep Troops, or Ships of
War in time of Peace, enter into any Agreement or
Compact with another State, or with a foreign Power,
or engage in War, unless actually invaded, or in such
imminent Danger as will not admit of Delay.

---

[1] This Lecture was Lecture X of the Lectures delivered before
the classes of the University Law School.

LECTURE. XII.

ARTICLE IX OF THE AMENDMENTS. The enumeration in the Constitution, of certain rights, shall not be construed to deny or disparage others retained by the people.

ARTICLE X OF THE AMENDMENTS. The powers not delegated to the United States by the Constitution, nor prohibited by it to the States, are reserved to the State respectively, or to the people.[1]

General considerations.

THE Constitution of the United States may be looked at under various views, and many classifications may be made of it, all of which tend to give clearer ideas of its scope and meaning. The most important arrangement and classification of its contents is into three divisions, which relate to the legislative, the executive, and the judicial powers.

I have considered the Second and Third Articles of the Constitution, as they refer to the subjects of the executive and the judiciary. Another classification of its provisions may be profitably made into first, the grants of powers to the Federal Government; second, the limitations upon the powers of that Government; and third, the limitations upon the powers of the States. In order to enable you to understand more clearly these limitations, it is necessary to state a few propositions in regard to the general theory of the constitutional powers of the Government of the United States.

---

[1] The Thirteenth, Fourteenth, and Fifteenth Amendments are also briefly alluded to in this lecture; but, as they are dismissed with the remark that they are " too important to be considered at the close of a lecture," they are not placed in this headnote. In the next, and concluding paper, they are treated more at length, and will be found in that headnote.

As a general rule, governments are unlimited in their powers. All free governments, perhaps all other governments, are entitled in some shape or other, to make laws, and to repeal, or amend them. This is called the legislative power of the government. There are, however, in the United States, two sets of governments, both occupying a part of the domain of the great functions of governments, including the executive, the legislative, and the judicial powers. The Government of the United States was created by the voluntary action of the people of the different States. When this was originally done there were thirteen States whose people united in forming the General Government called the United States of America. In doing this the States parted with all the powers of government which were thought necessary to establish that of the United States, but those which they did not thus surrender and give up to the National Government, were retained by each State as a part of its own system of political power. The powers thus ceded to the United States and parted with by the several States, are much the smaller part of the general functions of government of civil society, and it resulted that all the powers not conferred upon the United States were to remain, and did remain, with the States themselves. This purpose was so important that it was not left to the natural inference arising from the sources of its powers and the manner in which the Constitution was framed, but it is more than once referred to, and at least

LECTURE XII.
Relations between the State governments and the United States.

LECTURE XII.
Relations between
the State govern-
ment and the
United States. once expressly stated in the Constitution and amendments thereto. The eighteenth clause of the eighth section of the First Article of the Constitution closes the enumeration of the powers conferred upon Congress by the following language:—

"The Congress shall have power . . . to make all laws which shall be necessary and proper for carrying into execution the foregoing powers, and all other powers vested by this Constitution in the Government of the United States, or in any department or officer thereof."

Articles IX and X of the first set of amendments to the Constitution, made to give expression to the opinion of those who were jealous of the powers of the Federal Government, still more clearly state this view.

"Article IX. The enumeration in the Constitution of certain rights shall not be construed to deny or disparage others retained by the people.

"Article X. The powers not delegated to the United States by the Constitution, nor prohibited by it to the States, are reserved to the States respectively, or to the people."

Section 8 of the First Article is devoted to the grant of powers to the legislative branch of the Government of the United States; section 9 is devoted to the restrictions upon those powers, and section 10 to express limitations upon the powers of the States. If you will take the trouble to compare these limitations upon the powers of the States with those upon

the powers of the Federal Government in the Lecture XII.
preceding section, you will see that in many Relations between
the State govern-
instances they are the same, and of course ment and the
where that is the case they forbid entirely the United States.
exercise of the powers thus specified by either
the National or State Governments. Such is
the case in reference to the prohibition against
granting titles of nobility, and others to be
found in both sections.

The tenth section, to which I more especially Limitations upon
invite your attention, reads as follows:— the powers of the
States.
" Section 10. No State shall enter into any
treaty, alliance, or confederation; grant letters
of marque and reprisal; coin money; emit bills
of credit; make anything but gold and silver
coin a tender in payment of debts; pass any
bill of attainder, *ex post facto* law, or law impairing the obligation of contracts, or grant any
title of nobility.

" No State shall without the consent of Congress, lay any imposts or duties on imports or exports, except what may be absolutely necessary
for executing its inspection laws; and the net
produce of all duties and imposts, laid by any
State on imports or exports, shall be for the use
of the Treasury of the United States; and all such
laws shall be subject to the revision and control
of Congress.

" No State shall, without the consent of Congress, lay any duty of tonnage, keep troops, or
ships of war, in time of peace, enter into any
agreement or compact with another State, or
with a foreign power, or engage in war, unless

LECTURE XII.
Limitations upon
the powers of the
States.
Making treaties,
alliances, etc.

actually invaded, or in such imminent danger, as will not admit of delay."

The first of these items of prohibition, namely, against making treaties, alliances, or confederations, granting letters of marque and reprisal, and coining money, are directed to the exercise of powers which are in their essential nature appropriate alone to the sovereign power of the State. No government ought to have the power of making a treaty, or alliance, or a confederation with another government, unless it is in such a position of independence, and in full possession of all the faculties which will enable it to keep up its relations with other independent governments or to maintain a confederation or alliance with other sovereign powers. This prohibition was taken in substance from Article VI of the Articles of Confederation.

If one of the States of the Union could have made a treaty with France or Great Britain in the early days of our Government, or could have entered into a confederation with one of those powers, it is very obvious that the Government of the American Union would have been a rope of sand; temptations would have been offered by other nations to induce one or more of the States to withdraw from the Federal Union, which must in the struggle through which they passed in their early history have been successful. Indeed, during Washington's administration, constant efforts were made by France and by Great Britain to influence the conduct of our affairs upon the idea that our Government was

too weak to protect itself, and that it would be
open to the approaches which their ambition
and interest induced them to make. The late
civil war also presents an instance where, if the
States which attempted to secede could, in the
lawful exercise of the power to do so, have made
treaty arrangements or articles of confederation
with other powerful States of Europe before
they attempted to separate themselves from the
Union of the States, they would probably have
done so with fatal effect. And what they did
in the way of an alliance among themselves in
the attempt to create a confederacy between
several of the States is also expressly prohibited
by the language of this section that no State
shall, without the consent of Congress, "enter
into any agreement with another State, or with
a foreign power."

It is also provided that no State shall grant
letters of marque and reprisal. This form of
hostilities against a people and its government
has almost passed out of use among the nations
of the earth. A letter of marque and reprisal
is defined in the following terms: "A commission granted by the Government to a private
individual, to take the property of a foreign
State, or of the citizens or subjects of such State,
as a reparation for an injury committed by such
State, its citizens or subjects." [1]

It was a mode of asserting a remedy for a
supposed injustice, sometimes in the absence of

---

[1] Bouvier's Law Dictionary.

actual war, and frequently in the midst of war, as a means of inducing the private citizens of other nations to engage in the spoliation of the enemy. As it is fairly one of the war powers, and as, when exercised under the authority of the State against a nation with whom the United States was not at war, it might, and almost certainly would, lead to war against that State, it was forbidden to the States to exercise the authority to issue such commissions. It is easy to be seen that if each State of the Union were at liberty to so conduct itself toward any of the foreign nations of the world as to justify them in making war upon that State, the Federal Government must either permit such State to struggle in its own defence as best it could, or to be overrun, conquered, and subjected to the power of the hostile nation; or else it must intervene and protect the State. This latter alternative would leave the question of peace or war to the caprices and interests of a single State, a war which must involve the whole nation for the benefit of that State, without any control on the part of the nation over the causes which led to such a conflict. Hence, while the eighth section of this Article declares that Congress alone shall make war, the tenth section, which we are now considering, declares not only that a State shall not engage in war unless actually invaded, but to prevent the approach to such a condition of affairs refuses to the State the right to grant letters of marque and reprisal.

So also in regard to the coining of money, which by this clause is forbidden to the States, and which by another clause of the same Article is given in positive terms to the Congress of the United States, to wit, "to coin money, regulate the value thereof, and of foreign coins." This is a power, the exercise of which was in past times claimed as an attribute of sovereignty by all the semi-independent principalities of Europe. It is a sovereign power, and for wise reasons is expressly denied to the States.

In the same connection and for the same rea- sons the States are forbidden to make anything but gold or silver coin a tender in payment of debts, or to emit bills of credit. What was meant by the phrase "bills of credit" in this clause of the Constitution has been the subject of very considerable discussion. The constitutional meaning of the phrase was perhaps best defined in the case of *Craig* v. *State of Missouri*, 4 Pet. 410, 431. In the opinion of the court, delivered by Chief Justice Marshall, he asks, "What is a bill of credit? What did the Constitution mean to forbid?" To these questions he replies in the following language: "In its enlarged, and perhaps its literal sense, the term 'bill of credit' may comprehend any instrument by which a State engages to pay money at a future day; thus including a certificate given for money borrowed. But the language of the Constitution itself, and the mischief to be prevented, which we know from the history of our country, equally limit the interpretation of the terms. The word 'emit,' is never employed in describing those contracts by which a State binds itself to pay money at a future day for services actually received, or for money borrowed for present use; nor are instruments executed for such purposes, in common language, denominated 'bills of credit.' To 'emit bills of credit,' conveys to the mind the idea of issuing paper intended to circulate through the community, for its ordinary purposes, as money, which paper is redeemable at a future day. This is the sense in which the terms have been always understood."

He then goes into a history of the times previous to and during the revolution in regard to the excessive issues of paper money, much of which was never redeemed, and shows that it was the prevention of this evil which was aimed at by this constitutional provision.

Thus far, these provisions of section 10 are not among the classes of powers expressly forbidden to the Federal Government. How far that Government may make other things beside gold and silver coin a tender in payment of debts, and how far a State may organize banking corporations with the power to issue circulating notes, are questions of very great interest, and which have been very much discussed, with varying opinions, among the ablest and wisest statesmen and constitutional lawyers of the country. So far as the weight of judicial decisions may determine these questions, especially the decisions of the Supreme Court of the United

States, it may be said to be settled that the of credit in the way of circulating notes and to endow them with the capacity of being a tender in payment of debts; and that the States have the power to create banks and banking corporations with the power to issue such notes which do not depend upon the credit of the State for their value and which are not attempted to be made by the State a legal tender for debts, and that such laws are valid. It seems that the laws authorizing the States to create banks of issue are held not to violate the prohibition against emitting bills of credit, because it is not the State that emits those bills, and because for the bills thus issued the State is not responsible, as they are not issued or received on the credit of the State. In relation to some of the banks thus issuing circulating notes, in which the State owned a part of the stock but for the redemption of the notes of which the State was not legally liable, a closer question was raised, but it has been decided in favor of the validity of such issues. The exercise of this power of creating a bank with power to issue circulating notes, in which although the bank assumes the nature and character of a corporation doing business in the name of trustees and directors, yet the State itself is the sole owner of the capital stock, is more doubtful and probably would not be sustained at this day.[1]

Federal Government has the power to emit bills

Lecture XII.

Bills of credit.

---

[1] See on this subject *Briscoe* v. *Bank of the Commonwealth of Kentucky*, 11 Pet. 257 ; *Woodruff* v. *Trapnall*, 10 How. 190 ; *Curran* v. *Arkansas*, 15 How. 304.

The prohibition against passing bills of attainder is one which was intended to guard against a danger which has passed out of the memory of the present generation. Up to the time of the formation of this Constitution the Parliament of England had been in the habit by legislative enactments of declaring individuals attainted for treason, for murder, for conspiracies, and for other crimes, especially crimes against the Government. This declaration of attainder by the legislative body was accompanied, either impliedly or by the express terms of the bill, with a deprivation of all rights of property and of all capacity to transmit property by descent or acquire it in that manner, in addition to punishments such as death and other cruelties. This kind of proceeding was had, not in a court of justice, nor with a trial by jury, nor with any of the usual modes of ascertaining the guilt or innocence of the party accused, but the legislature, the Parliament, either with or without inquiry, or with such insufficient inquiry as they chose to make, generally in the absence of the victim, proceeded at once to make charges, decide upon the guilt of the party and announce the punishment, thus acting in all instances as the sovereign, the legislative, and judicial power at the same time. This was done without any regularly established mode of procedure or rules of decision. Our ancestors who had just come through the revolutionary struggle for independence, and who felt that most of them might have been subjected to this form of punishment by the Parliament of Great Britain, determined LECTURE XII. to eradicate this system entirely from the powers Bills of attainder. confided either to the Federal Government or to the States, and hence this prohibition.

There is also in this instrument, in addition to the prohibition of bills of attainder, the declaration in the second clause of the third section of Article III, that "no attainder of treason shall work corruption of blood, or forfeiture, except during the life of the person attainted," which probably has reference to the fact that attainder might be a mode of punishment under a judicial sentence, but even in that case it should not work corruption of blood or extend to forfeiture of property beyond the life of the person attainted.[1]

Ex post facto laws, which the States are here Ex post facto forbidden to pass, are laws intended to operate laws. in the way of punishing crimes, which are passed after the offence or crime for which the party is being tried was committed. It was at one time suggested that this kind of enactment, equally forbidden to the General Government and to the States, might be held to be any law which affected the rights of a person civilly or criminally after those rights had been acquired or established in accordance with existing laws. This, however, is a mistake, and the phrase " *ex post facto* laws " has application alone to laws which relate to crimes and criminal proceedings, because it was used in that limited

---

[1] See *Cummings* v. *Missouri*, 4 Wall. 277.

sense by our English ancestors long previous to the formation of the Constitution. The contemporary accounts of its adoption show that such was the sense in which the Convention understood it. And it was because it was understood that it did not forbid laws "impairing the obligation of contracts," that those words were added in the same clause.

This clause of the Constitution in regard to *ex post facto* laws was very early brought into question and came before the Supreme Court of the United States in the case of *Calder* v. *Bull*, 3 Dall. 386. Mr. Justice Chase, who seems to have spoken for the court on that occasion, although several other judges delivered separate opinions, takes a distinction between laws affecting civil rights, which may be retrospective, and those for the punishment of crime, which are *ex post facto ;* and as his definition has been frequently repeated and always with approval by the Supreme Court of the United States, and other courts, it is here quoted :

" I will state what laws I consider *ex post facto* laws, within the words and intent of the prohibition. 1st. Every law that makes an action done before the passing of the law, and which was innocent when done, criminal ; and punishes such action. 2d. Every law that aggravates a crime, or makes it greater than it was, when committed. 3d. Every law that changes the punishment, and inflicts a greater punishment, than the law annexed to the crime, when committed. 4th. Every law that alters the legal

rules of evidence, and receives less, or different,
testimony, than the law required at the time
of the commission of the offence, in order to
convict the offender.

"All these and similar laws are manifestly
unjust and oppressive. In my opinion, the true
distinction is between *ex post facto* laws and
retrospective laws. Every *ex post facto* law
must necessarily be retrospective; but every
retrospective law is not an *ex post facto* law:
the former, only, are prohibited. Every law
that takes away, or impairs, rights vested, agree-
able to existing laws, is retrospective, and is
generally unjust, and may be oppressive; and
it is a good general rule, that a law should have
no retrospect: but there are cases in which laws
may justly, and for the benefit of the community, and also of individuals, relate to a time
antecedent to their commencement; as statutes
of oblivion, or of pardon. They are certainly
retrospective, and literally both concerning, and
after, the facts committed.

"But I do not consider any law *ex post facto*,
within the prohibition, that mollifies the rigor
of the criminal law; but only those that create,
or aggravate, the crime; or increase the punishment, or change the rules of evidence, for the
purpose of conviction. Every law that is to
have an operation before the making thereof, as
to commence at an antecedent time; or to save
time from the statutes of limitations; or to
excuse acts which were unlawful, and before
committed, and the like, is retrospective. But

such laws may be proper or necessary, as the case may be. There is a great and apparent difference between making an unlawful act lawful, and the making an innocent action criminal, and punishing it as a crime.

"The expressions ' *ex post facto* laws' are technical; they had been in use long before the revolution, and had acquired an appropriate meaning, by legislators, lawyers, and authors. The celebrated and judicious Sir William Blackstone, in his Commentaries, considers an *ex post facto* law precisely in the same light as I have done. His opinion is confirmed by his successor, Mr. Wooddeson, and by the author of the Federalist, whom I esteem superior to both, for his extensive and accurate knowledge of the true principles of government." [1]

The prohibition that the States shall pass no law impairing the obligation of contracts is one of the clauses of the Constitution which has been the subject of as much judicial consideration as almost any part of that instrument. I have, however, devoted an entire lecture to that subject, and shall, therefore, say very little about it now. There is no such limitation upon the power of Congress; on the contrary, that body

---

[1] See also on this subject the case of *Watson v. Mercer*, 8 Pet. 88, 110 ; *Satterlee v. Matthewson*, 2 Pet. 380 ; *Kring v. Missouri*, 107 U. S. 221.

During the revolutionary war, bills of attainder and *ex post facto* acts of confiscation, were passed to a wide extent; and the evils resulting therefrom were supposed, in times of more cool reflection, to have outweighed any imagined good. 2 Story on Const. 237.

is expressly invested with the power to pass a LECTURE XII.
uniform system of bankruptcy, which in its es- Impairing the obligation of con-
sential nature has always been supposed to em- tracts.
brace the power of releasing the bankrupt from
the obligation of his contracts upon the surrender of all his property.   The contracts with
the obligations of which the States are forbidden
to interfere by this clause have by judicial decisions been held to be almost all classes of contracts
capable of judicial enforcement or judicial remedy,
contracts of States themselves whereby they have
granted for a valuable consideration rights to
private parties or to corporations, such as exemption from taxation, rights to carry on a particular kind of business, as banking powers and
others.   This prohibition extends without distinction to implied and express contracts, and
includes executory as well as executed contracts.
It is not, however, directed against a violation
of the contract by a party, but the declaration
is that " no State " *shall pass any law* impairing
the obligation of contracts.   In all instances in
which this provision is called in question it must
be in reference to a law of a State, and not to
the action of its judicial or executive powers.
The State as a State is not forbidden to violate
contracts, but it is forbidden to pass a law the
effect of which is to impair their obligation.[1]
With these general remarks on this subject I
must pass it for the present.

The prohibition that the State shall not grant Titles of nobility.

---

[1] *Railroad Company* v. *Rock*, 4 Wall. 177, 180.

any title of nobility may have had some signifi-
cance at the time of the formation of the Constitution of which we are not now fully sensible.
It is one of that class of provisions in that instrument by which the influence of powerful
individuals and of foreign nations in the domestic affairs of our Government was attempted to
be repelled in all the modes which its framers
could devise.   Thus no man in the public service was permitted to accept a present from any
foreign potentate or power, or to accept a title
of nobility, and no State was permitted to create or confer any such title.   These things
have passed very much away, and it has become
such a well settled practice, in the absence of
any attempt to exercise such powers for so long
a period, that it has made us indifferent and
thoughtless about it.   But the aspiration of
many of our wealthy families for social distinction, by making alliances of marriage or otherwise with the members of the nobility of foreign
States, leaves little doubt that, if patents of
nobility could be issued, either by the States or
the Federal Government, applications would be
sufficiently numerous for them, whatever may
be said of republican policy and of republican
simplicity.

Duties on imports
or exports.
The second clause of this section prohibits
certain acts of the States unless with the consent of Congress.   "No State shall, without
the consent of the Congress, lay any imposts or
duties on imports or exports, except what may
be absolutely necessary for executing its inspec-

tion laws." The word " imports " here has reference to goods imported from a foreign country,
and not to such as may be carried from one
State into another.[1]

But a State is prohibited from taxing goods
brought into it from neighboring States by that
provision of section 8 of the same Article which
declares that Congress shall regulate commerce
among the several States.[2]

As no attempt is known to have been made
by any of the States to levy directly or incidentally imposts or duties on goods imported from
foreign nations we need not say much about it,
except perhaps to refer to the case of *Brown* v.
Maryland. There an attempt was made to tax
goods which had been imported into Maryland
from abroad, but which had not been distributed
from the original packages, and it was held that
such goods were entitled to the character of
imports so long as they remained in the packages in which they were brought into this country, but that when these packages were broken
and the goods were used or offered for sale outside of such original packages, they had become
incorporated into the general property of the
State, and were liable to such taxation as the
State imposed on other property. The prohibition in regard to duties on exports, which, by
another clause, is also a limitation upon the power
of the Federal Government, makes it very clear

----

[1] *Brown* v. *Maryland*, 12 Wheat. 419 ; *Woodruff* v. *Parham*, 8
Wall. 123 ; *Hinson* v. *Lott*, 8 Wall. 148.

[2] See *Woodruff* v. *Parham* and *Hinson* v. *Lott*, *supra*.

that the Constitution intended thàt no product of a State which was in the process of exportation should be taxed either by a State or by the Federal Government; in other words, that the process of exporting the products of a State, the goods, chattels, and property of the people of the several States, should not be obstructed or hindered by any burden of taxation imposed by either State or Federal authority.

The Congress of the United States, during the late civil war, imposed a tax upon cotton and tobacco, which tax was not limited to those products when in the process of transportation, but was assessed on all the cotton and tobacco in the country. It was argued that because the larger part of these products was exported out of the country and sold to foreign nations, and because their production was limited to a particular part of the country, the tax was forbidden by the corresponding clause of the Constitution prohibiting Congress from levying a tax on exports. Although the question came at that time to the Supreme Court of the United States, it was not then decided, because of a division of opinion in that court. The recent cases, however, of *Coe* v. *Errol*, 116 U. S. 517, and *Turpin* v. *Burgess*, 117 U. S. 504, seem to decide that the objection was not valid, and hold that only such property as is in the actual process of exportation, and which has begun its voyage or its preparation for the voyage, can be said to be an export.

The clause which declares that "the net

produce of all duties and imposts, laid by any Lecture XII.
State on imports or exports, shall be for the use What is a duty on exports.
of the treasury of the United States," and that
"all such laws shall be subject to the revision
and control of the Congress," needs no comment, as no such duties or imposts have been
laid during the existence of the government.

The further provision that "no State shall, Duty on tonnage.
without the consent of Congress, lay any duty
of tonnage," has been the subject of frequent
decisions of the Supreme Court of the United
States. In many instances the States have
levied taxes and assessments on vessels engaged
in navigation in cases where they had a right
to make such assessments as on other property,
but unfortunately measured the amount of it
by the size of the vessel, taking her tonnage as
a mode of measurement; and, looking at the
literal language of such statutes, since they
impose a tax or duty of so much per ton or per
hundred tons, it is apparently a tonnage tax.
The question has been one of considerable difficulty, and the decisions are not perhaps always
in accord. But it may now be taken to be the
settled doctrine of the Supreme Court that only
a tax which may be said to be laid for the privilege of a vessel to enter a port can be held to
be a tonnage tax. The prohibition against the
States' levying a duty of tonnage is intended to
prevent any interference with commerce with
foreign nations or between one State and another,
and is not intended to prevent a rightful assessment to secure a compensation for services ren-

dered to vessels using the waters of a State, such as wharfage and the like. The question is considered and the authorities reviewed in a late case.[1] It was there held that in almost all cases relied on as showing that there was a reference to the tonnage capacity of the vessel as a measure of the tax there was an absence of any service rendered for which the assessment was a compensation, and generally the tax was held to be imposed for the privilege of entering and anchoring in the port.[2]

Then follows the provision that no State shall, without the consent of Congress, " keep troops, or ships of war, in time of peace, enter into any agreement or compact with another State, or with a foreign power, or engage in war, unless actually invaded, or in such imminent danger as will not admit of delay." These provisions need no explanation. They explain themselves. They are additional safeguards against the dangers mentioned under the first clause which we have just passed over, and are designed to incapacitate the States from making war against each other or against the General Government, or from putting themselves in a position to defy that government and overthrow its authority, withdrawing from them at the same time the power to do this successfully and discouraging the inclination to attempt it. They are prohibited from keeping troops or ships of war, thus dis-

---

[1] *Morgan's Steamship Co.* v. *Louisiana*, 455.

[2] See also *Cannon* v. *New Orleans*, 20 Wall. 577 ; *Packet Co.* v. *Keokuk*, 95 U. S. 80, 84.

abling them from any active belligerent operations; nor shall they enter into any agreement
or compact with any other State, meaning any
other State of this. Union, by which they are
deprived of the power of co-operation in any
hostile movement, either against a State or
against the Federal Government; nor shall they
do this with any foreign power, which would be
still more objectionable; nor shall they for any
reasons mentioned in reference to letters of
marque engage in war unless actually invaded,
or in such imminent danger as will not admit of
delay. That is to say, the only war power which
a State can exercise is one of defence, when
actually invaded, or in the most imminent danger
of such invasion. This last clause in regard to
imminent danger is perhaps best illustrated by
the wars with the Indian tribes, in which the
States have been compelled to organize forces of
their own to protect their inhabitants and citizens from the terrible onslaughts of the savages
who make no proclamation of war and whose
first intimation of hostilities is the destruction
of women and children who are unprepared and
unaware of their danger.

These provisions show the skill and wisdom
with which the framers of the original Constitution guarded against the exercise of such powers
by the States as might seriously endanger the
existence of the Federal Union.

The earliest amendments to that instrument,
namely, the first ten, passed almost immediately
after the formation of the Union, were intended

LECTURE XII.
The first ten
amendments.
to operate as restraints upon the national Government, and represent the fears of those whose distrust of it were greater than their fears from the power of the States. This distrust continued to be the prevailing sentiment of many politicians of the country until the recent civil war broke out in 1861. The actual events of that war, the circumstances which led to it, and its results, impressed upon the American people the fact that the main danger to the perpetuity of our national Government was to be found in the powers exercised by the States, and several amendments to the Constitution, the Thirteenth, Fourteenth, and Fifteenth, were almost exclusively devoted to limitations upon such powers. These are in themselves so important that I cannot in this lecture attempt to comment upon

The Thirteenth
Amendment.
them. It is sufficient to say that the Thirteenth abolishes slavery in all the States of the Union, its existence before that time being entirely dependent upon the laws of the several States, and it gives to Congress the power to enforce the prohibition by appropriate legislation. The

The Fourteenth
Amendment.
Fourteenth Amendment, after defining what citizenship of the United States is, makes these important limitations upon the powers of the States: "No State shall make or enforce any law which shall abridge the privileges or immunities of citizens of the United States; nor shall any State deprive any person of life, liberty, or property, without due process of law; nor deny to any person within its jurisdiction the equal protection of the laws."

The Fifteenth Amendment declares that "the right of citizens of the United States to vote shall not be denied or abridged by the United States or by any State on account of race, color, or previous condition of servitude."

These provisions of the amendments to the Constitution, adopted immediately after the close of the civil war as part of the system of reconstruction made necessary by that war, have been the subject of much discussion in the public prints, in both Houses of Congress, and of decisions of the Supreme Court of the United States. A moment's glance at them will show that they are too important to be considered at the close of a lecture already sufficiently long.

NOTES UPON LECTURE XII.

THIS lecture closes with a reference to the Thirteenth, Fourteenth, and Fifteenth Amendments, but without discussing them. They are treated in the Supplementary Paper, No. XIII, which is devoted to the consideration of subjects not discussed elsewhere.

In previous lectures, Mr. Justice Miller has referred to a class of powers which States may not exercise, because exclusively conferred upon Congress. The most prominent among these is the power to regulate commerce, which the Supreme Court, after considerable fluctuation, held, in a case in which the opinion was written by Mr. Justice Miller, to be so exclusively vested in Congress that a State could not legislate upon the subject. In the headnote, which was also prepared by him, the proposition is laid down that " a statute of a State, intended to regulate, or to tax, or to impose any other restriction upon the transmission of persons or property or telegraphic messages from one State to another, is not within that class of legislation which the States may enact in the absence of legislation by Congress; and such statutes are void, even

598

as to that part of such transaction which may be within the State." [1]

While the Constitution, by the tenth section of the First Article, took away from the States the power of passing bills of attainder and *ex post facto* laws, by the second paragraph in the third section of the Third Article it conferred upon Congress the " power to declare the punishment of treason," but added : " but no attainder shall work corruption of blood, or forfeiture, except during the life of the person attainted." As pertinent to the general subject of attainder, though not to the limitation of the powers of States, I will briefly notice the action of Congress and of the Supreme Court in respect of this power.

In 1861 Congress passed an act for the confiscation of property used in aid of the rebellion.[2] This was followed the next year by " an act to suppress insurrection, to punish treason and rebellion, to seize and confiscate the property of rebels, and for other purposes," [3] which made provision for the seizure, judicial confiscation, and sale of the property of persons giving aid and comfort to the rebellion. The latter act was accompanied by a joint resolution of Congress, also approved by the President, in which, after referring to that act, it was said : " Nor shall any punishment or proceedings under said act be

---

[1] *Wabash, St. Louis & Pacific Railway Co.* v. *Illinois*, 118 U. S. 557.

[2] Act of August 6, 1861, 12 Stat. 319 c. 60.

[3] Act of July 17, 1862, 12 Stat. 589 c. 195.

so construed as to work a forfeiture of the real estate of the offender beyond his natural life."[1]

The court held that the joint resolution was intended to protect the interest of the heirs only; and that the interest of the offender in the real estate could be seized and confiscated, leaving him without further interest or ownership in it.[2] But in a later case it held that if the offender was pardoned, a remainder was left in him after the confiscated life estate which he could dispose of.[3]

---

[1] Joint Resolution of July 17, 1862, 12 Stat. 627, No. 63.
[2] *Wallach* v. *Van Riswick*, 92 U. S. 202.
[3] *Illinois Central Railroad Co.* v. *Bosworth*, 133 U. S. 92.

XIII.

SUPPLEMENTARY: SUBJECTS NOT DIS-
CUSSED ELSEWHERE.

——∘∘⋆∘∘——

CONSTITUTION, ARTICLE I, SECTION 1. All legislative Powers herein granted shall be vested in a Congress of the United States, which shall consist of a Senate and House of Representatives.

ARTICLE I, SECTION 2, PARAGRAPHS 1, 2, AND 3. The House of Representatives shall be composed of Members chosen every second Year by the People of the several States, and the Electors in each State shall have the Qualifications requisite for Electors of the most numerous Branch of the State Legislature.

No Person shall be a Representative who shall not have attained to the Age of twenty-five Years, and been seven Years a Citizen of the United States, and who shall not, when elected, be an Inhabitant of that State in which he shall be chosen.

[Representatives and direct Taxes shall be apportioned among the several States which may be included within this Union, according to their respective Numbers, which shall be determined by adding to the whole Number of free Persons, including those bound to Service for a Term of Years, and excluding Indians not taxed, three-fifths of all other Persons.][1] The actual Enumeration shall be made within three Years after the first Meeting of the Congress of the United States, and within every subsequent Term of ten Years, in such Manner as they shall by Law direct. The Number of Representatives shall not exceed one for every thirty Thousand, but each State shall have

---

[1] The portion of this clause within brackets has been amended by the Fourteenth Amendment.

at Least one Representative; and until such enumeration shall be made, the State of New Hampshire shall be entitled to chuse three, Massachusetts eight, Rhode Island and Providence Plantations one, Connecticut five, New York six, New Jersey four, Pennsylvania eight, Delaware one, Maryland six, Virginia ten, North Carolina five, South Carolina five, and Georgia three.

ARTICLE I, SECTION 3. The Senate of the United States shall be composed of two Senators from each State, chosen by the Legislature thereof, for six Years; and each Senator shall have one Vote.

Immediately after they shall be assembled in Consequence of the first Election, they shall be divided as equally as may be into three Classes. The Seats of the Senators of the first Class shall be vacated at the Expiration of the second Year, of the second Class at the Expiration of the fourth Year, and of the third Class at the Expiration of the sixth Year, so that one-third may be chosen every second Year; and if Vacancies happen by Resignation, or otherwise, during the Recess of the Legislature of any State, the Executive thereof may make temporary Appointments until the next Meeting of the Legislature, which shall then fill such Vacancies.

ARTICLE I, SECTION 4, PARAGRAPHS 1 AND 2. The Times, Places and Manner of holding Elections for Senators and Representatives, shall be prescribed in each State by the Legislature thereof; but the Congress may at any time by Law make or alter such Regulations, except as to the places of chusing Senators.

The Congress shall assemble at least once in every Year, and such Meeting shall be on the first Monday in December, unless they shall by Law appoint a different Day.

ARTICLE I, SECTION 5, PARAGRAPHS 1 AND 2. Each House shall be the Judge of the Elections, Returns and Qualifications of its own Members, and a Majority of each shall constitute a Quorum to do Business; but a smaller Number may adjourn from day to day, and may be authorized to compel the Attendance of absent Members, in such Manner, and under such Penalties as each House may provide.

Each House may determine the Rules of its Proceedings, punish its Members for disorderly Behaviour, and, with the Concurrence of two-thirds, LECTURE XIII. expel a Member.

ARTICLE I, SECTION 8, PARAGRAPH 1 TO PARA-GRAPH 17. The Congress shall have Power

To lay and collect Taxes, Duties, Imposts and Excises, to pay the Debts and provide for the common Defence and general Welfare of the United States; but all Duties, Imposts and Excises shall be uniform throughout the United States;

To borrow Money on the credit of the United States;

To regulate Commerce with foreign Nations, and among the several States, and with the Indian Tribes;

To establish an uniform Rule of Naturalization, and uniform Laws on the subject of Bankruptcies throughout the United States;

To coin Money, regulate the Value thereof, and of foreign Coin, and fix the Standard of Weights and Measures;

To provide for the Punishment of counterfeiting the Securities and current Coin of the United States;

To establish Post Offices and post Roads;

To promote the progress of Science and useful Arts, by securing for limited Times to Authors and Inventors the exclusive Right to their respective Writings and Discoveries;

To constitute Tribunals inferior to the supreme Court;

To define and punish Piracies and Felonies committed on the high Seas, and Offences against the Law of Nations;

To declare War, grant Letters of Marque and Reprisal, and make Rules concerning Captures on Land and Water;

To raise and support Armies, but no Appropriation of Money to that Use shall be for a longer Term than two Years;

To provide and maintain a Navy;

To make Rules for the Government and Regulation of the land and naval Forces;

To provide for calling forth the Militia to execute the Laws of the Union, suppress Insurrections and repel Invasions;

To provide for organizing, arming, and disciplining, the Militia, and for governing such Part of them as may be employed in the Service of the United States, reserving to the States respectively, the Appointment of the Officers, and the Authority of training the Militia according to the Discipline prescribed by Congress;

To exercise exclusive Legislation in all Cases whatsoever, over such District (not exceeding ten Miles square) as may, by Cession of particular States, and the Acceptance of Congress, become the Seat of the Government of the United States, and to exercise like Authority over all Places purchased by the Consent of the Legislature of the State in which the same shall be, for the Erection of Forts, Magazines, Arsenals, Dock-yards, and other needful Buildings.

ARTICLE I, SECTION 9, PARAGRAPHS 1, 2, 3, 4. The Migration or Importation of such Persons as any of the States now existing shall think proper to admit, shall not be prohibited by the Congress prior to the Year one thousand eight hundred and eight, but a Tax or Duty may be imposed on such Importation, not exceeding ten dollars for each Person.

The Privilege of the Writ of Habeas Corpus shall not be suspended, unless when in Cases of Rebellion or Invasion the public Safety may require it.

No Bill of Attainder or ex post facto Law shall be passed.

No Capitation, or other direct, Tax shall be laid, unless in Proportion to the Census or Enumeration herein before directed to be taken.

ARTICLE II, SECTION 1, PARAGRAPHS 5 AND 7. In case of the Removal of the President from Office, or of his Death, Resignation, or Inability to discharge the Powers and Duties of the said Office, the same shall devolve on the Vice-President, and the Congress may by Law provide for the Case of Removal, Death, Resignation, or Inability, both of the President and Vice-President, declaring what Officer shall then act as President, and such Officer shall act accordingly, until the Disability be removed, or a President shall be elected.

Before he enter on the execution of his Office, he shall take the following Oath or Affirmation : —

" I do solemnly swear (or affirm) that I will faithfully execute the Office of President of the United States, and will to the best of my Ability, preserve, protect and defend the Constitution of the United States."

ARTICLE IV, SECTION 1. Full Faith and Credit LECTURE XIII.
shall be given in each State to the public Acts, Records, Supplementary.
and judicial Proceedings of every other State. And
the Congress may by general Laws prescribe the Manner in which such Acts, Records and Proceedings
shall be proved, and the Effect thereof.

ARTICLE IV, SECTION 2, PARAGRAPHS 2, 3. A Person charged in any State with Treason, Felony, or
other Crime, who shall flee from Justice, and be found
in another State, shall on Demand of the executive
Authority of the State from which he fled, be delivered
up, to be removed to the State having Jurisdiction of
the Crime.

No Person held to Service or Labour in one State,
under the Laws thereof, escaping into another, shall,
in Consequence of any Law or Regulation therein, be
discharged from such Service or Labour, but shall be
delivered up on Claim of the Party to whom such Service or Labour may be due.

ARTICLE IV, SECTION 3, PARAGRAPHS 1, 2. New
States may be admitted by the Congress into this
Union ; but no new State shall be formed or erected
within the Jurisdiction of any other State ; nor any
State be formed by the Junction of two or more
States, or Parts of States, without the Consent of the
Legislatures of the States concerned as well as of the
Congress.

The Congress shall have Power to dispose of and
make all needful Rules and Regulations respecting the
Territory or other Property belonging to the United
States ; and nothing in this Constitution shall be so
construed as to Prejudice any claims of the United
States, or of any particular State.

ARTICLE IV, SECTION 4. The United States shall
guarantee to every State in this Union a Republican
Form of Government, and shall protect each of them
against Invasion, and on Application of the Legislature, or of the Executive (when the Legislature cannot be convened) against domestic Violence.

ARTICLE VI, PARAGRAPHS 1, 2. All Debts contracted and Engagements entered into, before the
Adoption of this Constitution, shall be as valid against
the United States under this Constitution, as under
the Confederation.

This Constitution, and the Laws of the United
States which shall be made in Pursuance thereof ; and

all Treaties made, or which shall be made, under the authority of the United States, shall be the supreme Law of the Land ; and the Judges in every State shall be bound thereby, any Thing in the Constitution or Laws of any State to the Contrary notwithstanding.

FIRST AMENDMENT. Congress shall make no law respecting an establishment of religion, or prohibiting the free exercise thereof ; or abridging the freedom of speech, or of the press; or the right of the people peaceably to assemble, and to petition the Government for a redress of grievances.

SECOND AMENDMENT. A well regulated Militia, being necessary to the security of a free State, the right of the people to keep and bear Arms, shall not be infringed.

THIRD AMENDMENT. No Soldier shall, in time of peace, be quartered in any house, without the consent of the Owner, nor in time of war, but in a manner to be prescribed by law.

FOURTH AMENDMENT. The right of the people to be secure in their persons, houses, papers, and effects, against unreasonable searches and seizures, shall not be violated, and no Warrants shall issue, but upon probable cause, supported by Oath or affirmation, and particularly describing the place to be searched, and the persons or things to be seized.

FIFTH AMENDMENT. No person shall be held to answer for a capital, or otherwise infamous crime, unless on a presentment or indictment of a Grand Jury, except in cases arising in the land or naval forces, or in the Militia, when in actual service in time of War or public danger; nor shall any person be subject for the same offence to be twice put in jeopardy of life or limb; nor shall be compelled in any Criminal Case to be a witness against himself, nor be deprived of life, liberty, or property, without due process of law; nor shall private property be taken for public use, without just compensation.

EIGHTH AMENDMENT. Excessive bail shall not be required, nor excessive fines imposed, nor cruel and unusual punishments inflicted.

NINTH AMENDMENT. The enumeration in the Constitution, of certain rights, shall not be construed to deny or disparage others retained by the people.

TENTH AMENDMENT. The powers not delegated to the United States by the Constitution, nor prohibited

by it to the States, are reserved to the States respec- LECTURE XIII.
tively or to the people. Supplementary.

THIRTEENTH AMENDMENT. SECTION 1. Neither
slavery nor involuntary servitude, except as a punishment for crime whereof the party shall have been duly
convicted, shall exist within the United States, or any
place subject to their jurisdiction.

SECTION 2. Congress shall have power to enforce
this article by appropriate legislation.

FOURTEENTH AMENDMENT. SECTION 1. All persons born or naturalized in the United States, and
subject to the jurisdiction thereof, are citizens of the
United States and of the State wherein they reside.
No State shall make or enforce any law which shall
abridge the privileges or immunities of citizens of the
United States ; nor shall any State deprive any person
of life, liberty, or property, without due process of
law ; nor deny to any person within its jurisdiction
the equal protection of the laws.

SECTION 2. Representatives shall be apportioned
among the several States according to their respective
numbers, counting the whole number of persons in
each State, excluding Indians not taxed. But when
the right to vote at any election for the choice of Electors for President and Vice-President of the United
States, Representatives in Congress, the executive and
judicial officers of a State, or the members of the Legislature thereof, is denied to any of the male inhabitants of such State, being twenty-one years of age
and citizens of the United States, or in any way
abridged, except for participation in rebellion or
other crime, the basis of representation therein shall
be reduced in the proportion which the number of
such male citizens shall bear to the whole number of
male citizens twenty-one years of age in such State.

SECTION 3. No person shall be a Senator or Representative in Congress, or Elector of President and
Vice-President, or hold any office, civil or military,
under the United States, or under any State, who,
having previously taken an oath, as a member of Congress, or as an officer of the United States, or as a
member of any State Legislature, or as an executive or
judicial officer of any State, to support the Constitution of the United States, shall have engaged in insurrection or rebellion against the same, or given aid or
comfort to the enemies thereof. But Congress may,

by a vote of two-thirds of each House, remove such disability.

Section 4. The validity of the public debt of the United States, authorized by law, including debts incurred for payment of pensions and bounties for services in suppressing insurrection or rebellion, shall not be questioned. But neither the United States nor any State shall assume or pay any debt or obligation incurred in aid of insurrection or rebellion against the United States, or any claim for the loss or emancipation of any slave; but all such debts, obligations, and claims shall be held illegal and void.

Section 5. The Congress shall have power to enforce, by appropriate legislation, the provisions of this article.

Fifteenth Amendment. Section 1. The right of citizens of the United States to vote shall not be denied or abridged by the United States, or by any State, on account of race, color, or previous condition of servitude.

Section 2. The Congress shall have power to enforce this article by appropriate legislation.

Some of the minor provisions of the Constitution have not been treated by Mr. Justice Miller, or they have been touched upon only in a cursory way. It will be the aim of this supplementary paper to treat these subjects briefly, and in their order as they stand in that instrument.

1. Congress : its Organization and Parliamentary Powers.

Congress : its organization and parliamentary powers.

The legislative powers granted to the Union by the Constitution are, by section 1, Article I, " vested in a Congress of the United States, which shall consist of a Senate and House of Representatives."

In Lecture IV the separate powers confided

by the Constitution to the Senate and to the House of Representatives respectively were fully discussed. In other lectures the legislative powers reposed in them jointly, as "The Senate and the House of Representatives of the United States of America in Congress assembled," were treated in detail; and those which are denied to them and retained by the States were also pointed out and discussed in detail.

Lecture XIII. Supplementary. Congress: its organization and parliamentary powers.

From the opening of the Convention it was determined that, following the settled precedents of the English race, the power of the new legislative body to be created by it should be reposed in two Houses. It was not until the 25th of May, 1787, that a quorum of States was attained; and, as early as the 29th of that month, two projects were launched, which eventually resulted in the Constitution. The first of these was the Virginia plan in sixteen resolutions, offered by Edmund Randolph; and the second a draft for a Constitution, presented by Charles Pinckney of South Carolina. These papers will be found in the Appendix. Each made provision for a national legislature, to consist of two Houses; and in each it was provided that the members of the House of Representatives should be elected by the people.

The basis thus recommended for the House of Representatives was substantially adopted in section 2 of Article I of the Constitution, which provides that "the House of Representatives shall be composed of Members chosen every second Year by the People of the several States,

The House: how elected.

LECTURE XIII.
Supplementary.
The House: how
elected.

Number of mem-
bers.
and the Electors in each State shall have the Qualifications requisite for Electors of the most numerous Branch of the State Legislature."

As originally constituted, the House of Representatives consisted of sixty-five members, of whom the Constitution made the first apportionment; but, under further provision in the same section, an enumeration or census was taken, which was made the basis of a new apportionment. Once in each succeeding ten years, under the provisions of the same section, a new census or enumeration has been taken, and a new apportionment made by Congress. Under the last enumeration and apportionment[1] the House of Representatives consists of three hundred and fifty-six members, not including Delegates from the Territories. The District of Columbia also at one time enjoyed the privilege of being rep-

---

[1] 26 Stat. 735, c. 116. An act making an apportionment of Representatives in Congress among the several States under the Eleventh Census.

Be it enacted, etc., That after the third of March, eighteen hundred and ninety-three, the House of Representatives shall be composed of three hundred and fifty-six members, to be apportioned among the several States as follows: Alabama, nine; Arkansas, six; California, seven; Colorado, two; Connecticut, four; Delaware, one; Florida, two; Georgia, eleven; Idaho, one; Illinois, twenty-two; Indiana, thirteen; Iowa, eleven; Kansas, eight; Kentucky, eleven; Louisiana, six; Maine, four; Maryland, six; Massachusetts, thirteen; Michigan, twelve; Minnesota, seven; Mississippi, seven; Missouri, fifteen; Montana, one; Nebraska, six; Nevada, one; New Hampshire, two; New Jersey, eight; New York, thirty-four; North Carolina, nine; North Dakota, one; Ohio, twenty-one; Oregon, two; Pennsylvania, thirty; Rhode Island, two; South Carolina, seven; South Dakota, two; Tennessee, ten; Texas, thirteen; Vermont, two; Virginia, ten; Washington, two; West Virginia, four; Wisconsin, ten; Wyoming, one. [Approved February 7, 1891.]

resented in the House as a Territory, without
the right of voting. But this privilege, conferred at a late hour, was soon withdrawn.

The Senate was organized by the Constitution
on a very different basis from that thrown out
in either of the programmes. It was the result
of discussion and compromise. The equality of
representation of the small and the large States
contributed sensibly toward securing the assent
of the former to the Constitution, and thus aided
in bringing about the Union.

The third section of Article I contains two
clauses providing as follows: " The Senate of
the United States shall be composed of two
Senators from each State, chosen by the Legislature thereof, for six Years and each Senator
shall have one Vote." The first of these clauses
gives to the States the equality of representation
which each enjoyed under the Articles of Confederation. The second takes away the voting
by States, and puts that responsibility upon
each individual Senator. The same section, in
another paragraph, requires that each Senator
shall have attained the age of thirty years, that
he shall have been nine years a citizen of the
United States, and that, at the time of his election, he shall be an inhabitant of the State
which he represents.

The Senate is divided into three classes, as
nearly equally as possible, so that one-third shall
go out at the expiration of each Congress. The
first division was made under the provisions of
section 3, and as representatives from new States

have appeared they have successively been classified by. lot. At its inception it consisted of
twenty-six members. It now consists of eighty-
eight members.

The same section confers upon the House of
Representatives the power of choosing its Speaker
and other officers, and upon the Senate the power
of choosing its officers, and a President *pro tempore* in the absence of the Vice-President, who is
made its President by the Constitution, but
without a vote except when the Senate is equally
divided. In practice a President *pro tempore* is
usually elected, who serves in all absences of the
Vice-President until he resigns or is replaced by
another by vote of the Senate.

Article I, section 4, provides that " The Times,
Places and Manner of holding Elections for
Senators and Representatives shall be prescribed
in each State by the Legislature thereof; but
the Congress may at any time by Law make or
alter such Regulations, except as to the places
of choosing Senators."

This power was first exercised in 1842.[1] It
had become the custom in some of the States to
elect the entire State representation in the House
of Representatives on a general ticket, voted
upon as a whole throughout the State, thus
securing a solid delegation of one political faith.
To break up this custom Congress enacted that
when a State was entitled to more than one
member, the members should be elected by dis-

---

[1] Act of June 25, 1842, 5 Stat. 491, c. 47.

tricts composed of contiguous territory. This Lecture XIII.
system has been since retained.[1] In 1872 Con- Supplementary. How elected.
gress further provided that such elections should
take place on the Tuesday next after the first
Monday of November, 1876, and the like day of
that month in every second year thereafter,[2]
which is now the law.[3] It is further provided
that vacancies may be filled at such times as
State laws may prescribe,[4] and that all elections
shall be by ballot.[5]

The first legislation for regulating the election of Senators was in 1866.[6] The statute
then enacted is practically codified in the Revised Statutes.[7] The legislature of each State
chosen next preceding the expiration of the
time for which any Senator was elected to
represent the State in Congress, is on the second
Tuesday after its meeting and organization, to
elect a Senator in the manner pointed out by
that act. Provisions are also made for filling
vacancies.

Congress is required to assemble at least Day of meeting
once in each year on the first Monday in De- of Congress.
cember, unless it appoints by law a different
day. In 1867 it was enacted that there should
be a meeting of the Fortieth Congress and of
each succeeding Congress on the day on which

---

[1] Acts of August 30, 1856, 11 Stat. 150, c. 30; July 14, 1862, 12
Stat. 572, c. 170; March 11, 1868, 15 Stat. 41, c. 25; February 2,
1872, 17 Stat. 28, c. 11; Rev. Stat. § 23.

[2] Act of February 2, 1872, 17 Stat. 28, c. 11.

[3] Rev. Stat. § 25.   [4] Ib. § 26.   [5] Ib. § 27.

[6] Act of July 25, 1866, 14 Stat. 243, c. 245.

[7] Rev. Stat. §§ 14–19.

the term begins for which the Congress is elected (March 4) ;[1] but this act was repealed in 1871.[2]

The House is the judge of the election returns and qualifications of its own members. A majority constitutes a quorum, but a less number may adjourn from day to day.[3]

The second paragraph of section 5 confers upon each House the power " to determine the Rules of its Proceedings, punish its Members for disorderly Behaviour, and, with the Concurrence of two-thirds, expel a Member." We have already seen, in the comments on *Kilbourn* v. *Thompson*,[4] *ante*, 412, that the House, not being a judicial body, cannot convict for contempt, and cannot punish persons who are not members. The opinion in that case was written by Mr. Justice Miller. It practically overruled *Anderson* v. *Dunn*.[5]

The other provisions in that section are, that each House shall keep a journal, which shall be made public unless, in its judgment, secrecy is required ; that the yeas and nays may be called for by one-fifth of the members present, and that neither House, without the consent of the

---

[1] Act of January 22, 1867, 14 Stat. 378, c. 10.

[2] Act of April 20, 1871, 14 Stat. 12, c. 21, § 30.

[3] Rule XV, paragraph 3: " On the demand of any member, or at the suggestion of the Speaker, the names of members sufficient to make a quorum in the hall of the House who do not vote shall be noted by the clerk and recorded in the journal, and reported to the Speaker with the names of the members voting, and be counted and announced in determining the presence of a quorum to do business."

[4] 103 U. S. 168.   [5] 6 Wheat. 204.

other, shall adjourn for more than three days,
or to any other place than that in which the
two Houses shall be sitting.

Section 6 relates to the compensation and
privileges of members. The former is to be
determined by law, and the latter includes privilege from arrest[1] in all cases except treason,
felony, and breach of the peace during attendance at a session of Congress, going there and
returning thence; and also exemption from
being questioned elsewhere for speeches in debate. It also provides that no member can hold
an office created or of which the emoluments
were increased during the time for which he
was elected, and that no person can hold an
office under the United States, and be at the
same time a member of either House of Congress.

2. Powers conferred on Congress by Article I, Section 8.

A. Power to enact Bankrupt Laws.

Article I, section 8, conferring on Congress
power "to establish . . . uniform laws on the
subject of Bankruptcies throughout the United
States" was added to the draft of the Constitution as late as September 1, 1787, and on
Monday, the 3d September, it was adopted,
Connecticut alone voting in the negative. Mr.
Sherman of Connecticut gave as the reason for
his opposition " that bankruptcies were, in some

---

[1] See *Cox* v. *McClenachan*, 3 Dall. 478.

cases punishable with death by the laws of England, and he did not choose to grant a power by which that might be done here." The power to enact a bankrupt law was first exercised in 1800.[1] In 1803 that law was repealed.[2] In 1841[3] it was again exercised by an act which was repealed in 1843.[4] It was again exercised in 1867[5] by an act which, after being several times amended,[6] was finally repealed in 1878.[7]

The grant of this power to Congress does not divest the several States of the right to enact insolvent laws in the nature of bankrupt laws, both voluntary and involuntary, and to provide for the settlement of estates of insolvent persons by process of law, the distribution of their proceeds and the discharge of the debtors; but such exercise of power by a State is subject to be suspended by the enactment of a bankrupt law by Congress, and will remain suspended so long as such a law is in force; and a discharge so obtained through State proceedings does not operate upon the claim of a citizen of another State who has not proved his debt.[8]

---

[1] Act of April 4, 1800, 2 Stat. 19, c. 19.

[2] Act of December 19, 1803, 2 Stat. 248, c. 6.

[3] Act of August 19, 1841, 5 Stat. 440, c. 9.

[4] Act of March 3, 1843, 5 Stat. 614, c. 82.

[5] Act of March 2, 1867, 14 Stat. 517, c. 176.

[6] Act of July 27, 1868, 15 Stat. 227, c. 258; Act of February 13, 1873, 17 Stat. 436, c. 135; Act of March 3, 1873, 17 Stat. 509, c. 226, § 4; Act of June 8, 1872, 17 Stat. 334, c. 339; Act of March 3, 1873, 17 Stat. 577, c. 235; Act of June 22, 1874, 18 Stat. 178, c. 390; Act of July 26, 1876, 19 Stat. 102, c. 234.

[7] Act of June 7, 1878, 20 Stat. 99, c. 160.

[8] *Boese* v. *King,* 108 U. S. 379; *Baldwin* v. *Hale,* 1 Wall 223.

B. *Coinage: Bills of Credit: Weights and Measures.*

Mr. Pinckney's draft proposed to confer upon Congress the "power to borrow money and emit bills of credit," the power "to coin money and regulate the value of all coins," and the power "to fix the standard of weights and measures." In the discussions the power "to emit bills of credit" was stricken out by a vote of nine States to two. Otherwise, with some change of language, these powers were placed by the Convention in the Constitution. LECTURE XIII.
Supplementary.
Coinage.

That draft also contained a clause forbidding States to emit bills of credit. The Constitution, as completed, goes beyond this. It provides that "No State shall . . . coin money, emit bills of credit," etc. Bills of credit.

The people of the United States had greatly suffered from the over-issues of bills of credit having the character of legal tender, by the States, and the Convention made it clear that the power to make such issues in the future was to be taken away from them, as well as the power to coin money.[1]

The authority to fix the standard of weights and measures has been exercised by Congress only partially. It has provided a standard troy pound for the regulation of the coinage,[2] and it has authorized the use of the metric system throughout the United States.[3] Otherwise each State regulates this subject for itself. Weights and
measures.

---

[1] See *ante*, pp. 138, 139.   [2] Rev. Stat. § 3548.
[3] Rev. Stat. §§ 3569, 3570.

C. *Punishment for Counterfeiting.*

The Constitution further confers upon Congress the power " to provide for the punishment of counterfeiting the securities and current coin of the United States." It is held that this grant of power does not prevent a State from enacting laws to punish counterfeiting; and that, being bound to protect to other nations rights secured to them by the law of nations, Congress has the power to enact laws punishing the counterfeiting of foreign securities.[1]

D. *Post-office and Post-roads.*

Section 8, paragraph 7, confers power to "establish Post-offices and Post-roads." Mr. Pinckney's draft proposed to confer authority " to establish post-offices," without conferring any power over the means of maintaining communication between them. The essential words "and post-roads," under which the mail service of the country is carried on, were added during the discussion. Post routes are established by law, and the compensation for carriage over them fixed in the same way. And when a part of an established route is found to be impracticable, by reason of being almost or quite impassable, the Post-office Department may change that part without thereby creating a new route, not authorized by law.[2]

In one notable case Congress practically ter-

---

[1] *United States* v. *Arjona*, 120 U. S. 479.
[2] *United States* v. *Barlow*, 132 U. S. 271.

minated an important suit in equity by the exercise of this power.[1] The State of Virginia, having authorized a corporation to construct a bridge across the Ohio River at Wheeling, the State of Pennsylvania filed a bill in equity in the Supreme Court of the United States to enjoin its construction, upon the ground that it was an unconstitutional obstruction of a navigable river. As a result of proceedings, which are reported in several volumes of Howard, a writ of injunction issued from that court in June, 1854. Counsel then brought to the attention of the court that, in the Post-office Appropriation Act of 1852,[2] the bridge in controversy had been declared to be a lawful structure, and to be an "established post-road for the passage of the mails of the United States." The court said: "So far as this bridge created an obstruction to the free navigation of the river, in view of the previous acts of Congress, they are to be regarded as modified by this subsequent legislation; and, although it may still be an obstruction in fact, is not so in the contemplation of law. . . . We do not enter upon the question whether or not Congress possesses the power under the authority in the Constitution to establish ' post-offices and post-roads,' to legalize this bridge; for, conceding that no such powers can be derived from this clause, it must be admitted that it is, at least, necessarily included in the power con-

LECTURE XIII.

Supplementary.
Post-office and
Post-roads.

---

[1] *Pennsylvania* v. *Wheeling and Belmont Bridge Co.*, 9 How. 647; 11 How. 528 ; 13 How. 518 ; 18 How. 421.

[2] Act of August 31, 1852, 10 Stat. 110, 112, c. 111, §§ 6, 7.

ferred to regulate commerce among the several States." [1]

E. *Copyright, Patents and Trade Marks.*

Article I, section 8, paragraph 8. " To promote the progress of Science and useful Arts, by securing for limited Times to authors and Inventors the exclusive Right to their respective Writings and Discoveries." In regard to copyrights, Congress early exercised the power thus conferred,[2] and still does so. It is held that an author's right of property in his published works exists only under the provisions of the statutes thus enacted.[3]

The Act of March 3, 1891, amending the Revised Statutes, authorizes a copyright to be granted to a foreigner; but it provides in section 13 that " this act shall only apply to a citizen or subject of a foreign state or nation, when such foreign state or nation permits to citizens of the United States of America the benefit of copyright on substantially the same basis as its

---

[1] *Pennsylvania* v. *Wheeling and Belmont Bridge Co.*, 18 How. 421, 430.

[2] Act of May 31, 1790, 1 Stat. 124, c. 15 ; Act of April 29, 1802, 2 Stat. 171, c. 36 ; Act of February 3, 1831, 4 Stat. 436, c. 16 ; Act of August 10, 1846, 9 Stat. 106, c. 178, § 10 ; Act of March 3, 1855, 10 Stat. 685, c. 199, § 5 ; Act of August 18, 1858, 11 Stat. 138, c. 169 ; Act of February 5, 1859, 11 Stat. 380, c. 22, § 8 ; Act of February 18, 1867, 14 Stat. 395, c. 43 ; Act of July 8, 1870, 16 Stat. 198, c. 230, §§ 85–110 ; Rev. Stat. §§ 4948–4971 ; Act of June 18, 1874, 18 Stat. 78, c. 301 ; Act of March 3, 1879, 20 Stat. 359, c. 180, § 15 ; Act of August 1, 1882, 22 Stat. 181, c. 366.

[3] *Wheaton* v. *Peters*, 8 Pet. 591. See also *Banks* v. *Manchester*, 128 U. S. 244 ; *Callaghan* v. *Myers*, 128 U. S. 617 ; and *Burrow-Giles Lithographic Co.* v. *Sarony*, 111 U. S. 53.

own citizens; or when such foreign state or nation is a party to an international agreement which provides for reciprocity in the granting of copyright, by the terms of which agreement the United States of America may, at its pleasure, become a party to such agreement." [1]

Legislation was also had upon the subject of patents for inventions in the First Congress. The act was entitled "An act to promote the progress of useful arts." [2] As in the case of copyrights, etc., so here, after changes and amendments, the statutes were consolidated in 1871 [3] into one statute which embraced the three subjects of Patents, Copyrights and Trade Marks, and from thence was codified into the Revised Statutes. [4] The law as thus codified has been since amended. [5]

It has been held, over and over again, that unless a machine is novel, and unless it called for the inventive faculty to produce it, as distinguished from what existed before it, it is not patentable. It is also held that the discovery that a force of nature can be applied to a useful result is not patentable, unless some practicable way is pointed out for its application. [6]

The subject of trade marks is now classified with copyrights and patents in the legislation of

---

[1] 26 Stat. 1106, c. 565.

[2] Act of April 10, 1890, 1 Stat. 109, c. 7.

[3] Act of July 8, 1870, 16 Stat. 198, c. 230, §§ 1–76.

[4] Revised Stat. §§ 4883–4936.

[5] Act of February 4, 1887, 24 Stat. 387, c. 105.

[6] *O'Reilly* v. *Morse*, 15 How. 62; *The Telephone Cases*, 126 U. S. 1.

LECTURE XIII.
Supplementary.
Trade marks.

Congress, already referred to, subsequent to 1869. In the *Trade Mark Cases*,[1] which were decided at October Term, 1879, this legislation was before the Supreme Court, and it was held that a trade mark being " neither an invention, a discovery, nor a writing, within the meaning of the eighth clause of the eighth section of the First Article of the Constitution, and the legislation respecting it not being limited to the use of trade marks in ' commerce with foreign nations and among the several States, and with the Indian tribes,' " it was " void for want of constitutional authority."

But, although the right of property in it might not have been derived from legislation of Congress under its constitutional powers, it was clear, and was so held, that the right to such property had long been recognized by the common law and by the Chancery courts of England. Congress at once legislated under the powers conferred upon it by the commerce clause of the Constitution.[2] The title to such property is now sustained when the person who asserts ownership in it shows a just claim to protection.[3]

F.   *Piracies and Felonies on the High Seas.*

Piracy, etc.

Article I, section 8, paragraph 10, authorizes Congress " to define and punish Piracies and

---

[1] *Trade Mark Cases*, 100 U. S. 82, 92.

[2] Act of March 3, 1881, 21 Stat. 502, c. 138 ; Act of August 5, 1882, 22 Stat. 298, c. 393.

[3] *Canal Co.* v. *Clark*, 13 Wall. 311; *Menendez* v. *Holt*, 128 U. S. 514 ; *Corbin* v. *Gould*, 133 U. S. 308 ; *Liggett and Myers Tobacco Co.* v. *Finzer*, 128 U. S. 514.

Felonies committed on the high Seas, and
Offences against the Law of Nations." The Articles of Confederation conferred power " to appoint courts 'for the trial of piracies and felonies committed on the high seas." The Virginia draft extended this power by providing that Congress might " declare the law and punishment of piracies and felonies at sea ; " and the Constitution, as adopted, adds to those " offences against the law of nations." A foreign vessel, " by assuming a piratical character, is no longer included in the description of a foreign vessel ; " and the vessel, if the piratical act be committed " in an open road, may well be found by a jury to be on the seas." [1]

The provisions in the Act of Congress of August 18, 1856, codified in Title 72 of the Revised Statutes, which authorize the President to declare guano islands to be " appertaining to the United States, and which provide that crimes and offences committed on such islands shall be deemed to have been done or committed on the high seas on board a merchant ship or vessel belonging to the United States, and be punished according to the laws of the United States relating to such ships or vessels and offences on the high seas," was lately before the Supreme Court for construction. It was held that that act did " not assume to extend the admiralty jurisdiction over land, but merely extends the provisions of the statutes of the United States for the pun-

---

[1] *United States v. The Pirates,* 5 Wheat. 184, 198, 200.

ishment of offences upon the high seas to like offences upon guano islands, which the President has determined should be considered as appertaining to the United States;" and that a person charged with the offence of "murder committed on a guano island, which has been determined by the President to appertain to the United States, may be tried in the courts of the United States for the district into which the offender is first brought." [1]

G. *The National Defence.*

National defence. Article I, section 8, paragraphs 11, 12, 13, 14, 15, and 16 conferred upon Congress power " to declare War, grant Letters of Marque and Reprisal, and make Rules concerning Captures on Land and Water; to raise and support Armies, but no Appropriation of Money to that Use shall be for a longer Term than two Years; to provide and maintain a Navy; to make Rules for the Government and Regulation of the land and naval Forces; to provide for calling forth the Militia to execute the Laws of the Union, suppress Insurrections and repel Invasions; to provide for organizing, arming, and disciplining the Militia, and for governing such Part of them as may be employed in the Service of the United States, reserving to the States respectively, the Appointment of the Officers, and the Authority of training the Militia according to the Discipline prescribed by Congress."

---

[1] *Jones v. United States*, 137 U. S. 202.

These provisions relating to the means of national defence and self-protection are simple, and the most natural division of powers in a Federal Government. The provision as to appropriations for paying the land forces was not in either draft. It was put in by the Convention, undoubtedly prompted by the same jealousy of executive power which had established a similar custom in Great Britain. The Pinckney draft gave the United States power "to subdue a rebellion in any State on application of its legislature, and to call. forth the aid of the militia," not only "to execute the laws of the Union," "enforce treaties," and "repel invasions," but also "to suppress insurrections."

In the war of 1812 the right of the President to order State militia to duty outside the State was denied by the State of Massachusetts; but, in the much greater war of the rebellion, the militia of most of the Northern States was more than once ordered on duty outside of its own State, and responded without question or hesitation.

The power over the militia thus reserved to the States is so complete that a State may, unless restrained by its own constitution, enact laws to prevent any body of men whatever, other than the regularly organized volunteer militia of the State, and the troops of the United States, from associating themselves together as a military company or organization, or to drill or parade with arms in any place within the State, without the consent of the governor of the State.[1]

---

[1] *Presser* v. *Illinois*, 116 U. S. 252.

The power to declare war, and thus make active use of the other powers necessary, found its place in the Constitution from necessity. There could be no sovereignty without it. But the necessity for such active use can be made equally necessary by a declaration of war against the United States, as in the case of the war with Mexico, or by an active war against it, as in the war of the rebellion.

A state of war does not change the relation of a citizen to his government, or displace the civil authorities outside the theatre of conflict;[1] what it may do there depends upon the circumstances and exigencies of the case.[2]

H. *The District of Columbia.*

Article I, section 8, paragraph 17, authorizes Congress "to exercise exclusive Legislation in all Cases whatsoever, over such District (not exceeding ten Miles square) as may, by Cession of particular States, and the Acceptance of Congress, become the Seat of the Government of the United States, and to exercise like Authority over all Places purchased by the Consent of the Legislature of the State in which the Same shall be, for the Erection of Forts, Magazines, Arsenals, Dock Yards and other needful Buildings."

Under this authority the cession of the District of Columbia was made to the United States

---

[1] *Ex parte Milligan,* 4 Wall. 2.
[2] *Mitchel* v. *Harmony,* 13 How. 115.

by the States of Maryland and Virginia.[1] The Lecture XIII.
portion ceded by Virginia was subsequently Supplementary.
District of Colum-
retroceded to that State.[2] The local laws of bia.
each State existing at the time of the cession
remained in force, so far as they affected rights
of property, and except as changed by Congress.[3]
The municipal forms of government in the several municipalities also continued, except as
changed by Congress. For a short time a Territorial government was put in operation in the
District,[4] but this was soon discontinued,[5] and
the District is now only a municipal corporation.[6]
A most competent authority has questioned the
power of Congress to delegate the legislative
authority once acquired through this clause of
the Constitution.[7]

3. Restrictions in Section 9 upon the Power of Congress.

A. The African Slave Trade.

Article I, section 9. This section is entirely Slave trade.
taken up with statements of what Congress may
not do. All the important provisions in it have

---

[1] Act of July 16, 1790, 1 Stat. 130, c. 28; Act of March 3, 1791,
1 Stat. 214, c. 17; Proclamation of President Washington, January
24, 1791, 11 Stat. 751.

[2] Act of July 9, 1846, 9 Stat. 35, c. 35; President Polk's proclamation of September 7, 1846, 9 Stat. 1000.

[3] *Thaw* v. *Ritchie*, 136 U. S. 519.

[4] Act of February 21, 1871, 16 Stat. 419, c. 62.

[5] Act of June 20, 1874, 18 Stat. 116, c. 337.

[6] *Metropolitan Railroad Co.* v. *District of Columbia*, 132 U. S.
See *Geofroy* v. *Riggs*, 133 U. S. 258.

[7] Cooley's Principles of Constitutional Law, 90, 91.

been treated by Mr. Justice Miller. It only remains to notice a few of the less important ones. Paragraph 1 provides that " The Migration of Importation of such Persons as any of the States now existing shall think proper to admit, shall not be prohibited by the Congress prior to the Year one thousand eight hundred and eight, but a Tax or Duty may be imposed on such Importation, not exceeding ten dollars for each Person." This is a euphonious way of referring to the African slave trade, and it was a settlement by compromise of a question which caused some trouble in the Convention. The capitation tax was never imposed ; and, on the 2d of March, 1807, Congress prohibited the importation of slaves into any port or place within the jurisdiction of the United States from and after January 1, 1808.[1]

B. *Direct Taxes.*

Paragraph 4. " No Capitation, or other direct Tax, shall be laid, unless in Proportion to the Census or Enumeration hereinbefore directed to be taken." It has been held by the Supreme Court, in construing this clause of the Constitution, that " only capitation taxes as expressed in that instrument, and taxes on real estate" are direct taxes.[2] The same authority has settled that a carriage tax,[3] or an income

---

[1] Act of March 2, 1807, 2 Stat. 426, c. 22.
[2] *Springer* v. *United States*, 102 U. S. 586.
[3] *Hylton* v. *United States*, 3 Dall. 171.

tax,[1] or a tax on the circulation of banks,[2] or an internal revenue license tax,[3] is not a direct tax within the meaning of the Constitution. In 1861 Congress resorted to this mode of taxation, and enacted "that a direct tax of twenty millions of dollars be, and is hereby, annually laid upon the United States;[4] but in 1862, after one such tax had been assessed, it was suspended until April 1, 1865.[5] And in 1864 it was suspended until Congress should enact another law requiring it.[6] No such law was enacted; and during the late session of Congress the sums collected under the act of 1861 were restored to the States which paid them.[7]

LECTURE XIII.
Supplementary.
Direct taxes.

4. *Article II. The President.*

Section 1, paragraph 5. This paragraph confers upon the Vice-President the powers and functions of the President, in case of his removal, death, resignation, or inability. It was called into play four times during the first century of the Government — twice in consequence of the assassination of the President. The paragraph also authorizes Congress to declare what officer shall act as President in case of the removal, etc., of both President and Vice-President. The

Succession on the death of a President.

[1] *Pacific Insurance Co.* v. *Soule*, 7 Wall. 433.
[2] *Veazie Bank* v. *Fenno*, 8 Wall. 533.
[3] *License Tax Cases*, 5 Wall. 462.
[4] Act of August 5, 1861, 12 Stat. c. 45, § 8, p. 294.
[5] Act of July 1, 1862, 12 Stat. c. 119, § 119, p. 489.
[6] Act of June 30, 1864, 13 Stat. c. 173, § 173, p. 304.
[7] Act of March 2, 1891, 26 Stat. 822, c. 496.

LECTURE XIII.
Supplementary.
Succession on the
death of a Presi-
dent.
latest action of Congress in this matter confers
the power and duty in such case, first upon the
Secretary of State; then upon the Secretary
of the Treasury; then upon the Secretary of
War; then upon the Attorney General; then
upon the Postmaster General; then upon the
Secretary of the Navy; and, lastly, upon the
Secretary of the Interior.[1]   In the time of
Washington the Secretary of State, then called
Secretary for Foreign Affairs, was the ranking
officer of the Cabinet.   The others ranked according to the creation of the department over
which each presided.   Jefferson followed this rule
in all the departments, thus giving the Secretary
of State the ranking place.   The rule has been
steadily adhered to since, until Congress, for
some unknown reason, gave to the Attorney
General and the Postmaster General precedence
over the Secretary of the Navy in this statute.

Paragraph 7 of this section relates to the
oath of office to be taken by the President.   This
is usually taken in front of the Capitol, and in
the presence of both Houses of Congress.   In
President Hayes's case, however, as the fourth
of March fell upon Sunday, it was deemed wise,
in view of the peculiar circumstances, to have it
also administered at the Executive Mansion in
advance of its administration at the Capitol on
the fifth of March.

---

[1] Act of January 19, 1886, 24 Stat. 1, c. 4.

5. *Article IV. Interstate relations and duties. The Territories. Republican Form of Government.*

Article III, relating to judicial power, has been fully treated by Mr. Justice Miller in Lectures VII and VIII, leaving nothing further to be said. We will confine ourselves therefore to Article IV.

Lecture XIII.

A. *Judicial Proceedings and Public Acts and Records of a State.*

Section 1. "Full Faith and Credit shall be given in each State to the Public Acts, Records, and judicial Proceedings of every other State." It was held in a recent case, following a long line of decisions, that this "does not preclude inquiry into the jurisdiction of the court, in which a judgment is rendered over the subject matter or the parties affected by it, nor into the facts necessary to give such jurisdiction."[1] In a still more recent case[2] the matter came up in a novel form, the question being whether a judgment in a State court which was not responsive to the pleadings, rendered against a defendant who appeared, but took no part in the subsequent litigation which ended in the judgment, estopped him from contesting the matter on the merits in an action brought in another State. The court held that he was not estopped, and, in the course of its opinion, delivered by Mr. Justice Brewer, said: "The section of the Federal Con-

They are to have full faith and credit in other States.

---

[1] *Simmons.*v. *Saul,* 138 U. S. 439.
[2] *Reynolds* v. *Stockton,* 140 U. S. 254.

LECTURE XIII.
Supplementary.
They are to have
full faith and
credit in other
States.

stitution which is invoked by plaintiffs is section 1 of Article IV, which provides that 'full
faith and credit shall be given in each State
to the public acts, records, and judicial proceedings of every other State.' Under that section
the full faith and credit demanded is only that
faith and credit which the judicial proceedings
had in the other State in and of themselves
require. It does not demand that a judgment
rendered in a court of one State, without the
jurisdiction of the person, shall be recognized by
the courts of another State as valid, or that a
judgment rendered by a court which has jurisdiction of the person, but which is in no way
responsive to the issues tendered by the pleadings and is rendered in the actual absence of the
defendant, must be recognized as valid in the
courts of any other State. The requirements of
that section are fulfilled when a judgment rendered in a court of one State, which has jurisdiction of the subject matter and of the person, and
which is substantially responsive to the issues
presented by the pleadings, or is rendered under
such circumstances that it is apparent that the
defeated party was in fact heard on the matter
determined, is recognized and enforced in the
courts of another State. The scope of this constitutional provision has often been presented
to and considered by this court, although the
precise question here presented has not as yet
received its attention. It has been adjudged
that the constitutional provision does not make
a judgment rendered in one State a judgment in

another State upon which execution or other process may issue; that it does not forbid inquiry in the courts of the State to which the judgment is presented, as to the jurisdiction of the court in which it was rendered over the person, or in respect to the subject matter, or, if rendered in a proceeding *in rem*, its jurisdiction of the *res*. Without referring to the many cases in which this constitutional provision has been before this court, it is enough to notice the case of *Thompson* v. *Whitman*, 18 Wall. 457. The view developed in the opinion in that case, as well as in prior opinions cited therein, paves the way for inquiry into the question here presented. If the fact of a judgment rendered in a court of one State does not preclude inquiry in the courts of another, as to the jurisdiction of the court rendering the judgment over the person or the subject matter, it certainly also does not preclude inquiry as to whether the judgment so rendered was so far responsive to the issues tendered by the pleadings as to be a proper exercise of jurisdiction on the part of the court rendering it."

Another recent case[1] is instructive. One Bird, a citizen of Massachusetts, suspended payment March 2, 1885, Aaron Claflin & Co., a New York firm, being largely indebted to him. Butler, Hayden & Co., a Boston firm, citizens of Massachusetts, had a claim against Bird which, on the 6th of March they assigned to Fayer-

LECTURE XIII.
Supplementary.
They are to have full faith and credit in other States.

---

[1] *Cole* v. *Cunningham*, 133 U. S. 107.

LECTURE XIII.
Supplementary.
They are to have
full faith and
credit in other
States.

weather, a citizen of New York. On the 11th of March Fayerweather brought an action as such assignee against Bird as defendant, and Aaron Claflin & Co. as garnishees, to recover the amount of the assigned claim. On the 25th of March another similar suit was commenced by Fayerweather. The court found that these suits "were brought in a court of competent jurisdiction, and the attachments and proceedings were regular and in conformity with the laws of New York."

Subsequent to the commencement of these suits proceedings were had against Bird under the insolvent laws of Massachusetts, and on the 1st of June, 1885, assignees were duly appointed, to whom the insolvent's property was assigned. It was stated by the court in its opinion that "under these insolvent laws all preferences were avoided, and all attachments in favor of particular creditors dissolved."

On the 19th of June, 1885, the assignees filed a bill in equity in the Supreme Court of Massachusetts, to restrain Butler, Hayden & Co. from prosecuting the New York suits to judgment and to compel them to transfer to the assignees all the rights assigned to Fayerweather. The State court rendered the decree prayed for by the assignees; and that judgment being brought to the Supreme Court of the United States by writ of error, was affirmed by a majority of the court.

The opinion of the court was delivered by Chief Justice Fuller, who, in an opinion reviewing the authorities, said : —

"The question to be determined is, whether a decree of the Supreme Judicial Court of Massachusetts, restraining citizens of that Commonwealth from the prosecution of attachment suits in New York, brought by them for the purpose of evading the laws of their domicil, should be reversed upon the ground that such judicial action in Massachusetts was in violation of Article IV, sections 1 and 2, of the Constitution of the United States. . . . The Constitution did not mean to confer any new power upon the States, but simply to regulate the effect of their acknowledged jurisdiction over persons and things within their territory. It did not make the judgments of the States domestic judgments to all intents and purposes, but only gave a general validity, faith, and credit to them as evidence. No execution can be issued upon such judgments without a new suit in the tribunals of other States, and they enjoy, not the right of priority or privilege or lien which they have in the State where they are pronounced, but that only which the *lex fori* gives to them by its own laws, in their character of foreign judgments. . . . Great contrariety of State decision exists upon this general topic, and it may be fairly stated that, as between citizens of the State of the forum and the assignee appointed under the laws of another State, the claim of the former will be held superior to that of the latter by the courts of the former; while, as between the assignee and citizens of his own State and the State of the debtor, the laws of such State will

LECTURE XIII.
Supplementary.
They are to have
full faith and
credit in other
States.

ordinarily be applied in the State of the litigation, unless forbidden by, or inconsistent with,
the laws or policy of the latter. . . . In the
case at bar the attachment suits have not gone
to judgment, and the assignees in insolvency
have proceeded with due diligence as against
these creditors, citizens of Massachusetts, who
are seeking to evade the laws of their own
State; nor is there anything in the law or policy of New York opposed to the law or policy of
Massachusetts in the premises."

Mr. Justice Miller delivered a dissenting opinion in which Mr. Justice Field and Mr. Justice
Harlan concurred. He said: "The record introduced from the court of New York in this
case had the effect, in that State, to give Butler,
Hayden & Co. a lien on the indebtedness of
Aaron Claflin & Co. to their creditor, Bird,
which in that court would have ripened into a
judgment and been enforced. That was the
faith and credit which the laws of New York
gave to that proceeding, . . . and there was no
power in the courts of Massachusetts to inter-
rupt the course of these proceedings to the final
result. . . . When, therefore, Butler, Hayden &
Co. were sued in equity in the courts of Massachusetts, and there was produced the record of
these proceedings in the court of New York, the
question was presented to the courts of Massachusetts what effect they would give to those
proceedings. They did not give the effect which
the laws of New York gave to them. . . . It is
no answer to this to say that Butler, Hayden &

Co. were citizens of Massachusetts, and were LECTURE XIII. found within its jurisdiction. The higher law Supplementary. They are to have of the Constitution of the United States places full faith and this restraint upon the courts of Massachusetts credit in other States. in dealing even with her own citizens, and if her citizens have obtained rights in the courts of New York which have become a part of the records and judicial proceedings of those courts, no matter how the law under which those rights may be established may be opposed to the law of the State of Massachusetts, they are to be respected by the courts of Massachusetts because they are effectual over the parties and subject matter in New York, and because the Constitution of the United States and the Act of Congress of May 26, 1790,[1] assert the principle that the courts of Massachusetts must give full credit, by which is meant the same effect to the proceedings in New York, which that State gives to them."

B. *Surrender of Fugitives from Justice.*

Article IV, section 2, paragraph 2, providing Fugitives from for the surrender of fugitives from justice, is justice. found in the Articles of Confederation in substantially the same language. The legislation of Congress upon this subject will be found in sections 5278, 5279, of the Revised Statutes. The responsibility of determining whether the person demanded is a fugitive from the justice of the demanding State, rests with the Executive of the State or Territory in which the accused is

---

[1] 1 Stat. 122, c. 11. Rev. Stat. § 905.

found.[1] The case of the demanding State should be presented in some official form; either by official copy of an indictment, or by a complaint under oath. The right to demand surrender and the obligation to comply with the demand extend to all crimes and offences made punishable by the laws of the State where the offence was committed; but if the Governor of the State in which the accused is found refuses to surrender him, he cannot, through the judiciary department, be compelled to deliver him up.[2]

C. *Fugitive Slaves.*

Fugitive slaves.
Article IV, section 2, paragraph 3, of the same section provides for the surrender of fugitive slaves, and other persons " held to Service or Labor in one State, under the Laws thereof, escaping into another." It was taken from the proviso in the Sixth Article of the Ordinance of 1787 for the government of the Northwest Territory,[3] passed in Congress while the Convention was sitting.

D. *The Territories.*

The Territories.
Article IV, section 3, paragraph 2, respecting the power of Congress over the Territories, was carefully considered in a late case, and it was held that this power is general and plenary, arising from the right to acquire them. This right arises from the power of the Government

---

[1] *Ex parte Reggel,* 114 U. S. 642.

[2] *Kentucky* v. *Dennison,* 24 How. 66.

[3] Rev. Stat. 2d ed. p. 16.

to declare war and make treaties of peace, and LECTURE XIII.
in part from the power to make all needful rules Supplementary.
The Territories.
and regulations respecting the Territory or other
property of the United States. This plenary
power extends to the acts of the legislatures of
the Territories.[1]

In the case relating to the guano islands,
already referred to,[2] it was held that "by the
law of nations, when citizens or subjects of one
nation, in its name and by its authority, or with
its assent, take and hold actual, continuous, and
useful possession of territory unoccupied by any
other government or its citizens, the nation to
which they belong may exercise such jurisdiction
and for such period as it sees fit over territory
so acquired;" and that "courts of justice are
bound to take judicial notice of the territorial
extent of the jurisdiction exercised by the government whose laws they administer, or of its
recognition or denial of the sovereignty of a foreign power, as appearing from the public acts of
the legislature and executive, although those acts
are not formally put in evidence, nor in accord
with the pleadings;" and, further, that "the
island of Navassa, in the Caribbean Sea, must,
by reason of the action of the President," "be
considered as appertaining to the United States."

E. *Guaranty of a Republican Form of Government.*

Article IV, section 4. " The United States Republican form
shall guarantee to every State in this Union a of government.

---

[1] *Mormon Church* v. *United States*, 136 U. S. 1.
[2] *Jones* v. *United States*, 137 U. S. 202.

Republican Form of Government." No such provision was in the Articles of Confederation. It first appeared in the Virginia plan, of which it formed the eleventh resolution. A recent case, Chief Justice Fuller delivering the opinion, commented upon this as follows :

"By the Constitution, a republican form of government is guaranteed to every State in the Union, and the distinguishing feature of that form is the right of the people to choose their own officers for governmental administration, and pass their own laws in virtue of the legislative power reposed in representative bodies, whose legitimate acts may be said to be those of the people themselves ; but while the people are thus the source of political power, their governments, National and State, have been limited by written constitutions, and they have themselves thereby set bounds to their own power, as against the sudden impulses of mere majorities.

"In *Luther* v. *Borden*, 7 How. 1, it was held that the question which of the two opposing governments of Rhode Island, namely, the charter government or the government established by a voluntary convention, was the legitimate one, was a question for the determination of the political department, and when that department had decided, the courts were bound to take notice of the decision and follow it ; and also that, as the Supreme Court of Rhode Island, holding constitutional authority not in dispute, had decided the point, the well-settled rule applied that the courts of the United States

adopt and follow the decisions of the State Lecture XIII.
courts on questions which concern merely the Supplementary. Republican form
constitution and laws of the State. Mr. Web- of government.
ster's argument in that case took a wider
sweep and contained a masterly statement of the
American system of government, as recognizing
that the people are the source of all political
power, but that as the exercise of governmental
powers immediately by the people themselves is
impracticable, they must be exercised by representatives of the people; that the basis of representation is suffrage; that the right of suffrage
must be protected and its exercise prescribed by
previous law, and the results ascertained by
some certain rule; that through its regulated
exercise each man's power tells in the Constitution of the Government and in the enactment of
laws; that the people limit themselves in regard
to the qualifications of electors and the qualifications of the elected, and to certain forms for the
conduct of elections; that our liberty is the liberty secured by the regular action of popular
power, taking place and ascertained in accordance with legal and authentic modes; and that
the Constitution and laws do not proceed on the
ground of revolution or any right of revolution,
but on the idea of results achieved by orderly
action under the authority of existing governments, proceedings outside of which are not
contemplated by our institutions. Webster's
Works, vol. 6, p. 217." [1]

---

[1] *In re Duncan, Petitioner,* 139 U. S. 449, 461.

6. *Article V. Amendments to the Constitution.*

This article makes no provision for the withdrawal of its ratification by a State which has ratified the amendment, the withdrawal taking place before the necessary assent of three-fourths of the States is secured.

In the case of the Fourteenth Amendment there were some States which rejected the amendment and subsequently ratified it. Their votes were counted in making the necessary three-fourths. There were other States (New Jersey and Ohio) which ratified it and withdrew the ratification before the result was obtained. The votes of all were counted in making up the necessary two-thirds required by the Constitution.

In the case of the Fifteenth Amendment, one State attempted to withdraw its assent; but it was immaterial whether it was counted or not, as there were sufficient ratifying States without it.

The subject is considered further in connection with those amendments.

7. *Article VI. Debts of the United States. Supremacy of the Constitution.*

A. *Revolutionary Debt of the United States.*

Paragraph 1 provides for the assumption by the new Government of the existing debt of the old Government. This was done by an early act of Congress, in which, after reciting that "justice and the support of public credit require that provision should be made for fulfilling the engagements of the United States in respect to their foreign debt, and for funding their domestic debt upon equitable and satisfactory terms," legislative provisions were enacted which restored confidence and credit, and inspired faith in the new Government.   In a later section in the act, after reciting that "whereas a provision for the debts of the respective States by the United States, would be greatly conducive to an orderly, economical, and effectual arrangement of the public finances," a loan of $21,500,000 was proposed to the different States, to assist them in restoring their credit.[1]

LECTURE XIII.
Supplementary.
Revolutionary
debt of the United
States.

B.   *The Constitution the Supreme Law.*

Article VI, paragraph 2.   "This Constitution, and the Laws of the United States, which shall be made in Pursuance thereof; and all Treaties made, or which shall be made, under the authority of the United States, shall be the supreme Law of the Land."   It is elementary that a State statute, in conflict with a law of Congress upon a subject about which Congress may constitutionally legislate, is void.   So, too, a State statute is void if it relates to a subject which is vested exclusively in Congress by the

Supremacy of the
Constitution.

---

[1] Act of August 4, 1790, 1 Stat. 138, c. 34.   See also Act of August 10, 1790, 1 Stat. 180, c. 39 ; Act of August 12, 1790, 1 Stat. 186, c. 47 ; Act of December 27, 1700, 1 Stat. 188, c. 1 ; Act of May 8, 1792, 1 Stat. 281, c. 38 ; Act of March 2, 1793, 1 Stat. 338, c. 26 ; Act of May 30, 1794, 1 Stat. 370, c. 36 ; Act of January 28, 1795, 1 Stat. 410, c. 13 ; Act of February 19, 1796, 1 Stat. 448, c. 2 ; Act of March 3, 1797, 1 Stat. 516, c. 25.

Constitution.[1] A treaty, although its obligations in regard to the other party to it remain in force, is, as a part of the supreme law of the land, subject to be revoked or modified as to its municipal operation, by act of Congress, like any other law.[2]

8. *The First Ten Amendments.*

The first Congress proposed at its first session, in the manner prescribed by Article V of the Constitution, twelve amendments for the consideration of the several States. Ten of these were ratified by the States as shown in the margin.[3] The two which were never ratified are also printed in the margin.[4] The ratified articles

---

[1] *Head Money Cases*, 112 U. S. 580; *Wabash, St. Louis & Pacific Railway Co.* v. *Illinois*, 118 U. S. 557.

[2] *Head Money Cases*, 112 U. S. 580.

[3] By New Jersey, 20th November, 1789; by Maryland, 19th December, 1789; by North Carolina, 22d December, 1789; by South Carolina, 19th January, 1790; by New Hampshire, 25th January, 1790; by Delaware, 28th January, 1790; by Pennsylvania, 10th March, 1790; by New York, 27th March, 1790; by Rhode Island, 15th June, 1790; by Vermont, 3d November, 1791; by Virginia, 15th December, 1791.

[4] Article the First. After the first enumeration required by the First Article of the Constitution, there shall be one Representative for every thirty thousand, until the number shall amount to one hundred, after which, the proportion shall be so regulated by Congress, that there shall not be less than one hundred Representatives, nor less than one Representative for every forty thousand persons, until the number of Representatives shall amount to two hundred; after which the proportion shall be so regulated by Congress, that there shall not be less than two hundred Representatives, nor more than one Representative for every fifty thousand persons.

Article Second. No law, varying the compensation for the services of the Senators and Representatives, shall take effect, until an election of Representatives shall have intervened.

are known as the first ten amendments, and LECTURE XIII.
have been repeatedly held to be restraints upon Supplementary. The first ten
the power of Congress, and not restraints upon amendments.
the power of the States.

A. *Amendment I.*

This amendment provides that " Congress shall First Amendment.
make no law respecting an establishment of religion or prohibiting the free exercise thereof,"
etc.   In deciding the *Mormon Cases*, the Supreme
Court held that the pretence of a religious belief
in polygamy could not deprive Congress of the
power to prohibit it, as well as all other open
offences, against the enlightened sentiment of
mankind.[1]

B. *Amendment II.*

" A well regulated Militia, being necessary to Second Amend-
the security of a free State, the right of the ment.
people to bear Arms shall not be infringed."
This provision is a limitation only on the power
of Congress, and not upon the power of the
States; and, unless restrained by their own constitutions, State legislatures may enact statutes
to control and regulate all organizations, drilling
and parading of military bodies and associa-
tions, except those which are authorized by the
militia laws of the United States.[2]

---

[1] *Mormon Church* v. *United States,* 136 U. S. 1.   See also
Reynolds v. *United States,* 98 U. S. 145 ; *Murphy* v. *Ramsey,* 114
U. S. 15.

[2] *Presser* v. *Illinois,* 116 U. S. 252.

C. *Amendment III.*

" No Soldier shall, in time of peace, be quartered in any house, without the consent of the
owner, nor in time of war, but in a manner to
be prescribed by law." This amendment seems
to have been thought necessary. It does not
appear to have been the subject of judicial
exposition; and it is so thoroughly in accord
with all our ideas, that further comment is
unnecessary.

D. *Amendments IV and V.*

" The right of the people to be secure in their
persons, houses, papers, and effects, against unreasonable searches and seizures, shall not be
violated, and no warrants shall issue, but upon
probable cause, supported by oath or affirmation, and particularly describing the place to be
searched, and the persons or things to be
seized."

" No person shall be held to answer for a
capital, or otherwise infamous crime, unless on
a presentment or indictment of a Grand Jury,
except in cases arising in the land or naval
forces, or in the militia, when in actual service
in time of war or public danger; nor shall any
person be subject for the same offence to be
twice put in jeopardy of life or limb; nor shall
be compelled in any criminal case to be a witness against himself, nor be deprived of life,
liberty, or property, without due process of law;
nor shall private property be taken for public
use, without just compensation."

These two amendments were considered
together by the Supreme Court in a recent
case,[1] in which a section of an act to amend the
customs revenue laws,[2] which authorized a court
of the United States, in revenue cases, on motion
of the attorney for the Government, to require
the defendant to produce in court his private
books, invoices, and papers, or else the allegations of the Government be taken as confessed,
was brought before it for construction.

The court gave the case a careful consideration, and, in deciding it, delivered an opinion
which may be read with profit. The substance
of the decision was, that these provisions were
repugnant both to the Fourth and Fifth Amendments to the Constitution.

As to the Fourth Amendment, it was held
that no actual entry upon premises, and physi-
cal search for and seizure of papers, was necessary in order to constitute an unreasonable
search and seizure within the meaning of that
amendment; that a compulsory production of
them, to be used against their owner in a criminal or penal proceeding, or for a forfeiture, was
within the spirit and meaning of that amendment; and that it was equivalent to a compulsory production of papers, to make their non-
production a confession of the allegations which
it was pretended they would prove.

As to the Fifth Amendment, it was held that

---

[1] *Boyd* v. *The United States*, 116 U. S. 616.
[2] Act of June 22, 1874, c. 391, 18 Stat. 186.

a proceeding to forfeit a person's goods for an offence against the law, though civil in form, and whether *in rem* or *in personam* was in fact a criminal case within the meaning of the provision in that amendment, that "no person shall be compelled, in any criminal case, to be a witness against himself;" and that the seizure or compulsory production of a man's private papers, to be used in evidence against him, was equivalent to compelling him to be a witness against himself, and, in a prosecution for a crime, penalty, or forfeiture, was within the prohibition of that amendment.

As to both amendments, it was held that they related to the personal security of the citizen; that they nearly run into and mutually throw light upon each other; that when the thing forbidden in the Fifth Amendment — the compelling a man to be a witness against himself — is the object of a search and seizure of his private papers, it is an "unreasonable search and seizure," within the meaning of the Fourth Amendment; and that, as a rule, "constitutional provisions for the security of person and property should be liberally construed."

E. *Amendments VI and VII.*

The Sixth Amendment relates to jury trials in criminal cases, and the Seventh Amendment to jury trials in suits at the common law, where the value in controversy shall exceed twenty dollars. Both have been fully considered.

F. *Amendment VIII.*

"Excessive bail shall not be required, nor excessive fines imposed, nor cruel and unusual punishments inflicted." These provisions apply to National and not to State legislation.[1]

In *Kemmler's Case*,[2] where an attempt was made to convince the court that execution by the application of an electric current was a "cruel and unusual punishment within the intent of the Eighth Amendment," the court said: "The provision in reference to cruel and unusual punishments was taken from the well-known Act of Parliament of 1688, entitled 'An act declaring the rights and liberties of the subject, and settling the succession of the crown;' in which, after rehearsing various grounds of grievance, and, among others, that excessive bail hath been required of persons committed in criminal cases, to elude the benefits of the laws made for the liberty of the subject; and excessive fines have been imposed; and illegal and cruel punishments inflicted. This Declaration of Rights had reference to the acts of the executive and judicial departments of the government of England; but the language in question, as used in the constitution of the State of New York, was intended particularly to operate upon the legislature of the State, to whose control the punishment of crime was almost entirely confided. So that, if the punishment prescribed for an

LECTURE XIII. Supplementary. Eighth Amendment.

---

[1] *Pervear* v. *Commonwealth*, 5 Wall. 475.   [2] 136 U. S. 436.

offence against the laws of the State were manifestly cruel and unreasonable, as burning at the stake, crucifixion, breaking on the wheel, or the like, it would be the duty of the courts to adjudge such penalties to be within the constitutional prohibition. And we think this equally true of the Eighth Amendment, in its application to Congress."

G. *Amendment IX.*

"The enumeration in the Constitution, of certain rights, shall not be construed to deny or disparage others retained by the people." This principle of construction is manifestly just, and would doubtless have obtained, even if it had not been inserted in the Constitution.

H. *Amendment X.*

"The powers not delegated to the United States by the Constitution, nor prohibited by it to the States, are reserved to the States respectively or to the people." The old Articles of Confederation presented this principle of construction in a much broader shape. Article II provided that "Each State retains its sovereignty, freedom, and independence, and every power, jurisdiction, and right which is not, by this confederation, expressly delegated to the United States in Congress assembled." As originally adopted the Constitution contained no equivalent for this canon of construction. The Tenth Amendment was intended to serve as a compromise between the two extreme

views.   It will be observed that the controlling
word, "expressly," found in the Articles of Confederation, is omitted in the amendment.   Although the advocates of State's rights did not
fail to contend that the two were substantial
equivalents, notwithstanding the omission, their
views were never adopted by the judicial department, and it may now be said to be well
settled that Congress, under the operation of
the eighteenth paragraph of section 8, Article I,
which authorizes it "to make all laws which
shall be necessary and proper for carrying into
execution the foregoing powers," has by implication every power necessary and proper for
fully carrying into execution the powers expressly conferred.[1]   One of the latest expressions of the court on this point is as follows:
" A constitution, establishing a frame of government, declaring fundamental principles, and
creating a national sovereignty, and intended to
endure for ages, and to be adapted to the
various crises of human affairs, is not to be
interpreted with the strictness of a private
contract.   The Constitution of the United
States, by apt words of designation or general
description, marks the outlines of the powers
granted to the national legislature; but it does
not undertake, with the precision and detail of
a code of laws, to enumerate the subdivisions of
those powers, or to specify all the means by
which they may be carried into execution."

---

[1] *McCulloch v. Maryland*, 4 Wheat. 316.

Commenting upon the eighteenth paragraph of section 8, just cited, the court continued : " By the settled construction and the only reasonable interpretation of this clause, the words ' necessary and proper' are not limited to such measures as are absolutely and indispensably necessary, without which the powers granted must fail of execution; but they include all appropriate means which are conducive or adapted to the end to be accomplished, and which, in the judgment of Congress, will most advantageously effect it." And, referring to *McCulloch* v. *Maryland,* the court said : " The rule of interpretation thus laid down has been constantly adhered to and acted on by this court." [1]

9. *The Eleventh Amendment.*

This amendment, which relates to suits against States, has been already fully considered both in the lectures, and in the notes upon them. *Chisholm* v. *Georgia,*[2] was the direct and impelling cause for it. The States came out from the war of the revolution burdened with debt. Although Congress had made provision for taking care of a part of that debt, a large amount was still outstanding. When they learned that a State could be sued in the Federal courts, they hurried to make that an impossibility thereafter, Massachusetts taking the lead. The Eleventh Amendment, which effected that result, was

---

[1] *Legal Tender Case,* 110 U. S. 421, 439, 440, 441.
[2] 2 Dall. 419.

proposed by Congress March 5, 1794, and was Lecture XIII. Supplementary. Eleventh Amend-ment. proclaimed January 8, 1798. It is a little remarkable that the decision which made it necessary should have been practically overruled nearly a hundred years after it was made.[1]

10. *The Twelfth Amendment.*

This amendment grew out of the trouble in Twelfth Amend-ment. the election of Mr. Jefferson as President. It was proposed by Congress to the legislatures of the several States December 12, 1803, and was proclaimed as adopted September 25, 1804.

11. *The Thirteenth, Fourteenth, and Fifteenth Amendments.*

All these amendments were the outcome of Thirteenth, Four-teenth, and Fifteenth Amend-ments. the war and of the Reconstruction which fol-lowed it. The Thirteenth was proposed to the States by Congress by joint resolution dated February 1, 1865, before the close of the war, and was promulgated by the Secretary of State pursuant to law, as a part of the Constitution, December 18, 1865, having received the assent of the legislatures of twenty-seven States, being three-fourths of the States, thirty-six in all.[2]

The Fourteenth Amendment was submitted by Congress to the States June 16, 1866,[3] after the majority in that body and President John-son had separated on the question of reconstruc-tion. Mr. Seward, the Secretary of State, issued

---

[1] *Hans v. Louisiana*, 134 U. S. 1.   [2] See 13 Stat. 774, 775.
[3] 14 Stat. 358 ; Joint Resolution No. 48.

two promulgations of this amendment. The first was dated July 20, 1868.[1] It recited that no law " expressly or by conclusive implication, authorizes the Secretary of State to determine and decide doubtful questions as to the authenticity of the organization of State legislatures, or as to the power of any State legislature to recall a previous act or resolution of ratification of any amendment proposed to the Constitution." It then further recited that the assent of Arkansas, Florida, North Carolina, Louisiana, South Carolina, and Alabama had been given " by newly constituted and newly established bodies, avowing themselves to be and acting as the legislatures respectively" of those States; and that the assent of Ohio and New Jersey, once given, had been withdrawn by subsequent resolutions of their legislatures, and that it was " deemed a matter of doubt and uncertainty whether such resolutions are not irregular, invalid, and therefore ineffectual for withdrawing the consent of the said two States." The document closed by saying that " if the resolutions of the legislatures of Ohio and New Jersey, ratifying the aforesaid amendment, are to be deemed as remaining of full force and effect, . . . then the aforesaid amendment has been ratified."

This document, issued on the 20th. of June, 1868, was not accompanied by the order of publication required by the Act of April 20, 1818.[2]

---

[1] 15 Stat. 706; Proclamation No. 11.
[2] 3 Stat. 439, c. 80, § 2.

On the next day, July 21, 1868, Congress, by Lecture XIII. a joint resolution, resolved: [1] " Whereas the leg- Supplementary. islatures of the States of . . . New Jersey . . . Amendment how Ohio . . . Arkansas, Florida, North Carolina, ratified. Alabama, South Carolina, and Louisiana [naming twenty-nine States, including the Southern States supposed doubtful, and the Northern States which attempted to withdraw their ratificatioris] have ratified the Fourteenth Article of Amendment, . . . therefore *Resolved* . . . that said Fourteenth Article is hereby declared to be a part of the Constitution of the United States, and it shall be duly promulgated as such by the Secretary of State."

This seemed to solve Mr. Seward's doubts. On the 28th of July, 1868, he issued a second proclamation,[2] ordering the amendment published in the newspapers, and certifying that it had " been adopted " and that it had " become valid to all intents and purposes as a part of the Constitution of the United States." Since then many cases have been before the Supreme Court, involving the construction of this article; but in no one has any question been raised as to its ratification and incorporation into the Constitution.

In the case of the Fifteenth Amendment, the legislature of New York in 1870 attempted to withdraw the ratification given by its predecessor in 1869. The Secretary of State, Mr. Fish, in proclaiming the adoption of the amendment, said: " It appears from an official document on

---

[1] 15 Stat. 709.   [2] 15 Stat. 708.

file that the legislature of the State of New York has since passed resolutions claiming to withdraw the said ratification."[1]   In this case it would have made no difference in the result if the withdrawal had been treated as valid.

A. *The Thirteenth Amendment.*

Thirteenth Amendment relates to slavery.

This amendment relates entirely to slavery and involuntary servitude (which it abolishes) ; and, although by its reflex action, it establishes universal freedom in the United States, and Congress may probably pass laws directly enforcing its provisions, yet such legislative power extends only to the subject of slavery and its incidents; and the denial of equal accommodations in inns, public conveyances, and places of public amusement (which is forbidden by the sections in question), imposes no badge of slavery or involuntary servitude upon the party, but at most, infringes rights which are protected from State aggression by the Fourteenth Amendment.[2]

Mr. Justice Miller, in his opinion in the *Slaughter House Cases*, from which he quotes at length in Lecture VIII, makes this clear. In the headnote to that case, in the structure of which his hand is apparent, it is said of the three amendments which followed the war, that the main purpose of all was the freedom of the African race, the security and perpetuation of that freedom, and their protection from the

---

[1] 16 Stat. 1131.   [2] *Civil Rights Cases,* 109 U. S. 3.

oppressions of the white men who had formerly held them in slavery.

While the Thirteenth Article of Amendment was intended primarily to abolish African slavery, it equally forbids Mexican peonage or the Chinese coolie trade, when they amount to slavery or involuntary servitude; and the use of the word " servitude " is intended to prohibit all forms of involuntary slavery of whatever class or name.[1]

So, too, its effect is limited to matters subsequent to its adoption. A contract for the sale of a slave made before the war, was enforced in the courts after the adoption of this amendment;[2] and in another, and very recent case, a surviving partner, in possession of slaves and using them on the partnership plantation during the war, was held accountable for the value of their services.[3]

The first and second sections of the Civil Rights Act of March 1, 1875, are unconstitutional enactments as applied to the several States, not being authorized either by the Thirteenth or Fourteenth Amendments.[4]

B. *The Fourteenth Amendment.*

This amendment is a much larger matter. (1) It relates to citizenship: and (2) to the privileges and immunities of citizens. (3) It im-

---

1 *Slaughter House Cases*, 16 Wall. 36.
2 *Osborn* v. *Nicholson*, 13 Wall. 654.
3 *Clay* v. *Field*, 138 U. S. 464.
4 *Civil Rights Cases*, 109 U. S. 3.

LECTURE XIII.
Supplementary.
The Fourteenth
Amendment.
General consider-
ations.

poses limitations upon State power. (4) It deals with the apportionment of representation. (5) It excludes certain classes of persons from the exercise of certain political privileges: and (6) it forbids the invalidating of the public debt of the United States, or the assumption of any debt incurred in aid of the rebellion or any claim for the loss or emancipation of slaves. I shall attempt to classify the leading cases under these heads. Before doing this some general propositions, decided by the Supreme Court, should be stated, which are applicable to all.

That amendment was ordained to secure equal rights to all persons. To render its purpose effectual, Congress is vested with power to enforce its provisions by appropriate legislation. Such legislation must act, not upon the abstract thing denominated a State, but upon the persons who are its agents in the denial of the rights which were intended to be secured. Such is the Act of March 1, 1875, and it is fully authorized by the Constitution.[1]

On the other hand, it was not designed to interfere with the power of a State to protect the lives, liberty, and property of its citizens, nor with the exercise of that power in the adjudications of the courts of the State in administering the process provided by its laws. Therefore, when a person accused of crime within a State is subjected, like all other persons in the State, to the law in its regular course

---

[1] *Ex parte Virginia*, 100 U. S. 339.

of administration in courts of justice, the judgment so arrived at cannot be held to be an unrestrained and arbitrary exercise of power, and
therefore void.[1]

Nor can a State be deemed guilty of violating
its obligations under the Constitution because
its highest court, while acting within its jurisdiction, decides erroneously.[2]

In the *Civil Rights Cases*[3] it is held that this
amendment is prohibitory upon the States only,
and that the legislation authorized to be
adopted by Congress for enforcing it is not
direct legislation on the matters respecting
which the States are prohibited from making or
enforcing certain laws, or doing certain acts,
but is *corrective* legislation, such as may be
necessary or proper for counteracting and re-
dressing the effects of such laws or acts.

Nor does this amendment impair in any way
the police power of the States, nor limit the
subjects in relation to which it may be exercised
for the protection of its citizens.[4]

A municipal ordinance prohibiting from wash-
ing and ironing in public laundries and wash-
houses, within defined territorial limits, from ten
o'clock at night to six in the morning, is a purely
police regulation, within the competency of a
municipality possessed of the ordinary powers.[5]

---

[1] *In re Converse*, 137 U. S. 624.   [2] Ib.
[3] *Civil Rights Cases*, 109 U. S. 3.
[4] *Barbier* v. *Connolly*, 113 U. S. 27; *Soon Hing* v. *Crowley*,
113 U. S. 703.
[5] *Barbier* v. *Connolly*, 113 U. S. 27; see also *Powell* v. *Pennsylvania*, 127 U. S. 678.

LECTURE XIII.
Supplementary.
General consider-
ations.

Rights of citizen-
ship.

The guarantees of protection˙ extend to all persons within the territorial. jurisdiction of the United States, without regard to differences of race, color, or nationality;[1] and to corporations.[2]

It was not intended by it to compel the States to adopt an iron rule of equal taxation.[3]

1. *Citizenship.*

The Fourteenth Amendment did not radically change the whole theory of the relations of the State and Federal Governments to each other, and of both governments to the people. The same person may be at the same time a citizen of the United States and a citizen of the State.[4]

The right to practice law in the State courts is not a privilege or immunity of a citizen of the United States, within the meaning of the first section of the Fourteenth Article of Amendment of the Constitution of the United States. The power of a State to prescribe the qualifications for admission to the bar of its own courts is unaffected by that amendment, and the courts cannot inquire into the reasonableness or propriety of the rules it may prescribe.[5]

The right of suffrage was not necessarily one of the privileges or immunities of citizenship before the adoption of the Fourteenth Amend-

[1] *Yick Wo.* v. *Hopkins*, 118 U. S. 356.

[2] *Santa Clara County* v. *Southern Pacific Railroad*, 118 U. S. 394.

[3] *Bell Gap Railroad Co.* v. *Pennsylvania*, 134 U. S. 232.

[4] *In re Kemmler*, 136 U. S. 436, 448.

[5] *Bradwell* v. *The State*, 16 Wall. 130.

ment, and that amendment does not add to
these privileges and immunities. It simply furnishes additional guaranty for the protection of
such as the citizen already had. At the time of
the adoption of that amendment, suffrage was
not coextensive with the citizenship of the
States; nor was it at the time of the adoption
of the Constitution. Neither the Constitution
nor the Fourteenth Amendment made all citizens voters. A provision in a State Constitution which confines the right of voting to *male*
citizens of the United States, " is no violation of
the Federal Constitution. In such a State
women have no right to vote." [1]

The Fourteenth Amendment prohibits a State
from depriving any person of life, liberty, or
property, without due process of law, and from
denying to any person within its jurisdiction the
equal protection of the laws; but it adds nothing to the rights of one citizen as against
another. It simply furnishes an additional
guaranty against any encroachment by the
States upon the fundamental rights which belong to every citizen as a member of society.
The duty of protecting all its citizens in the
enjoyment of an equality of rights was originally assumed by the States, and it still remains
there. The only obligation resting upon the
United States is to see that the States do not
deny the right. This the amendment guarantees, but no more. The power of the National

---

[1] *Minor* v. *Happersett*, 21 Wall. 162.

Government is limited to the enforcement of
this guaranty.[1]

An Indian, born a member of one of the
Indian tribes within the United States, which
still exists and is recognized as a tribe by the
Government of the United States, who has
voluntarily separated himself from his tribe, and
taken up his residence among the white citizens
of a State, but who has not been naturalized, or
taxed, or recognized as a citizen, either by the
United States or by the State, is not a citizen of
the United States, within the meaning of the
first section of the Fourteenth Article of Amendment of the Constitution.[2]

The provision in the Fourteenth Amendment
that "no State shall make or enforce any law
which shall abridge the privileges or immunities
of citizens of the United States," does not prevent a State from passing such laws to regulate
the privileges and immunities of its own citizens
as do not abridge their privileges and immunities as citizens of the United States.[3]

Those subjects of the Emperor of China who
have the right to temporarily or permanently
reside within the United States, are entitled to
enjoy the protection guaranteed by the Constitution and afforded by the laws.[4]

Corporations are persons within the meaning
of the clauses of the Fourteenth Amendment to

---

[1] *United States* v. *Cruikshank*, 92 U. S. 542.
[2] *Elk* v. *Wilkins*, 112 U. S. 94.
[3] *Presser* v. *Illinois*, 116 U. S. 252.
[4] *Yick Wo* v. *Hopkins*, 118 U. S. 356.

the Constitution concerning the deprivation of property, and concerning the equal protection of the laws.[1]

LECTURE XIII.
Supplementary.
Rights of citizen-ship.

2. *Privileges and Immunities of Citizens.*

The privileges and immunities of citizens of the United States, as distinguished from the privileges and immunities of citizens of the States, are, indeed, protected by this amendment; but those are privileges and immunities arising out of the nature and essential character of the National Government, and granted or secured by the Constitution of the United States.[2]

Privileges and immunities which a State may not take away.

A trial by jury in suits at common law pending in the State courts is not a privilege or immunity of national citizenship, which the States are forbidden by the Fourteenth Amendment of the Constitution to abridge.[3]

3. *Limitations upon State Powers.*

The article provides that "no State shall make or enforce any law which shall abridge the privileges or immunities of citizens of the United States." That limitation we have already considered. It further provides: "nor shall any State deprive any person of life, liberty, or property, without due process of law; nor deny to any person within its jurisdiction the equal protection of the laws." On these prohibitions there are many decisions.

Limitations upon the powers of a State.

---

[1] *Santa Clara County* v. *Southern Pacific Railroad*, 118 U. S. 394, and *Pembina Mining Co.* v. *Pennsylvania*, 125 U. S. 181.

[2] *In re Kemmler*, 136 U. S. 436, 448.

[3] *Walker* v. *Sauvinet*, 92 U. S. 90.

In a very late case it was held, on careful consideration of a statute of California, providing for the widening of a street in San Francisco, that it provided due process of law for taking the property necessary for that purpose; and that mere errors in the administration of a State statute which was not repugnant to the Constitution, would not authorize the court to hold that the State had deprived, or was about to deprive a party of his property without due process of law.[1]

Law, in its regular course of administration through the courts of law, is due process of law, and, when it is secured by the law of the State, the requirements of the Fourteenth Amendment are satisfied. Due process of law, within the meaning of that amendment, is secured, if the laws operate on all alike, and do not subject the individual to an arbitrary exercise of the powers of government.[2]

When a person accused of crime within a State is subjected, like all other persons in the State, to the law in its regular course of administration in the courts of justice, the judgments so arrived at cannot be held to be such an unrestrained and arbitrary exercise of power as to be utterly void.[3]

The section of the act entitled " An act to protect all citizens in their civil and legal rights," approved March 1, 1875, 18 Stat. 335, c. 114,

---

[1] *Lent* v. *Tillson*, 140 U. S. 316.

[2] *Leeper* v. *Texas*, 139 U. S. 712.

[3] *In re Converse*, 137 U. S. 624.

which enacts that "no citizen, possessing all
other qualifications which are or may be prescribed by law, shall be disqualified from service
as grand or petit juror in any court of the United
States, or of any State on account of race, color,
or previous condition of servitude; and any officer
or other person, charged with any duty in the selection or summoning of jurors, who shall exclude or fail to summon any citizen for the cause
aforesaid, shall, on conviction thereof, be deemed
guilty of a misdemeanor, and be fined not more
than $5000," was examined and held author-
ized by the Thirteenth and Fourteenth Amendments of the Constitution. The inhibition
contained in the Fourteenth Amendment means
that no agency of the State, or of the officers or
agents by whom her powers are exerted, shall
deny to any person within her jurisdiction the
equal protection of the laws. Whoever by virtue
of his public position under a State government
deprives another of life, liberty, or property,
without due process of law, or denies or takes
away the equal protection of the laws, violates
that inhibition, and as he acts in the name of
and for the State, and is clothed with her power,
his act is her act. Otherwise the inhibition has
no meaning, and the State has clothed one of
her agents with power to annul or evade it.[1]

The State of Louisiana passed an act entitled
"An act to regulate proceedings in contestation
between persons claiming a judicial office."

---

[1] *Ex parte Virginia*, 100 U. S. 339.

LECTURE XIII.
Supplementary.
Fourteenth
Amendment.
Limitations upon
the powers of a
State.

Held, that the State, by proceedings under this act, which resulted in a judgment adverse to the title of the plaintiff in error to a certain judicial office, did not, through her judiciary, violate that clause of the Fourteenth Amendment to the Constitution of the United States which declares, " nor shall any State deprive any person of life, liberty, or property, without due process of law." [1]

Down to the time of the adoption of the Fourteenth Amendment, it was not supposed that statutes regulating the use, or even the price of the use, of private property necessarily deprived an owner of his property without due process of law. Under some circumstances they may, but not under all. The amendment does not change the law in this particular; it simply prevents the States from doing that which will operate as such deprivation. [2]

A law authorizing the imposition of a tax or assessment upon property according to its value does not infringe that provision of the Fourteenth Amendment to the Constitution, which declares that no State shall deprive any person of property without due process of law, if the owner has an opportunity to question the validity or the amount of it, either before that amount is determined, or in subsequent proceedings for its collection. [3]

A statute of a State, authorizing any person

---

[1] *Kennard* v. *Louisiana*, 92 U. S. 480.
[2] *Munn* v. *Illinois*, 94 U. S. 113.
[3] *Hagar* v. *Reclamation District*, 111 U. S. 701.

to erect and maintain on his own land a water- mill and mill-dam upon and across any stream not navigable, paying to the owners of lands flowed damages assessed in a judicial proceed- ing, does not deprive them of their property without due process of law, in violation of the Fourteenth Amendment.[1]

An act making water rates a charge upon lands in a municipality, prior to the lien of all incumbrances, does no violation, so far as it affects mortgages on such lands made after the passage of the act, to that portion of the Fourteenth Amendment to the Constitution which declares that no State shall deprive any person of property without due process of law.[2]

The statute of New Jersey of March 8, 1871, providing for the drainage of any tract of low or marshy land within the State, upon proceedings instituted by at least five owners of separate lots of land included in the tract, and for the assessment by commissioners, after notice and hearing, of the expenses upon all the owners, does not deprive them of their property without due process of law, nor deny to them the equal protection of the laws, within the meaning of the Fourteenth Amendment of the Constitution of the United States.[3]

A State statute for raising public revenue by the assessment and collection of taxes, which

---

[1] *Head* v. *Amoskeag Manufacturing Co.*, 113 U. S. 9.

[2] *Provident Institution for Savings* v. *Jersey City*, 113 U. S. 506.

[3] *Wurts* v. *Hoagland*, 114 U. S. 606.

LECTURE XIII.
Supplementary.
Fourteenth
Amendment.
Limitations upon
the powers of a
State.

gives notice of the proposed assessment to an owner of property to be affected, by requiring him at a time named to present a statement of his property, with his estimate of its value, to a designated official charged with the duty of receiving the statement, which fixes time and place for public sessions of other officials, at which this statement and estimate are to be considered, where the official valuation is to be made, and when and where the party interested has the right to be present and to be heard; and which affords him opportunity in a suit at law for the collection of the tax, to judicially contest the validity of the proceeding, does not necessarily deprive him of his property without "due process of law," within the meaning of the Fourteenth Amendment.[1]

A State law for the valuation of property and the assessment of taxes thereon, which provides for the classification of property, subject to its provisions, into different classes, which makes for one class one set of provisions as to modes and methods of ascertaining the value, and as to right of appeal, and different provisions for another class as to those subjects, but which provides for the impartial application of the same means and methods to all constituents of each class, so that the law shall operate equally and uniformly on all persons in similar circumstances, denies to no person affected by it "equal protection of the laws" within the meaning of

---

[1] *Kentucky Railroad Tax Cases*, 115 U. S. 321.

the Fourteenth Amendment to the Constitution of the United States.[1]

LECTURE XIII.
Supplementary.
Fourteenth
Amendment.
Limitations upon
the powers of a
state.

A statute of a State requiring every railroad corporation in the State to erect and maintain fences and cattle guards on the sides of its road, and, if it does not do so, making it liable in double the amount of damages occasioned thereby and done by its agents, cars, or engines to cattle or other animals on its road, does not deprive a railroad corporation, against which such double damages are recovered, of its property without due process of law, or deny it the equal protection of the laws in violation of the Fourteenth Article of Amendment.[2]

The provisions in the Fourteenth Amendment, that "no State shall deny to any person within its jurisdiction the equal protection of the laws," do not prohibit a State from requiring for the admission within its limits of a corporation of another State such conditions as it chooses.[3]

If the legislature of a State, in the exercise of its power of taxation, directs the expense of laying out, grading or repairing a street to be assessed upon the owners of lands benefited thereby; and determines the whole amount of the tax, and further determines what lands are benefited by the improvement; and provides for notice to and hearing of each owner, at some stage of the proceedings, upon the question what

---

[1] *Kentucky Railroad Tax Cases*, 115 U. S. 321.
[2] *Missouri Pacific Railway Co.* v. *Humes*, 115 U. S. 512.
[3] *Pembina Mining Co.* v. *Pennsylvania*, 125 U. S. 181.

LECTURE XIII.
Supplementary.
Fourteenth
Amendment.
Limitations upon
the powers of a
State.

proportion of the tax shall be assessed upon his land ; there is no taking of his property without due process of law, in violation of the Fourteenth Amendment.[1]

The statute of Kansas, which provides that "every railroad company organized or doing business in this State shall be liable for all damages done to any employé of such company, in consequence of any negligence of its agents, or by any mismanagement of its engineers or other employés, to any person sustaining such damage," does not deprive a railroad company of its property without due process of law; and does not deny to it the equal protection of the laws; and is not in conflict with the Fourteenth Amendment to the Constitution of the United States in either of these respects.[2]

The Kentucky statute of March 24, 1882, which authorizes the city government of Louisville to open and improve streets and assess the cost thereof on the owners of adjoining lots, does not deprive such owners of their property without due process of law, and does not deny them the equal protection of the laws, and is not repugnant to Section 1 of the Fourteenth Amendment to the Constitution of the United States.[3]

The provision in the Code of Iowa, Section 1289, which authorizes the recovery of "double the value of the stock killed or damages caused thereto," by a railroad, when the injury took place

---

[1] *Spencer* v. *Merchant*, 125 U. S. 345.

[2] *Missouri Pacific Railway Co.* v. *Mackey*, 127 U. S. 205.

[3] *Walston* v. *Nevin*, 128 U. S. 578.

at a point on the road where the corporation
had a right to erect a fence and failed to do so,
and when it was not " occasioned by the wilful
act of the owner or his agent," is not in conflict
with the Fourteenth Amendment to the Constitution, either as depriving the company of property without due process of law, or as denying
to it the equal protection of the laws.[1]

A tax which is imposed by a State statute
upon " the corporate franchise or business " of
all corporations incorporated under any law of
the State or of any other State or country, and
doing business within the State, and which is
measured by the extent of the dividends of the
corporation in the current year, is a tax upon
the right or privilege to be a corporation and to
do business within the State in a corporate
capacity, and is not a tax upon the privilege or
franchise which, when incorporated, the company may exercise ; and being thus construed,
its imposition upon the dividends of the company
does not violate the provisions of the statute
exempting bonds of the United States from
taxation, 12 Stat. 346, c. 33, § 2, although a
portion of the dividends may be derived from
interest on capital invested in such bonds.[2]

Such a tax is not in conflict with the last
clause of the first section of the Fourteenth
Amendment to the Constitution of the United
States, declaring that no State shall deprive any

---

[1] *Minneapolis & St. Louis Railway* v. *Beckwith*, 129 U. S. 26.
[2] *Home Insurance Company* v. *New York*, 134 U. S. 594.

LECTURE XIII.
Supplementary.
Fourteenth
Amendment.
Limitations upon
the powers of a
State.

person within its jurisdiction of the equal protection of the laws.[1]

The provisions in the Revised Statutes of
Texas, articles 1242–1245, which, as construed
by the highest court of the State, convert an
appearance by a defendant for the sole purpose
of questioning the jurisdiction of the court, into
a general appearance and submission to the
jurisdiction of the court, do not violate the provision in the Fourteenth Amendment to the
Constitution which forbids a State to deprive
any person of life, liberty, or property without
due process by law.[2]

No State can deprive particular persons or
classes of persons of equal and impartial justice
under the law, without violating the provisions
of the Fourteenth Amendment to the Constitution.[3]

State legislation, simply forbidding the defendant to come into court and challenge the validity
of service upon him in a personal action without
surrendering himself to the jurisdiction of the
court, but which does not attempt to restrain him
from fully protecting his person, his property, and
his rights against any attempt to enforce a judgment rendered without due process of law, is not
in violation of the Fourteenth Amendment.[4]

A person is not denied the equal protection of
the laws, nor deprived of liberty without due

---

[1] *Home Insurance Company* v. *New York*, 134 U. S. 594.

[2] *York* v. *Texas*, 137 U. S. 15.

[3] *Caldwell* v. *Texas*, 137 U. S. 692.

[4] *Kauffman* v. *Wootters*, 138 U. S. 285.

process of law, in violation of the Fourteenth Amendment, by being tried and sentenced to imprisonment by a judge who, although appointed by the governor without authority, is a judge *de facto* of a court *de jure*, by the law of the State as declared by its highest court.[1]

Lecture XIII.
Supplementary.
Fourteenth Amendment.
Limitations upon the powers of a state.

An ordinance passed by the city of New Orleans, under authority conferred by the legislature of Louisiana, prohibiting the keeping of any private market within six squares of any public market of the city, under penalty of being sentenced, upon conviction before a magistrate, to pay a fine of twenty-five dollars, and to be imprisoned for not more than thirty days if the fine is not paid, does not violate the Fourteenth Amendment to the Constitution.[2]

State Statutes regulating or prohibiting the sale of intoxicating liquors have been the subject of a great deal of litigation, and their constitutionality has been drawn in question. In most of the cases the question has been whether the statute before the court was or was not a regulation of commerce. That class of cases has already been noticed. There are, however, a few cases in which it has been claimed that the statute deprived the citizen of rights, privileges, or immunities protected by the Fourteenth Amendment.

Statutes regulating sales of intoxicating liquors not affected by this amendment.

It is well settled that the sale of spirituous and intoxicating liquors by retail, and in small

---

[1] *In re Manning*, 139 U. S. 504.
[2] *Natal* v. *Louisiana*, 139 U. S. 621.

LECTURE XIII.
Supplementary.
The Fourteenth
Amendment does
not affect statutes
regulating sales
of intoxicating
liquors.

quantities, may be regulated, or may be absolutely prohibited by State legislation, without violating the Constitution or laws of the United States.[1] Even a municipal corporation, when thereto duly authorized by the law of the State, may, in the exercise of the police power of the State, license or refuse to license persons to sell intoxicating liquors in that way,[2] without violatlating either the commerce clause of the Constitution or the Fourteenth Amendment.

The usual and ordinary legislation of the States, regulating or prohibiting the sale of intoxicating liquors, raised no question under the Constitution of the United States prior to the Fourteenth Amendment of that instrument. The right to sell intoxicating liquors is not one of the privileges and immunities of citizens of the United States, which by that amendment the States were forbidden to abridge.[3]

The restraining provisions of the Fourteenth Amendment are not infringed by the Statutes of Iowa authorizing its courts, when a person violates an injunction restraining him from selling intoxicating liquors, to punish him as for contempt by fine or imprisonment or both. Proceedings according to the common law for contempt of court are not subject to the right of trial by jury, and are "due process of law," within the meaning of the Fourteenth Amendment to the Constitution.[4]

---

[1] *Crowley* v. *Christensen*, 137 U. S. 86.   [2] Ib.
[3] *Bartemeyer* v. *Iowa*, 14 Wall. 21.
[4] *Eilenbecker* v. *Plymouth County*, 134 U. S. 31.

If a State deems the absolute prohibition of the manufacture and sale, within its limits, of intoxicating liquors for other than medical, scientific, and manufacturing purposes, to be necessary to the peace and security of society, the courts cannot, without usurping legislative functions, override the will of the people thus expressed. And if, in the judgment of the legislature, the manufacture of intoxicating liquors for the maker's own use, as a beverage, would tend to cripple, if it did not defeat, the effort to guard the community against the evils attendant upon the excessive use of such liquors, it is not for the courts, upon their views as to what is best and safest for the community, to disregard the legislative determination of that question. It cannot be said that Government interferes with or impairs any one's constitutional rights of liberty or of property, when it determines that the manufacture and sale of intoxicating drinks, for general or individual use as a beverage, are, or may become, hurtful to society, and constitute, therefore, a business in which no one may lawfully engage. This conclusion is unavoidable unless the Fourteenth Amendment of the Constitution takes from the States of the Union those powers of police that were reserved at the time the original constitution was adopted.[1]

Following *Mugler* v. *Kansas*, it was again held that a State has the right to prohibit or

LECTURE XIII. Supplementary. The Fourteenth Amendment does not affect statutes regulating sales of intoxicating liquors.

_____

[1] *Mugler* v. *Kansas*, 123 U. S. 623, 662, 663.

LECTURE XIII.
Supplementary.
The Fourteenth
Amendment does
not affect statutes
regulating sales
of intoxicating
liquors.
restrict the manufacture of intoxicating liquors within its limits; to prohibit all sale and traffic in them in the State; to inflict penalties for such manufacture and sale; and to provide regulations for the abatement, as a common nuisance, of the property used for such forbidden purposes; and that such legislation does not abridge the liberties or immunities of citizens of the United States, nor deprive any person of property without due process of law, nor contravene the provisions of the Fourteenth Amendment of the Constitution of the United States.[1]

The Act of August 8, 1890, 26 Stat. 313, c. 728, enacting "that all fermented, distilled, or other intoxicating liquors or liquids transported into any State or Territory, or remaining therein for use, consumption, sale, or storage therein, shall upon arrival in such State or Territory be subject to the operation and effect of the laws of such State or Territory enacted in the exercise of its police powers, to the same extent and in the same manner as though such liquids or liquors had been produced in such State or Territory, and shall not be exempt therefrom by reason of being introduced therein in original packages or otherwise," is a valid and constitutional exercise of the legislative power conferred upon Congress; and, after that act took effect, such liquors or liquids, introduced into a State or Territory from another State, whether in original packages or otherwise, became subject to the operation of

---

[1] *Kidd* v. *Pearson*, 128 U. S. 1.

such of its then existing laws as had been prop- Lecture XIII.
erly enacted in the exercise of its police powers, Supplementary.
The Fourteenth
among which was the statute in question as Amendment does
applied to the petitioner's offence.[1] not affect statutes
regulating sales
of intoxicating
liquors.

4. *The Apportionment of Representation.*

Before the war, or, to speak more accurately, Fourteenth
before the adoption of the Fourteenth Amend- Amendment.
Apportionment of
ment, the apportionment of representation representation.
among the States was determined " by adding
to the whole number of free persons, including
those bound to service for a term of years, and
excluding Indians not taxed, three-fifths of all
other persons." But when the slaves became
freemen, " five-fifths " of those denominated as
" all other persons " became subject to be counted
in the enumeration; and thus the war resulted
in increasing the political power of the South in
Congress. By the second section of the Fourteenth Amendment it was intended to protect
the emancipated slaves in the exercise of their
new political privileges.

5. *Exclusion from the Exercise of Political Privileges.*

On the 4th of July, 1868, President Johnson Political disa-
proclaimed a full pardon and amnesty "uncondi- bilities.
tionally and without reservation, to all and to
every person who directly or indirectly participated in the late insurrection or rebellion, excepting such person or persons as may be under
presentment or indictment in any court of the

---

[1] *In re Rahrer, Petitioner,* 140 U. S. 545.

United States having competent jurisdiction, upon a charge of treason or other felony."[1] A few days later the Fourteenth Amendment was proclaimed, by which certain classes of the persons covered by the proclamation of pardon were made ineligible for holding certain offices, unless Congress should, "by a vote of two-thirds of each House, remove such disability."

The index of volume 16 of the Statutes at Large, from page 1181 to page 1206, is taken up with the names of persons whose disabilities were so removed. On the 22d of May, 1872, Congress enacted, two-thirds concurring, " that all political disabilities imposed by the third section of the Fourteenth Article of Amendments of the Constitution of the United States are hereby removed from all persons whomsoever, except Senators and Representatives of the Thirty-sixth and Thirty-seventh Congresses, officers in the judicial, military, and naval service of the United States, heads of departments, and foreign ministers of the United States." [2]

The whole number thus excepted from the operation of the statute could not have been very large. Since its passage the disabilities of one hundred and sixty-nine of that number have been removed by special acts of Congress.

6. *Provisions as to Public Debts.*

The public debt. Little comment is necessary upon the provisions of section 4, relating to the public debt of

---

[1] 15 Stat. 702, 703.   [2] 17 Stat. 142, c. 93.

the United States, to debts incurred in aid of the rebellion, and to claims for the loss or emancipation of slaves. As to the former, it is sufficient to say that it was looked upon by those who regarded the emission of bills of credit in the form of circulating notes as unconstitutional, as a constitutional assumption of the debt so created. As to the latter, nothing need be said.

LECTURE XIII.
Supplementary.
The public debt.

C. *The Fifteenth Amendment.*

The Fifteenth Amendment to the Constitution does not confer the right of suffrage; but it invests citizens of the United States with the right of exemption from discrimination in the exercise of the elective franchise on account of their race, color, or previous condition of servitude, and empowers Congress to enforce that right by "appropriate legislation."

Fifteenth Amendment.

The power of Congress to legislate at all upon the subject of voting at State elections rests upon this amendment, and can be exercised by providing a punishment only when the wrongful refusal to receive the vote of a qualified elector at such elections is because of his race, color, or previous condition of servitude.

The third and fourth sections of the Act of May 31, 1870 (16 Stat. 140), not being confined in their operation to unlawful discrimination on account of race, color, or previous condition of servitude, are beyond the limit of the Fifteenth Amendment, and unauthorized.[1]

---

[1] *United States* v. *Reese*, 92 U. S. 214.

An indictment which charges in the first count that the defendants conspired to intimidate A. B., a citizen of African descent, in the exercise of his right to vote for a member of the Congress of the United States, and that in the execution of that conspiracy they beat, bruised, wounded, and otherwise maltreated him; and in the second count that they did this on account of his race, color, and previous condition of servitude, by going in disguise and assaulting him on the public highway and on his own premises, contains a sufficient description of an offence embraced within the provisions of §§ 5508, 5520, Rev. Stat.

Although it is true that the Fifteenth Amendment gives no affirmative right to the negro to vote, yet there are cases, some of which are stated by the court, in which it substantially confers that right upon him. *United States* v. *Reese*, 92 U. S. 214, qualified and explained.[1]

---

[1] *Ex parte Yarbrough*, 110 U. S. 65.

APPENDIX.

I.

[THE CONSTITUTION OF THE UNITED - STATES OF AMERICA.]

———oo⚬oo———

WE THE PEOPLE of the United States, in Order to form a more perfect Union, establish Justice, insure domes- tic Tranquility, provide for the common defence, promote the general Welfare, and secure the Blessings of Liberty to ourselves and our Posterity, do ordain and establish this CONSTITUTION for the United States of America.[1]

ARTICLE. I.

SECTION. 1. All legislative Powers herein granted shall be vested in a Congress of the United States, which shall consist of a Senate and House of Representatives.[2]

SECTION. 2. The House of Representatives shall be composed of Members chosen every second Year by the People of the several States, and the Electors in each State shall have the Qualifications requisite for Electors of the most numerous Branch of the State Legislature.[3]

No Person shall be a Representative who shall not have attained to the Age of twenty five Years, and been seven

---

[1] Chisholm v. Georgia, 2 Dall. 419; McCulloch v. Maryland, 4 Wheat. 316; Brown v. Maryland, 12 Wheat. 419; Barron v. The Mayor and City Council of Baltimore, 7 Pet. 243; Lane County v. Oregon, 7 Wall. 71; Texas v. White, 7 Wall. 700.

[2] Hayburn's Case, 2 Dall. 409 (notes); United States v. Harris, 106 U. S. 629; *In re* Neagle, 135 U. S. 1.

[3] *Ex parte* Yarbrough, 110 U. S. 651; *In re* Green, 134 U. S. 377.

Years a Citizen of the United States, and who shall not,
when elected, be an Inhabitant of that State in which he
shall be chosen.

Representatives and direct Taxes shall be apportioned
among the several States which may be included within
this Union, according to their respective Numbers, which
shall be determined by adding to the whole Number of
free Persons, including those bound to Service for a Term
of Years, and excluding Indians not taxed, three fifths
of all other Persons. The actual Enumeration shall be
made within three Years after the first Meeting of the
Congress of the United States, and within every subsequent Term of ten Years, in such Manner as they shall
by Law direct. The Number of Representatives shall
not exceed one for every thirty Thousand, but each State
shall have at Least one Representative; and until such
enumeration shall be made, the State of New Hampshire
shall be entitled to chuse three, Massachusetts eight,
Rhode-Island and Providence Plantations one, Connecticut five, New York six, New Jersey four, Pennsylvania
eight, Delaware one, Maryland six, Virginia ten, North
Carolina five, South Carolina five, and Georgia three.[1]

When vacancies happen in the Representation from
any State, the Executive Authority thereof shall issue
Writs of Election to fill such Vacancies.

The House of Representatives shall chuse their Speaker
and other Officers; and shall have the sole Power of
Impeachment.

SECTION. 3. The Senate of the United States shall be
composed of two Senators from each State, chosen by
the Legislature thereof, for six Years; and each Senator
shall have one Vote.

Immediately after they shall be assembled in Consequence of the first Election, they shall be divided as
equally as may be into three Classes. The Seats of the

---

[1] Dodge v. Woolsey, 18 How. 331; Loughborough v. Blake, 5 Wheat.
317; Pacific Insurance Co. v. Soule, 7 Wall. 433; Veazie Bank v. Fenno,
8 Wall. 533; Scholey v. Rew, 23 Wall. 331; De Treville v. Smalls, 98
U. S. 517; Springer v. United States, 102 U. S. 586.

Senators of the first Class shall be vacated at the Expiration of the second Year, of the second Class at the Expiration of the fourth Year, and of the third Class at the Expiration of the sixth Year, so that one third may be chosen every second Year; and if Vacancies happen by Resignation, or otherwise, during the Recess of the Legislature of any State, the Executive thereof may make temporary Appointments until the next Meeting of the Legislature, which shall then fill such Vacancies.

No Person shall be a Senator who shall not have attained to the Age of thirty Years, and been nine Years a Citizen of the United States, and who shall not, when elected, be an Inhabitant of that State for which he shall be chosen.

The Vice President of the United States shall be President of the Senate, but shall have no Vote, unless they be equally divided.

The Senate shall chuse their other Officers, and also a President pro tempore, in the Absence of the Vice President, or when he shall exercise the Office of President of the United States.

The Senate shall have the sole Power to try all Impeachments. When sitting for that Purpose, they shall be on Oath or Affirmation. When the President of the United States is tried, the Chief Justice shall preside: And no Person shall be convicted without the Concurrence of two thirds of the Members present.

Judgment in Cases of Impeachment shall not extend further than to removal from Office, and disqualification to hold and enjoy any Office of honor, Trust or Profit under the United States: but the Party convicted shall nevertheless be liable and subject to Indictment, Trial, Judgment and Punishment, according to Law.[1]

SECTION. 4. The Times, Places and Manner of holding Elections for Senators and Representatives, shall be prescribed in each State by the Legislature thereof; but the Congress may at any time by Law make or alter

---

[1] *In re* Green, 134 U. S. 377.

such Regulations, except as to the Places of chusing Senators.[1]

The Congress shall assemble at least once in every Year, and such Meeting shall be on the first Monday in December, unless they shall by Law appoint a different Day.

SECTION. 5. Each House shall be the Judge of the Elections, Returns and Qualifications of its own Members, and a Majority of each shall constitute a Quorum to do Business; but a smaller Number may adjourn from day to day, and may be authorized to compel the Attendance of absent Members, in such Manner, and under such Penalties as each House may provide.[2]

Each House may determine the Rules of its Proceedings, punish its Members for disorderly Behaviour, and, with the Concurrence of two thirds, expel a Member.[3]

Each House shall keep a Journal of its Proceedings, and from time to time publish the same, excepting such Parts as may in their Judgment require Secrecy; and the Yeas and Nays of the Members of either House on any question shall, at the desire of one fifth of those Present, be entered on the Journal.

Neither House, during the Session of Congress, shall, without the Consent of the other, adjourn for more than three days, nor to any other Place than that in which the two Houses shall be sitting.

SECTION. 6. The Senators and Representatives shall receive a Compensation for their Services, to be ascertained by Law, and paid out of the Treasury of the United States. They shall in all Cases, except Treason, Felony and Breach of the Peace, be privileged from Arrest during their Attendance at the Session of their respective Houses, and in going to and returning from the

---

[1] United States v. Reese, 92 U. S. 218; Ex parte Siebold, 100 U. S. 371; Ex parte Yarbrough, 110 U. S. 651; In re Coy, 127 U. S. 731; In re Neagle, 135 U. S. 1.

[2] In re Loney, 134 U. S. 372.

[3] Anderson v. Dunn, 6 Wheat. 204; Kilbourn v. Thompson, 103 U. S. 168.

same; and for any Speech or Debate in either House, they shall not be questioned in any other Place.[1]

No Senator or Representative shall, during the Time for which he was elected, be appointed to any civil Office under the Authority of the United States, which shall have been created, or the Emoluments whereof shall have been encreased, during such time; and no Person holding any Office under the United States, shall be a Member of either House during his Continuance in Office.

SECTION. 7. All Bills for raising Revenue shall originate in the House of Representatives; but the Senate may propose or concur with Amendments as on other Bills.

Every Bill which shall have passed the House of Representatives and the Senate, shall, before it become a Law, be presented to the President of the United States; If he approve he shall sign it, but if not he shall return it, with his Objections to that House in which it shall have originated, who shall enter the Objections at large on their Journal, and proceed to reconsider it. If after such Reconsideration two thirds of that House shall agree to pass the Bill, it shall be sent, together with the Objections, to the other House, by which it shall likewise be reconsidered, and if approved by two thirds of that House, it shall become a Law. But in all such Cases the Votes of both Houses shall be determined by yeas and Nays, and the Names of the Persons voting for and against the Bill shall be entered on the Journal of each House respectively. If any Bill shall not be returned by the President within ten Days (Sundays excepted) after it shall have been presented to him, the Same shall be a Law, in like Manner as if he had signed it, unless the Congress by their Adjournment prevent its Return, in which Case it shall not be a Law.[2]

Every Order, Resolution, or Vote to which the Con-

---

1 Coxe v. M'Clenachan, 3 Dall. 478; United States v. Cooper, 4 Dall. 341.

2 *In re* Neagle, 135 U. S. 1.

currence of the Senate and House of Representatives may be necessary (except on a question of Adjournment) shall be presented to the President of the United States; and before the Same shall take Effect, shall be approved by him, or being disapproved by him, shall be repassed by two thirds of the Senate and House of Representatives, according to the Rules and Limitations prescribed in the Case of a Bill.

SECTION. 8. The Congress shall have Power To lay and collect Taxes, Duties, Imposts and Excises, to pay the Debts and provide for the common Defence and general Welfare of the United States; but all Duties, Imposts and Excises shall be uniform throughout the United States;[1]

To borrow Money on the credit of the United States;[2]

To regulate Commerce with foreign Nations, and among the several States, and with the Indian Tribes;[3]

---

[1] Hylton v. United States, 3 Dall. 171; McCulloch v. Maryland, 4 Wheat. 316; Loughborough v. Blake, 5 Wheat. 317; Osborn v. Bank of the United States, 9 Wheat. 738; Weston v. City Council of Charleston, 2 Pet. 449; Dobbins v. The Commissioners of Erie County, 16 Pet. 435; License Cases, 5 How. 504; Cooley v. Board of Wardens of Port of Philadelphia, 12 How. 299; Dodge v. Woolsey, 18 How. 331; McGuire v. The Commonwealth, 3 Wall. 387; Van Allen v. The Assessors, 3 Wall. 573; Bradley v. The People, 4 Wall. 459; Pervear v. Commonwealth, 5 Wall. 475; Pacific Insurance Co. v. Soule, 7 Wall. 433; Woodruff v. Parham, 8 Wall. 123; Hinson v. Lott, 8 Wall. 148; Veazie Bank v. Fenno, 8 Wall. 533; The Collector v. Day, 11 Wall. 113; United States v. Singer, 15 Wall. 111; State tax on Foreign-held Bonds, 15 Wall. 300; United States v. Railroad Company, 17 Wall. 322; Railroad Company v. Peniston, 18 Wall. 5; Scholey v. Rew, 23 Wall. 331; Springer v. United States, 102 U. S. 586; Legal Tender Case, 110 U. S. 421; Edye v. Robertson, 112 U. S. 580; Van Brocklin v. Tennessee, 117 U. S. 151; License Tax Cases, 5 Wall. 462.

[2] McCulloch v. Maryland, 4 Wheat. 316; Osborn v. United States Bank, 9 Wheat. 738; Weston v. City Council of Charleston, 2 Pet. 449; Bank of Commerce v. New York City, 2 Black, 620; Bank Tax Case, 2 Wall. 200; The Banks v. The Mayor, 7 Wall. 16; Bank v. Supervisors, 7 Wall. 26; Hepburn v. Griswold, 8 Wall. 603; National Bank v. Commonwealth, 9 Wall. 353; Parker v. Davis, 12 Wall. 457; Legal Tender Case, 110 U. S. 421.

[3] Gibbons v. Ogden, 9 Wheat. 1; Brown v. Maryland, 12 Wheat. 419; Willson v. Black Bird Creek Marsh Company, 2 Pet. 245; Cherokee Nation v. Georgia, 5 Pet. 1; Worcester v. Georgia, 6 Pet. 515; City of New York v. Miln, 11 Pet. 102; United States v. Coombs, 12 Pet. 72;

Holmes v. Jennison, 14 Pet. 540; License Cases, 5 How. 504; Passenger Cases, 7 How. 283; Nathan v. Louisiana, 8 How. 73; Mager v. Grima, 8 How. 490; United States v. Marigold, 9 How. 560; Cooley v. Board of Wardens of the Port of Philadelphia, 12 How. 299; The Propeller Genesee Chief v. Fitzhugh, 12 How. 443; Pennslyvania v. The Wheeling Bridge Co., 13 How. 518; Veazie v. Moor, 14 How. 568; Smith v. Maryland, 18 How. 71; Pennsylvania v. Wheeling and Belmont Bridge Co., 18 How. 421; Sinnot v. Davenport, 22 How. 227; Foster v. Davenport, 22 How. 244; Conway v. Taylor's Executor, 1 Black, 603; Steamship Co. v. Joliffe, 2 Wall. 450; United States v. Holliday, 3 Wall. 407; Gilman v. Philadelphia, 3 Wall. 713; The Passaic Bridges, 3 Wall. 782; License Tax Cases, 5 Wall. 462; Steamship Company v. Port Wardens, 6 Wall. 31; Crandall v. Nevada, 6 Wall. 35; White's Bank v. Smith, 7 Wall. 646; Waring v. The Mayor, 8 Wall. 110; Paul v. Virginia, 8 Wall. 168; Thomson v. Pacific Railroad, 9 Wall. 579; Downham v. Alexandria Council, 10 Wall. 173; Ducat v. Chicago, 10 Wall. 410; The Clinton Bridge, 10 Wall. 454; The Daniel Ball, 10 Wall. 557; Liverpool Insurance Company v. Massachusetts, 10 Wall. 566; The Montello, 11 Wall. 411; Ward v. Maryland, 12 Wall. 418; Ex parte McNiel, 13 Wall. 236; State Freight Tax, 15 Wall. 232; State Tax on Railway Gross Receipts, 15 Wall. 284; Osborne v. Mobile, 16 Wall. 479; Railroad Company v. Fuller, 17 Wall. 560; Bartemeyer v. Iowa, 18 Wall. 129; The Delaware Railroad Tax, 18 Wall. 206; Peete v. Morgan, 19 Wall. 581; Railroad Company v. Richmond, 19 Wall. 584; Minor v. Happersett, 21 Wall. 162; Railroad Company v. Maryland, 21 Wall. 456; The Lottawanna, 21 Wall. 558; Welton v. Missouri, 91 U. S. 275; Henderson v. The Mayor of the City of New York, 92 U. S. 259; Chy Lung v. Freeman, 92 U. S. 275; South Carolina v. Georgia, 93 U. S. 4; Sherlock v. Alling, 93 U. S. 99; United States v. Forty-three Gallons of Whiskey, 93 U. S. 188; Foster v. Master and Wardens of the Port of New Orleans, 94 U. S. 246; Railroad Co. v. Husen, 95 U. S. 465; Pensacola Telegraph Co. v. Western Union Telegraph Co., 96 U. S. 1; Beer Co. v. Massachusetts, 97 U. S. 25; Cook v. Pennsylvania, 97 U. S. 566; Trade Mark Cases, 100 U. S. 82; Packet Co. v. St. Louis, 100 U. S. 423; Tiernan v. Rinker, 102 U. S. 123; Lord v. Goodall &c. Steamship Co., 102 U. S. 541; Wilson v. McNamee, 102 U. S. 572; Mobile County v. Kimball, 102 U. S. 691; Webber v. Virginia, 103 U. S. 344; Western Union Telegraph Co. v. Texas, 105 U. S. 460; Newport &c. Bridge Co. v. United States, 105 U. S. 470; People v. Compagnie Générale Translantique, 107 U. S. 59; Wiggins Ferry Co. v. East St. Louis, 107 U. S. 365; Escanaba Co. v. Chicago, 107 U. S. 678; Miller v. New York, 109 U. S. 385; Moran v. New Orleans, 112 U. S. 69; Foster v. Kansas, 112 U. S. 201; Head Money Cases, 112 U. S. 580; Cardwell v. American Bridge Co., 113 U. S. 205; Cooper Manufacturing Co. v. Ferguson, 113 U. S. 727; Gloucester Ferry Co. v. Pennsylvania, 114 U. S. 196; Brown v. Houston, 114 U. S. 622; Starin v. New York, 115 U. S. 248; Fisk v. Jefferson Police Jury, 116 U. S. 131; Stone v. Illinois Central Railroad Co., 116 U. S. 347; Stone v. New Orleans and Northeastern Railroad, 116 U. S. 352; Walling v. Michigan, 116 U. S. 446; Coe v. Errol, 116 U. S. 517; Pickard v. Pullman Southern Car Co, 117 U. S. 34; Tennessee v. Pullman Southern Car Co., 117 U. S. 51; Spraigue v. Thompson, 118 U. S. 90; Morgan Steamship

To establish an uniform Rule of Naturalization,[1] and uniform Laws on the subject of Bankruptcies throughout the United States;[2]

To coin Money, regulate the Value thereof, and of foreign Coin, and fix the Standard of Weights and Measures;[3]

To provide for the Punishment of counterfeiting the Securities and current Coin of the United States;[4]

To establish Post Offices and post Roads;[5]

Co. v. Louisiana, 118 U. S. 455; Wabash &c. Railway Co. v. Illinois, 118 U. S. 557; United States v. Arjona, 120 U. S. 479; Robbins v. Shelby County Taxing District, 120 U. S. 489; Corson v. Maryland, 120 U. S. 502; Fargo v. Michigan, 121 U. S. 230; Philadelphia and Southern Steamship Co. v. Pennsylvania, 122 U. S. 326: Western Union Telegraph Co. v. Pendleton, 122 U. S. 347; Sands v. Manistee River Improvement Co., 123 U. S. 288; Mugler v. Kansas, 123 U. S. 623; Smith v. Alabama, 124 U. S. 465; Willamette Iron Bridge Co. v. Hatch, 125 U. S. 1; Pembina Consolidated Mining Co. v. Pennsylvania, 125 U. S. 181; Bowman v. Chicago &c. Railway Co., 125 U. S. 465; California v. Central Pacific Railroad Co., 127 U. S. 1; Ratterman v. Western Union Telegraph Co., 127 U. S. 411; Leloup v. Port of Mobile, 127 U. S. 640; Kidd v. Pearson, 128 U. S. 1; Asher v. Texas, 128 U. S. 129; Stoutenburgh v. Hennick, 129 U. S. 141; Kimmish v. Ball, 129 U. S. 217; Western Union Telegraph Co. v. Alabama, 132 U. S. 472; Louisville, New Orleans &c. Railway Co. v. Mississippi, 133 U. S. 587; Leisy v. Hardin, 135 U. S. 100; Lyng v. Michigan, 135 U. S. 161; Cherokee Nation v. Southern Kansas Railway Co., 135 U. S. 641; McCall v. California, 136 U. S. 104; Norfolk and Western Railroad Co. v. Pennsylvania, 136 U. S. 114; Minnesota v. Barber, 136 U. S. 313; Crowley v. Christensen, 137 U. S. 86; Wheeler v. Jackson, 137 U. S. 245; Brimmer v. Rebman, 138 U. S. 78; Munn v. Illinois, 94 U. S. 113; Chicago, Burlington &c. Railroad v. Iowa, 94 U. S. 155; Peck v. North Western Railway, 94 U. S. 164.

[1] Collet v. Collet, 2 Dall. 294; Chirac v. Chirac, 2 Wheat. 259.

[2] Sturges v. Crowninshield, 4 Wheat. 122; McMillan v. McNeill, 4 Wheat. 209; Houston v. Moore, 5 Wheat. 1; Farmers' and Mechanics' Bank of Pennsylvania v. Smith, 6 Wheat. 131; Ogden v. Saunders, 12 Wheat. 213; Boyle v. Zacharie and Turner, 6 Pet. 348; Gassies v. Ballon, 6 Pet. 761; Beers v. Haughton, 9 Pet. 329; Suydam v. Broadnax, 14 Pet. 67; Cook v. Moffat, 5 How. 295; Dred Scott v. Sandford, 19 How. 393; In re Neagle, 135 U. S. 1.

[3] Briscoe v. The Bank of the Commonwealth of Kentucky, 11 Pet. 257; Fox v. Ohio, 5 How. 410; United States v. Marigold, 9 How. 560; Veazie Bank v. Fenno, 8 Wall. 533; Parker v. Davis, 12 Wall. 457; Legal Tender Case, 110 U. S. 421.

[4] Fox v. Ohio, 5 How. 410; United States v. Marigold, 9 How. 560.

[5] McCulloch v. Maryland, 4 Wheat. 316; Pennsylvania v. Wheeling and Belmont Bridge Co., 18 How. 421; Ex parte Jackson, 96 U. S. 727.

To promote the Progress of Science and useful Arts, by securing for limited Times to Authors and Inventors the exclusive Right to their respective Writings and Discoveries; [1]

To constitute Tribunals inferior to the supreme Court;

To define and punish Piracies and Felonies committed on the high Seas, and Offences against the Law of Nations; [2]

To declare War, grant Letters of Marque and Reprisal, and make Rules concerning Captures on Land and Water; [3]

To raise and support Armies, but no Appropriation of Money to that Use shall be for a longer Term than two Years; [4]

To provide and maintain a Navy; [5]

To make Rules for the Government and Regulation of the land and naval Forces;

To provide for calling forth the Militia to execute the Laws of the Union, suppress Insurrections and repel Invasions; [6]

To provide for organizing, arming, and disciplining, the Militia, and for governing such Part of them as may be employed in the Service of the United States, reserving to the States respectively, the Appointment of the

---

[1] Grant v. Raymond, 6 Pet. 218; Wheaton v. Peters, 8 Pet. 591; Trade Mark Cases, 100 U. S. 82; Burrow-Giles Lithographic Co. v. Sarony, 111 U. S. 53; Banks v. Manchester, 128 U. S. 244; Callaghan v. Myers, 128 U. S. 617.

[2] United States v. Palmer, 3 Wheat. 610; United States v. Wiltberger, 5 Wheat. 76; United States v. Smith, 5 Wheat. 153; United States v. Pirates, 5 Wheat. 184; United States v. Arjona, 120 U. S. 479.

[3] Brown v. United States, 8 Cranch, 110; American Insurance Co. v. Canter (356 bales cotton), 1 Pet. 511; Mrs. Alexander's Cotton, 2 Wall. 404; Miller v. United States, 11 Wall. 268; Tyler v. Defrees, 11 Wall. 331; Stewart v. Kahn, 11 Wall. 493; Hamilton v. Dillin, 21 Wall. 73; Lamar v. Browne, 92 U. S. 187; Prize Cases, 2 Black, 635.

[4] Crandall v. Nevada, 6 Wall. 35.

[5] United States v. Bevans, 3 Wheat. 336; Dynes v. Hoover, 20 How. 65.

[6] Houston v. Moore, 5 Wheat. 1; Martin v. Mott, 12 Wheat. 19; Luther v. Borden, 7 How. 1; Crandall v. Nevada, 6 Wall. 35; Texas v. White, 7 Wall. 700.

Officers, and the Authority of training the Militia according to the discipline prescribed by Congress;[1]

To exercise exclusive Legislation in all Cases whatsoever, over such District (not exceeding ten Miles square) as may, by Cession of particular States, and the Acceptance of Congress, become the Seat of the Government of the United States, and to exercise like Authority over all Places purchased by the Consent of the Legislature of the State in which the Same shall be, for the Erection of Forts, Magazines, Arsenals, dock-Yards, and other needful Buildings; — And[2]

To make all Laws which shall be necessary and proper for carrying into Execution the foregoing Powers, and all other Powers vested by this Constitution in the Government of the United States, or in any Department or Officer thereof.[3]

SECTION. 9. The Migration or Importation of such Persons as any of the States now existing shall think proper to admit, shall not be prohibited by the Congress prior to the Year one thousand eight hundred and eight,

---

[1] Houston v. Moore, 5 Wheat. 1; Martin v. Mott, 12 Wheat. 19; Luther v. Borden, 7 How. 1.

[2] Hepburn v. Ellzey, 2 Cranch, 444; Houston v. Moore, 5 Wheat. 1; Loughborough v. Blake, 5 Wheat. 317; Cohens v. Virginia, 6 Wheat. 264; American Insurance Co. v. Canter (356 bales cotton), 1 Pet. 511; Kendall, Postmaster-General, v. United States, 12 Pet. 524; Cross v. Harrison, 16 How. 164; Dred Scott v. Sandford, 19 How. 393; United States v. Dewitt, 9 Wall. 41; Dunphy v. Kleinsmith, 11 Wall. 610; Willard v. Presbury, 14 Wall. 676; Phillips v. Payne, 92 U. S. 130; United States v. Fox, 94 U. S. 315; National Bank v. Yankton County, 101 U. S. 129; Fort Leavenworth Railroad Co. v. Lowe, 114 U. S. 525; Van Brocklin v. Tennessee, 117 U. S. 151.

[3] McCulloch v. Maryland, 4 Wheat. 316; Wayman v. Southard, 10 Wheat. 1; Bank of United States v. Halstead, 10 Wheat. 51; Ableman v. Booth; United States v. Booth, 21 How. 506; Hepburn v. Griswold, 8 Wall. 603; National Bank v. Commonwealth, 9 Wall. 353; Thomson v. Pacific Railroad, 9 Wall. 579; Parker v. Davis (Legal Tender Cases) 12 Wall. 457; Railroad Company v. Johnson, 15 Wall. 195; Railroad Company v. Peniston, 18 Wall. 5; United States v. Harris, 106 U. S. 629; Legal Tender Case, 110 U. S. 421; Ex parte Yarbrough, 110 U. S. 651; United States v. Arjona, 120 U. S. 479; Stoutenburgh v. Hennick, 129 U. S. 141; In re Neagle, 135 U. S. 1.

but a Tax or duty may be imposed on such Importation,
not exceeding ten dollars for each Person.[1]

The Privilege of the Writ of Habeas Corpus shall not be suspended, unless when in Cases of Rebellion or Invasion the public Safety may require it.[2]

No Bill of Attainder or ex post facto Law shall be passed.[3]

No Capitation, or other direct, Tax shall be laid, unless in Proportion to the Census or Enumeration herein before directed to be taken.[4]

No Tax or Duty shall be laid on Articles exported from any State.[5]

No Preference shall be given by any Regulation of Commerce or Revenue to the Ports of one State over those of another: nor shall Vessels bound to, or from, one State, be obliged to enter, clear, or pay Duties in another.[6]

---

[1] Dred Scott v. Sandford, 19 How. 393; People v. Compagnie Générale Transatlantique, 107 U. S. 59.

[2] United States v. Hamilton, 3 Dall. 17; Hepburn v. Ellzey, 2 Cranch, 444; Ex parte Bollman and Swartwout, 4 Cranch, 75; Ex parte Kearney, 7 Wheat. 38; Ex parte Tobias Watkins, 3 Pet. 192; Ex parte Milburn, 9 Pet. 704; Holmes v. Jennison, 14 Pet. 540; Ex parte Dorr, 3 How. 103; Luther v. Borden, 7 How. 1; Ableman v. Booth; United States v. Booth, 21 How. 506; Ex parte Vallandigham, 1 Wall. 243; Ex parte Milligan, 4 Wall. 2; Ex parte McCardle, 7 Wall. 506; Ex parte Yerger, 8 Wall. 85; Tarble's Case, 13 Wall. 397; Ex parte Lange, 18 Wall. 163; Ex parte Parks, 93 U. S. 18; Ex parte Karstendick, 93 U. S. 396; Ex parte Virginia, 100 U. S. 339.

[3] Fletcher v. Peck, 6 Cranch, 87; Ogden v. Saunders, 12 Wheat. 213; Watson v. Mercer, 8 Pet. 88; Carpenter v. Pennsylvania, 17 How. 456; Locke v. New Orleans, 4 Wall. 172; Cummings v. Missouri, 4 Wall. 277; Ex parte Garland, 4 Wall. 333; Drehman v. Stifle, 8 Wall. 595; Klinger v. Missouri, 13 Wall. 257; Pierce v. Carskadon, 16 Wall. 234; In re Neagle, 135 U. S. 1; Cook v. United States, 138 U. S. 157.

[4] Loughborough v. Blake, 5 Wheat. 317; License Tax Cases, 5 Wall. 462; Pacific Insurance Co. v. Soule, 7 Wall. 433; Springer v. United States, 102 U. S. 586; Gibbons v. District of Columbia, 116 U. S. 404.

[5] Cooley v. Board of Wardens of Port of Philadelphia, 12 How. 299; Pacific Insurance Co. v. Soule, 7 Wall. 433; Pace v. Burgess, 92 U. S. 372; Turpin v. Burgess, 117 U. S. 504.

[6] Cooley v. Board of Wardens of the Port of Philadelphia, 12 How. 299; State of Pennsylvania v. Wheeling and Belmont Bridge Company, 18 How. 421; Munn v. Illinois, 94 U. S. 113; Packet Co. v. St. Louis, 100 U. S. 423; Packet Co. v. Catlettsburg, 105 U. S. 559; Gloucester Ferry Co. v. Pennsylvania, 114 U. S. 196; Walling v. Michigan, 116 U. S. 446; Morgan's Steamship Co. v. Louisiana, 118 U. S. 455; Johnson v. Chicago and Pacific Elevator Co., 119 U. S. 388.

No Money shall be drawn from the Treasury, but in Consequence of Appropriations made by Law; and a regular Statement and Account of the Receipts and Expenditures of all public Money shall be published from time to time.[1]

No Title of Nobility shall be granted by the United States: And no Person holding any Office or Profit or Trust under them, shall, without the Consent of the Congress, accept of any present, Emolument, Office, or Title, of any kind whatever, from any King, Prince, or foreign State.[2]

SECTION. 10. No State shall enter into any Treaty, Alliance, or Confederation; grant Letters of Marque and Reprisal; coin Money; emit Bills of Credit; make any Thing but gold and silver Coin a Tender in Payment of Debts; pass any Bill of Attainder, ex post facto Law, or Law impairing the Obligation of Contracts, or grant any Title of Nobility.[3]

---

[1] United States v. Guthrie, 17 How. 284.

[2] Brashear v. Mason, 6 How. 92.

[3] Van Horne's Lessee v. Dorrance, 2 Dall. 304; Commonwealth v. Franklin, 4 Dall. 255; Calder and wife v. Bull and wife, 3 Dall. 386; Cooper v. Telfair, 4 Dall. 14; Fletcher v. Peck, 6 Cranch, 87; New Jersey v. Wilson, 7 Cranch, 164; Sturges v. Crowninshield, 4 Wheat. 122; McMillan v. McNeil, 4 Wheat. 209; Dartmouth College v. Woodward, 4 Wheat. 518; Houston v. Moore, 5 Wheat. 1; Owings v. Speed, 5 Wheat. 420; Farmers and Mechanics' Bank v. Smith, 6 Wheat. 131; Green v. Biddle, 8 Wheat. 1; Ogden v. Saunders, 12 Wheat. 213; Mason v. Haile, 12 Wheat. 370; Satterlee v. Matthewson, 2 Pet. 380; Hart v. Lamphire, 3 Pet. 280; Craig v. Missouri, 4 Pet. 410; Providence Bank v. Billings and Pitman, 4 Pet. 514; Byrne v. Missouri, 8 Pet. 40; Watson v. Mercer, 8 Pet. 88; Mumma v. Potomac Company, 8 Pet. 281; Beers v. Haughton, 9 Pet. 329; Briscoe v. The Bank of the Commonwealth of Kentucky, 11 Pet. 257; The Proprietors of Charles River Bridge v. The Proprietors of Warren Bridge, 11 Pet. 420; Armstrong v. The Treasurer of Athens County, 16 Pet. 281; Bronson v. Kinzie, 1 How. 311; Gwin v. Breedlove, 2 How. 29; McCracken v. Hayward, 2 How. 608; Gordon v. Appeal Tax Court, 3 How. 133; Maryland v. Baltimore and Ohio R. R. Co., 3 How. 534; Neil, Moore & Co. v. Ohio, 3 How. 720; Cook v. Moffatt, 5 How. 295; Planters' Bank v. Sharp, 6 How. 301; West River Bridge Company v. Dix, 6 How. 507; Crawford v. Branch Bank of Mobile, 7 How. 279; Phalen v. Virginia, 8 How. 163; Woodruff v. Trapnall, 10 How. 190; Paup v. Drew, 10 How. 218; Baltimore and Susquehanna Railroad Co. v. Nesbit, 10 How. 395; Butler v. Pennsylvania, 10 How. 402; East Hartford v. Hartford Bridge Co., 10 How. 511; Achison v. Huddleson,

No State shall, without the Consent of the Congress,
lay any Imposts or Duties on Imports or Exports, except what may be absolutely necessary for executing its
inspection Laws: and the net Produce of all Duties and

---

12 How. 293; Darrington v. The Bank of Alabama, 13 How. 12; Richmond &c. Railroad Co. v. The Louisa Railroad Co., 13 How. 71; Trustees
for Vicennes University v. Indiana, 14 How. 268; Curran v. Arkansas,
15 How. 304; State Bank of Ohio v. Knoop, 16 How. 369; Carpenter v.
Pennsylvania, 17 How. 456; Dodge v. Woolsey, 18 How. 331; Mechanics'
&c. Bank v. Thomas, 18 How. 384; Beers v. Arkansas, 20 How. 527; As-
pinwall v. Commissioners of County of Daviess, 22 How. 364; Rector of
Christ Church, Philadelphia, v. County of Philadelphia, 24 How. 300;
Howard v. Bugbee, 24 How. 461; Jefferson Branch Bank v. Skelley,
1 Black, 436; Franklin Branch Bank v. Ohio, 1 Black, 474; Trustees of
the Wabash and Erie Canal Company v. Beers, 2 Black, 448; Gilman v.
City of Sheboygan, 2 Black, 510; Bridge Proprietors v. Hoboken Company, 1 Wall. 116; Hawthorne v. Calef, 2 Wall. 10; Florentine v. Barton, 2 Wall. 210; The Binghamton Bridge, 3 Wall. 51; The Turnpike
Company v. The State, 3 Wall. 210; McGee v. Mathis, 4 Wall. 143;
Locke v. New Orleans, 4 Wall. 172; Railroad Company v. Rock, 4 Wall.
177; Cummings v. Missouri, 4 Wall. 277; Ex parte Garland, 4 Wall. 333;
Von Hoffman v. City of Quincy, 4 Wall. 535; Williamson v. Suydam,
6 Wall. 723; Mulligan v. Corbins, 7 Wall. 487: Furman v. Nichol, 8 Wall.
44; Home of the Friendless v. Rouse, 8 Wall. 430; The Washington University v. Rouse, 8 Wall. 439; Butz v. City of Muscatine, 8 Wall. 575;
Drehman v. Stifle, 8 Wall. 595; Hepburn v. Griswold, 8 Wall. 603; Gut
v. The State, 9 Wall. 35; Chicago v. Sheldon, 9 Wall. 50; City of Ke-
nosha v. Lamson, 9 Wall. 477; Railroad Company v. McClure, 10 Wall.
511; Bethell v. Demaret, 10 Wall. 537; Parker v. Davis (The Legal
Tender Cases), 12 Wall. 457; Curtis v. Whitney, 13 Wall. 68; Pennsylvania College Cases, 13 Wall. 190; Wilmington Railroad v. Reid, Sheriff,
13 Wall. 264; Salt Company v. East Saginaw, 13 Wall. 373; White v.
Hart, 13 Wall. 646; Osborn v. Nicholson et al., 13 Wall. 654; Railroad
Company v. Johnson, 15 Wall. 195; Case of the State Tax on Foreign-
held Bonds, 15 Wall. 300; Tomlinson v. Jessup, 15 Wall. 454; Tomlinson
v. Branch, 15 Wall. 460; Miller v. The State, 15 Wall. 478; Holyoke
Company v. Lyman, 15 Wall. 500; Gunn v. Barry, 15 Wall. 610; Davis
v. Gray, 16 Wall. 204; Pierce v. Carskadon, 16 Wall. 234; Humphrey v.
Pegues, 16 Wall. 244; Walker v. Whitehead, 16 Wall. 314; Sohn v.
Waterson, 17 Wall. 596; Boyce v. Tabb, 18 Wall. 546; Barings v. Dab-
ney, 19 Wall. 1; Head v. The University, 19 Wall. 526; Pacific Rail-
road Co. v. Maguire, 20 Wall. 36; Garrison v. City of New York, 21
Wall. 196; Ochiltree v. Railroad Company, 21 Wall. 249; Erie Rail-
way v. Pennsylvania, 21 Wall. 492; Randall v. Kreiger, 23 Wall. 137;
Wilmington &c. Railroad v. King, Exr., 91 U. S. 3; County of Moultrie v.
Rockingham Ten Cent Savings Bank, 92 U. S. 631; Home Insurance
Company v. City Council of Augusta, 93 U. S. 116; West Wisconsin
Railroad v. Supervisors, 93 U. S. 595; Tennessee v. Sneed, 96 U. S. 69;
Williams v. Bruffy, 96 U. S. 176; Murray v. Charleston, 96 U. S. 432;

Imposts, laid by any State on Imports or Exports, shall be for the Use of the Treasury of the United States; and all such Laws shall be subject to the Revision and Controul of the Congress.[1]

Edwards v. Kearzey, 96 U. S. 595; Beer Co. v. Massachusetts, 97 U. S. 25; Keith v. Clark, 97 U. S. 454; Fertilizing Co. v. Hyde Park, 97 U. S. 659; Railroad Co. v. Georgia, 98 U. S. 359; University v. People, 99 U. S. 309; Packet Co. v. St. Louis, 100 U. S. 423; Vicksburg v. Tobin, 100 U. S. 430; Guy v. Baltimore, 100 U. S. 434; Kirtland v. Hotchkiss, 100 U. S. 491; Newton v. Commissioners, 100 U. S. 548; Railroad Co. v. Tennessee, 101 U. S. 337; Wright v. Nagle, 101 U. S. 791; Stone v. Mississippi, 101 U. S. 814; Railroad Co. v. Alabama, 101 U. S. 832; Louisiana v. New Orleans, 102 U. S. 203; Hartman v. Greenhow, 102 U. S. 672; Hall v. Wisconsin, 103 U. S. 5; Wolff v. New Orleans, 103 U. S. 358; Penniman's Case, 103 U. S. 714; Railroad Co. v. Hamersley, 104 U. S. 1; Asylum v. New Orleans, 105 U. S. 362; Guaranty Co. v. Board of Liquidation, 105 U. S. 622; Greenwood v. Freight Co., 105 U. S. 13; Kring v. Missouri, 107 U. S. 221; Antoni v. Greenhow, 107 U. S. 769; Ewell v. Daggs, 108 U. S. 144; Louisiana v. New Orleans, 109 U. S. 285; Gilfillan v. Union Canal Co., 109 U. S. 401; Hoff v. County of Jasper, 110 U. S. 53; Nelson v. St. Martin's Parish, 111 U. S. 716; Chicago Life Insurance Co. v. Needles, 113 U. S. 574; Virginia Coupon Cases, 114 U. S. 269; Amy v. Shelby County, 114 U. S. 387; Effinger v. Kenney, 115 U. S. 566; New Orleans Gas Co. v. Louisiana Light Co., 115 U. S. 650; Louisville Gas Co. v. Citizens' Gas Co., 115 U. S. 683; New Orleans Waterworks Co. v. Rivers, 115 U. S. 674; Fisk v. Jefferson Police Jury, 116 U. S. 131; Stone v. Farmers' Loan and Trust Co., 116 U. S. 307; Stone v. Illinois Central Railroad Co., 116 U. S. 347; Stone v. New Orleans & Northeastern Railroad, 116 U. S. 352; Royall v. Virginia, 116 U. S. 572; Hagood v. Southern, 117 U. S. 52; St. Tammany Waterworks v. New Orleans Water Works, 120 U. S. 64; United States v. Arjona, 120 U. S. 479; Church v. Kelsey, 121 U. S. 282; Lehigh Water Co. v. Easton, 121 U. S. 388; Seibert v. Lewis, 122 U. S. 284; New Orleans Waterworks Co. v. Louisiana Sugar Refining Co., 125 U. S. 18; Bank of Redemption v. Boston, 125 U. S. 60; Maynard v. Hill, 125 U. S. 190; Jaehne v. New York, 128 U. S. 189; Denny v. Bennett, 128 U. S. 489; Williamson v. New Jersey, 130 U. S. 189; Hunt v. Hunt, 131 U. S. appendix clxv; Freeland v. Williams, 131 U. S. 405; Campbell v. Wade, 132 U. S. 34; Pennsylvania Railroad Co. v. Miller, 132 U. S. 75; Crenshaw v. United States, 134 U. S. 99; Medley, Petitioner, 134 U. S. 160; McGahey v. Virginia, 135 U. S. 662; Bryan v. Virginia, 135 U. S. 662; Cuthbert v. Virginia, 135 U. S. 698; In re Brown, 135 U. S. 701; Hucless v. Childrey, 135 U. S. 709; Vashon v. Greenhow, 135 U. S. 713; Holden v. Minnesota, 137 U. S. 483; Sioux City Street Railway Co. v. Sioux City, 138 U. S. 98; Wheeling and Belmont Bridge Co. v. Wheeling Bridge Co., 138 U. S. 287.

[1] McCulloch v. Maryland, 4 Wheat. 316; Green v. Biddle, 8 Wheat. 1; Gibbons v. Ogden, 9 Wheat. 1; Brown v. Maryland, 12 Wheat. 419; Mager v. Grima, 8 How. 490; Cooley v. Board of Wardens of Port of

No State shall, without the Consent of Congress, lay
any Duty of Tonnage, keep Troops, or Ships of War in
time of Peace, enter into any Agreement or Compact with
another State, or with a foreign Power, or engage in War,·
unless actually invaded, or in such imminent Danger as
will not admit of delay.[1]

ARTICLE. II.

SECTION. 1. The executive Power shall be vested in
a President of the United States of America. He shall
hold his Office during the Term of four Years, and, together with the Vice President, chosen for the same
Term, be elected, as follows

Each State shall appoint, in such Manner as the
Legislature thereof may direct, a Number of Electors,
equal to the whole Number of Senators and Representatives to which the State may be entitled in the Congress:
but no Senator or Representative, or Person holding an
Office of Trust or Profit under the United States, shall
be appointed an Elector.[2]

Philadelphia *et al.*, 12 How. 299; Almy *v.* California, 24 How. 169;
License Tax Cases, 5 Wall. 462; Pervear *v.* Commonwealth, 5 Wall.
475; Steamship Co. *v.* Portwardens, 6 Wall. 31; Crandall *v.* Nevada,
6 Wall. 35; Waring *v.* The Mayor, 8 Wall. 110; Woodruff *v.* Parham, 8
Wall. 123; Hinson *v.* Lott, 8 Wall. 148; State Tonnage Tax Cases, 12
Wall. 204; State Tax on Railway Gross Receipts, 15 Wall. 284; Inman
Steamship Company *v.* Tinker, 94 U. S. 238; Cook *v.* Pennsylvania, 97
U. S. 566; Packet Co. *v.* Keokuk, 95 U. S. 80; Guy *v.* Baltimore, 100
U. S. 434; People *v.* Compagnie Générale Transatlantique, 107 U. S. 59;
Wiggins Ferry Co. *v.* East St. Louis, 107 U. S. 365; Brown *v.* Houston,
114 U. S. 622; Walling *v.* Michigan, 116 U. S. 446; Coe *v.* Errol, 116 U. S.
517; Turpin *v.* Burgess, 117 U. S. 504; Collet *v.* Collet, 2 Dall. 294.

[1] Green *v.* Biddle, 8 Wheat. 1; Poole *v.* The Lessee of Fleeger, 11 Pet.
185; Virginia *v.* West Virginia, 11 Wall. 39; Cooley *v.* Board of Wardens
of Port of Philadelphia, 12 How. 299; Peete *v.* Morgan, 19 Wall. 581;
Cannon *v.* New Orleans, 20 Wall. 577; Inman Steamship Company *v.*
Tinker, 94 U. S. 238; Transportation Co. *v.* Wheeling, 99 U. S. 273;
Packet Co. *v.* St. Louis, 100 U. S. 423; Guy *v.* Baltimore, 100 U. S. 434;
Packet Co. *v.* Keokuk, 95 U. S. 80; Vicksburg *v.* Tobin, 100 U. S. 430;
Packet Co. *v.* Catlettsburg, 105 U. S. 559; Transportation Co. *v.* Par-
kersburg, 107 U. S. 691; Morgan *v.* Louisiana, 118 U. S. 455; Huse *v.*
Glover, 119 U. S. 543; Ouachita Packet Co. *v.* Aiken, 121 U. S. 444;
Indiana *v.* Kentucky, 136 U. S. 479.

[2] Chisholm *v.* Georgia, 2 Dall. 419; Leitensdorfer *v.* Webb, 20 How.
176; *Ex parte* Siebold, 100 U. S. 371; *In re* Green, 134 U. S. 377.

The electors shall meet in their respective States, and vote by ballot for two Persons, of whom one at least shall not be an Inhabitant of the same State with themselves. And they shall make a List of all the Persons voted for, and of the Number of Votes for each; which List they shall sign and certify, and transmit sealed to the Seat of the Government of the United States, directed to the President of the Senate. The President of the Senate shall, in the Presence of the Senate and House of Representatives, open all the Certificates, and the Votes shall then be counted. The Person having the greatest Number of Votes shall be the President, if such Number be a Majority of the whole Number of Electors appointed; and if there be more than one who have such Majority, and have an equal Number of Votes, then the House of Representatives shall immediately chuse by Ballot one of them for President; and if no Person have a Majority, then from the five highest on the List the said House shall in like Manner chuse the President. But in chusing the President, the Votes shall be taken by States, the Representation from each State having one Vote; A quorum for this Purpose shall consist of a Member or Members from two-thirds of the States, and a Majority of all the States shall be necessary to a Choice. In every Case, after the Choice of the President, the Person having the greatest Number of Votes of the Electors shall be the Vice President. But if there should remain two or more who have equal Votes, the Senate shall chuse from them by Ballot the Vice President.[1]

The Congress may determine the Time of chusing the Electors, and the Day on which they shall give their Votes; which Day shall be the same throughout the United States.

No Person except a natural born Citizen, or a Citizen of the United States, at the time of the Adoption of this Constitution, shall be eligible to the Office of President; neither shall any Person be eligible to that Office who shall not have attained to the Age of thirty five

---

[1] This clause has been superseded by the Twelfth Amendment.

Years, and been fourteen Years a Resident within the
United States.[1]

In Case of the Removal of the President from Office, or of his Death, Resignation, or Inability to discharge the Powers and Duties of the said Office, the same shall devolve on the Vice President, and the Congress may by Law provide for the Case of Removal, Death, Resignation or Inability, both of the President and Vice President, declaring what Officer shall then act as President, and such Officer shall act accordingly, until the Disability be removed, or a President shall be elected.

The President shall, at stated Times, receive for his Services, a Compensation, which shall neither be encreased nor diminished during the Period for which he shall have been elected, and he shall not receive within that Period any other Emolument from the United States, or any of them.

Before he enter on the Execution of his Office, he shall take the following Oath or Affirmation: — "I do solemnly swear (or affirm) that I will faithfully execute the Office of President of the United States, and will to the best of my Ability, preserve, protect and defend the Constitution of the United States."

SECTION. 2. The President shall be Commander in Chief of the Army and Navy of the United States, and of the Militia of the several States, when called into the actual Service of the United States; he may require the Opinion, in writing, of the principal Officer in each of the executive Departments, upon any Subject relating to the Duties of their respective Offices, and he shall have Power to grant Reprieves and Pardons for Offences against the United States, except in Cases of Impeachment.[2]

---

[1] English v. The Trustees of the Sailors' Snug Harbor, 3 Pet. 99.

[2] Houston v. Moore, 5 Wheat. 1; United States v. Wilson, 7 Pet. 150; Ex parte Wells, 18 How. 307; Ex parte Garland, 4 Wall. 333; Armstrong's Foundry, 6 Wall. 766; Texas v. White, 7 Wall. 700; The Grapeshot, 9 Wall. 129; United States v. Padelford, 9 Wall. 531; United States v. Klein, 13 Wall. 128; Armstrong v. United States, 13 Wall. 154; Pargoud v. United States, 13 Wall. 156; Hamilton v. Dillin, 21 Wall. 73; Mechanics and Traders' Bank v. Union Bank, 22 Wall. 276; Lamar v. Browne, 92 U. S. 187; Wallach v. Van Riswick, 92 U. S. 202; In re Neagle, 135 U. S. 1.

He shall have Power, by and with the Advice and Consent of the Senate, to make Treaties, provided two-thirds of the Senators present concur; and he shall nominate, and by and with the Advice and Consent of the Senate, shall appoint Ambassadors, other public Ministers and Consuls, Judges of the supreme Court, and all other Officers of the United States, whose Appointments are not herein otherwise provided for, and which shall be established by Law: but the Congress may by Law vest the Appointment of such inferior Officers, as they think proper, in the President alone, in the Courts of Law, or in the Heads of Departments.[1]

The President shall have Power to fill up all Vacancies that may happen during the Recess of the Senate, by granting Commissions which shall expire at the End of their next Session.[2]

SECTION. 3. He shall from time to time give to the Congress Information of the State of the Union, and recommend to their Consideration such Measures as he shall judge necessary and expedient; he may, on extraordinary Occasions, convene both Houses, or either of them, and in Case of Disagreement between them, with Respect to the Time of Adjournment, he may adjourn them to such Time as he shall think proper; he shall receive Ambassadors and other public Ministers; he shall take Care that the Laws be faithfully executed, and shall Commission all the Officers of the United States.[3]

SECTION. 4. The President, Vice President and all civil

---

[1] Ware v. Hylton, 3 Dall. 199; Marbury v. Madison, 1 Cranch, 137; United States v. Kirkpatrick, 9 Wheat. 720; American Insurance Company v. Canter (356 bales cotton), 1 Pet. 511; Foster and Elam v. Neilson, 2 Pet. 253; Cherokee Nation v. State of Georgia, 5 Pet. 1; Patterson v. Winn, 5 Pet. 233; Worcester v. State of Georgia, 6 Pet. 515; City of New Orleans v. De Armas, 9 Pet. 224; United States v. Le Baron, 19 How. 73; Holden v. Joy, 17 Wall. 211; United States v. Germaine, 99 U. S. 508; Ex parte Siebold, 100 U. S. 371; United States v. Arjona, 120 U. S. 479; In re Neagle, 135 U. S. 1.

[2] The United States v. Kirkpatrick, 9 Wheat. 720; In re Neagle, 135 U. S. 1.

[3] Marbury v. Madison, 1 Cranch, 137; Kendall v. United States, 12 Pet. 524; Luther v. Borden, 7 How. 1; Mississippi v. Johnson, President, 4 Wall. 475; Stewart v. Kahn, 11 Wall. 493; In re Neagle, 135 U. S. 1.

Officers of the United States, shall be removed from Office on Impeachment for, and Conviction of, Treason, Bribery, or other high Crimes and Misdemeanors.

ARTICLE. III.

SECTION. 1. The judicial Power of the United States, shall be vested in one supreme Court, and in such inferior Courts as the Congress may from time to time ordain and establish. The Judges, both of the supreme and inferior Courts, shall hold their Offices during good Behaviour, and shall, at stated Times, receive for their Services, a Compensation, which shall not be diminished during their Continuance in Office.[1]

SECTION. 2. The Judicial Power shall extend to all Cases, in Law and Equity, arising under this Constitution, the Laws of the United States, and Treaties made, or which shall be made, under their Authority; — to all Cases affecting Ambassadors, other public Ministers and Consuls; — to all Cases of admiralty and maritime Jurisdiction; — to Controversies to which the United States shall be a party; — to Controversies between two or more States; — between a State and Citizens of another State; — between Citizens of different States, — between Citizens of the same State claiming Lands under Grants of different States, and between a State, or the Citizens thereof, and foreign States, Citizens or Subjects.[2]

---

[1] Chisholm v. Georgia, 2 Dall. 419; Stuart v. Laird, 1 Cranch, 299; United States v. Peters, 5 Cranch, 115; Durousseau v. United States, 6 Cranch, 308; Martin v. Hunter's Lessee, 1 Wheat. 304; Cohens v. Virginia, 6 Wheat. 264; Osborn v. United States Bank, 9 Wheat. 738; Benner v. Porter, 9 How. 235; United States v. Ritchie, 17 How. 525; Murray's Lessee v. Hoboken Land and Improvement Co., 18 How. 272; Ex parte Vallandigham, 1 Wall. 243; The Grapeshot, 9 Wall. 129; Mechanics' and Traders' Bank v. Union Bank of Louisiana, 22 Wall. 276; United States v. Union Pacific Railroad, 98 U. S. 569; Ames v. Kansas, 111 U. S. 449; In re Loney, 134 U. S. 372.

[2] United States v. Ravara, 2 Dall. 297; Georgia v. Brailsford, 2 Dall. 402; Hayburn's Case (note), 2 Dall. 410; Oswald v. New York, 2 Dall. 415; Chisholm v. Georgia, 2 Dall. 419; Glass v. Sloop Betsey, 3 Dall. 6; Bingham v. Cabott, 3 Dall. 19; Penhallow v. Doane's Administrator, 3 Dall. 54; United States v. La Vengeance, 3 Dall. 297; Hollingsworth v.

In all Cases affecting Ambassadors, other public Ministers and Consuls, and those in which a State shall be Party, the supreme Court shall have original Jurisdiction. In all the other Cases before mentioned, the supreme Court shall have appellate Jurisdiction, both as to Law

---

Virginia, 3 Dall. 378; Mossman v. Higginson, 4 Dall. 12; Abercrombie v. Dupuis, 1 Cranch, 343; Marbury v. Madison, 1 Cranch, 137; Hepburn v. Ellzey, 2 Cranch, 444; United States v. Moore, 3 Cranch, 159; Strawbridge v. Curtiss, 3 Cranch, 267; Ex parte Bollman, 4 Cranch, 75; Rose v. Himely, 4 Cranch, 241; Chappedelaine v. Dechenaux, 4 Cranch, 306; United States v. Schooner Betsey, 4 Cranch, 443; Hope Insurance Company v. Boardman, 5 Cranch, 57; Bank of United States v. Deveaux, 5 Cranch, 61; Hodgson v. Bowerbank, 5 Cranch, 303; Owings v. Norwood's Lessee, 5 Cranch, 344; Durousseau v. The United States, 6 Cranch, 307; United States v. Hudson and Goodwin, 7 Cranch, 32; Town of Pawlet v. Clark, 9 Cranch, 292; Martin v. Hunter's Lessee, 1 Wheat. 304; United States v. Coolidge, 1 Wheat. 415; Colson v. Lewis, 2 Wheat. 377; Gelston v. Hoyt, 3 Wheat. 246; United States v. Bevans, 3 Wheat. 336; Houston v. Moore, 5 Wheat. 1; Cohens v. Virginia, 6 Wheat. 264; Ex parte Kearney, 7 Wheat. 38; Matthews v. Zane, 7 Wheat. 164; Osborn v. United States Bank, 9 Wheat. 738; United States v. Ortega, 11 Wheat. 467; American Insurance Company v. Canter (356 bales of cotton), 1 Pet. 511; Jackson v. Twentyman, 2 Pet. 136; Cherokee Nation v. Georgia, 5 Pet. 1; New Jersey v. New York, 5 Pet. 283; Worcester v. Georgia, 6 Pet. 515; Davis v. Packard, 6 Pet. 41; United States v. Arredondo, 6 Pet. 691; Davis v. Packard, 7 Pet. 276; Breedlove v. Nicolet, 7 Pet. 413; Brown v. Keene, 8 Pet. 112; Davis v. Packard, 8 Pet. 312; City of New Orleans v. De Armas, 9 Pet. 224; Rhode Island v. Massachusetts, 12 Pet. 657; Bank of Augusta v. Earle, 13 Pet. 519; Commercial and Railroad Bank of Vicksburg v. Slocomb, 14 Pet. 60; Suydam v. Broadnax, 14 Pet. 67; Prigg v. Pennsylvania, 16 Pet. 539; Louisville, Cincinnati and Charleston Railroad Co. v. Letson, 2 How. 497; Cary v. Curtis, 3 How. 236; Waring v. Clark, 5 How. 441; New Jersey Steam Navigation Co. v. Merchants' Bank, 6 How. 344; Luther v. Borden, 7 How. 1; Sheldon v. Sill, 8 How. 441; The Propeller Genesee Chief v. Fitzhugh, 12 How. 443; Fretz v. Bull, 12 How. 466; Neves v. Scott, 13 How. 268; Pennsylvania v. The Wheeling &c. Bridge Company, 13 How. 518; Marshall v. Baltimore and Ohio Railroad Co., 16 How. 314; United States v. Guthrie, 17 How. 284; Smith v. Maryland, 18 How. 71; Jones v. League, 18 How. 76; Murray's Lessee v. Hoboken Land and Improvement Company, 18 How. 272; Dodge v. Woolsey, 18 How. 331; Dred Scott v. Sandford, 19 How. 393; Hyde v. Stone, 20 How. 170; Jackson v. Steamboat Magnolia, 20 How. 296; Irvine v. Marshall, 20 How. 558; Fenn v. Holme, 21 How. 481; Morewood v. Enequist, 23 How. 491; Kentucky v. Dennison, Governor, 24 How. 66; Ohio and Mississippi Railroad Company v. Wheeler, 1 Black, 286; The Steamer Saint Lawrence, 1 Black, 522; The Propeller Commerce, 1 Black, 574; Ex parte Vallandigham, 1 Wall. 243; Ex parte Milligan, 4 Wall. 2; The Moses Taylor, 4 Wall. 411; Mississippi v. Johnson, President, 4 Wall. 475; The Hine v. Trevor, 4 Wall. 555; Philadel-

and Fact, with such Exceptions, and under such Regulations as the Congress shall make.[1]

The Trial of all Crimes, except in Cases of Impeachment, shall be by Jury; and such Trial shall be held in the State where the said Crimes shall have been committed; but when not committed within any State, the

---

phia v. The Collector, 5 Wall. 720; Georgia v. Stanton, 6 Wall. 50; Payne v. Hook, 7 Wall. 425; The Alicia, 7 Wall. 571; Cowles v. Mercer County, 7 Wall. 118; The Belfast, 7 Wall. 624; *Ex parte* Yerger, 8 Wall. 85; Insurance Company v. Dunham, 11 Wall. 1; Virginia v. West Virginia, 11 Wall. 39; Coal Co. v. Blatchford, 11 Wall. 172; Railway Co. v. Whitton's Adm., 13 Wall. 270; Tarble's Case, 13 Wall. 397; Blyew v. United States, 13 Wall. 581; Davis v. Gray, 16 Wall. 203; Steamboat Co. v. Chase, 16 Wall. 522; Case of the Sewing Machine Companies, 18 Wall. 553; Insurance Co. v. Dunn, 19 Wall. 214; The Mohler, 21 Wall. 230; Insurance Company v. Morse, 20 Wall. 445; Vannevar v. Bryant, 21 Wall. 41; The Lottawanna, 21 Wall. 558; Gaines v. Fuentes, 92 U. S. 10; Muller v. Dows, 94 U. S. 444; Doyle v. Continental Insurance Company, 94 U. S. 535; United States v. Hall, 98 U. S. 343; United States v. Union Pacific Railroad Co., 98 U. S. 569; Tennessee v. Davis, 100 U. S. 257; *Ex parte* Boyd, 105 U. S. 647; New Hampshire v. Louisiana, 108 U. S. 76; New York v. Louisiana, 108 U. S. 76; Johnson v. Chicago &c. Elevator Co., 119 U. S. 388; Barron v. Burnside, 121 U. S. 186; De Saussure v. Gaillard, 127 U. S. 216; Wisconsin v. Pelican Insurance Co., 127 U. S. 265; Hans v. Louisiana, 134 U. S. 1; Johnson v. Risk, 137 U. S. 300; Cook County v. Calumet &c. Canal & Dock Co., 138 U. S. 635.

[1] Chisholm v. Georgia, 2 Dall. 419; Wiscart v. Dauchy, 3 Dall. 321; Marbury v. Madison, 1 Cranch, 137; *Ex parte* Bollman, 4 Cranch, 75; Durousseau v. United States, 6 Cranch, 307; Martin v. Hunter's Lessee, 1 Wheat. 304; Cohens v. Virginia, 6 Wheat. 264; *Ex parte* Kearney, 7 Wheat. 38; Wayman v. Southard, 10 Wheat. 1; Bank of the United States v. Halstead, 10 Wheat. 51; United States v. Ortega, 11 Wheat. 467; The Cherokee Nation v. Georgia, 5 Pet. 1; *Ex parte* Crane, 5 Pet. 189; New Jersey v. New York, 5 Pet. 283; Davis v. Packard, 7 Pet. 276; *Ex parte* Sibbald v. United States, 12 Pet. 488; Rhode Island v. Massachusetts, 12 Pet. 657; Pennsylvania v. The Wheeling &c. Bridge Company, 13 How. 518; *In re* Kaine, 14 How. 103; Ableman v. Booth; United States v. Booth, 21 How. 506; *Ex parte* Vallandingham, 1 Wall. 243; Kentucky v. Dennison, 24 How. 66; Freeborn v. Smith, 2 Wall. 160; *Ex parte* McCardle, 6 Wall. 318; *Ex parte* McCardle, 7 Wall. 506; Texas v. White, 7 Wall. 700: *Ex parte* Yerger, 8 Wall. 85; The Lucy, 8 Wall. 307; The Justices v. Murray, 9 Wall. 274; Pennsylvania v. Quicksilver Company, 10 Wall. 553; Virginia v. West Virginia, 11 Wall. 39; Murdock v. City of Memphis, 20 Wall. 590; Tennessee v. Davis, 100 U. S. 257; The Francis Wright, 105 U. S. 381; Börs v. Preston, 111 U. S. 252; Ames v. Kansas, 111 U. S. 449; Wisconsin v. Pelican Insurance Co., 127 U. S. 265; *In re* Baiz, 135 U. S. 403.

Trial shall be at such Place or Places as the Congress may by Law have directed.[1]

SECTION. 3. Treason against the United States, shall consist only in levying War against them, or in adhering to their Enemies, giving them Aid and Comfort. No Person shall be convicted of Treason unless on the Testimony of two Witnesses to the same overt Act, or on Confession in open Court.[2]

The Congress shall have Power to declare the Punishment of Treason, but no Attainder of Treason shall work Corruption of Blood, or Forfeiture except during the Life of the Person attainted.[3]

ARTICLE. IV.

SECTION. 1. Full Faith and Credit shall be given in each State to the public Acts, Records, and judicial Proceedings of every other State. And the Congress may by general Laws prescribe the Manner in which such Acts, Records and Proceedings shall be proved, and the Effect thereof.[4]

---

[1] United States v. Dawson, 15 How. 467; United States v. Jackalow, 1 Black, 484; Ex parte Milligan, 4 Wall. 2; Callan v. Wilson, 127 U. S. 540; Nashville, Chattanooga &c. Railway Co. v. Alabama, 128 U. S. 96; Eilenbecker v. District Court of Plymouth County, 134 U. S. 32; Jones v. United States, 137 U. S. 202; Cook v. United States, 138 U. S. 157.

[2] United States v. The Insurgents, 2 Dall. 335; United States v. Vigol, 2 Dall. 346; United States v. Mitchell, 2 Dall. 348; Ex parte Bollman and Swartwout, 4 Cranch, 75; United States v. Aaron Burr, 4 Cranch, 470.

[3] Bigelow v. Forest, 9 Wall. 339; Day v. Micou, 18 Wall. 156; Ex parte Lange, 18 Wall. 163; Wallach v. Van Riswick, 92 U. S. 202.

[4] Armstrong v. Carson's Executors, 2 Dall. 302; Mills v. Duryee, 7 Cranch, 481; Hampton v. McConnel, 3 Wheat. 234; Mayhew v. Thatcher, 6 Wheat. 129; Darby's Lessee v. Mayer, 10 Wheat. 465; United States v. Amedy, 11 Wheat. 392; Caldwell v. Carrington's Heirs, 9 Pet. 86; M'Elmoyle v. Cohen, 13 Pet. 312; Bank of Augusta v. Earle, 13 Pet. 519; Bank of the State of Alabama v. Dalton, 9 How. 522; D'Arcy v. Ketchum, 11 How. 165; Kentucky v. Dennison, Governor, &c., 24 How. 66; Christmas v. Russell, 5 Wall. 290; Green v. Van Buskirk, 7 Wall. 139; Paul v. Virginia, 8 Wall. 168; Cheever v. Wilson, 9 Wall. 108; Board of Public Works v. Columbia College, 17 Wall. 521; Thompson v. Whitman, 18 Wall. 457; Bonaparte v. Tax Court, 104 U. S. 592; Robertson v. Pickrell, 108 U. S. 608; Hanley v. Donoghue, 116 U. S. 1;

SECTION. 2. The Citizens of each State shall be en-titled to all Privileges and Immunities of Citizens in the several States.[1]

A person charged in any State with Treason, Felony, or other Crime, who shall flee from Justice, and be found in another State, shall on Demand of the executive Authority of the State from which he fled, be delivered up, to be removed to the State having Jurisdiction of the Crime.[2]

No Person held to Service or Labour in one State, under the Laws thereof, escaping into another, shall, in Consequence of any Law or Regulation therein, be dis-charged from such Service or Labour, but shall be delivered up on Claim of the Party to whom such Ser-vice or Labour may be due.[3]

SECTION. 3. New States may be admitted by the Con-gress into this Union; but no new State shall be formed or erected within the Jurisdiction of any other State;

Renaud *v.* Abbott, 116 U. S. 277; Chicago & Alton Railroad *v.* Wiggins Ferry Co., 119 U. S 615; Wisconsin *v.* Pelican Insurance Co., 127 U. S. 265; Cole *v.* Cunningham, 133 U. S. 107; Simmons *v.* Saul, 138 U. S. 439.

[1] Bank of United States *v.* Deveaux, 5 Cranch, 61; Gassies *v.* Ballou, 6 Pet. 761; Rhode Island *v.* Massachusetts, 12 Pet. 657; The Bank of Augusta *v.* Earle, 13 Pet. 519; Moore *v.* The People of the State of Illi-nois, 14 How. 13; Dodge *v.* Woolsey, 18 How. 331; Conner *v.* Elliott, 18 How. 591; Dred Scott *v.* Sandford. 19 How. 393; Crandall *v.* Nevada, 6 Wall. 35; Woodruff *v.* Parham, 8 Wall. 123; Paul *v.* Virginia, 8 Wall. 168; Downham *v.* Alexandria Council, 10 Wall. 173; Ducat *v.* Chicago, 10 Wall. 410; Liverpool Insurance Company *v.* Massachusetts, 10 Wall. 566; Ward *v.* Maryland, 12 Wall. 418; Slaughterhouse Cases, 16 Wall. 36; Bradwell *v.* The State, 16 Wall. 130; Minor *v.* Happersett, 21 Wall. 162; Chemung Bank *v.* Lowery, 93 U. S. 72; McCready *v.* Virginia, 94 U. S. 391; United States *v.* Harris, 106 U. S. 629; Brown *v.* Houston, 114 U. S. 622; Pembina Consolidated Mining Co. *v.* Pennsylvania, 125 U. S. 181; Kimmish *v.* Ball, 129 U. S. 217; Cole *v.* Cunningham, 133 U. S. 107; Norfolk and Western Railroad Co. *v.* Pennsylvania, 136 U. S. 114; Min-nesota *v.* Barber, 136 U. S. 313.

[2] Holmes *v.* Jennison, 14 Pet. 540; Kentucky *v.* Dennison, Governor, 24 How. 66; Taylor *v.* Taintor, 16 Wall. 366; Robb *v.* Connolly, 111 U. S. 624.

[3] Prigg *v.* Pennsylvania, 16 Pet. 539; Jones *v.* Van Zandt, 5 How. 215; Strader *v.* Graham, 10 How. 82; Moore *v.* The People of the State of Illi-nois, 14 How. 13; Dred Scott *v.* Sandford, 19 How. 393; Ableman *v.* Booth; United States *v.* Booth, 21 How. 506.

nor any State be formed by the Junction of two or more States, or Parts of States, without the Consent of the Legislatures of the States concerned as well as of the Congress.[1]

The Congress shall have Power to dispose of and make all needful Rules and Regulations respecting the Territory or other Property belonging to the United States; and nothing in this Constitution shall be so construed as to Prejudice any Claims of the United States, or of any particular State.[2]

SECTION. 4. The United States shall guarantee to every State in this Union a Republican Form of Government, and shall protect each of them against Invasion; and on Application of the Legislature, or of the Executive (when the Legislature cannot be convened) against domestic Violence.[3]

ARTICLE. V.

The Congress, whenever two thirds of both Houses shall deem it necessary, shall propose Amendments to this Constitution, or, on the Application of the Legislatures of two thirds of the several States, shall call a Convention for proposing Amendments, which, in either Case, shall be valid to all Intents and Purposes, as Part of this Constitution, when ratified by the Legislatures of three fourths of the several States, or by Conventions in three fourths thereof, as the one or the other Mode of Ratification may be proposed by the Congress; Provided

---

[1] American Insurance Company v. Canter (356 Bales of Cotton), 1 Pet. 511; Pollard's Lessee v. Hagan, 3 How. 212; Cross v. Harrison, 16 How. 164.

[2] McCulloch v. Maryland, 4 Wheat. 316; American Insurance Company v. Canter, 1 Pet. 511; United States v. Gratiot, 14 Pet. 526; United States v. Rogers, 4 How. 567; Cross v. Harrison, 16 How. 164; Mackey v. Coxe, 18 How. 100; Dred Scott v. Sandford, 19 How. 393; Freeborn v. Smith, 2 Wall. 160; Gibson v. Chouteau, 13 Wall. 92; Clinton v. Englebrecht, 13 Wall. 434; Beall v. New Mexico, 16 Wall. 535; United States v. Waddell, 112 U. S. 76; Van Brocklin v. Tennessee, 117 U. S. 151; Wisconsin Central Railroad Co. v. Price County, 133 U. S. 496; Mormon Church v. United States, 136 U. S. 1.

[3] Luther v. Borden, 7 How. 1; Texas v. White, 7 Wall. 700; Minor v. Happersett, 21 Wall. 162.

that no Amendment which may be made prior to the Year One thousand eight hundred and eight shall in any Manner affect the first and fourth Clauses in the Ninth Section of the first Article; and that no State, without its Consent, shall be deprived of its equal Suffrage in the Senate.

ARTICLE. VI.

All Debts contracted and Engagements entered into, before the Adoption of this Constitution, shall be as valid against the United States under this Constitution, as under the Confederation.[1]

This Constitution, and the Laws of the United. States which shall be made in Pursuance thereof; and all Treaties made, or which shall be made, under the Authority of the United States, shall be the supreme Law of the Land; and the Judges in every State shall be bound thereby, any Thing in the Constitution or Laws of any State to the Contrary notwithstanding.[2]

The Senators and Representatives before mentioned, and the Members of the several State Legislatures, and all executive and judicial Officers, both of the United States and of the several States, shall be bound by Oath or Affirmation, to support this Constitution; but no religious Test shall ever be required as a Qualification to any Office or public Trust under the United States.[3]

---

[1] Dred Scott v. Sandford, 19 How. 393.

[2] Hayburn's Case, 2 Dall. 409; Ware v. Hylton, 3 Dall. 199; Calder and Wife v. Bull and Wife, 3 Dall. 386; Marbury v. Madison, 1 Cranch, 137; Chirac v. Chirac, 2 Wheat. 259; McCulloch v. Maryland, 4 Wheat. 316; Society v. New Haven, 8 Wheat. 464; Gibbons v. Ogden, 9 Wheat. 1; Foster and Elam v. Neilson, 2 Pet. 253; Buckner v. Finley, 2 Pet. 586; Worcester v. Georgia, 6 Pet. 515; Kennett v. Chambers, 14 How. 38; Dodge v. Woolsey, 18 How. 331; Dred Scott v. Sandford, 19 How. 393; New York v. Dibble, 21 How. 366; Ableman v. Booth; United States v. Booth, 21 How. 506; Sinnot v. Davenport, 22 How. 227; Foster v. Davenport, 22 How. 244; Society for Savings v. Coite, 6 Wall. 594; Provident Institution v. Massachusetts. 6 Wall. 611; Haver v. Yaker, 9 Wall. 32; The Cherokee Tobacco, 11 Wall. 616; Hauenstein v. Lynham, 100 U. S. 483; Edye v. Robertson, 112 U. S. 580; Van Brocklin v. Tennessee, 117 U. S. 151; United States v. Rauscher, 119 U. S. 407; Whitney v. Robertson, 124 U. S. 190; The Chinese Exclusion Case, 130 U. S. 581; In re Neagle, 135 U. S. 1.

[3] Dodge v. Woolsey, 18 How. 331; Ex parte Garland, 4 Wall. 333; In re Neagle, 135 U. S. 1.

ARTICLE. VII.

The Ratification of the Conventions of nine States, shall be sufficient for the Establishment of this Constitution between the States so ratifying the Same.

The word "the", being interlined between the seventh and eighth Lines of the first Page, The Word "Thirty" being partly written on an Erazure in the fifteenth Line of the first Page, The Words "is tried" being interlined between the thirty second and thirty third Lines of the first Page and the Word "the" being interlined between the forty third and forty fourth Lines of the second Page.

[NOTE BY PRINTER.—The interlined and rewritten words, mentioned in the above explanation, are in this edition, printed in their proper places in the text.]

DONE in Convention by the Unanimous Consent of the States present the Seventeenth Day of September in the Year of our Lord one thousand seven hundred and Eighty seven and of the Independance of the United States of America the Twelfth **In Witness** whereof We have hereunto subscribed our Names,

G⁰: WASHINGTON — *Presidt.*
and deputy from Virginia

Attest WILLIAM JACKSON *Secretary*

New Hampshire { JOHN LANGDON
NICHOLAS GILMAN }

Massachusetts { NATHANIEL GORHAM
RUFUS KING

Connecticut { WM: SAML. JOHNSON
ROGER SHERMAN

New York . . . ALEXANDER HAMILTON

New Jersey { WIL: LIVINGSTON
DAVID BREARLEY.
WM. PATERSON.
JONA: DAYTON

Pennsylvania { B FRANKLIN
THOMAS MIFFLIN
ROBT. MORRIS
GEO. CLYMER
THOS. FITZ SIMONS
JARED INGERSOLL
JAMES WILSON
GOUV MORRIS

Delaware	GEO: READ GUNNING BEDFORD jun JOHN DICKINSON RICHARD BASSETT JACO: BROOM
Maryland	JAMES MCHENRY DAN OF ST THOS. JENIFER DANL CARROLL
Virginia	JOHN BLAIR— JAMES MADISON Jr.
North Carolina	WM: BLOUNT RICHD. DOBBS SPAIGHT. HU WILLIAMSON
South Carolina	J. RUTLEDGE CHARLES COTESWORTH PINCKNEY CHARLES PINCKNEY PIERCE BUTLER.
Georgia	WILLIAM FEW ABR BALDWIN

ARTICLES

IN

ADDITION TO, AND AMENDMENT OF

THE

CONSTITUTION OF THE UNITED STATES OF AMERICA,

PROPOSED BY CONGRESS AND RATIFIED BY THE LEGISLA-
TURES OF THE SEVERAL STATES, PURSUANT TO THE
FIFTH ARTICLE OF THE CONSTITUTION.

[ARTICLE I.][1]

Congress shall make no law respecting an establishment of religion, or prohibiting the free exercise thereof;

---

[1] Terrett *v.* Taylor, 9 Cranch, 43; Vidal *v.* Girard, 2 How. 127; *Ex parte*
Garland, 4 Wall. 333; United States *v.* Cruikshank, 92 U. S. 542; Reynolds *v.* United States, 98 U. S. 145; Presser *v.* Illinois, 116 U. S. 252;
Spies *v.* Illinois, 123 U. S. 131; Davis *v.* Beason, 133 U. S. 333; Eilenbecker *v.* District Court of Plymouth County, 134 U. S. 31; *In re* Neagle,
135 U. S. 1.

or abridging the freedom of speech, or of the press; or the right of the people peaceably to assemble, and to petition the Government for a redress of grievances.

[ARTICLE II.]

A well regulated Militia, being necessary to the security of a free State, the right of the people to keep and bear Arms, shall not be infringed.[1]

[ARTICLE III.]

No Soldier shall, in time of peace be quartered in any house without the consent of the Owner, nor in time of war, but in a manner to be prescribed by law.[2]

[ARTICLE IV.]

The right of the people to be secure in their persons, houses, papers, and effects, against unreasonable searches and seizures, shall not be violated, and no Warrants shall issue, but upon probable cause, supported by Oath or affirmation, and particularly describing the place to be searched, and the persons or things to be seized.[3]

[ARTICLE V.]

No person shall be held to answer for a capital, or otherwise infamous crime, unless on a presentment or indictment of a Grand Jury, except in cases arising in the land or naval forces, or in the Militia, when in actual service in time of War or public danger; nor shall any person be subject for the same offence to be twice put in jeopardy of life or limb; nor shall be compelled in any Criminal Case to be a witness against himself, nor be

---

[1] Presser v. Illinois, 116 U. S. 252; Spies v. Illinois, 123 U. S. 131; Eilenbecker v. District Court of Plymouth County, 134 U. S. 31.

[2] Spies v. Illinois, 123 U. S. 131; Eilenbecker v. District Court of Plymouth County, 134 U. S. 31.

[3] Smith v. Maryland, 18 How. 71; Murray's Lessee v. Hoboken Land and Improvement Company, 18 How. 272; Ex parte Milligan, 4 Wall. 2; Ex parte Jackson, 96 U. S. 727; Boyd v. United States, 116 U. S. 616; Spies v. Illinois, 123 U. S. 131; Eilenbecker v. District Court of Plymouth County, 134 U. S. 31.

deprived of life, liberty, or property, without due process
of law; nor shall private property be taken for public
use, without just compensation.[1]

[ARTICLE VI.]

In all criminal prosecutions, the accused shall enjoy the right to a speedy and public trial, by an impartial jury of the State and district wherein the crime shall have been committed, which district shall have been previously ascertained by law, and to be informed of the nature and cause of the accusation; to be confronted with the witnesses against him; to have compulsory process for obtaining Witnesses in his favor, and to have the Assistance of Counsel for his defence.[2]

---

[1] Houston v. Moore, 5 Wheat. 1; United States v. Perez, 9 Wheat. 579; Barron v. The City of Baltimore, 7 Pet. 243; Fox v. Ohio, 5 How. 410; West River Bridge Company v. Dix, 6 How. 507; Mitchell v. Harmony, 13 How. 115; Moore v. The People of the State of Illinois, 14 How. 13; Murray's Lessee v. Hoboken Land and Improvement Company, 18 How. 272; Dynes v. Hoover, 20 How. 65; Withers v. Buckley, 20 How. 84; Gilman v. The City of Sheboygan, 2 Black, 510; Ex parte Milligan, 4 Wall. 2; Twitchell v. The Commonwealth, 7 Wall. 321; Hepburn v. Griswold, 8 Wall. 603; Miller v. United States, 11 Wall. 268; Legal Tender Cases, 12 Wall. 457; Pumpelly v. Green Bay Co., 13 Wall. 166; Osborn v. Nicholson, 13 Wall. 654; Ex parte Lange, 18 Wall. 163; Minor v. Happersett, 21 Wall. 162; The Mohler, 21 Wall. 230; Secombe v. Milwaukee & St. Paul Railroad Co., 23 Wall. 108; Kohl v. United States, 91 U. S. 367; Davidson v. New Orleans, 96 U. S. 97; Sinking Fund Cases, 99 U. S. 700; Transportation Co. v. Chicago, 99 U. S. 635; Kelly v. Pittsburgh, 104 U. S. 78; United States v. Lee, 106 U. S. 196; Ex parte Wall, 107 U. S. 265; United States v. Jones, 109 U. S. 513; Ex parte Wilson, 114 U. S. 417; Boyd v. United States, 116 U. S. 616; Mackin v. United States, 117 U. S. 348; Ex parte Bain, 121 U. S. 1; Parkinson v. United States, 121 U. S. 281; Spies v. Illinois, 123 U. S. 131; Callau v. Wilson, 127 U. S. 540; United States v. De Walt, 128 U. S. 393; Eilenbecker v. District Court of Plymouth County, 134 U. S. 31; Louisville and Nashville Railroad Co. v. Woodson, 134 U. S. 614; Cherokee Nation v. Southern Kansas Railway, 135 U. S. 641; In re Kemmler, 136 U. S. 436.

[2] United States v. Cooper, 4 Dall. 341; United States v. Coolidge, 1 Wheat. 415; Ex parte Kearney, 7 Wheat. 38; United States v. Mills, 7 Pet. 142; Barron v. City of Baltimore, 7 Pet. 243; Fox v. Ohio, 5 How. 410; United States v. Dawson, 15 How. 467; Withers v. Buckley, 20 How. 84; United States v. Jackalow, 1 Black, 484; Ex parte Milligan, 4 Wall. 2; Twitchell v. The Commonwealth, 7 Wall. 321; Miller v. United States, 11 Wall. 268; United States v. Cook, 17 Wall. 168; Walker v. Sauvinet, 92 U. S. 90; United States v. Cruikshank, 92 U. S.

[ARTICLE VII.]

In suits at common law, where the value in controversy shall exceed twenty dollars, the right of trial by jury shall be preserved, and no fact tried by a jury shall be otherwise re-examined in any Court of the United States, than according to the rules of the common law.[1]

[ARTICLE VIII.]

Excessive bail shall not be required, nor excessive fines imposed, nor cruel and unusual punishments inflicted.[2]

[ARTICLE IX.]

The enumeration in the Constitution, of certain rights, shall not be construed to deny or disparage others retained by the people.[3]

[ARTICLE X.]

The powers not delegated to the United States by the Constitution, nor prohibited by it to the States, are reserved to the States respectively, or to the people.[4]

542; Reynolds *v.* United States, 98 U. S. 145; United States *v.* Union Pacific Railroad, 98 U. S. 569; Hayes *v.* Missouri, 120 U. S. 68; Spies *v.* Illinois, 123 U. S. 131; Brooks *v.* Missouri, 124 U. S. 394; Callan *v.* Wilson, 127 U. S. 540; Eilenbecker *v.* District Court of Plymouth County, 134 U. S. 31; Jones *v.* United States, 137 U. S. 202; Cook *v.* United States, 138 U. S. 157.

[1] United States *v.* La Vengeance, 3 Dall. 297; Whelan *v.* United States, 7 Cranch, 112; United States *v.* Schooner Betsey, 4 Cranch, 443; Bank of Columbia *v.* Okely, 4 Wheat. 235; Bank of Hamilton *v.* Dudley's Heirs, 2 Pet. 492; Parsons *v.* Bedford, 3 Pet. 433; Lessee of Livingston *v.* Moore, 7 Pet. 469; Webster *v.* Reid, 11 How. 437; Pennsylvania *v.* The Wheeling &c. Bridge Co., 13 How. 518; Dodge *v.* Woolsey, 18 How. 331; The Justices *v.* Murray, 9 Wall. 274; Edwards *v.* Elliot, 21 Wall. 532; Walker *v.* Sauvinet, 92 U. S. 90; Pearson *v.* Yewdall, 95 U. S. 294; McElrath *v.* United States, 102 U. S. 426; Barton *v.* Barbour, 104 U. S. 126; Spies *v.* Illinois, 123 U. S. 131; Arkansas Land and Cattle Co. *v.* Mann, 130 U. S. 69; Eilenbecker *v.* District Court of Plymouth County, 134 U. S. 31.

[2] Pervear *v.* Commonwealth, 5 Wall. 475; Spies *v.* Illinois, 123 U. S. 131; Eilenbecker *v.* District Court of Plymouth County, 134 U. S. 31; *In re* Kemmler, 136 U. S. 436.

[3] Lessee of Livingston *v.* Moore, 7 Pet. 469; Spies *v.* Illinois, 123 U. S. 131.

[4] Chisholm *v.* Georgia, 2 Dall. 419; Hollingsworth *v.* Virginia, 3 Dall. 378; Martin *v.* Hunter's Lessee, 1 Wheat. 304; McCulloch *v.* Maryland,

[ARTICLE XI.]

The Judicial power of the United States shall not be Appendix.
construed to extend to any suit in law or equity, com- The Constitution.
menced or prosecuted against one of the United States
by Citizens of another State, or by Citizens or Subjects
of any Foreign State.[1]

[ARTICLE XII.]

The Electors shall meet in their respective states, and
vote by ballot for President and Vice President, one of
whom, at least, shall not be an inhabitant of the same
state with themselves ; they shall name in their ballots
the person voted for as President, and in distinct ballots
the person voted for as Vice-President, and they shall
make distinct lists of all persons voted for as President,
and of all persons voted for as Vice-President, and of the
number of votes for each, which lists they shall sign and
certify, and transmit sealed to the seat of the government of the United States, directed to the President of
the Senate ; — The President of the Senate shall, in pres-

---

4 Wheat. 316; Anderson v. Dunn, 6 Wheat. 204; Cohens v. Virginia, 6
Wheat. 264; Osborn v. United States Bank, 9 Wheat. 738; Buckner v.
Finley, 2 Pet. 586; Dodge v. Woolsey, 18 How. 331; Ableman v. Booth,
21 How. 506; The Collector v. Day, 11 Wall. 113; Claflin v. Houseman,
93 U. S. 130; Inman Steamship Co. v. Tinker, 94 U. S. 238; United States
v. Harris, 106 U. S. 629; Civil Rights Cases, 109 U. S. 3; Spies v. Illinois,
123 U. S. 131.

1 Georgia v. Brailsford et al., 2 Dall. 402; Chisholm v. Georgia, 2
Dall. 419; Hollingsworth v. Virginia, 3 Dall. 378; Bingham v. Cabot, 3
Dall. 382; United States v. Peters, 5 Cranch, 115; Cohens v. Virginia,
6 Wheat. 264; Osborn v. United States Bank, 9 Wheat. 738; United
States Bank v. The Planters' Bank, 9 Wheat. 904; The Governor of
Georgia v. Juan Madrazo, 1 Pet. 110; Cherokee Nation v. Georgia, 5 Pet. 1;
Briscoe v. The Bank of the Commonwealth of Kentucky, 11 Pet. 257;
Curran v. Arkansas, 15 How. 304; Davis v. Gray, 16 Wall. 203; Ten-
nessee v. Davis, 100 U. S. 257; New Hampshire v. Louisiana, 108 U. S.
76; New York v. Louisiana, 108 U. S. 76; Clark v. Barnard, 108 U. S.
436; Virginia Coupon Cases, 114 U. S. 269; Hagood v. Southern, 117
U. S. 52; Rolston v. Missouri Fund Commissioners, 120 U. S. 390; In re
Ayers, 123 U. S. 443; Wisconsin v. Pelican Insurance Co., 127 U. S. 265;
Lincoln County v. Luning, 133 U. S. 529; Christian v. Atlantic & North
Carolina Railroad Co., 133 U. S. 233; Hans v. Louisiana, 134 U. S. 1;
North Carolina v. Temple, 134 U. S. 22; Louisiana ex rel. New York
Guaranty &c. Co. v. Steele, 134 U. S. 230.

ence of the Senate and House of Representatives, open
all the certificates and the votes shall then be counted;
—The person having the greatest number of votes for
President, shall be the President, if such number be a
majority of the whole number of Electors appointed;
and if no person have such majority, then from the persons having the highest numbers not exceeding three on
the list of those voted for as President, the House of
Representatives shall choose immediately, by ballot, the
President. But in choosing the President, the votes
shall be taken by states, the representation from each
state having one vote; a quorum for this purpose shall
consist of a member or members from two-thirds of the
states, and a majority of all the states shall be necessary
to a choice. And if the House of Representatives shall
not choose a President whenever the right of choice shall
devolve upon them, before the fourth day of March next
following, then the Vice-President shall act as President,
as in the case of the death or other constitutional disability
of the President. The person having the greatest number of votes as Vice-President, shall be the Vice-President, if such number be a majority of the whole number
of Electors appointed, and if no person have a majority,
then from the two highest numbers on the list, the Senate shall choose the Vice-President; a quorum for the
purpose shall consist of two-thirds of the whole number
of Senators, and a majority of the whole number shall be
necessary to a choice. But no person constitutionally
ineligible to the office of President shall be eligible to
that of Vice-President of the United States.[1]

[Article XIII.]

Section 1. Neither slavery nor involuntary servitude,
except as a punishment for crime whereof the party shall
have been duly convicted, shall exist within the United
States, or any place subject to their jurisdiction.

---

[1] *In re* Green, 134 U. S. 377.

SECTION 2. Congress shall have power to enforce this article by appropriate legislation.[1]

[ARTICLE XIV.]

SECTION 1. All persons born or naturalized in the United States, and subject to the jurisdiction thereof, are citizens of the United States and of the State wherein they reside. No State shall make or enforce any law which shall abridge the privileges or immunities of citizens of the United States ; nor shall any State deprive any person of life, liberty, or property, without due process of law ; nor deny to any person within its jurisdiction the equal protection of the laws.[2]

---

[1] Dred Scott v. Sandford, 19 How. 393; Osborn v. Nicholson, 13 Wall. 654; Slaughterhouse Cases, 16 Wall. 36; Ex parte Virginia, 100 U. S. 339; United States v. Harris, 106 U. S. 629; Civil Rights Case, 109 U. S. 3.

[2] Slaughterhouse Cases, 16 Wall. 36; Bradwell v. The State, 16 Wall. 130; Bartemeyer v. Iowa, 18 Wall. 129; Minor v. Happersett, 21 Wall. 162; United States v. Cruikshank, 92 U. S. 542: Davidson v. New Orleans, 96 U. S. 97: Railroad Co. v. Richmond, 96 U. S. 521; Strauder v. West Virginia, 100 U. S. 303; Virginia v. Rives, 100 U. S. 313; Ex parte Virginia, 100 U. S. 339; Missouri v. Lewis, 101 U. S. 22; Springer v. United States, 102 U. S. 586; Kelly v. Pittsburgh, 104 U. S. 78; Bush v. Kentucky, 107 U. S. 110; Pace v. Alabama, 106 U. S. 583; United States v. Harris, 106 U. S. 629; Gross v. United States Mortgage Co., 108 U. S. 477; Vance v. Vance, 108 U. S. 514; Civil Rights Cases, 109 U. S. 3; United States v. Gale, 109 U. S 65; Louisiana v. New Orleans, 109 U. S. 285; Hurtado v. California, 110 U. S. 516; Ex parte Yarbrough, 110 U. S. 651; Hagar v. Reclamation District, 111 U. S. 701; Elk v. Wilkins, 112 U. S. 94; Foster v. Kansas, 112 U. S. 205; Head v. Amoskeag Manufacturing Co., 113 U. S. 9; Barbier v. Connolly, 113 U. S. 27; Provident Institution for Savings v. Mayor &c. of Jersey City, 113 U. S. 506; Soon Hing v. Crowley. 113 U. S. 703; Wurts v. Hoagland, 114 U. S. 606; Kentucky Railroad Tax Cases, 115 U. S. 321; Missouri Pacific Railway Co. v. Humes, 115 U. S. 512; Campbell v. Holt, 115 U. S 620; Brown v. Grant, 116 U. S. 207; Presser v. Illinois, 116 U. S. 252; Stone v. Farmers' Loan and Trust Co., 116 U. S. 307; Arrowsmith v. Harmoning, 118 U. S. 194; Yick Wo v. Hopkins, 118 U. S. 356; Santa Clara County v. Southern Pacific Railroad, 118 U. S. 394; Philadelphia Fire Association v. New York, 119 U. S. 110; Home Insurance Co. v. New York, 119 U. S. 129; Schmidt v. Cobb, 119 U. S. 286; Kerr v. Illinois, 119 U. S. 436; Hayes v. Missouri, 120 U. S. 68; Baldwin v. Franks, 120 U. S. 678; Church v. Kelsey, 121 U. S. 282; Spies v. Illinois, 123 U. S. 131; Sands v. Manistee River Improvement Co., 123 U. S. 288; Mugler v. Kansas, 123 U. S. 623; Great Falls Manufacturing Co. v. Attorney-General, 124

SECTION 2. Representatives shall be apportioned among the several States according to their respective numbers, counting the whole number of persons in each State, excluding Indians not taxed. But when the right to vote at any election for the choice of electors for President and Vice-President of the United States, Representatives in Congress, the Executive and Judicial officers of a State, or the members of the Legislature thereof, is denied to any of the male inhabitants of such State, being twenty-one years of age, and citizens of the United States, or in any way abridged, except for participation in rebellion, or other crime, the basis of representation therein shall be reduced in the proportion which the number of such male citizens shall bear to the whole number of male citizens twenty-one years of age in such State.[1]

SECTION 3. No person shall be a Senator or Representative in Congress, or elector of President and Vice President, or hold any office, civil or military, under the United States, or under any State, who, having pre-

---

U. S. 581; Pembina Consolidated Mining Co. v. Pennsylvania, 125 U. S. 181; Spencer v. Merchant, 125 U. S. 345; Dow v. Beidelman, 125 U. S. 680; California v. Central Pacific Railroad Co., 127 U. S. 1; Ro Bards v. Lamb, 127 U. S. 58; Missouri Pacific Railway Co. v. Mackey, 127 U. S. 205; Minneapolis and St. Louis Railway Co. v. Herrick, 127 U. S. 210; Powell v. Pennsylvania, 127 U. S. 678; Mahon v. Justices, 127 U. S. 700; Kidd v. Pearson, 128 U. S. 1; Nashville, Chattanooga &c. Railway Co. v. Alabama, 128 U. S. 96; Walston v. Nevin, 128 U. S. 578; Minneapolis and St. Louis Railway v. Beckwith, 129 U. S. 26; Dent v. West Virginia, 129 U. S. 114; Huling v. Kaw Valley Railway &c. Co., 130 U. S. 559; Freeland v. Williams, 131 U. S. 405; Cross v. North Carolina, 132 U. S. 131; Pennie v. Reis, 132 U. S. 464; Sugg v. Thornton, 132 U. S. 524; Palmer v. McMahon, 133 U. S. 660; Eilenbecker v. District Court of Plymouth County, 134 U. S. 31; Bell's Gap Railroad Co. v. Pennsylvania, 134 U. S. 232; Chicago, Milwaukee &c. Railway Co. v. Minnesota, 134 U. S. 418; Minneapolis Eastern Railway Co. v. Minnesota, 134 U. S. 467; Home Insurance Co. v. New York, 134 U. S. 594; Louisville and Nashville Railroad Co. v. Woodson, 134 U. S. 614; Norfolk and Western Railroad Co. v. Pennsylvania, 136 U. S. 114; In re Kemmler, 136 U. S. 436; York v. Texas, 137 U. S. 15; Crowley v. Christensen, 137 U. S. 86; Wheeler v. Jackson, 137 U. S. 245; Holden v. Minnesota, 137 U. S. 483; In re Converse, 137 U. S. 624; Caldwell v. Texas, 137 U. S. 692; Kauffman v. Wootters, 138 U. S. 285; Leeper v. Texas, 139 U. S. 462; In re Manning, 139 U. S. 504; Natal v. Louisiana, 139 U. S. 621.

[1] Slaughterhouse Cases, 16 Wall. 36.

viously taken an oath, as a member of Congress, or as an Appendix.
officer of the United States, or as a member of any State The Constitution.
legislature, or as an executive or judicial officer of any
State, to support the Constitution of the United States,
shall have engaged in insurrection or rebellion against
the same, or given aid or comfort to the enemies thereof.
But Congress may by a vote of two-thirds of each House,
remove such disability.

Section 4. The validity of the public debt of the
United States, authorized by law, including debts incurred for payment of pensions and bounties for services
in suppressing insurrection or rebellion, shall not be
questioned. But neither the United States nor any
State shall assume or pay any debt or obligation incurred
in aid of insurrection or rebellion against the United
States, or any claim for the loss or emancipation of any
slave; but all such debts, obligations and claims shall be
held illegal and void.

Section 5. The Congress shall have power to enforce,
by appropriate legislation, the provisions of this article.[1]

[Article XV.]

Section 1. The right of citizens of the United States
to vote shall not be denied or abridged by the United
States or by any State on account of race, color, or previous condition of servitude.

Section 2. The Congress shall have power to enforce
this article by appropriate legislation.[2]

---

[1] Crandall v. Nevada, 6 Wall. 35; Paul v. Virginia, 8 Wall. 168; Ward
v. Maryland, 12 Wall. 418; Slaughterhouse Cases, 16 Wall. 36; Bradwell
v. The State, 16 Wall. 130; Bartemeyer v. Iowa, 18 Wall. 129; Minor v.
Happersett, 21 Wall. 162; Walker v. Sauvinet, 92 U. S. 90; Kennard v.
Louisiana, ex rel. Morgan, 92 U. S. 480; United States v. Cruikshank, 92
U. S. 542; Munn v. Illinois, 94 U. S. 113; Virginia v. Rives, 100 U. S.
313; Strauder v. West Virginia, 100 U. S. 303; United States v. Harris,
106 U. S. 629; Civil Rights Cases, 109 U. S. 3.

[2] Minor v. Happersett, 21 Wall. 162; United States v. Reese, 92 U. S.
214; United States v. Cruikshank, 92 U. S. 542; Neal v. Delaware, 103
U. S. 370; United States v. Harris, 106 U. S. 629; Ex parte Yarbrough,
110 U. S. 651.

UNITED STATES OF AMERICA.

DEPARTMENT OF STATE.

To all to whom these presents shall come, Greeting:

I certify that the documents hereto annexed are true copies, from the Archives of this Department, of the Constitution of the United States of America with the amendments; and that said copy has been carefully compared with the original and found to be correct in text, letter and punctuation.

In testimony whereof I, William F. Wharton, Acting Secretary of State of the United States, have hereunto subscribed my name and caused the seal of the [SEAL.] Department of State to be affixed.

Done at the City of Washington, this 15th day of June, A.D., 1891, and of the Independence of the United States of America the one hundred and fifteenth.

WILLIAM F. WHARTON.

II.

[ARTICLES OF CONFEDERATION—1777.]

To all to whom these Presents shall come, we the undersigned Delegates of the States affixed to our Names send greeting.

Whereas the Delegates of the United States of America in Congress assembled did on the fifteenth day of November in the Year of our Lord One Thousand Seven Hundred and Seventyseven, and in the Second Year of the Independence of America agree to certain articles of Confederation and perpetual Union between the States of Newhampshire, Massachusetts-bay, Rhodeisland and Providence Plantations, Connecticut, New York, New Jersey, Pennsylvania, Delaware, Maryland, Virginia, North-Carolina, South-Carolina and Georgia in the Words following, viz.

" *Articles of Confederation and perpetual Union between the States of Newhampshire, Massachusetts-bay, Rhode-island and Providence Plantations, Connecticut, New-York, New-Jersey, Pennsylvania, Delaware, Maryland, Virginia, North-Carolina, South-Carolina and Georgia.*

ARTICLE I. The Stile of this confederacy shall be " The United States of America."

ARTICLE II. Each State retains its sovereignty, freedom and independence, and every Power, Jurisdiction and right, which is not by this confederation expressly delegated to the United States, in Congress assembled.

ARTICLE III. The said states hereby severally enter into a firm league of friendship with each other, for their common defence, the security of their Liberties, and their mutual and general welfare, binding themselves to assist each other, against all force offered to, or attacks made upon them, or any of them, on account of religion, sovereignty, trade, or any other pretence whatever.

ARTICLE IV. The better to secure and perpetuate mutual friendship and intercourse among the people of the different states in this union, the free inhabitants of each of these states, paupers, vagabonds and fugitives from justice excepted, shall be entitled to all privileges and immunities of free citizens in the several states ; and the people of each state shall have free ingress and regress to and from any other state, and shall enjoy therein all the privileges of trade and commerce, subject to the same duties, impositions and restrictions as the inhabitants thereof respectively, provided that such restriction shall not extend so far as to prevent the removal of property imported into any state, to any other state of which the Owner is an inhabitant; provided also that no imposition, duties or restriction shall be laid by any state, on the property of the united states, or either of them.

If any Person guilty of, or charged with treason, felony, or other high misdemeanor in any state, shall flee from Justice, and be found in any of the united states, he shall upon demand of the Governor or executive power, of the state from which he fled, be delivered up and removed to the state having jurisdiction of his offence.

Full faith and credit shall be given in each of these states to the records, acts and judicial proceedings of the courts and magistrates of every other state.

ARTICLE V. For the more convenient management of the general interests of the united states, delegates shall be annually appointed in such manner as the legislature of each state shall direct, to meet in Congress on the first Monday in November, in every year, with a power reserved to each state, to recall its delegates, or any of them, at any time within the year, and to send others in their stead, for the remainder of the Year.

No state shall be represented in Congress by less than two, nor by more than seven Members; and no person shall be capable of being a delegate for more than three years in any term of six years; nor shall any person, being a delegate, be capable of holding any office under the united states, for which he, or another for his benefit receives any salary, fees or emolument of any kind.

Each state shall maintain its own delegates in a meeting of the states, and while they act as members of the committee of the states.

In determining questions in the united states, in Congress assembled, each state shall have one vote.

Freedom of speech and debate in Congress shall not be impeached or questioned in any Court, or place out of Congress, and the members of congress shall be protected in their persons from arrests and imprisonments, during the time of their going to and from, and attendance on Congress, except for treason, felony, or breach of the peace.

ARTICLE VI. No state without the consent of the united states in congress assembled, shall send any embassy to, or receive any embassy from, or enter into any conference, agreement, alliance or treaty with any King prince or state; nor shall any person holding any office of profit or trust under the united states, or any of them, accept of any present, emolument, office or title of any kind whatever from any king, prince or foreign state; nor shall the united states in congress assembled, or any of them, grant any title of nobility.

No two or more states shall enter into any treaty, confederation or alliance whatever between them, with- out the consent of the united states in congress as- sembled, specifying accurately the purposes for which the same is to be entered into, and how long it shall continue.

No state shall lay any imposts or duties, which may interfere with any stipulations in treaties, entered into by the united states in congress assembled, with any king, prince or state, in pursuance of any treaties already proposed by congress, to the courts of France and Spain.

No vessels of war shall be kept up in time of peace by any state, except such number only, as shall be deemed necessary by the united states in congress assembled, for the defence of such state, or its trade; nor shall any body of forces be kept up by any state, in time of peace, except such number only, as in the judgment of the united states, in congress assembled, shall be deemed requisite to garrison the forts necessary for the defence of such state; but every state shall always keep up a well regulated and disciplined militia, sufficiently armed and accoutred, and shall provide and constantly have ready for use, in public stores, a 'due number of field pieces and tents, and a proper quantity of arms, ammunition and camp equipage.

No state shall engage in any war without the consent of the united states in congress assembled, unless such state be actually invaded by enemies, or shall have re- ceived certain advice of a resolution being formed by some nation of Indians to invade such state, and the dan- ger is so imminent as not to admit of a delay, till the united states in congress assembled can be consulted: nor shall any state grant commissions to any ships or vessels of war, nor letters of marque or reprisal, except it be after a declaration of war by the united states in congress assembled, and then only against the kingdom or state and the subjects thereof, against which war has been so declared, and under such regulations as shall be established by the united states in congress assembled, unless such state be infested by pirates, in which case vessels of war may be fitted out for that occasion, and kept so long as the danger shall continue, or until the united states in congress assembled shall determine otherwise.

ARTICLE VII. When land-forces are raised by any state for the common defence, all officers of or under the rank of colonel, shall be appointed by the legislature of each state respectively by whom such forces shall be raised, or in such manner as such state shall direct, and all vacancies shall be filled up by the state which first made the appointment.

ARTICLE VIII. All charges of war, and all other expenses that shall be incurred for the common defence or general welfare, and allowed by the united states in congress assembled, shall be defrayed out of a common treasury, which shall be supplied by the several states, in proportion to the value of all land within each state, granted to or surveyed for any Person, as such land and the buildings and improvements thereon shall be estimated according to such mode as the united states in congress assembled, shall from time to time direct and appoint.

The taxes for paying that proportion shall be laid and levied by the authority and direction of the legislatures of the several states within the time agreed upon by the united states in congress assembled.

ARTICLE IX. The united states in congress assembled, shall have the sole and exclusive right and power of determining on peace and war, except in the cases mentioned in the sixth article — of sending and receiving ambassadors — entering into treaties and alliances, provided that no treaty of commerce shall be made whereby the legislative power of the respective states shall be restrained from imposing such imposts and duties on foreigners, as their own people are subjected to, or from prohibiting the exportation or importation of any species of goods or commodities whatsoever — of establishing rules for deciding in all cases, what captures on land or water shall be legal, and in what manner prizes taken by land or naval forces in the service of the united states shall be divided or appropriated — of granting letters of marque and reprisal in times of peace — ap_ pointing courts for the trial of piracies and felonies com. mitted on the high seas and establishing courts for receiving and determining finally appeals in all cases of captures, provided that no member of congress shall be appointed a judge of any of the said courts.

The united states in congress assembled shall also be the last resort on appeal in all disputes and differences now subsisting or that hereafter may arise between two or more states concerning boundary, jurisdiction or any other cause whatever; which authority shall always be exercised in the manner following. Whenever the legis. lative or executive authority or lawful agent of any state in controversy with another shall present a peti- tion to congress, stating the matter in question and praying for a hearing, notice thereof shall be given by order of congress to the legislative or executive author- ity of the other state in controversy, and a day assigned for the appearance of the parties by their lawful agents, who shall then be directed to appoint by joint consent, commissioners or judges to constitute a court for hearing and determining the matter in question : but if they can- not agree, congress shall name three persons out of each of the united states, and from the list of such persons each party shall alternately strike out one, the peti- tioners beginning, until the number shall be reduced to thirteen; and from that number not less than seven, nor more than nine names as congress shall direct, shall in the presence of congress be drawn out by lot, and the persons whose names shall be so drawn or any five of them, shall be commissioners or judges, to hear and finally determine the controversy, so always as a major part of the judges who shall hear the cause shall agree

in the determination : and if either party shall neglect
to attend at the day appointed, without showing reasons,
which congress shall judge sufficient, or being present
shall refuse to strike, the congress shall proceed to nominate three persons out of each state, and the secretary of
congress shall strike in behalf of such party absent or
refusing ; and the judgment and sentence of the court to
be appointed, in the manner before prescribed, shall be
final and conclusive ; and if any of the parties shall refuse to submit to the authority of such court, or to
appear or defend their claim or cause, the court shall
nevertheless proceed to pronounce sentence, or judgment,
which shall in like manner be final and decisive, the
judgment or sentence and other proceedings being in
either case transmitted to congress, and lodged among
the acts of congress for the security of the parties concerned : provided that every commissioner, before he sits
in judgment, shall take an oath to be administered by
one of the judges of the supreme or superior court of
the state, where the cause shall be tried, " well and
truly to hear and determine the matter in question, according to the best of his judgment, without favour,
affection or hope of reward : " provided also that no
state shall be deprived of territory for the benefit of the
united states.

All controversies concerning the private right of soil
claimed under different grants of two or more states,
whose jurisdictions as they may respect such lands, and
the states which passed such grants are adjusted, the
said grants or either of them being at the same time
claimed to have originated antecedent to such settlement
of jurisdiction, shall on the petition of either party to
the congress of the united states, be finally determined
as near as may be in the same manner as is before prescribed for deciding disputes respecting territorial jurisdiction between different states.

The united states in congress assembled shall also
have the sole and exclusive right and power of regulating the alloy and value of coin struck by their own
authority, or by that of the respective states — fixing

the standard of weights and measures throughout the united states, — regulating the trade and managing all affairs with the Indians, not members of any of the states, provided that the legislative right of any state within its own limits be not infringed or violated — establishing and regulating post-offices from one state to another, throughout all the united states, and exacting such postage on the papers passing thro' the same as may be requisite to defray the expenses of the said office — appointing all officers of the land forces, in the service of the united states, excepting regimental officers — appointing all the officers of the naval forces, and commissioning all officers whatever in the service of the united states — making rules for the government and regulation of the said land and naval forces, and directing their operations.

The united states in congress assembled shall have authority to appoint a committee, to sit in the recess of congress, to be denominated "a committee of the states," and to consist of one delegate from each state, and to appoint such other committees and civil officers as may be necessary for managing the general affairs of the united states under their direction — to appoint one of their number to preside, provided that no person be allowed to serve in the office of president more than one year in any term of three years ; to ascertain the necessary sums of Money to be raised for the service of the united states, and to appropriate and apply the same for defraying the public expenses — to borrow money, or emit bills on the credit of the united states, transmitting every half year to the respective states an account of the sums of money so borrowed or emitted, — to build and equip a navy — to agree upon the number of land forces, and to make requisitions from each state for its quota, in proportion to the number of white inhabitants in such state; which requisition shall be binding; and thereupon the legislature of each state shall appoint the regimental officers, raise the men and cloath, arm and equip them in a soldier like manner, at the expense of the united states, and the officers and men so cloathed, armed and equipped shall march to the place appointed, and within the time agreed on by the united states in congress assembled: But if the united states in congress assembled shall, on consideration of circumstances judge proper that any state should not raise men, or should raise a smaller number than its quota, and that any other state should raise a greater number of men than the quota thereof, such extra number shall be raised, officered, cloathed, armed and equipped in the same manner as the quota of such state, unless the legislature of such state shall judge that such extra number cannot be safely spared out of the same, in which case they shall raise officer, cloath, arm and equip as many of such extra number as they judge can be safely spared. And the officers and men so cloathed, armed and equipped, shall march to the place appointed, and within the time agreed on by the united states in congress assembled.

The united states in congress assembled shall never engage in a war, nor grant letters of marque and reprisal in time of peace, nor enter into any treaties or alliances, nor coin money, nor regulate the value thereof, nor ascertain the sums and expenses necessary for the defence and welfare of the united states, or any of them, nor emit bills, nor borrow money on the credit of the united states, nor appropriate money, nor agree upon the number of vessels of war, to be built or purchased, or the number of land or sea forces to be raised, nor appoint a commander in chief of army or navy, unless nine states assent to the same: nor shall a question on any other point, except for adjourning from day to day be determined, unless by the votes of a majority of the united states in congress assembled.

The congress of the united states shall have power to adjourn to any time within the year, and to any place within the united states, so that no period of adjournment be for a longer duration than the space of six Months, and shall publish the Journal of their proceedings monthly, except such parts thereof relating to treaties, alliances or military operations, as in their judgment require secrecy; and the yeas and nays of the delegates of each state on any question shall be entered on the journal, when it is desired by any delegate; and the delegates of a state, or any of them, at his or their request shall be furnished with a transcript of the said Journal, except such parts as are above excepted, to lay before the legislatures of the several states.

ARTICLE X. The committee of the states, or any nine of them, shall be authorized to execute, in the recess of congress, such of the powers of congress as the united states in congress assembled, by the consent of nine states, shall from time to time think expedient to vest them with; provided that no power be delegated to the said committee, for the exercise of which, by the articles of confederation, the voice of nine states in the congress of the united states assembled is requisite.

ARTICLE XI. Canada acceding to this confederation, and joining in the measures of the united states, shall be admitted into, and entitled to all the advantages of this union: but no other colony shall be admitted into the same, unless such admission be agreed to by nine states.

ARTICLE XII. All bills of credit emitted, monies borrowed and debt contracted by, or under the authority of congress, before the assembling of the united states, in pursuance of the present confederation, shall be deemed and considered as a charge against the united states, for payment and satisfaction whereof the said united states, and the public faith are hereby solemnly pledged.

ARTICLE XIII. Every state shall abide by the determinations of the united states in congress assembled, on all questions which by this confederation are submitted to them. And the Articles of this confederation shall be inviolably observed by every state, and the union shall be perpetual; nor shall any alteration at any time hereafter be made in any of them; unless such alteration be agreed to in a congress of the united states, and be afterwards confirmed by the legislatures of every state.

And whereas it has pleased the Great Governor of

the World to incline the hearts of the legislatures we
respectively represent in congress, to approve of, and to
authorize us to ratify the said articles of confederation
and perpetual union. Know ye that we the undersigned delegates, by virtue of the power and authority
to us given for that purpose, do by these presents, in the
name and in behalf of our respective constituents, fully
and entirely ratify and confirm each and every of the said
articles of confederation and perpetual union, and all and
singular the matters and things therein contained : And
we do further solemnly plight and engage the faith of our
respective constituents, that they shall abide by the determinations of the united states in congress assembled,
on all questions, which by the said confederation, are
submitted to them. And that the articles thereof shall
be inviolably observed by the states we repectively
represent, and that the union shall be perpetual.

In witness whereof we have hereunto set our hands
in Congress. Done at Philadelphia in the State of
Pennsylvania the ninth Day of July in the Year of
our Lord one Thousand seven Hundred and Seventy-
eight, and in the third Year of the independence of
America.

On the part & behalf of the State of New Hampshire

JOSIAH BARTLETT   JOHN WENTWORTH, Junr
                                  August 8th, 1778.

On the part and behalf of the State of Massachusetts Bay

JOHN HANCOCK   FRANCIS DANA
SAMUEL ADAMS   JAMES LOVELL
ELBRIDGE GERRY   SAMUEL HOLTEN

*On the part and behalf of the State of Rhode Island and
Providence Plantations*

WILLIAM ELLERY   JOHN COLLINS
HENRY MARCHANT

On the part and behalf of the State of Connecticut

ROGER SHERMAN
SAMUEL HUNTINGTON
OLIVER WOLCOTT

TITUS HOSMER
ANDREW ADAMS

On the part and Behalf of the State of New York

JAS. DUANE
FRA. LEWIS

WM. DUER,
GOUV. MORRIS.

*On the part and in Behalf of the State of New Jersey,
Novr. 26, 1778.*

JNO. WITHERSPOON

NATHL. SCUDDER.

On the part and behalf of the State of Pennslyvania

ROBT. MORRIS,
DANIEL ROBERDEAU
JONA. BAYARD SMITH

WILLIAM CLINGAN,
JOSEPH REED, 22d July, 1778.

On the part & behalf of the State of Delaware

THO. M'KEAN, Feby. 12, 1779. NICHOLAS VAN DYKE,
JOHN DICKINSON–May 5th, 1779.

On the part and behalf of the State of Maryland

JOHN HANSON, March 1, 1781. DANIEL CARROLL, do.

On the Part and Behalf of the State of Virginia

RICHARD HENRY LEE
JOHN BANISTER
THOMAS ADAMS

JNO. HARVIE
FRANCIS LIGHTFOOT LEE.

On the part and Behalf of the State of No. Carolina

JOHN PENN July 21st. 1778.   JNO. WILLIAMS
CORNS. HARNETT

On the part & behalf of the State of South Carolina

HENRY LAURENS,
WILLIAM HENRY DRAYTON
JNO. MATHEWS

RICHD. HUTSON,
THOS. HEYWARD, Junr.

On the part & behalf of the State of Georgia

JNO. WALTON, 24th July 1778. EDWD. LANGWORTHY.
EDWD. TELFAIR

Endorsed :—Act of Confederation of the United States
of America.

UNITED STATES OF AMERICA.

DEPARTMENT OF STATE.

To all to whom these presents shall come, Greeting:

I certify That the document hereto annexed is a true copy, from the Archives of this Department, of the original Articles of Confederation as engrossed and signed in Congress.

In testimony whereof I, William F. Wharton, Acting Secretary of State of the United States, have hereunto subscribed my name and caused the seal of the [SEAL.] Department of State to be affixed.

Done at the City of Washington this 12th day of June, A.D., 1891, and of the Independence of the United States of America the one hundred and fifteenth.

WILLIAM F. WHARTON.

III.

RESOLUTIONS,

OFFERED BY MR. EDMUND RANDOLPH TO THE CONVENTION, MAY 29, 1787.

1. Resolved, that the Articles of the Confederation ought to be so corrected and enlarged, as to accomplish the objects proposed by their institution, namely, *common defence*, security of Liberty and *general welfare*.

2. Resolved, therefore, that the right of suffrage, in the National Legislature, ought to be proportioned to the quotas of contribution, or to the number of free inhabitants, as the one or the other may seem best, in different cases.

3. Resolved, that the National Legislature ought to consist of *two branches*.

4. Resolved, that the members of the *first* branch of the National Legislature ought to be elected by the people of the several States, every   for the term

of   to be of the age of   years at least; to re.
ceive liberal stipends, by which they may be compensated
for the devotion of their time to publick service; to be
in-eligible to any office established by a particular state,
or under the authority of the United States (except
those peculiarly belonging to the functions of the first
branch) during the term of service and for the space of
        after its expiration; to be incapable of re-elec-
tion for the space of   after the expiration of their
term of service; and to be subject to recal.

5. Resolved, that the Members of the $\frac{\text{Second}}{2d}$ branch
of the National Legislature ought to be elected by those
of the first, out of a proper number of persons nominated
by the individual Legislatures; to be of the age of
years, at least; to hold their offices for a term sufficient
to ensure their independency; to receive liberal stipend,
by which they may be compensated for the devotion of
their time to the publick service; and to be ineligible to
any office established by a particular state, or under the
authority of the United States (except those peculiarly
belonging to the functions of the second branch) during
the term of service; and for the space of   after
the expiration thereof.

6. Resolved, that each branch ought to possess the
right of originating acts; that the Nat'l Leg. ought to
be empowered to enjoy the *Legislative right vested in
Congress,* by the Confederation; and moreover to Legislate in all cases to which the separate States are incompetent, or in which the harmony of the United States
may be interrupted by the exercise of individual legislation; to negative all laws passed by the several States,
contravening, in the opinion of . . . . the Nat'l Leg'e,
the Articles of Union, or any Treaty subsisting under
the authority of the Union; and to call forth the force
of the Union against any member of the Union, failing
to fulfil its duty under the Articles thereof.

7. Resolved, that a National *Executive* be instituted,
to be chosen by the Nat'l Leg'e for the term of   years,
to receive punctually, at stated times, a fixed compensa-

tion for the services rendered, in which no increase or diminution shall be made, so as to affect the Magistracy existing at the time of the increase or diminution; to be ineligible a second time; and that, besides a general authority to execute the National laws, it ought to enjoy the executive rights vested in Congress by the confederation.

8. Resolved, that the executive, and a convenient number of the national Judiciary, ought to compose a *Council of revision*, with authority to examine every act of the National Legislature, before it shall operate, and every act of a particular Legislature before a negative thereon shall be final; and that the dissent of the said Council shall amount to a rejection, unless the act of the National Legislature be again passed, or that of a particular Legislature be again negatived by   of the Members of each branch.

9. Resolved, that a National Judiciary be established to hold their offices during good behaviour, and to receive punctually, at stated times, fixed compensation for their services, in which no increase or diminution shall be made, so as to affect the persons actually in office at the time of such increase or diminution. That the jurisdiction of the Inferior Tribunals, shall be, to hear and determine, in the first instance, and of the Supreme tribunal to hear and determine, in the denier resort,

all piracies and felonies on the high seas; captures from an enemy; cases in which foreigners, or Citizens of other States, applying to such jurisdictions may be interested, or which respect the Collection of the National Revenue; impeachments of any National officer; and questions which involve the National peace or harmony.

10. Resolved, that provision ought to be made for the *admission of States*, lawfully arising within the limits of the United States, whether from a voluntary junction of government and territory, or otherwise, with the consent of a number of voices in the National Legislatures less than the whole.

11. Resolved, that a Republican Government, and the

territory of each state (except in the instance of a voluntary junction of Government and territory) ought to be guaranteed by the United States to each State.

12. Resolved, that provision ought to be made for the continuance of a Congress, and their authorities and privileges, until a given day, after the reform of the Articles of Union shall be adopted, and for the completion of all their engagements.

13. That provision ought to be made for the amendment of the articles of Union, whensoever it shall seem necessary; and that the assent of the National Legislature ought not to be required thereto.

14. Resolved, that the Legislative, Executive, and Judiciary powers within the several States ought to be bound by oath to support the articles of Union.

15. Resolved, that the Amendments, which shall be offered to the Confederation by the Convention, ought, at a proper time or times, after the approbation of Congress, to be submitted to an assembly or assemblies of representatives, recommended by the several Legislatures, to be expressly chosen by the people to consider and decide thereon.

UNITED STATES OF AMERICA.

DEPARTMENT OF STATE.

To all to whom these presents shall come, Greeting:

I certify That the document hereto annexed is a true copy, from the Archives of this Department, of Randolph's resolutions of May 29, 1787, as found among the papers of David Brearley, one of the members of the Convention, furnished by his executor General Bloomfield.

In testimony whereof I, William F. Wharton, Acting Secretary of State of the United States, have hereunto subscribed my name and caused the seal of the

[SEAL.] Department of State to be affixed.

Done at the City of Washington, this 12th day of June, A.D., 1891, and of the Independence of the United States of America the one hundred and fifteenth.

WILLIAM F. WHARTON.

IV.

THE PINCKNEY PLAN,

Submitted May 29, 1787.

Appendix.
Pinckney's Draft. We the people of the States of New Hampshire, Massachusetts, Rhode Island & Providence Plantations, Connecticut, New York, New Jersey, Pensylvania, Delaware, Maryland, Virginia, North Carolina, South Carolina, and Georgia, do ordain, declare, and establish the following constitution for the Government of ourselves and posterity.

Article 1.

The Stile of this Government shall be the United States of America, and the Government shall consist of supreme legislative, Executive and judicial powers.

2.

The Legislative power shall be vested in a Congress, to consist of two separate Houses; one to be called the House of Delegates; and the other the Senate, who shall meet on the   day of   in every year.

3.

The Members of the House of Delegates shall be chosen every   year by the people of the several States; and the qualification of the electors shall be the same as those of the electors in the several States for their Legislatures. Each member shall have been a citizen of the United States for   years; shall be of   years of age, and a resident in the State he is chosen for until a census of the people shall be taken in the manner herein after mentioned. The House of Delegates shall consist of   to be chosen from the different States in the following proportions: For New Hampshire   for Massachusetts,   for Rhode Island,   for Connecticut   for New York,   for New Jersey,   for Pensylvania,   for Delaware,   for Maryland,   for Virginia,

for North Carolina, for South Carolina, for Georgia, and the Legislature shall hereafter regulate the
number of Delegates by the number of inhabitants, according to the provisions herein after made, at the rate of one
for every Thousand. All money Bills of every kind
shall originate in the House of Delegates, and shall not
be altered by the Senate. The House of Delegates shall
exclusively possess the power of impeachment, and shall
choose its own officers; and vacancies therein shall be
supplied by the Executive authority of the State in the
representation from which they shall happen.

4.

The Senate shall be elected and chosen by the House
of Delegates; which House, immediately after their
meeting, shall choose by ballot Senators from among
the Citizens and residents of New Hampshire, from
among those of Massachusetts, from among those of
Rhode Island, from among those of Connecticut,
from among those of New York, from among those
of New Jersey, from among those of Pensylvania,
from among those of Delaware, from among
those of Maryland, from among those of Virginia,
from among those of North Carolina, from among
those of South Carolina, from among those of Georgia — The Senators chosen from New Hampshire,
Massachusetts, Rhode Island and Connecticut, shall form
one class; those from New York, New Jersey, Pensylvania, and Delaware, one Class; – – – and those from
Maryland, Virginia, North Carolina, South Carolina, &
Georgia, one class. The House of Delegates shall
number these classes one, two, and three; and fix the
times of their service by Lot. The first class shall serve
for years; the second for years; & the third
for years. As their times of service expire, the
House of Delegates shall fill them up by Elections for
years; and they shall fill all vacancies that arise
from Death, or resignation, for the time of service remaining of the Members so dying or resigning. Each
Senator shall be years of age at least; shall have been

a Citizen of the United States $\frac{four}{4}$ years before his election; and shall be a resident of the State he is chosen from.   The Senate shall choose its own Officers

5.

Each State shall prescribe the time and manner of holding elections by the people for the House of Delegates; and the House of Delegates shall be the judges of the Elections, returns, and qualifications of their Members.

In each House a Majority shall constitute a quorum to do business. Freedom of Speech and Debate in the Legislature shall not be impeached, or questioned, in any place out of it; and the members of both Houses shall in all cases, except for Treason, felony, or breach of the Peace, be free from arrest during their attendance of Congress, and in going to and returning from it. Both Houses shall keep Journals of their proceedings, and publish them, except on Secret occasions; and the yeas and nays may be entered thereon at the desire of one-of the Members present. Neither House, without the consent of the other, shall adjourn for more than days, nor to any place but where they are sitting

The Members of each house shall not be eligible to, or capable of holding any office under the Union, during the time for which they have been respectively elected, nor the Members of the Senate for one year after. The Members of each House shall be paid for their services by the States which they represent. Every Bill, which shall have passed the Legislature, shall be presented to the President of the United States for his revision; if he approves it he shall sign it; but if he does not approve it, he shall return it, with his objections, to the House it originated in; which House, if two-thirds of the Members present, notwithstanding the President's objections, agree to pass it, shall send it to the other House, with the President's objections; where, if two-thirds of the Members present also agree to pass it, the same shall become a law; and all bills sent to the Presi-

dent, and not returned by him within   days, shall be
Laws, unless the Legislature, by their adjournment,
prevent their return; in which case they shall not be
laws.

6.

The Legislature of the United States shall have the
power to lay and collect taxes, duties, imposts and excises; To regulate commerce with all Nations and among
the several States : —

To borrow money and emit bills of credit ;

To establish post offices ;

To raise Armies ;

To build and equip Fleets ;

To pass laws for Arming, organizing and disciplining the
Militia of the United States ;

To subdue a rebellion in any State, on application of
is Legislature ;

To coin Money, & regulate the value of all coins, and fix
the standard of weights and measures ;

To provide such Dock yards and arsenals, and erect such
Fortifications as may be necessary for the United States,
and to exercise exclusive jurisdiction therein ;

To appoint a Treasurer, by ballot ;

To constitute Tribunals inferior to the Supreme Court ;

To establish Post & Military roads ;

To establish and provide for a National University at
the seat of the Government of the United States ;

To establish uniform rules of Naturalization ;

To provide for the establishment of a seat of Government for the United States, not exceeding   miles
square, in which they shall have exclusive jurisdiction ;

To make rules concerning captures from an Enemy ;

To declare the Law and punishment of piracies and felonies at Sea, and of counterfeiting Coin, and of all
offences against the Laws of Nations ;

To call forth the aid of the Militia to execute the laws
of the Union, enforce Treaties, suppress insurrections,
& repel invasions ;

And to make all laws for carrying the foregoing powers
into execution.

The Legislature of the United States shall have the power to declare the punishment of treason, which shall consist only in levying War against the United States, or any of them, or in adhering to their Enemies. No person shall be convicted of Treason but by the Testimony of two Witnesses.

The proportion of direct Taxation shall be regulated by the whole number of inhabitants of every description; which number shall, within   years after the first meeting of the Legislature, and within the term of every year after, be taken in the manner to be prescribed by the Legislature

No Tax shall be laid on articles exported from the States; nor capitation Tax, but in proportion to the census before directed.

All Laws regulating commerce shall require the assent of two thirds of the Members present in each House.

The United States shall not grant any title of Nobility.

The Legislature of the United States shall pass no Law on the subject of Religion; nor touching nor abridging the Liberty of the press; nor shall the privilege of the writ of Habeas Corpus ever be suspended, except in case of Rebellion or invasion.

All acts made by the Legislature of the United States, pursuant to this Constitution, and all Treaties made under the authority of the United States, shall be the supreme Law of the Land; and all Judges shall be bound to consider them as such in their decisions.

7.

The Senate shall have the sole and exclusive power to declare War; and to make Treaties; and to appoint Ambassadors and other Ministers, to Foreign Nations; and Judges of the Supreme Court.

They shall have the exclusive power to regulate the Manner of deciding all disputes and controversies now subsisting or which may arise, between the States, respecting Jurisdiction or territory.

8.

The Executive power of the United States shall be vested in a President of the United States of America, which shall be his Stile; and his title shall be His Excellency. He shall be elected for   years; and shall reeligible.

He shall from time to time give information to the Legislature, of the State of the Union, and recommend to their consideration the measures he may think necessary. He shall take care that the Laws of the United States be duly executed. He shall commission all the officers of the United States; and, except as to Ambassadors, other Ministers, and Judges of the Supreme Court, he shall nominate, and, with the consent of the Senate, appoint, all other officers of the United States. He shall receive publick Ministers from Foreign Nations; and may correspond with the Executives of the different States. He shall have power to grant pardons and reprieves, except in impeachments. He shall be commander in chief of the Army and Navy of the United States, and of the Militia of the several States; and shall receive a compensation which shall not be increased or diminished during his continuance in office. At entering on the duties of his office, he shall take an oath faithfully to execute the duties of a President of the United States. He shall be removed from his office on impeachment by the House of Delegates, and conviction in the Supreme Court, of Treason, bribery, or corruption. In case of his removal, Death, resignation, or disability, the President of the Senate shall exercise the duties of his office until another President be chosen, and in case of the Death of the President of the Senate, the Speaker of the House of Delegates shall do so.

9.

The Legislature of the United States shall have the power, and it shall be their duty, to establish such Courts of Law, Equity & admiralty, as shall be necessary. The Judges of the Courts shall hold their offices during good behavior; and receive a compensation which shall not be increased or diminished during their continuance in office. One of these Courts shall be termed the Supreme Court, whose jurisdiction shall extend to all cases arising under the Laws of the United States, or affecting A‑bassadors, other publick Ministers and Consuls; to the trial of impeachment of officers of the United States; to all cases of admiralty & Maritime jurisdiction. In cases of impeachment affecting Ambassadors, and other publick Ministers, this jurisdiction shall be original; and in all the other cases appellate.

All Criminal offences (except in cases of impeachment) shall be tried in the State where they shall be committed. The trials shall be open & publick, and be by Jury.

10.

Immediately after the first Census of the people of the United States, the House of Delegates shall apportion the Senate by electing for each State, out of the Citizens resident therein, one Senator for every   Members such State shall have in the House of Delegates. Each State shall be entitled to have at least one Member in the Senate.

11.

No State shall grant Letters of Marque & reprisal, or enter into treaty, or alliance, or Confederation; nor grant any title of Nobility; nor, without the consent of the Legislature of the United States, lay any Impost on imports; nor keep Troops or Ships of War in time of Peace; nor enter into compacts with other States or Foreign Powers, or emit Bills of Credit, or make any thing but Gold, Silver or Copper, a tender in payment of debts; nor engage in War, except for self defence when actually invaded, or the danger of invasion is so great as not to admit of a delay, until the Government of the United States can be informed thereof. And to render these prohibitions effectual, the Legislature of the United States shall have the power to revise the Laws of the several States that may be supposed to

infringe the powers exclusively delegated by this Constitution to Congress, and to negative and annul such as
do.

12.

The Citizens of each State shall be entitled to all privileges and immunities of Citizens in the several States.
Any person, charged with crimes in any State, fleeing
from justice to another, shall, on demand of the Executive of the State from which he Fled, be delivered up,
and removed to the State having jurisdiction of the
offence.

13.

Full faith shall be given, in each State, to the acts of
the Legislature and to the records and judicial proceedings of the Courts and Magistrates of every State.

14.

The Legislature shall have power to admit New States
into the Union on the same terms with the original
States; provided two thirds of the Members present in
both Houses agree.

15.

On the application of the Legislature of a State, the
United States shall protect it against domestick insurrection.

16.

If two thirds of the Legislatures of the States apply
for the same, the Legislature of the United States shall
call a Convention for the purpose of amending the Constitution: Or, Should Congress, with the consent of two
thirds of each House, propose to the States amendments
to the same, the agreement of two thirds of the Legislatures of the States shall be sufficient to make the said
amendments parts of the Constitution.

The Ratification of the　　　　Conventions of
States shall be sufficient for organizing this Constitution.

UNITED STATES OF AMERICA.

DEPARTMENT OF STATE.

Appendix.
Pinckney's Draft.

To all to whom these presents shall come, Greeting:

I certify That the document hereto annexed is a true copy, from the Archives of this Department, of Pinckney's plan of government of May 29, 1787, as furnished by himself for publication under the Resolution of Congress of March 27, 1818, directing the publication and distribution of the Journal and proceedings of the Convention which formed the Constitution of the United States.

In testimony whereof I, William F. Wharton, Acting Secretary of State of the United States, have hereunto subscribed my name and caused the seal of the

[SEAL.] Department of State to be affixed.

Done at the City of Washington, this 12th day of June, A.D., 1891, and of the Independence of the United States of America the one hundred and fifteenth.

WILLIAM F. WHARTON.

INDEX.

ACCUSED PARTIES
    cannot be tried for a crime not stated in the indictment, 509.
    have a right to be confronted with the witnesses, 509.
    and to compulsory process to secure their attendance, 510.

ACTIVE, THE
    case of, 42.

ADMIRALTY AND MARITIME JURISDICTION. [See *Colonial Admiralty*
    Courts : Prize Courts of the Revolution.]
    early exercise of, more limited than now, 132.
    its extension, 110, 133.
    this extension constitutional, 134.
    extent of it under the Constitution, 326.

ADMISSION OF NEW STATES, 131.

ALIENS. [See *Citizenship : Naturalization.*]

AMBASSADORS. [See *Citizenship.*]
    jurisdiction of the Supreme Court over cases affecting, 325, 361.
    evidence in support of a claim to this right, 362, 426.

AMENDMENTS TO THE CONSTITUTION
    the first ten amendments, 91.
    unratified articles, 91 n.
    eleventh amendment, 92 n., 331 n., 363, 379, 423, 652.
    twelfth amendment, 149, 653.
    thirteenth amendment, 406, 653.
    fourteenth amendment, 407, 653.
    fifteenth amendment, 408, 653.
    whether a ratification once given can be withdrawn, 642, 653.

AMPHICTYONIC COUNCILS
    not a federal government, 78 n.

ANNAPOLIS, CONVENTION OF
    convened through the action of Virginia, 6.

APPOINTMENT. [See *Senate.*]
    where the power of appointment is vested, 156.
    the annoyance it caused to Washington, 177.

SOVEREIGN POWERS

the Congress of the Confederation claimed and exercised them, 57.

some such powers never possessed by the States, 36.

SOVEREIGNTY OF THE PEOPLE

de Tocqueville's views as to, 89 n.

SPEAKER. [See *House of Commons : House of Representatives.*]

SPIRITUOUS LIQUORS. [See *Intoxicating Liquors : Regulation of Commerce.*]

STATES. [See *Sovereign Powers.*]

difference between their government and the Federal government, 103.

held that they can be sued in Federal courts, 379.

subsequent proceedings resulting in the Eleventh Amendment, 380-382.

suits against, under Articles of Confederation, 421-423.

Chisholm v. *Georgia* overruled, 423.

limits imposed upon the States, 577.

STATES' RIGHTS

theory of construction, 23, 117.

STEAM VESSELS. [See *Regulation of Commerce.*]

STORY, JUSTICE

his opinion in *Martin* v. *Hunter*, 102 n.

his opinion in *Parsons* v. *Bedford*, 497.

STRONG, JUSTICE

his opinion in *Knox* v. *Lee*, 136.

SUFFRAGE. [See *Citizenship.*]

extension of, 106.

SUPREME COURT

its functions in construing the Constitution, 315.

only one Supreme Court, and it cannot be abolished by Congress, 338.

its judges hold office during good behavior, 340, 343.

its original jurisdiction, 344.

its appellate jurisdiction, 345.

its history and influence, 374.

is the head of the Judicial Department, 376.

its constitutional decisions not binding on the Executive, 377.

its organization and its chief justices, 378.

when its justices have been employed on civil duties, 378, 420.

it may issue a writ of prohibition, 427.

its justices protected when travelling on circuit, 428.

SURRENDER OF OFFENDERS. [See *Fugitives from Justice.*]

SUSANNA, THE

the judgment reviewed and sustained, 121.

SWISS CONFEDERATION
  its disadvantages, 87 n.

TANEY, CHIEF JUSTICE
  his opinion in *United States* v. *Ferreira*, 354.